A Critical
INTRODUCTION
to the
NEW TESTAMENT

A Critical
INTRODUCTION
to the
NEW TESTAMENT

*Interpreting the Message and
Meaning of Jesus Christ*

CARL R. HOLLADAY

Abingdon Press / Nashville

A CRITICAL INTRODUCTION TO THE NEW TESTAMENT
INTERPRETING THE MESSAGE AND MEANING OF JESUS CHRIST

Copyright © 2005 by Abingdon Press

Library of Congress Cataloging-in-Publication Data

Holladay, Carl R.
  A critical introduction to the New Testament : interpreting the message and meaning of Jesus Christ / Carl R. Holladay.
    p. cm.
  Includes bibliographical references and index.
  ISBN 0-687-08569-1 (adhesive perfect binding : alk. paper)
  1. Bible. N.T.—Criticism, interpretation, etc. I. Title.

  BS2361.3.H65 2005
  225.6'1—dc22

2004030675

ISBN-13: 978-0-687-08569-9

09 10 11 12 13 14—10 9 8 7 6 5 4

MANUFACTURED IN THE UNITED STATES OF AMERICA

For
Sarah Elizabeth Holladay
and
James Patrick Holladay

Contents

Maps, Diagrams & Images ix

Preface xi

Abbreviations. xv

Introduction. 1

PART 1   **Theology and Scripture**

Chapter 1   The New Testament as Theological Writings 9
Chapter 2   The Shape of the Canon 26

PART 2   **The Gospels: Narrative Traditions about Jesus**

Chapter 3   Relating the Gospels to Each Other 39
Chapter 4   From Jesus to the Gospels 58
Chapter 5   From the Gospels to Jesus 77
Chapter 6   The Gospel of Mark 104
Chapter 7   The Gospel of Matthew 128
Chapter 8   The Gospel of Luke 158
Chapter 9   The Gospel of John 190

PART 3   **The Story of Jesus Continued: The Church's Origin and Expansion**

Chapter 10   The Acts of the Apostles 225

PART 4   **The Pauline Letters and Hebrews**

Chapter 11   Reading the Pauline Letters 263
Chapter 12   The Thessalonian Letters 289

Contents

Chapter 13   The Corinthian Letters 303
Chapter 14   Galatians 333
Chapter 15   Romans 348
Chapter 16   Philippians 370
Chapter 17   Philemon 383
Chapter 18   Colossians 392
Chapter 19   Ephesians 409
Chapter 20   The Pastoral Letters 420
Chapter 21   Hebrews 445

PART 5   **The Catholic Letters**

               Introduction to the Catholic Letters 469
Chapter 22   James 471
Chapter 23   First Peter 484
               Introduction to Jude and Second Peter 501
Chapter 24   Jude 503
Chapter 25   Second Peter 510
Chapter 26   The Letters of John 519

PART 6   **Jesus in the Apocalyptic Imagination**

Chapter 27   Revelation 535

PART 7   **The Formation of the New Testament Canon**

Chapter 28   The Christian Scriptures: Witnesses to Christ and the
               Church's Faith 571

Index 597

Maps, Diagrams & Images

Map: The Eastern Early Roman Empire xxiii
Diagram: "Doing Theology" Tetrahedron 20
Diagram: Augustine's View of the Gospels 41
Diagram: Single (Common) Source Model 44
Diagram: Miscellaneous Sources 45
Diagram: Two Gospel Hypothesis 46
Diagram: Two Source Hypothesis 47
Diagram: Four Source Hypothesis 47
Diagram: Traditional Model of the "Tunnel Period" 70
Diagram: Form Critical Model of the "Tunnel Period" 72
Diagram: Rabbinic Transmission Model of the "Tunnel Period" 73
Map: Palestine at the Time of Jesus 105
Image: Woodcut of the Evangelist Mark (1541) 109
Diagram: The Gospel of Mark (Column Chart) 124
Diagram: Matthew's Interpretation of Mark 132
Image: Woodcut of the Evangelist Matthew (1541) 136
Diagram: The Gospel of Matthew (Column Chart) 154
Diagram: Luke's Interpretation of Mark 162
Map: Setting for Luke's Travel Narrative (Jesus' Journey to Jerusalem) 164
Image: Woodcut of the Evangelist Luke (1541) 168
Image: Woodcut of The Women at Jesus' Tomb on Easter Morning (1563) 185
Diagram: The Gospel of Luke (Column Chart) 186
Map: The Geography of John's Gospel (Jesus' Journey in John 4) 193
Diagram: The Length of Jesus' Ministry in John 194
Image: P75 (3d-cent. papyrus; the end of Luke and the beginning of John) 200
Image: P52 (the oldest NT manuscript [ca. 125 C.E.]) 200
Image: Woodcut of the Evangelist John (1541) 202
Diagram: The Gospel of John (Column Chart) 218
Map: Early Expansion of Christianity (Syria and Cilicia) 230
Image: Woodcut of the Coming of the Spirit on Pentecost in Acts 2 (1569) . . . 231

Map: The Eastern Mediterranean in Paul's Time 235
Diagram: The Speeches in Acts 236
Map: Homelands of the Pentecost Pilgrims in Acts 2:9–11 244
Map: Early Expansion of Christianity into Asia Minor 252
Image: Woodcut of Saul's Conversion in Acts 9 (1695) 255
Diagram: The Acts of the Apostles (Column Chart) 256
Image: Oxyrhynchus Papyrus No. 115, Letter of Consolation (2d cent. c.e.) . . . 266
Image: Papyrus Letter from Theon to His Father (2d or 3d cent. c.e.) 267
Image: Woodcut of the Apostle Paul (1477) 271
Image: Woodcut of Paul at His Writing Desk (1536) 274
Diagram: Suggested Pauline Chronology 276
Diagram: Chronology of Paul's Life and Letters (Chart) 279
Map: Via Egnatia (The Aegean Region) 291
Image: Woodcut of the Apostle Paul with Two Swords (Matthias Flacius, 1549) . . 297
Map: The Aegean Region 309
Image: Woodcut of the Apostle Paul (Lucas Cranach, 1550) 319
Map: Galatia 335
Image: Woodcut of Saul's Heavenly Vision on the Damascus Road (1477) 342
Image: Woodcut of Phoebe, a Deacon of the Church at Cenchreae (1547) 362
Map: Main Roadways of Asia Minor (and the Lycus Valley) 395
Map: The Eastern Mediterranean (Geographical Setting of the Pastorals) 423
Image: Woodcut of the Author of the Letter to the Hebrews at His Writing
    Desk (1695) 455
Image: Woodcut of James Delivering His Letter to a Courier (1547) 478
Map: Asia Minor (Roman Provinces Addressed in 1 Peter) 488
Image: Woodcut of the Apostle Peter (Lucas Cranach, 1550) 491
Image: Woodcut of the Apostle John Sending a Letter by a Courier (1547) 526
Image: The New Jerusalem in Rev 21 (Caspar Luiken, 1712) 540
Map: The Seven Churches of Revelation 542
Diagram: The Book of Revelation (Column Chart) 546
Image: The Opening of the Seventh Seal in Rev 8 (Caspar Luiken, 1712) 554
Image: The Slain Lamb Receives the Scroll in Rev 5 (Caspar Luiken, 1712) . . . 556
Image: Satan's Defeat in Rev 20 (Caspar Luiken, 1712) 562

Preface

The idea for this book began in 1997 when Rex Matthews, then Senior Editor for Academic Books at Abingdon Press, invited me to write a theological introduction to the New Testament. What was needed, Rex insisted, was an introductory text for theology students, ministers, and Bible teachers that would treat the usual historical and literary questions but that would give special attention to theological issues.

I was intrigued with the suggestion, but little did I realize that the project would occupy my attention for the next five to six years. I drafted the requisite book proposal, which was vetted among several New Testament professors in North America who regularly teach introductory courses in seminaries. Jouette Bassler (Perkins School of Theology at Southern Methodist University), Charles Cousar (Columbia Theological Seminary), and Richard Hays (Duke Divinity School) read the proposal and offered many helpful suggestions. Also at an early stage, my Emory colleague Fred Craddock offered insightful suggestions about how to conceive the project.

Further refinement occurred in a grant proposal, which I submitted to the Association for Theological Schools (ATS) in Pittsburgh. Shortly before, thanks to the initiatives of James L. Waits, Executive Director of ATS, and Daniel Aleshire, Associate Director of ATS, the Henry Luce III Fellows in Theology program had been established under the auspices of the Henry Luce Foundation, Inc., with the enthusiastic support of then-President John W. Cook. Once established, the program was nurtured under the creative leadership of Michael Gilligan, Program Director for Theology. From the outset, these fellowships were intended to fund projects with an explicit theological dimension that had potential for enriching the life of the church and its ministries. These two foci—theology and church—figured centrally in my conception of the project.

Although I had over twenty years of experience teaching New Testament introduction at Yale Divinity School and Candler School of Theology, I had to rethink basic questions of pedagogy. What, for example, do ministers really need to know about the New Testament to relate it meaningfully to their own life of faith and the communities of faith they serve? I also had to rethink the genre of New Testament introduction. What should such a work actually look like? Should it be organized around the familiar "W's"—Who wrote each document? When? Where? To whom? Why? If standard literary and historical questions were to be treated but not given the same weight as in traditional introductions, what would this mean? And if greater attention were given to the theological dimension of the New Testament, what form should it take?

To my great delight, I was awarded a Luce Fellowship to work on the project during a 1999–2000 sabbatical year granted by Emory. I interpreted this as a strong endorsement of my project, and I remain indebted to ATS and the Luce Foundation for their support. Rather than simply writing up my lecture notes from previous years, however, I felt an obligation genuinely to rethink the task of introducing the New Testament to theology students in the changed environment of the twenty-first century. Working on the book has been an intriguing intellectual challenge, since it has required me to broaden my own horizons of theological understanding and yet tackle a question at the heart of my own academic discipline. One of the great values of the Luce Fellowship program was being able to attend for three consecutive years a seminar comprising recipients of awards from other theological disciplines—the first year as a newcomer, the second year as a presenter, and the third year as a "veteran." Preparing a presentation for this group of engaging, diverse scholars at the Luce Conference, held at the Center for Theological Inquiry at Princeton Theological Seminary in November 2000, required me to engage in interdisciplinary conversation with other scholars, most of whom were not specialists in New Testament studies but just as passionate for its theological claims as I.

Coupled with the Luce Seminar was another interdisciplinary experience—The Consultation on Teaching the Bible in the Twenty-First Century—sponsored by Lilly Endowment, Inc., and offered for three consecutive years at Wabash College in Crawfordsville, Indiana. From 1998–2000, some thirty biblical scholars, roughly fifteen from Hebrew Bible and fifteen from the New Testament, met for a week of intensive discussion of issues related to teaching the Bible in colleges, universities, and seminaries. Before this diverse, and sometimes raucous, group of colleagues comprising Jewish and Christian scholars, women and men who represented several ethnic groups and taught in a variety of settings throughout North America, I presented my project. The interchange was lively, and questions from persons teaching in settings quite different from a mainline Protestant seminary required me to think through my project at an even deeper level. I am grateful to the Lilly Endowment for funding this consultation, to Raymond Williams, Director of the Wabash Center, and to Gary Anderson (Harvard Divinity School) and Richard Hays for convening the biblical group; also to each of the participants for many lively conversations that allowed me to discuss what I was doing.

Yet another context that has shaped my project is the institution where I teach—Candler School of Theology at Emory University. Since coming to Emory in 1980, I have benefited immensely from the engaging collegiality that characterizes Candler. Monthly faculty colloquia allow another form of interdisciplinary discussion, and, once again, I used this venue to discuss my project. As usual, the conversation was focused, lively, and constructive, and the feedback from my Candler colleagues was very useful.

Beyond these formal meetings, I have benefited from ongoing discussions with my Emory New Testament colleagues: Michael Brown, Luke Johnson, Steve Kraftchick, Gail O'Day, Vernon Robbins, Walter Wilson, and, of course, Emeritus Professor Hendrikus Boers. One of the monthly New Testament colloquia, attended by faculty and graduate students, provided another forum for presentation and critique. Besides this were ongoing conversations in offices, hallways, and over lunch.

Other Emory colleagues have also been valuable conversation partners: Don Saliers, Walt Lowe, David Pacini, and Joy McDougall on theological aspects of the project; Lewis Ayres on the formation of the New Testament canon; and Brooks Holifield and Jonathan Strom on different aspects of history of interpretation. Another emeritus colleague, Robert Kysar, also kindly offered comments relating to the Fourth Gospel. As in so many other respects, my Old Testament colleague John Hayes, with whom I have coauthored other books, has been a valuable, and always entertaining, conversation partner, especially on matters of the history of biblical interpretation as well as protocols of editing and publishing. Thanks are also in order to the remarkable staff at Candler's Pitts Theology Library and to its Librarian, Patrick Graham, for their assistance and cooperation at every stage of the project. I also owe a word of thanks to two Candler deans, Kevin LaGree and Russell Richey, for supporting the project and providing sabbatical time and institutional resources at critical junctures.

Another advantage of working at Emory is having access to master's level theology students at Candler and doctoral students in the Graduate Division of Religion. Both settings have provided me wonderful research assistants. At an early stage, Patrick Gray, Scott Shauf, and John Weaver worked carefully through several chapters and provided critical feedback and research assistance. I have also drawn on the expertise of doctoral students' dissertation research: Greg Stevenson and Lynn Huber on Revelation, and Patrick Gray and Bryan Whitfield on Hebrews. At a later stage, two other New Testament doctoral students, Derek Olsen and James (Bru) Wallace, provided invaluable assistance in researching bibliographical and other details, editing, and compiling lists of abbreviations and indices. Derek's expertise with computers has been a marvelous resource, and I gratefully acknowledge his assistance in producing a number of the diagrams. So reliable and resourceful has Bru been at every stage that early on I dubbed him *Jacobus Factotum*—appropriate enough, I thought, given his Christian name. As the endnotes reveal, a doctoral seminar on the Gospels offered in the spring of 2002 provided an occasion to think through some basic questions. From this seminar I have drawn on the work of William Wright and Bart Bruehler. From the School of Theology, Andy Guffey has also been a resourceful assistant, especially in providing several of the diagrams for the book, but also in many editorial details. I am also grateful to Edward McMinn, an M.Div. student enrolled in my New Testament Interpretation class, for focusing his experienced editorial eye on the manuscript and producing pages of suggested revisions and corrections.

In the final stages of the project, Bo Adams provided invaluable editorial assistance and computer expertise. Brad Storin also assisted with editorial work but his main contribution was the compilation of the index. To both I owe special gratitude.

A number of church venues have also been important testing grounds for several ideas in the book. Among the most prominent is my own congregation, Northlake

Church of Christ in Atlanta, where I regularly teach adult Bible classes. Several of the chapters were composed while teaching the same material at the Northlake church, as well as before sermon seminars and workshops offered under the auspices of Candler and also at Rochester College in Rochester, Michigan; Pepperdine University in Malibu, California; and Austin Graduate School of Theology in Austin, Texas. An invitation to give the W. B. West, Jr. Lectures at Harding Graduate School of Religion in Memphis, Tennessee in November 2002 also afforded an opportunity to give a public lecture titled "Introducing the New Testament Theologically" and to engage in a profitable discussion with another group of energetic theology students.

A number of professional colleagues at other institutions have also been kind enough to read parts of the manuscript or individual chapters, including Richard Hays, David Moessner (University of Dubuque Theological Seminary), James Thompson (Abilene Christian University), Jeff Peterson (Austin Graduate School of Theology), Christopher Rowland (Oxford University), and Birger Gerhardsson (Lund University). An invitation from Gregory Sterling at the University of Notre Dame enabled me to present a lecture on the project to the faculty and students at the School of Theology, from which I received valuable feedback. I am especially indebted to two of my former teachers, both of whom are now emeritus professors: Abraham J. Malherbe, Emeritus Buckingham Professor of New Testament Criticism and Interpretation at Yale Divinity School, and C. F. D. Moule, Emeritus Lady Margaret's Professor of Divinity in the University of Cambridge. Each was willing to look at the entire manuscript and offer detailed comments and corrections, and I have sought to incorporate their suggestions into the final manuscript. To each of them I am indebted in quite different ways for putting me on the path to New Testament scholarship and for encouraging me and nurturing my work over the years.

A special word of thanks to the editorial staff at Abingdon Press: to John Kutsko and Bob Ratcliff for their willingness to be innovative and to deploy precious editorial resources to the project; to Kathy Armistead and Tim West for superb editorial oversight and copy editing; to all four for their commitment to excellence and quality.

Atlanta
February 28, 2005

Abbreviations

1 Apol.	Justin Martyr, *Apologia i* (*First Apology*)
1 Clem.	*1 Clement*
1 En.	*1 Enoch* (*Ethiopic Apocalypse*)
1QH	Qumran *Hodayot* (*Thanksgiving Hymns*)
1QM	Qumran *Milḥamah* (*War Scroll*)
1QpHab	Qumran *Pesher Habakkuk*
1QS	Qumran *Serek Hayaḥad* (*Rule of the Community*)
1QSb	Qumran *Rule of the Blessings* (Appendix b to 1QS)
2 Bar.	*2 Baruch* (*Syriac Apocalypse*)
2 Clem.	*2 Clement*
2 En.	*2 Enoch* (*Slavonic Apocalypse*)
3 Bar.	*3 Baruch* (*Greek Apocalypse*)
4 Ezra	*4 Ezra*
11QMelch	Qumran *Melchizedek*
AB	Anchor Bible
ABD	*Anchor Bible Dictionary*
ABRL	Anchor Bible Reference Library
ANF	*Ante-Nicene Fathers*
Acts Pet.	*Acts of Peter*
Ag.	Aeschylus, *Agamemnon*
Alex.	Lucian, *Alexander* (*Pseudomantis* / *Alexander the False Prophet*)
An.	Tertullian, *De anima* (*The Soul*)
Ann.	Tacitus, *Annales* (*Annals*)
Ant.	Josephus, *Jewish Antiquities*
Antichr.	Hippolytus, *De antichristo* (*Concerning the Antichrist*)
Antid.	Isocrates, *Antidosis* (*Or. 15*)
Apoc. Ab.	*Apocalypse of Abraham*
Apoc. Pet.	*Apocalypse of Peter*
Apocr. Ezek.	*Apocryphon of Ezekiel*

Apol.	Tertullian, *Apologeticus* (*Apology*)
Arist.	Plutarch, *Aristides*
Ascen. Isa.	*Mart. Ascen. Isa.* 6–11 (*Martyrdom and Ascension of Isaiah*)
Autol.	Theophilus, *Ad Autolycum* (*To Autolycus*)
Bapt.	Tertullian, *De baptismo* (*Baptism*)
Barn.	*Barnabas* (*Epistle of Barnabas*)
B.C.E.	Before the Common Era
BDAG	Bauer, W., F. W. Danker, W. F. Arndt, and F. W. Gingrich. *A Greek-English Lexicon of the New Testament and Other Early Christian Literature.* 3d ed. (Chicago: University of Chicago Press, 2000)
Bruce, *Canon*	F. F. Bruce, *The Canon of Scripture* (Downers Grove: InterVarsity Press, 1988)
C. Ar.	Athanasius, *Orationes contra Arianos* (*Orations against the Arians*)
Catech.	Cyril of Jerusalem, *Catecheses* (*Catechetical Instructions*)
CD	Qumran Cairo Genizah copy of the *Damascus Document*
C.E.	Common Era
Cels.	Origen, *Contra Celsum* (*Against Celsus*)
cf.	compare
ch(s).	chapter(s)
Cher.	Philo, *De cherubim* (*On the Cherubim*)
Chron.	Eusebius of Caesarea, *Chronicon* (*Chronicle*)
Civ.	Augustine, *De civitate Dei* (*The City of God*)
Claud.	Suetonius, *Divus Claudius* (*The Divine Claudius*)
col(s).	column(s)
Comm. Dan.	Hippolytus, *Commentarium in Danielem* (*Commentary on Daniel*)
Comm. Gen.	Origen, *Commentarii in Genesim* (*Commentary on Genesis*)
Comm. Jo.	Origen, *Commentarii in evangelium Joannis* (*Commentary on the Gospel of John*)
Comm. Matt.	Origen, *Commentarium in evangelium Matthaei* (*Commentary on the Gospel of Matthew*)
Comm. Phlm.	Jerome, *Commentariorum in Epistulam ad Philemonem liber* (*Commentary on the Epistle to Philemon*)
Comm. Ps.	Jerome, *Commentarioli in Psalmos* (*Commentary on Psalms*)
Comm. Rom.	Origen, *Commentarii in Romanos* (*Commentary on Romans*)
Comm. ser. Matt.	Origen, *Commentarium series in evangelium Matthaei* (*Commentary on Matthew 22:34–27:63*)
Comm. Tit.	Jerome, *Commentariorum in Epistulam ad Titum liber* (*Commentary on the Epistle to Titus*)
Conf.	Philo, *De confusione linguarum* (*On the Confusion of Tongues*)
Cons.	Augustine, *De consensu evangelistarum* (*Harmony of the Gospels*)
Const. Ap.	*Constitutiones apostolicae* (*Apostolic Constitutions*)
Contempl.	Philo, *De vita contemplativa* (*On the Contemplative Life*)
Cult. fem.	Tertullian, *De cultu feminarum* (*The Apparel of Women*)
De or.	Cicero, *De oratore* (*On Oratory*)

Dial.	Justin Martyr, *Dialogus cum Tryphone* (*Dialogue with Trypho*)
Did.	*Didache* (*The Teaching of the Lord to the Gentiles Through the Twelve Apostles*)
Diogn.	*Diognetus* (*The Epistle to Diognetus*)
Div. quaest. LXXXIII	Augustine, *De diversis quaestionibus LXXXIII* (*Eighty-three Different Questions*)
Doctr. chr.	Augustine, *De doctrina christiana* (*Christian Instruction*)
Dom.	Suetonius, *Domitianus* (*Domitian*)
Ecl.	Clement of Alexandria, *Eclogae propheticae* (*Extracts from the Prophets*)
e.g.	for example (Latin *exempli gratia*)
enl.	enlarged
Ep.	Cyprian of Carthage, *Epistulae* (*Epistles*)
Ep.	Pliny the Younger, *Epistulae* (*The Letters of Pliny*)
Ep.	Seneca, *Epistulae morales* (*Moral Essays*)
Ep. Apos.	*Epistle to the Apostles*
Ep. fest.	Athanasius, *Epistulae festales* (*Festal Letters*)
Ep. Tra.	Pliny the Younger, *Epistulae ad Trajanum* (*Letters to Trajan*)
Epist.	Basil, *Epistulae* (*Epistles*)
Epist.	Jerome, *Epistulae* (*Epistles*)
Eth. nic.	Aristotle, *Ethica nichomachea* (*Nichomachean Ethics*)
Exc.	Clement of Alexandria, *Excerpta ex Theodoto* (*Excerpts from Theodotus*)
ff.	folio pages
fl.	flourished, e.g., Clement of Rome fl. ca. 96 C.E.
Fid. Grat.	Ambrose, *De fide ad Gratianum* (*On the Faith, to Gratian*)
FTMT	Fortress Texts in Modern Theology
Gk.	Greek
Gig.	Philo, *De gigantibus* (*On Giants*)
Gorg.	Plato, *Gorgias*
Gos. Heb.	*Gospel of the Hebrews*
Gos. Thom.	*Gospel of Thomas*
Gos. Truth	*Gospel of Truth*
GP	Burton Throckmorton, ed., *Gospel Parallels: A Comparison of the Synoptic Gospels* (5th ed.; Nashville: Nelson, 1992)
Haer.	Hippolytus, *Refutatio omnium haeresium* (*Refutation of All Heresies*)
Haer.	Irenaeus, *Adversus haereses* (*Against Heresies*)
Herm.	Hermas
Herm.	Tertullian, *Adversus Hermogenem* (*Against Hermogenes*)
Herm. *Mand.*	Shepherd of Hermas, *Mandate*
Herm. *Sim.*	Shepherd of Hermas, *Similitude*
Herm. *Vis.*	Shepherd of Hermas, *Vision*
Hist.	Tacitus, *Historiae* (*The Histories*)
Hist. eccl.	Eusebius of Caesarea, *Historia ecclesiastica* (*Ecclesiastical History*)
Hist. eccl.	Sozomen, *Historia ecclesiastica* (*Ecclesiastical History*)

Hom.	Jerome, *Homiliae* (*Homilies*)
Hom. 2 Cor.	John Chrysostom, *Homiliae in epistulam ii ad Corinthios* (*Homilies on 2 Corinthians*)
Hom. Act.	John Chrysostom, *Homiliae in Acta apostolorum* (*Homilies on the Acts of the Apostles*)
Hom. Ezech.	Origen, *Homiliae in Ezechielem* (*Homilies on Ezekiel*)
Hom. Jer.	Origen, *Homiliae in Jeremiam* (*Homilies on Jeremiah*)
Hom. Luc.	Origen, *Homiliae in Lucam* (*Homilies on Luke*)
Hom. Matt.	John Chrysostom, *Homiliae in Matthaeum* (*Homilies on Matthew*)
Hom. Phlm.	John Chrysostom, *Homiliae in epistulam ad Philemonem* (*Homilies on the Epistle to Philemon*)
Hypoth.	Philo, *Hypothetica*
i.e.	that is (Latin *id est*)
Ign.	Ignatius
Ign. Eph.	Ignatius, *To the Ephesians*
Ign. Magn.	Ignatius, *To the Magnesians*
Ign. Phld.	Ignatius, *To the Philadelphians*
Ign. Pol.	Ignatius, *To Polycarp*
Ign. Rom.	Ignatius, *To the Romans*
Ign. Smyrn.	Ignatius, *To the Smyrnaeans*
Ign. Trall.	Ignatius, *To the Trallians*
Jos. Asen.	*Joseph and Aseneth*
Jov.	Jerome, *Adversus Jovinianum libri II* (*Against Jovian, 2 Books*)
Jub.	*Jubilees*
KJV	King James Version
LCL	Loeb Classical Library
Leg.	Athenagoras, *Legatio pro Christianis* (*A Plea for the Christians*)
Leg.	Plato, *Leges* (*Laws*)
Leg. alleg.	Philo, *Legum allegoriae* (*Allegorical Interpretation*)
lit.	literally
LJCE	David Friedrich Strauss, *The Life of Jesus Critically Examined* (ed. Peter Hodgson; trans. George Eliot; Philadelphia: Fortress,1972; reprinted Sigler Press, 2002)
LW	*Luther's Works: American Edition* (ed. Jaroslav Pelikan and Helmut T. Lehmann; St. Louis: Concordia; Philadelphia: Muhlenberg/Fortress, 1955–1996)
LXX	*Septuagint* (Greek translation of the OT)
m. 'Abot	Mishnah *Avot* (*The Fathers*)
m. Sanh.	Mishnah *Sanhedrin*
Mag. mor.	Aristotle, *Magna moralia* (*Great Ethics*)
Marc.	Tertullian, *Adversus Marcionem* (*Against Marcion*)
Mart. Pol.	*Martyrdom of Polycarp*
Mem.	Xenophon, *Memorabilia*

Metaph.	Aristotle, *Metaphysica* (*Metaphysics*)
Metzger, *Canon*	Bruce M. Metzger, *The Canon of the New Testament: Its Origin, Development, and Significance* (Oxford: Clarendon Press, 1997)
Mon.	Tertullian, *De monogamia* (*Monogamy*)
NA²⁷	Nestle-Aland, *Novum Testamentum Graece* (27th ed.; Stuttgart: Deutsche Bibelgesellschaft, 2001)
Nat.	Pliny the Elder, *Naturalis historia* (*Natural History*)
Nat.	Seneca, *Naturales quaestiones* (*Natural Questions*)
Nat. d.	Cicero, *De natura deorum* (*On the Nature of the Gods*)
NEB	New English Bible
Nero	Suetonius, *Nero*
NHC	Nag Hammadi Codices
NIV	New International Version
NJB	New Jerusalem Bible
*NPNF*¹	*Nicene and Post-Nicene Fathers*, Series 1
*NPNF*²	*Nicene and Post-Nicene Fathers*, Series 2
NRSV	New Revised Standard Version
NT	New Testament
NTA	*New Testament Apocrypha* (ed. E. Hennecke and W. Schneemelcher; trans. R. McL. Wilson; 2 vols; London: Lutterworth, 1963-65)
NTL	New Testament Library
Oct.	Minucius Felix, *Octavius*
op. cit.	in the work cited (Latin *opere citato*)
Orat.	Tatian, *Oratio ad Graecas* (*Oration to the Greeks*)
Or. Brut.	Cicero, *Orator ad M. Brutum* (*Orator*)
OT	Old Testament
OTP	*The Old Testament Pseudepigrapha* (ed. J. H. Charlesworth; 2 vols.; New York: Doubleday, 1983–1985)
p(p).	page(s)
Paed.	Clement of Alexandria, *Paedagogus* (*Christ the Educator*)
Paen.	Ambrose, *De paenitentia* (*On Repentance*)
Pan.	Epiphanius, *Panarion* (*Adversus haereses* / *Refutation of All Heresies*)
Pan.	Pliny the Younger, *Panegyricus*
Panath.	Isocrates, *Panathenaicus* (*Or.* 12)
Pecc. merit.	Augustine, *De peccatorum meritis et remissione* (*Guilt and Remission of Sins*)
Pelag.	Jerome, *Adversus Pelagianos dialogi III* (*Dialogues against the Pelagians, Three Books*)
Peregr.	Lucian, *De morte Peregrini* (*The Passing of Peregrinus*)
PG	Patrologia graeca (ed. J.-P. Migne; 162 vols.; Paris, 1857–1886)
Phil.	Isocrates, *Philippus* (*Or.* 5)
PL	Patrologia latina (ed. J.-P. Migne; 217 vols.; Paris, 1844–1864)
Pol.	Polycarp
Pol.	Aristotle, *Politica* (*Politics*)

Pol. *Phil.*	Polycarp, *To the Philippians*
P. Oxy.	Oxyrhynchus Papyri
Praem.	Philo, *De praemiis et poenis* (*On Rewards and Punishments*)
Praescr.	Tertullian, *De praescriptione haereticorum* (*Prescription against Heretics*)
Prax.	Tertullian, *Adversus Praxean* (*Against Praxeas*)
Pre. Pet.	*Kerygma Petrou* (*Preaching of Peter*)
Preachings of Peter	*Kerygmata Petrou* (*The Preachings of Peter*)
Princ.	Origen, *De principiis* (*Peri archōn* / *First Principles*)
Prob.	Philo, *Quod omnis probus liber sit* (*That Every Good Person Is Free*)
Protr.	Clement of Alexandria, *Protrepticus* (*Exhortation to the Greeks*)
Pss. Sol.	*Psalms of Solomon*
Pud.	Tertullian, *De pudicitia* (*Modesty*)
Quis div.	Clement of Alexandria, *Quis dives salvetur* (*Salvation of the Rich*)
REB	Revised English Bible
Res.	Tertullian, *De resurrectione carnis* (*The Resurrection of the Flesh*)
Resp.	Plato, *Respublica* (*Republic*)
rev.	revised (by)
RGG[3]	*Religion in Geschichte und Gegenwart* (ed. K. Galling; 7 vols.; 3d ed.; Tübingen, 1957–1965)
Rhet.	Aristotle, *Rhetorica* (*Rhetoric*)
RSV	Revised Standard Version
Sacr.	Ambrose, *De sacramentis* (*The Sacraments*)
Sat.	Juvenal, *Satirae* (*Satires*)
SBT	Studies in Biblical Theology
Scorp.	Tertullian, *Scorpiace* (*Antidote for the Scorpion's Sting*)
Sel. Exod.	Origen, *Selecta in Exodum* (*Excerpted Comments on Exodus*)
Sel. Ps.	Origen, *Selecta in Psalmos* (*Excerpted Comments on Psalms*)
Sera	Plutarch, *De sera numinis vindicta* (*On the Delays of the Divine Vengeance*)
Serm.	Augustine, *Sermones* (*Sermons*)
Sib. Or.	*Sibylline Oracles*
Silv.	Statius, *Silvae*
Somn.	Philo, *De somniis* (*On Dreams*)
Soph.	Isocrates, *In sophistas* (*Or. 13*)
SPNT	Studies on Personalities of the New Testament
Stromata	Clement of Alexandria, *Stromata* (*Miscellanies*)
Superst.	Plutarch, *De superstitione* (*On Superstition*)
suppl.	supplemented (by) or supplement
Symp.	Methodius of Olympus, *Symposium* (*Convivium decem virginum*)
T. Dan	*Testaments of the Twelve Patriarchs* (=*T. 12 Patr.*), *Testament of Dan*
T. Gad	*T. 12 Patr.*, *Testament of Gad*
T. Jud.	*T. 12 Patr.*, *Testament of Judah*
T. Levi	*T. 12 Patr.*, *Testament of Levi*
T. Mos.	*Testament of Moses*

T. Naph.	*T. 12 Patr.*, *Testament of Naphtali*
T. Reu.	*T. 12 Patr.*, *Testament of Reuben*
Theron, *Tradition*	Daniel J. Theron, *Evidence of Tradition* (Grand Rapids: Baker, 1957)
Tim.	Plato, *Timaeus*
Tract. ep. Jo.	Augustine, *In epistulam Johannis ad Parthos tractatus* (*Tractates on the First Epistle of John*)
Trin.	Didymus, *De Trinitate* (*On the Trinity*)
Trin.	Hilary of Poitiers, *De Trinitate* (*On the Trinity*)
UBS[4]	United Bible Societies, *Greek New Testament* (4th ed.; Stuttgart: Deutsche Bibelgesellschaft, 2001)
Ux.	Tertullian, *Ad uxorem* (*To His Wife*)
Virg.	Tertullian, *De virginibus velandis* (*The Veiling of Virgins*)
Vir. ill.	Jerome, *De viris illustribus* (*Concerning Illustrious Men*)
WA	Weimar edition of Luther's words (WA = Weimar Ausgabe), *D. Martin Luthers Werke: Kritische Gesamtausgabe* (69 vols.; Weimar: Böhlau, 1883–1997)

Biblical Books

Old Testament

Gen	Genesis	Isa	Isaiah
Exod	Exodus	Jer	Jeremiah
Lev	Leviticus	Lam	Lamentations
Num	Numbers	Ezek	Ezekiel
Deut	Deuteronomy	Dan	Daniel
Josh	Joshua	Hos	Hosea
Judg	Judges	Joel	Joel
Ruth	Ruth	Amos	Amos
1–2 Sam	1–2 Samuel	Obad	Obadiah
1–2 Kgs	1–2 Kings	Jonah	Jonah
1–2 Chr	1–2 Chronicles	Mic	Micah
Ezra	Ezra	Nah	Nahum
Neh	Nehemiah	Hab	Habakkuk
Esth	Esther	Zeph	Zephaniah
Job	Job	Hag	Haggai
Ps(s)	Psalms	Zech	Zechariah
Prov	Proverbs	Mal	Malachi
Eccl	Ecclesiastes		
Song (or Cant)	Song of Songs (Song of Solomon, or Canticles)		

Old Testament Apocrypha (OT pseudepigrapha cited in the text are included in master list above)

Bar	Baruch
Add Dan	Additions to Daniel
Pr Azar	Prayer of Azariah
Bel	Bel and the Dragon
Sg Three	Song of the Three Young Men
Sus	Susanna
1–2 Esd	1–2 Esdras
Add Esth	Additions to Esther
Ep Jer	Epistle of Jeremiah
Jdt	Judith
1–2 Macc	1–2 Maccabees
3–4 Macc	3–4 Maccabees
Pr Man	Prayer of Manasseh
Ps 151	Psalm 151
Sir	Sirach/Ecclesiasticus
Tob	Tobit
Wis	Wisdom of Solomon

New Testament

Matt	Matthew	1–2 Thess	1–2 Thessalonians
Mark	Mark	1–2 Tim	1–2 Timothy
Luke	Luke	Titus	Titus
John	John	Phlm	Philemon
Acts	Acts	Heb	Hebrews
Rom	Romans	Jas	James
1–2 Cor	1–2 Corinthians	1–2 Pet	1–2 Peter
Gal	Galatians	1–2–3 John	1–2–3 John
Eph	Ephesians	Jude	Jude
Phil	Philippians	Rev	Revelation
Col	Colossians		

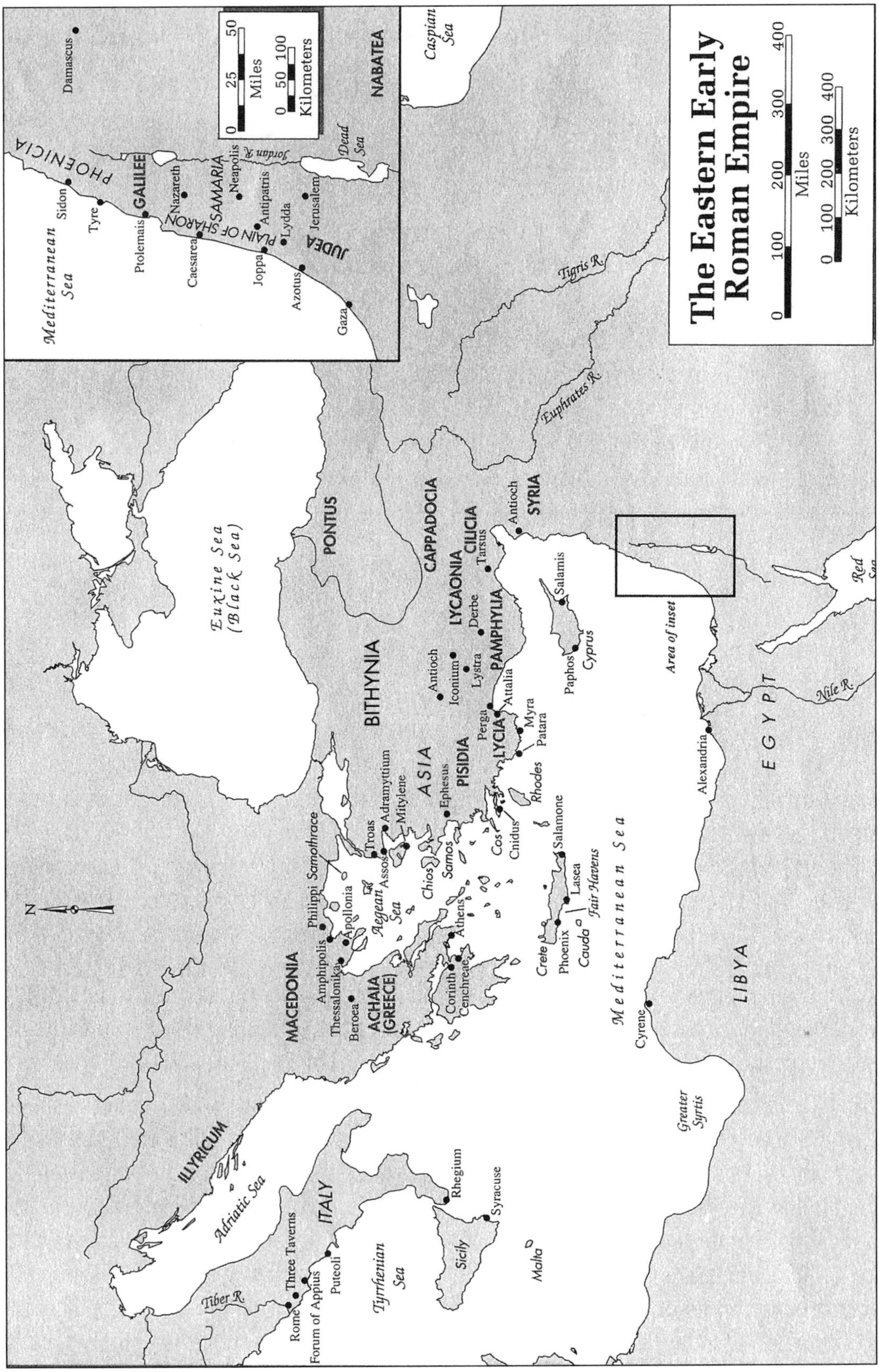

The Eastern Early Roman Empire
0 100 200 300 400
Miles
0 100 200 300 400
Kilometers
0 25 50
Miles
0 50 100
Kilometers
Mediterranean Sea
PHOENICIA
Sidon
Tyre
Ptolemais
GALILEE
Nazareth
Caesarea
PLAIN OF SHARON
SAMARIA
Neapolis
Antipatris
Lydda
Joppa
Azotus
Gaza
JUDEA
Jerusalem
Jordan R.
Dead Sea
Damascus
NABATEA
Caspian Sea
Tigris R.
Euphrates R.
Euxine Sea (Black Sea)
PONTUS
CAPPADOCIA
BITHYNIA
LYCAONIA
CILICIA
Tarsus
Antioch
SYRIA
Derbe
Lystra
Iconium
Antioch
PAMPHYLIA
Attalia
Perga
LYCIA
Myra
Patara
PISIDIA
ASIA
Ephesus
Adramyttium
Mitylene
Troas
Assos
Samothrace
Philippi
Apollonia
Amphipolis
Thessalonika
Beroea
MACEDONIA
ACHAIA (GREECE)
Aegean Sea
Chios
Samos
Athens
Corinth
Cenchreae
Cos
Cnidus
Rhodes
Salamone
Crete
Lasea
Fair Havens
Phoenix
Cauda
Cyprus
Salamis
Paphos
Area of inset
Alexandria
EGYPT
Nile R.
Red Sea
LIBYA
Cyrene
Greater Syrtis
Mediterranean Sea
ILLYRICUM
Adriatic Sea
ITALY
Rome
Three Taverns
Forum of Appius
Puteoli
Tiber R.
Tyrrhenian Sea
Rhegium
Syracuse
Sicily
Malta
N

Introduction

In this book I introduce readers to the twenty-seven writings of the New Testament. Although I presuppose little or no previous knowledge of these writings on the reader's part, I recognize that many readers have grown up with these texts. They may have been introduced to the New Testament through children's Bible story books and through a lifetime of hearing the stories read, taught, and preached in church. I have written for those who have read them many times but also for those who are reading them for the first time—and for those in between. Regardless of how familiar we are with these writings, we still need to be introduced to them in various settings.

Anyone writing such a book recognizes that the best "introduction" is to read the New Testament itself. There is no substitute for this direct encounter with these classic texts of the church. And yet, because these texts have been read for centuries and have exercised such vast influence within the Christian church and the broader culture, they have acquired a tradition of scholarly and popular interpretation that is of great interest to readers, especially students of the Bible. I have sought to acquaint readers not only with the contents of the New Testament but also with critical issues of interpretation. This is what is meant by labeling the work as a "critical introduction." It is introductory in the sense that it provides basic, elementary information about these writings and the centuries-long conversation that has been conducted about them. But it is critical in that it deals with interpretive issues relating to the literary, historical, social, and religious dimensions of the New Testament.

As the subtitle suggests, I have written this work for those interested in "interpreting the message and meaning of Jesus Christ." Much of the first four writings—the Gospels—concentrates on Jesus' teaching. But the remaining twenty-three writings also deal in different ways with the message of Jesus, both what he proclaimed as well as what was proclaimed about him. And if all twenty-seven writings are about anything, they are certainly about what the phrase "Jesus Christ" signifies. In this sense, each New Testament writing is an exercise in meaning-making. Regardless of differences in literary genre and historical-social settings out of which the writings arose, each one grapples with the meaning of Jesus Christ in its multiple dimensions. Often New Testament writers are trying to convey what Jesus meant when he spoke and taught. Others are more concerned to write about the meaning of his death and resurrection. They vigorously examine such questions as: What are the implications of early Christian claims that Jesus died and rose again on the third day? What metaphorical language best captures the meaning of this "Christ event"?

One of my major goals in the book is to explore the religious and theological dimensions of the New Testament writings. This does not mean neglecting or even minimizing the historical and literary questions normally treated in New Testament introductions. But it does mean approaching them differently. I am interested in the latter questions primarily as a way of getting at the former. In my discussion of each writing, I have tried to identify what is at stake theologically: how the "message" of the writing illuminates the religious convictions shared by the author(s) and reader(s).

I have devoted most of the book to the individual New Testament writings themselves. In some cases I have treated an individual writing—in others, a group of writings together. In every case, I have tried to orient the reader to the writings without providing a substitute for actually reading them. For reasons that I outline in the second chapter, I treat the writings roughly in the order in which they appear in the table of contents of our modern Bibles: first, the Gospels, then Acts, followed by the Pauline letters, the Letter to the Hebrews, the seven Catholic Letters, and Revelation. Within each category, I sometimes rearrange the order of treatment for reasons that I explain at the beginning of each section or chapter.

Throughout the book, I have given considerable attention to how the New Testament has been read and interpreted through the centuries. While this dimension is usually referred to as the "history of interpretation," it is more than mere historical review. Because the message and meaning of these writings over time have heavily influenced how readers in successive generations regard them, attending to this "afterlife" of the texts helps illuminate their religious and theological dimensions. I hope this benefits not only seminary students, who usually take courses in New Testament introduction or interpretation at roughly the same time they are being introduced to the history of the Christian church or to the history of Christian thought and doctrine, but also others who may not be as familiar with the role that New Testament writings have played in shaping the church's thought as well as that of the larger culture in the last two millennia.

Trying to write an introductory text that is also comprehensive is a delicate balancing act. This aim is complicated by my desire to address multiple audiences: undergraduate students enrolled in courses in the history and literature of early Christianity; seminary students being introduced to the New Testament, sometimes in courses lasting a quarter, a semester, or an academic year; ministers engaged in weekly interpretation and study of these writings with their congregations; and Bible school teachers and other serious students seeking to understand these writings themselves even as they help others understand them.

Several features of the book are more easily understandable in light of these multiple goals.

First a word about its length. For some thirty years, I have taught New Testament introduction to seminary students. In many other church and academic settings I have taught individual New Testament writings and themes. I cannot remember that students in any of these settings have complained about receiving too much material. On the contrary, regardless of how much I give them, they usually ask for more. Consequently, in each chapter I have tried to include what I regard as essential introductory information for understanding the writing or topic being discussed.

My desire to be comprehensive resulted in a printed manuscript of 900 pages, filled with detailed footnotes, extensive annotated bibliographies, numerous charts, diagrams, maps, and illustrative images. Over the years, I have found these to be invaluable resources for teaching the New Testament. Consequently, I have included them.

To make the volume both affordable and manageable, the editors and I decided to offer a printed edition that contains the essential introductory information. This we have designated the Standard Edition. The discussion is ample; the illustrations, charts, and diagrams are numerous; the notes are minimal; and the bibliography is highly selective. Our aim is to give substantive introductory material that is informative, inviting, and interesting. We assume that readers who come to this material will have already read the relevant New Testament writing(s). My hope is that the discussion will prompt them to return to the biblical text and read it with even more interest, curiosity, and imagination than before.

Recognizing that virtually every writing or topic discussed in the Standard Edition has deeper levels of complexity, we have included additional resource material in the Expanded CD-ROM Version of the book. This is indicated within the text of the Standard Edition by a parenthetical notation referring the reader to the CD and giving the appropriate page number(s). For example, in the discussion of the synoptic problem in chapter 3, after a brief discussion of the hypothetical sayings source "Q," the reader who is interested in seeing a complete listing of passages that constitute Q is referred to pages 55–59 in the CD, which contain the table "Probable Contents of Q." Similarly, in chapter 15 (Romans), the reader who desires a more complete discussion of the problematic topic "the righteousness of God" is referred to the fuller discussion on pages 499–502 in the CD, "Righteousness of God: Ambiguity within Biblical Thought."

Supplementing the basic bibliographies given at the end of each chapter in the Standard Edition are the lengthy annotated bibliographies found in the Expanded CD-ROM Version. In these annotations I have given my evaluation of the relevant literature and how I see the overall scholarly debate. I also try to indicate the bibliographical sources that have been especially helpful to me in writing that chapter. In the chapters devoted to the New Testament writings themselves, I have devoted separate categories to "Commentaries" and "Books and Articles" to assist users in finding the resources they need for further study. I have also placed an asterisk beside items that I especially recommend for purchase. These are typically bibliographical items that have an introductory focus or that have become widely accepted as standard reading material. These recommendations are intended to assist students, ministers, church librarians, and others in building their own libraries. In making these recommendations, I have tried to ask whether an individual item would have genuine lasting value, that is, whether it would be worth consulting and re-consulting over time.

While the Standard Edition contains some endnotes following each chapter, the Expanded CD Version contains the complete set of annotations on each chapter.

These endnotes are rich in primary references, especially to patristic authors. But they also contain numerous references to the Old and New Testaments, as well as to the Old Testament apocryphal and pseudepigraphical writings, early Christian apocrypha, and classical texts from antiquity. In several places, for example, chapter 3 (Relating the Gospels to Each Other), I have gathered in the endnotes carefully chosen references to illustrate different problems. Instructors who need examples of significant differences or agreements within the Synoptic Gospels, or well-known examples of Minor Agreements, will find passages in the endnotes that can serve as the focus for discussion groups. Similarly, I have placed in the endnotes much of the technical discussion relating to such questions as the Pauline authorship of the disputed letters, especially the Pastoral Letters.

Some additional diagrams and illustrations are also found in the Expanded CD Version, along with the two appendices containing ancient canonical lists and patristic testimony relating to the Gospels. The comprehensive index included in the CD is designed to assist readers in doing computer searches. By gathering into a single index significant proper names, topics, and technical terms, we have sought to provide a comprehensive "map" of the Expanded Version.

We have tried to make the CD as user-friendly as possible by providing the full, expanded text of the book in PDF format. The user simply needs to have the widely available Adobe Acrobat Reader software installed (a link to download the software is provided on the CD) to access the full text. From the main menu, the user can go directly to the detailed table of contents, browse the full text, or view the full text's index. The table of contents is linked to the text, so the user is able to click on the heading, sub-heading, or sub-sub-heading within each chapter and be taken to the corresponding section of the text. In the "Browse" section, the user is provided with lists of the images, maps, and diagrams, as well as a list of the CD Exclusives, which are links to fuller discussions of sections within the Standard Edition of the text corresponding to the parenthetical notations within the text. The "Browse" section also allows a user to go directly to a page number, perform a full-text search within individual chapters, and print a page or specified set of pages directly.

We have designed the Standard Edition and the Expanded CD Version to be used in tandem. Working from the Standard Edition, the user is able to find the desired information in the CD quickly. For example, one might read about the synoptic problem in the Standard Edition of the text and want to learn more about the hypothetical document "Q." The user could then go to the Expanded CD Version, click on "Browse," select the CD Extra that corresponds to the parenthetical notation within the Standard Edition, and be taken to the precise point where the Expanded CD Version supplements the Standard Edition's discussion of "Q." By embedding the Standard Edition within the Expanded Version, we have made it possible to find one's way in both editions of the book.

Deciding what should be included in the respective editions of the book has not been easy. By no means does the CD contain only advanced technical discussion. Much of this is found in the Standard Edition. But neither does the Standard Edition contain the "wheat" from which the "chaff" of the Expanded Version has been removed. Plenty of rich, detailed discussion occurs in the CD. Parts of it are supplemental, but much of it is just as basic as the material in the Standard Edition. The Standard Edition and the Expanded Version should be used in relation to each other: the former to give basic orientation and information; the latter to amplify the discussion; both to enrich each other.

Designing the book in this manner represents a bold editorial move by Abingdon Press. In some ways, it represents the changing face of academic publishing. This decision recognizes the degree to which all learning is being transformed by improved and constantly changing technologies. While there were several considerations in making this decision, our main concern is pedagogical: to find efficient, interesting, and illuminating ways to interpret the message and meaning of Jesus Christ through the use of a critical introduction to the New Testament.

[For discussion of the arrangement and contents of the full, expanded text, see Expanded CD Version pp. 1–4: *Introduction*]

Part 1

THEOLOGY
AND
SCRIPTURE

Chapter 1

The New Testament as Theological Writings

"Christian theology is the fully reflective understanding of the Christian witness of faith as decisive for human existence."

Schubert Ogden

"[The New Testament writings] are theological as actualizations of the unique revelation that preceded them."

Willi Marxsen

Theology may be thought of in different ways. If we ask someone, "What is your theology?" we are probably asking about that person's religious beliefs. In the strictest sense, we would be asking what the person believes about God, since "theology" technically means "discourse about God."[1] But the term can include beliefs about other divine or semidivine beings, such as angels or devils. It can also encompass beliefs about human beings: whether we are inherently good or evil; why we behave the way we do; how we deal with our sins; how we relate to God and neighbor; and what happens to us when we die. These are only a few of the standard topics—theological loci—encompassed by the term "theology."

But how do we arrive at what we believe? How do we come to have a theology? Quite simply, by doing theology. By shifting the verb from having to doing, we point to the process through which we arrive at our theological beliefs. When we subscribe to a particular creed, we may be struck by its simple formulation. How we have come to adopt it, however, may not be so simple. We may have undergone a period of religious instruction to learn about the elements that comprise the statement of faith. Prior to that, we may have undergone a radical conversion experience or perhaps have come to faith more gradually. In either case, religious conversion has a ripple effect that touches all aspects of our lives, simplifying them in some respects, complicating them in others. The process of moving from "believing in" to "believing that" may turn out to be quite complex.

We might also reflect for a moment on how a statement of faith arises. We may be impressed by its cadence, its smoothly turned phrases, and even its poetic quality, but this surface simplicity masks the rich, often long, history that led to its formulation. Seemingly simple combinations of words may have resulted from lengthy church controversies that turned on a single word or phrase, or even on a single letter. Competing formulations may have created deep divisions within the church that caused sharp debates and required the convening of church councils. Statements of faith have usually arisen from a long, complex process in which the church as a whole struggled to express its "belief in" as "belief that."

Whether we think of an individual believer who comes to faith or of an entire church that formulates its beliefs in a creedal statement, the process of clarifying belief may be thought of as doing theology. But why the verb "doing"? Why not simply "having"? Because to have a theology means that we have made some decisions about certain things to believe. To that extent, they are fixed decisions. Even if we find ourselves rolling them over in our heads in light of different life experiences, they are still reference points to which we return. How we think about them may change, but the fundamental item of belief remains constant. Taken together, these beliefs frame our house of faith.

Life is never static, however, and faith remains dynamic by responding to new questions. We find that the points of belief to which we have committed ourselves, perhaps many years ago, constantly need clarification. To say that we believe in God the Father may express our fundamental belief in God, but we find ourselves asking whether "the Father" is the only, or even the best, way of attributing reality to God. We may ask, "What does this metaphor actually mean?" or "Are there less traditional but equally profound ways of expressing our faith in God?" These questions may be prompted by life around us, by our conversations with other believers, and by struggles within the church over what language is most appropriate for talking about God. As we pursue these questions openly, we seek to clarify, refine, and enrich our basic convictions. In doing so, we may draw on many resources as we do theology.

The questions that prompt us to do theology arise from many quarters. They may derive from our own personal quests, but they often arise within the church. Perhaps our congregation is trying to decide an issue relating to its own life together. Our denomination may be facing an issue with broad ramifications for church policy and for the ways people think about themselves, their fellow Christians, and how they will speak about God, Christ, and the Spirit. However these questions originate, we find ourselves trying to think about them in light of our faith commitments. We find them challenging our faith as well as requiring a response from our faith.

Responding *faithfully* means more than simply repeating our statements of faith. We talk with others to clarify what we believe and to formulate our faith in light of these newly raised issues. We also find ourselves reading—going to our church libraries as well as our public libraries—to educate ourselves further about these issues. What we read may vary widely, ranging from the works of Christians who lived centuries ago to the writings of contemporary theologians. We find ourselves praying alone and with others as we try to discern what is at stake for faith and life. In short, we use virtually every resource imaginable as we seek to clarify what and how we believe about a particular issue.

The process of theological discernment is not a theoretical process. It is not as though we simply sit down and think. That we do, but we also act. We talk with others; we do research; we pray; we worship; we continue to make a living; we go to movies, art galleries, and sports events. Through this tangle of events and experiences we try to gain greater clarity about our beliefs. As we give shape to our thoughts, we put them into words and behave in ways that express those beliefs. All of this is involved in doing theology. What makes it "doing"? The ongoing activity. What makes it theology? That it is ultimately about God and from God.

To say that we formulate patterns of behavior that reflect our beliefs introduces yet a third dimension: *living* our theology. In one sense, this behavioral element is inseparable from *having* and *doing* theology. Even as we do theology we are expressing our faith in action. Still, we can distinguish this third element as a discrete aspect of theology. At the risk of gross oversimplification, we can say that *having* a theology is an essentially cognitive act. At a critical point, it is a matter of intellectual assent. *Doing* theology, while involving cognitive activity, may be thought of as an essentially practical act. It involves specific practices that have been developed over time as the church has related faith to life.

While doing theology may appear to be intuitive, random, and even somewhat unpredictable, it actually implies certain well-defined theological practices that have been shaped in a variety of contexts, including churches, schools, homes, and various public institutions. To take just one example, biblical interpretation has occurred for centuries, yielding its own set of rules and practices that are widely recognized, even if they are practiced differently. Or, when we engage in thought, we use principles of logic and common sense that constitute a set of assumptions that is widely shared, even among archrivals. We all recognize inconsistency as something we avoid rather than strive for. And so on. Without developing an entire taxonomy of theological practices, we can see how doing theology both presupposes and utilizes such practices. They include cognitive activity, but they include much more.

In contrast to having a theology and doing theology, living a theology is behavioral in a way that neither of the other two is. As indicated earlier, it includes patterns of behavior that are consonant with our beliefs but also are expressive of them. Typically this aspect of theology encompasses the field of ethics: how we behave as individuals and as communities of faith. Behavior should be understood to encompass both thoughts and actions. Forming attitudes can be thought of as a behavior, even though the most conspicuous forms of behavior are those that express our underlying attitudes. By patterns of behavior, however, we refer primarily to how we act: how we worship, both in public and private; what we say; how we relate to others, whether we embrace or exclude them, protect or harm them; how we form communities or institutions that serve to promote our faith; how we form families; how we play; and how we rejoice and mourn.

These behaviors along with many others are the means by which theology is lived. If there were some way to consider our behaviors comprehensively and look for consistent themes in how we behave, we would discover the theology that lies behind them. If we have any doubt about how closely correlated having a theology and living a theology are, we need to consider only some of its more conspicuous examples. In the ancient world, the members of the Qumran community, who separated themselves from what they regarded as the corrupt religious leadership associated with the temple in Jerusalem, expressed their theology in quite remarkable behavioral patterns. They lived together as a sectarian community, they engaged in certain communal practices, they followed their own calendar, they worshiped in a certain way, and they read the Jewish Bible in a distinctive way. This example simply confirms what we already know at an experiential level: that the theology we have and the theology we live are inseparably connected. In fact, each affects the other quite dramatically.

To say that theology is discourse about God suggests that there is an underlying reality—God—who serves as more than the topic of theology. When we say that we believe in God, we are doing more than setting the conversation topic; we are identifying God as our conversation partner. Behind every confession of faith is belief in the Living God, even if this is expressed in a Trinitarian form that also encompasses Christ the Son and the Holy Spirit. When we engage in doing theology, we are doing more than thinking and talking about God. Through it all, we are trying to make sense of God, the Someone beyond us all. To say that God transcends us suggests that God exists independently of any one of us. Taken seriously, this means that God is not something or someone we construct in our heads, even if we think constantly about God. Trying to understand who God is and to discern how God is present and active in the world is the central task of theology. The Living God is the primary Subject of theology, serving both as the One whom we adore and the One whom we discuss. It is possible to think and talk about God with great sophistication and yet not believe in God. Thought and conversation about God, however, take a different form when they stem from belief in God. At the heart of theology, in any of its forms—having, doing, and living—is the Living God who is finally the source and goal of our intellectual longing.

Christian Theology: Believing in Christ

To speak of *Christian* theology narrows the focus of our discussion, for it implies that God has been revealed through the figure Jesus Christ. Classic formulations of this belief, such as "God was in Christ reconciling the world to God's Self" (2 Cor 5:19; my translation), render more precisely the ways God is present in the world. Among the most pressing questions is how to think of Jesus Christ in relation to God. Naturally it is a question Christian believers have considered from many different angles over the centuries: Is Christ God? If so, in what sense? How do their essential natures compare? Has Christ always been God, or was this a status he had to attain?

"God at work in Christ" suggests the notion of delegated authority, in which one person carries out the work of someone in a higher position. Whether Christ is thought of in highly personal terms, such as God's Son, or in less personal terms, such as God's *Logos*, he is seen as the one through whom God's work is accomplished. To the extent that Christ is privy to God's desires, he provides clues to who God is.

Understanding how God has been revealed in Jesus Christ and how God has been experienced as present in the world through Jesus Christ is the special task of

Christian theology. Among the many resources available to anyone engaged in this task, the twenty-seven writings of the New Testament (NT) occupy a unique position. With a few possible exceptions, they are the earliest writings that reflect this distinctive perspective. Eventually they acquired canonical status throughout the church, which means that they were regarded as uniquely normative in a way that other writings were not. As the title New Testament suggests, they were intended to be read alongside the Old Testament and thus were given a privileged status among the many early Christian writings.

It is fully appropriate to approach the NT as a set of writings that bear witness to "God at work in Christ." If they are about anything, they are surely about this. Rather than trying to prove that God exists or that God has been active in the world, they assume both. They do not assume that God has been *generally* present in the world, but rather that God's tracks are most visibly present in Israel—its people and their history—as abundantly illustrated in the Jewish Scriptures. This earlier story of how God chose Israel and nurtured their growth as God's people is regarded by the NT writers as a prelude to the story of Jesus Christ. The Jewish Scriptures are seen as earlier chapters of a larger story that continues into the time of Jesus Christ. The NT writings express it in different ways, but they confidently place Jesus Christ in Israel's line of succession leading all the way back to Adam and including such notable figures as Abraham, Isaac, Jacob, Joseph, Moses, and David. They regard Jesus Christ, however, as more than another link in the chain of successors. They see him as the culmination of the line—the last link in the chain.

For the NT writers, the Jewish Scriptures are more than a collection of proof texts that point forward to a future Messiah. Rather, they unfold the history of God's people as a series of ups and downs, as alternating cycles of obedience and disobedience, of exile and return. Reading the Jewish Scriptures as recurring cycles in which God's people are alternately faithful and unfaithful and in which God is constantly faithful, early Christians saw patterns of behavior in Israel's past that were repeated in later generations. Bondage in Egypt led to the exodus, but newfound freedom became bondage in the wilderness. Deliverance from the wilderness led to the promised land, but the promise gave way to an unanticipated monarchy. Capture gave way to exile, and exile to return. Through it all, Israel saw deliverers appear and reappear and experienced salvation time and again. Early Christians saw these "types" continued in the story of Jesus and his followers, a story that presented its own version of obedience and disobedience, rejection and restoration.

"God at work in Christ" aptly captures the NT's angle of vision: The God who was powerfully at work in creation, in the call of Abraham, and in the many ups and downs of Israel's turbulent love affair with God once again appears in Jesus Christ. This basic claim is filled out in two directions by the NT writers. They identify persons and events in both the remote and recent past that led up to the story of Jesus. They compare Jesus favorably with figures such as Moses and David; for these writers, John the Baptist is seen as Jesus' immediate predecessor. They also carry the story forward beyond the time of Jesus' death to show how his disciples continue the work he began.

The NT writers naturally focus on Jesus himself—what he did and said and what was done to him. The death of Jesus—including the circumstances that led to his death and reactions to it by both friend and foe—occupies much of their attention. At a deeper level, the NT writers probe the significance of Jesus' death, often struggling to find appropriate metaphors to express its significance. One of the most poignant and profound metaphors, sacrifice, is developed in several different directions.

For all of their preoccupation with Jesus' death, the NT writers extend the Jesus story into the period beyond his death. In doing so, they reveal a fundamental presupposition of all NT writings: God raised Jesus from the dead. This may be expressed in the formulaic language of preaching, confession, prayer, and singing, or it may take the form of a proposition that is defended in the heat of debate. Either way, the NT writers are expressing their conviction that after Jesus died, he experienced a form of aliveness that was unique and God-given. Early Christians placed Jesus' resurrection in a different category from other afterlife experiences, such as the ascensions of Enoch and Elijah or instances of a person being restored to life (cf. 1 Kgs 17:7–24; 2 Kgs 4:8–37; John 11). What set Jesus apart from these other figures, in their view, was that he experienced both death and life in a way no one else had—he truly died, yet he experienced an unprecedented form of new life.

Early Christians attributed the miracle of Jesus' new life to God. The language they use to describe it varies, yet they frequently describe the event in the passive voice: *Jesus was raised* (see, however, Mark 8:31; 9:9, 31; Acts 10:41; 1 Thess 4:14). When they express this conviction in the active voice, God is the subject: "God raised Jesus from the dead." They do not claim that Jesus raised himself. By such careful and consistent use of language, either when expressing their own beliefs or when reporting the beliefs of other early Christians, the NT writers attest the theological conviction that Jesus experienced newness of life uniquely as God's gift. As an instance of divine intervention, Jesus' resurrection occurred by God's power.

Convinced of Jesus' resurrection, NT writers also report that Jesus' disciples continued to experience his presence as more than the memory of a dead friend or revered teacher. How the disciples experience Jesus' continued presence takes different forms, as we see in the variety of ways the NT writers report these experiences. They consistently claim, however, that Jesus is among them as a living, active presence who motivates, teaches, guides, and comforts them.

Not surprisingly, the NT writers devote a lot of attention to what Jesus *continues to do* after his death. Like God, Jesus is for them not only the object of reflection but also an energizing presence among them. He too is both conversation topic and conversation partner. Early Christians pray to him, but they also talk about him. We see the story of Jesus continued in narrative form in the Acts of the Apostles, in which Jesus' disciples emerge as a movement with enough visibility and continuity to be recognized as a distinct religious community. In other parts of the NT we also see evidence of the continued presence of Jesus, often where communities of believers who confess him as Lord are trying to shape their lives in ways that express this faith. Typically, they work with both a backward and a forward perspective informed by their belief in Jesus Christ. Jesus' life, death, and resurrection have become pivotal reference points for them. Looking back, early Christians remembered these events and shaped them into memorable accounts that embodied their memory of his deeds and words and what made them significant.

Something about these events also defined their perception of the future. We find early Christians looking forward to the end of time when God would once again intervene decisively in history. As we might expect, this event is also variously understood in the NT, but Jesus Christ is expected to play a decisive role in the events relating to the end of history. Often designated as Jesus' second coming, this event becomes a significant conviction informing and shaping Christian behavior. The extent to which Jesus himself is responsible for these views of the future and the role he is to play in them are much debated. Even so, it is a conviction that finds expression in various NT writings, which suggests that it was a widely held conviction among early Christians. In this way, the Jesus story acquired an afterlife that was expected to continue until the end of time.

Because "God at work in Christ" encompasses much more than the actual lifetime of the first-century figure Jesus of Nazareth, Christian theology takes into account what happened before and after Jesus lived. Jesus as a figure of the past occupies a central place in Christian theology, but so does Jesus as a figure who transcends the past. To speak of Jesus as Savior entails thinking about Jesus' death as a past event with consequences that continue into the present and future, but it also requires us to think of his saving work as something unbounded by time, as that which occurs continuously.

Theology, then, is something we do as we bring our convictions about God to consciousness and express them in language drawn from our own time and experience. As these beliefs take definite form, we may be said to have a theology. Having a theology results from doing theology, and living a theology results from both. When Jesus Christ becomes the primary lens through which we view God, we do theology in a specifically Christian mode. We find ourselves pressed to clarify a wide range of questions, many of them having to do with how Jesus Christ relates to God and how this set of beliefs is actualized in living communities of faith—how belief in Christ is lived.

The Theological Conversation

To say that God is the object of our theological reflection need not mean that God is passive. On the contrary, God is better seen as the One who triggers our theological reflection. We can be actively in relation to God at many levels: responding to God's call, praising God in prayer and song, asking for God's forgiveness, seeking God's guidance for our lives, and enlisting God's mercy for the sick and needy. These representative actions of faith are prompted by God even though we actually do them.

When we say that the central task of theology is to understand who God is and to discern God's presence and action in the world, we are affirming the reality of the Living God within our midst. When we claim that "God is at work in Christ," we are affirming the reality of the Living Christ in our world. What stands behind all of our theological reflections, then, are Living Realities whose Spirit prompts us to express our faith.

Returning to the metaphor of conversation, we can think of theology as a conversation we have *about* God based on an ongoing conversation we have *with* God. What we say and think about God derives ultimately from our experience of the Living

God. Yet theological reflection involves more than notes from a journal in which we have recorded impressions of our encounters with God. However profound such encounters may be, they do not occur in a vacuum. Nor do we reflect on them by drawing on images and resources that we alone generate, however fertile our minds may be. If we stand within the tradition of Israel and the church, Scripture provides a rich resource for us. In many ways, the Jewish Scriptures are the record of the conversation between God and Israel from the time of Israel's emergence as a people. At the very least, they illuminate that conversation.

If we imagine a person or a community of faith engaging in theological reflection, seeking to articulate their understanding of their religious experience, we can envision this as a conversation taking place between the believer or community of believers and God. Although this relationship can be understood in many different ways and the conversation between the believer and God can take many different forms, this "I-Thou" relationship is the driving force of all theological reflection. At the heart of theology is "believing in."

When we look at the experience of Israel and the church as reflected in the Jewish and Christian Scriptures, we can identify several distinct elements that inform and help give shape to their theological reflection. While these elements are not always easily distinguished from each other, each one is distinctive enough to be considered separately.

Text and Tradition

By "text," we mean a written text that has come to be regarded as uniquely normative by a community of faith. By "tradition," we mean a set of interpretations and practices that have developed around a text, but also that may extend beyond the text. Tradition may also include interpretations, stories, and liturgies that grow out of the life of the people and form around their central beliefs. We should not distinguish too sharply between text and tradition since traditions of interpretation based on a sacred text may themselves later be regarded as sacred texts. Even so, the basic distinction can be made.

Text. It is not necessary to rehearse how sacred texts emerged within ancient Israel and then gave rise to sets of interpretation, even though this is a fascinating story. By the mid-first century C.E. when the earliest NT writings began to appear, the Jewish Scriptures were already widely accepted by Jews as a sacred text. This was especially the case with the first five books—the Torah—and to some extent the other two main sections, the Prophets and the Writings. Since Christianity originated as a reform movement within first-century Judaism, it inherited the Jewish Scriptures as its sacred text. Luke's story of Jesus in the synagogue at Nazareth, reading a text from Isaiah, then interpreting it for his audience, captures the image of Jesus as an interpreter of Scripture (Luke 4:16–30). The NT writers frequently refer to the Jewish Scriptures, and this frequency of usage provides some gauge of the authority attached to them. This is clearly reflected in the formula often used by the NT writers to introduce scriptural texts, "It is written," a phrase that is the functional equivalent of "God says."

The extent to which Scripture informed the earliest stages of Christian theological reflection is seen in 1 Cor 15:3–5, a four-part summary of Christian belief that predates Paul. Two parts—the death and resurrection of Christ—are said to have occurred "in accordance with the scriptures." While we do not know which scriptural texts are in view, we catch glimpses elsewhere in the NT of how early Christians used Scripture to make sense of these two central tenets of their belief. How they did so is by no means uniform or simple. We find them quoting from all three sections of the Jewish Bible, even though they use some parts more frequently than others. Their interpretations are often highly creative, even puzzling to modern readers, but no more imaginative or puzzling than interpretations we find in other first-century religious groups. Without trying to summarize the complex process of early Christian scriptural interpretation, here we can simply note how central an activity it was for them. For Jesus and his early followers, the Jewish Scriptures provided one of the most important resources for theological reflection available to them.

Tradition. Rarely, if ever, do readers confront texts that have not been interpreted previously. When readers are aware of these interpretations, they take them into account as they read and interpret the texts afresh. In the NT we also see evidence that traditions of interpretation had already begun to develop around the Jewish Scriptures. These traditions became an important resource for early Christian theological reflection.

One form of scriptural interpretation occurs when a text is translated from one language into another. By the first century C.E., the Jewish Scriptures had already been translated from Hebrew into Greek, and this Greek translation, the Septuagint (LXX), was widely used both inside and outside Palestine. Naturally it served as the Bible for Greek-speaking Jews, and it could be found in Jewish synagogues all over the Mediterranean world, especially those where Greek was the primary language. Even though the NT writers show some familiarity with the Hebrew text of the Jewish Scriptures, they primarily use the LXX. Those places where the LXX renders the Hebrew text more as an interpretation than a strict translation are instances of tradition. And when the NT makes use of such passages in the LXX, it is drawing on tradition.

Another form of tradition is represented by a genre of texts called biblical paraphrases. Unlike translations, these writings take a biblical text and amplify it, sometimes by changing the text, sometimes by adding details or even episodes not found in the biblical text. What results is a more fully expanded version of the text. Classic examples of this genre are *Jubilees*, the Qumran text *Genesis Apocryphon*, and Aramaic translations or paraphrases of the OT known as Targums.

However, tradition-dependent works are more commonly identified with interpretations or collections of interpretations based on a text, rather than free translations or expanded paraphrases of a text that reflect some interpretive perspective. Perhaps best known in this regard are the rabbinic interpretations of the Jewish Scriptures collected in the Babylonian and Palestinian (Jerusalem) Talmuds. Even though the collecting and editing of these interpretations occurred well after the NT period, many of them likely derived from this period or even earlier. They may well serve as resources for early Christian theological reflection.

As noted earlier, tradition can be understood in a broader sense than simply that of traditions of text interpretations. In ancient Israel, worship practices gave rise to traditions, as did certain persons or events. Legends and lore might be connected to Israel's sacred text, but they might also arise independently of it.

Context

Understood as the setting within which theological reflection occurs, context can be understood broadly or narrowly. Broadly speaking, it includes all of those elements that define a given society: time and place, as well as political, social, economic, and religious realities that are expressed in institutional forms such as monarchies, families, clans, schools, museums, banks, and temples. Narrowly speaking, it refers to recognizable social settings that are usually defined by an institutional structure. An educational or catechetical setting implies the existence of a school; a liturgical setting implies a temple, sanctuary, or church where people worship; and a forensic setting usually suggests a law court or some legal setting in which conflicts are adjudicated. These are only a few of the social settings within which one might imagine theological reflection taking place. To some extent, they will be microcosms of the broader cultural setting, yet each setting will have its own dynamic and rules that govern behavior. Language is used one way in a liturgical setting, for example, and in quite another way in a forensic setting.

Context exercises a decisive influence on theological reflection. Distinct forms of theological language, such as hymns, prayers, confessions, readings, and sermons, develop within different liturgical settings. Since each genre expresses a slightly different aspect of the "I-Thou" conversation, each develops a distinctive literary shape. The lines between them may be slightly blurred, yet we can tell the difference between a prayer and a sermon, a Scripture reading and a confession of faith.

If we think of the different settings in which people do theology, we can imagine scribes or other religious professionals engaging in religious debate; worshipers reciting prayers or even formulating new prayers; religious teachers explaining various facets of their beliefs to students and to other teachers; parents instructing their children in their faith, telling them stories and answering their children's questions; and preachers proclaiming their beliefs in formally gathered religious communities or in more casual settings, such as marketplaces, shops, or homes. These are only some of the many contexts in which theological reflection is done. For our purposes, what is important is to recognize how each setting informs the theological reflection that is done in that setting and how the setting gives distinctive shape to such reflection.

Interpreter

At the center of theological reflection is the "I-Thou" conversation that takes place between the believer and God. It is the believer, however, who seeks to discern the presence and activity of God in the world and, by using contemporary language, to articulate how this occurs. The believer may receive insight from God, but it is the believer, not God, who finally must put such insight into words. Humans do theology; God prompts it.

As we have seen, believers may draw on numerous resources in giving shape to their theological understanding. Primary among these are the text that the believer's community of faith holds sacred and the body of interpretations that have formed around it. To give precision to our theological beliefs, we enter into conversation both with the text and the tradition, drawing on both for images, ideas, and themes that help us give shape to what we believe. At one level, our task is to retrieve relevant materials from the text and tradition and accurately describe them. At another level, however, we employ what we find there to assist us in expressing our beliefs in our own words. In the former case, our task is descriptive; in the latter case, it is constructive.

To do the latter, we draw heavily on our own context. We use the language of our own time and relevant ideas from many fields of study, such as art, literature, history, and philosophy, to assist us in articulating our faith. We may also draw on the world around us—popular culture in all of its fascinating varieties, proverbial wisdom that has been transmitted through families or schools, and conversations from a variety of settings. Taken as a whole, our context provides a rich supply of images and ideas on which we can draw to do theology.

Regardless of the form that our theological reflection finally takes, it bears our own imprint. We may have drawn on numerous resources to help us shape our beliefs, but we finally put our beliefs into our own words. As our theology passes through the sieve of our own personality, it becomes a reflection of who we are. Because theological formulations bear the signature of their chief architects, it is possible to characterize them accordingly. When we speak of Pauline theology or Johannine theology in the NT, we are recognizing the close connection between these interpreters and their theological formulations.

The creative role of the interpreter should be noted. It is the interpreter who brings all of the pieces together and shapes them into meaningful theological language. It is the interpreter who engages in theological sense-making, and the interpretation that emerges is usually more than the sum of the many parts that have gone into it. Even the least imaginative interpreter who simply collects texts and traditions and draws more or less haphazardly on the larger context leaves an imprint on the final interpretation. The very act of pulling together disparate strands of material and arranging them in some identifiable sequence can be a creative one.

Summary

If doing theology is the process through which we formulate what we believe, we now see that it results from the interplay of several distinct elements. We may say that *Christian theological reflection results when interpreters, either an individual believer or a community of believers, engage in conversation with a sacred text and tradition, broadly construed, in order to make sense of, and give formal expression to, their experience and understanding of "God at work in Christ" within a specific context.*

Understood this way, theology is not something that we can easily extract from the NT writings. As we have already noted, in one sense they all derive from a

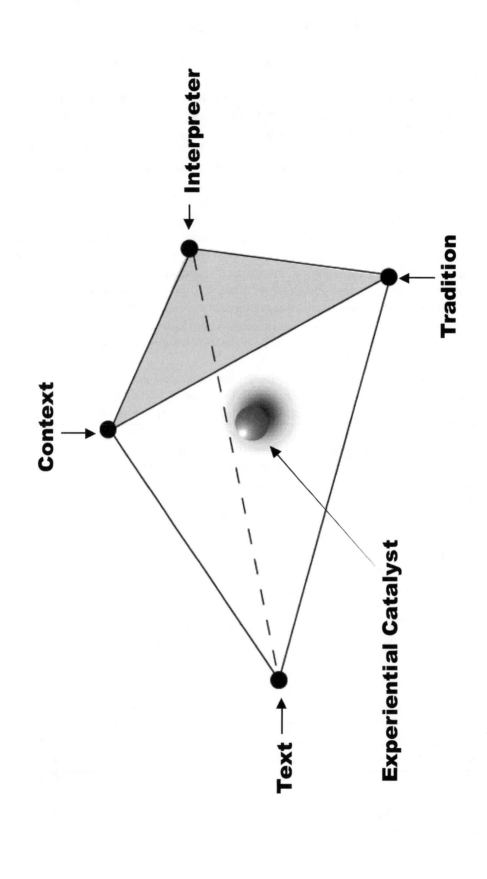

conviction that "God is at work in Christ." In their various ways, they work out the implications of this conviction and develop theological formulations appropriate to their audience and setting. In this sense, they are pervasively theological. But where do we locate their theology? We have access to it only through the final form of the texts that comprise the NT canon, but how does it reside there? Is it something that can be extracted from the text? Getting at the theology of the NT, or more important, getting at how the NT writers do theology, requires more than sifting through these texts and finding how they develop various theological themes, such as Christology, soteriology, and eschatology. This may be a helpful way of summarizing major theological emphases or perspectives in the text, but it fails to do justice to the richness and complexity of the process of theological sense-making that has gone into producing the text.

It is now widely recognized that the NT writings, like their OT counterparts, have often gone through several stages of editorial redaction, although to a lesser degree. Even though we have only the final form of the text, scholars have been able to identify earlier strata within the text. They have also made plausible suggestions about its earlier stages of formation. The NT writers often use telltale formulaic expressions to indicate that they are drawing on earlier material that they inherited from their predecessors. In such cases it is necessary to distinguish between the theological outlook that is reflected in this earlier material and that of the author or final editor. It might be argued that when a NT author uses the earlier material, it becomes part of the author's theological formulation. Even so, we flatten the process of theological reflection if we fail to distinguish between earlier traditions and an author's later reappropriation of those traditions. At the very least we should be attentive to the process through which an author appropriates and further develops earlier theological formulations.

There is another reason why it is sometimes difficult to extract the theology of a text from its final edited form. Quite often there are theological claims within a single text that are in tension with each other. This may occur because one part of the text draws on an earlier tradition whose outlook is not fully compatible with that of the author or final editor. In such cases, diverse theological viewpoints have not been fully integrated. In other cases, tensions within a text may exist because the author has not resolved them completely. Whenever this occurs, it becomes difficult to summarize the position of the text or the author under the rubric, "the author's theology of *x*." An author may include a theological formulation without having fully embraced it or incorporated it into his or her overall theological point of view. Other formulations, by contrast, may be much more fully developed and worked out with much greater consistency.

To speak of the theology of Matthew, for example, or of any other Gospel may be more problematic than it seems. Such language may imply that all of the theological formulations and claims within the Gospel can be attached to a specific individual or community of faith. It may also suggest a much more unified picture than a detailed analysis of the text actually yields. Finally, it may obscure a far more complex process of theological sense-making than we imagine.

Because NT writings display a consistent interest in behavior, it is also necessary to take into account how these texts yield a lived theology. This is not simply a matter of identifying ethical instructions in the various writings or even identifying underlying ethical norms that are expressed in various ways. It is rather to identify the ways belief and behavior are connected, to explore the dynamic relationship between them, and to account for the distinctive ethical concerns in each writing. Taking into account the ethical dimension of NT writings requires us to take seriously the NT's pervasive interest in the "lived life."

Catalysts for Theological Reflection

In the model of theological reflection we have sketched above, we have identified several crucial elements: the interpreter (individual believer or community of believers) in an "I-Thou" conversation with the Living God, informed by a conversation with text and tradition set within a specific context construed either broadly or narrowly.

This process is usually triggered by some specific event. It may be some crisis within the life of the believer or the community—an unexpected death, a breach of trust, a broken relationship, or an argument. It may be a crisis within the larger society—a war; a famine, an earthquake, or some other natural disaster; repressive measures taken by a hostile government against one's religious group; or an economic crisis. It may be a question asked by someone inside or outside the community—a question about a text, a religious practice, or a belief. It need not be a crisis at all. It may be a celebration—the coronation of a king, a sick child getting well, or some memorable achievement or accomplishment. It may be a combination of several of these elements.

Without trying to catalog all the possible catalysts or classify them according to types, suffice it to say that the process of theological reflection is usually set in motion by some specific event or pressing question. Something triggers it. The act of doing theology may grow out of the interpreter's "I-Thou" relationship, and it may severely test this relationship. In any case, something happens to send the interpreter back to the text and its tradition of interpretations, to the larger context and its store of images and ideas, to family and friends with their accumulated wisdom and advice.

One triggering question may lead to many others. One triggering event may tip the first domino in a series of other triggering events. Whatever the case may be, what often gives focus to the theological reflection is a single driving question or set of questions that forms the interpreter's agenda.

In some NT writings, the triggering event or question can be identified quite easily. Some of the Pauline letters reveal quite clearly the circumstances that prompted their writing. In other cases, what gave rise to certain writings is not as clear. It is difficult to determine precisely what triggered the writing of the four Gospels, although we can make educated guesses. Each NT writing differs in the degree to which it reveals its triggering event, and yet we usually can read between the lines well enough to get a fairly good idea.

Jesus the Catalyst

In one sense, the figure Jesus is the primary catalyst for early Christian theological reflection. For all of their complexity and ambiguity, the four Gospels portray Jesus as a highly controversial figure who questioned some cherished assumptions and challenged venerable institutions of his Jewish contemporaries. By all accounts, the circumstances surrounding his death were complicated enough to generate questions at a number of levels: Who bore responsibility for putting him to death? What were the charges against him? How did his disciples and members of his family react? How did his death relate to what he had said and done during his ministry? Had he foreseen his death? How could he be a crucified Messiah?

From the NT we also get glimpses of the crisis that Jesus' death created among his followers. If he was alive with God, in what sense was he now present among them? How should they carry on his mission of preaching and healing? Could they expect him to return and to be among them in the near future? How were they to deal with questions of succession and continuity? Should the circle of twelve apostles be reconstituted by appointing a replacement, or should they continue without replacing Judas?

One of the most pressing set of questions had to do with Jesus' relationship to the Jewish people. He appears to have confined his ministry, for the most part, to his fellow Israelites in Palestine. Should his followers continue this mission, or should they reach out to non-Jews, especially outside Palestine? The relationship between Christ and Israel is dealt with extensively in Paul's writings, especially Romans and Galatians. It is Paul especially who develops a theological rationale for preaching to the Gentiles. How Jewish and Gentile Christians should relate to each other becomes a pressing question in the early decades of the church's existence, yet the question is asked and answered with close reference to the figure Jesus.

Summary and Conclusion

In outlining the process through which theological reflection occurs, our primary frame of reference has been the NT, but this process can be amply illustrated in the OT as well. It should have become clear that this process did not end when the last NT writer died. Instead, it is a process that has characterized both Israel and the church since their inceptions and that has continued in subsequent generations. In fact, the efforts of Jewish and Christian interpreters down to the present time reflect this model. However, since our explicit interest is the NT, we will confine our summarizing remarks to Christian theological reflection.

All Christian interpreters, in some sense, anchor their interpretive experience in "what God has done in Christ." The driving force of Christian interpretation is the initial "believing in," the "I-Thou" conversation that occurs between the believer and God, who is revealed in Christ and experienced through the Spirit. The Jewish Scriptures supplemented by the NT now comprise the Christian Bible, an indispensable resource for Christian theological reflection. In addition, the centuries of interpretation of both Testaments constitute the tradition on which Christian interpreters also draw. These earlier interpretations may represent viewpoints that modern Christian interpreters find difficult to understand or even regard as outmoded, but they also contain rich insights on which we continue to draw.

Context also represents a critical element in the process of theological reflection in every age. When interpreters compare their contexts with those of their predecessors, they may find that these respective contexts vastly differ in some respects or that they are virtually unchanged in others. The social and political contexts of much of the twenty-first-century world differ radically from that of the Mediterranean world in the first century. Yet such specific contexts as worship and teaching may bear close resemblance, regardless of the number of centuries separating the two worlds. Even so, the ways in which interpreters reflect their context, draw on it, and are shaped by it remain very much the same. We can usually detect in our modern setting the various patterns of relating to contexts, all the way from uncritical acceptance to radical rejection, that were also present in the ancient world.

Like our predecessors, our theological reflection is usually set in motion by some event, question, or crisis. Because these occur in every generation and in different settings, the need for theological reflection never ceases. In some cases, the things that trigger our theological reflections closely resemble those things that triggered the NT writings. In other cases, the questions that drive us to seek fresh answers are completely new. For many of our questions, we search in vain in both the biblical text and the tradition of biblical interpretations for precedents that provide much help.

For all the differences between our situation and that of the biblical writers, our way of doing theology is similar to theirs. As modern interpreters, we find that we stand in a long line of biblical interpreters who have struggled to make sense of God's action in Christ very much as we do. We are part of a hermeneutical continuum—a succession of interpreters who over many generations have been engaged in a common task. When we enter into conversation with the text and tradition to help us discern how God through Christ is both present and active in our world, and when we do so with an informed understanding of our larger and smaller contexts, we are engaged in theological sense-making much as our predecessors were. In one sense, we are their successors; in another sense, their partners.

The task before us is to recognize the NT writings not only as a set of theological formulations resulting from this process, but also as vital witnesses to the process itself. Given its final, edited form, each writing may be thought of as a set of theological interpretations frozen in time, as it were. If we are successful in "thawing" these writings, we will be able to expose the elements that we have discussed and see their dynamic interaction. This in turn will enable us to understand better the theological sense-making of early Christians. We will have a much better understanding not only of what the NT writers believed but also of how they did theology.

Note

1. The Greek word *theologos* combines two words: *theos*, "god," and *logos* from *legō*, "to speak." A *theologos* is thus someone who discourses about a god or the gods. See Aristotle, *Metaph.* 1000[a]9.

Bibliography

Boers, Hendrikus. *What Is New Testament Theology? The Rise of Criticism and the Problem of a Theology of the New Testament.* Philadelphia: Fortress, 1979.

Fowl, Stephen E. *Engaging Scripture: A Model for Theological Interpretation.* Oxford: Blackwell, 1998.

Lindbeck, George. *The Nature of Doctrine: Religion and Theology in a Postliberal Age.* Philadelphia: Westminster, 1984.

Ogden, Schubert. "Doing Theology Today." Pages 417–36 in *Doing Theology in Today's World: Essays in Honor of Kenneth S. Kantzer.* Edited by John D. Woodbridge and Thomas E. McComiskey. Grand Rapids: Zondervan, 1991.

Via, Dan O. *What Is New Testament Theology?* Guides to Biblical Scholarship. New Testament Series. Minneapolis: Fortress, 2002.

Watson, Francis. *Text, Church and World: Biblical Interpretation in Theological Perspective.* Grand Rapids: Eerdmans, 1994.

Chapter 2

The Shape of the Canon

"The canon was not the result of a series of contests; rather, canonical books were separated from others by the intuitive insight of the Church."

Brooke Foss Westcott

"There is a difference between a collection of authoritative books and an authoritative collection of books."

Bruce M. Metzger

When we compare the Bibles used within Orthodox Christianity, the Roman Catholic Church, and Protestant churches, we find considerable variation in the choice and arrangement of the books that comprise the Old Testament. Their New Testaments, by contrast, are virtually identical.[1] Each has twenty-seven writings arranged in the same order. So familiar is this NT "table of contents" that it may seem self-evident why these writings were selected over other early Christian writings or even why they were arranged this way. Yet some basic questions are worth asking: Why did these twenty-seven writings emerge as the church's book? Why this particular arrangement? When did it occur? What (and whom) does it privilege? In what ways does it shape our understanding of the church and the gospel it proclaims?

We can begin by stating the obvious. The first four books are named after individuals, purportedly their authors. Two of them—Matthew and John—are apostles; the other two—Mark and Luke—are not apostles but belong to the wider circle of "apostolic followers." Unlike the first four books, the title "Acts of the Apostles" appears to describe its contents rather than its author. Only by reading it do we learn that it reports apostolic acts *after* Jesus' death and resurrection. Next come the letters attributed to Paul: nine letters addressed to churches followed by four letters addressed to individuals. Naming these writings after their addressees rather than their author is reasonable, since there are so many of them. Why they are arranged in this order, however, is not so obvious. It is not geographic—there is no discernible pattern of movement from east to west or vice versa, or from large cities to smaller, less renowned cities. Nor are they arranged in chronological order, since 1 Thessalonians, or perhaps

Galatians, is the earliest letter Paul wrote. If anything, they appear to be arranged according to their descending length. The three individuals addressed are persons close to Paul, although in different ways.

Placing Hebrews next represents a break in the pattern. Even though Hebrews makes no claim to Pauline authorship, it was associated with Paul quite early and was often attributed to him. Its placement here signals this borderline status. Next come seven writings named after individuals who are the authors rather than the addressees of the letters. In the cases of James, Peter, and Jude the names of the authors are mentioned in the opening greeting, but John is not mentioned specifically in the three letters attributed to him. Even though the identities of James and Jude remain imprecise, what all four of these named individuals have in common is their proximity to Jesus' inner circle, either as apostles or family members.

Revelation is attributed to the figure "John" (Rev 1:1, 4, 9), yet the title of the writing derives from its content stated in the opening verse. Since Revelation deals with the "last things," it comes last although its placement in the final position may relate to its disputed status within the canon.

There is a clear logic to the overall arrangement. Since narrative traditions about Jesus are preserved in the four Gospels, they come first. Acts provides a natural sequel to the Gospels, since it begins where they left off—with the risen Lord's appearing to the disciples. Tracing the rise and spread of the church from Jerusalem to Rome through the heroic efforts of Peter and Paul, Acts is suitably placed before the thirteen letters attributed to Paul. As already noted, the placement of Hebrews indicates its liminal status. Why the letters attributed to members of Jesus' circle come next is not as clear. They could have been placed earlier, closer to the Gospel narratives whose authorship was similarly conceived. With its dramatic vision of the new heaven, the new earth, and the new Jerusalem, Revelation forms a fitting conclusion to the collection.

This familiar arrangement might appear sensible to us, but it was by no means accepted universally in the early church. In fact, there was considerable variety in the arrangement of the NT writings by early Christian writers, whose testimony can be quite illuminating in showing how they regarded these writings and what they saw as important issues in deciding their proper arrangement.[2] [**For the following discussion, see Expanded CD Version pp. 871–81:** *Appendix 1: Canonical Lists*]

Some Fourth-Century Arrangements

The first time a list of twenty-seven writings appears that contains exactly the same writings as our NT canon is in 367 C.E. when Athanasius, bishop of Alexandria (ca. 296–373), issued his *Thirty-Ninth Festal Letter*.[3] In Athanasius's list, the four Gospels come first, in the following order: Matthew, Mark, Luke, and John. Acts is mentioned next, followed by the "seven so-called catholic epistles of the apostles . . . one of James, two of Peter, three of John, and, after these, one of Jude." As noted earlier, this arrangement is plausible since these letters are attributed to persons close to Jesus who are prominently featured in Acts. Then come "fourteen epistles of the apostle Paul," listed in the following order: Romans, 1–2 Corinthians, Galatians, Ephesians, Philippians, Colossians, 1–2 Thessalonians, Hebrews, 1–2 Timothy, Titus, and Philemon. By placing Paul's writings in this position, Athanasius acknowledges his importance in the early church but also separates him from the inner circle of Jesus' followers. Also worth noting is Athanasius's inclusion of Hebrews within the Pauline writings at the end of the letters addressed to churches and before those addressed to individuals. Mentioned last is the Apocalypse of John.

Athanasius also lists "other books outside these, which are not indeed included in the canon, but have been appointed from the time of the fathers to be read to those who are recent converts to our company and wish to be instructed in the word of true religion."[4] These include the Wisdom of Solomon, Sirach, Esther, Judith, Tobit, the so-called Teachings of the Apostles (*Didache*), and the Shepherd (of Hermas). By mentioning the latter two writings, Athanasius tacitly acknowledges a principle of selectivity among Christian writings. Along with the other Jewish writings mentioned, these Christian works are regarded as recommended reading; they do not qualify as required reading for the church. This is an important distinction.

From roughly the same period comes the canonical list issued by the Council of Laodicea about 363 C.E.[5] It also begins with the four Gospels—Matthew, Mark, Luke, and John. Like Athanasius, this list puts Acts next, followed by the seven Catholic Letters listed in the same order. It also attributes fourteen letters to Paul, including Hebrews, which comes immediately after the Thessalonian letters. Unlike Athanasius, however, the Laodicea list omits Revelation.

The canonical list that most resembles our modern arrangement of the NT is that of the Third Council of Carthage (397 C.E.).[6] Five distinct groupings are evident: the four Gospels, Acts, the Pauline letters (including Hebrews), the Catholic Letters (in a slightly different order: 1–2 Peter, 1–2–3 John, James, and Jude), and Revelation. Unlike the previous lists, this list from the Council of Carthage, which probably reflects a decision of an earlier council at Hippo in 393, acknowledges Hebrews as a special case to be distinguished from the thirteen letters attributed to Paul. Accordingly, it falls at the end of the Pauline group. The rationale for the arrangement of the Catholic Letters is to list first the letters attributed to apostolic figures—Peter and John—and then those attributed to Jesus' brothers—James and Jude.

Even though these fourth-century witnesses differ in some fundamental respects, they are fairly uniform in their understanding of the limits of the canon. *Where* the books belong in the list is still disputed, but there is general agreement concerning *which* books should be included. As we might expect, we find a more confused picture when we move to an earlier period.

Earlier Arrangements

The earliest known list of NT writings is found in the Muratorian Fragment, generally dated to the late second century C.E. and named after Lodovico Antonio Muratori, an Italian Jesuit who discovered the list in a seventh- or eighth-century manuscript and published it in 1740.[7] Eighty-five lines of the list survive, but its beginning is missing and perhaps its ending as well.[8] Beginning with a brief mention of an unnamed book, almost certainly Mark, the Muratorian Fragment then mentions Luke, calling it "the third book of the gospel" and attributing it to Luke the physician, Paul's traveling companion. The "fourth [book] of the Gospels" is said to come from John, "one of the disciples," and is linked with the Johannine letters. The fragment next mentions "the acts of all the apostles" written in "one book" by Luke, who is said to have described the things that "were done in his own presence." The fragment also notes that Acts omits Peter's passion and Paul's departure from "the city [of Rome] for Spain."

Next mentioned are the "letters of Paul," which show "from which place and for which cause they were directed." We are told that Paul wrote "first of all" to the Corinthians, admonishing against the schism of heresy; then to the Galatians, forbidding circumcision; then to the Romans he wrote "at greater length . . . pointing out with a series of Scripture quotations that Christ is their main theme also."[9] Paul is said to have imitated John by writing to seven churches by name and in the following order: Corinthians (two letters), Ephesians, Philippians, Colossians, Galatians, Thessalonians (two letters), and Romans. Then are mentioned Paul's letters to individuals: Philemon, Titus, and Timothy (two letters). Also included is a letter (from Paul) to the Laodiceans, mentioned in Col 4:16, and another letter to the Alexandrians, (both?) said to have been "forged [in Paul's name] in accordance with Marcion's heresy." The Fragment also reports that there were other letters "which cannot be received into the catholic church."

The list then mentions the Letter of Jude and the two with the superscription "John," which are accepted in the catholic church. Also mentioned is the Wisdom of Solomon, "written by Solomon's friends in his honor." It then reports that the Apocalypses of John and Peter are accepted, but notes that "some of our people" do not want it (presumably only the Apocalypse of Peter) "to be read in church." The Shepherd of Hermas, said to have been recently composed, is mentioned next. We are told that it "may be read indeed but cannot be given out [published?] to the people in church." The fragment concludes with a list of writings that are prohibited from being read. Nothing from Arsinous, Valentinus, or Miltiades can be accepted. Also excluded is a book of psalms composed for Marcion, along with writings of Basilides and the founder of the Cataphrygians of Asia.

The Muratorian Fragment reflects a state of affairs far less settled than what we find in the fourth-century lists. If we assume that it began by mentioning Matthew and Mark, we have a list that follows a structure roughly resembling our current canon: four Gospels, Acts, the Pauline letters (nine addressed to churches, four to individuals), some other letters attributed to Jude and John, and finally the Apocalypse of John. Hebrews, James, 1–2 Peter, and one Johannine epistle, probably 3 John, are not mentioned at all. The thirteen Pauline letters already form a well-defined group, and they are to be distinguished from other letters attributed to Paul that were associated with "Marcion's heresy." Worth noting is its mention of the *Apocalypse of Peter*, a writing that apparently had wide circulation among churches during the second century in spite of objections raised in some circles.[10] The inclusion of the Wisdom of Solomon without any qualification or disclaimer shows that the canonical boundaries were still somewhat fluid. As Athanasius later recognized, the Shepherd of Hermas has edificatory value, but it belongs to the category of writings that cannot be recommended for use by the universal church.

If Athanasius represents the situation in Alexandria in the late fourth century, Origen (ca. 185–254 C.E.) gives us an Alexandrian voice from a century earlier. His views on the Gospels, which are summarized in his *Commentary on Matthew*, are reported by Eusebius (ca. 260–340 C.E.).[11] Worth noting is Origen's insistence on "only four [undisputed] Gospels," which clearly implies the existence of other Gospels that had been rejected. His listing also appears to be chronological: Matthew was written "first," followed by Mark, Luke, and "last of all" John. Nor does he merely list the names of the books; he also reports other information to help secure their trustworthiness: Matthew's status as a tax collector who became an apostle and his facility with the Hebrew language, enabling him to address his Gospel to Jewish Christians; Mark's apostolic connection through Peter; and Luke's apostolic connection through Paul, which explains why his Gospel was addressed to Gentile Christians. Thus, by Origen's time a biographical profile of the Gospel authors had already begun to develop. In addition, information pertaining to the setting of each Gospel, such as the language of composition and its addressees, had also begun to be collected.

Eusebius, having read Origen's *Commentary on John*, reports Origen's views on "the epistles of the apostles."[12] Here Origen reports what he knows about letters written by Paul, Peter, and John. Noting that Paul wrote only to some of his churches, Origen also says that some of his letters consist of "only a few lines." Origen is willing to vouch for 1 Peter but not for 2 Peter, since its status was doubtful. He identifies the author of the Fourth Gospel with the unnamed figure mentioned in John 13:23 (see John 19:26–27; 20:1–10; 21:7, 20–24; cf. 19:35) and also attributes to him Revelation and 1 John, and possibly 2–3 John. Despite questions about these latter two letters, Origen clearly envisions a Johannine corpus comprising the Fourth Gospel, Revelation, and 1 John. By treating Hebrews in a separate category, Origen acknowledges its problematic status.[13]

Origen's remarks do not give us his comprehensive views about which writings belong to the NT canon. His failure to mention such writings as Acts or James does not necessarily mean that he regarded them as noncanonical. Yet these remarks are quite informative. They show us a fixed fourfold Gospel as well as other writings attached to the names of three other apostolic figures—Paul, Peter, and John. Origen's remarks also reflect the disputed status of certain writings, such as 2 Peter and 2–3 John, and Hebrews, to some extent. **[See Expanded CD Version pp. 30–31: *Later Testimony*]**

Significance of Different Arrangements

This review by no means exhausts the early church's views about which writings belonged to the NT and how they should be arranged, but it does show that the "table of contents" we find in our Bibles was by no means universally accepted in the early church. By the fourth century, a broad consensus had been reached on some issues.

The number and arrangement of the four Gospels were widely agreed upon, as was the placement of Acts in the next position. Whether the Catholic Letters or Paul's letters came next was debated, but there was broad agreement about which writings belonged to each group. Disputes continued about some of the Catholic Letters, but almost everyone agreed that James, 1 Peter, and 1 John belonged to this group. As for Paul's letters, the main question was whether Hebrews belonged with them, and thus whether there were thirteen or fourteen Pauline writings. Apart from this, the arrangement was fairly well settled: first the letters addressed to churches followed by letters to individuals. The status of Revelation continued to be disputed, but when it was included, it was placed last.

Also revealing is the extent to which these witnesses are aware of other writings that compete for the church's attention. In almost every case, these witnesses are aware of a circle of writings around the NT whose existence must be acknowledged but whose value must be distinguished in some way. The distinction between "required" and "recommended" must have been made quite early, suggesting that from the outset the NT writings had to win approval within a wider field of competition. It is also remarkable that, apart from the nucleus of writings that were widely accepted as normative, canonical boundaries could be somewhat fluid. Modern readers are sometimes surprised to learn that writings such as the Shepherd of Hermas, the *Apocalypse of Peter,* or the Wisdom of Solomon were regarded as canonical in some quarters.

As the limits of the NT canon gradually became established, questions remained about the arrangement of the writings. Some important issues were at stake here, since the arrangement of the books affected not only the order in which they were to be read but also how each writing was read. Grouping Matthew, Mark, and Luke together already recognizes the similarities in their treatment of Jesus, hence their later designation as Synoptic Gospels that "see together" the Jesus story. Putting John in the fourth position recognizes its distinctiveness and probably its relatively late date. Placing Matthew before Mark and Luke gives it priority in shaping the church's understanding of Jesus' life and teachings. This helps explain, for example, the church's preference for Matthew's version of the Lord's Prayer.

The positioning of the Catholic Letters also had important consequences. As noted earlier, since these letters were attributed to the apostolic figures Peter and John, or to Jesus' brothers James and Jude, they found a natural place close to the Gospels and Acts. Had they remained there, individual letters such as James and 1 Peter might have been read quite differently. Their influence on the church—and the church's perception of them—also might have been quite different. But Paul's letters won the third slot after the Gospels and Acts, doubtless reflecting the powerful influence he exercised in this formative period but also ensuring his importance for subsequent generations of readers. Within the Pauline writings, the position of each letter became an important consideration. By placing Hebrews after the Pauline writings addressed to churches, the church could read it more easily as a Pauline letter. This in turn influenced the church's perception of Paul and also affected how Hebrews was perceived by the church. In the Muratorian Fragment, the two Corinthian letters head the list of Pauline writings addressed to churches, and Romans comes at the end of the list. This arrangement conforms to the order in which the author of the Fragment thought the letters were written. By the time of Athanasius, however, Romans had begun to be listed first among the Pauline letters and remained in that position in most of the canonical lists. This meant that Romans had an influential role in shaping the church's perception of Paul and his thought, not only in relation to the other Pauline letters but also to the other NT writings as well. The canonical ordering reflected the importance of Romans and also ensured that it would continue to have a dominant role within the church.

Even when the seven Catholic Letters are grouped together, and the disputed status of several of them is no longer an issue, it is still not altogether clear how they should be read. Should 1–2 Peter be read together since they purportedly have the same author? What about the Johannine letters? Was Origen right to link them with the Fourth Gospel and the Apocalypse so they could all be read as letters of John the apostle? Should James be read first within the group or come further down in the list? What about Jude? Should it be read with James as another writing by one of Jesus' brothers?

What does it mean to read Revelation last? Placing it last certainly underscores its preoccupation with the end time. In this position, it forms a fitting conclusion not only to the NT but also to the Christian Bible comprising both Testaments. The biblical story that began with creation ends with a vision of the new heaven, the new earth, and the new Jerusalem. Other NT writings also deal with "last things," but their views concerning the end time can easily be muffled because they are buried in the middle of the canon rather than heard as the final chorus. What effect would it have had if the church as a whole followed the Council of Laodicea and Cyril of Jerusalem (ca. 315–387 C.E.) (and even the doubting Eusebius) in omitting Revelation? We might even ask what the effect would have been if Revelation had been placed earlier in the canon, for example, in the first position—ahead of the Gospels—or even between Paul and the Catholic Letters?

As it turns out, the arrangement of the NT writings in our Bible may not be as value-neutral as it appears. What emerges is a list that reflects both theological victories and defeats. What we call the apocryphal gospels clearly lost, since they were not only excluded but also parodied by several of the witnesses we have reviewed. Other writings, such as the *Didache* and the Shepherd of Hermas, also lost, though not entirely, since their value continued to be recognized. Among the four Gospels, Mark lost in the sense that it was overshadowed by, and thus tended to be read in the light of, Matthew. The other three Gospels appear to have received much greater attention than Mark. The earliest known commentary on Mark dates from the first half of the seventh century, while the other three Gospels received extensive commentary treatment much earlier. Within the Pauline letters, Romans and Galatians came to exercise far greater influence than the shorter Pauline letters, such as 1–2 Thessalonians, Colossians, and Ephesians. Paul looks quite different when read primarily through the lens of Romans and Galatians as opposed to some of his other letters.

How we order the NT writings is a decision of enormous consequence. When we read the NT writings in the canonical order adopted in most modern Bibles, we should be aware of the theological significance of this arrangement and the theological value judgments that it represents. As the preceding review indicates, there is nothing sacred about any single canonical arrangement. The church may have delimited the number of canonical writings, but it did not make a comparable judgment about their order—at least, not explicitly. To be sure, some of its decisions, such as consistently placing the four Gospels first, reflect clear theological convictions. We do well to ask what such decisions meant for the church theologically and whether something is lost when we veer from that judgment. In the following treatment, I generally follow the canonical arrangement, although I believe there is good reason to diverge from it in some respects. In what follows, I offer an explanation for the order in which I introduce the NT writings.

Order of Treatment

In the following pages, the narrative traditions about Jesus are treated first, even though there is broad scholarly agreement that they are chronologically quite late. Each of the four Gospels in its final edited form probably dates from the latter third of the first century C.E. or later. By contrast, one of Paul's letters, either 1 Thessalonians or Galatians, is probably the earliest NT writing (ca. 50–52 C.E.), although some scholars regard the Letter of James as equally early. Since Jesus is the central figure of the NT, the narrative traditions about him logically come first. Even if they are relatively late chronologically, they contain many traditions that predate Paul. Thus, even on chronological grounds, a case can be made for treating the Gospels first. More important, they define the contours of the figure who is presupposed by the other NT writings, even though little explicit reference is made in these other writings to Gospel traditions about Jesus.

Before treating the Gospels individually, I have included three preliminary chapters. The first chapter, "Relating the Gospels to Each Other," examines some of the ways the church has dealt with the problem of "one Jesus and four Gospels." Since the modern debate has focused on how the first three Gospels are related to each other—the Synoptic Problem—this is dealt with first. Some account is given of the major scholarly options and how they arose. A separate section treats the relationship between the Synoptic Gospels and the Gospel of John. The next chapter, "From Jesus to the Gospels," focuses on the pre-Gospel period, the time between Jesus and the first written Gospel. It is intended to help readers envision this "tunnel period" and develop an understanding of some of the main models used to explain how the Gospel tradition was formed. A third chapter, "From the Gospels to Jesus," examines how the church accesses Jesus through its reading of the four canonical Gospels. Because the Gospels present important variations in their portraits of Jesus, eventually the question emerges, "Who was Jesus?" So important is this question, both to the early and to the modern church, that it receives separate treatment.

In treating each Gospel, however, I diverge somewhat from the canonical order. Mark is treated first because of widespread scholarly support for seeing it as the earliest Gospel. While Markan priority still remains a controversial claim, it enjoys strong support. Since there is such support for thinking that Matthew and Luke used Mark independently as a source, along with other sources no longer extant, there is good reason to regard Matthew and Luke as "second editions" of Mark. Even though I believe that Matthew and Luke have used Mark in the composition of their Gospels, each has reinterpreted Mark quite significantly. Which "second edition" appeared first is not known. More important than trying to determine which appeared first is recognizing the distinctive interpretive directions Matthew and Luke followed. As in the canonical lists and witnesses mentioned earlier, John is discussed fourth, not only because it reflects such a different construal of the Jesus story but also because it appears to be largely independent of the synoptic tradition. It is also probably later chronologically.

Early Christian writers knew that the Gospel of Luke and the Acts of the Apostles were written by the same person, who was often identified as Luke the physician, Paul's companion. Even so, Acts became separated from Luke in the canonical "table of contents." As noted earlier, this placement was logical since Acts began where the Gospels ended. Moreover, rehearsing the apostolic preaching of Peter and John in Jerusalem and the subsequent mission of Paul outside Palestine, which eventually ended in Rome, provided a broad geographical and chronological background against which to read the other NT writings. Other considerations also came into play. By featuring Peter and Paul alongside each other, and both within the framework of other apostolic activity, Acts formed a natural bridge between the Gospels and Paul's letters. Similarly, placing Paul between Acts and the Catholic Letters displayed a plurality of "apostolic" witnesses bound together by their common faith in Jesus Christ. Although Acts is the second volume of a two-volume work, I devote a separate chapter to it rather than include it in the chapter on the Gospel of Luke. At the beginning of the chapter on Acts, attention is given to the close literary and theological connections with the Gospel of Luke.

The Pauline writings are dealt with next but not in their canonical order. Since 1 Thessalonians is probably the earliest Pauline letter (and thereby probably the earliest writing in the NT), it is discussed first. The Pauline authorship of 2 Thessalonians is disputed by many scholars, but since I consider the letter as Pauline these two letters are paired together here as they are in early canonical lists. Then follow the two Corinthian letters, which are treated in a single chapter as well. Because the second letter is probably composed of several shorter letters, some attention is given to how the overall correspondence between Paul and the Corinthian church unfolded. Galatians comes next, followed by Romans, in their apparent chronological order. They address some of the same issues, although in quite different ways.

The following four letters—Philippians, Philemon, Colossians, and Ephesians— are discussed together because they are all addressed to churches[14] and were written from prison. There is an ongoing scholarly debate about where Paul was imprisoned, the most conventional suggestion being Rome. In the following discussion, however, I conclude that Philippians was probably written from an Ephesian imprisonment, otherwise unreported in the NT. If so, it would fall chronologically earlier, probably sometime between the Thessalonian letters and the Corinthian letters. Next come Philemon, Colossians, and Ephesians, the other prison letters. Given the close connections between Philemon and Colossians, I treat them as letters written from Paul's Roman imprisonment. Because of the close similarity in content and outlook between Colossians and Ephesians, these two letters are probably connected literarily. I regard Colossians as the earlier letter and Ephesians as an expanded version of Colossians— or, at the very least, as a freshly conceived letter operating out of the same framework as Colossians. By taking all four prison letters together, the numerous critical questions about their authorship, date, and place of composition can be considered together.

Next come the letters attributed to Paul, which are addressed to his coworkers Timothy and Titus. They are usually referred to as the Pastoral Letters because they deal with matters relating to pastoral duties and ecclesiastical order. Their similarity in language, style, and overall outlook distinguishes them as a group from the other Pauline letters. Since their direct Pauline authorship is seriously contested, some attention is given to this important issue. In turn, each letter is discussed separately in the following order: Titus, 1 Timothy, and 2 Timothy. A concluding section is devoted to their overall theological vision. Here, the Pastoral Letters are seen as writings that do not come directly from Paul, but from Paul's followers, hence, as post-Pauline writings both in content and spirit.

The Letter to the Hebrews is covered next, not because it is a Pauline writing but because it was so regarded from a very early period. In some ways it reflects a Pauline outlook, and the church for centuries read it that way. Even though Hebrews is now widely believed to be non-Pauline, it is taken up here in the position where it fell in many canonical lists—at the edge of the Pauline letters. Since Hebrews was long held to be Pauline by the church and consequently shaped ecclesiastical opinion about Paul, some attention is given to the relationship between Hebrews and Paul's thought.

As we have already seen, the Catholic Letters—James, 1–2 Peter, 1–2–3 John, and Jude—were grouped together from a very early date. Once again, I have rearranged them slightly. James and 1 Peter are discussed first because they represent distinct witnesses from circles close to Jesus. Following the broad scholarly consensus that Jude preceded 2 Peter, and that the author of 2 Peter recast Jude into a fresh theological statement addressing a different situation, Jude is treated before 2 Peter, which is then seen as a "second edition" of Jude. The three letters of John are taken together since they reflect a similar outlook and were possibly written by the same author. Even though the letters of John stem from the same circles as the Fourth Gospel and constitute important witnesses to the Johannine tradition within early Christianity, I devote a separate chapter to them because they reflect a later stage of development in which the Johannine community became divided. As such, they present an illuminating case study in practical theology.

Following the usual canonical arrangement, the Johannine Apocalypse comes last, not because it was the latest NT composition, although it was likely composed near the end of the first century. The church thought it made sense to place Revelation last because of its final, grand vision of the reconstituted heaven and earth. Although Revelation and the Gospel of John were often attributed to John the apostle, here they are separated because of broad scholarly support for their separate authorship. Revelation presents a distinctive theological vision that requires attention in its own right.

A concluding chapter addresses several issues that surface throughout the earlier chapters. Questions addressed here include: How did the NT writings become theologically normative for the church? What criteria were used for determining canonicity? What considerations should the contemporary church take into account as it seeks to hear the Word of God through this collection of writings? Also addressed are questions relating to their status as authoritative writings for Christian communities of faith.

This is the right place to deal with these questions—after we have let each writing or group of writings speak for itself.

Notes

1. For the most part, a uniform NT canon is used within all branches of Christianity, but there are some exceptions. In the Ethiopian (Abyssinian) Church, for example, the usual twenty-seven NT writings are canonical, but four additional sets of writings are included in a "broader canon." Furthermore, churches can give varying levels of importance to each of the twenty-seven writings, which results in different *de facto* canons. See chapter 28, "The Christian Scriptures: Witnesses to Christ and the Church's Faith."

2. In the remarks that follow, I draw on Appendix 1, "Ancient Canonical Lists," and Appendix 2, "Early Christian Views of the Gospels," which are found in the Expanded CD Version, pp. 871-89.

3. The letter is contained in Appendix 1. Also see *NPNF*[2] 4:551–52.

4. F. F. Bruce, *The Canon of Scripture* (Downers Grove: InterVarsity, 1988), 209.

5. See Appendix 1. See Canon 60 in *NPNF*[2] 14:159; also Bruce, *Canon*, 210.

6. See Appendix 1. See *NPNF*[2] 14:454.

7. A fourth-century date for the Muratorian Fragment is argued by Geoffrey Mark Hahneman, *The Muratorian Fragment and the Development of the Canon* (Oxford: Clarendon Press, 1992). While his comprehensive argument has convinced some scholars, it has not been decisive in overturning the traditional second-century date. See E. Ferguson's review in *Journal of Theological Studies* 44 (1993): 691–97; also his "Canon Muratori: Date and Provenance," *Studia Patristica* 17.2 (Oxford: Pergamon, 1982), 677–83. For a comprehensive refutation of Hahneman's position, see Joseph Verheyden, "The Canon Muratori: A Matter of Dispute," in *The Biblical Canons* (ed. J.-M. Auwers and H. J. de Jonge; Leuven: University Press/Peeters, 2003), 487–556.

8. For the complete text of the Muratorian Fragment, see Appendix 1.

9. Here I follow the translation of Daniel J. Theron, *Evidence of Tradition* (Grand Rapids: Baker, 1957), 111.

10. Clement of Alexandria believed that *Apoc. Pet.* was written by Peter. See *Ecl.* 41.1–3; 48.1.

11. *Hist. eccl.* 6.25.3–6. See Appendix 1

12. *Hist. eccl.* 6.25.7–10. See Appendix 1.

13. *Hist. eccl.* 6.25.11–12. See Appendix 1.

14. The Letter to Philemon is included since it is addressed to Philemon, Apphia, Archippus, and "to the church in your house" (v. 2).

Bibliography

Auwers, J.-M., and H. J. de Jonge, eds. *The Biblical Canons*. Bibliotheca Ephemeridum Theologicarum Lovaniensium 163. Leuven: University Press/Peeters, 2003.

Barton, John. *Holy Writings, Sacred Text: The Canon in Early Christianity*. Louisville: Westminster John Knox, 1997.

Bruce, F. F. *The Canon of Scripture*. Downers Grove: InterVarsity, 1988.

Campenhausen, Hans von. *The Formation of the Christian Bible*. Translated by John Austin Baker. London: Black, 1972.

Gamble, Harry Y. *Books and Readers in the Early Church: A History of Early Christian Texts*. New Haven: Yale University Press, 1995.

McDonald, Lee Martin. *The Formation of the Christian Biblical Canon*. Rev. and exp. ed. Peabody: Hendrickson, 1995.

Part 2

THE GOSPELS: NARRATIVE TRADITIONS ABOUT JESUS

Chapter 3

Relating the Gospels
to Each Other

"If it is necessary to have not one but several accounts of the one life of Jesus which must be the foundation of all Christian belief, it is as good as admitting that none of them is perfect."

Oscar Cullmann

Anyone who reads the four canonical Gospels, even casually, is struck by how much alike Matthew, Mark, and Luke are and how different they are from John's Gospel. Because the first three Gospels are so similar in both content and arrangement, they are called the Synoptic Gospels. The term *synoptic* transliterates the Greek *synoptikos*, which means "seeing the whole together" or "taking a comprehensive view." When applied to the first three Gospels, it suggests that they tend to see the story of Jesus alike. The canonical arrangement, with John in the fourth position, underscores its difference in outlook, content, and overall sequence. The early church easily recognized the sharp differences between John and the other three canonical Gospels. By characterizing the Fourth Gospel as the "spiritual Gospel" or seeing it as an effort to supplement the physical aspects of Jesus' life, early Christian writers sought to account for the theological distance separating John and the Synoptic Gospels. **[See Expanded CD Version pp. 41–43: *The Need for a Theory Relating the Gospels to Each Other*] [For the following discussion, see Expanded CD Version pp. 883–89: *Appendix 2: Patristic Comments on the Gospels*]**

Strategies for Relating the Gospels to Each Other

Harmonization

Over the centuries, Christian readers have developed different strategies for relating the Gospels to each other. One of the most common is *harmonizing* the Gospels. Typically, this means taking passages from the different Gospels related to the same theme and developing an explanation that brings them into harmony with each other. An early example of this approach is Augustine's comprehensive work *De consensu evangelistarum*, written about 400 C.E. This title is usually translated *Harmony of the Gospels* but could be rendered more aptly as *Concerning the Agreement of the Evangelists*.[1] Writing in response to critics of the church who had pointed to discrepancies in the Gospels, Augustine moves through the Gospel narratives, using Matthew as the primary reference point. **[See Expanded CD Version p. 43: *Augustine's Harmonization: Some Examples*]**

Another early example of Gospel harmonization is Tatian's *Diatessaron* (ca. 150–160 C.E.), which wove the four Gospels into a single account using the Gospel of John as a basic narrative framework. Other harmonies appeared in the patristic and medieval period, but they became especially popular during the sixteenth century, when more than thirty harmonies were published in different languages. One of the most notable was John Calvin's *Commentary on a Harmony of the Evangelists, Matthew, Mark, and Luke* (1555).[2] The use of Gospel harmonies has continued well into the modern period.[3] Even though these harmonies may present material common to several Gospels in vertical or horizontal parallel columns, they resemble their earlier counterpart, the *Diatessaron*, by combining all four accounts into a single life of Christ.

Sometimes harmonization took the form of allegorical interpretation in which readers found additional levels of meaning beyond the literal sense of the text. Commenting on the differences in the Gospel accounts of Jesus' movements immediately after his temptation by Satan (Matt 4:11–13; Mark 1:13–15; Luke 4:13–16), Origen acknowledges discrepancies at the level of their literal meaning but insists that "the truth of these accounts lies in the spiritual meanings."[4] "The meaning of [the four evangelists'] historical accounts would be found to be harmonious," Origen insists, "once it was understood."[5] The intention of the four evangelists, in Origen's view, was "to speak the truth spiritually and materially at the same time where that was possible but, where it was not possible in both ways, to prefer the spiritual to the material."[6] When discrepancies could not be resolved, the reader is expected to look for the spiritual truth within them: "The spiritual truth is often preserved in the material falsehood, so to speak."[7]

Literary Comparison and Diachronic Reconstruction (Literary Dependence)

In this approach, the four Gospels are closely compared with each other and explanations are offered based on how the Gospels are related to each other *diachronically*, in other words, "through time." This means that the four Gospels are placed in some chronological sequence and their different parts are compared with each other accordingly.

Although this strategy has become especially prominent since the eighteenth century, it was anticipated in the early church. Augustine believed that the canonical order of the Gospels—Matthew, Mark, Luke, and John—reflects their chronological order.[8] Matthew wrote first—in Hebrew—followed by Mark, Luke, and John, all of whom wrote in Greek. Furthermore, Augustine apparently thought that after Matthew, each evangelist wrote fully aware of the work of his predecessor(s).[9] He believed that Mark composed an epitome of Matthew.[10] Precisely how Augustine thought Luke was related to Mark is less clear. Even so, Augustine's view of the relationship between the Gospels is usually understood as follows:

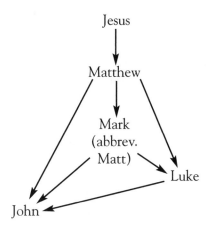

According to one tradition, Clement of Alexandria believed that the two Gospels containing genealogies—Matthew and Luke—were written first, that Mark next recorded traditions traceable to Peter, and that finally John, aware of the other three Gospels, wrote his "spiritual Gospel."[11]

Even though patristic authors could envision an evangelist's taking into account the work of his predecessors, this way of relating the Gospels to each other received further refinement in the modern period. For a variety of reasons, the value of stories and sayings in the Gospels for reconstructing the life of Jesus became a special concern. It became increasingly important for scholars to engage in *literary comparison* of the Gospels for the purpose of determining the relative reliability of what they reported. This in turn meant that a higher priority was placed on the early dating of traditions reported in the Gospels. *Literary comparison* was carried out in conjunction with *diachronic reconstruction*. The Gospels and their component traditions were envisioned as having been formed over a period of time.

Trying to account for the origin and development of four Gospels not only entailed developing an understanding of what preceded them, but it also raised the question of how they were related to each other. Did all four Gospels stem independently from an early, common source, either an oral or written Gospel? Or were they dependent on each other in some way? Was the form of dependence exclusively literary? Should we imagine one evangelist writing his Gospel with nothing other than a complete written Gospel before him? Or should we imagine an author working with both written and oral traditions, some rather complete, others incomplete?

As these questions became more pressing over time, problems relating to the Gospel of John became distinct from those relating to the Synoptic Gospels. Even though some reconstructions took into account the origin and development of all four canonical Gospels and how they in turn shed light on the figure Jesus, special attention was given to the Synoptic Problem: clarifying how the first three canonical Gospels are related to each other.

The Synoptic Problem

In relating the Synoptic Gospels to each other, several considerations must be taken into account: (1) extensive agreement in wording; (2) similarities in the sequence of events; and (3) distinctive features of content and arrangement within each Gospel.

Agreement in Wording[12]

In some cases, parallel passages in all three Synoptic Gospels display close similarity.[13] In other cases, parallel passages in two of the three Synoptic Gospels agree, with the other Gospel offering no comparable parallel or significant agreement.[14] In still other cases, there are rather remarkable verbal agreements, especially in the material—mostly sayings of Jesus—found only in Matthew and Luke.[15] In some of the sayings material, two of the three Synoptic Gospels agree against the third.[16]

While the patterns of verbal agreement are not uniform, some explanation is required to account for the extent of overall verbal similarity. One of the most striking instances of almost verbatim agreement in wording occurs in the Matthean and Lukan accounts of John the Baptist's preaching.

Matt 3:7–10	Luke 3:7–9
(7) But when he saw many Pharisees and Sadducees coming for baptism, he said to them, "You brood of vipers! Who warned you to flee from the wrath to come? (8) Bear fruit worthy of repentance. (9) Do not presume to say to yourselves, 'We have Abraham as our ancestor'; for I tell you, God is able from these stones to raise up children to Abraham. (10) Even now the ax is lying at the root of the trees; every tree therefore that does not bear good fruit is cut down and thrown into the fire."	(7) John said to the crowds that came out to be baptized by him, "You brood of vipers! Who warned you to flee from the wrath to come? (8) Bear fruits worthy of repentance. Do not begin to say to yourselves, 'We have Abraham as our ancestor'; for I tell you, God is able from these stones to raise up children to Abraham. (9) Even now the ax is lying at the root of the trees; every tree therefore that does not bear good fruit is cut down and thrown into the fire."

Sequence of Events

While each of the Synoptic Gospels presents a distinctive storyline in some respects, all three display a common overall conception of Jesus' ministry: an initial Galilean period of ministry is followed by a brief period in Judea and Jerusalem, where Jesus meets resistance, is crucified, and is raised on the third day.

The Synoptic Gospels display rather remarkable agreement in the order of events that occur during the first part of Jesus' Galilean ministry, especially in certain sections of material. For example, at the beginning of Jesus' ministry, the appearance of John the Baptist, John's preaching, and Jesus' baptism, temptations, and initial preaching in Galilee all occur in the same order (Matt 3:1–4:17; Mark 1:1–15; Luke 3:1–4:15). Later in Jesus' Galilean ministry, the events beginning in Caesarea Philippi occur in the same order: teaching about discipleship, the transfiguration, healing of the boy with a spirit, the second prediction of the passion, and the dispute about greatness (Matt 16:13–18:5; Mark 8:27–9:37; Luke 9:18–48).[17] In the latter two-thirds of their respective narratives, Matthew and Mark report events in the same order (Matt 13:53–28:20 and Mark 6:1–16:8). With few exceptions, the Synoptic Gospels also present the events of Jesus' final week in the same sequence.[18]

An event in one Gospel may be reported in a different sequence in another Gospel. In Mark's Gospel, for example, Jesus' rejection at Nazareth occurs well into his Galilean ministry (Mark 6:1–6), whereas in Luke's Gospel this event inaugurates his Galilean ministry (Luke 4:14–30). Or one of the Synoptic Gospels may report a sequence of sayings or events not found in the other two. Luke's Travel Narrative (9:51–19:27) has no counterpart in Matthew and Mark.[19] Matthew's Sermon on the Mount (Matt 5–7) and Luke's Sermon on the Plain (Luke 6:20–49) have no counterpart in Mark.

Another consistent pattern has also been detected: when Matthew and Luke depart from Mark's order, they tend to follow independent paths. Either may relate a series of sayings or events in a distinctive arrangement, but when this happens neither Matthew nor Luke tends to agree with each other against Mark. Rather, when one diverges from Mark's order, the other tends to follow an order that agrees with Mark.[20]

In spite of some disparities in the sequence of events, some explanation is required for those sections in each Synoptic Gospel in which the same set of events is reported in roughly the same order.

Differences

Some notable differences are also encountered in the Synoptic Gospels. Matthew and Luke include a birth and infancy narrative, whereas Mark does not. Matthew and Luke's respective accounts of Jesus' early life are quite different, however. Luke's interest in presenting John the Baptist and Jesus as parallel figures is absent in Matthew. Mary is the center of attention in Luke's birth and infancy story, whereas Matthew focuses more on Joseph. The overall mood of each account is quite different: Luke's is more buoyant, while Matthew's is more ominous and foreboding. In Luke, Jesus' family resides in Nazareth; in Matthew, Bethlehem.

Similarly, whereas Mark ends abruptly, without reporting any appearances by the risen Lord, Matthew and Luke supply more detailed endings to their respective Gospels. Here, too, they differ significantly. In Luke, the risen Lord's appearances occur in or near Jerusalem, while Matthew locates them in Galilee. Each account has unique elements: the bribing of the soldiers in Matt 28:11–15 and Jesus' conversation with the two disciples en route to Emmaus and his appearance to the other disciples in Luke 24:13–49. Unlike Matthew, Luke reports Jesus' ascension (Luke 24:50–53).

Within their respective narratives, each Gospel differs significantly from the other two, not only in content and order but also in theme and emphasis. Matthew's account is notable for the five discourses that are interspersed throughout the narrative (chs. 5–7, 10, 13, 18, 23–25). Mark portrays the death of John the Baptist in greater detail than Matthew or Luke (Mark 6:17–29; cf. Matt 14:3–12; Luke 3:19–20). In Luke, Jesus' Sermon on the Plain (6:20–49) serves as a shorter counterpart to Matthew's Sermon on the Mount (Matt 5–7). Especially remarkable in Luke is the lengthy Travel Narrative, occupying almost a third of the Gospel (9:51–19:27).

Possible Explanations

Broadly speaking, three types of explanations have been offered to account for this pattern of similarities and differences.

Single (or Common) Source Theories

According to these theories, we should envision an early, single source, either oral or written, to which each of the Synoptic Gospels (and even John) is independently traceable. Similarities of wording and sequence are thus explained as deriving from a common original. Differences are explained as the result of each evangelist's having drawn on different parts of the common source or tradition. Differences may also be attributable to each evangelist's distinctive style or special theological interests. The fundamental framework of these theories may be diagrammed as follows:

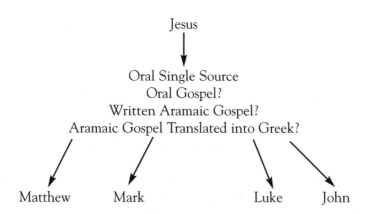

The original single source has been thought of in various ways. Some have seen it as an original oral tradition that informed the apostles' teaching and was eventually written first in Aramaic and later translated into Greek. Others have envisioned a single written Gospel, originally composed in Aramaic and perhaps later translated into Greek. Whatever form this original Gospel might have taken, it has been given various designations, such as Ur-Gospel (i.e., an original Gospel). Some propose that this may have been a Gospel referred to in patristic authors but no longer extant, such as the *Gospel of the Hebrews*.

The common feature of this model is an original source, in whatever form, on which each Gospel draws more or less independently.

Miscellaneous Sources[21]

An alternative view sees a variety of traditions, both oral and written, existing after Jesus' death. Imagined here are many types of material, including Jesus' teachings in the form of sayings or longer discourses, stories about Jesus in many different forms, and accounts of his trial and death. Other forms of narrative similar to the Lukan Travel Narrative, or even groups of miracle stories, may also have begun to take shape.

Rather than drawing on an already well-formulated single source, each evangelist is seen as an editor who collected miscellaneous sources and shaped them into his Gospel narrative. This view, sometimes known as the "fragments" hypothesis, may be diagrammed as follows:

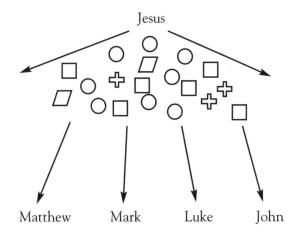

Jesus

Matthew   Mark   Luke   John

Literary Dependence Theories[22]

According to this model, oral and written traditions about Jesus were given narrative shape initially by one of the evangelists. Once this was done, the first Gospel became a literary source used directly by at least one, and probably both, of the other two synoptic evangelists, and maybe even the Fourth Evangelist. In addition to the use of the Gospels themselves as literary sources, this model also envisions the possibility of other oral and written sources on which the evangelists could draw directly. What distinguishes this model from the previous two models is the way *complete* Gospel narratives or other extended written documents are envisioned as direct sources on which an evangelist could draw. Distinctive about this approach are the various possibilities for *literary dependence* that are envisioned among the canonical Gospels. **[See Expanded CD Version pp. 49–51: *Possible Literary Relationships: Diagrams*]**

Whichever relationship is envisioned, agreements of wording and order are attributable to one evangelist's directly borrowing from another. Differences in content and order occur when an evangelist modifies his source or supplements it with material from other sources.

Widely Held Views

While single source theories were popular in the eighteenth and early nineteenth centuries, they no longer enjoy widespread support. The hypothetical nature of the original source posed a problem, even though ancient gospels no longer extant, such as the *Gospel of the Hebrews*, were proposed as possible candidates. Upon closer inspection, these theories were unable to account for extensive similarities in wording and order found in the Synoptic Gospels. More specifically, they failed to account for the numerous ways that the Synoptic Gospels *related to each other*.

Miscellaneous source theories proved helpful in prompting scholars to think about the variety of forms in which traditions about Jesus probably circulated in the post-Easter period. But they also proved inadequate in explaining the patterns of agreement in content and order of events.

Literary dependence theories, however, have been more widely received. Besides the preface to Luke's Gospel, which specifically mentions his use of previous written sources (Luke 1:1–4), patristic authors mention various relationships of literary dependence among the evangelists. While ancient precedent is an important consideration, literary dependence theories, which envision *one evangelist copying directly from another*, have gained favor over the last two centuries because they provide more satisfying explanations for the verbatim agreements and the similarities in the order of events. Since literary dependence does not preclude authorial creativity, theories developed out of this model are also able to explain differences in content, order, and theological emphasis.

Of the numerous possible literary relationships that can be imagined among the Synoptic Gospels, two have received special prominence: the Two Gospel Hypothesis and the Two Source (or Two Document) Hypothesis.

Two Gospel Hypothesis

This hypothesis received its classic formulation by Johann Jakob Griesbach in 1789–1790, although it had been proposed earlier.[23] According to this view, Matthew was the first Gospel, which was then used as a source by Luke; at a third stage, Mark used both Matthew and Luke alternately as sources to compose his abbreviated Gospel. This relationship among the Synoptic Gospels is conceived in the following way:

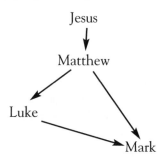

Providing an attractive alternative to Augustine's theory of Gospel origins, the Two Gospel (or Griesbach) Hypothesis gained support from several influential scholars in the nineteenth century, including David Friedrich Strauss and Ferdinand Christian Baur. It fell out of favor in the late nineteenth and early twentieth centuries. In a somewhat modified form, it gained renewed support in the late twentieth century. Its more recent proponents prefer the label "Two Gospel" because only two extant canonical Gospels—no other outside, hypothetical sources—are required to explain the composition of the third Gospel.

Two Source Hypothesis

This view has three distinguishing features: (1) Mark is the earliest Gospel; (2) Matthew and Luke used Mark independently; and (3) a second source, no longer extant—Q (*Quelle*, "source")—was used independently by Matthew and Luke. It can be diagrammed as follows:

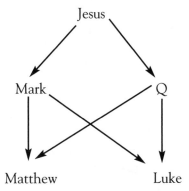

In this form the Two Source Hypothesis primarily accounts for the material that Matthew, Mark, and Luke have in common, also referred to as the Triple Tradition. It is also able to account for the material, consisting mostly of Jesus' sayings, that Matthew and Luke have in common but that is not found in Mark: the Double Tradition, which is also designated Q. It does not, however, account for the material unique to Matthew and Luke. Accordingly, a further refinement was developed to take into account the unique material on which Matthew and Luke drew respectively—M and L—thus yielding a variation called the Four Source Hypothesis. It can be diagrammed as follows:

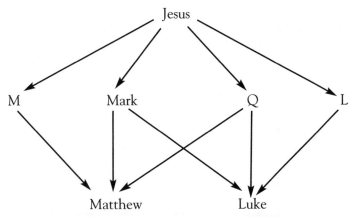

Just as the Two Gospel Hypothesis broke new ground in proposing Luke as the second Gospel directly dependent on Matthew, and Mark as derived from Matthew and Luke, the Two Source Hypothesis was an even bolder departure. Proposing Mark as the earliest Gospel challenged the centuries-old consensus of Matthean priority. Positing a hypothetical second source that Matthew and Luke used alongside Mark was also an innovative formulation.

While different features of the Two Source Hypothesis began to be formulated in the late eighteenth and early nineteenth centuries, it received its essential formulation from Christian Hermann Weisse in 1838. Its appeal was strengthened even more by Heinrich Julius Holtzmann's detailed analysis, initially published in 1863 and later modified in 1886, which focused especially on Markan priority and was based primarily on internal evidence. Further refinements occurred in the late nineteenth and early twentieth centuries that enabled it to gain widespread scholarly support among both Protestant and Roman Catholic biblical scholars in Europe and North America. Among the many works that appeared in support of this view, one of the most influential was Burnett Hillman Streeter's *The Four Gospels: A Study of Origins*, first published in 1924.

Since the Two Source Hypothesis has received such widespread scholarly support, some of its major features are worth noting.

Markan Priority. We can begin with two widely acknowledged observations about the Synoptic Gospels: (1) Most of Mark is contained in Matthew and Luke.[24] (2) The material common to Matthew, Mark, and Luke reveals a core storyline behind all three. Neither of these observations requires Mark to be the first Gospel. Either could be explained just as easily if one assumed that Matthew or even Luke was the first Gospel, and that Mark was derived from one or both.

Other considerations have convinced many scholars that Mark is the earliest Gospel and that Matthew and Luke were derived from Mark. While these considerations may not be uniformly persuasive, especially when any one of them is taken alone, they have cumulative force. Taken together, they suggest that *it is more plausible to imagine Mark as the source from which Matthew and Luke were derived than to imagine either Matthew or Luke as the source from which the other two Synoptic Gospels, in whatever combination, were derived.*

Among the most prominent considerations are the following:

(1) The order of events. Even though a core storyline can be seen behind all three Synoptic Gospels, both Matthew and Luke sometimes diverge from Mark's storyline. Yet when this happens, Matthew and Luke rarely, if ever, agree against Mark in the order of events that they construct. While this pattern does not prove Markan priority, it can be explained if Matthew and Luke are both following Mark's basic storyline but working independently when they diverge from it. If Matthew and Luke ever agreed against Mark in their order of events, this would suggest that one copied the other or that both followed another source besides Mark.

(2) Differences within the Triple Tradition suggesting that Matthew and Luke modified Mark.

(a) Stylistic changes. In a number of cases Mark's grammar or style is matched by more felicitous phrasing in the parallel accounts of Matthew and Luke. Sometimes their improvements are similar, at other times they differ. One of the most notable examples concerns the use of the historical present, a grammatical idiom more typical of Latin (and English) than Greek, in which the present tense of a verb expresses past action. In Mark this idiom occurs about 150 times (excluding its use in parables). When Matthew provides a parallel, he changes Mark's historical present to an alternate construction about 75 percent of the time; in Lukan parallels, Mark's historical presents are almost always rendered with a suitable replacement.[25] Another consistent pattern emerges around Mark's tendency to use the coordinating conjunction "and" (*kai*) to link clauses and sentences. In parallel passages in which this occurs, Matthew and Luke tend to replace *kai* with other grammatical constructions, such as a milder adversative conjunction (*de*), various forms of participial clauses, or alternate phraseology.[26]

(b) Redundancies. Mark's literary style is sometimes characterized as "pleonastic," referring to the tendency to repeat phrases rather than employ a lean writing style. Over 200 instances of Mark's use of redundant (or duplicate) expressions have been identified. It is more common for such repetitive phrases to be absent in the parallel accounts of Matthew or Luke (or both) than for them to be retained or amplified. One of the most familiar examples occurs in Mark 1:32, in which people are said to have brought those who were sick to Jesus "that evening, at sundown." Instead of repeating this pleonastic mention of the time of day, Matthew preserves one half, "that evening" (Matt 8:16), while Luke retains the other half, "as the sun was setting" (Luke 4:40).[27] Since Matthew and Luke used a more sophisticated Greek style than Mark, these differences can be explained as resulting from their tendency to tighten Mark's pleonastic prose.

(c) Problematic statements. Some of Mark's statements, which appear to be problematic for various reasons, are found in a less objectionable form in the parallel accounts of Matthew and Luke. Mark 6:5 reports that Jesus "*could do* no deed of power [in his hometown]," whereas Matt 13:58 says that Jesus "*did not do* many deeds of power there" (emphasis added). It is easier to imagine Matthew changing Mark's statement about Jesus' *inability* to work miracles to a statement about his *unwillingness* to do so than vice versa. In several passages, Mark highlights the disciples' lack of understanding (e.g., Mark 4:13). These negative comments are often absent or toned down in the Matthean and Lukan parallels (Matt 13:18; Luke 8:11; also cf. Mark 6:51–52 and Matt 14:32–33). Mark 2:26 incorrectly identifies Abiathar (instead of his father Ahimelech) as high priest when David entered the temple to eat the bread of the presence (1 Sam 21:1–6; cf. 30:7). The reference to Abiathar is omitted in the parallel accounts (Matt 12:4; Luke 6:4), thereby producing a correct text. It is easier to imagine Matthew and Luke correcting Mark's simple mistake than to think that Mark would introduce an error into a factually correct story.

In each of the aforementioned instances, it is easier to explain the differences in the Triple Tradition if one assumes that Mark came first and was used (and corrected) independently by Matthew and Luke.

Q: The Sayings Source. The material common to Matthew and Luke but absent in Mark is commonly designated Q.[28] This material, which is also called the Double Tradition, consists of some 230 verses. It includes primarily sayings of Jesus, although it contains some narrative material.* [See **Expanded CD Version pp. 55–59:** *Probable Contents of Q: A Chart*]

Whether Q is best thought of as a single document consisting mostly of Jesus' sayings or as a more fluid set of oral and written traditions that nevertheless reflect an identifiable, continuous stream of early Christianity remains disputed. In either case, in the Two Source Hypothesis, Q is a source used independently by Matthew and Luke. If so, the close verbal similarities found in the Double Tradition are easily explained.[29] Rather than Matthew's drawing on Luke, or vice versa, they are drawing on a common source. When they agree verbatim, they are representing Q verbatim. When they differ in wording, they are modifying their Q source.

In spite of the extensive similarities in wording in much of the Double Tradition, this material is employed differently in Matthew and Luke. In Matthew, many of these sayings are found in the five discourses of Jesus (chs. 5–7, 10, 13, 18, and 23–25). In Luke, much of Q is distributed in two sections: the section of teaching beginning with the Sermon on the Plain (6:20–8:3) and the Travel Narrative (9:51–19:27).

Rather than being randomly distributed by Matthew and Luke, these Q sayings sometimes appear in Matthew and Luke in clusters in which the sayings are arranged in roughly the same order. For example, sayings in Luke 6:20–49 are spread throughout their Matthean counterpart, the Sermon on the Mount (chs. 5–7), but they occur in roughly the same order in which they are found in Luke.[30]

Scholars have noted other instances in which the order of Q sayings in their Lukan form is more or less retained in Matthew. As one might expect, the patterns of clustering are sometimes irregular and sayings can occur in a different order. Even so, enough uniformity exists in certain clusters of Q sayings to suggest that Matthew and Luke drew on a written sayings source, although not slavishly.

Another argument for the existence of Q is the presence of doublets—sayings or episodes that are reported twice in Matthew and Luke.[31] In several instances, the doublet consists of one occurrence with a parallel in Mark and a second occurrence with a parallel in Q.[32] The presence of these doublets can be readily explained if Matthew and Luke were drawing on two separate sources—Mark and Q—and trying to report both faithfully.

Even though Q is a hypothetical source, the probability that such a source existed was increased by the 1945–1946 discovery of the *Gospel of Thomas* in Nag Hammadi, Egypt. This Gnostic gospel, which records 114 sayings of Jesus without placing them in a larger narrative framework, was composed later than Q, probably in the early second century C.E., yet it provides an early literary analogue for Q. It shows, at the very least, that a document like Q circulated within early Christianity and that it is quite conceivable that such a document existed several decades earlier. [See **Expanded CD Version pp. 60–61:** *The Theology of Q*]

Efforts by scholars to date Q, to construct a profile of the "Q community," and to detect different strata within Q on the basis of which separate editions or recensions of Q can be identified (Q^1, Q^2, and Q^3) have been controversial. Since Q

---

*The accepted scholarly form for citing Q is based on the Lukan versification. Thus, Q 3:7–9 refers to the Lukan formulation in Luke 3:7–9, and its parallel is Matt 3:7–10.

represents one of the earliest strata of traditions traceable to Jesus, dating perhaps to about 50 C.E., the energy devoted to these tasks is understandable. Searching for earlier strata of Q and correlating these various strata with specific communities of faith and the different Christologies of those communities can be problematic both methodologically and theologically. Identifying editorial stages based on literary markers in the text or anachronistic clues that point to different time periods for the editorial activity can be difficult enough, even when working with writings such as the OT prophets. It becomes far more subjective when one is working with a hypothetical writing. Such editorial reconstruction can also become problematic when theological biases influence or even dictate the principles for deciding what is early or late.

M & L: The Special Material in Matthew and Luke. M and L are used to designate the material unique to Matthew and Luke. Much of this special material is concentrated in their respective birth and infancy narratives (Matt 1–2; Luke 1–2) and resurrection accounts (Matt 28; Luke 24). Unique sayings or episodes are also found throughout the Matthean and Lukan narratives. Much of the L material is located in the Lukan Travel Narrative (9:51–19:27), although a number of unique episodes occur in the Lukan Passion Narrative, for example, Jesus' conversation with the wailing women (23:27–31) and the criminals being crucified with him (23:39–43). Similarly unique episodes occur in Matthew, for example, the death of Judas (Matt 27:3–10).

Certain theological tendencies are also evident within this unique material. This is clear when reviewing the contents of the special material in both Matthew and Luke. [**See Expanded CD Version pp. 62–66: *M & L: Contents and Distinguishing Features***]

Without further comparative material it is difficult to posit a single written M or L source. The exact nature of the unique material at Matthew and Luke's disposal must remain an open question, although it is entirely conceivable that it was a mixture of oral and written traditions. [**See Expanded CD Version pp. 66–69: *Multiple Stage Development Hypothesis* and *The Ongoing Debate: Two Gospel or Two Source Hypothesis***]

The Gospel of John and the Synoptic Gospels

While much scholarly attention has been devoted to the Synoptic Problem, an equally pressing question for readers of the Gospels is how the Fourth Gospel relates to the Synoptic Gospels. Unlike Luke, the Fourth Gospel's prologue mentions no literary predecessors nor does it state that the author had investigated earlier accounts of Jesus' life (see Luke 1:1–4). Toward the end of the Gospel, John reflects an awareness of other traditions and especially notes how extensive they are (20:30; 21:25). The storyline of John's Gospel differs so radically from that of the Synoptic Gospels that it is impossible to see it as a "second edition" of any of them. We are thus unable to think of the author of the Fourth Gospel using one of the Synoptic Gospels as a source in the same way Matthew and Luke might have used Mark.

Similarities between John and the Synoptics

A number of John's stories are found in the Synoptic Gospels. Among the most prominent are the following: the cleansing of the temple (2:13–25; see Mark 11:11–17; Matt 21:10–17; Luke 19:45–46); feeding the 5,000 (6:1–15; see Mark 6:32–44; Matt 14:13–21; Luke 9:10–17); walking on the water (6:16–21; see Mark 6:45–52; Matt 14:22–33); Mary's anointing of Jesus (12:1–8; see Mark 14:3–9; Matt 26:6–13; Luke 7:36–50); and the triumphal entry into Jerusalem (12:12–19; see Mark 11:1–10; Matt 21:1–9; Luke 19:28–40). Besides these direct parallels, other Johannine stories closely resemble synoptic stories, for example, the healing of the official's son (4:46–54; see the healing of the centurion's servant in Matt 8:5–13; Luke 7:1–10); the Sabbath healing of the man who had been sick thirty-eight years (5:1–9; see the healing of the paralytic in Mark 2:1–12; Matt 9:1–8; Luke 5:17–26; the healing of the man with the withered hand in Mark 3:1–6; Matt. 12:9–14; Luke 6:6–11; the healing of the crippled woman on the Sabbath in Luke 13:10–17; and the healing of the man with dropsy in Luke 14:1–6); Peter's confession (6:66–71; see Mark 8:27–33; Matt 16:13–23; Luke 9:18–22); and the healing of the man born blind (ch. 9; see the healing of the blind man in Mark 8:22–26 and Bartimaeus in Mark 10:46–52; see also Matt 20:29–34; Luke 18:35–43).

Along with these narrative episodes are a number of Jesus' sayings that also echo the synoptic tradition: "a prophet has no honor in the prophet's own country" (4:44; see Mark 6:4); "those who love their life lose it" (12:25; see Mark 8:35; Matt 16:25; Luke 9:24); "whoever receives me receives him who sent me" (13:20; see Mark 9:37; Matt 18:5; Luke 9:48); "ask and you will receive" (16:24; see Matt 7:7–8; Luke 11:9–10); and "save me from this hour" (12:27; see Mark 14:33–36; Matt 26:39; Luke 22:42). John the Baptist's testimony about Jesus (1:26–27) has very close parallels in the Synoptic Gospels (see Mark 1:7–8; Matt 3:11–12; Luke 3:16; also John the Baptist's use of the bridegroom image in 3:29–30; cf. Mark 2:19–20; Matt 9:15; Luke 5:34–35).

Especially in John's Passion Narrative, which technically begins in 18:1 but actually begins as early as 11:47, there is close resemblance to the synoptic Passion Narrative not only in terms of the episodes reported but also in their sequence. Admittedly, John's account shows considerable variation from the Synoptics. For example, John places the plot to kill Jesus (11:45–57) and Mary's anointing of Jesus (12:1–8) before the triumphal entry (cf. Mark 14:1–9). Yet from Jesus' betrayal and arrest (18:1–12) onward, John's account follows the Markan sequence fairly closely (compare John 18:1–19:42 and Mark 14:43–15:47). John's account exhibits many distinctive elements, but there is an undisputed family resemblance with Mark's account.

Traditions Unique to John

Just as each of the Synoptics, especially Matthew and Luke, report material unique to them, so does John. The Synoptic Gospels have no stories comparable to Jesus' encounter with Nicodemus (ch. 3), his conversation with the Samaritan woman (ch. 4), the raising of Lazarus (ch. 11), or the washing of the disciples' feet (13:1–11), let alone the Johannine prologue (1:1–18) and several of the post-Easter episodes (chs. 20–21). Equally distinctive are the Johannine discourses, both their form and content. Discourses or dialogues about eternal life (ch. 3), living water (ch. 4), manna from heaven (ch. 6), the good shepherd (ch. 10), the resurrection and the life (ch. 11), and especially the Farewell Discourse (chs. 14–17) are without parallel in the Synoptics. Also distinctive are the highly stylized "I am" declarations that occur repeatedly in John (e.g., 6:35, 41, 48, 51). These declarations, as well as his distinctive geographical and chronological framework for the Jesus story, represent uniquely Johannine constructions.

Sources and Theories of Composition

To account for the distinctiveness of the Fourth Gospel, interpreters have suggested numerous possible sources that John used. They have also proposed various theories of composition. **[See Expanded CD Version p. 71: *Eusebius's Theory of Gospels Composition*]**

Several things seem clear. First, John knows a Jesus tradition independent of the synoptic tradition. This is clear from the numerous episodes and sayings that are unknown to the synoptic tradition (see those listed above, for a start). Second, John knows one or more of the Synoptic Gospels in written form, probably Mark or Luke, or a common oral tradition. Because John and the Synoptic Gospels have so many episodes and sayings in common, especially in the Passion Narrative, it is difficult to believe that John was unaware of them in some synoptic form. We can easily imagine a common tradition out of which both the Synoptic Gospels and John have drawn, and there is no reason that parts of it could not have been written down. It is harder to imagine his actually having written copies of either Mark or Luke, partly because he departs so radically from each of them, but also because each has material that would have been quite useful to him.

As for other literary sources at his disposal, the following seem possible: (1) a version of the Passion Narrative containing many of the distinctive elements we find in John, for example, Jesus washing the disciples' feet, some elements of Jesus' trial, and certain features of the crucifixion account itself; (2) a signs source that contained a collection of miracle stories attributed to Jesus, especially emphasizing Jesus' power as a miracle worker and miracles as a basis for faith; (3) a sayings source with a list of "I am" declarations, either as a simple series of declarations, or, more likely, as a series of expanded reflections or homilies in which Jesus develops each metaphor— for example, light, water, or bread—to interpret himself and his mission; and (4) a stories source with material about John the Baptist and his relation to Jesus, but also including various controversy stories (e.g., 5:9b–18; 7:14–24) as well as encounters between Jesus and individuals such as Nicodemus, the Samaritan woman, and Lazarus, Mary, and Martha.

The presence of literary seams in the Gospel of John suggests that it has gone through several editorial stages. This is most obviously the case with chapter 21, which is best read as an epilogue added later. This was certainly the case with the story of the woman taken in adultery (7:53–8:11). It is less likely that the prologue was a later addition, although it might well have been. Chapters 5–7, as they stand, exhibit no logical chronological sequence. At some stage they must have been given their current arrangement for some editorial reason not easily recognizable to us.

However plausible or implausible this imagined reconstruction of the tradition John inherited might appear, it suggests that he had a rich variety of traditions at his disposal and that the task before him was not a simple one. In certain ways John faced a challenge similar to that of Luke in writing Acts. He was heading into uncharted waters, and the boldness of his literary and theological vision is seen both by the direction he took the Jesus tradition and how he took it there. [See **Expanded CD Version p. 72**: *Augustine's Evaluation of John's Achievement*]

Notes

1. This is William Wright's observation in a paper prepared for an Emory doctoral seminar on the Gospels, Feb. 19, 2002. The following treatment draws on Wright's paper, "St. Augustine's *De consensu evangelistarum*."

2. See Harvey K. McArthur, *The Quest Through the Centuries: The Search for the Historical Jesus* (Philadelphia: Fortress, 1966), especially his chapter on sixteenth-century Gospel harmonies (85–101) and the appendix (157–64), which gives a comprehensive list of sixteenth-century harmonies with annotations.

3. See A. T. Robertson, *A Harmony of the Gospels for Students of the Life of Christ* (New York: Harper, 1922); more recently, Robert L. Thomas and Stanley N. Gundry, *The NIV Harmony of the Gospels: With Explanations and Essays, Using the Text of the New International Version* (San Francisco: Harper and Row, 1988). This is a revised edition of John Broadus and A. T. Robertson, *Harmony of the Gospels* (New York: Harper, 1950).

4. *Comm. Jo.* 10.10. His exposition of the four accounts is in 10.1–20, in which he discusses the synoptic accounts in connection with John 2:1, 12–15.

5. *Comm. Jo.* 10.18.

6. *Comm. Jo.* 10.20.

7. *Comm. Jo.* 10.20.

8. *Cons.* 1.2.3. Similarly, Origen (Eusebius, *Hist. eccl.* 6.25.4–6). Eusebius also posits a similar order of composition (see *Hist. eccl.* 3.24.5–15). Also, cf. Irenaeus, *Haer.* 3.1.1.

9. *Cons.* 1.2.4. Even though each Gospel has a distinct sequence of events, Augustine insists that this should *not* be taken to mean that "each individual writer chose to write in ignorance of what his predecessor had done" (*NPNF*[1] 6:78). Some have argued, on the basis of other passages in *De consensu*, that Augustine thought Mark knew both Matthew and Luke. See *Cons.* 4.10.11; also 1.3.6.

10. *Cons.* 1.2.4.

11. Eusebius, *Hist. eccl.* 6.14.5–7.

12. In the following notes, GP stands for Burton H. Throckmorton, Jr., ed., *Gospel Parallels: A Comparison of the Synoptic Gospels* (5th ed.; Nashville: Nelson, 1992). Reference is made to the section number (§).

13. Some of the more prominent examples are: Jesus heals a leper (Matt 8:1–4; Mark 1:40–45; Luke 5:12–16; GP § 45); Jesus heals the paralytic (Matt 9:1–8; Mark 2:1–12; Luke 5:17–26; GP § 52); the call of Levi/Matthew (Matt 9:9; Mark 2:14; Luke 5:27; GP § 53); the conditions of discipleship (Matt 16:24–28; Mark 8:34–9:1; Luke 9:23–27; GP § 123); Jesus blesses the children (Matt 19:13–15; Mark 10:13–16; Luke 18:15–17; GP § 188); questions about Jesus' authority (Matt 21:23–27; Mark 11:27–33; Luke 20:1–8; GP § 202); the parable of the wicked tenants (Matt 21:33–46; Mark 12:1–12; Luke 20:9–19; GP § 204); Jesus' dispute with the Sadducees about the resurrection (Matt 22:23–33; Mark 12:18–27; Luke 20:27–40; GP § 207); and the signs of the end of the age (Matt 24:4–8; Mark 13:5–8; Luke 21:8–11; GP § 214).

14. Examples of significant agreements between Matthew and Mark include: the call of the first disciples (Matt 4:18–22; Mark 1:16–20; GP § 11); the feeding of the 4,000 (Matt 15:32–39; Mark 8:1–10; GP § 118); the traitor (Matt 26:20–25; Mark 14:17–21; GP § 235); and Jesus in Gethsemane (Matt 26:36–46; Mark 14:32–42; GP § 239). Significant agreements between Mark and Luke include: Jesus in the synagogue at Capernaum (Mark 1:21–28; Luke 4:31–37; GP § 12); the Gerasene demoniac (Mark 5:1–20; Luke 8:26–39; GP § 106); the report of another exorcist (Mark 9:38–41; Luke 9:49–50; GP § 130); and the widow's gift (Mark 12:41–44; Luke 21:1–4; GP § 212).

15. Some prominent examples are: John's preaching of repentance (Matt 3:7–10; Luke 3:7–9; GP § 2); John's preaching about baptism with the Holy Spirit and fire (Matt 3:11*b*–12; Luke 3:16*b*–17; GP § 4); Jesus' teaching about prayer (Matt 7:7–11; Luke 11:9–13; GP § 38); Jesus' message to John the Baptist (Matt 11:4–6; Luke 7:22–23; GP § 64); the return of the unclean spirit (Matt 12:43–45; Luke 11:24–26; GP § 88); and the lament over Jerusalem (Matt 23:37–39; Luke 13:34–35; GP § 211).

16. For example, Jesus' teaching about greatness in service (Matt 20:24–28; Mark 10:41–45; against Luke 22:24–27; GP § 192) and Jesus' denunciation of the scribes (Mark 12:38–40; Luke 20:46–47; against Matt 23:6–13; GP § 210).

17. One exception is Matt 8–10, which diverges in some respects from the Markan order (cf. Mark 1:40–6:13). In Luke, several passages do not follow Mark's order: rejection at Nazareth (Luke 4:16–30; cf. Mark 6:1–6); the call of the first disciples (Luke 5:1–11; cf. Mark 1:16–20); the call of the Twelve (Luke 6:12–16; cf. Mark 3:13–19*a*); the woman with the ointment (?) (Luke 7:36–50; cf. Mark 14:3–9); Jesus' true family (Luke 8:19–21; cf. Mark 3:31–35); the lawyer's question (?) (Luke 10:25–28; cf. Mark 12:28–31); the Beelzebul controversy (Luke 11:14–23; cf. Mark 3:22–27); blasphemous speech (Luke 12:10; cf. Mark 3:28–29); the betrayal foretold (Luke 22:21–23; cf. Mark 14:18–21); greatness in the kingdom (Luke 22:24–30; cf. Mark 10:42–45); and Peter's denial (Luke 22:54–65; cf. Mark 14:66–72).

18. See Matt 19:1–28:10; Mark 10:1–16:8; and Luke 18:15–24:12. In Matthew, the cleansing of the temple occurs on the same day as the triumphal entry (Matt 21:10–17; similarly Luke 19:45–46); in Mark, the cleansing of the temple takes place on the following day (Mark 11:12–19). Even so, Mark, Matthew, and Luke report the same sequence: the cleansing of the temple follows the triumphal entry. For differences between Luke and Mark, see previous note.

19. There is a small portion of Markan material (Mark 10:13–52) in Luke 18:15–43.

20. For example, some of the material in Mark 1:40–6:14 is found in a different order in Matt 8–10. Much of this Markan material, however, is presented in roughly the same order in Luke (see esp. Luke 5:12–19; 8:4–9:50).

21. One version of this view was held by F. D. E. Schleiermacher (1768–1834), who used the term *diēgēsis* from Luke 1:1, meaning "narrative" or "account," to designate his theory.

22. Literary dependence theories are sometimes designated "utilization" hypotheses, signifying that the evangelists directly utilized the written narratives of their counterparts.

23. Henry Owen, *Observations on the Four Gospels* (London, 1764) and Anton Friedrich Büsching, *Die vier Evangelisten mit ihren eigenen Worten zusammengesetzt und mit Erklärung versehen* (Hamburg, 1766).

24. Mark contains 661 verses. Ninety percent of them are found in Matthew; 65 percent of them occur in Luke. There are very few Markan verses that are without parallel in either Matthew or Luke. The most notable examples are two healing miracles—the deaf mute (Mark 7:31–37) and the blind man of Bethsaida (Mark 8:22–26)—and the parable of the seed growing secretly (Mark 4:26–29; also Mark 3:20–21; 13:35*b*–36; 14:51–52).

25. For example, Mark's frequent use of "he says" (*legei*) or "they say" (*legousin*) usually appears in Matthew or Luke as "he said" (*eipen*) or "they said" (*eipan*).

26. Many of these changes are not evident in English translations.

27. Advocates of the Griesbach hypothesis argue that this is an instance in which Mark conflates Matthew and Luke.

28. "Q" is derived from *Quelle*, the German word for "source." Since the late nineteenth century, Q has been used by scholars to designate the non-Markan hypothetical source used by Matthew and Luke. An early sayings source (in Aramaic or Greek) common to Matthew and Luke was proposed by Christian Hermann Weisse (1838). A less well-defined sayings source that stemmed from an original oral Gospel

55

had already been suggested by Johann Gottfried Eichhorn (1794), who, for this reason, has been identified as the originator of the idea of a sayings source that scholars later identified as Q.

29. Some of the most conspicuous examples of close verbal agreement are: Matt 6:24 & Luke 16:13; Matt 7:7–11 & Luke 11:9–13; Matt 11:25–27 & Luke 10:21–22; and Matt 23:37–39 & Luke 13:34–35. There are, however, a number of instances in which the wording is quite different: Luke 6:29 & Matt 5:39–40; Luke 11:44 & Matt 23:27; Luke 12:2–9 & Matt 10:26–33; and Luke 16:16–17 & Matt 11:12–13 and 5:18.

30. See especially Luke 6:20–21 (Matt 5:1–3, 6); Luke 6:22–23 (Matt 5:11–12); Luke 6:27–28 (Matt 5:44); Luke 6:41–42 (Matt 7:3–5); Luke 6:43–44 (Matt 7:18–20); Luke 6:46 (Matt 7:21); and Luke 6:47–49 (Matt 7:24–27). A similar pattern is seen in the cluster of sayings in Luke 7:1–10, 18–23, 24–26, 27, 28, 31–35. While they are distributed differently in Matthew, they appear in the same order. The pattern is repeated in Q 11:14–23, 24–26, 39–52.

31. Some scholars distinguish between "doublets" (instances within a given Gospel in which a saying or episode is simply repeated) and "double traditions" (double occurrences in which one is drawn from Mark, the other from Q). Here, no such distinction is made. Doublet simply means a double occurrence of a saying or episode within the same Gospel. Such doublets occur twenty-two times in Matthew (3:2 & 4:17; 3:10 & 7:19; 4:23 & 9:35; 5:29–30 & 18:8–9; 5:32 & 19:9; 7:16–18 & 12:33–35; 9:13 & 12:7; 9:27–31 & 20:29–34; 9:32–34 & 12:22–24; 10:15 & 11:24; 10:22a & 24:9b; 10:22b & 24:13; 10:38 & 16:24; 10:39 & 16:25; 12:38–39 & 16:1–2; 12:39 & 16:4; 13:12 & 25:29; 16:19 & 18:18; 17:20 & 21:21; 19:30 & 20:16; 20:26–27 & 23:11; 24:42 & 25:13). Eleven doublets occur in Luke (8:16 & 11:33; 8:17 & 12:2; 8:18 & 19:26; 9:3 & 10:4; 9:23 & 14:27; 9:24 & 17:33; 9:26 & 12:9; 9:46 & 22:24; 11:43 & 20:46; 12:11–12 & 21:14–15; 14:11 & 18:14). One doublet occurs in Mark (9:35 & 10:43–44), though some scholars also identify two others (6:34–44 & 8:1–10; 9:36 & 10:16).

32. The following examples may be noted. The "lighting the lamp" saying, which occurs in Luke 8:16, is found in Mark 4:21; the same saying in Luke 11:33 is found in Q (Matt 5:15). Similarly, the "nothing is hidden" saying, which occurs in Luke 8:17, is found in Mark 4:22; its second occurrence in Luke 12:2 is found in Q (Matt 10:26). In Matthew, Jesus' pronouncement concerning divorce occurs twice: once with a Markan parallel (Matt 19:9; Mark 10:11–12), and again in a Q passage (Matt 5:32; Luke 16:18). Jesus' saying about self-denial in Matthew 16:24 has its parallel in Mark 8:34 (cf. Luke 9:23); its other occurrence (Matt 10:37–38) is found in Q (Luke 14:26–27).

Bibliography

Dungan, David Laird. *A History of the Synoptic Problem: The Canon, the Text, the Composition, and the Interpretation of the Gospels.* The Anchor Bible Reference Library. New York: Doubleday, 1999.

Goodacre, Mark S. *The Synoptic Problem: A Way Through the Maze.* Biblical Seminar 80. London: Sheffield (Continuum), 2001; repr. Edinburgh: T&T Clark (Continuum), 2004.

Hengel, Martin. *The Four Gospels and the One Gospel of Jesus Christ: An Investigation of the Collection and Origin of the Canonical Gospels.* Translated by John Bowden. London: SCM Press, 2000.

Nickle, Keith F. *The Synoptic Gospels: An Introduction.* Louisville: Westminster John Knox, 2001.

Stein, Robert H. *Studying the Synoptic Gospels: Origin and Interpretation.* 2d ed. Grand Rapids: Baker, 2001. Rev. ed. of *The Synoptic Problem* (1987).

Tuckett, Christopher M. "Synoptic Problem." Pages 263–70 in vol. 6 of *The Anchor Bible Dictionary.* Edited by David Noel Freedman. 6 vols. New York: Doubleday, 1992.

Q

Catchpole, David R. *The Quest for Q*. Edinburgh: T&T Clark, 1993.

Kloppenborg Verbin, John S. *Excavating Q: The History and Setting of the Sayings Gospel*. Minneapolis: Fortress, 2000.

Robinson, James McConkey, Paul Hoffmann, and John S. Kloppenborg. *The Critical Edition of Q: Synopsis Including the Gospels of Matthew and Luke, Mark and Thomas with English, German, and French Translations of Q and Thomas*. Leuven: Peeters, 2000.

Tuckett, Christopher M. *Q and the History of Early Christianity: Studies on Q*. Edinburgh/Peabody: T&T Clark/Hendrickson, 1996.

Synopses in English

Aland, K. *Synopsis of the Four Gospels*. 7th ed. Stuttgart: United Bible Societies, 1984.

Throckmorton, Burton H., Jr. *Gospel Parallels*. Based on 9th ed. of the Huck-Lietzmann Greek Synopsis (1936). 5th ed. Nashville: Nelson, 1992.

Online Resources

The New Testament Gateway at http://www.ntgateway.com.

Chapter 4

From Jesus to the Gospels

"We must recognize that a literary work or fragment of tradition is a primary source for the historical situation out of which it arose, and is only a secondary source for the historical details concerning which it gives information."

Rudolf Bultmann

The four decades between the death of Jesus and the appearance of the first written Gospel are a shadowy period, full of many unknowns. Some shafts of light are provided by the letters of Paul that began to appear in the early 50s C.E. Paul's use of the tradition reporting Jesus' institution of the Lord's Supper (1 Cor 11:23–26) and his appeal to Jesus' sayings (1 Thess 4:15; 1 Cor 7:10; 9:14) give some indication of how the Gospel tradition was being remembered and appropriated in the life of the church. Although some glimpses are provided in other NT writings (e.g., Acts 20:35), for the most part scholarly reconstructions of the period prior to the Gospels are derived by working backward from the written Gospels themselves. Such reconstructions are, in other words, exercises in scholarly imagination. [**See Expanded CD Version pp. 82–83:** *Glimpses from Acts of Early Church Teachings*]

Centers of Activity Rather than Stages of Development

The formation of the Gospel tradition is sometimes conceived in distinct stages. In the earliest stage, Palestinian Christianity, which was centered in Jerusalem, formed the defining context in which the apostles and other close associates of Jesus—whose first language was Aramaic—played a major role in shaping the Jesus tradition. A second stage occurred when the church's memory of Jesus began to be recast into Greek. Since this was done in Jewish settings, such as synagogues in Jerusalem populated by Diaspora Jews (Acts 6:1, 9) and in Diaspora synagogues, this second phase is characterized as Hellenistic Jewish Christianity. Since this stage sees a shift from Aramaic to Greek as the primary language in which Jesus was remembered as the church moved away from Jerusalem, it is a transitional stage both linguistically and geographically. A third stage set in when the church moved into settings that were thoroughly Gentile. In this transition from Hellenistic Jewish to Gentile Christianity, the Jesus tradition experienced yet another set of changes as the gospel was recast to make it intelligible to those with very little, if any, knowledge of Jewish Scripture and tradition. In such Gentile settings outside Palestine, certain titles used of Jesus, such as "Lord," would acquire new connotations even as other titles, such as "Son of Man," which would have had little meaning to Gentiles, would have gradually disappeared.

It is now difficult to use this three-stage developmental model in explaining the formation of the Gospel tradition. For one thing, it presupposes a sharp distinction between Aramaic-speaking, Palestinian Judaism and Greek-speaking, Diaspora Judaism that no longer holds. We now know that first-century Palestine was more thoroughly hellenized than once thought. To assume that the earliest stage of the Jesus tradition was exclusively Aramaic-speaking is no longer possible. The three-stage developmental model also ignores or oversimplifies conceptual, linguistic continuities and discontinuities that co-existed at each "stage." Forms of Jewish Christianity continued to flourish well after the first century and provided numerous settings in which the Jesus tradition could be preserved and modified.

But we can think of *centers* in which the Jesus tradition would have taken shape. From the NT writings and other early Christian writings it is evident that Jerusalem was one of the most prominent and, in many ways, the originating center. Its role shifted dramatically with the events surrounding the Jewish-Roman War in 66–70 C.E., which culminated in the destruction of the Jerusalem temple and prompted Christians to flee from the city. Other prominent centers of Christian activity are also known, including Antioch of Syria, Ephesus, and Rome. Other cities or regions left untreated by Acts, such as Alexandria in Egypt and Edessa in Osroëne (northwest Mesopotamia), also became vital repositories for the Jesus tradition, at least later on.

Different sets of circumstances characterized each center. We can imagine circles of Aramaic-speaking Christians in Jerusalem preserving, even writing down, Jesus' teachings in Aramaic. Yet it is just as plausible to imagine circles of Greek-speaking Jewish Christians in Jerusalem preserving the Jesus tradition in Greek. One language may have been more prominent in a center that tended to be monolingual, while other centers may have been bilingual, even trilingual. Aramaic forms of the Jesus tradition were not confined to Jerusalem, and Greek versions of Jesus' stories and deeds were not necessarily a later overlay that received distinctive shape only in Diaspora centers.

What has been characterized as a rabbinic mode of transmitting the Jesus tradition, in which disciples memorized the teachings of their master and sought faithfully to preserve them in both spirit and form, might well have been operative in one center but not in others. Followers of Jesus under the leadership of an influential figure, such as one of the original disciples, might have been organized as a formal school devoted to Scripture study and systematic examination of Jesus' teachings. Such "Christian scribes" would have interpreted the teachings of Jesus utilizing rabbinic methods of Scripture interpretation. They might also have utilized a distinctive literary style and organizational structures that made the Jesus tradition more memorable.

It is just as plausible to imagine another center that was more charismatic in outlook. Informed by a strong sense of the Spirit's presence, disciples located there may have understood Jesus to be present in their midst, actively revealing new truth to them. Such a center may have been less concerned with preserving earlier forms of the Jesus tradition intact than with adapting them to new circumstances. Here too the center may have reflected the outlook of an influential Christian teacher, perhaps an apostle or an apostolic associate, who operated with a different sense of what fidelity to Jesus meant.

Other centers may have blended the rabbinic and charismatic models or even have operated with quite different models.

Life Settings in Which the Jesus Tradition Took Shape

Even with radical differences in outlook and in modes of preserving the Jesus tradition, the various centers probably had many things in common. Certain "life settings," such as gathering for worship, giving instruction in the faith, proclaiming the gospel to others, and defending the faith before different adversaries, would have existed in every center, as well as in many localities throughout the Mediterranean. From ritual studies and sociological analysis of religious behavior of individuals and communities, we know that the dynamics within different "life settings" yield "rules" that shape the use of sacred texts and traditions. Prayers and hymns celebrating the saving work of Christ would be used in liturgical settings, even though they might be reused in catechetical and homiletical settings. Conversely, communities of faith might collect sayings and teachings of Jesus primarily for the purpose of instructing new members, and yet use these collections of sayings in their public preaching and recite them in worship. Even allowing for fluid "life settings," we can think of each one as a formative context in which parts of the Jesus tradition were shaped.

Worship

Some glimpses into early Christian worship are provided in the NT (e.g., Acts 2:42–47; 4:23–37; 20:7–12; 1 Cor 11:2–34; 14:1–40) and early patristic sources.[1] Christians regularly gathered for worship to confess their faith, sing, pray, hear Scripture read and proclaimed, and celebrate the Lord's Supper. In such settings a variety of traditions relating to Jesus would have been recalled, such as his model prayer (Matt 6:9–13; Luke 11:2–4) and the words with which he instituted the Eucharist (1 Cor 11:23–26; Mark 14:22–25; Matt 26:26–29; Luke 22:15–20; cf. 1 Cor 10:16–17). Along with creedal summaries through which the church confessed its faith (e.g., 1 Cor 15:3–6; 1 Tim 3:16) and hymns that celebrated the work of Christ (Phil 2:5–11; Col 1:15–20; Rev 5:12; 7:12; 11:17–18), we can also imagine early Christian communities recalling Jesus' sayings, parables, and teachings, his interpretations of Scripture, episodes from his ministry, the circumstances that led to his death and resurrection, and stories of his post-resurrection appearances. Much of the early Jesus tradition may well have been shaped by its usage in Christian worship.

Teaching

Teachers figure prominently in lists of leadership roles mentioned in the NT (e.g., 1 Cor 12:28; Eph 4:11), and they are often differentiated from other groups such as prophets, evangelists, and bishops in a manner suggesting that they constituted a separate form of ministry. Even so, teaching would have been an indispensable part of the work of persons operating in these several roles. Whether a "scribe who has been trained for the kingdom of heaven" (Matt 13:52) was a common phenomenon is difficult to say, but the phrase suggests a specialized role in which one might have labored as a Christian teacher.

Teaching as a "life setting" should not be thought of in a monochromatic fashion. A teacher's personality, the backgrounds of students, the formality or informality of instruction, the location of teaching—rural or urban, synagogue or school, public or private—defined the contours of any given setting. Regardless of the different configurations of teaching contexts, there is good reason to think that much of the Jesus tradition was shaped in catechetical settings. The organizational structure of the Gospel of Matthew, for example, with its tendency to report units of tradition in groups of threes, fives, and sevens, has led some scholars to posit a "school of St. Matthew."[2] The distinctive form of Scripture interpretation found in Matthew, which closely resembles pesher interpretation at Qumran, might easily have been perfected in such a setting.

Also in such settings we can imagine that Jesus' sayings, parables, and teachings were collected and preserved, along with the many stories that were told about Jesus. It would have been sensible to gather Jesus' miracle stories or stories that had a controversial element into separate collections. Sayings or stories with common forms, such as parables, or having common themes, such as the kingdom of heaven, could also have been collected. Searching for biblical passages that could be linked to Jesus' messiahship would constitute another discrete activity. Collecting such "proof texts" or OT *testimonia* about Jesus in such settings could help explain their frequent occurrence in NT writings.

Preaching

The sermons reported in Acts, for all of their variety, show Peter, Paul, and others proclaiming Jesus in ways that recall the Gospel tradition. In some cases these sermons have a midrashic texture, with a heavy emphasis on OT passages that prove Jesus' messiahship (e.g., Acts 2, 13). Others rehearse the OT story as a prelude to Jesus Christ, noting how the fate of certain OT figures, such as Moses, anticipated Israel's rejection of Jesus Christ as God's duly appointed leader (Acts 7:2–53; also Acts 3:17–26). Still others provide brief narrative summaries of the Jesus story, which is amplified more fully in the canonical Gospels (Acts 10:34–43).

Elsewhere in the NT we find aspects of the Jesus story being appropriated for Christian proclamation and teaching. In 2 Pet 1:16–21, Jesus' transfiguration is cited to show that the "prophetic message" of Christian proclamation is borne by duly authorized witnesses, such as Peter himself, who heard the same divine voice that Jesus heard when he was declared God's Son.

Given the emphasis on Jesus' death and resurrection in early Christian preaching, the prominence of the Passion Narrative in all four Gospels is understandable. As Christians proclaimed Jesus' death as "good news," they had to answer questions relating to his trial and crucifixion: How could someone who was crucified have been God's Messiah? What were the actual charges brought against him at his trial? How did his inner circle of disciples conduct themselves during his trial and crucifixion? What accounts for Judas's betrayal of Jesus?

Early Christians were required to develop a coherent account of what happened during the weeks that led up to Jesus' death in Jerusalem. The story of Jesus' passion was laced with OT interpretation, since this was the framework within which early Christians had to make sense of Jesus' crucifixion. Throughout this sequence of events, Christian preachers would correlate OT passages with different aspects of the Passion Narrative. While the demands of preaching may not have been the only catalyst that prompted early Christians to develop a coherent narrative of Jesus' final days, they certainly constituted one important motivation.

Literary Forms within the Jesus Tradition

As varied as the centers of Christian activity might have been, there emerged some distinctive literary forms through which the Jesus tradition was transmitted. Broadly speaking, three types of material can be identified: (1) sayings and teachings of Jesus; (2) stories about Jesus; and (3) narratives relating to the beginning and end of his ministry: the birth and infancy stories and the Passion Narrative.

Sayings and Teachings

Traditions relating to what Jesus taught took different forms that often overlap.

Logia (literally, "sayings") *or Individual Sayings.* Typically characterized by their brief, memorable form, logia sometimes resemble proverbial sayings, for example, "Prophets are not without honor, except in their hometown" (Mark 6:4; cf. Luke 4:24; John 4:44). Other brief sayings—aphorisms—draw less on the cumulative wisdom of the past and more from an individual sage's own wisdom and insight. Aphorisms can be in the form of a statement (Matt 10:24–25), a question (Mark 8:36–38), or an imperative (Luke 13:24). In some cases, sayings are pronouncements attached to a specific title, for example, "[T]he Son of Man has authority on earth to forgive sins" (Mark 2:10). By the time they were incorporated into a written Gospel, such individual sayings may have been grouped together according to a theme or catchword (e.g., Luke 16:10–13).

Parables. Mark 4:34 reports that Jesus "did not speak to [his disciples] except in parables." While it is difficult to define a parable (Greek *parabolē*) precisely, the following formulation may serve as a working definition: "a narrative or saying of varying length, designed to illustrate a truth especially through comparison or simile."[3] Jesus' use of parables may reflect influence from the OT, in which the Hebrew term *mashal* designates certain forms of figurative speech (Judg 14:10–18; 1 Sam 10:12; Ezek 17:2–24; also cf. 2 Sam 12:1–25).

No parables as such are recorded in John's Gospel, but the term is frequently used in the Synoptic Gospels: Matthew (seventeen times), Mark (thirteen times), and Luke (eighteen times). Parables may be quite long—for example, the parable of the ten pounds (Luke 19:11–27)—or brief (Luke 4:23: "Doctor, cure yourself!"). Some scholars distinguish between short metaphorical parable sayings (Matt 5:14b; 15:14)—the similitude, an amplified form of comparison (Luke 13:20–21; Matt 11:16–17)—and full-fledged parables in which a comparison is made using a longer story (Matt 20:1–16). If there is one recurrent theme connected with Jesus' parables, it is the kingdom of God/heaven (*basileia tou theou/tou ouranou*, e.g., Mark 4:11, 26–32). Even stories that are not technically called parables, for example, the story of the rich man and Lazarus (Luke 16:19–31), belong to the same general category of amplified stories that were told by Jesus to illustrate different aspects of his teaching.

Midrash or Scripture Interpretation. The Gospels often portray Jesus interpreting Scripture. In his inaugural address at Nazareth in Luke 4:16–30, Jesus' use of Isa 61:1–2 figures prominently. In other cases, Jesus cites brief OT passages and relates them to his ministry. In the episode of Jesus' cleansing the temple, he is reported as quoting Isa 56:7 (cf. Mark 11:17). In the parable of the wicked tenant, the "rejected stone" passage of Ps 118:22–23 figures centrally in his teaching. Similarly, Jesus adduces Ps 110:1 as proof of his messiahship (Mark 12:36). In some cases, especially in the Fourth Gospel, Jesus' use of the OT draws heavily on familiar themes, such as the exodus and manna in the wilderness (John 6) or the role of the good shepherd (John 10). Jesus also makes explicit appeal to Scripture in the Fourth Gospel (e.g., John 13:18).

Apocalyptic Teachings. Individual sayings of Jesus frequently carry apocalyptic overtones.[4] These may relate to the role of the Son of Man at the end time (Mark 9:1) or to other dimensions of apocalyptic thought (e.g., Luke 11:17–23; 12:49–56). A conspicuous cluster of such teachings occurs in the so-called "little apocalypses" in the Synoptic Gospels (Mark 13; Luke 21; Matt 24). In these discourses, all three of which are located at the same point in Jesus' ministry, Jesus sketches a vision of the future as it relates to the impending destruction of the Jerusalem temple.

Stories about Jesus

Episodes reporting Jesus' deeds occur in different forms. Among the more prominent are the following:

Miracle Stories. Stories in which Jesus performs a "sign" (*sēmeion*), "wonder" (*teras*), or "power" (*dynamis*) frequently occur in all four Gospels. Many of them are healing stories, and among this group a significant number are exorcism stories in which Jesus casts out a demon or performs some similar act that suppresses or evicts evil spirits. Others are "nature miracles" in which Jesus' actions defy the natural order in some way, for example, stilling the storm (Mark 4:35–41) or walking on the water (Mark 6:45–52). Like the parables, miracle stories can be quite lengthy and elaborate, for example, the Gerasene demoniac (Mark 5:1–20), or very brief, for example, the healing of Peter's mother-in-law (Mark 1:29–31).

From the extensive scholarly research on miracle stories, a fairly distinct literary form of a healing story has been identified, sometimes with three or more of the following elements: (1) introductory setup; (2) appearance of Jesus; (3) appearance of the afflicted person and a description of the person's malady; (4) encounter between Jesus and the afflicted person; (5) the miracle; (6) outcome of the miracle, for example, the astonishment of the crowd or a sign that the person has been healed; and (7) conclusion.

Controversy Stories. Other episodes are built around some point of conflict, often between Jesus and some named adversaries, such as Pharisees, scribes, or Sadducees. The conflict may arise over some word or action of Jesus or his disciples, for example, plucking grain on the Sabbath (Mark 2:23–28). Out of the controversy, some aspect of Jesus' mission will be highlighted or clarified, and often the story may conclude with a pronouncement that clinches the theological point of the story, for example, "the Son of Man is lord even of the sabbath" (Mark 2:28). As with miracle stories, controversy stories in which different aspects of Jesus' teaching are clarified can be grouped together in the written Gospels (e.g., Mark 12:13–40).

Pronouncement Stories. Stories about Jesus that feature some striking pronouncement, especially at the conclusion of the story, constitute another category. In earlier scholarly discussions, this type of story was referred to as a "paradigm" (Martin Dibelius) or "apophthegm" [English equivalent: apotegm] (Rudolf Bultmann), but the label "pronouncement story" (Vincent Taylor) eventually won the day. Such stories resemble the *chreia*, a brief story common in the Greco-Roman world that was often told of a sage and featured a memorable saying.[5]

In some cases these pronouncement stories may blend with the previous two types of stories. The pronouncement may relate to a miracle that Jesus has performed (Mark 3:1–6) or stem from some controversy in which he has been involved (e.g., Mark 2:15–17). Pronouncements may also occur in other settings (Mark 3:31–35; 12:13–17; Matt 8:18–22; Luke 11:27–28). Although Jesus' predictions of his death and resurrection are not technically related to specific stories, they nevertheless qualify as pronouncements (Mark 8:31; 9:31; 10:32–34).

Commissioning Stories. Reminiscent of certain OT stories that feature the commissioning of someone called by God (e.g., Gen 12:1–4; Exod 3:1–4:17; 1 Sam 3:1–14; Isa 6; Jer 1:1–10), certain episodes in the Gospels (and Acts) report Jesus' calling the apostles (Matt 10:1–4; Mark 3:16–19; Luke 6:13–16) or commissioning other disciples (Luke 10:1–12, 17–24). Among the most dramatic of the commissioning stories is the call and conversion of Saul of Tarsus (Acts 9, 22, 26).

Hero Stories. Although stories in the previous categories often portray Jesus in a heroic manner, a number of stories in the Gospels resemble stories from the ancient world that were used to herald the deeds of heroic, semidivine, and divine figures. Sometimes referred to as "legends" (Dibelius, Bultmann), such stories feature extraordinary aspects of Jesus' life that relate to his divine status. The birth stories of Matthew and Luke, which report the miraculous circumstances of Jesus' birth and the extraordinary events that occurred thereafter, are reminiscent of similar OT stories as well as legends known from the Greco-Roman world. At other places in the Gospels, when extraordinary cosmic occurrences occur, for example, in relation to Jesus' death (Matt 27:51–54), we find elements of such heroic stories. Other heroic stories include the temptation (Mark 1:12–13; Matt 4:1–11; Luke 4:1–13), the transfiguration (Mark

9:2–9; Matt 17:1–13; Luke 9:28–36), and most notably the resurrection and post-Easter appearances (Mark 16; Matt 28; Luke 24; John 20–21).

The Passion Narrative

All four Gospels display similarities in content and sequence within the Passion Narratives (Mark 14–15; Matt 26–27; Luke 22–23; John 18–19). For this reason, scholars have concluded that this part of the Gospel tradition took shape relatively early. It also appears to have been fairly uniform in the various Christian centers. How early it began to be written down is unknown, but it constituted a core tradition within early Christian communities. As the Passion Narrative was incorporated into each of the written canonical Gospels, it acquired some distinctive theological emphases. In Luke's Gospel, for example, the innocence of Jesus is a recurring motif in the Passion Narrative to a degree that distinguishes it from the other Gospels.

From the Jesus Tradition to Written Gospel

With the gradual passing of Jesus' closest associates—the apostles, other disciples, members of his family, and others who knew him directly—it became necessary to preserve their memories of Jesus in a more permanent form. Combined with this urge to replace eyewitness testimony with written accounts of Jesus' ministry were the practical needs of his disciples. Instructing new converts, strengthening the faith of those who had been disciples for a while, and responding to outside critics created the need to organize and record the diverse elements of the Jesus tradition. The preface to Luke's Gospel attests the need to produce a reliable account of Jesus' words and deeds so that Theophilus could be assured of the truth of what he had been taught (Luke 1:1–4). John's Gospel echoes similar sentiments when its concluding purpose statement accents the desire to foster faith, probably in the double sense of enabling readers to "begin believing" and to "continue believing" (John 20:30–31).

Pressure to create written accounts of Jesus' life and ministry also may have come from other sources. The aftermath of the Jewish revolt in 66–70 C.E. not only saw the reconfiguration of Pharisaic Judaism but also significant changes within Palestinian Christianity. The destruction of the Jerusalem temple differentiated followers of Jesus from other Jewish groups in Palestine. Clarifying their newly discovered identity caused Christian groups to rethink elements of the Jesus tradition. In what sense, for example, had Jesus foreseen the crisis of 70 C.E.? Could he now be seen as the new locus of God's presence and hence a replacement of the temple? Such pressing questions became guiding interpretive principles for retelling the Jesus story.

Yet another impulse may have been provided by the inherent desire to create a literary legacy. While many of the earliest traditions about Jesus may have originally been preserved in Aramaic form, each of the canonical Gospels was written in Greek—most, if not all of them, by Jewish Christians. A rich literary legacy already existed among Greek-speaking Jews, both inside and outside Palestine. From the third century B.C.E., Hellenistic Jews had become adept at retelling the story of Israel, utilizing different Greek literary genres ranging from various forms of historical narrative to epic and tragic poetry. During the first century C.E., Philo of Alexandria and Flavius Josephus continued this literary legacy by producing voluminous works in different genres for their respective audiences. When the four evangelists undertook to render the Jesus story into narrative form, they were continuing a literary tradition that had become well established among other Hellenistic Jews.

Some Considerations

While centers of Christian activity existed in different regions of the Roman Empire, they shared some common convictions and influences.

Jesus as Living Presence. Belief in Jesus' resurrection was expressed in different ways. Jesus could be envisioned as exalted to God's right hand (e.g., Heb 1:3–4; 12:2). In the apocalyptic vision of John the Seer, Jesus was seen as the slain Lamb of God now standing alongside the enthroned God and making intercession for the persecuted saints (e.g., Rev 5:6–10). However differently the risen Lord may have been envisioned, churches in different regions nevertheless regarded him as a living presence in their midst. This presence may have been experienced in a number of ways, for example, through his teaching (Matt 28:18–20) or through the Spirit understood as Advocate (John 13–17). Either way, churches experienced Christ both as a figure of the past and the present, even as a figure of the future. This ongoing awareness of Christ's presence must be considered a vital element in the composition of the Gospels.

Related to this awareness of Christ's continuing presence is prophetic activity that occurred within early Christian communities. Christian prophets constituted a recognizable group within early Christianity (1 Cor 12:28; 14:1–40; Acts 13:1–3). Infused by the Spirit, inspired prophets such as Paul could operate with a self-consciousness that Christ spoke through them (2 Cor 13:3). The capacity to confess Jesus as Lord could even be seen as a Spirit-endowed impulse (1 Cor 12:3). Whether the authors and editors of the Gospels operated with a prophetic self-consciousness is difficult to say, yet they doubtless had traditions about Jesus at their disposal that were attributed to prophetic revelations. They might well have had versions of Jesus' sayings or teachings, or even stories about Jesus, that had been received and transmitted by Christian prophets who saw themselves as speaking on behalf of Christ himself.

The Twelve Apostles. Jesus' appointing the Twelve occupies a prominent place in the Synoptic Gospels (Matt 10:1–4; Mark 3:16–19; Luke 6:13–16; cf. Acts 1:12–26). Even though the Twelve figure less prominently in John's Gospel (John 6:66–71; 20:24), close associates of Jesus, such as the beloved disciple (John 19:26; 20:2; 21:7, 20) and Peter (e.g., John 13:6–38; 18:1–27; 20:2–10; 21:1–19), belong to Jesus' inner circle. The role of the Twelve as authenticating witnesses to Christ's resurrection is firmly established in some of the earliest strata of Christian tradition (1 Cor 15:5).

None of the four canonical Gospels is explicitly attributed to one of the Twelve. Even so, the First and Fourth Gospels were quickly attributed to the apostles Matthew and John. It also became important for the church to link the Second and Third Gospels with apostolic figures—Mark to Peter, and Luke to Paul. These patterns of apostolic attribution point to the importance of the Twelve as a crucial ingredient in understanding the composition of the Gospels. In Acts, the Twelve are located in Jerusalem and remain there during the first formative years of the church, serving as an authoritative body along with the elders (cf. Acts 15:4). Whether this picture from Acts represents a highly idealized account or whether it portrays actual conditions in Jerusalem during the first decades of the church remains hotly contested. At the minimum it suggests that the Twelve occupied a unique role in preserving and transmitting the Jesus tradition. To what extent the Twelve or other individuals constituted a *collegium* that actively shaped the Jesus tradition remains an open question. It is hard to imagine the composition of the Gospels having occurred in a manner that either ignored or bypassed Jesus' inner circle of followers. Given the prominence attached to certain members of the apostolic circle, for example, Peter and John, and later to the exceptional apostle Paul, we can easily imagine certain centers of Christian activity being dominated by the person, reputation, or legend of one of the Twelve. This was almost certainly the case with the apostle John, regardless of whether the Fourth Gospel and the Johannine letters (or the Apocalypse) were actually composed by him directly.

Mobility and Speed of Transmission. In imagining the circumstances that existed prior to the composition of the written Gospels, we should note how quickly information could spread through the Mediterranean world in the first century. People from different social groups traveled frequently throughout the Roman Empire. Paul's letters reveal a well-traveled apostle, often accompanied by a diverse entourage of followers, and a network of churches that were in contact with each other through the use of letters and couriers. This picture is confirmed, even enhanced, by Acts.

What this means for Gospel composition is that the Jesus tradition could have spread quickly throughout the Mediterranean region, even in directions not reported by Acts, such as Egypt and eastern Syria and Mesopotamia. The sayings, teachings, and stories comprising the Jesus tradition were not necessarily confined to Jerusalem or to Galilee, the center of his ministry. They could have spread from Jerusalem just as quickly as his followers traveled to other areas, which seems to have occurred quite early. Acts reports such dispersion from Judea to Samaria (8:1–3) and an important thrust into Antioch of Syria shortly thereafter (11:26).

Writing the First Gospel

When Mark began to compose the first Gospel, several decades had elapsed since Jesus' death and resurrection. During this time, a relatively coherent narrative account of Jesus' trial and crucifixion had developed and probably circulated in several Christian centers. Traditions relating to Jesus existed in various forms. Oral accounts of his words and deeds were still circulating, but many of these probably had been recorded and collected into groups. We can well imagine collections of sayings, parables, miracle stories, and controversy stories at Mark's disposal. Some of them may have been well organized around certain themes or locations, while others may have been only loosely organized.

Other traditions relating to Jesus would have included a strong scriptural component. We can easily imagine collections of proof texts or OT *testimonia* that were thought to have been fulfilled in Jesus. These might also have been accompanied by midrashic interpretations, even in written form, which sought to clarify the connections between the OT texts and events or aspects of Jesus' ministry. It is also reasonable to believe that Mark might have consulted the Greek Scriptures independently and even developed his own interpretations. We know this to have been true of the three other evangelists.

Whether this reconstruction adequately represents the oral and written resources at Mark's disposal, it gives some idea of the state of the Jesus tradition when he began his composition. Since writing is a creative act in which the author not only collects and arranges material but also shapes it towards specific ends, we can think of Mark as an intentional author working with a well-defined theological vision that is expressed through his narrative. This is in contrast to some earlier, form critical views that saw Mark as someone without firm literary or theological purposes who merely collected traditions about Jesus and arranged them like "pearls on a string."

At what points in the narrative Mark is responsible for creating the story is difficult to say. His creativity is already evident in the first verse, "The beginning of the good news of Jesus Christ, the Son of God" (1:1). Prior to Mark, "gospel" (*euangelion*) had been used in the church, especially by Paul, to express the essential content of early Christian preaching (e.g., 1 Cor 15:1–11). The term may still have that connotation in Mark 1:1, but when he placed it in this introductory position, the way was open for "gospel" to acquire another meaning—a narrative account of Jesus' life and ministry. Mark is often credited with originating the gospel genre, which was to have a productive, multifaceted legacy.

Writing Other Gospels

We have no firm evidence that Mark had even a rough draft of an earlier Gospel at his disposal. Some scholars believe that he may have had access to Q or to a list of sayings similar to Q, but this remains a conjecture. Matthew and Luke were in a different position. Luke informs us that he knew of earlier accounts of Jesus and took them into account in composing the Third Gospel (Luke 1:1–3).

In many ways, traditions relating to Jesus to which the other evangelists had access must have resembled those at Mark's disposal: reminiscences from eyewitnesses or those who had known eyewitnesses; assorted oral traditions; and some written traditions, for example, collections of written sayings, stories, and OT *testimonia*. We are confident that Matthew and Luke possessed a comprehensive list of sayings material, Q, which had an ordered sequence by the time they received it. In addition to this, each had a wide range of stories and sayings uniquely his own. Whether these stemmed from the specific locale in which each evangelist was working, or whether they derived from other locales and were collected through the evangelist's own research, is impossible to say.

As for OT interpretations relating to Jesus, Matthew and Luke were able to see how Mark had incorporated these into his narrative. Like Mark, each of them had access to the Greek Scriptures, and as they composed their narratives, they developed independent interpretations of OT passages. The "formula quotations" in Matthew represent the evangelist's own distinctive form of OT quotation, or they may stem from a special school of pesher interpretation located in the area in which he was operating.

Even though Matthew and Luke possessed different sets of resources relating to the Jesus tradition, like Mark, they too exercised their own creativity in shaping their narratives. Their narratives reflect not only their distinct literary styles but also their distinctive theological visions. In each case, the Jesus story has not only been rethought but also retold toward specific literary and theological ends.

As for the Fourth Evangelist, we have already noted some of the similarities and differences between John and the Synoptic Gospels. We have also sketched the probable form of the Jesus tradition at the Fourth Evangelist's disposal. Like his synoptic counterparts, John probably had access to collections of sayings, miracle stories, controversy stories, and the Passion Narrative, and yet their distinctive literary form in the Fourth Gospel is easily apparent. Whatever the form of traditions at John's disposal, no one can seriously doubt the boldness of his theological vision. Reflecting extraordinary confidence as Christ's own voice, the Fourth Evangelist not only speaks about Christ but for Christ. By recasting the Jesus tradition in such dramatic fashion, John redefined the gospel genre.

Locating the Gospels in Certain Centers

While we can imagine different centers where the Jesus tradition was preserved, it is more difficult to assign each Gospel to a particular location. Quite early, Mark was located in Rome since it supposedly contained the reminiscences of Peter. Some early traditions located Matthew in Palestine, Luke in Antioch of Syria, and John in Ephesus. None of these can be confidently asserted, even though each location is entirely plausible. It does not matter, finally, where each Gospel originated, although such localized attributions influence how we think of certain cities or regions as the centers in which the formation of the Gospel tradition occurred.

Quite often the Gospels are presented as though they were written to churches in specific locales. Scholars often speak confidently of the Matthean, Markan, Lukan, and Johannine communities as not only the context from which each Gospel arose but also as their primary addressees. Recently, however, some scholars have questioned whether the addressees of the Gospels should be so confined. They have suggested instead that the Gospels, for all their variety in outlook and content, may have been written to the larger church.

Before the Written Gospels: The "Tunnel Period"

Now that we have looked at several considerations relating to the transition from Jesus to the Gospels, we can examine three models that have been used to envision what occurred during this period.

Traditional Model

According to this model, which was developed during the patristic period, the Gospels are directly traceable to named figures related to Jesus. To the First and Fourth

Gospels were attached the names of Jesus' apostles, members of the Twelve; to the Second and Third Gospels were given the names of persons who were close associates with two other apostolic figures: Mark as Peter's interpreter, and Luke as Paul's traveling companion. From the patristic evidence that we discussed in the previous chapters, especially that collected in Appendix 2 [**see Expanded CD Version pp. 883–89**], we can see how important it was for each Gospel to have an apostolic connection. Since each could be traced to an eyewitness or a close associate of an eyewitness, this meant that the Gospels could be linked directly with Jesus. The sayings and deeds recorded in them could thus be read as reliable eyewitness accounts.

Over the centuries, as scholars began to evaluate the titles ascribing the Gospels to apostles or apostolic associates, they discovered that these titles were relatively late. Other considerations, such as the language and style of each Gospel, raised doubts about apostolic authorship. If Matthew, for example, was a Galilean tax collector who presumably spoke Aramaic, how can we explain the excellent Greek style in the First Gospel? If the Fourth Gospel was written by the apostle John, why the indirect, coy references to the "beloved disciple" rather than to the apostle himself?

The traditional model may be diagrammed as follows:[6]

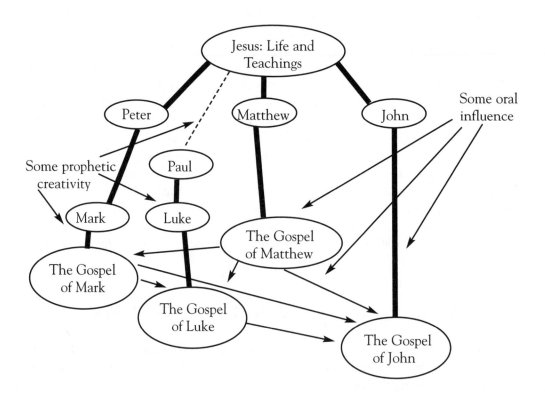

The Form Critical Model

From the seventeenth century onward, traditional authorship of the Gospels was questioned. Alternative explanations were developed as more intensive investigation of the Gospels was done. Scholarly tools and resources, such as Gospel synopses, were developed to expedite close comparison of the Gospels. In the late nineteenth and especially in the early twentieth centuries, form critical analysis was applied to the Gospels. This approach had already been used successfully in OT research, for example, by Hermann Gunkel (1862–1932) in his analysis of Genesis and the psalms.

Through the pioneering work of German scholars such as Karl Ludwig Schmidt (1891–1956), Martin Dibelius (1883–1947), and Rudolf Bultmann (1884–1976), form critical theories of the formation of the Gospels were developed. The foundation had already been laid by earlier scholars such as J. G. Herder (1744–1803), J. G. Eichhorn (1752–1827), F. D. E. Schleiermacher (1768–1834), and others who had conceptualized in greater detail what had occurred during the pre-Gospel period. Several assumptions informed form critical analysis:

(1) During the formative period shortly after Jesus' death, stories about Jesus and sayings attributed to him were collected by *communities of believers* in different locations. Imagined were clusters of Christians in various places who actively sought to preserve the Jesus tradition.

(2) To account for the great variety of forms in which materials were preserved, scholars postulated *theological shaping* of the Jesus tradition. This was seen as a period when the traditions circulated in a fluid form, which meant that the form of sayings and stories would undergo considerable change.

(3) Form critics focused on various *literary forms*—different kinds of sayings and stories, such as miracle stories or pronouncement stories.

(4) This meant that form critics were more interested in *small units of material*—pericopes—than the Gospels as a whole.

(5) Form critics were also interested in the *life setting* (German: *Sitz im Leben*) in which the materials were used. They assumed that the shape of a particular story—its form—was closely related to how it was used—its function. The settings in which form and function were interrelated became differentiated, for example, worship, teaching, preaching, and defense.

(6) Those who finally brought these materials together into single narratives were *anonymous editors* who strung materials together into loosely conceived narratives about Jesus.

(7) Form criticism was motivated by the desire to find the *earliest form of the saying or story*. Great emphasis was placed on reconstructing how certain sayings or stories developed over time.

(8) Form critics were interested in reconstructing the *tradition history* of individual units.

The form critical model was developed in close conjunction with Jesus studies. Theories for relating the Gospels to each other were developed as a way of reconstructing the historical Jesus. Many form critics assumed that if they could get to the original form of a saying or story, they could reach "bedrock" tradition about Jesus.

Although some scholars were skeptical about their ability to find much core material, they were convinced that reconstructing the history of the Jesus tradition would enable them to track the development of the kerygma, or proclamation about Jesus. Even if they could not locate the Word of God in Jesus' actual words and deeds, they could at least find it within the transmission of those Jesus traditions.

As some opponents of form criticism have observed, theological motives are clearly visible in constructing this model. By conceiving the "tunnel period" as a time when anonymous individuals and communities were "traditors"—those who transmitted the tradition—form critics created a chasm between Jesus and the first or second generation of his disciples. By imagining a time of great fluidity, form critics could account for the great variation one finds in the Gospels, but this also led to decreased confidence in the historical reliability of the Gospel reports. The form critical model may be diagrammed as follows:

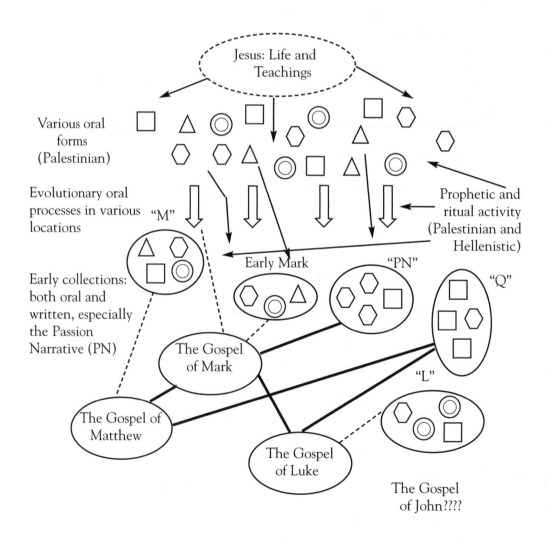

The Rabbinic Transmission Model

As an alternative to the form critical model, Scandinavian scholar Birger Gerhardsson developed a model that used the formation and transmission of rabbinic traditions as an analogy. Gerhardsson readily conceded that the crystallization and final editing of the Mishnah, Tosefta, and the two Talmuds occurred much later than the composition of the Gospels. But he postulated that the methods of transmitting rabbinic teachings, some of which were traceable to first-century C.E. rabbis such as Hillel and Shammai, illuminate how the Gospel tradition developed.

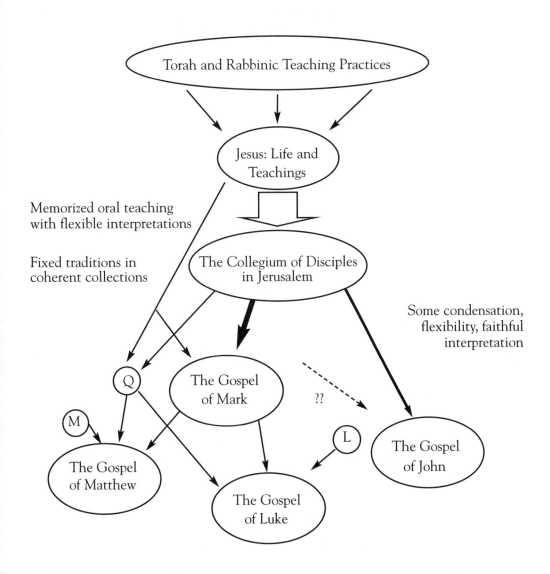

According to Gerhardsson, Jesus actively taught his disciples using materials in both fixed and flexible forms. The transmission of these traditions occurred in a manner analogous to rabbinic methods of transmitting haggadic materials—stories rather than legal (halakic) texts. Emphasis would have been placed on accuracy in transmitting the tradition and fidelity in preserving it. Another key element of Gerhardsson's model is the presence of a *collegium*, a group of Jesus' disciples, perhaps the Twelve or even a larger circle of disciples, who had responsibility for the collection, preservation, and transmission of the tradition.

Another Scandinavian scholar, Harald Riesenfeld, proposed that Jesus taught his disciples to memorize a Holy Word, perhaps an early gospel that was recited primarily, if not exclusively, in early Christian worship.

In developing this model, Gerhardsson concurred with many scholars in accepting the Two Source Hypothesis. But he differed with many of them in his conception of what happened prior to the composition of the first Gospel, which he believed to be Mark.

The implications of the rabbinic model are clear. It would ensure much greater continuity between Jesus and his immediate circle of followers. It would also engender greater confidence in the reliability of the form in which his sayings and deeds were remembered and written down.[7]

Summary

Still other models have been proposed, but these represent some of the main options. The availability of different models is a reminder that each of them is a hypothesis that attempts to explain what we actually find in the four canonical Gospels. Rather than assuming that only one model was operative during the "tunnel period," perhaps we should envision different models at work in different locations.

Notes

1. *Did.* 9.1–10.7; 14.1; Justin, *1 Apol.* 1.67.1–3, 7; Pliny, *Ep. Tra.* 10.96; Tertullian, *Apol.* 39.1–5; *An.* 9.4; Clement of Alexandria, *Strom.* 6.14.113.3; *Paed.* 3.11.80.4.

2. Krister Stendahl, *The School of St. Matthew and Its Use of the Old Testament.* 1st American ed., Philadelphia: Fortress, 1968; 1st Sigler ed., Ramsey: Sigler, 1991.

3. BDAG, 759.

4. See the discussion of apocalyptic in chapter 27 on Revelation.

5. See Xenophon, *Mem.* 3.13.

6. I am indebted to Bart Bruehler for the following diagrams, which were produced in a paper on "The Formation of the Gospel Tradition" for an Emory doctoral seminar on the Gospels, April 16, 2002.

7. For this brief description of the Rabbinic Transmission Model, I gratefully acknowledge clarifications provided by Prof. Birger Gerhardsson, Lund University, Sweden, in a letter dated September 29, 2003.

Bibliography

Bailey, James L., and Lyle D. Vander Broek. *Literary Forms in the New Testament: A Handbook.* Louisville: Westminster/John Knox, 1992.

Bauckham, Richard, ed. *The Gospels for All Christians: Rethinking the Gospel Audiences*. Edinburgh: T&T Clark, 1998.

Bultmann, Rudolf. *History of the Synoptic Tradition*. Translated by John Marsh from the 2d German edition (1931). Rev. ed. New York: Harper, 1968 (1963).

Dahl, Nils. *Jesus in the Memory of the Early Church*. Minneapolis: Augsburg, 1976.

Dibelius, Martin. *From Tradition to Gospel*. Library of Theological Translations. Translated by Bertram Lee Woolf from the rev. 2d German edition. London: Clarke, 1971.

Gerhardsson, Birger. *The Reliability of the Gospel Tradition*. Peabody: Hendrickson, 2001.

Nickle, Keith. "Gospel Beginnings." Pages 1–43 in *The Synoptic Gospels*. Rev. and expanded. Louisville: Westminster John Knox, 2001 (1980).

Miracles

Fuller, Reginald H. *Interpreting the Miracles*. London: SCM, 1963.

Kee, Howard C. *Miracle in the Early Christian World*. New Haven: Yale University Press, 1983.

Theissen, Gerd. *The Miracle Stories of the Early Christian Tradition*. Translated by F. McDonagh. Philadelphia: Fortress, 1983.

Parables

Dodd, C. H. *The Parables of the Kingdom*. Rev. ed. New York: Scribner's, 1961.

Donahue, John R. *The Gospel in Parable: Metaphor, Narrative, and Theology in the Synoptic Gospels*. Philadelphia: Fortress, 1988.

Hultgren, Arland J. *The Parables of Jesus: A Commentary*. Grand Rapids: Eerdmans, 2000.

Jeremias, Joachim. *The Parables of Jesus*. Rev. ed. Translated by S. H. Hooke from the 8th German ed. (1970). London: SCM, 1972.

Scott, Bernard Brandon. *Hear Then the Parable: A Commentary on the Parables of Jesus*. Minneapolis: Fortress, 1989.

Chapter 5

From the Gospels to Jesus

"There is no historical task which so reveals a [person's] true self as the writing of a Life of Jesus."

Albert Schweitzer

"There is pathos in the discovery of each succeeding study of the 'historical Jesus' that what its immediate predecessors had thought to be a path for genuine access to the figure turned out to be just another blind alley."

Hans Frei

"There have been many quests for the Jesus of history, but there has never been a wholly disinterested one. . . . What must not be overlooked is the likelihood that Jesus himself is responsible for the scholars' failure to classify him precisely."

Leander E. Keck

From the time the four Gospels appeared in the late first century, they have served as indispensable resources for the church. They have figured prominently in the church's internal disputes as well as in its defense to outside critics. Just as the Gospels quickly occupied a central role in the church's public worship, so did they also exercise a formative role in shaping individual Christian piety. Within a very short time, the church embraced four complementary Gospels as its definitive accounts of Jesus. It did so, recognizing the theological problems posed by the existence of four Gospels. While the church tried several options for relating the Gospels to each other, such as combining them into a single gospel (Tatian), privileging one or more over the others (certain Gnostic groups), and adopting a single, radically edited gospel (Marcion), it never tried to dispense with them altogether.

Although the Gospels exercised steady influence on the church through the early, medieval, and early modern periods, the last three hundred years have witnessed particularly important developments. The emergence of English Deism in the late seventeenth and early eighteenth centuries introduced a negative view of revealed religion and valued a form of rational thought that dramatically altered how the Gospels were read at both scholarly and popular levels. With this shift in attitude toward the Gospels, perceptions of Jesus also changed. Eighteenth-century Enlightenment suspicion of authority, both civic and ecclesiastical, along with the promotion of free inquiry, also directly affected the study of the Gospels. Anti-ecclesiastical bias often took an explicitly antidogmatic form. Studies of Jesus and the Gospels were often motivated by the desire to break free of dogmatic formulations, such as that of Chalcedon's Christ as "truly God and truly man . . . one and the same Christ . . . recognized in two natures."[1] What were perceived as dogmatic accretions were usually attributed to the church's undue fascination with Greek philosophical categories and were thought to camouflage the early church's simple faith in Jesus. What was needed was to remove the shackles of doctrinal belief in order to rediscover the pristine faith that had started it all. The "Jesus of history," it was thought, had been smothered by the "Christ of faith."

The potential effects of revisionist efforts formulated in this matter were evident, especially to church authorities. Investigators who proceeded to examine the church's core beliefs thus justified their efforts in the name of free inquiry. Quite often those who took the initiative were firmly located within the church as pastors, priests, and church-affiliated professors. Yet just as often their investigations moved them towards the church's edge, and sometimes well outside its gates.

Especially worth noting is how much interest the Gospels generated during this period of social, political, and ecclesiastical change. One of the gauges of the Gospels' increased popularity is the conspicuous amount of attention devoted to studying the life of Jesus. Although this period saw the appearance of hundreds, if not thousands, of works devoted to Jesus, this literary activity was not without precedent.

Medieval Lives of Jesus

During the medieval period, there appeared several lengthy works that focused on Jesus.[2] One of the most popular was *The Meditations on the Life of Christ*, published about 1300 and once attributed to the Italian Franciscan theologian St. Bonaventure (ca. 1217–1274). Written as a contemplative work, the *Meditations* imaginatively reconstructs the course of Jesus' life as a way of inviting the reader to identify with Christ. That the life rather than the teachings of Christ is the primary focus is seen in the way the work draws heavily on the narrative portions of the Gospels to the virtual exclusion of Jesus' discourses. Another life of Jesus that achieved wide circulation in Europe was *Concerning the Deeds of the Lord Savior* (*De Gestis Domini Salvatoris*), written in Italy by Simone Fidati between 1338 and 1348. Comprising fifteen books and following a loosely chronological and topical arrangement, the work draws exclusively from biblical sources and provides edifying comments. In contrast to the *Meditations*, Fidati featured Jesus' discourses. Even more popular than these two works was *The Life of Christ* (*Vita Christi*), a lengthy work of some 2,500 octavo pages composed in Mainz about 1350 by the Carthusian monk Ludolf of Saxony (ca. 1300–1378). The work appeared in numerous Latin editions and was translated into several languages. Based mainly on Matthew and John, Ludolf's *Vita* takes on the qualities of a harmonization. Along with the biblical text Ludolf provides commentary based on the well-established scheme of a fourfold meaning. He also quotes from more than eighty earlier authors, both Christian and secular, and draws on apocryphal material about Jesus.

Although these earlier works from the medieval period had a distinct devotional focus, they nevertheless belong to the Life of Jesus genre. Their authors had to make some critical decisions about how to relate the four Gospels to each other, as well as what other literary sources to use. For all of their differences in emphasis and scope, they did not draw a sharp distinction between what they read in the Gospels and their own reconstructed lives of Jesus. Instead, they generally assumed the reliability of the Gospel accounts. Their motivation for producing works that unfolded a unified life of Jesus was not to provide more historically reliable accounts but rather to produce works that were useful for meditation.

The Modern Period

Reimarus: Rationalistic Historiography

From around 1750 onward, the study of Jesus often achieved high visibility because of controversial publications. Between 1774 and 1778, Gotthold Ephraim Lessing (1729–1781) published a collection of seven extended excerpts from the 4,000-page treatise by Hermann Samuel Reimarus (1694–1768) titled "An Apology or Defense of the Rational Worship of God." Written between 1744 and 1767 while Reimarus served as Professor of Hebrew and Oriental Languages in Hamburg, this work was a sustained attack on revealed religion. Because Reimarus's work constituted such a radical challenge to traditional Christian belief, he declined to publish it during his lifetime. After Reimarus's death, however, his son-in-law Lessing decided to publish portions of the larger work anonymously. Since Lessing had taken an earlier draft of the fragments to Wolfenbüttel, near Braunschweig in Lower Saxony, they became known as the Wolfenbüttel Fragments.

Among the most controversial was the seventh—and longest—fragment, "The Aims of Jesus and His Disciples," in which Reimarus subjected the Gospels to a thoroughly rational analysis. Reflecting his strong confidence in human reason, Reimarus insisted that the informed reader must ask at every point, "Can this be accepted by a rational mind?"[3] For Reimarus, the credibility of the Gospel narratives is best determined by whether they demonstrate logical consistency. By this he usually meant the absence of contradiction either within a single evangelist, among the four evangelists, or between the evangelists and other NT writers. His typical interpretive method is to identify an implausible feature of the Gospel accounts, expose it, and then propose a more reasonable explanation.

As an overall explanation of how the Gospels originated, Reimarus thinks it more reasonable to believe that the apostles freely invented much of what is reported in the Gospels than to assume that in every case they faithfully reported what Jesus said and did or what happened to him. He is forced to this position not so much by an inherent skepticism but rather by implausible features that he finds within the Gospel narratives. His method of approach might be characterized as thoroughgoing rationalism—historical reconstruction based on a consistently rational reading of the Gospels. **[See Expanded CD Version pp. 106–7: *Reimarus's Approach to the Gospels*]**

While Reimarus may appear as an eccentric, radical critic from another epoch, his legacy was lasting. Certain themes from his analysis continued to find their way into Gospel research. His sharp distinction between Jesus' intentions, as expressed in his words and deeds recorded in the Gospels, and the apostles' later construal of Jesus' message and mission may not have been retained by later scholars in precisely that form, but the perceived gap between the historical figure Jesus and the Gospel reports about Jesus continued to inform scholarly investigations. Similarly, his contention that the Gospel accounts reflect the apostles' own theological outlook, which had been formed in a post-Easter setting, was also seminal. While scholars differ widely about the extent to which this has occurred in each evangelist, it is still widely assumed that the Gospels, in varying degrees, reflect the outlook of the post-Easter church. Even his thoroughgoing rationalism is evident in later Gospel research. Proposing plausible historical reconstructions to account for perceived discrepancies within the Gospel narratives has become a staple of Life of Jesus research.

Not surprisingly, these highly unorthodox views prompted immediate public responses, most notably from the Hamburg pastor J. M. Goeze (1717–1786). The intrigue surrounding the publication of these anonymous fragments intensified the publicity, and the true identity of their author did not become known until 1814, when Reimarus's son presented a copy of his father's "Defense" to the university library in Göttingen.

Strauss: Dialectical-Mythic Interpretation

Some fifty years later, similar furor was created by the 1835–1836 publication of the two-volume *The Life of Jesus Critically Examined* by David Friedrich Strauss (1808–1874). Originally from Ludwigsburg near Stuttgart, Strauss studied under Ferdinand Christian Baur in Tübingen from 1825 to 1830 and, after completing his doctorate, heard G. W. F. Hegel lecture in Berlin just prior to the latter's death on November 14, 1831. While Strauss had worked on his *Life of Jesus* for several years, he wrote the manuscript in just over a year while living in Tübingen.

Like Reimarus, Strauss employed reason in his interpretation of the Gospels, relying heavily on the principle of consistency. But unlike Reimarus, Strauss was less interested in impugning the motives of the evangelists or in providing a more plausible historical reconstruction of Christian origins, especially one that undercut the overall credibility of the Christian message. Rejecting traditional theism that allowed for God's intervention in human affairs, Strauss operated instead with a form of pantheism in which God and the world were indistinguishable, "permanently and immoveably [*sic*] united."[4]

For Strauss, the ultimate truthfulness of the Christian faith does not depend on the historical reliability of the gospel story but rests instead on the philosophical cogency of its dogmatic content. Once the historical status of Jesus is eliminated as the linchpin of faith, Strauss is able to examine the Gospel texts and assess their historical reliability more freely.

In one way, Strauss's method of reading the Gospels resembled Reimarus's version of rationalistic historiography. Gospel stories that are inconsistent either within themselves or with other accounts are historically problematic.[5] In addition, events that were contrary to "the known and universal laws which govern the course of events" can also be recognized as non-historical.[6]

In other respects, however, Strauss moved well beyond Reimarus, most notably in his appropriation of Hegelian dialectic in shaping his exegetical method and his use of myth as a hermeneutical category. Because these two elements are integrally connected, Strauss's hermeneutical approach may be characterized as *dialectical-mythic interpretation*. [See Expanded CD Version pp. 108–9: *Strauss's Dialectical-Mythic Approach to the Gospels*]

In spite of its comprehensive, penetrating analysis of the Gospels and highly nuanced methodological approach, Strauss's *Life of Jesus* provoked a storm of controversy. Its publication resulted in Strauss's dismissal from his Tübingen professorship, and when he was appointed to another professorial post in Zürich, he met such stiff resistance from the clergy in the city that his appointment was aborted. Thereafter, he was unable to obtain a professorship but continued to pursue his scholarly work privately. Strauss's *Life of Jesus* generated numerous negative reviews to which he wrote a comprehensive response in 1837. In the third edition (1838), Strauss made concessions to his critics, granting some historical reliability to the Fourth Gospel. He eventually retracted these concessions in the fourth edition of 1840 and reaffirmed the views formulated in the first edition.

Strauss's own turbulent life gives some indication of the seismic impact of his *Life of Jesus*, but its residual effect was even greater in shaping the subsequent scholarly debate. For one thing, he forced later interpreters to clarify the relationship between historical inquiry and religious (or dogmatic) truth. They had to ask: Does the truth of the Gospels—and their claims about Jesus—depend on the historical veracity of what they report? Second, his appropriation of the category of myth, which had earlier been used to interpret OT stories, introduced a way of reading Gospel stories that found a prominent successor in Rudolf Bultmann a century later. While Bultmann moved beyond Strauss in both his understanding and application of myth, it nevertheless functioned as a central element of his hermeneutical program of demythologizing the Gospel stories. Third, Strauss squarely confronted the difficulties posed by the Fourth Gospel in Life of Jesus research. During his career Strauss equivocated in his views about the overall reliability of the Fourth Gospel as a source for constructing a life of Jesus, but he eventually returned to his initial position that its highly mythical construal of Jesus is of a different order from that of the Synoptic Gospels. Fourth, Strauss anticipated twentieth-century form criticism in his views of the pre-Gospel oral period as a time of immense creativity both literarily and theologically.

Renan: Romantic History and the "Fifth Gospel"

No less dramatic was the impact of the much slimmer *The Life of Jesus* written by Ernest Renan (1823–1892), which was first published in French in 1863.[7] Written as the first of an eight-volume work titled *The History of the Origins of Christianity*, this work achieved immediate renown. Over 60,000 copies were sold within a few months of its initial publication. It was immediately translated into English (1864) and into several European languages as well. Well into the twentieth century, Renan's *Life of Jesus* continued to be read widely as a literary classic.

Renan trained for the Roman Catholic priesthood but eventually left in order to pursue the study of philosophy. He became an accomplished linguist, historian, and social critic. Under the auspices of the French government, he traveled to Italy and eventually conducted two explorations in Syria (1860, 1864–1865).

Through his travels in the Middle East, Renan became fascinated with the people and land of Palestine. While there he composed a draft of his *Life of Jesus*, which is interlaced with graphic, moving descriptions of the places he visited. "The striking agreement of the texts with the places, the marvelous harmony of the Gospel ideal with the country which served it as a framework," prompted Renan's famous remark, "I had before my eyes a fifth Gospel, torn, but still legible."[8] With studied attention to the details of ordinary life in Palestine, Renan crafted his *Life of Jesus* to take its readers along with him into the Galilean hills and lead them through the streets of Palestinian villages. Through this mental journey, Renan transports readers into Jesus' own time and place, for example, to Nazareth,

> a small town in a hollow, opening broadly at the summit of the group of mountains which close the plain of Esdraelon on the north. . . . The cold there is sharp in winter, and the climate very healthy . . . no place in the world was so well adapted for dreams of perfect happiness. . . . The people (today) are amiable and cheerful; the gardens fresh and green . . . the beauty of the women who meet [at the fountain] in the evening . . . is still most strikingly preserved. . . . No doubt Mary was there almost every day, and took her place with her jar on her shoulder in the file of her companions who have remained unknown.[9]

Renan's *Life of Jesus* is notable for its pathos and sentimentalism, as well as for the way it embroiders the Gospel accounts with fanciful details and fictional scenes. Not the least of its admirable qualities is its simple, seductive prose, a far cry from the technical analysis of Strauss or even of Reimarus. Renan portrayed Jesus as an ordinary man, born to simple, hardworking parents, so the work appealed to a wide variety of people, especially since he prepared a second version that was more affordable than the first.

The simple elegance of Renan's work can all too easily mask the brilliance of its conception and the masterly way in which it was executed. Renan brought to the work an impressive scholarly grasp of the ancient world and Near Eastern religion and languages, to say nothing of the field of biblical scholarship. His introductory chapter provides a thorough, albeit highly idealized, review of biblical history, as well as a comprehensive, informed survey of literary sources that inform the work. Besides the biblical sources, these include Philo, Josephus, the Talmud, and apocryphal writings such as *1 Enoch* and the *Sibylline Oracles*, as well as early Christian sources. Renan also gives an informed, nuanced account of the prehistory of the Gospels, laying out his own theory of the formation of the Gospel tradition. He is especially attentive to the problems posed by the Fourth Gospel, and his decision to draw on all four canonical Gospels in constructing his *Life of Jesus* is well conceived. He accepts neither the Synoptic Gospels nor the Fourth Gospel uncritically. Reflecting a thorough grasp of the terrain of each Gospel, Renan sees the Matthean discourses as being more authentic than their narrative framework, and, by contrast, prefers the Johannine framework over the Johannine discourses, which he sees as creative theological reflections by the aged apostle John, yet shaped by the "school of John." For Renan, the problem posed by Jesus and his portrayal in the Fourth Gospel is not unlike that of Socrates and his two "biographers," Xenophon and Plato. Recognizing that Xenophon's treatment of Socrates is probably more historically accurate, Renan nevertheless embraces Plato's *Dialogues*. Like the Synoptic Gospels' portrait of Jesus, Xenophon offers a "clear, transparent, impersonal compilation," while Plato's *Dialogues* reflects Socrates' "vigorous individuality." Given a choice between the "dialogues" of Plato and the "discourses" of Xenophon, any discriminating reader, Renan insists, would choose Plato over Xenophon: "Does Plato . . . teach us nothing about Socrates?"[10]

Like the works of his predecessors, Renan's *Life of Jesus* triggered visceral responses. His decision to "banish miracle from history" invited a storm of protest,[11] as did his elimination of other legendary elements of the Gospel stories, such as the birth and infancy accounts of Matthew and Luke and numerous features of the Passion Narrative.[12] Renan's *Life of Jesus* may have upset many, but it also introduced a variation of the genre that has had a long life: the masterly written popular biography, composed by a technically well-trained scholar, using imaginative reconstruction informed by the "fifth Gospel," the Holy Land.

Farrar: Orthodox Historiography

In Great Britain, the orthodox response to Renan was Frederic William Farrar's *The Life of Christ*, published in 1874.[13] Like its French counterpart, Farrar's work was based on a trip to the Holy Land, which he made in 1870 under the sponsorship of his enterprising publisher, Cassell. Farrar's literary style was no match for Renan's easy-flowing prose; in fact, his rather massive tome was widely criticized for its rhetorical excesses and pious sentimentalism. Cassell had taken the British pulse correctly, however, and Farrar's *Life* was an immediate success. Over the next twenty-five years the work went through numerous printings, was published in lavishly illustrated editions, and was translated into several European languages, as well as Russian and Japanese. Before long, it had gone through more than thirty editions and sold over 100,000 copies.

Like Renan, Farrar brought to his *Life* impressive scholarly credentials, having been educated at King's College, London, and Trinity College, Cambridge. Unlike Renan, however, he was a distinguished cleric, eventually becoming Canon of Westminster and Rector of St. Margaret's (1876) and Dean of Canterbury (1895). His linguistic and philological gifts are evident throughout the work, as is his familiarity with the relevant ancient sources and contemporary technical scholarship, including the earlier works of Strauss and Renan. In keeping with his orthodox outlook, Farrar draws on conservative biblical scholarship, for example, in defending the apostolic authorship of John. He confidently uses the Johannine storyline as the framework for constructing his *Life*, although he confronts the difficulties posed by integrating the four Gospels into a single coherent story. His theory of the formation of the Gospel tradition is elaborated in neither the detail nor the sophistication of Renan's work. His alignment with orthodox Christian faith is obvious at every turn: "I can still say respecting every fundamental doctrine of the Christian faith, *Manet immota fides* ('Faith remains unmoved')."[14] Scoffing at those who read the birth and infancy stories in Matthew and Luke as "palpable mythology," he also dismisses those who "scarcely conceal their misgiving" toward those who accept Christ's miracles.[15]

Where Renan had been skeptical, Farrar was affirming, for he wrote "as a believer to believers, as a Christian to Christians."[16] Like Renan, Farrar had been transformed by his experience in the Holy Land, where "many things came home to me, for the first time, with a reality and vividness unknown before."[17] Farrar, too, wanted to help "the simple and the unlearned to understand and enter into the human surroundings of the life of the Son of God."[18] Distancing himself from Strauss and Renan, he insisted that his readers would not find in his *Life* "brilliant combinations of mythic cloud tinged by the sunset imagination of some decadent belief."[19] They could, however, expect the Holy Land—and, by extension, Jesus himself—to come alive as they read:

> He who has seen the children of Nazareth in their red caftans, and bright tunics of silk or cloth, girded with a many-coloured sash, and sometimes covered with a loose outer jacket of white or blue—he who has watched their noisy and merry games, and heard their ringing laughter as they wander about the hills of their little native vale, or play in bands on the hill-side beside their sweet and abundant fountain, may perhaps form some conception of how Jesus looked and played when He too was a child.[20]

Schweitzer: Thoroughgoing Eschatology (and Wrede: Radical Skepticism)

The publication of Albert Schweitzer's *The Quest of the Historical Jesus* in 1906 was a defining moment in modern Life of Jesus research.[21] The original German title *Von Reimarus zu Wrede* defined the chronological limits of the work. Schweitzer began with Reimarus's "The Aims of Jesus and His Disciples," convinced that it was the first genuinely historical treatment of Jesus and the Gospel tradition. "Before Reimarus," Schweitzer wrote, "no one had attempted to form a historical conception of the life of Jesus."[22] What especially commended Reimarus to Schweitzer, however, was his recognition of the eschatological dimension of Jesus' preaching.

Schweitzer concluded his treatment with William Wrede's *The Messianic Secret in the Gospels: An Investigation of the Gospel of Mark*, which was published in German in 1901. Wrede's groundbreaking work marked an appropriate stopping point because it denied Jesus' messianic consciousness and held that Jesus operated without any clear sense of being the eschatological Son of Man destined to return soon to vindicate the cause of his people. Arguing instead that Mark's messianic portrait of Jesus, with its numerous secrecy motifs, reflected a post-Easter perspective, Wrede insisted that Mark's Gospel should be read not as a straightforward historical account of Jesus' life but as a heavily biased theological work. As such, it could not be used as a reliable source for constructing a historical account of the life of Jesus.

What Reimarus had originally seen quite clearly—that Jesus was an eschatological preacher of repentance and the kingdom of God—Wrede denied. By setting his investigation within the Reimarus-Wrede framework, Schweitzer was able to propose his own version of the life of Jesus, which heavily accented both his messianic consciousness and his eschatological mission. Acknowledging his indebtedness to Johannes Weiss's brief but programmatic study, *Jesus' Proclamation of the Kingdom of God*, first published in German in 1892, Schweitzer drew attention to what many previous lives of Jesus had largely ignored—the strong eschatological overtones of the Synoptic Gospels. (Following Strauss, Schweitzer excluded the Gospel of John as of little, if any, historical value in investigating the life of Jesus.) For Schweitzer, Jesus' usage of Son of Man imagery to designate the Messiah whose coming would occur soon was traceable to the historical Jesus. He also insisted that Jesus' proclamation of the kingdom of God should be understood as God's coming reign, triggered by the Messiah's parousia and accompanied by final judgment. The kingdom of God was not, in other words, a moral ideal to be realized—the kingdom of God on earth—as it had often been depicted. It was instead an eschatological reality.

In sharp contrast to Wrede, Schweitzer believed that Jesus operated with messianic self-awareness that began to develop as early as the time of his baptism. During his ministry in Galilee, which Schweitzer believed lasted only a few weeks, Jesus taught and performed miracles. Schweitzer argued that when Jesus sent his disciples on their preaching mission (Mark 6:7–13), he fully believed that the Son of Man would appear and that the kingdom of God would arrive before they returned (cf. Matt 10:23). When this did not happen, Jesus accommodated his views to this first "postponement of the parousia."[23] Gradually, Jesus became convinced that he himself was the Son of Man whom God had entrusted to initiate the coming kingdom. Even though Jesus tried to keep his messianic identity secret, Peter's confession at Caesarea Philippi effectively revealed it; the experience of the transfiguration merely confirmed it. When Jesus finally went to Jerusalem to die, he did so confident that he was the Son of Man and that he would be fully vindicated by God. He was crucified in the full consciousness that he was God's messianic Son of Man.

While Schweitzer spelled out his view of "thoroughgoing eschatology" in the first edition of his book, he sharpened it even further in the second edition that appeared in 1913, which was substantially revised and expanded. Even though Schweitzer retracted the famous passage that portrayed Jesus as flinging himself on the wheel of fate and being crushed as it ran over him,[24] he remained convinced that this eschatological dimension of Jesus' teaching, which was so pervasive in the Synoptic Gospels, had largely been ignored by most nineteenth-century lives of Jesus. Reimarus had seen it clearly, Schweitzer insisted, as had several others, such as Strauss and later Weiss, but most had not. Schweitzer moves beyond them all in sharpening the eschatological edge of Jesus' messianic mission.

When William Montgomery's English translation of Schweitzer's original German edition appeared, the title *The Quest of the Historical Jesus* was drawn from a line in the final chapter in the book.[25] The phrase became far more than the title of a justly famous book, however; it defined a whole era in the study of the Gospels, which began in earnest in the eighteenth century and continues unabated today. What made the title apt for Schweitzer's study was the way it captured the spirit of investigations of the Gospels that began with Reimarus. What distinguished these studies from the medieval lives mentioned earlier was their thoroughly historical approach. They were reading the Gospels not so much as witnesses to the church's faith but as sources for investigating and reconstructing "what actually happened" in the life of Jesus. In this way, investigators sought to get behind the "Christ of faith"—the Jesus as confessed in the creeds—and the layers of Greek philosophical language that had accumulated around the simple belief in Jesus of Nazareth.

Part of the brilliance of Schweitzer's book, however, was the way it exposed the "mirror syndrome" in nineteenth-century lives of Jesus. After reviewing critically more than a hundred (mostly German) lives of Jesus, Schweitzer concluded that "each epoch . . . found its reflection in Jesus" and that "there is no historical task which so reveals a [person's] true self as the writing of a Life of Jesus."[26] Lives of Jesus based on nineteenth-century liberal theology turned out looking like the liberal theologians who had written them. In these accounts Jesus emerged as a preacher of ethical ideals, fully rational in outlook, not given to eschatological enthusiasm or spiritual excess. The kingdom of God that Jesus preached was an ideal society that could be realized on earth by straight-thinking, morally minded disciples. [See **Expanded CD Version pp. 114–15:** *Schweitzer's View of Jesus*]

By exposing investigators' tendencies to create Jesus in their own image, Schweitzer's groundbreaking work had a chastening effect on subsequent efforts to grasp the significance of Jesus. It was also useful in clarifying some of the differences among the various approaches to the Gospels and the study of Jesus.

Kähler: The Historic, Biblical (Dogmatic) Christ

"The entire Life-of-Jesus movement [is] a blind alley." So wrote Martin Kähler (1835–1912), a University of Halle systematic theologian, in his provocative essay "The So-called Historical [*historische*] Jesus and the Historic [*geschichtliche*], Biblical Christ," which first appeared in 1892.[27] Whereas Schweitzer (later) faulted his predecessors for failing to see what he saw clearly, Kähler questioned the validity of the entire enterprise, both in principle and in practice.

Standing firmly within the Lutheran tradition, which accented the powerful presence of Christ mediated through the preached word of God, Kähler denied history a determinative role in validating the witness of the gospel. The gospel neither derives its power from historical certitude nor can it be adequately grasped in purely historical terms. Christianity has an inescapably historical dimension since Jesus was a historical figure of the past, but history is neither its essence nor its power. To search for Jesus *purus putus homo,* "a man pure and simple," is to look for something that never existed;[28] and when a historical reconstruction of such a figure appears—a "historical Jesus"—it exists only in the mind of the investigator, who thus assumes the role of a "fifth evangelist."[29] The Jesus of the Christian faith, who from the beginning was experienced, confessed, and preached by the church, is both a historical and transhistorical figure. To peel away the latter (Jesus the Christ) to get at the former (Jesus the man) is, in principle, impossible since both were inextricably connected from the outset. To attempt to do so destroys both, and in the process, authentic Christian faith self-destructs. It is in this sense that "the historical Jesus of modern authors conceals from us the living Christ."[30]

Kähler also argued that besides being theologically impermissible, Life of Jesus research was also flawed in practice. The vagaries of historical research disqualify it as a certifying norm for authentic faith. Since even the best scholarly reconstructions always represent a working consensus rather than final, unchanging results, they cannot serve as a necessary foundation for genuine faith. To give historical knowledge such a determinative role would also mean that ordinary believers—nonspecialists—could only access faith indirectly. While historical knowledge can enlighten faith, it does not—and cannot—create faith, much less certify it.

Instead of the historical Jesus—either the elusive figure of the past "as he was" or the historian's reconstructed Jesus—Kähler opts for the "historic, biblical Christ." Capitalizing on the distinction in German between *historisch*, which is rendered in English as "historical" (in the sense of "event-ness"), and *geschichtlich*, rendered as "historic" (in the sense of existential significance), Kähler wants to capture the unique dimension of Christ that is embedded within the biblical narrative, especially the Gospels. As the Christ woven into the texture of the Gospels, he is the "biblical Christ." This is the Christ who is preached, who is experienced in worship, and who lives within the church. Through the medium of the Bible, this Christ is accessible to specialist and nonspecialist alike.

By framing his argument in this manner, Kähler aligns himself with orthodox Christianity and its various creedal expressions. Readily acknowledging the distance between the dogmatic language of the Gospels and later creedal formulations, Kähler nevertheless prefers dogmatic construals of Christ, whether biblical or creedal, to imaginative, psychological, historical, and quasi-historical construals that pass themselves off as definitive accounts of "the *real* Jesus."[31] He writes:

> The Jesus of the "Life-of-Jesus movement" is merely a modern example of human creativity, and not an iota better than the notorious dogmatic Christ of Byzantine Christology. One is as far removed from the real Christ as is the other. In this respect historicism is just as arbitrary, just as humanly arrogant, just as impertinent and "faithlessly gnostic" as that dogmatism which in its day was also considered modern.[32]

Kähler insists that the Gospels are not historical sources that can yield a historically reconstructed Jesus; they do, however, represent *perfectio respectu finis*, "perfection with respect to purpose."[33] They are perfectly suited for what they were intended to do: they present the church's preaching of Christ and, in so doing, they contain, proclaim, and mediate Christ.

Bultmann: The Kerygmatic Christ

No single figure had a more profound impact on Gospel studies and scholarly study of Jesus in the early twentieth century than Rudolf Bultmann (1884–1976), NT professor at Marburg from 1921 to 1951. An early formulation of his views was published in 1926 under the German title *Jesus*, which appeared in the series "Immortals:

The Spiritual Heroes of Humanity in Their Life and Work." An English translation, *Jesus and the Word*, was published in 1934.[34] The English title aptly captured the work's distinctive focus: "The subject of this book is . . . not the life or the personality of Jesus, but only his teaching, his message."[35] Like others, Bultmann had felt the chilling effect of Schweitzer's *Quest* and regarded "what [had] been written in the last hundred and fifty years on the life of Jesus, his personality and the development of his inner life, [as] fantastic and romantic."[36]

Bultmann had already laid the groundwork for the Jesus book in *The History of the Synoptic Tradition* (1st German ed., 1921),[37] a pioneering form critical analysis in which he unfolded his theory of the formation of the synoptic tradition. Sharply distinguishing between the earliest stage of the tradition—Palestinian, Aramaic-speaking Christianity—and the later stage of Hellenistic, Gentile Christianity, Bultmann concluded that "everything in the synoptics which for reasons of language or content can have originated only in Hellenistic Christianity must be excluded as a source for the teaching of Jesus."[38] Even within the Palestinian traditions it was possible to distinguish layers of tradition, and "whatever betrays the specific interests of the church or reveals characteristics of later development must be rejected as secondary."[39] Using form critical analysis, Bultmann detected layers within the synoptic accounts of Jesus' teaching and confidently correlated each layer with different stages in the development of the tradition.[40] The goal of his literary excavation was to reach bedrock Jesus teaching; even then, however, he admitted that "we have no absolute assurance that the exact words of this oldest layer were really spoken by Jesus."[41] Bearing such a heavy post-Easter imprint, the Synoptic Gospels provide *direct evidence* of the church's proclamation but only *indirect evidence* of Jesus' proclamation. Thus emerged Bultmann's general skepticism concerning what can be confidently known about what Jesus *actually* said and taught. Even with these qualifications, he proceeded confidently: "It is precisely this complex of ideas in the oldest layer of the synoptic tradition which is the object of our consideration."[42]

It was through Jesus' teaching, then, that Bultmann gained access, not to his personality—since this was unrecoverable and, in any case, inconsequential—but to his *work*. What should ultimately interest anyone in such figures as Plato, Jesus, Dante, or Luther is not their personality but their work. Moreover, "[i]n the case of those who like Jesus have worked through the medium of *word*, what they purposed can be reproduced only as a group of sayings, of ideas—as *teaching*."[43] Jesus' "purpose can be comprehended only as teaching."[44]

Bultmann thus narrows the Gospel lens through which he views Jesus. Like Schweitzer and Strauss, he excluded John: "The Gospel of John cannot be taken into account at all as a source for the teaching of Jesus, and it is not referred to in this book."[45] Eliminating the synoptic narrative material represents yet a further reduction, even if the grounds for doing so—lack of interest in Jesus' personality—were judged to be dubious by many of Bultmann's critics, who wondered why one's work can only be accessed through one's words, as opposed to one's deeds and words together. The relevant "data base" is reduced even further by his theory of synoptic origins:

> What the [synoptic] sources offer us is first of all the message of the early Christian community, which for the most part the church freely attributed to Jesus. This naturally gives

no proof that all the words which are put into his mouth were actually spoken by him. As can be easily proved, many sayings originated in the church itself; others were modi-fied by the church.[46]

[See Expanded CD Version pp. 117–19: *Bultmann's Jesus: Eschatology and Demythologizing*]

So methodical was Bultmann's exegetical and form critical analysis, so encom-passing and penetrating were his theological insights, that in many important ways he set the agenda for Gospels research and NT scholarship generally in the twentieth cen-tury. His tendency to reduce if not eliminate the human figure Jesus from the kerygma became a target for his critics, and his successors felt the need to reconnect Jesus with history, or at least to find ways of establishing continuity between the figure Jesus—both his life and teaching—and the church's preaching. What came to be perceived as Bultmann's excessive skepticism concerning what can be known not only about Jesus' personality and life but also his teachings prompted his successors to articulate more clearly criteria for determining the authenticity of Jesus' words. Bultmann had begun the process; others saw the need to refine it.

After Bultmann: The New Quest and the Recovery of History

Bultmann's efforts to articulate a meaningful Christology within the social-political turbulence of early twentieth-century Europe had far-reaching effects well beyond Europe. He capitalized on advances in form critical analysis of the Gospels and increasing scholarly confidence in the Two Source Hypothesis. No one doubted the critical sophistication of Bultmann's interpretation of the Synoptic Gospels and the Fourth Gospel, even though a number of his views were later modified or even aban-doned. What especially commended his critical analysis, however, was the breadth and depth of his theological vision. Combining strands of dialectical theology with elements of existential philosophy, Bultmann crafted a version of the Christian message that provided many believers a suitable alternative to nineteenth-century liberal theology that was neither naively uncritical nor existentially disappointing.

Ernst Käsemann. Much of the latter half of the twentieth century was spent responding to Bultmann's agenda. Especially among Bultmann's own students, dissat-isfaction surfaced, perhaps most vocally in the work of Ernst Käsemann (1906–1998), Professor of New Testament at Tübingen from 1959 to 1970. In a now-famous lecture delivered in 1953 at a gathering of Bultmann's former students, the "old Marburgers," eventually published as "The Problem of the Historical Jesus," Käsemann challenged his teacher's virtual exclusion of the historical Jesus in his reformulation of the Christian kerygma.[47] Relinquishing all interest in the earthly Jesus, Käsemann insisted, fails to recognize a central element of early Christian belief—"the identity between the exalted and the humiliated Lord"[48]—and also threatens to produce a docetic kerygma emptied of any meaningful, recognizable content. Establishing some theologically legit-imate continuity between the earthly Jesus and the church's preaching, far from being a false problem, arises naturally from the particularity of Jesus' existence: "[T]he problem of the historical Jesus is not our invention, but the riddle which [Jesus] himself sets us."[49]

Günther Bornkamm. In many ways, *Jesus of Nazareth,* which was first published in German in 1956 by another Bultmann student, Günther Bornkamm (1905–1990), responded to Käsemann's call for a critically rendered historical Jesus.[50] In Bornkamm's words, "the aim of this book [is] to give an historical presentation of Jesus and his message."[51] The opening line of the book, "No one is any longer in the position to write a life of Jesus,"[52] signaled Bornkamm's recognition that Schweitzer's *Quest* had not only "erected [the Life of Jesus movement's] memorial" but also "delivered its funeral oration."[53] Well aware of the extent to which historical reminiscence and ecclesial interpretation were interwoven into the Gospels, Bornkamm saw this as a challenge for historically sensitive interpretation. But it was more than that: the strong imprint of the church's faith on Jesus' message exposed the process of early Christian hermeneutics. In one sense, post-Easter language that crept into Jesus' parables, for instance, is anachronistic—it belongs to a later period. In another sense, such recasting of Jesus' original sayings shows how the church appropriated Jesus' teachings for its own time and place. A notable example is the parable of the wicked tenants (Mark 12:1–12; Matt 21:33–46; Luke 20:9–19), in which Jesus recounts how tenants of a vineyard reject a series of emissaries sent by the owner to collect a share of the produce and finally seize and kill the owner's son, which then prompts the owner's rejection of the tenants. The Markan and Lukan accounts speak of the owner's "beloved son" who is seized, killed, and thrown out of the vineyard (Mark 12:6; Luke 20:13). Even the casual reader can spot this thinly veiled reference to Jesus and recognize how the church's story of Jesus' divine commissioning and ultimate rejection has become a post-Easter template through which the story has been retold.

Far from denigrating historical-critical research on the Gospels, Bornkamm defends it as necessary, given the irreducibly historical nature of the material. While admitting that "faith cannot and should not be dependent on the change and uncertainty of historical research," neither should anyone "despise the help of historical research to illumine the truth with which each of us should be concerned."[54] Rather than radically separating history and kerygma, as Bultmann had done, Bornkamm defined his task as seeking "the history *in* the Kerygma of the Gospels, and in this history to seek the Kerygma."[55] **[See Expanded CD Version pp. 121–22: *Bornkamm's "Historical" Jesus*]**

What Käsemann called for, Bornkamm supplied—an account of Jesus that gives substantial content to his historical existence without lapsing into the romantic, psychologically oriented biographical treatments of the earlier quest. The figure Jesus—both his teachings and his earthly life—infuse Bornkamm's construal of the Christian kerygma. Like Bultmann, Bornkamm is fully attentive to the critical challenges of differentiating between authentic and inauthentic sayings or traditions, but the result is a more humanly framed figure. Not only Jesus' sayings, but also the numerous episodes narrated in synoptic pericopes, mediate the richness and immediacy of the earthly Jesus. Indeed, each episode in its own way encapsulates the whole gospel story as it confronts readers and listeners with Jesus, who as both prophet and rabbi exudes authority and immediacy, even as he issues the call to faith.

James M. Robinson. It was James M. Robinson, Professor of New Testament at Claremont School of Theology, who saw what a seismic shift the work of Käsemann and Bornkamm represented. He marked the moment by publishing *A New Quest of the Historical Jesus* in 1959, thereby naming a new stage in the discussion.[56] Robinson was careful to frame his vision of the "New Quest" as a way to move beyond Bultmann's programmatic formulation, particularly in Germany. In doing so, he recognized that other versions of the quest continued within French and Anglo-Saxon scholarship. Although Robinson originally meant "New Quest" in a somewhat limited sense, the phrase caught on and eventually came to characterize the post-Bultmannian era generally.

Robinson rightly included Ernst Fuchs (1903–1983) and Hans Conzelmann (1915–1989), along with Käsemann and Bornkamm, among Bultmann's students who sought to move the discussion forward. Standing within this same tradition, Robinson constructed his own proposal for demonstrating continuity between the human Jesus and later kerygmatic formulations.

Like his fellow post-Bultmannians, Robinson sees the Christian kerygma as having an indispensable historical core. "A new quest must be undertaken," he writes, "because the *kerygma* claims to mediate an existential encounter with a historical person, Jesus, who can also be encountered through the mediation of modern historiography."[57] By "modern historiography" Robinson means a historical approach with a much richer understanding of history than the nineteenth-century positivistic version. Such an approach must also work with an understanding of the human self that recognizes our capacity to study, organize, and reconstruct the past within legitimate limits, and yet one that allows us to experience new self-understanding as we encounter figures from the past who also transcend the past. Historiography so formulated would make it possible "to test the validity of the *kerygma*'s identification of *its* understanding of existence with *Jesus'* existence."[58]

Rather than eschewing critical methods used to differentiate between authentic and inauthentic sayings of Jesus, Robinson calls for greater refinement of those methods. Sayings that are "conceivable in terms of Jesus' Jewish, Palestinian background," yet that do not show unmistakable signs of "the distinctive views of the Church" or that the Church is not likely to have initiated, are probably authentic.[59] Rather than boldly claiming access to a rich supply of new sources, Robinson prefers more imaginative, theologically sensitive interpretation of the standard, old sources. He does recognize, however, the potential importance of the then-newly discovered Gnostic sources, especially the *Gospel of Thomas*.

Robinson's firm commitment to an inescapably history-based kergyma and his confidence in the use of modern historiography place him squarely within the "New Quest." Indeed, this short but seminal work helped make him one of its principal architects.

More Recent Developments

Criteria of Authenticity

Reimarus had already detected elements in the Gospels that he thought reflected a post-Easter perspective, for example, the Trinitarian formula used by Jesus in Matthew's version of the Great Commission (Matt 28:19–20). Scholars ever since have noted the presence of such material throughout the Gospels and have sought to find ways to differentiate between what can actually be traced to Jesus himself and those elements that originated after Jesus' death. For Bultmann, material that could convincingly be traced to Hellenistic Gentile Christianity as opposed to what originated within Palestinian Aramaic-speaking Christianity constituted post-Easter material. Any material, for that matter, that reflected the later church's outlook as opposed to that of Jesus himself was also probably inauthentic. Similar criteria for distinguishing authentic from inauthentic sayings of Jesus were used by other scholars.

As greater attention was given to Jesus' teachings, the need for more clearly defined criteria increased. One of the clearest—and earliest—formulations of criteria for determining the authenticity of Jesus' sayings was developed by Norman Perrin (1920–1976) in *Rediscovering the Teaching of Jesus* (1967).[60] Three criteria were identified.

The Criterion of Dissimilarity. In Perrin's formulation, "the earliest form of a saying we can reach may be regarded as authentic if it can be shown to be dissimilar to characteristic emphases both of ancient Judaism and of the early Church."[61] While scholars readily admitted that Jesus' teaching had much in common with contemporary Jewish teaching—for example, with the first-century rabbinic teachers Hillel and Shammai—words of Jesus that were *not* traceable to such sources—that were distinctively original—were judged authentic. Similarly, any words of Jesus that do not reflect "characteristic emphases" of the early church could be accepted as genuine. An often-cited example is Jesus' use of "Abba" in addressing God (Mark 14:36). Since there is no clear precedent for this way of addressing God in prayer within ancient Judaism, it probably originated with Jesus himself. If so, the other instances of such language elsewhere in the NT (Rom 8:15; Gal 4:6) probably derived from Jesus. Other examples of authentic teachings or emphases established by this criterion are distinctive elements of Jesus' parables, his vision of the kingdom of God, and the Lord's Prayer.

New Testament biblical critics readily admitted that this criterion—sometimes referred to as the negative criterion—became a very small sieve through which Jesus' sayings were filtered. As with any teacher, no matter how extraordinary or original, Jesus would have absorbed much of his contemporary Jewish culture, including the wisdom of Jewish sages and similar teaching reflected in biblical and non-biblical Jewish writings. The large portion of Jesus' teaching that overlapped with that of his Jewish contemporaries is thus eliminated by the criterion of dissimilarity, not because it is unimportant but because it is not demonstrably original.

The Criterion of Coherence. As Perrin formulated it, "material from the earliest strata of the tradition may be accepted as authentic if it can be shown to cohere with material established as authentic by means of the criterion of dissimilarity."[62] Once an aspect of Jesus' teaching is shown to be genuinely distinctive, the biblical critic is then in a position to identify other sayings that closely resonate with such teaching. This second layer of material would not easily pass the test of dissimilarity since it is not, strictly speaking, unique. But if it shows no clear signs of ecclesial bias or as having derived from some other source, it can reasonably be regarded as authentic. By applying this criterion to Saying 82 from the *Gospel of Thomas*—"He that is near me is near the fire; he that is far from me is far from the Kingdom"—Joachim Jeremias argued that this logion has "the ring of a genuine saying of Jesus."[63]

The Criterion of Multiple Attestation. "This is a proposal," Perrin writes, "to accept as authentic material which is attested in all, or most, of the sources which can be discerned behind the synoptic gospels."[64] Presupposed here is a theory of the origin of the Gospels in which distinguishable strands of Jesus tradition can be identified. How these strands are understood depends on one's theory of Gospel origins. In the Two Source Hypothesis, Mark and Q would constitute two distinct, independent sources and so would, by extension, the materials unique to Matthew and Luke—M and L. Assuming that the Fourth Gospel is largely, if not wholly, independent of the Synoptic Gospels, it would constitute yet another strand of the Jesus tradition. Sayings material or even certain motifs that appear in streams of the Jesus tradition thought to have been independent of each other, and thus not subject to lateral influence, are judged to be authentic when they tend to converge in the way they report Jesus' teachings or characterize his actions.

Evaluation of the Criteria. As formulated by Perrin, the three criteria can be differentiated from each other, and their cumulative impact is assumed. The criterion of dissimilarity is seen as the most rigorous, while the other two criteria allow room for more authentic material to be recognized. The latter two criteria thus build on the first one, and all three are used interdependently. Even so, their actual application in specific cases can often be quite subjective, and both their conception and usage have been sharply criticized by some scholars. One complaint is how narrowly the first criterion constricts the pool of possible authentic Jesus sayings. To require that every saying must clear the hurdle of dissimilarity first and only then include additional sayings that meet the other two criteria is seen by some as unnecessarily restrictive. Some complain that eliminating on the front end so much of Jesus' teaching that he might have shared with his Jewish contemporaries results in a distorted picture, however "scientifically based" it might appear. Some also ask whether such a restrictive criterion would be applied to any other extraordinary teacher from antiquity, such as Socrates or Hillel.

Other Criteria

In an effort to overcome the perceived restrictiveness of these criteria, some scholars have suggested additional criteria. These have been summarized by Graham Stanton.[65] First is the criterion of *embarrassment*. Elements of the Jesus tradition that would have been embarrassing to his followers, and thus not easily explainable as having originated from them, probably derive from Jesus himself or the pre-Easter period. Examples might include charges that Jesus was out of his mind (Mark 3:21), Peter's behavior during Jesus' trial (Mark 14:53–72 and parallels), and the tradition of Judas's betrayal (Mark 14:10–11, 17–21, 43–52 and parallels). Second is the criterion of *historical plausibility*. Rather than excluding what Jesus had in common with his Jewish environment, this criterion seeks to evaluate these common elements and judge as authentic material that can be plausibly attributed to Jesus, given what we know of the social and political context of first-century Palestine. It is an effort to rectify what is perceived to be the grotesque narrowing of Jesus' teaching. Third is the criterion of *aftermath*. In view here is some appreciation of cause and effect in evaluating the teachings and actions of Jesus. If certain features of the later Jesus movement call for some historical explanation, it is permissible to analyze what is reported about Jesus' words and actions in order to find what might have caused certain results. For example, if one judges the eschatological sayings of Jesus to be inauthentic, how can one explain the defining presence of imminent eschatology in so many later strands of Christian tradition, such as Paul's letters, 1 Peter, Revelation, and Hebrews? [See Expanded CD Version pp. 125–27: *The Jesus Seminar and Its Legacy*]

The Difficulty of Finding Patterns and Directions

Whatever inhibiting influence Schweitzer's *Quest* may have had in the early twentieth century appears to have vanished. Scholarly studies of Jesus have regularly appeared since the middle of the century. Some of them came in the wake of Bultmann's pioneering work, but others conceived their task in different terms. What has characterized the last several decades as much as anything else is the fragmented state of Jesus studies. Even among the post-Bultmannians, it is difficult to detect consistent patterns or directions of research.

Finding a way to organize Life of Jesus research has posed a challenge in its own right. One of the popular ways of doing so is to distinguish at least four discrete stages: (1) The Old Quest—the nineteenth century and earlier; (2) No Quest—the period immediately following Schweitzer, thus the early twentieth century; (3) The New Quest—the fresh initiative inaugurated by Käsemann and continued by Bornkamm and other members of the Bultmann school; and (4) The Third Quest—the latter part of the twentieth century, a period characterized by multiple emphases.[66]

As with all stage theory, this way of conceiving the overall movement recognizes certain defining moments, such as the publication of Schweitzer's *Quest* in 1906 or Käsemann's famous lecture of 1953. While this scheme provides a broad interpretive framework, it also obscures and distorts the picture. Even the pre-1900 period requires differentiation. By no means do all of the nineteenth-century works of Jesus constitute a monolith. Reimarus and Strauss operated with quite different agendas and achieved equally different results. Neither of them was guilty of the "mirror syndrome" in the same way that many of the liberal lives of Jesus were. Moreover, Schweitzer himself is guilty of the "mirror syndrome" found in his predecessors and yet marks a new beginning. It is just as important to differentiate the work that occurred between 1900 and 1950. As Robinson rightly observed, French and Anglo-Saxon research on Jesus often went its own way. Even within the German tradition, scholars took quite different paths.

Similar complexity marks the period from 1950 to 2000. In many ways, much of what occurred between 1800 and 1950 tends to be repeated during this period. Critics of the Jesus Seminar, for example, Luke T. Johnson in *The Real Jesus* (1996),[67] have observed that its non-eschatological Jesus, given to countercultural, aphoristic teaching and committed to social justice, egalitarianism, and nonviolence, simply mirrors the values and the social, political, and religious visions of its members. The Jesus Seminar is thus charged with "modernizing" Jesus as did many nineteenth-century scholars who wrote about Jesus. [See Expanded CD Version pp. 128–29: *Recent Studies on the Historical Jesus*]

Lessons Learned

Among the many lessons learned from Schweitzer's *Quest,* perhaps one of the most enduring is how he was able to engage in hard-nosed, often devastating critique of another scholar, yet spot fresh insights in that scholar's work and even appropriate some of his constructive findings. The scholarly positions that Schweitzer treated ranged from the bizarre to the brilliant, but everyone agreed that something was truly at stake in the debate. It was assumed that vigorous, intellectual debate actually moved the discussion forward. At this juncture, it is worth asking where three centuries of debate have now brought us.

The Gospels as the Voice of the Church

The Enlightenment's legacy of historical consciousness constitutes one of the defining features of Life of Jesus research. This inevitably meant that critics would evaluate the Gospels in terms of their usefulness as reliable sources for historical investigation. It also meant that critics would look for the earliest sources. Consequently, they eliminated John as late and too theologically imaginative. Eventually Mark was seen as the earliest Gospel, and its primitive, realistic narrative appeared to provide bedrock historical reminiscence. Yet even Mark was seen to have a heavy theological slant.

It is now clear that the Gospels bear the imprint of the church's faith. Since they were written some forty to seventy years after Jesus' death, it is only to be expected that they reflect a post-Easter perspective. This does not mean that the evangelists fail to distinguish between the time before and after Easter; it only means that the experience of Jesus' death and resurrection had such dramatic impact that it colored everything they remembered and reported about what happened before Easter. The pre-Easter Jesus was filtered through their post-Easter experience.

Recognizing this helps us to understand why the Gospels look as they do. For all of their differences in emphasis and outlook, each Gospel sees the final stage of Jesus' life as the point toward which the story inexorably moves, thereby establishing the perspective through which everything that was said and done earlier was remembered. Jesus' passion, death, and resurrection thus become the lens through which the church looked backward so that it could tell the story of Jesus from its beginning forward. Rather than displaying features usually associated with biographies, such as descriptions of physical appearance or formative early life experiences, the Gospels focus sharply on Jesus' messianic identity, mission, and message. These dictate not only what the Gospels report about Jesus but also how sayings and episodes are reported. Through carefully devised rhetorical strategies in which material about Jesus is selected, arranged, and presented from a distinctive theological viewpoint, each Gospel to varying degrees presents a "strong reading" of Jesus. None of the Gospels pretends to give an objective, neutral account of Jesus; instead, each asserts a richly imagined theological vision of Jesus. The Gospels are written "from faith to faith." They originate within the church, are written from the church's perspective, and promote the church's vision of Jesus.

As portraits of Jesus painted by admiring artists, the Gospels reflect the disciples' devout fidelity to Jesus' teaching, and yet we discover the evangelists exercising rather remarkable freedom in reporting those teachings.[68] For this reason, consistent themes run through Jesus' message, especially in the Synoptic Gospels but also in the Fourth Gospel, yet they are not reported with uniform precision. Readers who equate faithful reporting of Jesus' message with invariable, verbatim reminiscence have repeatedly been disappointed with what they find in the Gospels.

The Problematic Role of History

No one saw the dilemma more clearly than Strauss: How are history and faith related? Scholars who produced liberal lives of Jesus thought they were engaged in objective historiography until Schweitzer exposed their illusion. Yet history also served Schweitzer's agenda. Bultmann ultimately proved to be a threat to some because his Jesus was too loosely connected with historical reality. Many of his students sought to correct this by forging new ways of connecting the Jesus of history with the Christ of faith. More recently, scholars have proceeded with a newfound confidence in history, sometimes blithely unaware of its limitations or even of its ambiguous role in certifying faith. Attempts to link history and theology more closely have had mixed results. Kähler's ghost still hovers over the current debate, haunting those trying to underpin dogmatic confession with historical claims.

Learning to Live with the Fourth Gospel

As Schweitzer saw it, Life of Jesus critics faced an either/or: either the Synoptic Gospels or the Fourth Gospel. The last three centuries have seen virtually every possibility tested. Strauss (finally) excluded John as a useful historical source, and Schweitzer followed suit. Schleiermacher, by contrast, embraced John and excluded the Synoptics, even if his Jesus was conceived more philosophically than historically.[69] Renan embraced the synoptic discourses and some of the Johannine narrative, while mostly rejecting the synoptic narrative and the Johannine discourses. Recent investigators, for example, Sanders and Wright, bracket the Fourth Gospel, effectively eliminating it from consideration. British scholars from Westcott to Dodd have argued for historically reliable core traditions in John, yet it continues to be ignored by many scholars.[70] Paula Fredriksen argues against the grain of much scholarly opinion when she finds reliable traditions in John, especially in the Passion Narrative, which can be usefully integrated with synoptic tradition to reconstruct the historical Jesus.[71] By taking this contrarian position, Fredriksen challenges the next generation of scholars to heed Dodd's earlier call for discriminating use of the Fourth Gospel in Life of Jesus research.

Critically Embracing the Mythic Dimension of the Gospels

Once the pervasively theological character of the Gospels registers with us, we are in a much better position to appreciate the distinctive character of the *rhetoric of faith* through which they are expressed. This recognition, in turn, helps us grasp the significance of the imaginative framework within which the evangelists set the story of Jesus. To borrow a phrase from Hans Frei, the Gospels can be read as "realistic narratives."[72] In sharp contrast to some other ancient narratives that rehearse the exploits of heroic, even semidivine or divine figures, the Gospels depict Jesus within an easily recognizable, everyday world in which weddings occur, sick people get well but sometimes die, and religious experts debate points of scribal law. They set Jesus within a world with which readers in every time and place can readily identify. Ordinary people encounter Jesus and express emotions that run the gamut of human experience, all the way from despair and disappointment to ecstatic joy and confident hope. Jesus' words and deeds are reported within a storyline of everyday human experience with which readers have regularly and immediately connected. In the story as a whole as well as within individual episodes, readers have been able to recognize themselves or at least imagine that they are somehow being addressed, even summoned. They feel the same magnetic pull toward Jesus that his followers within the story display.

At another level, however, the Gospels depict a world that transcends the ordinary, everyday world experienced by many readers. It is a world punctuated by dramatic divine epiphanies, often through the medium of angels or other heaven-sent messengers. Sometimes the voice of God breaks earth's silence, usually from above. Even if God remains an invisible speaker, not given to pictorial description, the divine presence is never far away. Malevolent figures also figure prominently in this world—Satan, evil personified, and demonic figures usually depicted as Satan's minions, either his direct representatives or his allies. It is also a world characterized by dramatic reversals of the ordinary: healings, especially exorcisms; raising the dead; stilling storms; walking on water; seemingly unexpected earthquakes and eclipses; and after-death appearances.

How to characterize this dimension of the Jesus story has always presented a challenge. It has been variously designated as transhistorical, mythic, or supernatural. Critics have thus explained the Gospels as religious sagas in which historical and transhistorical strands of material have been interwoven. Another interpretive strategy has been to identify these "nonrealistic" elements with the Jewish apocalyptic outlook that became especially dominant from the mid-second century B.C.E. until at least the second century C.E. Belief in resurrection is particularly prominent within apocalyptic literature, although heavenly visions, angelic figures, divine mediators, and satanic and demonic figures are also common elements of this worldview. Not every aspect of the Gospels framework can be traced exclusively to Jewish apocalyptic, however, since divine epiphanies, angels, miraculous healing, raising the dead, and other seeming reversals of nature's course are also reported throughout the OT. Variations of these phenomena are also found outside Judaism in the ancient Mediterranean world.

Regardless of the sources that informed the conceptual framework of the Gospels, the peculiar blend of realistic and transrealistic narrative is one of their distinctive theological elements. It is the vehicle through which the evangelists articulate their theological vision of Jesus.

Even if we name this transrealistic dimension as mythic or supernatural, we still must decide how to appropriate it within our own world of meaning. The strategies developed over the last three centuries may not represent all the options, but they remain illuminating for twenty-first century NT interpreters.

The Peril of Modernizing Jesus

Schweitzer's "mirror syndrome" was aptly captured in the title of Henry J. Cadbury's book *The Peril of Modernizing Jesus*, published in 1937.[73] As Schweitzer observed, after a while nineteenth-century lives of Jesus all began to read alike. They may have been cast in different terms, but the same plot was told and retold, usually with predictable results. Jesus was created in the image of the scholar who studied him. Scholars may have taken this lesson to heart for a while, but recent studies of Jesus tend to repeat the mistakes of the earlier liberal lives. An eschatological Jesus remains as problematic for many twenty-first-century people as he was for earlier generations. As the previous debate showed, our image of Jesus directly relates to the way he functions as a moral agent and paradigm for Christians. If we understand eschatology in a strictly chronological sense, Jesus' moral teachings easily become an "interim ethic" that is difficult to extend into later centuries. Equally troubling was the tendency to isolate Jesus from his Jewish or Greco-Roman surroundings, as Adolf Harnack (1851–1930) did, for example.[74] In his view, someone who embodied the essence of God had to be insulated from his cultural environment. Here we see doctrinal conviction—belief in the incarnation—shaping one's image of Jesus, thereby detaching—and thus distancing—Jesus from his past as well as his contemporary culture. It is another form of modernizing Jesus.

Devising Critical Methods Appropriate to the Study of the Gospels

The quest for the historical Jesus has been deeply intertwined with the development of critical methods for studying the Gospels. This has taken many forms: developing theories to explain the formation of the Gospel tradition, solving the Synoptic Problem, and formulating such approaches as source, form, and redaction criticism. As scholars became increasingly aware of the difficulty in distinguishing between authentic and inauthentic sayings of Jesus, it was necessary to define criteria of authenticity that were both compelling and practical. As critical methods were developed, these criteria were not only refined but also criticized. Each one has had strong advocates and equally strong critics. With the proliferation of critical methods, however, it is always worth asking whether due allowance has been made for the originative role of the figure Jesus himself. Just as the shapers of the Jesus tradition can easily become anonymous members of the community, so can Jesus become a faceless figure. Somehow methods of Gospel criticism must be devised that take into account the extraordinary force of Jesus' own personality and his life as an arena of God's activity.

Respecting the Narrative Structure of the Gospels

As part of the church's legacy, we have four narrative accounts of Jesus. They comprise sayings material, episodes relating his activity, and extended sections devoted to his final days in Jerusalem, plus other narratives such as the birth and infancy stories. Among other things, the last three centuries have shown how difficult it is to formulate a portrait of Jesus that does justice to all of these elements. Again, various strategies have been followed: focusing on his teachings to the exclusion of his deeds (Bultmann); excluding certain sections, such as the resurrection accounts (Schleiermacher); and attempting to incorporate most of these components (Bornkamm).

While the Fourth Gospel differs quite remarkably from the Synoptic Gospels, all four Gospels share a common conviction: Jesus is best understood when readers experience the *whole* story. The challenge is to be attentive to how the sayings and the deeds are interconnected, and how these, taken together, are connected with the storyline that culminates in Jesus' death and resurrection. In some respects the four evangelists arrange materials quite differently, but they agree in seeing a single logic underlying the story from beginning to end. Taking our cue from the Gospels themselves, it is always profitable to ask how they relate Good Friday and Easter to each other, and why.

Grasping the Message and Meaning of Jesus

Schweitzer perceptively saw the close connection between Jesus' messianic consciousness and his eschatological preaching of the kingdom of God. If the last three centuries have shown anything, it is the persistence of these three topics: the kingdom of God, Jesus' messiahship, and eschatology. Widely differing views have been offered on all three, and, as we have seen, these issues continue to dominate scholarly discussion. Here again, the relationship between the Synoptic Gospels and John becomes a critical consideration. Exclude the Fourth Gospel, and the message and meaning of Jesus look one way. Include it, and they look quite different. Even if we grant that the Johannine discourses are creatively shaped theological discourses, are they of no value in our formulation of Jesus' message and mission? Renan's question, "Is Plato of no value in understanding Socrates?" continues to haunt modern investigations.

Notes

1. Henry Bettenson, *Documents of the Christian Church* (2d ed.; London: Oxford University Press, 1963), 73.

2. For the following, see Harvey K. McArthur, *The Quest Through the Centuries: The Search for the Historical Jesus* (Philadelphia: Fortress, 1966), 57–84.

3. Charles H. Talbert, ed., *Reimarus: Fragments* (trans. Ralph S. Fraser; Philadelphia: Fortress, 1970), 171.

4. David Friedrich Strauss, *The Life of Jesus Critically Examined* (ed. Peter C. Hodgson; trans. George Eliot; Philadelphia: Fortress, 1972), 79. Abbreviated in the following notes as *LJCE*.

5. "An account which shall be regarded as historically valid, must neither be inconsistent with itself, nor in contradiction with other accounts" (*LJCE*, 88).

6. *LJCE*, 88. Specifically, this includes the laws of causation, succession, and psychology.

7. References here are taken from Ernest Renan, *The Life of Jesus*, with an Introduction by John Haynes Holmes (The Modern Library Edition; trans. Charles E. Wilbour; New York: Modern Library [Random House], 1927; repr. 1955).

8. Renan, *Life of Jesus*, 61.

9. Renan, *Life of Jesus*, 85–86.

10. Renan, *Life of Jesus*, 48.

11. Renan, *Life of Jesus*, 59.

12. Renan, *Life of Jesus*, 50, n.1.

13. The edition cited here is Frederic W. Farrar, *The Life of Christ* (2 vols.; London: Cassell, Petter & Galpin, n.d.); see also Daniel Pals, *The Victorian 'Lives' of Jesus* (San Antonia: Trinity, 1982), 77–85.

14. Farrar, *Life of Christ*, v.

15. Farrar, *Life of Christ*, vi.

16. Farrar, *Life of Christ*, v.

17. Farrar, *Life of Christ*, iv.

18. Farrar, *Life of Christ*, iv.

19. Farrar, *Life of Christ*, v.

20. Farrar, *Life of Christ*, 47.

21. William Montgomery's widely used English translation of the 1906 German edition appeared in 1910. The edition cited here is Albert Schweitzer, *The Quest of the Historical Jesus* (First Complete Edition; ed. John Bowden; Minneapolis: Fortress, 2001), which provides an improved revision of Montgomery's translation. This new English edition is based on the second German edition of 1913 (reproduced with few alterations in the ninth German edition of 1984), which contained substantial revisions of the 1906 edition as well as additional new chapters updating the discussion. Unless otherwise indicated, the following quotations are from the Fortress edition.

22. Schweitzer, *Quest*, 14.

23. Schweitzer, *Quest*, 328.

24. In Montgomery's translation based on the first German edition, the passage says: "Soon after [John the Baptist's proclamation] comes Jesus, and in the knowledge that He is the coming Son of Man lays hold of the wheel of the world to set it moving on that last revolution which is to bring all ordinary history to a close. It refuses to turn, and He throws Himself upon it. Then it does turn; and crushes Him. Instead of bringing in the eschatological conditions, He has destroyed them. The wheel rolls onward, and the mangled body of the one immeasurably great Man, who was strong enough to think of Himself as the spiritual ruler of mankind and to bend history to His purpose, is hanging upon it still. That is His victory and His reign." See Albert Schweitzer, *The Quest of the Historical Jesus: A Critical Study of Its Progress from Reimarus to Wrede* (Baltimore: The Johns Hopkins University Press, 1998), 370–71.

25. Schweitzer, *Quest*, 478.

26. Schweitzer, *Quest*, 6.

27. Martin Kähler, *The So-called Historical Jesus and the Historic, Biblical Christ* (Seminar Editions; ed. and trans. Carl E. Braaten; Philadelphia: Fortress, 1964). Braaten's edition is based on the 1896 edition (Leipzig: Deichert), which was reissued in 1956 (Munich: Christian Kaiser Verlag). Although the essay appeared with three other essays in 1896, it was paired with only the first of these essays ("Do Christians Value the Bible Because It Contains Historical Documents?") in the 1956 edition. The following quotations are taken from Braaten's edition.

28. Kähler, *The So-called Historical Jesus*, 103.

29. Kähler, *The So-called Historical Jesus*, 62.

30. Kähler, *The So-called Historical Jesus*, 43.

31. Kähler, *The So-called Historical Jesus*, 57.

32. Kähler, *The So-called Historical Jesus*, 43.

33. Kähler, *The So-called Historical Jesus*, 127.

34. Rudolf Bultmann, *Jesus and the Word* (trans. Louise Pettibone Smith and Erminie Huntress Lantero; New York: Scribner's, 1934; repr. 1962).

35. Bultmann, *Jesus and the Word*, 12.

36. Bultmann, *Jesus and the Word*, 8.

37. Rudolf Bultmann, *The History of the Synoptic Tradition* (trans. John Marsh; rev. ed.; Oxford/New York: Blackwell/Harper, 1968). Marsh's translation was based on the second German edition (Göttingen: Vandenhoeck & Ruprecht, 1931). The second English edition (1968) included corrections and additions from the 1962 supplement.

38. Bultmann, *Jesus and the Word*, 13.

39. Bultmann, *Jesus and the Word*, 13.

40. Bultmann, *Jesus and the Word*, 12–13.

41. Bultmann, *Jesus and the Word*, 13.

42. Bultmann, *Jesus and the Word*, 14.

43. Bultmann, *Jesus and the Word*, 10.

44. Bultmann, *Jesus and the Word*, 10.

45. Bultmann, *Jesus and the Word*, 12.

46. Bultmann, *Jesus and the Word*, 12.

47. Ernst Käsemann, "The Problem of the Historical Jesus," in *Essays on New Testament Themes* (trans. W. J. Montague; SBT 41; London: SCM, 1964), 15–47.

48. Käsemann, "Problem," 46.

49. Käsemann, "Problem," 46.

50. Günther Bornkamm, *Jesus of Nazareth* (trans. Irene and Fraser McLuskey, with James M. Robinson; New York: Harper & Row, 1960). This English translation is based on the third German edition (1959). The first German edition was published in 1956.

51. Bornkamm, *Jesus*, 14.

52. Bornkamm, *Jesus*, 13.

53. Bornkamm, *Jesus*, 13.

54. Bornkamm, *Jesus*, 9.

55. Bornkamm, *Jesus*, 21.

56. James M. Robinson, *A New Quest of the Historical Jesus* (SBT 25; London: SCM, 1959; repr. 1966).

57. Robinson, *New Quest*, 94.

58. Robinson, *New Quest*, 94.

59. Robinson, *New Quest*, 104.

60. Norman Perrin, *Rediscovering the Teaching of Jesus* (NTL; London: SCM, 1967).

61. Perrin, *Rediscovering*, 39.

62. Perrin, *Rediscovering*, 43.

63. Joachim Jeremias, *Unknown Sayings of Jesus* (trans. R. H. Fuller; London: SPCK, 1957), 54–55.

64. Perrin, *Rediscovering*, 45.

65. Graham Stanton, *The Gospels and Jesus* (2d ed.; Oxford: Oxford University Press, 2002), 174–77.

66. "Third Quest" was coined by N. T. Wright, *Jesus and the Victory of God* (Minneapolis: Fortress, 1996), xiv, to designate a particular stream of the quest which "regards Jesus as an eschatological prophet announcing the long-awaited kingdom, and which undertakes serious historiography around that point." Its broader use to designate "*all* current study of Jesus" (xv) appears to be well established.

67. Luke Timothy Johnson, *The Real Jesus: The Misguided Quest for the Historical Jesus and the Truth of the Traditional Gospels* (San Francisco: HarperSanFrancisco, 1996; repr. 1997).

68. See Bornkamm, *Jesus*, 17.

69. See Friedrich Schleiermacher, *The Life of Jesus* (ed. Jack C. Verheyden; trans. S. Maclean Gilmour; Philadelphia: Fortress, 1975), esp. xxxi–xxxii.

70. See C. H. Dodd, *Historical Tradition in the Fourth Gospel* (Cambridge: University Press, 1963; repr. 1999).

71. Paula Fredriksen, *Jesus of Nazareth, King of the Jews: A Jewish Life and the Emergence of Christianity* (New York: Vintage [Random House], 2000).

72. Hans Frei, *The Eclipse of Biblical Narrative* (New Haven: Yale University Press, 1974), 10–16.

73. Henry J. Cadbury, *The Peril of Modernizing Jesus* (New York: Macmillan, 1937).

74. See Adolf von Harnack, *What Is Christianity?* (trans. Thomas Bailey Saunders; FTMT; Philadelphia: Fortress, 1986).

Bibliography

Becker, Jürgen. *Jesus of Nazareth*. Translated by James E. Crouch. New York: de Gruyter, 1998.

Betz, Otto. *What Do We Know About Jesus?* Philadelphia: Westminster, 1968.

Bockmuehl, Markus. *This Jesus: Martyr, Lord, Messiah*. Edinburgh: T&T Clark, 1994.

———, ed. *The Cambridge Companion to Jesus*. Cambridge: Cambridge University Press, 2001.

Boers, Hendrikus. *Who Was Jesus? The Historical Jesus and the Synoptic Gospels*. San Francisco: Harper, 1989.

Borg, Marcus J. *Jesus: A New Vision: Spirit, Culture, and the Life of Discipleship*. San Francisco: HarperCollins, 1991 (1987).

———. *Jesus in Contemporary Scholarship*. Valley Forge: Trinity, 1994.

Bornkamm, Günther. *Jesus of Nazareth*. Translated by Irene and Fraser McLuskey, with James M. Robinson. New York: Harper, 1960.

Bultmann, Rudolf. *Jesus and the Word*. Translated by Louise Pettibone Smith and Erminie Huntress Lantero. New York: Scribner's, 1958 (1st Ger. ed. 1926; ET 1934).

———. *Jesus Christ and Mythology*. New York: Scribner's, 1958.

Burridge, Richard A. *What Are the Gospels? A Comparison with Graeco-Roman Biography*. Society for New Testament Studies Monograph Series 70. Cambridge: Cambridge University Press, 1992; repr. 1995; 2d ed. Grand Rapids: Eerdmans, 2004.

Cadbury, Henry J. *The Peril of Modernizing Jesus*. The Lowell Lectures. New York: Macmillan, 1937.

Crossan, John Dominic. *The Historical Jesus: The Life of a Mediterranean Jewish Peasant*. San Francisco: HarperSanFrancisco, 1991.

de Jonge, Marinus. *God's Final Envoy: Early Christology and Jesus' Own View of His Mission*. Grand Rapids: Eerdmans, 1998.

———. *Jesus, The Servant-Messiah*. New Haven: Yale University Press, 1991.

Dodd, C. H. *The Founder of Christianity*. New York: Macmillan, 1970; London: Collins, 1971.

Dunn, James D. G. *Jesus Remembered*. Vol. 1 of *Christianity in the Making*. Grand Rapids: Eerdmans, 2003.

Fredriksen, Paula. *Jesus of Nazareth, King of the Jews: A Jewish Life and the Emergence of Christianity*. New York: Knopf (distributed by Random House), 1999.

Gnilka, Joachim. *Jesus of Nazareth: Message and History*. Translated by Siegfried S. Schatzmann. Peabody: Hendrickson, 1997 (1993).

Hengel, Martin. *The Four Gospels and the One Gospel of Jesus Christ: An Investigation of the Collection and Origin of the Canonical Gospels*. Translated by John Bowden. London: SCM, 2000.

Johnson, Luke Timothy. *The Real Jesus: The Misguided Quest for the Historical Jesus and the Truth of the Traditional Gospels*. San Francisco: HarperCollins, 1996.

Kähler, Martin. *The So-called Historical Jesus and the Historic, Biblical Christ*. Translated by Carl E. Braaten. Seminar Editions. Philadelphia: Fortress, 1964 (1896).

Keck, Leander E. *Who Is Jesus? History in Perfect Tense*. Studies on Personalities of the New Testament. Columbia: University of South Carolina Press, 2000.

McArthur, Harvey K., ed. *In Search of the Historical Jesus*. Scribner Source Books in Religion. New York: Scribner's, 1969.

McKnight, Edgar V. *Jesus Christ in History and Scripture: A Poetic and Sectarian Perspective*. Macon: Mercer University Press, 1999.

Meier, John P. *A Marginal Jew: Rethinking the Historical Jesus*. 3 vols. *Volume 1: The Roots of the Problem and the Person* (1991); *Volume 2: Mentor, Message, and Miracles* (1994); *Volume 3: Companions and Competitors* (2001). Anchor Bible Reference Library. New York: Doubleday, 1991–2001.

Meyer, Ben F. *The Aims of Jesus*. Princeton Theological Monograph Series 48. San Jose: Pickwick, 2002 (1979).

Miller, Robert J., ed. *The Complete Gospels*. Annotated Scholars Version. Rev. ed. Santa Rosa: Polebridge, 1994 (1992).

Pelikan, Jaroslav. *Jesus Through the Centuries: His Place in the History of Culture*. New Haven: Yale University Press, 1985.

Powell, Mark Allan. *Jesus as a Figure in History: How Modern Historians View the Man from Galilee*. Louisville: Westminster John Knox, 1998.

Robinson, James M. *A New Quest of the Historical Jesus*. Studies in Biblical Theology 25. London: SCM, 1966 (1959).

Sanders, E. P. *The Historical Figure of Jesus*. London: Penguin Books, 1993.

Schweitzer, Albert. *The Quest of the Historical Jesus. First Complete Edition*. Edited by John Bowden. Based on the translation of the first German edition in 1906 by William Montgomery, revised by J. R. Coates, Susan Cupitt, and John Bowden. Minneapolis: Fortress, 2001.

Stanton, Graham. *The Gospels and Jesus*. 2d ed. Oxford: Oxford University Press, 2002.

Strauss, David Friedrich. *The Life of Jesus Critically Examined*. Translated by George Eliot from the fourth German ed. (1840). Edited with an introduction by Peter Hodgson. Lives of Jesus Series. Philadelphia: Fortress, 1972; repr. by Sigler Press, 2002 (1835–1836).

Stuhlmacher, Peter. *Jesus of Nazareth—Christ of Faith*. Translated by Siegfried S. Schatzmann. Peabody: Hendrickson, 1993.

Vermes, Geza. *Jesus the Jew: A Historian's Reading of the Gospels*. London/Philadelphia: Collins/Fortress, 1973.

Witherington, Ben. *The Jesus Quest: The Third Search for the Jew of Nazareth*. 2d ed. Downers Grove: InterVarsity, 1997 (1995).

———. *Jesus the Sage: The Pilgrimage of Wisdom*. Minneapolis: Fortress, 1994.

Wright, N. T. *Christian Origins and the Question of God: Volume 1: The New Testament and the People of God* (1992); *Volume 2: Jesus and the Victory of God* (1996); *Volume 3: The Resurrection and the Son of God* (2003). Minneapolis: Fortress, 1992–2003.

Chapter 6

The Gospel of Mark

"A religion which denies that God is hidden is not true."

Blaise Pascal

"Our knowledge of God begins in all seriousness with the knowledge of the hiddenness of God."

Karl Barth

Often read as a simple, straightforward account of Jesus' life, Mark is now widely regarded as one of the subtlest, most enigmatic of the Gospels. Early readers of Mark saw that it was far from simple. Some were so mystified by its abrupt ending that two alternate conclusions were devised to bring neater closure to the story. The opening verse also presents a puzzle. Did it always contain the phrase "the Son of God"? Some scholars have wondered whether 1:1 was originally the title of the whole book or perhaps a vestige of an original, longer beginning that is now lost.

Within the Gospel itself, some readers found other literary puzzles. Struggling to understand why Mark (1:2) would attribute a line from Mal 3:1 to the prophet Isaiah, Jerome (ca. 345–420 C.E.) candidly admits, "Informed as he is in spiritual matters, [Mark] is uninformed here, and credits to one prophet of Holy Writ what is written by another."[1] Readers have long been puzzled by other features of Mark's narrative as well. In 5:1–2, after crossing the Sea of Galilee, Jesus steps out of the boat in the "country of the Gerasenes," some thirty miles from the sea! To no one's surprise, fidgeting scribes substituted more plausible place names, for example, Gadarenes. The death of John the Baptist (6:14–29) appears to interrupt the narrative; 6:30 more sensibly follows 6:13. Later in chapter 6, after Jesus walks on the water, the disciples land their boat at Gennesaret, on the northwest coast of the Sea of Galilee, whereas earlier they had taken a northeasterly course toward Bethsaida (6:45, 53). It was doubtless problems like these that prompted Papias, bishop of Hierapolis (ca. 60–130 C.E.), to report that Mark "wrote accurately, though not in order."[2]

PALESTINE AT THE TIME OF JESUS

SCALE OF MILES
0   5   10   15   20   25   30

Besides these literary puzzles, we are also struck by Mark's overall portrait of Jesus, the only figure in the Gospel who deserves to be called a character in a literary sense. To say that Jesus is an elusive figure in Mark is an understatement. Not that he remains hidden from view, for he is very much a public figure. But even though Jesus does his work out in the open, he is not an open book easily read by those whom he encounters. The highest level of recognition is expressed by God, first as a private revelation to Jesus (and presumably John the Baptist) at his baptism (1:9–11), then to Peter, James, and John at the transfiguration (9:2–8). By having these two confessions originate in heaven, Mark renders them as theophanies, appearances by God. Strategically located at the beginning of the two main sections of the Gospel, each episode reaffirms what the reader learns in the opening verse and anticipates what Jesus himself knows (14:62) and what the Roman centurion recognizes at the crucifixion: Jesus is the Son of God (1:1; 15:39).

Those on earth who come closest to this level of recognition (apart from the centurion and the young man in the tomb) are members of the demonic order—the unclean spirits—whom Jesus encounters in several of the healing stories. Their confessional language echoes that of God (1:24; 3:11; 5:7). It also stands in sharp contrast to the failure of Jesus' own disciples to understand what he says or does. To reinforce the point, Mark includes specific examples of disciples who failed to grasp Jesus' mission, even naming names—Peter (8:27–33; 14:26–31, 66–72), James and John (10:35–40), and Judas (14:43–50). At the final hour, Mark tells us, "all of them deserted him and fled" (14:50). The lone exceptions are the Galilean women (15:40–41; 16:1–8) and possibly Joseph of Arimathea (15:42–47), although they never use confessional language comparable to that of the unclean spirits.

Mark's sketch of the public character of Jesus' ministry, all the way from Galilee to Jerusalem, actually sets in bold relief this surprising range of responses. What should have been obvious is not so obvious, and the problem is compounded by the numerous times Jesus tries to suppress his identity. Frequently, Jesus tries to impose silence on those who encounter him, regardless of their level of recognition: the demonic order (1:25, 34; 3:11–12); those whom he healed or who saw him heal others (1:44; 5:43; 7:36; 8:26); and his own disciples (8:30; 9:9). Taken together, these "messianic secret" passages reflect a distinctively Markan viewpoint, whether he is reporting Jesus' actual words or an interpretive perspective developed later by the church. The effect is the same. Rather than publicize his true identity, the Markan Jesus tries to hide it.

That he is not just speaking tongue-in-cheek is reflected in another distinctive element in Mark's Gospel—Jesus' use of parables in which we also find this tendency to conceal rather than reveal. They do so by underscoring how elusive "the secret [or mystery] of the kingdom of God" is (4:11). Even insiders, those whom Jesus calls and who are constantly with him, often fail to comprehend this mystery although they have received constant private instruction about it (4:34). Seeing what he does in episode after episode and listening to how he challenges cherished assumptions of his hearers, we are perplexed by this elusive side of Jesus, this tendency to keep his true identity and mission hidden.

When scholars characterize Mark as mysterious revelation or apocalyptic drama, they are not trying to complicate what is simple. Rather, they are inviting us to experience the Gospel of Mark as a subtly written narrative that seriously probes the question, "Who was Jesus?" **[See Expanded CD Version pp. 149–52:** *Mark as the Second Gospel* **and** *From Second Gospel to First Gospel*]

Giving Shape to the Jesus Story

Up close, Mark's Gospel may appear to be loosely organized, but seen from a distance it reflects a clear, logical storyline: Jesus, the anointed Son of God, moves from an impressive ministry of teaching and healing in Galilee to Judea and Jerusalem, where he enacts the destiny of the suffering Son of Man. Even so, scholars have found it difficult to agree on a clear organizing principle in Mark. They have outlined the story according to geography, chronology, theme, or even as stages of a drama. The following structure may be suggested: a cluster of inaugural events (1:1–15); Jesus' ministry of healing and teaching in Galilee (1:16–8:26); the moment of truth at Caesarea Philippi (8:27–9:1); moving from the transfiguration to Judea and Trans-jordan where the disciples listen to Jesus (9:2–10:52); Jesus' passion predictions fulfilled in Jerusalem (11:1–16:8).

When we read Mark along with the other Gospels, we are first struck by its comparative brevity. Mark is roughly 60 percent the length of Matthew and Luke. Mark lacks some of the most memorable parts of its longer counterparts. It has no birth story, no genealogy, no resurrection appearances, and no ascension. It devotes much less space to pivotal moments in Jesus' life, such as his baptism (1:9–11) and temptation (1:12–13), although it gives more detailed accounts of certain episodes, such as the death of John the Baptist (6:14–29). Compared with the longer opening and closing sections of Matthew and Luke, Mark has an abrupt beginning and ending.

Mark appears to give less space to the content of Jesus' teaching than its synoptic counterparts, and in certain respects this is correct. Mark records fewer parables than Matthew and Luke, and we find no digest of Jesus' teaching comparable to Matthew's Sermon on the Mount (Matt 5–7) or Luke's Sermon on the Plain (Luke 6:20–49). Even so, Mark gives an impressive amount of space to what Jesus taught. We find blocks of teaching clustered in chapter 4 (parables), chapters 9–10 (teachings directed primarily to the disciples), and chapter 13 (the apocalyptic discourse). Interwoven with the cycles of controversy stories in chapters 2 and 12 is a substantial amount of teaching. Compared with the amount of additional teaching we find in Matthew and Luke, Mark certainly gives less attention to the content of Jesus' teaching, but the overall percentage of Mark's available space devoted to teaching is by no means slight. Even with these qualifications, however, Mark's account of Jesus' actual teachings is briefer than that of Matthew and Luke.

Some of Mark's harsher critics have characterized his narrative as cluttered and disorganized, which seems to have been the point of Papias's phrase mentioned earlier: "however, not in order." There is an unmistakable rough-edged quality to Mark's narrative. His Greek is far from polished and well below the literary standards of other, more stylistically accomplished NT authors such as Matthew, Luke, or the author of Hebrews. Rather than establishing tight connections between individual episodes or larger parts of the narrative, Mark uses simple coordinating words such as "and," "again," or "immediately" (*euthys*, used over forty times) to link his episodes. This creates minimal causal connection between events, although it does move the story along. Such usage may reflect a storyteller's lively narrative style in which stories are told excitedly one after another and in which a high premium is placed on well-chosen, unforgettable images, such as Jesus "in the stern, asleep on the cushion" (4:38) or crowds sitting on "green grass" in groups of hundreds and fifties (6:39–40). In many ways, reading Mark is like watching a slideshow or a quick-action TV episode in which the camera cuts rapidly from scene to scene with very few pauses.

Yet there are signs that Mark has done more than assemble a collection of stories like pearls on a string. His literary artistry is reflected, for example, in his use of *hybrid stories*, in which one story encloses another, smaller story. Numerous examples of this distinctive Markan literary technique occur: Jesus' encounter with Jerusalem scribes about Beelzebul (3:22–30) within the story of Jesus with his family (3:19b–21, 31–35); healing the hemorrhaging woman (5:24b–34) within the story of the raising of Jairus's daughter (5:21–24a, 35–43); the cleansing of the temple (11:15–19) within the story of the cursing of the fig tree (11:12–14, 20–25); the anointing at Bethany (14:3–9) within the account of the plan to arrest Jesus (14:1–2, 10–11); and Jesus before the high priest (14:55–65) within the story of Peter's denial (14:53–54, 66–72). Other examples also occur, although the seams may not be as clear.[3]

Rather than reflecting a clumsy storytelling technique, the inner stories usually serve a literary purpose: an episode begins, time is needed for certain things to occur, the second story fills the time gap, and the first episode is resumed. In the healing of Jairus's daughter (5:21–43), pausing to relate the healing of the hemorrhaging woman (5:24b–34) dramatizes Jesus' delay in reaching the little girl, thereby heightening the effect of the desperate question in 5:35: "Your daughter is dead. Why trouble the teacher any further?" Coming on the heels of the Gerasene demoniac story, which was far more impressive than earlier exorcisms, this double miracle extends the image of Jesus as healer even further: He can both heal the sick and raise the dead. Placing these three episodes immediately prior to Jesus' rejection at Nazareth renders his hometown's lackluster response even less forgivable.

Mark displays similar literary artistry by enclosing the cleansing of the temple (11:15–19) within the cursing of the fig tree and its interpretation (11:12–14, 20–24) to make a theological point: The withered fig tree symbolizes the fate of the temple.

Further evidence of Mark's literary purpose is his use of well-placed *summaries*. Not only do they allow the reader to pause and catch up, but they also render previously narrated episodes as samples of more widespread activity. The three summaries of healings in 1:32–34; 3:7–12; and 6:53–56 extend the scope of Jesus' healing ministry numerically and geographically (see 6:6b–13, esp. 12–13). The parables summary of 4:33–34 alerts readers to a host of unreported parables. These and other transitional summaries reveal that Mark knows more than he tells (1:39; 4:1–2; 6:6b; 10:1). Readers would easily conclude that Jesus' ministry included far more than what Mark actually reports.

Mark has also made the overall story more coherent by including *narrative arrows* that direct the reader's attention forward. As early as 2:20, he anticipates a time when "the bridegroom is taken away." The conspiracy of the Pharisees and Herodians "to destroy him" (3:6) serves as an omen for events in chapters 14–15. The three highly stylized passion predictions in 8:31–33; 9:30–32; and 10:32–34 are fulfilled in the Passion Narrative. Mark's literary foresight is also seen elsewhere. In 1:14 the arrest of John the Baptist anticipates his death in 6:14–29; in 4:1 Jesus can get into a boat because earlier preparations were made in 3:9.

By looking closely at the shape of Mark's narrative, we see that he has not only received the Jesus tradition, but has also shaped it. His story still has its rough edges, but it is far more coherent than the disconnected set of traditions he inherited. Mark's Gospel may be uneven in places, but it is a single, creatively constructed story—a remarkable literary achievement. **[See Expanded CD Version pp. 154–58: *The Plot of Mark's Story: A Summary of Mark's Gospel*]**

A woodcut depicting the evangelist Mark, with his attribute, the lion (Rev 4:7); taken from a 1541 printing of Martin Luther's German translation of the New Testament. From the Digital Image Archive of The Richard C. Kessler Reformation Collection, Pitts Theology Library, Candler School of Theology, Emory University, Atlanta, Georgia.

Jesus in Mark

As noted earlier, there is only one real character in the story—Jesus—and while Mark considers aspects of how God is present and at work in the world, the primary lens through which he does so is the figure Jesus. To state it more formally, Mark's primary interest is Christology.

Is it correct to characterize Mark's Jesus as *charismatic teacher*? Yes and no. Yes, in the sense that this phrase combines two key elements of the Markan portrait: Jesus' deeds of power and his teachings. No, because it oversimplifies what we find in Mark's richly textured narrative.

What Jesus Does

We find Jesus engaged in a dazzling array of activities in Mark: proclaiming God's good news, calling disciples, teaching in synagogues, healing the sick, exorcising demons, confronting named and unnamed opponents from all sides, speaking parables, subduing nature, and feeding the hungry, all while traveling both on land and on sea. Even when Jesus reaches Jerusalem (ch. 11), he remains the protagonist, though much of the Passion Narrative (chs. 14–15) is less about what he did than what others did to him.

Without flattening the narrative too much, we can say that Jesus emerges as a preacher who consistently engaged in two activities: teaching and performing miracles. We recognize the hazard of distinguishing too neatly between what Jesus does and what he says. In some cases miracle stories are also occasions for Jesus to teach. Quite often such stories conclude with a pronouncement in which Jesus utters a saying that clarifies some aspect of his identity or mission. His healing of the paralytic, for example, prompts him to explain how he, as Son of Man, has the authority to forgive sins—like God, no less (2:7–11).

Preaching. At the outset, Mark introduces Jesus as the preacher of God's good news (1:14–15). He takes over this role from John the Baptist (1:4, 7), and continues it (1:38–39, 45), even as he hands it over to his disciples (3:14; 6:12). If there is an overarching theme to his preaching, it is "the kingdom of God" (*hē basileia tou theou*; 4:11, 26, 30; 9:1, 47; 10:14–15, 23–25; 12:34; 14:25; cf. 15:43). Variously rendered as "God's reign," "God's rule," or "God's dominion," the phrase suggests a sphere in which God is the defining reality and in which the pursuit of God's purposes guides everything. So closely is it identified with both the person and preaching of Jesus that his presence makes it "near" or "at hand." What "kingdom of God" signifies is unfolded through Mark's presentation of Jesus' teaching and his wondrous powers.

Teaching. The image of teacher may suggest other images—perhaps a court philosopher, a teacher with his own academy, or wandering philosopher; a rabbi with disciples gathered around him discussing Torah; or a sage who speaks words of wisdom or utters and collects proverbs. No single one of these images captures fully Jesus the Teacher in Mark, though elements of each are present.

Considering how much Jesus travels in Mark, he is certainly an itinerant teacher. Galilee and its environs define his primary sphere of activity, an admittedly limited geographical locale when compared with some other itinerant philosophers who traveled throughout the Mediterranean world. Even so, his teaching is not confined to one place, for we find him teaching in synagogues, homes, and other private settings, and out in open spaces. How he teaches is equally varied. Much of his teaching occurs in controversial settings in which he engages opponents who perceive him as a threat to the status quo. In these controversy stories he often makes shocking pronouncements in which he clarifies some aspect of his identity or mission. Much of his teaching is directed to his inner circle of followers: the Twelve and a larger circle of unnamed disciples (see esp. chs. 9–10).

One of the most persistent features we find in early traditions about Jesus is his use of *parables*. At the end of the parables discourse in chapter 4, Mark reports that Jesus "did not speak to [the crowds] except in parables" (4:34). Closely related are other instances of metaphorical speech that are not specifically identified as parables (2:21–22; 9:49–50; 13:28–29). That Jesus spoke in parables is clear; how and why he did so is far less clear.

Jesus' parables stop people in their tracks, inviting them to look again at how they see the world. What puzzles us, especially if we come to Mark with the naïve view that parables are simple stories told to illuminate some aspect of the kingdom of God, is Jesus' insistence that parables are primarily designed *not for insiders but for outsiders*; and, as if that were not enough, employing the language of Isa 6:9–10, he uses them *to obscure rather than enlighten*—to close the blinds rather than open them (4:11–12).

Compared with Matthew and Luke, Mark only gives us a handful of parables (3:23–27; 4:1–34; 12:1–12; 13:28; cf. 7:17), but enough to show that, for him, they function like two-way mirrors. If we look at them one way, we only see images of ourselves; the stories simply mirror our everyday lives. But looked at another way, they enable us to "see through" the story to what life in the kingdom of God is really about. Parables show that God's territory is not always visible to us, even when we are standing near it. One thing is for sure: we have to open our ears (and eyes) to "get it" (cf. 4:9, 23).

Also worth noting is how the parable of the sower in Mark provides the key to understanding all the others (4:1–9, 13–20). The word, the proclamation of God's good news, falls on many types of ears. It competes against demonic diversions, superficial commitments, and the lure of other gods. Yet occasionally it takes root and bears incredible yields. As the narrative unfolds we witness the unpredictability of people's responses to God's good news.

By using parables to expound the mystery of God's kingdom (ch. 4), Jesus clarifies what it means to confront God in God's own space and on God's own terms. The few parables that Mark recounts reveal many dimensions of God: hiddenness, ambiguity, subtle presence, dramatic surprise, sternness, and utter reliability. But all the parables reveal the heart of God by illuminating the space God occupies and declaring a way of being and behaving in the world appropriate to God's dominion.

As prominent as Jesus' parables are in Mark, they represent only a small slice of his teaching. Quite often Mark's stories conclude with a saying in which Jesus makes a stunning pronouncement. These occur in different settings but they typically illuminate some aspect of Jesus' identity or mission: he claims God's power to forgive sin

(2:7–11); his mission is not to the righteous but to sinners (2:17); he redefines how the Sabbath should be understood—it should serve us, not we it (2:27–28); and his true family includes not his blood kin, but those who serve God (3:35). Taken as a group and along with the parables, these *pronouncement stories* enable Jesus to explain in his own terms who he is and what he does.

Much of Jesus' teaching occurs in *controversy stories* in which Jesus engages opponents in debate. As one would expect, sometimes his miracles prompt controversy (2:1–12; 3:1–6), but more often controversy erupts in other settings, usually ones in which some action or word of Jesus challenges conventional assumptions, practices, or institutions: when he violates accepted social convention by dining with tax collectors and sinners (2:15–17); when his disciples do not fast (2:18); when he breaks Sabbath observance (2:23–28; see 3:1–6); when he relaxes rules relating to ritual uncleanness (7:1–8); and when he confronts temple abuses (11:15–19). The cumulative effect of these stories is to reinforce the image of Jesus as someone who challenges convention.

One reading of 2:1–3:6 sees a cycle of five such controversy stories whose repetition hammers home this point. By placing this cycle of stories so early in the narrative, Mark introduces Jesus as a provocative figure who boldly sparks controversy, a role that only increases as the narrative progresses. This is especially seen in chapter 12, in which Jesus answers certain stock questions put to him by named groups of adversaries—Pharisees, Herodians, Sadducees, and scribes: How should we regard civil authority (12:13–17)? Is there a resurrection (12:18–27)? What is the great commandment (12:28–34)? Who is David's true successor (12:35–37)? Here Mark gives us a set of "position papers" that distinguish Jesus from other religious teachers.

However varied these controversies are, they show Jesus not only as a herald of a grand vision, but also as someone who confronts people where they are. He jolts, argues, explains, cajoles, and clarifies in order to expose the complex tapestry of the kingdom of God. Like every visionary teacher, Jesus' ultimate purpose is to make disciples. A note of urgency is sounded throughout his teaching. Insisting that God's reign is near, already interrupting and even upsetting normal routines of life, Jesus confronts his hearers with God's presence by bringing them into God's own space and time. God surrounds them, he insists, and requires an immediate response.

Some of Jesus' most intense teaching occurs in chapters 8–10 and is prompted by Peter's (and the other disciples') profound misunderstanding of his messiahship. His three passion predictions are dramatic teaching moments that prompt him to give *instructions about discipleship* (8:31–32; 9:30–32; 10:32–34). With the divine voice at the transfiguration having commanded Peter, James, and John to "listen to him," Jesus descends from the mount as the Teacher par excellence (9:9). While some of the teaching in chapters 9–10 is directed to the crowds, most of it is directed to his circle of disciples. In 9:33–10:45 Jesus sketches in detail what is expected of disciples who take their cue from the suffering Son of Man.

Yet another dimension of his teaching is reflected in chapter 13, the *apocalyptic discourse* whose distinctive literary form has earned it the name "the little apocalypse." Unlike other sets of teaching in the Gospel, with the possible exception of the parable discourse in chapter 4, this chapter constitutes a single discourse delivered by Jesus on the Mount of Olives to Peter, James, John, and Andrew as they faced the temple.

Since this discourse anticipates the temple's destruction (13:2, 14) and the religious, political, and social chaos that followed, it shows one way early Christians dealt with this monumental crisis: Jesus not only foresaw it, he triggered it (11:12-24; 14:58)! But he also looked beyond this crisis and saw a far greater reality replacing it: the coming kingdom of God, already begun, but finally to be ushered in by the triumphant Son of Man, who will gather to himself a new, universal community (13:23-27). Many false claimants will try to fill the vacuum created by the temple's destruction, Jesus assures his disciples, and serious social upheaval, turmoil, and pain will occur in the interim, but he expects his disciples to endure—to be alert and stay awake (13:32-37).

Given its placement in the narrative—it is Jesus' last word prior to his death—the apocalyptic discourse looms large in Mark. By looking forward rather than backward, it establishes the horizon of expectations for the events of chapters 14-16. What transpires from 14:1 onward, with all of its tragic elements—the leaders' conspiracy, Judas's betrayal, Peter's denial, the disciples' desertion, and God's nonintervention—will nevertheless give way to a newly built temple (14:58), a new way to experience God's presence through Jesus Christ. This risen Christ will once again gather disciples in Galilee (16:7), and from there will emerge a worldwide witness to God's "good news" (13:10). Through all the chaos and disappointment emerges an ongoing community of disciples devoted to the suffering Son of Man, who remember the woman's anointing of Jesus (14:3-9), who preserve his memory in the Eucharist (14:22-25), who testify boldly in the face of stiff resistance (13:9-13), and who finally look to the coming Son of Man for their ultimate vindication (13:24-27).

Miracles. Closely related, but hardly separable from his teaching, are the numerous "deeds of power" (*dynameis*) that Jesus performs throughout the story. Sixteen such stories are recorded by Mark, most of them clustered in chapters 1-8. Twelve of these are healing stories, a weighting that strongly tilts Mark's portrait of Jesus in the direction of a compassionate healer who reaches out to those afflicted with physical and psychological maladies. Since four of the miracle stories are exorcisms, Mark's image of Jesus as healer has a special dimension. Demons may not be the adversary in every healing episode, but they occur frequently enough for Jesus to be cast regularly in the role of exorcist (1:39).

Some of the healing stories are set in mundane circumstances, but others show Jesus as the enemy of Satan and the demonic order, whose grip on humanity is most visibly seen in debilitating and otherwise inexplicable illnesses. Whether Jesus is confronting people with "unclean spirits," either those who experience seizures (1:21-28) or behave as crazed outcasts unaware of their own strength and the threat they pose to society (5:1-20), he is more than a medicine man gathering herbs and stirring potions. Rather, he is Satan's archenemy, engaged in a titanic struggle with the whole demonic order. Not surprisingly, when charged with being in league with Beelzebul, the prince of demons, Jesus retorts by insisting that a kingdom divided against itself cannot stand (3:24).

The miracle stories are often reported in clusters. This suggests that soon after the death of Jesus such stories were probably grouped together in cycles and that Mark received them in this form. Even so, he has positioned them carefully in the narrative to achieve maximum effect. By giving the set of four miracle stories in 1:21-2:12 top billing, Mark privileges the image of Jesus as healer at the outset. This image of Jesus the wonder-worker is further reinforced by the second cycle of miracle stories in 4:35–5:43 and a shorter cycle in 6:34–56.

Besides noting the frequency of miracle stories in Mark, we should also observe where they occur and how they function within the narrative. The three stories that occur immediately after the parables in chapter 4 sharpen the profile of Jesus as miracle worker. Stilling the storm shows Jesus dealing with the chaos of nature (4:35–41); the earlier healing stories pale in comparison to Jesus' healing the Gerasene demoniac (5:1–20), an exorcism story written in all capital letters. The story of raising Jairus's daughter, which encloses the healing of the woman with a hemorrhage, demonstrates his power to overcome both sickness and death (5:21–43).

Still other miracle stories occur after Jesus' rejection at Nazareth: feeding the 5,000 (6:34–44), walking on water (6:45–52), healing the daughter of the Syrophoenician woman (7:24–30), healing the deaf mute (7:31–37), feeding the 4,000 (8:1–10), and healing the blind man at Bethsaida (8:22–26). Each of these miracles advances the story in different ways, depending upon its function within the narrative. The two feeding stories extend Jesus' power beyond healing and place him within the tradition of Moses, who feeds the multitudes in the wilderness. Jesus' encounter with the Syrophoenician woman takes him into Gentile territory, thereby crossing an important symbolic boundary. This doubtless enabled later readers of Mark's Gospel to justify their preaching mission to non-Jews. Only two instances of curing the blind occur (8:22–26; 10:46–52), both immediately after stunning instances of incomprehension on the part of the disciples. Their symbolic function is widely recognized: the recipients of Jesus' mercy "see" in ways that his own disciples do not.

Jesus' miracles amplify different aspects of his identity. Among other things, they provide an arena for Jesus to engage Satan and the demonic order in "hand-to-hand combat." The exorcisms, in particular, become occasions when Jesus triumphs over the "unclean spirits" and when some of the clearest confessional moments occur. In these contexts, he is recognized by the demons as "Son of God" (3:11; 5:7), "God's Holy One" (1:24), and perhaps by the Syrophoenician woman as Lord (7:28). Healing stories also become occasions when Jesus identifies himself as the Son of Man who boldly claims God's power to forgive sins (2:6–11); as the one who redefines the Sabbath (3:1–6); as the Lord who performs acts of mercy (5:19); as the powerful Teacher who subdues unclean spirits (9:17, 25–27); and as the Son of David who acts as a merciful rather than militant king (10:46–52). By stilling the storm (4:35–41), he is the authoritative Teacher whom even the winds and sea obey. The two miraculous feedings (6:34–44; 8:1–10) call up images of Moses and Elijah, who were associated with similar feats in Israel (Exod 16:13–35; Num 11:1–35; Ps 78:17–31; 1 Kgs 17:8–16; 2 Kgs 4:1–7, 38–44), and anticipate their appearance on the Mount of Transfiguration (9:2–9).

In Mark there is no simple correlation between miracles and faith. When they are connected, faith typically precedes the miracle (5:34, 36; 9:23–24, 29; 10:47–48, 52; possibly 7:28–29). People do not believe in Jesus because he performs miracles (as in John's Gospel); Jesus performs miracles when people believe. Miracles may expose the absence of faith (4:40) or faith may arise in the absence of miracles (15:39).

Miracles cause amazement and may even prompt people to "glorify God" (2:12); but they can also stir fear in people's hearts (5:15, 33). One thing they consistently do is serve as catalysts for further proclamation (1:44–45; 5:14–20; 7:36). So powerful are they that people ignore Jesus' commands to silence (1:45; 7:36). They also stir controversy (3:1–6).

In spite of the many roles miracles play in Mark's Gospel, they mainly amplify Mark's portrait of Jesus. More than anything else, they are dramatic expressions of God's power. They show God interrupting time and space to effect the divine purpose through Jesus. They present two competing kingdoms—the kingdom of God, in which Jesus and the Holy Spirit are active, and the kingdom of Satan, in which his minions, the demonic order, do their work. Jesus is seen as bringing the fight to Satan's border and posing a frontal challenge to his dominion over humanity. To state it technically, miracles function as part of Mark's Christology.

Who Jesus Is

One way of getting at Mark's Jesus is to look at the ways Jesus speaks of himself as well as the ways others talk to him or about him—in short, by examining the titles used in Mark's narrative. This is not a simple task because several titles with different nuances occur in Mark. Some titles are clearer than others and may signify different things in different parts of the narrative. It is widely recognized that Mark's Jesus is far more than the sum total of all the titles used in the Gospel.

We see this, for example, in the way Mark crafts his stories to suggest certain images without attaching them to a specific title. Taken as a whole, the miracles call up images of Elijah and Elisha, who also heal the sick, raise people from the dead, perform miraculous feedings, and triumph over nature (1 Kgs 17–19; 2 Kgs 1–6). Such associations, in turn, lend credibility to questioners who wonder whether Jesus is Elijah come back from heaven (8:28; 9:1–13). But they also provide an opportunity to identify John the Baptist, not Jesus, as Elijah *redivivus* (9:13). For all of these echoes of the OT prophetic tradition, however, Mark's Jesus is not clothed in prophetic garb, even though he once refers to himself as a "prophet without honor" (6:4). If there is a prophet in Mark, it is John the Baptist (1:1–8).

As noted earlier, Moses imagery can be seen behind such stories as feeding the multitudes. These images are prominent enough to keep us from being surprised to find Jesus compared with Elijah and Moses in the transfiguration story (9:2–8). And having been assured by God of his unique identity as Son, Jesus descends from the Mount of Transfiguration only to begin a period of teaching (chs. 9–10) reminiscent of the Deuteronomic Moses. And yet the image of Jesus as a new Moses is not exploited by Mark.

Son of David. When blind Bartimaeus addresses Jesus as "Son of David" (10:47–48), he expresses the messianic hopes that were often associated with David. Similar expectations of a newly established Davidic kingdom surface at the triumphal entry (11:9–10, paraphrasing Ps 118:25–26). Jesus' interpretation of Ps 110 in Mark 12:35–37 shows that he was later identified by his followers as David's lord rather than merely his son. The imagery of messianic king figures prominently in Mark's account of the trial and crucifixion (15:2, 9, 12, 18, 26, 32). The language is sometimes straightforward, sometimes highly ironic—Mark's way of presenting both popular and official perceptions. Yet through it all a fundamental theological truth emerges: Jesus *is* messianic king, but in a radically different sense than those who tried and crucified him imagined. Even so, the image of Jesus as king remains relatively undeveloped in Mark. Jesus wears royal garb only in an ironic sense (15:16–20). To be sure, he is a figure who possesses awe-inspiring authority, but not because he acts like a king.

Teacher. Jesus' authority in Mark usually derives from his role as charismatic teacher. Because Jesus' teaching and miracles are so closely intertwined, it is hard to say which establishes his authority more firmly. In the Capernaum synagogue episode, when Jesus first teaches the audience and then exorcises the unclean spirit (1:21–28), we see how closely these two roles are blended. What impresses the bystanders is his teaching (1:27). The point of the story is clear: since the demons yield to his authoritative word, the people interpret his power to heal as an extension of his power to teach.

The image of Jesus as teacher is perhaps the most persistent single image found in Mark. Fifteen times Mark uses the term "teach" (*didaskō*) with specific reference to Jesus (1:21–22; 2:13; 4:1–2; 6:2, 6, 34; 8:31; 9:31; 10:1; 11:17; 12:14, 35; 14:49). "Teacher" (*didaskalos*) is the title most frequently used by people who address Jesus in Mark. "Teacher" is not used as a confessional title, however, since it occurs on the lips of so many different characters: disciples (4:38; 9:38; 10:35; 13:1), a potential disciple (10:17, 20), "some people" (5:35; 9:17), Jesus' adversaries (12:14, 19, 32), even Jesus himself (14:14). A similar pattern of usage is also reflected in the closely related term "Rabbi," used by Peter (9:5; 11:21), Judas (14:45), and Bartimaeus (10:51). "Teacher" functions as the primary image around which Mark organizes Jesus' activity. From day to day, from situation to situation, people experience Jesus first and foremost as teacher—a wonder-working teacher, to be sure, but a teacher nonetheless. Because of its indiscriminate usage in Mark, "Teacher" does not signify deep, confessional recognition. It captures one dimension of who Jesus is, but acknowledging Jesus as Teacher is only entry-level recognition.

For higher orders of recognition, we come to "Son of God" and "Son of Man," both highly freighted expressions in Mark.

Son of God. The title "Son of God," which was probably part of the original wording of the opening verse (1:1), figures prominently in setting the reader's expectations in Mark. The divine pronouncement at Jesus' baptism, with subtle echoes of Ps 2:7 and Isa 42:1 and possibly even Abraham's sacrifice of Isaac (Gen 22), dramatically reinforces the portrait of Jesus as a duly anointed king, adopted as God's Son, yet still an obedient servant and child (1:11). His healings, most notably his exorcisms, prompt the unclean spirits to recognize him as Son of God (3:11), a confession written in even bolder type in the Gerasene demoniac story (5:7). In the healing episode at the Capernaum synagogue, the unclean spirit recognizes Jesus as "the Holy One of God" (1:24). While this image shifts the metaphor slightly, it is part of the same constellation of ideas.

Like Jesus' baptism, the transfiguration is a carefully placed theophany in which the divine voice properly identifies Jesus as God's Son. It is more than a private event, however, and it advances the story by claiming that Jesus as God's Son truly surpasses Moses and Elijah, who symbolically represent the law and the prophets. While the title "Son of God" does not appear in the parable of the wicked tenants (12:1–12), the "beloved son" (12:6), the heir who is finally killed, is clearly a parabolic figure for Jesus. The sonship of Jesus also comes to expression in Gethsemane when he prays to God, "Abba, Father" (14:36). A variation of Son of God, "Son of the Blessed One" (14:61), also surfaces at the trial when the high priest presses Jesus to identify himself. And finally, the well-known confession of the Roman centurion uses this title (15:39).

For Mark, "Son of God" represents the summit of confessional recognition. The opening verse (assuming its originality) is the thesis statement that drives Mark to compose the Gospel in the first place, and it informs every compositional decision he makes. Witnesses are lined up in impressive order, God being the chief witness who speaks twice. The demonic order, doubtless including Satan himself, also reaches this level of understanding, as does the centurion. This title also reflects Jesus' own self-understanding (at least in Mark's view), as his prayer in the garden (14:36) and his answer to the high priest attest (14:62). That no one else in the narrative ever really reaches this level of understanding—the Twelve, the other disciples, Jesus' family, his opponents, the crowds, or his accusers—is testimony to just how high Mark set the bar for grasping Jesus' identity as "Son of God."

Son of Man. The closely related expression "Son of Man" has an equally strategic role in Mark, even though it functions in a different way from "Son of God." In the Galilean ministry it occurs twice, both times on the lips of Jesus, to clarify some aspect of his behavior. The first time, in the healing of the paralytic (2:1–10), he clearly refers to his own actions when he boldly claims, "so that you may know that the Son of Man has authority on earth to forgive sins. . ." (2:10). In the second instance, the story of plucking grain on the Sabbath (2:23–28), Jesus doubtless refers to himself when he claims that "the Son of Man is lord even of the sabbath" (2:28). What is remarkable about both instances is how Jesus uses the term. Rather than saying, "I am the Son of Man, and thus forgive sins or redefine how the Sabbath is understood," he uses the third person form of expression. It looks as though he is referring to someone else, yet his usage is clearly self-referential.

What is meant by the expression, both here and later in the narrative, is much debated. Most likely, its usage here is informed by the enigmatic Son of Man figure in Dan 7:13–14, though its precise connotation is not at all clear. Even if the term can be understood as a highly poetic way of describing a human being, it should not be read simply as a title expressing Jesus' humanity. "Son of Man" is not the opposite of "Son of God," as though the former expresses his humanity while the latter expresses his divinity. In both 2:10 and 2:28 the term is associated with bold strokes of authority. Whether Jesus is using a relatively neutral title that he empowers by claiming authority to forgive sins and redefine the Sabbath or is appropriating a title already endowed with power is hard to tell. In either case, for Mark, it serves to expose yet another dimension of Jesus' identity.

Jesus' use of the expression "Son of Man" increases dramatically in chapters 9–16. His exchange with Peter at Caesarea Philippi forces the question of his messianic identity (8:29), and Peter's confession appears both clear and unequivocal. But it is short-lived clarity. In the first of three highly stylized predictions (8:31–33; 9:31–32; 10:32–34), Jesus anticipates the end of the story when his suffering, rejection by the leaders, death, and resurrection are narrated in unfolding stages. As before, he uses the term "Son of Man" of himself, but no longer does it connote authority; instead, for the first time it is linked with a destiny that entails suffering and death. Perhaps its association with heavenly grandeur and triumph, as suggested by Dan 7:13–14, accounts for the utter disbelief expressed by Peter. In any case, Peter's refusal to take Jesus at his word lands him in Satan's kingdom, a move that effectively erases the earlier confession. What follows is a sharp profile of discipleship that takes its cue from the suffering Son of Man, whose example will illustrate a paradoxical truth: to avoid death at all costs may reflect a distorted view of life; to die for the right reason may be the fullest expression of life.

Before he is finished, however, Jesus speaks of the Son of Man in yet a third way: as one who will later come in angelic glory to dispense justice and usher in God's kingdom. And this is expected to occur within the lifetime of some of those in the audience (9:1). The Son of Man's role as eschatological judge especially comes to the fore in the apocalyptic discourse (ch. 13), in which Jesus looks into the future and sees the Son of Man coming in power and glory to gather the faithful (13:24–27). It is less clear that Jesus is referring to himself here, but his statement in 9:1 makes this very probable. This discourse looks beyond the end of the book, even beyond the resurrection, to a time when God, through Jesus, will vindicate the cause of the saints.

Jesus' use of "Son of Man" is so unusual that it is difficult to tell when he is using the term to refer to himself. The three passion predictions are self-referential, and probably so are the other uses. Cryptic though they are, these uses reveal a figure who, on the one hand, identifies himself with the powerful, heavenly figure of Dan 7 as he exercises his role as God's herald, challenging the religious, social, and political order, but who, on the other hand, modulates this understanding of raw power by reinterpreting the Son of Man as a figure destined to suffer and die. And what authorizes him to assume the future role of eschatological judge is his experience of suffering, humiliation, and death. By experiencing God's forsakenness, Jesus takes his stand with every human being who lives in death's shadow and only then experiences the miracle of God's new life. It is in this sense that his death is redemptive (10:45).

For Mark, true knowledge of Jesus entails recognizing him as "Son of God" and "Son of Man," and, by extension, as "Messiah." Though each title reveals different aspects of Jesus' identity and functions in different ways in the narrative, they form a constellation of images with a single center: the figure Jesus. Seeing how this central figure is refracted in each image constitutes full-fledged faith for Mark. This occurs most graphically in the scene before the high priest (14:53–65). Asked if he is the "Messiah, the Son of the Blessed One," Jesus answers, "I am." Declaring himself to be both, he goes on to predict the coming of the "Son of Man seated at the right hand of the Power." By drawing on Dan 7 and Ps 110, Jesus etches more sharply the profile of the messianic king exalted by God (14:61–62). The convergence of all these images creates the "circuit overload" that prompts the high priest to cry, "Blasphemy!" (14:64). The high estimation of Jesus throughout Mark is doubtless reflected in the two instances in which he refers to himself as "Lord" (5:19; 11:3; see 2:28; 12:36-37).

Summary

By now, the hazard of trying to reduce Mark's Christology to a single image, such as charismatic teacher, should be obvious. In virtually every paragraph of the Gospel, some claim about Jesus is being made. It is difficult to extract Mark's Jesus from the narrative because it is so deeply embedded there. Still, some images are more prominent than others. While there are echoes of the Elijah/Elisha stories as well as stories about Moses, Mark's Jesus is neither prophet nor lawgiver. We see royal imagery surface in the uses of "Son of David" and the interchanges at the trial when Jesus is depicted as King of the Jews, but Mark's Jesus is no king, at least not in any ordinary sense. At one level he is a charismatic teacher who gains a hearing in first-century Palestine, but his interruption of Palestinian life is perceived at many levels. At a much higher level, he is a particular blend of Messiah, Son of God, and Son of Man whose true identity is best discerned in the richness of the story that unfolds between chapters 1 and 16. Very few characters in the story actually reach this level of understanding. To this extent, Jesus remains a highly enigmatic, elusive figure in Mark.

Discipleship

One of the most well-known features of Mark is its portrayal of the disciples. Early in the narrative, Jesus spends time gathering a circle of disciples. Jesus' first official act is to call Peter, Andrew, James, and John (1:16–20) and then Levi (2:13–14). After the first cycle of miracle and controversy stories, Jesus appoints the Twelve (3:13–19). Thereafter his disciples are always close by, sometimes participating in events, sometimes being taught by him. He commissions them to replicate his own mission of teaching and healing (6:7–13), presumably in the same region, and they return with apparent success (6:30).

Early in the narrative, Jesus' disciples display signs of dullness (4:13, 40–41). Their situation worsens as the narrative progresses. The more Jesus instructs them, the less they seem to understand. His feeding of the 5,000 and his walking on the water leave them puzzled (6:51–52), and their puzzlement only increases (7:18). A repeat of the mass feeding and an encounter with the Pharisees (8:1–13) send the disciples into a downward spiral of incomprehension (8:14–21). Their blindness and deafness now fulfill Isaiah's words earlier directed to outsiders (4:12; Isa 6:9–10). As ironic symbolism, Jesus' healing of the blind man at Bethsaida (8:22–26) serves as a dramatic counterpoint to the disciples' blindness.

The contrasting responses of the demonic order and the disciples constitute two parallel tracks that run throughout the Galilean ministry. The demons rightly perceive Jesus' identity: God's Son, God's Holy One, and the one in whom God is really at work. The disciples, by contrast, move from light to darkness. Naturally, Jesus' adversaries—Pharisees, scribes, and the like—fail to recognize him as Messiah, but this simply provides a pattern of obduracy alongside which the disciples' behavior can be seen. These twin tracks of proper and improper identification, of full and partial knowledge, lead to Caesarea Philippi, where the question of Jesus' identity becomes urgent.

Even though Peter is the principal speaker during the conversation en route to Caesarea Philippi, in his confession and subsequent rebuke by Jesus he exemplifies the disciples' attitude. All three passion predictions are addressed specifically to the disciples, and Mark notes their stunned disbelief (9:32). The third time, their disbelief takes the form of James and John's misguided ambition (10:35–43).

Jesus continues to instruct the disciples after the transfiguration (9:2–13). As he moves toward Jerusalem, his instruction intensifies (9:14–10:52).

The triumphal entry begins with two disciples' complying with Jesus' request to fetch a colt (11:1–10). As events begin to involve Jesus and other groups, such as the Pharisees, Sadducees, and scribes, the disciples still remain in the picture (11:11, 14). A disciple's question about the temple's future is the occasion for the apocalyptic discourse in chapter 13, which is addressed to Peter, James, John, and Andrew (13:3). Jesus observes Passover with the disciples (14:14–16), further identified as the Twelve (14:17), and Judas's infamous role as betrayer is also documented (14:10–11, 20–21). Appropriating Zech 13:7, Jesus predicts that all the disciples will become deserters (14:26–31), which naturally prompts storms of protest on their part. The narcoleptic behavior of Peter, James, and John in Gethsemane understandably irritates the Son of Man, whose hour has come (14:41–42). Judas's betrayal provides the disciples their cue to fulfill Jesus' earlier prediction that they would all become deserters (14:50). Peter's threefold denial (14:66–72) is yet another instance in which his actions symbolize those of the entire group. The only sympathetic figures who are around at the crucifixion are the otherwise unknown Simon of Cyrene (15:21–24), the Roman centurion (15:39), the women from Galilee (15:40–41), Joseph of Arimathea (15:42–47), and the fleet-footed young man who appears at the tomb and gives the definitive interpretation of what has happened (16:6–7; cf. 14:51).

Depending on how negatively scholars read this overall portrayal, they have described the disciples as obtuse, dim-witted, and hardheaded. It is admittedly difficult to find redemptive elements in Mark's portrait of the disciples. This is not to say that Mark sees no future for them, for there are hints that the disciples will outlive their infamy and successfully resume their role as those called to carry on Jesus' ministry of teaching and healing (6:6b–13, 30). They will bear witness to the gospel in the face of stiff resistance (13:9–13). Mark's account of the Lord's Supper (14:22–25) may even envision the disciples celebrating future Eucharists (cf. Matt 26:29). They are doubtless envisioned as agents of the Gentile mission (13:10; 14:9). The promise of an appearance of the risen Lord to the disciples in Galilee (16:7) strikes a hopeful chord. It implies that the disciples will come out of hiding, return to Galilee where they were first called, and become convinced that Jesus was right when he predicted that he would be raised. It is a faint image of the risen Lord commissioning them as witnesses, but it is there.

Mark knows that the disciples recovered from their shameful failure and desertion. This is clear not only from the hints in the narrative referred to above, but also because he includes so much teaching about discipleship. Jesus' teachings in chapters 9–10 and in the apocalyptic discourse in chapter 13 are valuable primarily as instructions to the circle of disciples responsible for proclaiming the gospel after Jesus' death and resurrection and continuing his ministry of teaching and healing. These teachings presuppose that responsible forms of discipleship have arisen from the ashes of disappointment depicted in the narrative of Mark.

What, then, should we make of Mark's portrait of the disciples' behavior? There must have been some truth to his portrait, even if it is exaggerated. Several possibilities have been suggested: Mark's portrait of the disciples shows his understanding of how fragile discipleship is—that it is not something to be taken for granted—or it functions as part of the "messianic secret" theme as yet another indication of the degree to which Jesus' identity remained hidden.

It is also possible that Mark's portrait of the disciples simply reinforces his Christology. As we have already seen, Mark's portrait of Jesus is sketched at different levels, and for Mark the highest order of recognition occurs when Jesus' identity and mission are understood to embrace his dramatic demonstrations of power—his teachings and his miracles—as well as his embodiment of redemptive suffering as it was experienced during his final days. As the narrative moves forward, both the divine voice and the voices of his closest followers become silent—God at the cross and the disciples in the events leading up to the cross. It is this sense of utter alienation that Mark's narrative captures so well. What makes it even more poignant is that those in the best position to translate their recognition into overt support fail to do so.

The genius of Mark's story is how well he understands the gap between "Jesus" and "Christ, the Son of God" (1:1). The disciples' behavior attests that being close to the events does not produce automatic recognition; it may even hinder recognition. Mark's story shows that the confession embodied in 1:1 is not formulaic. Grasping the full force of the claim that Jesus the Teacher, proclaimer of God's good news, is much more—Messiah, Son of God, Son of Man—in a radically new sense is neither easy nor predictable. As the parables show, this level of recognition breaks through at the most unexpected times and in the least expected ways, as both the demons and the Roman centurion attest. By highlighting this lack of recognition among the disciples, Mark reveals, perhaps better than any of the Gospels, the genuine ambiguity of faith.

Mark's Theological Achievement

No Gospel explores the mystery of faith in Jesus Christ more profoundly than Mark. Jesus' ministry may have begun with two private events—his baptism and temptation—but from the beginning of his Galilean ministry until his execution, he preached "God's good news" of the kingdom and taught and performed powerful deeds—all out in the open so people could both see and hear him. Even his resurrection slipped from the shadows—it is announced to three women by a conspicuously dressed young man sitting in the tomb vacated by Jesus.

The Jesus we meet in Mark speaks for God. He is the "Lord" for whom John prepares the way and the "Son" whom God calls beloved at two critical moments in the story: his baptism and transfiguration. These, and a cluster of other honorific titles, are used of him and by him. Together with what he does and says from episode to episode, these titles project an image of someone with dazzling power who threatens the religious establishment in Palestine every bit as much as he offers hope and healing to the sick, dying, and those who live at society's edges. All of this he does as God's duly anointed representative—the messianic king.

Yet what is obvious to the reader (or listener) of Mark's Gospel, who has a panoramic view of the entire drama, is not so obvious to those who seemingly have the best seats in the house. From the outset Mark sketches the cosmic framework within which the story can only be understood: the heavens are ripped open, the Spirit descends, God's voice is heard, and immediately Jesus is in the middle of a contest in which the Spirit is pitted against Satan before an audience of wild beasts and angels. Grasping this larger framework is itself an act of faith because it breaks the boundaries of ordinary human experience, at least for many modern readers. And yet, only if the world is seen this way, Mark insists, can the story of Jesus be told meaningfully.

From start to finish, this is the story of Jesus Christ, the Son of God—so the opening verse tells us, so the Roman centurion confesses at the end. But those who recognize this constitute a distinct minority: God, of course; the unclean spirits and other representatives of the demonic order, on several occasions; and Peter initially, but finally not. Most conspicuously, Jesus' own disciples—the Twelve and the larger circle of disciples—fail to penetrate the mystery of Jesus' true identity and mission, even though they were constantly with him and taught by him privately.

This is the paradox Mark relentlessly explores: being close to Jesus fails to ensure faith; it even prevents it. Those who heard his teaching most directly understood it the least. Especially was this true of his thrice-repeated prediction of his suffering, death, and resurrection.

It is in this sense that Jesus is an elusive figure in Mark. He performs dramatic miracles, then silences those healed or those who witnessed the healing. He speaks in parables, not to clarify but to obscure. His favorite way of referring to himself—Son of Man—is utterly baffling, as the continuing scholarly debate shows.

Thus what is done in plain view turns out to be quite unclear, which accounts for Mark's highly developed sense of the ironic. Two carefully placed stories of blind people being healed merely underscore the blindness of Jesus' disciples. Jesus the messianic king is only recognized as such by Pilate and the other nameless participants in his trial and crucifixion who jeeringly hail him "King of the Jews," speaking what for Mark is truth but not in ways they understand. Jesus' cleansing of the temple is neatly wrapped within the story of the cursing of the fig tree, which is Mark's way of symbolizing the lethal effect Jesus had on this venerable institution. Most whimsical of all is his treatment of the "young man" who flees the scene of Jesus' betrayal naked but shows up again in the empty tomb to give the definitive interpretation of the events of Passion Week. He alone of all the characters in the Gospel knows that Jesus is risen. By recognizing the full truth of the threefold passion prediction, the young man utters a confession surpassing even that of the Roman centurion.

Faith in Jesus Christ for Mark is by no means something that happens easily or automatically. It is not even something that Jesus himself can guarantee to happen within his disciples. But it is not for that reason incapable of being experienced, for clearly Mark envisions that the disciples will do so later. They will carry out the mission to the Gentiles, bear bold witness in the face of stiff resistance, and even continue Jesus' own ministry of teaching and healing. But theirs is a faith that arises from misunderstanding, desertion, and fear. **[See Expanded CD Version pp. 171–73:** *The Controversial Ending of Mark*]

Chapter 1	**Chapter 2**	**Chapter 3**	**Chapter 4**
JUDEA/GALILEE	GALILEE	GALILEE	GALILEE
Prologue (1:1-15) - John the Baptist (2-8) - Baptism of Jesus (9-11) – FIRST THEOPHANY - Temptation (12-13) - Preaching: Kingdom of God near (14-15) 1. Call of Peter, Andrew, James & John (16-20) 2. Exorcism of unclean spirit in Capernaum synagogue (21-28) **M** 3. Healing Peter's mother-in-law (29-31) **M** 4. Summary of healings (32-34) **S** 5. Jesus at prayer (35-38) 6. Transition (39) 7. Healing of leper (40-45) **M**	1. Healing of paralytic (2:1-12) **M & C** 2. Call of Levi (13-14) 3. Eating with sinners (15-17) **C & P** 4. Questions about fasting: wedding, old & new cloth & wineskins (18-22) **C & T** 5. Grainfield on Sabbath – "Lord of Sabbath" (23-28) **C & P**	1. Healing man with withered hand (3:1-6) **M, P, & C** 2. Summary of healings (7-12) **S** 3. Appointment of the Twelve (13-19) 4. Beelzebul controversy (20-30) **C & T** 5. Jesus' true family (31-35) **P**	1. *Transition* (1) 2. Parable of sower (2-9) **T** 3. Purpose of parables (10-12) 4. Interpretation of parable of sower (13-20) **T** 5. Lamp under bushel (21-25) **T** 6. Parable of seed growing secretly (26-29) **T** 7. Parable of mustard seed (30-32) **T** 8. Summary: Use of parables (33-34) **S** 9. Stilling of storm (4:35-41) **M**

Chapter 9	**Chapter 10**	**Chapter 11**	**Chapter 12**
GALILEE	JUDEA & TRANS-JORDAN	JERUSALEM	JERUSALEM: TEACHINGS
1. Prediction of coming Son of Man (1). 2. Transfiguration (2-8) - SECOND THEOPHANY 3. Sequel – Coming of Elijah (9-13) 4. Healing of epileptic boy (14-29) **M** 5. *Transition* (30) 6. Second Passion Prediction (30-32) TEACHINGS: 7. Who is greatest? (33-37) **T** 8. Who is with us? (38-41) **T** 9. Eliminating obstacles (42-48) **T** 10. Salt (49-50) **T**	1. *Transition* (1) TEACHINGS (cont.): 2. Divorce (2-12) **T** 3. Children (13-16) **T** 4. Rich man & eternal life (17-22) **T** 5. Burden of wealth (23-27) **T** 6. Leaving everything (28-31) **T** 7. Third Passion Prediction (32-34) 8. James & John: Misplaced ambition (35-40) **T** 9. Servant leaders (41-45) **T** 10. Healing blind Bartimaeus (46-52) **M**	1. Palm Sunday: triumphal entry (1-10) 2. Entry to Temple (11) 3. Cursing fig tree (12-14) 4. Cleansing Temple (15-19) 5. Lesson of fig tree (20-[26]) 6. Temple opposition: question about Jesus' authority (27-33) **C**	1. Parable of wicked tenants (1-12) **T** 2. Paying taxes: Jesus vs. Pharisees & Herodians (13-17) **C & T** 3. Resurrection: J vs. Sadducees (18-27) **C & T** 4. First commandment: Jesus vs. scribe (28-34) **C & T** 5. Who's David's Son? Jesus vs. scribes (35-37) **C & T** 6. Warning vs. scribes (38-40) **T** 7. Widow's offering (41-44) **T**

Chapter 5	Chapter 6	Chapter 7	Chapter 8
GALILEE	GALILEE	GALILEE	GALILEE
1. Healing Gerasene demoniac (1-20) **M** 2. Raising Jairus's daughter (21-24) **M** 3. Healing woman with hemorrhage (25-34) **M** 4. Raising Jairus's daughter, cont. (35-43) **M**	1. Rejection at Nazareth (1-6a) 2. *Transition* (6b) 3. Mission of the Twelve (7-13) 4. Death of John the Baptist (14-29) 5. Return of the Twelve (30-33) 6. Feeding the 5000 (34-44) **M** 7. Walking on water (45-52) **M** 8. Summary of healings (53-56) **S**	1. Tradition of elders; opposition by Jeru. Pharisees & scribes (1-13) **C & T** 2. Parable: what defiles (14-[16]) **T** 3. Parable interpretation (17-23) **T** 4. Exorcism: daughter of Syro-Phoenician woman (24-30) **M** 5. Healing deaf mute (31-37) **M**	1. Feeding the 4000 (1-10) **M** 2. Pharisees demand sign (11-13) **C** 3. Teaching: beware leaven of Phar. & Herod (14-21) **T** 4. Healing blind man at Bethsaida (8:22-26) **M** CAESAREA PHILIPPI 1. Peter confesses Jesus as Messiah (27-30) 2. <u>First Passion Prediction:</u> Jesus predicts his death and resurr.; Peter objects (31-33) 3. Jesus instructs disciples about Messianic sufferings (8:34-38) **T**

Chapter 13	Chapter 14	Chapter 15	Chapter 16
JERUSALEM: APOCALYPTIC DISCOURSE	JERUSALEM: PASSION NARRATIVE	JERUSALEM: PASSION NARRATIVE (cont.)	JERUSALEM
1. Predicts Temple destruction (1-2) **T** 2. Signs to look for (3-8) **T** 3. Persecution and resistance foretold (9-13) **T** 4. Desolating sacrilege (14-20) **T** 5. False messiahs (21-23) **T** 6. Coming of Son of Man (24-27) **T** 7. Lesson of fig tree (28-29) **T** 8. Day & hour unknown (30-32) **T** 9. Warning: be alert, keep awake (33-37) **T**	1. Plot to kill Jesus (1-2) 2. Anointing at Bethany (3-9) **T** 3. Judas agrees to betray Jesus (10-11) 4. Passover with disciples (12-21) 5. Institution of Lord's Supper (22-25) 6. Jesus predicts denial by Peter & other apostles (26-31) 7. Jesus prays in Gethsemane (32-42) 8. Betrayal & arrest (43-52) 9. Jesus before the council (53-65) 10. Peter's denial (66-72)	1. Jesus before Pilate (1-5) 2. Pilate hands Jesus over to be crucified (6-15) 3. Soldiers mock Jesus (16-20) 4. Crucifixion (21-32) 5. Death of Jesus (33-39) 6. Women followers (40-41) 7. Burial (42-47)	1. Empty tomb (1-8) [[Shorter Ending]] [[Longer Ending: 1. Jesus appears to Mary Magdalene (9-11) 2. Jesus appears to two disciples (12-13) 3. Jesus commissions disciples (14-18) 4. Jesus ascends (19-20)]]

Legend:

C = Controversy Story
M = Miracle Story
P = Pronouncement Story
S = Summary
T = Teaching Material

Notes

1. *Hom.* 75.
2. Eusebius, *Hist. eccl.* 3.39.15.
3. Mark 2:5*b*–10*a* within 2:1–5*a* and 10*b*–12; 3:4–5*a* within 3:1–3 and 5*b*–6; 6:14–29 within 6:6*b*–13 and 30; 15:16–20 within 15:6–15 and 21–32.

Bibliography

Commentaries

Gundry, Robert H. *Mark: A Commentary on His Apology for the Cross.* Grand Rapids: Eerdmans, 1993.

Hooker, Morna D. *The Gospel According to St. Mark.* Black's New Testament Commentaries. London: Black, 1991.

Juel, Donald. *Mark.* Augsburg Commentary on the New Testament. Minneapolis: Augsburg, 1990.

Nineham, Dennis E. *The Gospel of St. Mark.* Pelican Gospel Commentaries. Harmondsworth: Penguin, 1963. Republished in Westminster Pelican Commentaries. Philadelphia: Westminster, 1977.

Perkins, Pheme. "The Gospel of Mark: Introduction, Commentary, and Reflections." Pages 507–733 in vol. 8 of *The New Interpreter's Bible.* Edited by Leander E. Keck. 12 vols. Nashville: Abingdon, 1995.

Schweizer, Eduard. *The Good News According to Mark.* Richmond: John Knox, 1970.

Taylor, Vincent. *The Gospel According to St. Mark.* 2d ed. London/New York: Macmillan/St. Martin's, 1966.

Other Resources

Anderson, Janice Capel, and Stephen D. Moore. *Mark & Method: New Approaches in Biblical Studies.* Minneapolis: Fortress, 1992.

Best, Ernest. *Mark: The Gospel as Story.* Edinburgh: T&T Clark, 1983.

Collins, Adela Yarbro. *The Beginning of the Gospel: Probings of Mark in Context.* Minneapolis: Fortress, 1992.

Juel, Donald. *A Master of Surprise: Mark Interpreted.* Minneapolis: Fortress, 1994.

Kingsbury, Jack D. *The Christology of Mark's Gospel.* Philadelphia: Fortress, 1983.

———. *Conflict in Mark: Jesus, Authorities, Disciples.* Minneapolis: Fortress, 1989.

Malbon, Elizabeth S. *Hearing Mark: A Listener's Guide.* Harrisburg: Trinity, 2002.

———. *In the Company of Jesus: Characters in Mark's Gospel.* Louisville: Westminster John Knox, 2000.

Matera, Frank J. *What Are They Saying About Mark?* New York: Paulist, 1987.

Rhoads, David M., and Donald Michie. *Mark as Story: An Introduction to the Narrative of a Gospel.* Philadelphia: Fortress, 1982.

Telford, William. *The Interpretation of Mark.* 2d ed. Studies in New Testament Interpretation. Edinburgh: T&T Clark, 1995.

————. *The Theology of the Gospel of Mark.* New Testament Theology. Cambridge: Cambridge University Press, 1999.

MARK IN THE HISTORY OF INTERPRETATION

Black, C. Clifton. *Mark: Images of an Apostolic Interpreter.* Studies on Personalities of the New Testament. Columbia: University of South Carolina Press, 1994; repr. Minneapolis: Fortress, 2001.

Kealy, Sean P. *Mark's Gospel: A History of Its Interpretation From the Beginning Until 1979.* New York: Paulist, 1982.

Schildgen, Brenda Deen. *Power and Prejudice: The Reception of the Gospel of Mark.* Detroit: Wayne State University Press, 1999.

Chapter 7

The Gospel of Matthew

"The Gospel of Matthew, all things considered, is the most important book of Christianity—the most important book that has ever been written."

Ernest Renan

irst-time visitors to Orthodox churches are often struck by the wealth of pictorial images adorning the sanctuary. Biblical personalities along with distinguished saints of the church gaze at observers from the iconostasis and stained glass windows, but surely one of the most overwhelming images is the enthroned Christ—the Pantocrator—often positioned in the center of the ceiling. As a symbol of Christ's eternal presence, this icon hovers over the church as it worships. Much about this image may be remote. The facial features and clothing may well suggest a figure from the ancient past, yet this positioning of Christ renders him ever present. Typically, the seated Christ is framed by three Greek letters—O, Ω, and N—or *ho ōn*, "the one who is." Unbounded by time, Christ presides from his exalted position as the Lord of the church who encompasses past, present, and future. This is the Christ of Matthew's Gospel.

From the opening genealogy, which traces Jesus' lineage through forty-two generations (1:17), and the birth story that "took place in this way" (1:18), to the concluding scene in which the events leading up to the Great Commission are reported as past actions (28:16–18), Matthew's glance is backward-looking. He even looks beyond what happened in the life and ministry of Jesus to earlier times. "For all the prophets and the law prophesied until John came," Jesus says to the crowds as he explains the role of John the Baptist within the overall story (11:13). The biblical period gives way to John the Baptist, who in turn points the way to Jesus.

Yet for all of Matthew's emphasis on past events, he frequently blurs the distinction between past and present. It is well known, for example, that he alone of the four evangelists uses the term "church" (*ekklēsia*, 16:18; 18:15–17). Since there was no church as such during the time of Jesus' ministry, Matthew's use of the term is anachronistic even though he is technically correct to envisage its *future* founding and Jesus' teaching about church discipline as a *future* need. Even so, Matthew's own setting, in which the church is a present reality, blends easily into the earlier period of Jesus. This poses no theological problem for Matthew because as Lord of the church Jesus bridges past and present.

Another memorable instance in which Matthew blurs time distinctions occurs in his account of the death of Jesus (27:45–54). After reporting that Jesus expired and the temple veil was torn from top to bottom—an image symbolizing Jesus' death as giving access to God's presence—Matthew declares that "the tombs also were opened, and many bodies of the saints who had fallen asleep were raised" (v. 52). He further reports that after Jesus' resurrection, these saints "came out of the tombs and entered the holy city and appeared to many" (v. 53). With his use of "saints," a later designation for Christians used only here in his Gospel, Matthew easily moves from his own time—the period of the church—to the earlier period of Jesus' passion and death. Projecting back to the time of Jesus' death what is so obviously a future event—the final resurrection of Christians—may strike us as a jarring collision of tenses. But this, along with the reported earthquake (27:51), is Matthew's way of signifying the momentous impact of Jesus' death: It shakes the cosmos and redefines time.

One effect of Matthew's viewing all time as *the Lord's present* is to structure the narrative with two audiences in view. While Jesus' teachings may be addressed to smaller groups of listeners identified throughout the narrative, they extend beyond the time of Jesus' ministry and speak directly to the church. No matter how many generations separate readers from the text, Jesus' words transcend their original setting. When we hear Jesus speak in Matthew we are hearing the Lord of the church who is always present "where two or three are gathered" (18:20).

The ability to tell an ancient story that reaches across time and enables readers to experience Jesus not so much as a distinguished figure from the past whose teachings survive but rather as their living Teacher reflects Matthew's own inspired genius as a teacher. This timeless quality helps explain the Gospel's enduring popularity through the centuries.

The First Gospel

The church felt Matthew's magnetic power quite early. By the early second century, its formative influence is already seen in Ignatius (ca. 35–107 C.E.), bishop of Antioch, who in his seven letters addressed to churches in western Asia Minor and Rome and to Polycarp cited Matthew more often than any other Gospel. Toward the end of the second century Matthew encountered competition from the Gospel of John, but even then remained the preferred Gospel for most Christians. Its widespread popularity in both the East and West is reflected in the steady stream of commentaries in Greek and Latin from the third century onward. One of the earliest is also the longest: Origen's commentary comprising twenty-five books, roughly half of which survive, written in his sixties at Caesarea. Matthew also received serious treatment by John Chrysostom (ca. 347–407 C.E.) and Jerome (ca. 345–420 C.E.).

In early canonical lists, Matthew is typically mentioned first among the four Gospels, which automatically gave it pride of place among all the NT writings. Its early composition and its apostolic authorship were closely connected, a view well expressed by Origen (ca. 185–254 C.E.): ". . . first was written [the Gospel] according to Matthew, who was once a tax collector but afterwards an apostle of Jesus Christ, who published it for those who from Judaism came to believe, composed as it was in the Hebrew language."[1] Since Matthew's own call is recorded in the Gospel (9:9; cf. Mark 2:14; also cf. Matt 10:3 and parallels), this somehow made it easier to claim that it was the first written Gospel.

If we ask why Matthew became the First Gospel, part of the answer must be its didactic quality. It shows all the signs of having been composed by someone familiar with teaching techniques and learning strategies. Matthew's fondness for grouping items in threes, fives, sevens, or even tens is seen throughout the narrative. The list of names in the opening genealogy is more manageable as three groups of fourteen generations, even though the numbers have to be juggled a bit (1:17). Jesus' five discourses are carefully distributed throughout the narrative: the Sermon on the Mount (chs. 5–7), the discourse on mission (ch. 10), the parables discourse (ch. 13), the discourse on church teachings (ch. 18), and the final discourse comprising the polemic against the scribes and Pharisees (ch. 23), the apocalyptic discourse (ch. 24), and the parables of judgment (ch. 25). Since these discourses interrupt the narrative flow, Matthew uses the concluding formula "Now when Jesus had finished saying these things" (or some variation thereof) to ease the reader back into the narrative (7:28–29; 11:1; 13:53; 19:1; 26:1). Within each discourse are found similar organizational patterns: seven prophetic "woes" comprise the polemical discourse in chapter 23; three parables about final judgment occur in chapter 25; and the parables discourse in chapter 13 is structured around seven parables, three of which are grouped together. In the Sermon on the Mount, Matthew groups material into easily remembered units and skillfully employs rhetorical devices such as repetition and antithesis.

Whatever we make of these and many other features of Matthew's Gospel, they clearly suggest an organized mind at work. But more than that, they reflect the mind of a teacher, someone interested in composing a narrative about Jesus that could also serve as a handbook for the church. This suggests that Matthew was composed with the church's needs in mind. So pervasive is this catechetical interest that one scholar saw Matthew as a converted rabbi—a plausible suggestion because of the numerous formulaic expressions and teaching devices typical of rabbinic teaching.

Another reason Matthew's Gospel was ranked first relates to the story he tells, and especially *how* he tells it. If there was ever a case in which the content of the story helps explain its popularity, this is it. Matthew attracted readers who wanted a grandly conceived, complete account of Jesus' life and teaching. But Matthew provided more than a comprehensive collection of Jesus' words; it was a story so methodically conceived, so meticulously arranged, and so carefully told that it became etched indelibly in the church's memory. It was a Gospel from which the church could learn, but with its generous supply of memorable stories and teachings it was also a Gospel suited for teaching others. Usage—repeated, widespread usage—ensured Matthew's popularity. It became the First Gospel because it consistently whetted the church's appetite to learn more about—and from—Jesus the Messiah.

Matthew as a Second Edition of Mark

For centuries, the view expressed in Origen's statement above prevailed. Also worth noting is his claim that the Gospel was written for Jewish readers "in the Hebrew language" (*grammasin Hebraikois*). A century earlier Papias (ca. 60–130 C.E.) had written that "Matthew compiled the oracles in the Hebrew language [*Hebraidi dialektō ta logia*], but everyone interpreted them as he was able."[2] Much about this cryptic statement is unclear: What are the oracles? Is the language Hebrew or Aramaic? How were they interpreted? Scholars still puzzle over these questions, but the view that Matthew was originally composed in Hebrew for Jewish readers was also held by Irenaeus (ca. 130–200 C.E.),[3] Eusebius (ca. 260–340 C.E.),[4] and John Chrysostom,[5] and it continued to be held for centuries.

To claim that Matthew was written in Hebrew enhanced its authority. This would make it much more amenable to a Palestinian setting, and it would put us closer to the very words of Jesus, who probably spoke Aramaic, a dialect of Hebrew. But as early as the sixteenth century, John Calvin observed that Matthew's OT quotations are based not on the Hebrew text but on a Greek translation. Naturally this raised doubts about the theory of Hebrew composition. And no text of Matthew or even fragments of Matthean texts survived in Hebrew, only the Greek text. The possibility that the First Gospel was originally written in Greek raised doubts about Matthean authorship since an apostle from Palestine probably would have written in Aramaic.

As noted earlier in chapter 3, when scholars in the eighteenth and nineteenth centuries began comparing the Gospels more closely, they became convinced that Mark's storyline lay behind both Matthew and Luke. This became especially clear in the Passion Narrative, in which virtually every episode in Mark also occurs in Matthew, and in the same order. Close comparison of the two accounts suggests that Matthew depended on Mark rather than vice versa. One of the clearest examples occurs in the trial before the council in which the chief priests taunt Jesus to prophesy and ask, "Who is it that struck you?" The question only makes sense if Jesus is blindfolded, a detail not found in Matthew but present in the Markan account (cf. Matt 26:66–68; Mark 14:65; also Luke 22:63–65). Here Matthew presupposes knowledge of Mark.

To think of Matthew as a second edition of Mark implies that he has drawn his main storyline from Mark: a Galilean ministry (4:12–18:35) followed by a ministry in the Transjordan and Judea (chs. 19–20) that culminates in Jerusalem (chs. 21–27). Important events, such as the rejection at Nazareth (13:54–58; cf. Mark 6:1–6*a*), the death of John the Baptist (14:1–12; cf. Mark 6:14–29), and the confession at Caesarea Philippi (16:13–20; cf. Mark 8:27–30) occur in the same sequence and at roughly the same points in the storyline. Seldom does Matthew omit episodes found in Mark (although see, for example, the healing of the blind man at Bethsaida [Mark 8:22–26]). In a highly oversimplified sense, we can imagine Matthew taking the Markan storyline, adding an expanded introduction (chs. 1–2) and conclusion (ch. 28), and inserting the five main discourses throughout the narrative.

MATTHEW'S INTERPRETATION OF MARK

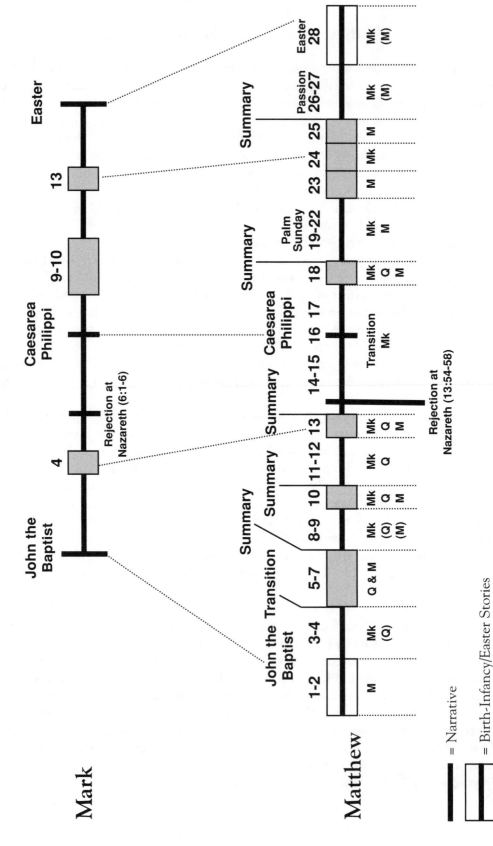

Occasionally Matthew adds narrative episodes to the Markan narrative. One of the most prominent examples is his account of the death of Judas (27:3–10), which interrupts the narrative sequence of the trial before Pilate and is chronologically out of sequence. Matthew also expands certain Markan episodes, such as the baptism of Jesus, the temptation, and the confession at Caesarea Philippi. In some cases he abbreviates Markan episodes, for example, the stilling of the storm (8:18, 23–27; cf. Mark 4:35–41) and the Gerasene demoniac (8:28–34; cf. Mark 5:1–20).

With these editorial changes, Matthew tends to tighten the Markan framework. Where Mark connects episodes with a simple coordinating word, such as the conjunction "and" or the adverb "immediately," Matthew makes the chronological and spatial connections between episodes more explicit. Where Mark reports, "Again he began to teach beside the sea" (4:1), Matthew says, "That same day Jesus went out of the house and sat beside the sea" (13:1). In other instances Matthew turns Mark's simple sentences into complex sentences (cf. Matt 12:46; Mark 3:31). Like Mark, Matthew makes effective use of summaries to move the narrative along, but he provides additional summaries at key junctures in the narrative (e.g., Matt 4:17; 16:21; also, the summaries concluding the five discourses). The overall effect is to produce a smoother, more tightly conceived narrative written in a more sophisticated Greek style.

These changes affect the way the reader experiences the story of Jesus. In Mark, episodes are often reported in rapid-fire succession to produce a narrative that moves quickly. Mark's frequent use of "immediately" reinforces this sense of rapid movement. In sharp contrast, we do not experience this race car effect in Matthew. Instead, the story is interrupted at five key points for Jesus to deliver fairly lengthy discourses. By inserting these "speed bumps," Matthew requires the reader to slow down every now and then to listen to Rabbi Jesus, sometimes at length. In moving from Mark to Matthew, we experience a shift from a dramatic narrative to a didactic narrative in which the teachings of Jesus are focal.

We misread Matthew if we see it only as a complex set of editorial changes and expansions of Mark—simply as a second edition. Of greater importance is to see what happens theologically when Matthew reinterprets Mark in a new setting. Rather than looking at the whole Gospel, we will examine the first part of the Gospel (chs. 1–10) to illustrate how Matthew's editorial changes reveal some of his distinctive theological ideas.

Before doing this, however, let us look at some critical components that influence Matthew's theological sense-making: the tradition he received and his context.

The Tradition Matthew Received

At least three sets of sources lay before Matthew as he began composing his Gospel: the Gospel of Mark, the sayings source Q, and the material unique to Matthew—M. Scholars have deduced this by carefully comparing Matthew with Mark and Luke. These sources should be seen as three different sets of witnesses to Jesus. **[See Expanded CD Version pp. 186–88: *Matthew's Use of Mark, Q, and M*]**

In what form Matthew received these traditions is not known. He probably had the Gospel of Mark, and possibly the sayings source Q, in written form. Whether the latter was already a unified written collection or was still a relatively unorganized collection of written and oral material is difficult to say. Some of the material in M was probably already written down—perhaps collected in units, such as pairs or small groups of parables—but much of M may derive from oral tradition. Even in those cases in which Matthew drew on oral tradition, for example, the six antitheses (5:21–48), he is responsible for the final literary shape of the material.

Matthew's Use of the Old Testament

Mark's Gospel already expresses the firm conviction that Jesus fulfills Scripture's messianic expectations. Matthew retains many of Mark's Scripture quotations and allusions, although he appropriates them freely. For example, he edits Mark's opening Scripture citation to make its attribution to the prophet Isaiah correct (Matt 3:3; cf. Mark 1:2–3). Interpreting Jesus in the light of certain OT passages, such as Ps 110:1, was already firmly embedded in the Jesus story well before Mark received it (Matt 22:41–45; Mark 12:35–37a; Luke 20:41–44). Pre-Markan tradition had also probably applied Ps 118:22–23 to Jesus as the "stone rejected by the builders" that became the cornerstone (Matt 21:42; Mark 12:10–11; Luke 20:17–18).

Matthew takes what he finds in Mark in new directions. One of the most well-known examples of Matthew's enthusiastic appropriation of the OT occurs in his account of Jesus' entry into Jerusalem. Mark's account of the story is straightforward, with no explicit reference to the OT until the end, when the crowds' acclamation is expressed in terms of Ps 118:26 (Mark 11:1–10). Matthew, by contrast, sees deeper significance in Mark's mention of the two disciples' fetching a colt upon which Jesus would ride into Jerusalem. For Matthew the event signified the arrival of the messianic king, an interpretation supported by Isa 62:11 and Zech 9:9: "'Tell the daughter of Zion, Look, your king is coming to you, humble, and mounted on a donkey, and on a colt, the foal of a donkey'" (Matt 21:5). What Matthew, or his source, fails to realize, however, is that the Hebrew text employs the rhetorical device of parallelism, in which a line is repeated in different words to express the same meaning. Thus, "a colt, the foal of a donkey" is simply a poetic way of repeating the first mention of "donkey" (Zech 9:9). Instead of seeing one animal in the OT passage, Matthew sees two, and to make the story fit the passage he mentions not one (as do Mark and Luke) but two animals (Matt 21:2, 7). Also worth noting is Matthew's omission of "triumphant and victorious" from Zech 9:9 and his retention of "humble" to emphasize the nonpolitical nature of Jesus' messianic character. This is in keeping with his emphasis elsewhere on Jesus' role as the Suffering Servant of Isaiah (Matt 12:18–21; cf. Isa 42:1–4).

This use of the OT to interpret the significance of Jesus' entry into Jerusalem is but one of fourteen instances in which Matthew employs *formula quotations*, one of the most distinctive features of his Gospel (1:22–23a; 2:5b–6; 2:15b; 2:17–18; 2:23b; 3:3; 4:14–16; 8:17; 12:17–21; 13:14–15; 13:35; 21:4–5; 26:56 [see 26:54]; 27:9–10). Their common feature is an introductory formula that links a particular episode to an OT passage. Some of these will be discussed later, but here several observations can be made.

First, Matthew has gone beyond Mark by identifying moments in the Jesus story that can be correlated with OT passages. In some cases the OT passages are promises that anticipate fulfillment at some later date, such as Isaiah's prediction of Emmanuel's birth (Isa 7:14; Matt 1:22–23; similarly Matt 2:6 quoting Mic 5:2 and 2 Sam 5:2). In other cases, rather than fulfilling an OT promise, an event may allude to a vivid OT image. Thus Herod's slaughter of the infants (Matt 2:16–18) prompts Matthew to think of the weeping mother Rachel in Jer 31:15.

Second, the formula quotations typically express Matthew's theological perspective. In two cases, the formula occurs on the lips of Jesus himself—Matthew's way of aligning his own interpretive practice with that of Jesus (13:14–15; 26:54–56). Through this elaborate scheme of fulfilled promises, Matthew extends the interpretive work that Jesus himself began. His exegetical practice of reading the Jesus story as the fulfillment of the OT may be drawn from Mark but it is traced ultimately to Jesus.

As Matthew reconceives the Jesus story, he is in conversation with two distinct sets of traditions: (1) the Jesus traditions preserved in Mark, Q, and M, and (2) the OT. Naturally both sets of traditions intersect since the Jesus traditions he inherited had already begun to make use of the OT. But Matthew engages in a separate conversation with the OT, and both conversations—the one with the Jesus tradition and the one with the OT—inform his theological work.

Matthew's Context

There is broad scholarly agreement that Matthew's Gospel arose in a setting with a strong Jewish presence—one in which the church was living "across the street" from the synagogue, perhaps in the same city or region. But several questions concerning the relationship between church and synagogue remain unanswered. Did the church consist mainly of Jews who had recently become followers of Jesus? Or did it include a large number of converted Gentiles, thus forming a community with diverse ethnic backgrounds? Or should we even think of a single community? Would it be better to think of smaller groups of disciples, loosely organized perhaps, scattered through the towns and countryside of a given region? Does it make sense, in other words, to speak of *the* Matthean church as though it was an identifiable community of believers, even if it was larger than a single congregation?

Even though Matthew is not addressed to a specific church, it provides some clues about the situation out of which it arose. Quite revealing is the highly polemical tone throughout the Gospel, particularly in Jesus' denunciation of the scribes and Pharisees in chapter 23. Even if Matthew's characterization of them is a caricature, his description suggests a serious level of conflict between them and Jesus, and by extension, between them and Jesus' followers, the church. Even though Jesus' other conflicts with Jewish groups are not pitched this high rhetorically, they are nevertheless quite sharp (see Matt 11:20–24). Add to this Matthew's references to "their synagogues" (4:23; 10:17; 13:54; see 23:34) or "their scribes" and his negative portrayals of the

A woodcut depiction of the evangelist Matthew receiving inspiration from the Holy Spirit shown as a dove. Matthew is shown with his attribute, the third living creature with a face like a human (Rev 4:7). From the Digital Image Archive of The Richard C. Kessler Reformation Collection, Pitts Theology Library, Candler School of Theology, Emory University, Atlanta, Georgia.

synagogue (6:2, 5; 23:6). A high level of acrimony is also suggested by the unusually harsh condemnation of the Jewish people reflected in their cry at Jesus' trial, a cry reported only by Matthew: "His blood be on us and on our children!" (27:25).

Because these polemical elements are not present to the same degree in Mark, they probably mirror the sharp conflict that existed between the Matthean church and its Jewish opponents. Whether it was still going on at the time Matthew was written or whether a sharp breach had already occurred is uncertain. Some scholars contend that Matthew and his church were still within the fold of Judaism, while others argue that a parting of the ways had already occurred. The overall tone of the rhetoric and the shape of Matthew's response make it probable that the Matthean church had separated from the synagogue, that it consisted of both Jews and Gentiles, and that it was now carving out a new identity within this changed situation.

Of the possible geographical locales where this might have occurred, Syria is the most likely. A strong Jewish community had existed in Antioch of Syria for some time, and Christianity took hold there quite early. From other sources we know of Antioch's importance as a center of Christian mission (Acts 11; Gal 2). A Syrian origin is also suggested by the fact that Ignatius, bishop of Antioch, made such heavy use of Matthew.

Given this construal of Matthew's context, we can envision his theological agenda. To make sense of its break with the synagogue, Matthew's church had to decide how to relate to its Jewish heritage. Since the church took its cue from Jesus, Matthew had to clarify Jesus' own relationship to Torah. Because the synagogue and the church shared the same Scripture, Matthew rightly pitched the battle on the field of Scripture interpretation. If Jesus' primary conflict was with Israel, he had to be presented as the embodiment of Israel's hopes expressed in Scripture. Naturally this required Matthew to reinforce Mark's claims that Jesus is Messiah, Son of God, Son of Man, and Son of David, and develop them even further.

Matthew's theological work also has a practical dimension. In helping his community shape a new identity, he had to address the needs of congregations consisting of Jews and Gentiles. This meant expanding the Markan emphasis on the Gentile mission and clarifying Jesus' own attitude toward Gentiles, especially regarding how Jesus preached to them. Matthew also had to meet the church's practical needs, such as learning how to pray, to practice genuine piety, to continue Jesus' ministry of teaching and healing, to deal with disputes among church members, and related questions of congregational practice. Such needs required a church handbook roughly equivalent to the Qumran *Rule of the Community* or *Manual of Discipline*.

Put briefly, Matthew's task was to help the Christian community define itself over against the synagogue. This may be a negative form of definition—trying to shape an alternative worldview and lifestyle in opposition to traditions and practices from which one has separated—but this is the challenge that Matthew faced.

The Shape of Matthew's Story

Deciding how to read the Matthean storyline depends on the weight one gives to the five discourses that loom so large in the Gospel. If these are heavily accented,

Matthew will be seen as an extended narrative interrupted by five major discourses, each concluding with a formulaic summary that helps move the story along. Some evidence for recognizing the five discourse structure of Matthew may be provided in an early Greek fragment, possibly dated as early as the second century, that reads, "Matthew curbs the audacity of the Jews checking them in five books as it were with bridles."[6] Read this way, Matthew alternates between narrative and discourse, with the "five books" dominating the overall story. One advantage of this organizational scheme is the prominence it gives to the five discourses, which for a long time were seen as Matthew's answer to the five books of Moses. On this view, Matthew is read as a Christian Pentateuch presenting the teachings of Jesus, the new Moses.

While this way of reading Matthew is attractive in some respects, it also creates some interpretive problems. It is not certain, for example, that chapters 23–25 comprise a single discourse, even though they are grouped together. And privileging the five discourses tends to render chapters 1–2 and 26–28 as prologue and epilogue rather than seeing them as central parts of a continuous narrative.

An alternative arrangement takes its cue from the two formulaic summaries in 4:17 and 16:21, with their recurrent phrase, "From that time Jesus began to. . . ." In the first instance he began "to proclaim," in the second instance "to show." Arranged this way, Matthew consists of three major sections: 1:1–4:16—The Person of Jesus Messiah; 4:17–16:20—The Proclamation of Jesus Messiah; and 16:21–28:20—The Revelation of Jesus Messiah through His Passion and Resurrection.

This arrangement also has some attractive features but it overlooks some basic elements within the narrative. In the second section, Jesus does far more than proclaim, although his teachings are prominent in this section. The expanded rehearsal of miracle stories in chapters 8–9 falls within this section, and Jesus' conflict with Israel, which intensifies from chapter 10 onward, is not fully reflected in this scheme. Similarly, the final section is both more and less than revelation.

Any arrangement of Matthew must give full weight to the five discourses and the extent to which they dominate the narrative, but Matthew's narrative flow must be preserved as well. As a general organizational principle, the two-stage ministry moving from Galilee to Judea should be kept in mind.

Matthew's Theological Reshaping of the Tradition

Having identified elements of Matthew's received tradition and the probable context that prompted him to reimagine the Jesus story, we now look at two examples of his theologizing. They are useful because they illustrate how Matthew converses with different elements of the Jesus tradition and with the OT. In both cases, we focus especially on Matthew's reinterpretation of Mark.

How the Story Begins

In Mark, it only takes twenty verses to get Jesus to the Capernaum synagogue where he teaches and heals the man with the unclean spirit (Mark 1:21–28). After this, miracle stories follow in rapid-fire succession. By contrast, it takes Matthew *seven chapters* to get to Jesus' first miracle story (8:1–4)! Earlier, Matthew summarizes Jesus' miracle-working activity, but this summary does not occur until the end of chapter 4 (vv. 23–25). Whereas Mark is eager to show Jesus the miracle-working teacher in action, Matthew delays this display of power (chs. 8–9). Like Mark, Matthew appreciates Jesus as one whose teaching stops people in their tracks. In Matthew, however, it is not through Jesus' miracles but through his inaugural sermon that the crowds first experience the rhetorical power that distinguishes him from "their scribes" (cf. Mark 1:27 and Matt 7:28–29).

Everything from Matt 1:1 forward prepares the way for Jesus' first sermon. Echoes of Moses are heard in the birth story: a baby destined to become Israel's preeminent teacher receives divine protection from a king willing to slaughter children to protect his throne. Echoes of Exodus are also heard in the extended period of testing in the wilderness (forty years for Israel; forty days and nights for Jesus). In sharp contrast to disobedient Israel, Jesus emerges from the temptations as the obedient Son. For him the wilderness experience was not a time to declare his independence from God, to play games with God, or to entertain visions of worldly power. Instead it was a time to test his identity as God's duly appointed Son—an identity confirmed at his baptism—and a time to discern whether the one speaking to him was really God or Satan masquerading as God.

Matthew places Jesus within a bloodline that extends all the way back to Abraham and includes King David (1:6). Unlike Moses, whose authority is traceable to priestly descent (Exod 6:14–25), Jesus belongs to a royal line befitting one who will eventually enjoy universal dominion (28:18–20). Matthew doubtless knows Moses' towering stature (see Deut 34), yet he ascribes to Jesus honorific titles never attributed to Moses in the Bible: Messiah (1:16–18; 2:4), Emmanuel (1:23), Lord (e.g., 7:21), and Beloved Son (3:17). The temptations show Jesus as thoroughly obedient in a way Moses was not (Num 20:9–13; 27:12–14; Deut 32:51). Matthew's account of Jesus' birth is more extraordinary than the Exodus account of Moses' birth (Exod 1–2).

The events surrounding Jesus' birth reflect a repeated pattern of divine fulfillment. They connect the dots of biblical promises that yield a clear image of Jesus the Messiah: his virgin birth and the name Emmanuel (1:23; cf. Isa 7:14); his birth in Bethlehem (2:5–6; cf. Mic 5:2); his escape to Egypt (2:15; cf. Hos 11:1); the slaughter of the infants (2:17–18; cf. Jer 31:15); and establishing residence in Nazareth (2:23; possibly Isa 11:1; Zech 3:8; 6:12). The dots were always there in Scripture, Matthew would insist, awaiting the arrival of a single figure who would make it possible for an astute interpreter to connect them.

Matthew's amplified account of Jesus' baptism by John the Baptist reveals Jesus' instinctive inclination to "fulfill all righteousness" (3:15). This uniquely qualifies him to speak as an authority on righteousness. The term "righteousness" (*dikaiosynē*) occurs six times in Matthew, but not once in Mark (besides Matt 3:15, see 5:6, 10, 20; 6:1, 33; 21:32). Mark uses "righteous" twice (2:17; 6:20). Matthew retains one of them (9:13) and adds eighteen more (e.g., 1:19; 5:45; 10:41).

Galilee also has symbolic significance for Matthew, who remembers it as the location of the tribes of Zebulun and Naphtali, thus exposing another dot: Isa 9:1–2 refers to "Galilee of the nations [Gentiles]," the place where darkness would give way to light. Jesus thus begins his ministry in the place where Gentile hopes for inclusion within God's people had lain dormant for centuries. Jesus' unconventional genealogy, after all, includes four Gentile women (1:3, 5, 6; Bathsheba had become a Gentile as "the wife of Uriah" the Hittite), all prominently mentioned. Jesus' own genealogy already anticipates the newly constituted people, consisting of both Jews and Gentiles, that would emerge from his "bloodline"—a universal church all of whose members are "children of Abraham" (cf. 1:1).

These expectations begin to be realized as people from predominantly Gentile areas (the Decapolis, probably Syria and Transjordan) and from Jewish areas (Judea, Jerusalem) stream to Jesus (4:23–25). This universal crowd forms the audience for Jesus' programmatic sermon, which recalls Moses' sermons in Deuteronomy. Rather than speaking as a new Moses, Jesus now speaks as the authoritative interpreter of God's will who surpasses Moses. As an inaugural address, the Sermon on the Mount introduces themes to be repeated throughout the story: blessings of life in the kingdom of heaven (5:1–12); exemplary witness (5:13–16); righteousness that exceeds both Jewish and Gentile expectations by recognizing Torah's deeper demands (5:17–48); being genuinely religious in giving alms, praying, and fasting (6:1–18); living in the security of God's promise (6:19–34); and enacting righteousness by "doing the will of God" (7:1–27). While the sermon has a strong Jewish flavor, it is equally critical of Jewish and Gentile behavior. Ultimately, it addresses everyone. [See Expanded CD Version pp. 194–98: *Another Example of Matthew's Theologizing:* Chapters 8–10]

Matthew's Theological Vision

Given the context of his audience, how does Matthew respond? First, he produces a *new foundation narrative* for his readers. Even though Matthew already possesses Mark, it is no longer adequate for the changed situation his readers face. Second, taking the Jesus tradition he knows from Mark, Q, and M, he shapes a *new vision of Jesus*. Drawing on Mark's portrait of Jesus, he develops an understanding of Jesus that would be suitable for Christians defining themselves over against the synagogue. Third, he fashions a *new identity* for his readers as they self-consciously become a new people. Fourth, he sketches a *new ethic* appropriate to life in the kingdom of heaven.

A New Foundation Narrative

For Matthew's church to survive in its new situation, it must have an account of the Jesus story that relates them to their past and makes sense of their present. Mark's Gospel does neither of these successfully for this new group of readers, although it makes a start. Matthew attends to the first need by expanding the limits of the salvation story in which Jesus is the central figure and by linking his readers more directly to that story. He attends to the second need by shaping a narrative that addresses the practical needs of the church, one that rehearses the gospel the church proclaims and gives concrete instructions for church life—a narrative that is both gospel and church handbook.

One of the most obvious ways Matthew broadens the scope of salvation history is in the opening genealogy (1:1–17). While this may not be as dramatic an opening as Mark's, it has the effect of pushing the beginning of the Jesus story back to the time of Abraham. Its immediate purpose is to establish an appropriate pedigree for Jesus the Messiah, but since the church is so clearly linked to Jesus, its founder (16:18), it is the church's genealogy as well. This point is reinforced by Jesus' insistence that his real family includes his disciples who do the heavenly Father's will (12:46–50).

By thinking of the "prophets and the law" as the predecessors of John the Baptist (11:13), Jesus fills out the earlier stages of the salvation story. With the formula quotations scattered throughout the narrative, Matthew weaves even more threads into this tapestry. Each fulfillment knits Jesus' story ever more tightly with Israel's story. The story also extends into the future. Jesus' disciples can expect to share in Israel's destiny at the end time, "the renewal of all things," when they will sit on thrones judging the twelve tribes of Israel (19:28).

Jewish Christians might easily understand their lineage as one leading from Christ through David to Abraham, but what about Gentile Christians? Matthew is equally attentive to their links to the family tree. As already noted, the prominent mention of Gentiles in the genealogy links Gentile Christians with Jesus' own lineage. And Matthew showcases OT passages that envision the inclusion of Gentiles within the people of God (4:15–16; 12:18). This point is reinforced in the story of healing the centurion's servant, when Jesus pointedly declares that Gentiles would participate in the messianic banquet with Jews (8:11–12). It would be hard to think of a more dramatic way to incorporate Gentile Christians within Israel's distinguished history.

By enlarging the scope of God's story of salvation, Matthew makes a fundamental theological contribution. With this new foundation narrative in hand, both Jewish and Gentile Christians are in a much better position to see their separate stories as part of God's larger story.

Matthew's Gospel also anchors the church in another way: It serves as a "community rule" for the church's ongoing life and practice. By including a comprehensive digest of Jesus' teachings, the Gospel supplies the church with useful materials for catechetical instruction. The church is able to experience the presence of Jesus through his teachings. But the church also receives from the Gospel concrete instructions about Christian practices: prayer, almsgiving, and fasting. Recognizing the need for actual models of Christian practice, Matthew includes the Lord's Prayer (6:9–13). Well aware of the tensions that churches experience and the fractiousness of church members, Matthew offers protocols for dealing with internal differences (18:15–20). Surrounding these instructions with Jesus' teachings about forgiveness suggests that Matthew probably had considerable experience living among congregations of believers.

A church reading Matthew would be anchored historically and socially. It would have a clear sense of its founder, of who he was and is and where he came from. It would know why it should regard Jesus as an authoritative teacher. And the church would have received instruction about its ritual practice: how it should pray, give alms, and fast. It would also have been informed about the significance of baptism and the Eucharist. The church would have a way of reading the OT that would connect it to Israel's larger story through Jesus. The church would have a clear sense of the future and its role in that future. It would have instructions about how to face the end time and what to do during the interim. The church would certainly have a clear profile of the "others" against whom it defines itself: scribes, Pharisees, and Sadducees. It would also know how to relate to certain institutions, most notably the synagogue.

A New Vision of Jesus

Jesus as Lord of the Church. A church engaged in deep and painful conflict with a competing religious tradition needs a clear sense of its own authority. This requires an even clearer sense about the One from whom its authority derives, especially when the debate has focused on the legitimate identity and authority of this figure. Matthew responds to this need by taking Mark's audacious set of claims about Jesus the Messiah and ratcheting them up even higher. Matthew's Jesus emerges as a more authoritative figure who occupies an exalted status from the moment the narrative begins until its concluding scene, which clearly signals that his role as exalted Lord is not limited to the period of his earthly ministry but continues into the period of the church.

The opening genealogy lends considerable authority to Jesus as it traces his lineage to Abraham. Its mention of the Son of David accents royal elements in the lineage and anticipates the way Matthew creatively expands this image as the narrative unfolds. The overall thrust of the birth narrative is in the same direction. Joseph is identified as "son of David" (1:20), and one of the formula quotations promises that "from you [Bethlehem] shall come a ruler" (2:6). The wise men ask, "Where is the child who has been born king of the Jews?" (2:2), and they pay homage to him and bring gifts fit for a king (2:11). It soon becomes clear why the infant Jesus is so well traveled. The birth narrative explains how Jesus of Nazareth *first* came from Bethlehem, the city of David, and only later came to live in Nazareth. It is now widely recognized that the birth narrative answers the two questions Who? and From Where? Jesus is the Davidic king from Bethlehem and is now "God with us."

The image of Jesus as the Son of David is already a prominent feature of Mark, and Matthew retains these stories: the healing of Bartimaeus (Mark 10:46–52 & Matt 20:29–34); the entry into Jerusalem (Mark 11:1–10 & Matt 21:1–9); and the debate about David's Son (Mark 12:35–37a & Matt 22:41–46). But Matthew further develops this image either by adding to Mark's story or by altering it. In the healing of the two blind men (Matt 9:27–31), a Matthean addition, Jesus is addressed as "Son of David." In other instances Matthew changes the Markan account by adding references to Son of David that are not found in Mark (Matt 12:22–24; cf. Mark 3:19b–22; Matt 15:21–28; cf. Mark 7:24–30). Even more significant is the fact that the four stories Matthew relates prior to Jesus' entry into Jerusalem are all healing stories. Here people experience the messianic king through his acts of mercy, not through military or political power. This stands in sharp contrast to the image of the messianic Son of David found in the *Psalms of Solomon*, a Jewish writing from the first century B.C.E. that responds to the Roman capture of Jerusalem by envisioning the Lord Messiah as a militant figure establishing dominion with a "rod of discipline" (18:6–7).

One of Matthew's subtlest changes of Mark occurs in his account of the mocking by the soldiers. In Mark, Jesus is clothed with a purple cloak and receives a crown of thorns (15:17). In Matthew, Jesus is clothed with a scarlet robe and receives a crown of thorns, but he also is given a "reed in his right hand" before he is finally mocked as "King of the Jews" (Matt 27:27–31). Matthew thus portrays Jesus with a royal robe, royal crown, and a royal scepter, thereby signaling to the reader that the messianic king is being handed over to death.

In Mark, the title "Son of David" appears as a relatively minor christological motif. In Matthew, it becomes a major theme because it coveys the royal, exalted status of the central cultic figure within the Matthean church.

As in Mark, so also in Matthew, Jesus' transcendent status is conveyed through the dynamic interplay of two other titles: Son of God and Son of Man. According to one scholar, these titles may be seen as two centers of an ellipse that frames Matthew's portrait of Christ.

As we know from Mark, Jesus' baptism and transfiguration were seen as pivotal moments in which God acknowledged Jesus as Son. By standardizing the divine voice in both episodes so that God proclaims, "This is my Son, the Beloved" (Matt 3:17; 17:5), Matthew makes both events more public. Like Mark, Matthew retains the centurion's confession at the crucifixion, although it occurs on the lips of the centurion *and his companions* (27:54). This makes the recognition of Jesus as Son of God a more public event than it is in Mark. In Matthew's abbreviated version of the Gerasene demoniac, Jesus is addressed as Son of God by *two* demoniacs (Matt 8:28–34). When Peter adds "Son of the living God" to his confession of Jesus as Messiah (16:16), he gives Jesus a chance to attribute this revealed knowledge to "my Father in heaven" (16:17). From Q Matthew knows a much fuller account of the temptations in which Jesus' Sonship figures prominently, but unlike Luke, Matthew joins this story directly to the baptism rather than to a genealogy. Having been declared Son of God at his baptism, Jesus proves his vocation by emerging from the temptations as a genuinely obedient Son.

One of the most distinctive episodes, however, in which Matthew conveys his understanding of Jesus' Sonship occurs in 11:25–30. In this passage Jesus prays to the Father, explains the interior of the Father-Son relationship, and extends an invitation to discipleship. Here Matthew draws on Q (Luke 10:21–22), but the conclusion comes from M. Addressing God as Father echoes the Lord's Prayer (6:9–13) and anticipates the prayer in Gethsemane (26:39; cf. Mark 14:36), but these words, with their distinctive Johannine sound (John 3:35; 10:14–15; 17:25), expose a remarkably intimate self-understanding of his relationship with the Father. By asserting mutual knowledge between the Son and the Father, Jesus lays claim to his unique role as Revealer of God's will. This role may derive from his filial obedience as reflected in the temptations and later in Gethsemane. By claiming the Father's full authority, Jesus issues an invitation earlier associated with divine Wisdom (Sir 24:19; 51:23). As God's Son, Jesus invites disciples to experience his knowledge of the Father as revealed in his reinterpretation of Torah.

Even though Matthew is more explicit in portraying Jesus as Son of God, as the one who comes from God and who lives an obedient life before God, like Mark he rarely reports instances in which people address Jesus as Son of God in a confessional sense. The two demoniacs do, as does Peter. But as in Mark, Peter's confession is short-lived, even though this knowledge was a divine revelation. If anything, Jesus' response to the high priest who asks if he is "the Messiah, the Son of God" is less direct than it is in Mark (26:63; Mark 14:62). Matthew is far more willing to convey the disciples' recognition of Jesus as Son of God, as seen in the walking on the water episode in which the disciples worshiped Jesus, saying, "Truly you are the Son of God" (14:33). Matthew's narrative proclaims Jesus as Son of God through editorial comment and through Jesus' own words and actions. It goes well beyond Mark in claiming that Jesus' own disciples, not just the demons and Roman centurion, achieve this level of recognition.

Matthew knows from Mark that Son of Man is the title Jesus uses to refer to himself, always in the third person, never as a predicate nominative. He also follows Mark in never placing the title on the lips of someone else as a confessional title used to identify Jesus. Matthew retains most of the Markan references to Son of Man but he also adds a significant number from Q (Matt 8:20; cf. Luke 9:58; Matt 11:19; cf. Luke 7:34; Matt 12:32; cf. Luke 12:10; Matt 12:40; cf. Luke 11:30; Matt 24:27; cf. Luke 17:24; Matt 24:37, 39; cf. Luke 17:26, 30; Matt 24:44; cf. Luke 12:40). This suggests that Q's emphasis on Jesus as Son of Man reinforces the Markan portrait for Matthew. In several places, Matthew alters Mark by adding references to Son of Man (16:13, 28; 17:12), and in other places he supplies uniquely Matthean references (10:23; 13:37, 41; 19:28; 25:31). He thus draws on all three streams of the Jesus tradition in portraying Jesus as Son of Man.

Matthew also retains the three general categories of usage for Son of Man found in Mark: (1) as a general term of self-reference describing various aspects of his person and mission, such as his homelessness (8:20), his power to forgive sins (9:6), his daily ritual of eating and drinking (11:19), his being Lord of the Sabbath (12:8), and his role as the one who sows the seed (13:37) and who gives his life as a ransom for others (20:28); (2) as the one who will suffer and die at his enemies' hands (12:40; 17:9, 12, 22; 20:18; 26:2, 24, 45); and (3) as the eschatological judge (10:23; 13:41; 16:27–28; 19:28; 24:27, 30, 37, 39, 44; 25:31; 26:64).

Rather than altering substantially the Markan understanding of Son of Man, Matthew amplifies it. Like "Son of God," it remains for him an enormously important title for conveying Jesus' exalted status as the one who makes audacious claims for himself, as the suffering Servant who will follow the way of the cross, and as the one who, as exalted Lord, will exercise final judgment.

When evaluating Matthew's use of "Lord" in reference to Jesus, we first notice that he uses it much more frequently than Mark. In a few instances in Mark, Jesus uses the term self-referentially (Mark 5:19; 11:3), and when it is used as a form of address, it seems to have the meaning "Sir" (Mark 7:28). But in Matthew it occurs more frequently as a way of addressing Jesus both in the context of healing stories (8:2, 6; 9:28; 15:22, 25, 27; 17:15; 20:30, 31, 33) and in contexts in which he is addressed by the disciples (8:21, 25; 26:22), especially Peter (14:28, 30; 16:22; 18:21). While some of these uses may be equivalent to "Sir," not all of them can be; for example, the Canaanite woman addresses Jesus as "Lord, Son of David." Nor is it likely that in the last judgment people would mean "Sir" when addressing the Judge as "Lord" (Matt 25:37, 44). Similarly, when Jesus chides those who address him superficially as "Lord, Lord" (7:21–22), the title can be meaningful only if a genuine use of the term would signify true discipleship.

These usages, combined with Matthew's usage of "Son of God" and "Son of Man," contribute even further to the authoritative image of Jesus in the Gospel.

Whether all of these streams converge in the final scene in which Jesus, gathered with his disciples, issues the Great Commission is a matter of debate (28:18–20). The only one of them mentioned specifically is "the Son" in the Trinitarian formula for baptism. But we can hardly ignore the unparalleled scope of Jesus' final claim: "All authority in heaven and on earth has been given to me" (v. 18). The disciples' worshipful posture (apart from those who doubted) also reinforces Jesus' exalted status. This claim to authority also recalls a similar, though less universal, claim to unique revelatory knowledge of the Father in his earlier prayer (Matt 11:25–27). Given the strong similarity of this language to Dan 7:13–14, in which "dominion and glory and kingship" are given to the Son of Man so that "all peoples, nations, and languages should serve him," it is very difficult to escape the conclusion that Jesus from the Galilean mountains is laying full claim to the universal authority of the Danielic Son of Man. Stretching the promise of his continued presence until "the end of the age" is quite resonant with Dan 7:14: "His dominion is an everlasting dominion that shall not pass away, and his kingship is one that shall never be destroyed."

While Son (of God) is the only title specifically mentioned, the related images of Jesus as Lord and exalted Son of Man appear to inform the scene as well. This final, climactic scene serves as a stream into which all three of these christological tributaries flow. Looking back, we can see that the narrative has been moving towards this point from the beginning, and by signaling the theme of God's presence through Christ at both beginning and end, Matthew further reinforces the point (Matt 1:23; 28:20).

Just as Matthew enhances Jesus' authority through his use of christological titles, so also he achieves this throughout the narrative. He makes Jesus' miracle stories more impressive by noting that they occur instantly (Matt 8:13; cf. Luke 7:10; Matt 9:22; cf. Mark 5:34; Matt 15:28; cf. Mark 7:30; Matt 17:18; cf. Mark 9:27). In Matthew, Jesus' feeding miracles benefit larger numbers of people (Matt 14:20–21; cf. Mark 6:43; Matt 15:37–38; cf. Mark 8:8–9). Whereas Mark suggests that Jesus was *unable* to perform many miracles at Nazareth (Mark 6:5), Matthew reports that he was *unwilling* to do so (Matt 13:58). Matthew also enhances Jesus' authority by omitting instances in Mark in which people flagrantly disobey Jesus' commands (Mark 1:44–45; cf. Matt 8:4; Mark 7:36; cf. Matt 15:30–31). Still, Jesus' orders can be ignored (Matt 9:30–31).

Whether Matthew's portrayal of Jesus' emotional status vis-à-vis Mark also enhances his authority is subject to debate. Even so, his changes are worth noting. For example, Matthew eliminates Mark's references to Jesus' pity (Matt 8:3; cf. Mark 1:41), sternness (Matt 8:3b; cf. Mark 1:43; Matt 12:16; cf. Mark 3:12), and indignation (Matt 19:14; cf. Mark 10:14). And yet he retains Mark's references to Jesus' compassion

(Matt 14:14; cf. Mark 6:34; Matt 15:32; cf. Mark 8:2) and even adds new ones (Matt 9:36; although cf. Mark 6:34; Matt 20:34; cf. Mark 10:51–52).

Jesus' authoritative status also extends to his relationship with his disciples. When Jesus calls the first disciples, they respond quickly and decisively. Twice Matthew tells us that "immediately they left . . . and followed him" (Matt 4:18–22; cf. Mark 1:16–20). As disciples, they do more than learn from Jesus; they worship him (Matt 14:33; cf. Mark 6:51–52; Matt 28:9, 17). Similar reverence is shown at the transfiguration when Peter, James, and John respond to the heavenly voice by being gripped with fear and falling to the ground, only to have Jesus, God's Beloved, reassure them (Matt 17:5–7; cf. Mark 9:6–8).

The Jesus of Matthew's Gospel thus enacts his role as the exalted Lord of the church who, as it were, presides over the church like the Pantocrator in Orthodox church ceilings. In every way—through editorial comment, through characters who interact with Jesus, through Jesus' own words and actions—Matthew develops this understanding of Jesus steadily throughout the narrative. It reaches its grand conclusion in the final scene when readers are assured of the continued presence of the Lord within their midst—even until the end of the age. For a church in transition, seeking to develop a new identity independent of the synagogue, this image both centers and anchors the church. There can be little doubt about who authorizes and presides over the church.

Jesus the Messianic Teacher. Matthew knows from Mark the image of Jesus as a charismatic teacher, but he gives it a different valence. Like Mark, he frequently portrays Jesus engaged in teaching, although he actually describes Jesus as teaching less often than Mark (nine times vs. fifteen times). Still, he records a much larger body of Jesus' teaching than Mark. Compare Matthew's seventeen parables to Mark's six.

Matthew's Jesus is always the Teacher, but what exactly does this mean? One passage goes to the heart of the matter: Jesus' opening comments in chapter 23, in which he utters seven prophetic "woes" against the scribes and Pharisees. Jesus first observes that the scribes and Pharisees sit on Moses' seat, by which he means that they are the official interpreters of Moses' teachings. Follow their teaching, he insists, but do not emulate their behavior. Why? They are pompous and pretentious and do not practice what they preach. As for Jesus' disciples (and the crowds), they are not to be called "rabbi" because, he says, "you have one teacher [*didaskalos*] and you are all brothers" (*adelphoi*). Nor are they to call any human being "father," since they have only one Father, who is in heaven. Their sole instructor (*kathēgētēs*) is Jesus himself, the Messiah (*ho Christos*).

Once again, Matthew's use of church language is telling. To refer to the disciples as "brother(s)" doubtless reflects his own situation. As elsewhere, he is thinking of how church members relate to each other (5:22–24; 7:3–5; 18:15, 21, 35). Mark nowhere uses the term "brother" in this way. As Matthew sees it, the church's ultimate loyalty is to God, and their only teacher is the one who is present among them: Jesus, whom they confess as Messiah. As seen earlier, Jesus can serve as God's sole interpreter and can call disciples to learn from him because as God's Son he is uniquely positioned to reveal God's mysteries (11:25–30).

Jesus' authority to teach the church derives from his messianic status. Matthew draws a consistent distinction between those who recognize Jesus merely as teacher and those who recognize him as messianic Teacher. This is in marked contrast to Mark, in which, as we saw earlier, the title Teacher is used indiscriminately as a form of address. All sorts of people—enemies and friends, disciples and non-disciples—address Jesus as Teacher in Mark. Not so in Matthew, in which Jesus is addressed as Teacher only by scribes, Pharisees, or others who have not yet become disciples (8:19; 9:11; 12:38; 17:24; 19:16; 22:16, 24, 36). Once Jesus uses the term in reference to himself (26:18), but for him it is inseparably attached to Messiah (23:8–10).

One of the most graphic illustrations of Matthew's perspective is his account of Jesus' conversation with his disciples prior to the Last Supper (26:20–25). When he warns of an impending betrayal by one of them, they respond, "Surely not I, Lord?" The final word from Judas, however, is "Surely not I, Rabbi?" Judas recognizes Jesus as Teacher but not as Lord (see also 26:49). With this telltale form of address, Matthew excludes Judas from the circle of true disciples and places him with Jesus' other detractors who recognize him only as a teacher, nothing more. This distinction is absent in Mark's account (14:17–21).

When Jesus teaches in Matthew, he does not do so as an ordinary rabbi or even as a new Moses. When Matthew's Jesus says six times, "You have heard it said . . ., but I say to you . . .," he is not assuming Moses' seat, he is trumping Moses (5:21–48). He now speaks as Son of God, a unique status revealed at his baptism (3:13–17) and confirmed at the temptations (4:1–11). He alone can reveal the Father because he alone knows the Father (11:25–30). When Jesus is asked by Jewish leaders where he received his authority to teach, the correct answer is "from heaven" (21:23–27). It is Jesus the Lord who speaks in the Sermon on the Mount, who determines entrance into the kingdom of heaven (7:21–23), who insists that *his* words be obeyed (7:24–27). The authority that astonishes the crowd who hears this teaching has unparalleled weight because it derives from Jesus the Messiah, Lord, and Son of God.

All the teachings Matthew reports must be read as teachings of Jesus the messianic Teacher: his five discourses, his other parables and pronouncements, and his many other instructions to the disciples and the crowds. And when he finally transfers his teaching authority to his disciples, he does so as the exalted Lord who has universal authority (28:18–20).

Jesus as the One Who Perfects the Law and the Prophets. Once we recognize Jesus' status as messianic Teacher as the major premise of Matthew's Gospel, we are in a better position to appreciate how Matthew sees Jesus' relationship to Torah, or more broadly, to the Jewish Scriptures as a whole.

We return to our earlier discussion for our first clue: "Do whatever [the scribes and Pharisees] teach you and follow it," he says to the disciples and crowds (23:3).

This should come as no surprise, given his programmatic declaration in the Sermon on the Mount:

Do not think that I have come to abolish the law or the prophets; I have come not to abolish but to fulfill. For truly I tell you, until heaven and earth pass away, not one letter, not one stroke of a letter, will pass from the law until all is accomplished. Therefore, whoever breaks one of the least of these commandments, and teaches others to do the same, will be called least in the kingdom of heaven; but whoever does them and teaches them will be called great in the kingdom of heaven. For I tell you, unless your righteousness exceeds that of the scribes and Pharisees, you will never enter the kingdom of heaven. (5:17–20)

Two things should be noted here. First is *Jesus' unqualified affirmation of the law and the prophets.* As messianic Teacher, Jesus does not set aside Scripture's demands; he fulfills these demands by perfecting or completing them. He is the one (to return to our earlier metaphor) who makes it possible to connect the dots in Scripture, who finally makes it possible to understand the *full* meaning of Scripture—its promises, expectations, and hidden allusions. He provides the key that unlocks Scripture's hidden meanings (11:25–26). He also perfects Scripture by providing a more satisfactory interpretation of its deeper demands and expectations.

Second, we should note *Jesus' assertion of the permanent validity of the law and the prophets* (5:18). The law and the prophets set the expectations for life in the kingdom, and their commandments, even the most trivial, are to be obeyed (v. 19). What undergirds the Golden Rule, "In everything do to others as you would have them do to you" (7:12), is not Jesus' own genius as a teacher, but "the law and the prophets." The superior righteousness he calls for is recognition of the abiding authority of the law and the prophets and unqualified submission to them. His own instinctive urge to "fulfill all righteousness" (that is, to do what is fully right) at his baptism (3:13–17) exemplifies his deepest respect for God's expectations as expressed in Scripture. Where scribal and Pharisaic practice had tried to finesse Scripture's demands, Jesus requires even more scrupulous observance (cf. 23:13–36). What each of the six antitheses has in common is Jesus' claim that the underlying attitude, the unexpressed act, is more important than the act itself. Get the underlying motive right, Jesus insists, and right action naturally follows.

Matthew's Jesus consistently upholds the importance of Jewish observances prescribed by Torah. He does not denounce the practices themselves, only their abuse (6:1–18; 23:23). Especially revealing is the way Matthew treats Mark's discussion of Jewish dietary practices (Matt 15:1–20; Mark 7:1–23). Whereas Mark interprets Jesus' teachings to mean that "he declared all foods clean" (7:19), thus suspending Jewish dietary regulations, Matthew omits the phrase, thereby upholding such regulations.

What does this mean for Matthew's readers? They may have parted ways with the synagogue, but not with Scripture. The law and the prophets are not to be set aside but taken even more seriously. They are to be interpreted, however, in light of Jesus' more demanding interpretation. As the church's "pulpit Bible," the law and the prophets are to be venerated, but are now understood through the words of Jesus the messianic Teacher. The church possesses the Scriptures as they always did, but now they have a definitive way of reading them from God's chosen Revealer.

As for their religious practices, Matthew's Jewish readers will doubtless be expected to continue observing traditional forms of Jewish piety, such as prayer, almsgiving, and fasting. They will also continue to observe dietary regulations and probably to circumcise their male children, although Matthew never addresses this latter question directly.

Matthew affirms the continuing validity of the law and the prophets in a way that sharply distinguishes him from other NT writers, such as Paul, for whom Torah was more problematic as a basis for Christian living (cf. Rom 10:4; but cf. Rom 8:3–4). He is especially distant from later Christians, such as Marcion (died ca. 160 C.E.), who looked for ways to reject the Jewish Scriptures wholesale.

A New Identity

When Matthew retells the Markan parable of the wicked tenants, he reports Jesus saying to the temple leadership, "The kingdom of God will be taken away from you and given to a people [*ethnos*] that produces the fruits of the kingdom" (21:43). There can be little doubt that Matthew's readers would see themselves as this people through whom God's rule has now been redirected. And why? They are now the community over whom Jesus the messianic king presides and with whom he resides. This should be seen as a redirection of God's reign rather than supersession, because this new people consists of Jews who still retained their Jewish identity and Gentiles who saw themselves as stemming from the same family tree—Gentiles whose hopes for inclusion within God's people had been embedded within Scripture for centuries. They do not see themselves as the "Israel of God," to use Paul's metaphor (Gal 6:16), thus as neither the "new Israel" nor the "true Israel." Their new identity has been forged by their conflict with Israel, a conflict they see extending back into Jesus' ministry. As the readers of Matthew's Gospel read their foundation narrative, they see how early Israel's resistance to Jesus set in, how continuous it was, and finally how complete it became.

As people to whom the "kingdom of God" has been given and who offer the prospect of producing the "fruits of the kingdom," they can now see themselves as the primary locus of God's kingly rule, the people who live in order to enact Jesus' prayer that God's kingdom come and God's will be done (6:9–10), who become the "salt of the earth" and "the light of the world" (5:13–16) as they seek to transform the earth into a place where God's desires are carried out. Like their founder Jesus and his predecessor John, their message can be summed up in a few words: "Repent, for the kingdom of heaven has come near" (3:2; 4:17). From their foundation narrative they know how often Jesus spoke of the "kingdom of heaven" (thirty-two times), or, because of his respect for the divine name, the less preferred "kingdom of God" (four times), sometimes in the same breath (19:23–24). From his many pronouncements they know the kingdom of heaven as a dynamic reality already breaking in (10:7), dramatically visible in Jesus' own powerful words and miracles. They get glimpses of it when Jesus exorcises demons (12:28). They associate its good news with Jesus' healing miracles (4:23; 9:35). They also know it as a future hope, a reality they will not fully experience until the coming of the Son of Man (16:28).

As they live in the interim between the "already" and the "not yet," Matthew's readers are far from clueless about the kingdom because Jesus has revealed its mysteries to them through his parables (13:11). They know what the "kingdom of heaven is like": it springs up in surprising places (13:1–23); it must compete with powerful, demonic forces (13:19; 12:22–32); it is often an invisible presence in the world, yet has phenomenal transforming power (13:31–33); it is worth pursuing at all costs (13:44–46); it attracts all sorts of folks—every kind of fish—but God does the final sorting (13:38, 41, 43, 47–50); you get in by becoming a child (18:1–4); you stay in by being childlike (19:14); you are rebuked when you angle for position and power (20:21); some people try to block your entry (23:13); riches can keep you out (19:23–24); it is surprising who gets in and who does not (8:11–12; 20:1–16; 21:31; 22:1–24; 25:1–46); it is where true blessedness can be found (5:3, 10); you get in by being genuinely obedient, not by mouthing titles, even honored ones (7:21); you must behave appropriately and responsibly to stay in (5:19–20); to stay in is to enjoy an incredible banquet (8:11); it requires uncalculating forgiveness (18:21–35); it sometimes means unusual levels of sacrifice (19:12); it requires vigilant preparation (25:1–13), responsible use of our gifts (25:14–30), and attending to basic human needs (25:31–36), and failure to do these things places us under God's judgment, where we experience the severe side of God; and so compelling is its good news that it will break through all national boundaries and be proclaimed to the whole world (24:14; 28:18–20).

Matthew peppers his narrative with enough images from his own readers' experience for them to construct, even deepen, their own sense of identity: they are Jesus' true family (12:46–50); the church (16:18; 18:18); a community of brothers (and sisters) gathered before the heavenly Father listening to their sole Rabbi Jesus interpret Torah and reveal the will of the Father (23:8–10); and saints destined to share Jesus' resurrection who, in their encounter with his death, already begin their witness to his words and deeds, his life and death (27:52–53).

There is also another side of their new identity. Since this identity has been forged in the heat of intense conflict, it acquires a razor-sharp edge. Matthew has also given his readers a picture of the "other" whose profile is all too clear. They know scribes, Pharisees, and Sadducees, as well as the several groups of leaders whose power base is the temple, as their enemies (9:34; 12:14; 21:45–46; 23:1–36). While they can envision some crossovers—scribes, for example, who enlist in the service of the kingdom (13:52)—they mainly see them as "that group" in "their synagogues." The church must always be wary of these "blind guides" (15:14); to follow them is to risk falling into a ditch. The church must not be seduced by their teaching, which has the corrupting power of yeast (16:5–12), although their practice condemns them more than their preaching (ch. 23). But Matthew's rhetoric gets the better of him when he places the blame for Jesus' death on the "people as a whole," who cry out, "His blood be on us and on our children!" (27:25), a line destined to have tragic consequences when Christians would later seek biblical warrant for anti-Semitism.

Here we experience one of the most enduring paradoxes of Matthew's Gospel. From Papias onward, people thought Matthew was written for Jewish readers, and even reported that it was written in the Hebrew language. Like no other Gospel, it affirms the validity of the law and the prophets, appreciates their enduring value, and sees the Jewish Scriptures as the indispensable framework for understanding Jesus. And yet its sharply polemical context has yielded the inevitable religious caricatures that reduce the riches and nuances of historical and social realities to manageable stereotypes. In retrospect this may have been necessary in helping the church construct its new identity, but we now recognize the price at which this new identity was purchased.

A New Ethic

While much of Jesus' teaching in Matthew is done metaphorically through parables and a host of memorable images and pictures, much of it is done in other ways as well. What it means to be a disciple is portrayed both in narrative episodes and direct discourses, which is to say, within the story itself. To get some sense of the full range of expectations of discipleship, one must observe the characters in the story as well as listen to their words and the words of Jesus.

Being a Disciple. As in Mark, the twelve apostles constitute Jesus' inner circle (4:18–22; 9:9; 10:1–4). As his designated emissaries (10:5–15), they receive special instruction (11:1). They are often, though not always, the disciples in view in various episodes and conversations throughout the story. While there is a larger circle of unnamed disciples, the Twelve are seen as the vital link between Jesus and the church. To them is granted special prominence after the resurrection and to them, now eleven, the risen Lord gives the Great Commission (28:18–20). As carriers of the Jesus tradition, they guarantee continuity between the time of Jesus and the time of the church. The power to "bind and loose" that Jesus promises Peter (16:19) is also extended to them (18:18), which means that they will finally exercise Jesus' full teaching authority.

Like Jesus, the disciples occupy an exalted position in Matthew. This becomes especially evident in Matthew's revisions of Mark. Where Mark reports their lack of understanding, Matthew may alter it (Matt 16:12; cf. Mark 8:21; Matt 13:18–19; cf. Mark 4:13) or omit it (Matt 14:32–33; cf. Mark 6:51–52); he may even report instances of understanding where Mark does not (Matt 17:12–13; cf. Mark 9:13). Matthew transfers the ambition of James and John to their mother (Matt 20:20; Mark 10:35). Even so, Matthew does not idealize the disciples beyond recognition. They still exhibit fear and anxiety (14:26) and "little faith" (8:26; 14:31; 16:8), and Peter's misunderstanding is still attributed to demonic motives (Matt 16:23). Matthew also reports Peter's threefold denial (26:69–75) and the disciples' wholesale desertion of Jesus (26:56). Even in the triumphant concluding scene, "some doubted" (28:17). The disciples emerge not as stick figures in Matthew, but as real human beings who experience the full range of emotions associated with the life of faith, who can be decisive when they are called but fearful when they confront danger. Like anyone else, they need reassurance (19:27–30). They strike a more sympathetic pose than Mark's obtuse disciples—they are people with whom church members can truly identify.

Emulating Jesus. In Matthew, Jesus emerges as a figure eminently worthy of imitation. As such, he serves as a model for the church. One of his first official acts reflects his instinctive urge to submit to God's righteousness (3:15), and from start to finish he displays exemplary obedience before God (4:1–11; 26:36–46). He willingly follows the way of suffering that leads to death and expects his disciples to "take up their cross" and be willing to die (10:38; 16:24–26). Even though his official mission, and that of his disciples, is to "the lost sheep of the house of Israel" (10:6), he already begins to cross ethnic boundaries during his mission and will eventually inaugurate a universal mission (28:18–20). His many miracles of healing show him to be the compassionate messianic king, and his disciples are expected to follow him by enacting missions of mercy (10:8; 25:31–46). His exemplary function becomes explicit in his declaration that the "disciple [is] to be like the teacher" (10:24). How disciples act will determine what recommendation Jesus makes to the Father (10:32–33).

Listening to Jesus. Matthew well knows that to be a disciple is to be a learner, and he brings this image to full flower. The central thrust of Jesus' invitation is to "learn from me" (11:28–30), and in Matthew disciples learn by listening. We have already noted how disciples learn about life in the kingdom by "having ears to hear" the subtle lessons of the parables (13:9). But the major discourses that are assembled and reported by Matthew constitute Jesus' real curriculum, for they touch on the major themes of his mission. **[See Expanded CD Version pp. 210–11:** *Jesus' Teaching: Matthew's Five Discourses***]**

Righteousness and Obedience. It is hard to miss Matthew's insistent call for disciples to practice righteousness. As noted earlier, Matthew emphasizes righteousness in a way Mark does not. Whereas Mark never mentions righteousness, Matthew does so seven times, five times in the Sermon on the Mount. Matthew's nineteen uses of "righteous" contrast with Mark's two uses. Striving first for the "kingdom of God and [God's] righteousness" is a paramount concern (6:33). In his programmatic statement about the law and the prophets, Jesus calls disciples to exhibit righteousness superior to that of the scribes and Pharisees. In calling for righteousness to be a way of life, Jesus is urging behavior that he exemplifies (3:13–17).

Coupled with his call for righteousness is the repeated insistence on obedience. Jesus' final word to his apostles is to enlist disciples who are taught "to obey everything that I have commanded you" (28:20). To be a disciple in the Matthean church is to be obedient to all of Jesus' commandments. When asked what is the greatest commandment, Matthew's Jesus reaffirms what is expressed in Mark: wholehearted love of God and self-directed love of neighbor. He goes beyond Mark in concluding, "On these two commandments hang all the law and the prophets" (Matt 22:34–40; cf. Mark 12:28–34). Scrupulous adherence to the deeper demands of Torah produces lives of enacted love. Concretely, this means feeding the hungry, extending hospitality to the stranger, clothing the naked, taking care of the sick, and visiting those in prison (25:31–36).

As Emmanuel, Jesus identifies so closely with humanity that doing these things for others is to do them for him. But if disciples fail to live for others, Jesus, the exalted Son of Man, will exclude them from eternal life. Not every religious act done in the Lord's name qualifies as genuine obedience. One can prophesy, exorcise demons, and perform miracles, even in the Lord's name, and yet fail to be truly obedient to God (7:21–23). The litmus test of obedience is whether disciples "produce the fruits of the kingdom" (21:43)—whether they exhibit the qualities of life Jesus sketches in his parables of the kingdom. Matthew insists on the direct correlation between inner disposition and outward acts: good trees bear good fruit, evil trees evil fruit (7:15–20), the point repeatedly made in the six antitheses (5:21–48). Obedience does not take the form of superficial piety (6:1–18) or public display of religious behavior (ch. 23), but attending to the weightier demands of Torah: justice, mercy, and faith (23:23). To honor God from the heart outward requires inward devotion to Torah's deep demands (15:1–20).

For Matthew, actions are decisive indicators of true discipleship. Doing must accompany hearing. Listening closely to Jesus' interpretation of Torah and his other teachings points disciples to the superior righteousness he demands. To be a true disciple in Matthew's church is to be an obedient student of Jesus (28:20).

1-2	3-4	5	6	7
Judea, Egypt, Naz.	Judea & Galilee			
		Discourse # 1: Sermon on the Mount – T		
Genealogy (1:1-17) Birth of Jesus (1:18-25) Visit of Wise Men (2:1-12) Escape to Egypt (2:13-15) Massacre of Infants (2:16-18) Trip to Nazareth (2:19-23)	Proclamation of JB (3:1-12) Baptism of Jesus (3:13-17) Temptation (4:1-11) Galilean ministry begins (4:12-17) Jesus calls Pet., A, Js, & Jn (4:18-22) Summary: Jesus' teaching & healing (4:23-25) **S**	Beatitudes (1-12) Salt & light (13-16) Fulfilling Law & Prophets (17-20) Anger & reconcili-ation (21-26) Adultery (27-32) Oaths (33-37) Non-retaliation (38-42) Love for enemies (43-48)	Piety (1) Giving alms (2-4) Praying (5-15) [Lord's Prayer (9-13)] Fasting (16-18) True treasures (19-21) Healthy eye, 2 masters (22-24) Anxiety & Kgdm of God (25-34)	Judging others (1-5) Profaning the holy (6) Ask, seek, knock (7-11) Do to others (7:12) Narrow & wide gate (13-14) False prophets (15-20) Doing God's will (21-23) Wise & foolish man (24-27) Summary (28-29) **S**

12	13	14	15	16
			Galilee	
	Discourse # 3: Parables -T			
Plucking grain on Sabbath (1-8) **C/P** Heal. man w/ withd. hand (9-14) **M** Jesus as God's Servant (15-21) Healing demoniac: Jesus & Beelzebul (22-32) **M** Tree/ fruit (33-37) **T** J's sign (38-42)**C/T** Return of unclean spirit (43-45) **T** J's family(46-50) **P**	Sower (1-23) Weeds among wheat (24-30) Mstrd seed (31-32) Yeast (33) Use of par. (34-35) Weeds explained (36-43) Hidden treas. & pearl (44-46) Dragnet (47-50) Treasures new and old (51-52) Summary (13:53) **S**	Rejection at Nazareth (13:54-58) **C** Death of JB (1-12) Feeding 5000 (13-21) **M** Walking on water (22-33) **M** Healing sick in Gennesaret (34-36) **M**	Tradition of elders (1-9) **C & T** Things that defile (10-20) **T** Healing Canaanite woman's daughter (21-28) **M** Healing many people (29-31) **M** Feeding 4000 (32-39) **M**	Demand sign (1-4) **C** Yeast of Pharisees and Sadd. (5-12) **T** Caesarea Philippi: Peter's confession (13-20) First passion prediction (21-23) Teaching about discipleship (24-26) **T** Coming Son of Man (27-28) **T**

21	22	23	24	25
			Jerusalem	
		Discourse # 5: Polemic vs. S. & Phar. End-Time, Judgment - T		
Triumphal entry (1-11) Cleansing Temple (12-17) Cursing fig tree (18-22) Jesus' authority questioned (23-27) **C** Parable of two sons (28-32) **T** Parable of wicked tenants (33-44) **T** Response (45-46)	Parable of wedding banquet (1-14) **T** Paying taxes (15-22) **C & T** Resurrection (23-33) **C & T** Greatest commandment (34-40) **C & T** David's Son (41-46) **C & T**	Warnings (1-12) Seven woes against Scribes & Pharisees (13-36) Lament over Jerusalem (37-39)	End of Temple (1-2) Signs of end (3-8) Persecutions foretold (9-14) Des. Sacril. (15-28) Coming of Son of Man (29-31) Fig tree (32-35) Must watch (36-44) Parable of faithful & wise slave (45-51)	Ten bridesmaids (1-13) Talents (14-30) Judgment of Gentiles (31-46) Summary (26:1) **S**

8	9	10	11
Galilee			
Healing the leper (1-4) **M** Healing centurion's servant (5-13) **M** Healing Peter's mother-in-law (14-17) **M** Would-be followers of Jesus (18-22) **P** Stilling the storm (23-27) **M** Healing the Gadarene demoniacs (8:28-9:1) **M**	Healing the paralytic (2-8) **M** Call of Matthew (9) Tax collectors and sinners (10-13) **C/P** Fasting questioned (14-17) **T** Raising leader's daughter & healing woman (18-26) **M** Healing two blind men (27-31) **M** Healing mute demoniac (9:32-34) **M** Great harvest, few laborers (9:35-38) **T**	**Discourse # 2: Mission - T** The Twelve (1-4) Sending the Twelve (5-15) Coming Trials (16-23) Disciple & teacher (24-25) Not fearing (26-33) Cost of discipleship (34-39) Hospitality (40-42) Summary (11:1) **S**	Messengers from JB (2-6) JB as Elijah (7-19) **T** Woes to unrepentant cities (20-24) **T** Jesus as Wisdom reveals Father's secrets (25-27) **T** Wisdom's invitation: "Come unto me" (28-30) **T**

17	18	19	20
		Transjordan & Judea	
Transfiguration (1-13) Healing boy with demon (14-20) **M** Second passion prediction (22-23) Jesus & Temple tax (24-27)	**Discourse # 4: Community Rules - T** True greatness (1-4) Temptations to sin (6-9) Parable of lost sheep (10-14) Disciplining church members (15-20) Forgiveness (21-22) Parable of unforgiving servant (23-35) Summary (19:1-2) **S**	Summary (1-2) **S** Teaching about divorce (3-9) **T** Kingdom eunuchs (10-12) **T** Blessing children (13-15) **T** Rich young man (16-22) **T** Teaching disciples about riches (23-30) **T**	Parable of workers in vineyard (1-16) **T** Third passion prediction (17-19) James & John's Mother's request (20-28) **T** Healing two blind men (29-34) **M**

26	27	28	
		Judea & Galilee	
Plot vs. Jesus (1-5) Anointing at Bethany (6-13) **T** Judas plans (14-16) Passover (17-25) Eucharist (26-30) Peter's denial foretold (31-35) Gethsemane (36-46) Betrayal and arrest (47-56) Jesus before the high priest (57-68) Peter's denial of Jesus (69-75)	Before Pilate (1-2) Judas' death (3-10) Pilate's ?'s (11-14) Barabbas (15-23) Pilate hands Jesus over to be crucified (24-26) Soldiers mock Jesus (27-31) Crucifixion (32-44) J's death (45-56) Burial (57-61) Guard at tomb (62-66)	Resurrection (1-10) Report of guard (11-15) Commissioning of disciples in Galilee (16-20)	

Legend:
C= Controversy Story
M = Miracle Story
P = Pronouncement Story
S = Summary
T = Teaching Material

Notes

1. Eusebius, *Hist. eccl.* 6.25.4.
2. Eusebius, *Hist. eccl.* 3.39.16.
3. *Haer.* 3.1.1–2.
4. *Hist. eccl.* 3.24.6; cf. 5.10.3.
5. *Hom. Matt.* 1.7.
6. See W. D. Davies, *The Setting of the Sermon on the Mount* (Cambridge: Cambridge University Press, 1964), 14 n. 5.

Bibliography

Commentaries

Davies, William D., and Dale C. Allison. *A Critical and Exegetical Commentary on the Gospel According to Saint Matthew.* International Critical Commentary. 3 vols. Edinburgh: T&T Clark, 1988–1997.

Hagner, Donald A. *Matthew.* Word Biblical Commentary 33. 2 vols. Dallas: Word, 1993–1995.

Luz, Ulrich. *Matthew 1–7: A Commentary.* Translation by W. C. Linss. Minneapolis: Augsburg, 1989; *Matthew 8–20: A Commentary.* Minneapolis: Augsburg, 2003.

Schweizer, Eduard. *The Good News According to Matthew.* Translated by David E. Green. Atlanta: John Knox, 1975.

Other Resources

Aune, David E., ed. *The Gospel of Matthew in Current Study.* Grand Rapids: Eerdmans, 2001.

Kingsbury, Jack D. *Matthew as Story.* 2d ed. Philadelphia: Fortress, 1988.

———. *Matthew: Structure, Christology, Kingdom.* Philadelphia: Fortress, 1975; London: SPCK, 1976.

Luz, Ulrich. *Matthew in History: Interpretation, Influence, and Effects.* Minneapolis: Fortress, 1994.

———. *The Theology of the Gospel of Matthew.* New Testament Theology. Translated by J. Bradford Robinson. Cambridge: Cambridge University Press, 1995; repr. 2002.

Minear, Paul. *Matthew: The Teacher's Gospel.* New York: Pilgrim, 1982; repr. Eugene: Wipf and Stock, 2003.

Riches, John. *Matthew.* New Testament Guides. Sheffield: Sheffield Academic Press, 1996; repr. 1997.

Senior, Donald. *What Are They Saying about Matthew?* Rev. ed. New York: Paulist, 1996.

Stanton, Graham. *A Gospel for a New People: Studies in Matthew.* Edinburgh: T&T Clark, 1992.

————. *The Interpretation of Matthew.* Issues in Religion and Theology 3. Philadelphia/London: Fortress/SPCK, 1983.

SERMON ON THE MOUNT

Allison, Dale C. *The Sermon on the Mount: Inspiring the Moral Imagination.* New York: Crossroad, 1999.

Betz, Hans D. *The Sermon on the Mount: A Commentary on the Sermon on the Mount, Including the Sermon on the Plain (Matthew 5:3–7:27 and Luke 6:20–49).* Hermeneia. Edited by Adela Yarbro Collins. Minneapolis: Fortress, 1995.

Davies, W. D. *The Setting of the Sermon on the Mount.* Cambridge: Cambridge University Press, 1964.

————. *The Sermon on the Mount.* Cambridge: Cambridge University Press, 1966; repr. 1969–1990.

Guelich, Robert A. *The Sermon on the Mount: A Foundation for Understanding.* Waco: Word, 1982.

Chapter 8

The Gospel of Luke

"Luke had something of the poet in his make-up and an artist's ability to depict in vivid pen-portraits the men and women who inhabit his pages."

G. B. Caird

Even though the Third Gospel nowhere names its author, early readers of the New Testament deduced that it was Luke. From the opening verses in Acts, they knew that Luke's Gospel was the first of a two-volume work. They also concluded that both works were written by the same author because of their similar style and vocabulary. Noticing the author's several uses of "we" in Acts when reporting events in Paul's ministry (16:10–17; 20:5–15; 21:1–18; 27:1–28:16), they concluded that the author was a companion of Paul. From the circle of co-workers mentioned by Paul in his letters, they identified Luke as the one who had been with Paul continuously and thus as most likely to have written the "we's" (cf. 2 Tim. 4:11). They also identified him as "the beloved physician" who was with Paul when he wrote Colossians (Col 4:14; cf. Phlm 24). Their reading of Acts suggested that Luke did not belong to the original circle of apostles but was connected to the apostolic tradition only through Paul. Their perception of Luke as a "follower of the apostle(s)" rather than as someone who was part of the original apostolic circle was reinforced by the preface to the Gospel, in which the author acknowledges that he is at least one generation removed from "those who from the beginning were eyewitnesses and servants of the word" (Luke 1:1–4).

By connecting these biblical references, early readers of the NT confidently concluded that Luke, the "beloved physician" and constant companion of Paul, had written the Third Gospel. Reflecting this view, the Christian scribe who copied $\mathfrak{P}^{75}$, the earliest surviving manuscript of the Gospel (late second or early third century C.E.), concluded the Gospel by inscribing the title "Gospel according to Luke" (*euangelion kata Loukan*). As the tradition about Luke developed, other hunches emerged, for example, that Luke was the person who was "famous among all the churches for his proclaiming the good news" (2 Cor 8:18) or that he was the Lucius mentioned in Rom 16:21. Some also reasoned that if Luke had been with Paul, why not with Jesus as well? In one later tradition, Luke (and Mark) was included among the seventy disciples whom Jesus sent out during his ministry (Luke 10:1–12). [**See Expanded CD Version pp. 220-23:** *The Church's Use of Luke* **and** *Early Traditions about Luke the Author*]

Luke's Theological Work

Luke is the only synoptic evangelist who supplies a preface telling us why he wrote and describing the state of the tradition that he inherited (Luke 1:1–4). He also provides a similar, though shorter, preface to Acts that not only links it to the Gospel of Luke, but also helps us understand how the two are connected (Acts 1:1–5).

Luke acknowledges that many had earlier attempted what he now wishes to do better. He does not name his literary predecessors, but we can confidently identify one of them as the Gospel of Mark. By mentioning "those who from the beginning were eyewitnesses and servants of the word" (1:2), Luke identifies the links in the chain of tradition to which he is indebted. Whether he is thinking of two stages in the tradition—the apostolic eyewitnesses and a later circle of preachers and teachers who carried their work forward—or whether he thinks these two groups belong to the same period is not certain. Either way, Luke does not claim a place among the original circle of Jesus' followers, but he does place himself squarely within the tradition directly traceable to Jesus through earlier eyewitnesses.

To say that he investigated "everything carefully from the very first" is typical of prefaces we find in other ancient works, especially historical writings, in which the author emphasizes the extensive research that has gone into the writing of the narrative. That Luke is now providing his own "orderly account" implies some dissatisfaction with the work of his predecessors. Taken together, these two statements tell us that Luke wants to supply an account that is comprehensive and coherent.

We learn more about Luke's purpose from the end of the preface, where he addresses "most excellent Theophilus," the same person addressed at the beginning of Acts. Apart from these two references, Theophilus is otherwise unmentioned in the NT. Whether he was Luke's patron (probably the case) or whether the name, which means "lover of God," is a literary fiction inviting any devout Christian to read the narrative is not certain. Here again Luke employs a literary convention, widely used in antiquity, through which an author gains credibility for his work by dedicating it to a prominent person. An example is found in Josephus (ca. 37–100 C.E.), who mentions his patron Epaphroditus at the beginning of his *Jewish Antiquities*.

More important than identifying the otherwise unknown addressee is Luke's remark that he writes so that Theophilus might "know the truth [*asphaleia*] concerning the things about which [he has] been instructed" (1:4). Whether this means that Theophilus is an interested inquirer wanting to know more about Christianity or that he is already a Christian who wants to be reassured in his faith is not clear; probably the latter is correct. In either case, Luke's concern is to provide an account of events that his reader(s) will find reliable. No doubt this means that Luke wants to get his facts straight and record them accurately, but it means more than this. By identifying the focus of his research as "the events that have been fulfilled among us," Luke reveals his theological interests. If we understand "fulfill" in its technical sense of how Scripture's expectations become realized in certain events (e.g., Luke 4:21; 24:44; Acts 1:16; 3:18; 13:27), Luke's statement is quite revealing. It suggests that he is not merely interested in chronicling "events that have occurred in our midst" but rather in constructing a narrative that shows how God's purposes have been realized in those events. Luke is writing a purposeful theological narrative in which God is the primary actor.

The Shape of Luke's Story: Using Earlier Traditions about Jesus

While Luke does not name the sources he used in compiling his Gospel, they probably included the Gospel of Mark, the sayings source Q, and the materials found only in Luke, which are commonly designated L. We do not know whether L consisted mostly of written or oral materials or the extent to which Luke created them. The designation L simply means that they are materials unique to Luke, nothing more. Neither are we very confident about *how* Luke used these sources.

Luke possibly proceeded in a manner similar to Matthew—using the Gospel of Mark as his basic source, supplying a longer beginning and ending mostly from material unique to him, and interweaving material from Q and L into Mark's main narrative to produce a revised edition of Mark. But whereas Matthew, with rare exception, retained most of Mark's narrative and generally followed the Markan sequence of events, Luke did not. Two fairly sizeable portions of Mark (6:45–8:26 and 9:41–10:12), along with scattered verses from Mark (6:19–29; 8:32, 33; 9:9b–13, 28–29; 10:35–40; 11:12–14, 20–25 [26]), are absent in Luke. These omissions suggest that Luke exercised considerable freedom in his use of Mark (and probably other sources as well).

Some scholars doubt that Luke used Mark as a basic storyline into which he inserted fresh material at various points. Alternatively, they have observed that a relatively coherent narrative is produced when the material unique to Luke (L) is combined with the material Luke has in common with Matthew but that is not found in Mark (Q). They have suggested that Luke compiled an original draft of his Gospel (Proto-Luke) from these two sources (or perhaps used an already composed earlier draft) and at a later stage obtained a copy of Mark's Gospel, which he used to supplement his first draft. Since he already had a relatively complete Gospel, he did not need to retain as much of Mark. This would explain why so much of Mark did not make it into Luke's Gospel. While this view of a two-stage composition has been accepted by some scholars, it does not enjoy as much support as the first view. Still other proposals have sought to explain Luke's complex pattern of writing.

Which of these theories of composition one adopts can affect the interpretation of certain passages. For example, if one adopts the first view, Jesus' inaugural sermon at Nazareth (4:16–30) is seen as Luke's retelling of the rejection at Nazareth episode in Mark 6:1–6. In this case, Luke takes a relatively minor episode in Mark, moves it forward to an earlier point in the story, and reinterprets it as a programmatic event. According to the second view, however, Luke could have used another story about

Jesus' preaching in his hometown synagogue as the basis for the Nazareth inaugural, and later, when he found a similar story in Mark, omitted it as a needless repetition. Either way, Luke emerges as a remarkably creative interpreter of the traditions he inherited.

Regardless of one's theory of Lukan composition, the distinctive features of Luke's storyline, especially compared with Mark and Matthew, should be noted. Of particular interest in determining the contours of Luke's theology is how he used the traditions at his disposal to write his Gospel.

The Birth Stories (Chs. 1–2)

Like Matthew, Luke is dissatisfied with Mark's decision to begin the Jesus story with John's ministry. It is conceivable, however, that an earlier edition of Luke's Gospel began at chapter 3, given the formal style of its opening verses and the placement of John's ministry within a broader political context. Although Marcion omitted the first two chapters of Luke's Gospel, our canonical version contains them with their memorable birth story and the episode of the precocious lad instructing his teachers in the temple (2:41–52).

Since the birth stories of Matthew and Luke have become so closely intertwined in popular consciousness, it is difficult for us to read them on their own terms. This is illustrated vividly every Christmas when nativity scenes routinely combine Matthew's wise men with Luke's manger scene. The practice of weaving the two into a single story has an ancient precedent, occurring as early as Tatian's *Diatessaron* (ca. 150–160 C.E.).

To recall how different Luke's opening chapters are from Matthew's, we should note the carefully structured form of Luke's narrative. After the preface (1:1–4) come two dramatic announcements by the angel Gabriel: first to Zechariah the birth of John the Baptist (1:5–25), and then to Mary the birth of Jesus (1:26–38). Mary's visit to her relative Elizabeth provides the occasion for her hymn of praise (1:46–55; commonly known as the Magnificat, the first word of the hymn in Latin), which has its counterpart in Zechariah's equally lyrical prophecy spoken after the birth of John (1:67–79; commonly called the Benedictus, the Latin word for "blessed," the first word of the prophecy). In each case the main characters, Mary and Zechariah, interpret the significance of their respective announcements from Gabriel. Like the double announcements, the births of John and Jesus exhibit a parallel structure (1:57–66; 2:1–20). As expected, Jesus' birth is told in greater detail. By recounting Jesus' circumcision and presentation in the temple, Luke lets two other interpreters—Simeon and Anna—make sense of these events (2:21–38). By reporting Jesus' instructing his teachers in the temple—"my Father's house"—Luke further underscores his status as God's Son.

While Luke and Matthew agree on some details, including Jesus' birth to the Virgin Mary in Bethlehem, the city of David, they also differ in some notable respects. In Luke's birth story, we find no genealogy (Luke locates it between Jesus' baptism and temptation in 3:23–28), no visit of the wise men, no slaughter of the infants, and no escape to Egypt. In Matthew the angel appears to Joseph, in Luke to Mary. This difference in focus—Matthew on Joseph, Luke on Mary—characterizes the respective accounts.

LUKE'S INTERPRETATION OF MARK

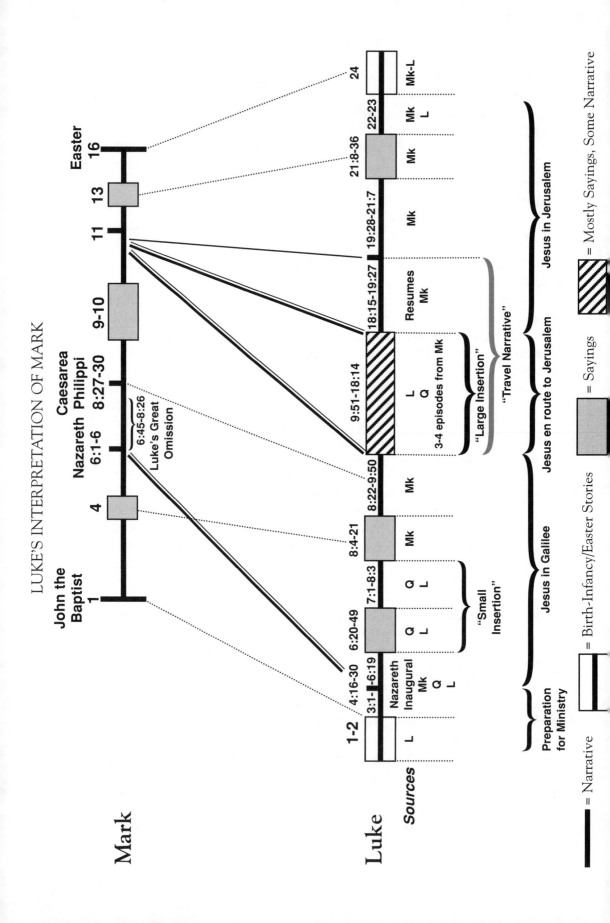

The overall mood of each account is also quite different. Matthew is ominous and foreboding: a murderous king threatened by the birth of a child, conniving and conspiring to protect his throne; terrified young parents fleeing the country, waiting until the coast is clear enough to return to the land of Israel and eventually make their home in (not return to) Nazareth. Luke's narrative, by contrast, is buoyant, filled with songs and prayers of rejoicing—no slain infants, no terrifying kings, no plots, and no fugitives. An air of high expectation pervades Luke's story as all the participants interpret two separate but closely related births quite positively. They all see a bright future, although one fraught with controversy and conflict.

Virtually everything found in Luke 1–2 is drawn from L, which suggests that Luke (like Matthew) was working with a distinctive set of traditions relating to Jesus' birth, infancy, and childhood. Regardless of the source of Luke's account, these first two chapters should be read as an integral part of his overall portrait of Jesus.

The Galilean Ministry (3:1–9:50)

In this section, Luke tends to follow the Markan storyline, with some notable exceptions. [**See Expanded CD Version pp. 228–29:** ***The Galilean Ministry: Luke and Mark Compared***]

The Travel Narrative: Jesus' Journey from Galilee to Jerusalem (9:51–19:27)

Luke generally follows the first half of Mark's storyline, taking the story through the transfiguration (Luke 9:28–36; Mark 9:2–8), Jesus' second passion prediction (Luke 9:43b–45; Mark 9:30–32), and some of the teachings that follow (Luke 9:46–50; Mark 9:33–41). Whereas Mark then proceeds to report Jesus' teachings to his disciples, the third passion prediction, and the healing of Bartimaeus in 9:42–10:52, Luke takes the story in a different direction. At this point begins Luke's Travel Narrative, an extended section that takes up roughly one-third of the entire Gospel (9:51–19:27). Mark notes Jesus' movement from Galilee to Judea, but *it takes only one verse to get him there* (cf. Mark 9:33; 10:1). In a highly oversimplified sense, we might think of Luke snipping Mark's story between 9:50 and 10:1 and inserting his nine-chapter Travel Narrative, which arrives at the same point Mark reaches by the end of chapter 10: the final passion prediction (Luke 18:31–34; Mark 10:32–34) and healing the blind beggar at Jericho (Luke 18:35–43; Mark 10:46–52).

Luke dramatizes this shift in the storyline with the opening line, "When the days drew near for him to be taken up, he set his face to go to Jerusalem" (9:51). Even though it is a long, meandering journey in which Jesus winds his way from Galilee through Samaria and finally to Judea, Luke repeatedly reminds the reader that Jesus' ultimate destination is Jerusalem (9:53; 13:33–34; 17:11; 18:31; 19:11). Finally, Luke marks the end of the section by reporting Jesus' arrival in Jerusalem (19:28).

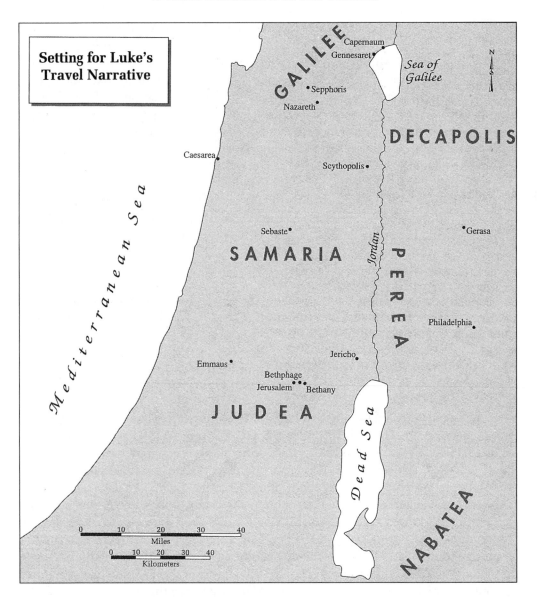

Like Matthew's five discourses, Luke's Travel Narrative showcases Jesus' teachings, often employing the same material:

- the Lord's prayer (Luke 11:1–4; Matt 6:9–13);
- teachings about prayer (Luke 11:9–13; Matt 7:7–11);
- teachings about light (Luke 11:33–36; Matt 5:15; 6:22–23);
- woes to the Pharisees (Luke 11:37–12:1; Matt 23);
- mission teachings (Luke 12:2–12; Matt 10:26–33);
- teachings about anxiety (Luke 12:22–34; Matt 6:25–33);
- being watchful (Luke 12:35–46; Matt 24:43–51);
- causing division (Luke 12:49–56; Matt 10:34–36);
- settling with one's accuser (Luke 12:57–59; Matt 5:25–26);

- parables of the mustard seed and yeast (Luke 13:18–21; Matt 13:31–33);
- the narrow door (Luke 13:22–30; Matt 7:13–14);
- the lament over Jerusalem (Luke 13:34–35; Matt 23:37–39);
- the cost of discipleship (Luke 14:25–26; Matt 10:37–38);
- the parable of the lost sheep (Luke 15:1–7; Matt 18:12–14);
- the permanence of the law (Luke 16:17; Matt 5:18);
- teaching about divorce (Luke 16:18; Matt 5:32);
- occasions for stumbling (Luke 17:1–2; Matt 18:6–7);
- teaching about forgiveness (Luke 17:3–4; Matt 18:15); and
- the day of the Son of Man (Luke 17:22–37; Matt 24:26–28).

The above list indicates the extent to which Luke has drawn from Q in composing the Travel Narrative. But he has also included considerable material from L, most of it teaching. In the Travel Narrative are ten parables found only in Luke:

- the good Samaritan (10:29–37);
- the friend at midnight (11:5–8);
- the rich fool (12:13–21);
- the fig tree (13:6–9);
- the lost coin (15:8–10);
- the prodigal son (15:11–32);
- the dishonest manager (16:1–9);
- the rich man and Lazarus (16:19–31);
- the widow and the unjust judge (18:1–8); and
- the Pharisee and the publican (18:9–14).

Luke also reports three healing miracles from L: the crippled woman (13:10–17); the man with dropsy (14:1–6); and the ten lepers (17:12–19). Only rarely does Luke include in the Travel Narrative material drawn from Mark (see Luke 10:25–28 and Mark 12:28–31; Luke 11:14–23 and Mark 3:22–27; Luke 13:18–19 and Mark 4:30–32).

Especially worth noting is the occurrence of Jesus' passion prediction toward the end of the Travel Narrative (18:31–34). This prediction probably occurs in Judea since Luke reports it just before Jesus reaches Jericho (18:35). As compared with Mark, where the three passion predictions are closely compressed in the narrative (8:31; 9:31; 10:32–34; the first two occur in Galilee and the third in Judea), Luke's inclusion of the Travel Narrative creates considerable distance between the first two predictions (9:21–22, 43–45) and the final prediction (18:31–33). This may explain why Luke supplies an additional passion prediction toward the end of the Travel Narrative (17:25).

The Jerusalem Section (19:28–24:53)

In the final section of Luke's Gospel—Jesus' last days in Jerusalem—Luke resumes the Markan storyline. Luke generally follows Mark's sequence of events from the time Jesus enters Jerusalem, although he feels quite free to omit episodes that had great symbolic significance for Mark (the cursing of the fig tree); to relocate episodes to other parts of his narrative (the anointing at Bethany); and to rearrange Mark's order (Jesus' prediction of Peter's denial at the Last Supper and the events of Jesus' trial). Along with these editorial changes of Mark, Luke also freely supplements the Markan account with L material (Jesus' prediction of Jerusalem's destruction, Jesus' appearance before

Herod, and the procession of wailing women). There is little evidence of Luke's use of Q in the last third of his Gospel (see Luke 22:28–30 and Matt 19:28). [See Expanded CD Version pp. 232–33: *Jesus in Jerusalem: How Luke Modifies Mark's Narrative*]

Comparable to what we find elsewhere, Luke displays considerable independence from Mark in reporting Jesus' final days in Jerusalem.

Among many other changes, Luke's account of "Gethsemane" is much shorter than that of Mark and Matthew (Luke 22:40–46; cf. Mark 14:32–42; Matt 26:36–46). It does not name any disciples (Matthew and Mark single out Peter for criticism), and Luke is more generous towards the disciples, who fell asleep "because of grief" (Luke 22:45). In the betrayal episode (Luke 22:47–53), only Luke reports that Jesus healed the amputated ear of the high priest's slave (Luke 22:51).

Luke offers a considerably revised account of Jesus' trial. According to Mark, Jesus' trial before the Sanhedrin took place the evening he was betrayed (Mark 14:53–65). Mark also places Peter's denial in that same evening and uses the cock's crowing to mark the beginning of morning (Mark 14:68, 72). Once morning comes, a second session of the council occurs (Mark 15:1), which results in Jesus' being handed over to Pilate (Mark 15:2–5). Perhaps recognizing the oddity, or even illegality, of an evening session before the Sanhedrin, Luke reverses Mark's order. After the betrayal by Judas on the Mount of Olives, Jesus is brought the same night to the high priest's house but not before the Sanhedrin (Luke 22:54). Since it was night, it was appropriate for Luke to report Peter's denial next, and for the crowing cock to mark the beginning of day (Luke 22:54b–62). But, according to Luke, only "when day came" (Luke 22:66) did the Sanhedrin meet, and they met for only one session. The exchanges between Jesus and the high priest, found in Mark's account of the Sanhedrin's evening meeting, Luke reports in this morning session (Luke 22:67–71). As in Mark, the Sanhedrin session results in Jesus' being handed over to Pilate (Luke 23:1).

Luke's account of the trial before Pilate reproduces the core of Mark's account but amplifies it considerably. Among other things, Luke's version provides an occasion for Pilate to declare Jesus' innocence (Luke 23:4). The following session, in which Jesus appears before Herod, is unique to Luke (Luke 23:6–16) and, once again, Luke emphasizes Jesus' innocence (Luke 23:13–15). Luke gives an abbreviated account of Pilate's release of Barabbas (Luke 23:17–25) and omits entirely Mark's account of the soldiers' mocking of Jesus (Mark 15:16–20). And yet Luke's description of Jesus' journey to the cross is fuller than Mark's (cf. Luke 23:25–32 and Mark 15:21): The funeral procession of wailing women underscores the tragedy of an innocent death.

Luke's free interpretation also continues in his account of the crucifixion and death of Jesus. As in Mark and Matthew, Jesus is crucified between two criminals (Luke 23:32), but the words from Jesus' mouth are words of forgiveness (Luke 23:34, a disputed text; cf. NRSV notes) and salvation (Luke 23:43). In Luke's death scene, Jesus speaks confidently to the Father (Luke 23:46; cf. Ps 31:5) rather than uttering the familiar words of protest and lament, "My God, my God, why have you forsaken me?" (cf. Mark 15:34–37; Matt 27:46–50; cf. Ps 22:1). As before, Luke continues to emphasize Jesus' innocence (Luke 23:41, 47). In reporting Jesus' burial and the events of Easter morning, Luke follows Mark, yet continues to chart his own course. The remaining events that Luke reports on Easter morning are all unique to his Gospel.

The Things That Have Been Fulfilled Among Us: Luke's Use of Scripture

Besides earlier traditions about Jesus, Luke also makes extensive use of the Jewish Scriptures in constructing his account. As was the case with Matthew, the Jesus traditions Luke received from Mark already reflect the conviction that Jesus "fulfilled Scripture." All three synoptic evangelists agree that Jesus met the expectations Scripture created in the minds of readers who were looking for the Messiah. Like Mark and Matthew, Luke takes the "one crying in the wilderness" mentioned in Isa 40:3 to refer to John the Baptist (Luke 3:4; cf. Mark 1:3; Matt 3:3). Like Matthew, Luke omits the first part of the OT quotation in Mark that comes from Mal 3:1, thereby making the attribution of the quotation to Isaiah technically correct. Unlike Mark and Matthew, however, Luke extends the quotation from Isa 40 to include verses 4–5, whose geographical reordering symbolizes the social reordering that will occur when God's salvation becomes truly universal (Luke 3:5–6). Here we can imagine Luke with two texts in front of him: Mark's Gospel, with its use of the OT, and his own copy of Scripture, which he reads independently of Mark. This is typical of what we find throughout Luke-Acts: two conversations occurring at the same time, one with the Jesus tradition, the other with Scripture. Both conversations interact with each other, yet each occurs in its own right. Recognizing this dual conversation gives us some insight into how Luke does theology.

It is easy enough to identify Mark's uses of the OT taken over by Luke more or less unchanged. A clear example is the interpretation of Ps 110:1 in Mark 12:35–37, in which Jesus argues that when God speaks to "my Lord," the addressee must be someone other than David. Both Matthew and Luke retain this story virtually unchanged at the same point in the Passion Narrative (Matt 22:41–46; Luke 20:41–44). Luke and Matthew also adopt Mark's use of Isa 6:9–10 to explain why people fail to understand Jesus' parabolic teaching, although Matthew gives a fuller version of the OT passage than either Mark or Luke (Mark 4:12; Luke 8:10; Matt 13:13–15).

Whereas Matthew advances beyond Mark's use of the OT by supplying a rich assortment of formula quotations, Luke goes in another direction. Like Matthew, Luke is eager to correlate OT passages with aspects of Jesus' life and teachings. Luke's reading of Scripture, however, does not appear to be as mechanical as Matthew's method of Scripture interpretation, which is often a form of one-to-one correspondence that identifies an event in Jesus' life, such as his ministry in Galilee, as the fulfillment of an OT quotation (see Matt 4:12–17). Some of this occurs in Luke-Acts, for example, when Peter says in the Pentecost sermon, "This is what was spoken through the prophet Joel" (Acts 2:16). Pentecost is thus understood as the set of events envisioned in the prophecy of Joel 2:28–32.

On the whole, Luke reads Scripture more subtly than Matthew. In the birth stories, for example, he adopts a biblical writing style that reminds his reader(s) of the earlier biblical story and prompts them to read the story of Jesus as a continuation of that story. Luke narrates the birth of John the Baptist and Jesus using language that recalls the OT accounts of the births of Isaac, Samson, and Samuel. He does so,

A woodcut depicting the evangelist Luke receiving inspiration from the Madonna and child, with his attribute, the ox (Rev 4:7); taken from a 1541 printing of Martin Luther's German translation of the New Testament. From the Digital Image Archive of The Richard C. Kessler Reformation Collection, Pitts Theology Library, Candler School of Theology, Emory University, Atlanta, Georgia.

however, without ever mentioning these characters by name or citing texts from Genesis, Judges, or 1 Samuel. To an ear attuned to Scripture, Mary's Magnificat would recall Hannah's song at Samuel's birth (1 Sam 2:1–10), just as Zechariah's prophecy would resonate with prayers in the Psalter blessing God (Pss 41:13; 72:18; 106:48). A similar echo effect occurs in Luke's use of prophetic imagery to depict Jesus. In the Nazareth inaugural, Jesus introduces Elijah and Elisha as prophetic figures with whom he identifies (Luke 4:16–30). Luke reinforces the prophetic role of Jesus by recounting a pair of miracle stories with strong OT echoes. Jesus' healing of the centurion's servant recalls Elisha's healing of Naaman, the Syrian commander who had leprosy (Luke 7:1–10; 2 Kgs 5:1–14). His raising of the widow's son at Nain recalls Elijah's raising of the widow's son at Zarephath (Luke 7:11–17; 1 Kgs 17:17–24). Neither story mentions Elisha or Elijah specifically. Luke is creating his own biblical story not by the use of fulfillment quotations, as Matthew does, but by subtly crafting a narrative that presents Jesus as the fulfillment of Israel's hopes. **[See Expanded CD Version p. 236:** *Jesus as an Interpreter of Scripture and the Use of the OT in Acts*]

Luke's Context

As with the other Synoptic Gospels, it is difficult to determine the specific context within which Luke was written. This has not kept interpreters from suggesting plausible settings for Luke. Quite early, Luke was seen as the evangelist who wrote for Gentiles. He was identified as "Luke the physician," who actively participated in Paul's mission to the Gentiles (cf. Col 4:14; Phlm 24). This perception developed not only because of Luke's explicit interest in Gentiles (1:79; 2:32; 3:6; 24:47), but also because of his tendency to avoid Semitic expressions. In Luke's account of Jesus' entry into Jerusalem (19:36–40), for example, he omits the occurrences of "Hosanna" found in Mark 11:9–10, both of which are retained by Matthew (21:9). Where Mark feels compelled to explain Jewish words or customs that might be unfamiliar to non-Jewish readers, Luke simply omits them. Mark's "Abba, Father" becomes "Father" in Luke (Mark 14:36; Luke 22:42). The name Golgotha, which Matthew and Mark explain as meaning "the place of a skull" (Mark 15:22; Matt 27:33), is omitted by Luke, who simply reports that Jesus was crucified at "the place that is called The Skull" (Luke 23:33).

We find some rather confident assertions in early Christian writings about Luke's context, for example, in the early prologue to the Gospel mentioned previously, which says that "Luke was a Syrian of Antioch." This extrabiblical text, whose date and provenance are disputed, also reports that whereas Matthew was composed in Judea and Mark in Italy, Luke "under inspiration of the Holy Spirit wrote this Gospel in the regions of Achaia" for Greek believers.[1] Some other early traditions suggest that Luke's Gospel was composed in Rome or Bithynia.

In spite of the relative antiquity of these proposals, they are guesses. Luke-Acts provides no clear indicators of the geographical location from which Luke wrote. As to the time of composition, we are on slightly firmer ground. Luke's preface places the work at least a generation or two from the time of Jesus, but how much later is hard to say. Luke's use of Mark would imply an interval of several decades between the death of Jesus and the time of composition. Probably the best clue for dating Luke's Gospel is the reference in 21:20 to "Jerusalem surrounded by armies." Since this language is reminiscent of earlier biblical descriptions of assaults made on Jerusalem by foreign armies (see 2 Kgs 8:12; Isa 29:3; Jer 6:6–8), it does not necessarily reflect knowledge of Vespasian's siege of Jerusalem in 68 C.E. and its fall under Titus in 70, but such knowledge on Luke's part is highly probable. When Luke speaks of these events as "days of vengeance" (Luke 21:22), it sounds as though he is interpreting the destruction of Jerusalem within a larger timetable for determining when the Son of Man would come (Luke 21:25–33). Luke's presumed knowledge of the destruction of Jerusalem in 70 suggests that Luke-Acts was written in the last quarter of the first century C.E.

Luke's Questions

One way of identifying Luke's context is by trying to determine his purpose in writing. This may be done by identifying his audience. As we have seen, the view that Luke wrote for Gentiles surfaced quite early and became widely accepted. But is this so clear? Luke-Acts is, after all, heavily steeped in the language of Scripture, and many of Luke's midrashic interpretations are quite complicated. They would be difficult for non-Jews to follow unless they had a fairly close acquaintance with the OT.

Based on Luke's remarks in the preface, we might think of a catechetical setting in which efforts are made to instruct new converts. But, unlike Matthew, Luke's Gospel does not show the same concerns for pedagogy that would suggest a "school of St. Luke" comparable to what some scholars have seen as the context out of which Matthew arose. Because of its interest in the Gentile mission, seen, for example, in Jesus' sending of the seventy (Luke 10), the risen Lord's remarks in 24:44–49, and the missionary thrust of Acts, some have proposed a missionary purpose for the work, suggesting that it was written to convince people of the truth of Christianity and bring them to faith. While Luke-Acts has been useful in missionary settings, Luke's remarks in the preface suggest edification more than evangelism. Still other contexts have been suggested: a legal setting, in which some account of the origins and development of Christianity was required to show Roman authorities that it was politically innocuous, if not socially beneficial; or a polemical setting, in which the church was defining itself against the synagogue and needed to establish continuity with earlier Jewish history either to defend itself against the charge of novelty or to promote its legitimacy as a religious movement having ancient origins.

Rather than thinking about Luke's purpose in the usual ways, however, we can put the question a little differently. We can ask what theological questions drive Luke's investigation; or how his narrative reveals what problems he is trying to make sense of theologically. Or, to put it in terms of the Lukan preface, we can ask about what Theophilus or someone like him would need reassurance.

When Will the Son of Man Come?

According to one widely held view, the major theological question addressed by Luke is the delay of the Parousia. In the early decades of the Christian movement,

Jesus' promise to return within the lifetime of first-generation believers seemed realistic. But as the generation of eyewitnesses began to die and a new generation arose, some Christians began to believe that Jesus would not return soon. This required them to adjust their timetable for calculating when the end of time and the "coming of the Son of Man" would occur. This meant postponing the expected date of the Parousia and finding a way to make sense of the unexpected interval within which Christians were living.

To meet this challenge, Luke rethought the Jesus tradition and devised a new way of thinking about the periods through which the story of salvation had moved. The first period was the time of Israel, the time of the "law and the prophets," which ran through the time of John the Baptist, who was seen as the last in a long line of OT prophets. After John's death, stage two began: the time of Jesus, which included his ministry, death, and resurrection. This was then followed by the third period, the time of the church, which began after Easter with the events of Pentecost and was to continue into the indefinite future. This historical scheme of three periods of salvation history enabled Christians to locate themselves within God's larger purpose. They looked back on the time of Jesus as *past history* and positioned themselves within the period of the church in which their ongoing history was unfolding. By constructing a story of the church that explained how the early Christian mission moved beyond Israel to include the Gentiles, Luke pointed the way to an open-ended future.

According to this reconstruction, Luke's main contribution was to create a three-period scheme of salvation history as a framework within which Christians could both understand and proclaim their story. By softening the eschatological urgency of Jesus' message and the early church's preaching, Luke enabled third-generation Christians to explain why Jesus had not yet returned. He had not done so, they could argue, because in his earlier preaching he had not promised to return quickly.

Why is this a plausible reading of Luke's theological purpose? It mainly derives from a comparative reading of Mark and Luke. One of the most telling differences occurs at the opening of Jesus' apocalyptic discourse in the temple (Mark 13; Luke 21; Matt 24). Predicting that "Not one stone will be left here upon another," Jesus prompts his disciples to ask when this would occur (Mark 13:4). He replies, "Beware that no one leads you astray. Many will come in my name and say, 'I am he!' and they will lead many astray. When you hear of wars and rumors of wars, do not be alarmed; this must take place, but the end is still to come" (Mark 13:5–7; similarly Matt 24:4–6).

Luke's version of Jesus' apocalyptic discourse begins with the same interchange between Jesus and his disciples in the temple, but Jesus' response to the disciples' question has some important differences (italicized in the following quotation): "Beware that you are not led astray; for many will come in my name and say, 'I am he!' and, *'The time is near!'* Do not go after them. When you hear of wars and insurrections, do not be terrified; for these things must take place *first, but the end will not follow immediately*" (Luke 21:8–9). Grouping people who say it is the eleventh hour with false messiahs, Luke's Jesus envisions an interval of time before the end during which certain things must occur first. This is a stalling device found in other NT writings that try to keep fanatics at bay: "The end is not as near as you think," the response runs, "several events must happen first before the end comes" (see 2 Thess 2:3).

Another telling difference occurs in Jesus' trial before the Sanhedrin. In Mark's account, when asked by the high priest if he is "the Messiah, the Son of the Blessed One," Jesus replies, "I am." Then drawing on imagery from Dan 7:13 and Ps 110:1, he predicts that "'you will see the Son of Man seated at the right hand of the Power,' and '*coming with the clouds of heaven*'" (Mark 14:61–62; similarly Matt 26:64). In Luke, Jesus responds to the high priest's question less directly: "If I tell you, you will not believe; and if I question you, you will not answer." Dropping the cloud imagery from Dan 7:13, Jesus then says, "But from now on the Son of Man will be seated at the right hand of the power of God" (Luke 22:67–69). Mark envisions a *future coming* of the Son of Man, whereas Luke speaks only of his *future enthronement*. **[See Expanded CD Version pp. 239–41:** *Other Passages Relating to Lukan Eschatology*]

Luke shares with Mark and Matthew a view of the future shaped by Jesus' messianic destiny. Luke can scarcely think about the future, whether near or distant, apart from the Son of Man. Even though Luke draws heavily on Mark's understanding of the future, he does not adopt it unchanged (cf. Luke 23:26–32). He makes adjustments to Mark, and some of these changes have a postponing effect. Luke is aware of people who are overly excited about the end and keen to circle an early date on the calendar. He squarely confronts the question "When?" He answers, "Not yet," since he insists that certain things must first occur. But neither does he answer, "Never," nor even, "Not for a very long time." Luke may place the coming of the Son of Man at a more distant point in the future, but it is not completely out of sight. He repeatedly reports Jesus' warnings of judgment coupled with calls for repentance and vigilance (9:26–27; 10:13–16; 12:8–10; 17:20–37). He even warns that the Son of Man will come at an unexpected hour (12:35–40; also cf. 12:45–46). He also includes other possible references to the nearness of the end (10:9, 11; 11:30; 18:8; 21:32). Luke provides enough hints that his generation would live to see the Son of Man's coming to keep his readers from slipping into comfortable hibernation.

Why Must God's Messiah Suffer?

Theophilus may have needed reassurance about the time of Christ's coming, but this was not the only pressing theological question for Luke. If we examine some of the questions raised about Jesus by characters in Luke's narrative, we find that certain christological questions were also driving Luke's theological project.

If we compare Luke's treatment of Jesus with that of Mark, we see them posing two different questions. For Mark, the overarching question is, "Who is Jesus?" Jesus' true identity is the abiding mystery in Mark. Luke is puzzled by a different question: Why must the Messiah suffer? The Messiah is destined "to be raised and enter glory," but why must the road to exaltation and glory lead through suffering and death? This is the abiding mystery in Luke. Finding a convincing answer to this question is one of Luke's major preoccupations.

Luke's answer can be simply put: *Scripture requires it.* Jesus, God's Messiah, must experience betrayal, suffering, and death en route to resurrection, exaltation, and glory because this is the destiny laid out for him in Scripture. We should note the logic of Luke's argument: not "Jesus suffers and dies *although* he is God's Messiah," but "Jesus suffers and dies *because* he is God's Messiah." As Luke sees it, Jesus' suffering and death are necessary aspects of his messiahship.

Already in Mark's version of Jesus' three passion predictions, we find this emphasis on the necessity of his suffering and death (8:31; 9:31; 10:33–34). Equally clear from Mark is the disciples' difficulty comprehending the connection between messiahship and suffering. When Jesus insists on the necessity of messianic suffering, Peter violently objects and the disciples scratch their heads. In Luke's version of the passion predictions (9:21–22, 43–45; 18:31–34; he adds a fourth in 17:25), he also reports the disciples' puzzlement.

Unlike Mark and Matthew, however, Luke explains that Jesus' passion is necessary because it meets Scripture's expectations: "We are going up to Jerusalem, and everything that is written about the Son of Man by the prophets will be accomplished" (Luke 18:31). We find a similar emphasis in Luke's Easter narrative when the risen Lord chides the two Emmaus travelers for being "slow of heart to believe all that the prophets have declared!" (24:25). Luke then expresses his own view through the lips of the risen Lord: It was "necessary that the Messiah should suffer these things and *then* enter into his glory." Using "Moses and all the prophets," Jesus then explains how his fate in Jerusalem had been anticipated "in all the scriptures." Later, he expands this explanation to include all the disciples. Once again the risen Lord insists that his suffering and death were divine necessities—Scripture had to be fulfilled. The events to follow in Acts—the universal proclamation of repentance and forgiveness—are also required by Scripture (24:44–49).

That Luke thinks Jesus' suffering, death, and resurrection, as well as the events they trigger—the beginning and expansion of the church—were already anticipated in Scripture is clear. Not so clear, however, is where the Jewish Scriptures speak of these things. Where, for example, does Scripture say that God's Messiah must suffer and die, much less be raised from the dead? Luke is irritatingly silent on this question, especially in the Gospel. When Jesus insists that his trip to Jerusalem was being made in order to accomplish "everything that is written about the Son of Man by the prophets" (18:31), Luke gives no scriptural support. Nor, for that matter, does the risen Lord give chapter and verse. Instead, his view is much broader: the entire Jewish canon—"the law of Moses, the prophets, and the psalms"—testifies to the necessity of the Messiah's suffering (24:44).

Nowhere does the OT speak of a suffering *Messiah*, nor do any Jewish writings that Luke could have known. How are we to understand Luke's claim? The answer lies in his use of two biblical images for interpreting Jesus: Isaiah's Suffering Servant and God's rejected prophet.

Suffering Servant. The Suffering Servant in Isa 40–66 should not be understood as a suffering *Messiah*, although later Jewish interpreters applied the title "Messiah" to the Isaianic Servant. Even so, at a very early stage the language of Isaiah's Servant Songs was applied to Jesus, for example, by the heavenly voice at Jesus' baptism (Mark 1:11). Luke repeats this usage (Luke 3:22) but further enhances the image of Jesus as God's Servant. This occurs most dramatically when Luke, in a passage unique to his Gospel, reports Jesus' actually quoting from the fourth Servant Song, "And he was counted among the lawless" (Isa 53:12), and claiming its fulfillment "in me" (Luke 22:37). A fuller explanation of how Jesus can be understood as the Servant of Isa 53 is given in Acts 8, in which this text plays a central role in the conversion of the Ethiopian eunuch. To these explicit appropriations of Isa 53 by Luke should also be added his use of Isa 61 in the Nazareth inaugural, another text whose fulfillment Jesus claims "today" (Luke 4:21). Other echoes of God's promise to restore Israel through Jesus are heard elsewhere in Luke, and they are framed in language drawn from Isa 40–66 (Luke 2:25, 29–32; 3:4–6).

From Luke's use of these Isaiah texts emerges the image of Jesus, God's Messiah, the one anointed with God's Spirit who is also to be identified as God's righteous Servant. In him lie the hopes of both Jews and Gentiles, for he is destined to bring God's salvation to universal expression. He will do so, however, at the cost of his own life.

Prophet. Closely related is the image of Jesus the prophet, which especially comes to the fore in the Nazareth inaugural when Jesus aligns himself with Elijah and Elisha. As Luke's narrative unfolds from chapter 4 forward, he accents Jesus' prophetic role, moving it well beyond what we find in Mark. We will treat the prophetic image of Jesus more fully in a later section dealing with Luke's Christology. Here we simply note how it relates to Luke's distinctive notion of the suffering Messiah.

The Lukan Jesus is not merely God's prophet, but *God's rejected prophet*, a point reinforced by interpreting Jesus as the new Moses (Acts 3:22–23; 7:37–53). As God's chosen messenger, Jesus experiences rejection within Israel and ultimately death at the hands of Israel's leaders. These experiences Luke understands as sufferings the Messiah must endure. To the question of why Jesus, as God's Messiah, must suffer and be rejected, Luke replies: That was the fate of Jesus' prophetic predecessors, and now he re-enacts that fate once again. Anyone who had read the Scriptures carefully and in their entirety, Luke insists, should have seen that suffering would be the inevitable fate of God's messianic prophet. What becomes dramatically visible in Luke's Gospel is further amplified in Acts as Peter, Philip, Stephen, and Paul reiterate this claim in their speeches.

Another way of posing Luke's question is to ask, "Why did Jesus die?" It is well known that Luke omitted Mark's answer, "For the Son of Man came not to be served but to serve, and to give his life a ransom for many" (Mark 10:45; cf. Luke 22:24–27). Some scholars regard this omission as evidence of Luke's failure to reflect deeply on the significance of Jesus' death. They readily acknowledge Jesus' conversation with his disciples at the Last Supper, in which he said that his body "is given for you" and his blood is "poured out for you" (Luke 22:19–20). They also concede that Luke encapsulates his view of Jesus' mission through the words addressed to Zacchaeus, "The Son of Man came to seek out and to save the lost" (Luke 19:10). But since Luke nowhere employs a metaphor equivalent to "ransom" to explain why Jesus died, some scholars think his understanding of Jesus' death is theologically anemic.

Compared with Paul's extensive theological reflection on the death of Jesus and the numerous metaphors he employs to express its salvific effects, Luke's sparse comments about the purpose of Jesus' death are meager indeed. But does Luke supply a poor answer to Paul's (and Mark's) question? Perhaps he is posing a different question or answering their question in a different way. After all, Jesus' death can be explained from one of two viewpoints: God's or ours. To explain it primarily in terms of how it benefits others is one possibility, and various theories of atonement follow that path. But Luke seeks an explanation from God's side. To explain Jesus' death as a divine necessity, as something Scripture requires of God's Messiah, is no less daunting a task. In all fairness, neither Mark nor Paul addresses the theological problem of a suffering Messiah in precisely the way Luke does. This is a distinctively Lukan notion. The cross stands at the center of Paul's Christology and he rightly sees the scandal of Jesus' suffering and death (Gal 3:13–14), but he does not pose the problem the way Luke does: suffering and death as necessary functions of Jesus' messianic identity.

By recognizing how fundamental these christological questions are to Luke, we are in a better position to appreciate the role Scripture interpretation plays in his overall narrative. His elaborate system of biblical interpretation, which is based on a scheme of promise fulfillment, is largely driven by pressure to explain why the Messiah had to suffer and die.

Who Are God's People?

A third question also drives Luke's investigation: How does God deliver on the promise originally made to Abraham that "all nations would be blessed through him"? Naturally this question is related to questions about Jesus' role as God's Messiah, but it extends further. The overarching question is how Gentiles eventually emerge as the heirs to God's promise. Already in Luke's Gospel the groundwork is laid for answering this question, but especially in Acts we see Luke narrating how a new people of God is formed in response to the proclamation of the gospel about Jesus. In one sense, it is the story of how God's promise extends from Jerusalem to Rome, but this does not necessarily mean that it is the story of how Gentiles replace Jews as the people of God. Luke carefully shows how the gospel is preached first to Jews, then to Gentiles, but he also portrays people from each group accepting and rejecting the gospel. Even so, by the end of Acts Luke clearly envisions that the church will experience its most promising outreach through the Gentile mission.

Much of Luke's interpretive effort goes into constructing a plausible understanding of the story of God's dealings with Israel from its earliest stages, beginning with Abraham, Isaac, Jacob, and Joseph and continuing through the time of Moses, Israel's conquest of Canaan, and the period of the monarchy. How Luke understands the main links in this story is revealed in his rehearsal of the biblical story in Stephen's speech in Acts 7 and its continuation in Paul's speech in Acts 13. One of Luke's main theological contributions is to pick up the thread of Israel's story at the point where it ends in the Jewish Scriptures and carry it forward to the time of John the Baptist and Jesus. Luke was not the first to see the story of John and Jesus as the continuation of the OT story, but he was the first to develop the connection on such a grand scale. Through elaborate interpretation of the OT, Luke constructs an understanding of the biblical story that sees God's promise to Abraham continued through Israel's history down to the time of David and that sees Jesus as the heir to David's throne (Acts 13:16–25). As the one whom God anointed to continue the Davidic line through which the promise to Abraham would come to fulfillment, Jesus carries God's story forward as the embodiment of the divine promise that salvation would eventually include both Jews and Gentiles (Luke 1:55, 68–79; Acts 28:29).

How Jesus fits into God's larger story and his role in achieving God's original purpose are interconnected concerns for Luke. The thrust of his Gospel is to show how Scripture in its entirety reaches its fulfillment in Jesus. By constructing a plausible retelling of Scripture that reveals a grand narrative extending from Abraham through Christ, Luke lays the groundwork for explaining the church's origin and mission.

Aspects of Luke's Theology

In outlining the questions that drive Luke's project, we have already touched on some of his answers. Now we look at how Luke understands Jesus as God's Messiah and the message he preached. How Luke thinks about Jesus and his preaching is closely connected with other questions as well. How Luke thinks about the end time, for example, cannot easily be separated from how he thinks about Jesus. How he explains the mission to the Gentiles is vitally connected to his understanding of Jesus as the one through whom God's promise to Abraham comes true.

Jesus in Luke: God's Messiah

Luke's Christology exhibits a rich complexity that is difficult to comprehend through individual titles or overarching themes. Yet, as with the other Gospels, we cannot avoid looking at the images and titles used by and of Jesus in the Gospel of Luke. In addition to this, we can look at how Luke's shaping of his story has contributed to his overall portrait of Jesus. **[See Expanded CD Version pp. 245–50: Christological Titles in Luke]**

It is difficult to gather all of the images Luke uses for Jesus into a single, coherent picture. Jesus' preferred self-designation, as in Mark and Matthew, remains "Son of Man," an expression used in at least three ways but always connoting heavenly authority. Luke also uses "Son of God" to designate Jesus' unique relationship to the Father, and his birth story underscores Jesus' divine paternity (1:35). Through his ministry, Jesus is experienced by people as a teacher, and they address him as such, but his disciples see him as more than this. We find them addressing him as "Master," and on several occasions calling him "Lord," the term frequently used in the Septuagint for God. Even if the precise nuance of this form of address is not altogether clear, there can be no doubt about those dozen or so narrative uses in which Luke reveals his post-Easter belief in Jesus as "Lord." He even allows Elizabeth, well in advance of Easter, to confess her faith in Jesus by referring to Mary as "the mother of *my Lord*" (1:43, emphasis added).

That Jesus receives David's royal mantle is abundantly clear in Luke, and his kingly role receives repeated emphasis. He is recognized by the blind beggar as the Son of David and enters Jerusalem hailed as the "king who comes in the name of the Lord" (19:38). Yet Luke is careful to avoid political overtones in his portrayal of Jesus as king in the Passion Narrative, omitting Mark's reference to Jesus' purple cloak and crown of thorns and significantly reducing Mark's numerous references to Jesus as "King of the

Jews." Jesus' messianic status is closely related to Luke's use of Davidic imagery for Jesus, but Luke does not think of Messiah and Son of David as two circles that coincide with each other. The anointing Jesus receives at Nazareth is a prophetic anointing that inaugurates his ministry of preaching and healing.

Luke's repeated use of the unusual expression "the Lord's Messiah" or "the Messiah of God" reflects his conviction that Jesus is God's duly appointed representative. For Luke, Messiah is not Jesus' name but his uniquely designated role. Acting in the role of God's Chosen One, Jesus does several things: He brings God's salvation and redemption and thus acts as Savior; he announces the good news of the kingdom of God, thereby re-establishing the prospect of fulfilling the Abrahamic promise through the Davidic lineage and enacting the prophetic vision of Jubilee when people are healed, liberated, and given hope; he enacts the prophetic vision of preaching and healing, transferring it to ever-expanding circles of disciples; he exercises the Son of Man's lordly authority both in his ministry to people and in his vision of the future, insisting on the greatest paradox of all—that this lordly status entails suffering and death; and he comports himself in a way that prompts people to address, and probably confess, him as "Lord." While others may confess him as "Teacher," his disciples recognize him as something more: as "Master," and probably as "Lord" also.

Which of these images best captures Luke's understanding of Jesus? None of them alone. If one were forced to choose a single image around which Luke organizes the others, the best choice would probably be Messiah, understood broadly as a figure who receives God's anointing for a special task. Luke does not always distinguish sharply between the titles since he sometimes uses them together, often without clear differentiation (Luke 1:31–33, 35; 2:11). He can speak of Jesus as "God's Messiah" in one breath (Luke 9:20) and describe the necessity of the Son of Man's suffering in another (Luke 9:21–22; also 22:67–70). We are on firmer ground if we think of Luke portraying Jesus as God's Messiah who combines several identities and who, through those identities, plays several interrelated roles. He is both messianic prophet and messianic king. In one capacity, he stands in the tradition of Elijah, Elisha, and Moses as the one who proclaims God's good news, pronouncing both blessings and woes; in the other capacity, he is like other "sons of God" in Israel's history, a king who wears the mantle of David, who both embodies and extends God's kingly rule, bringing to fruition the promise originally made to Abraham. Yet central to both roles is his identity as the Son of Man who speaks and acts with God's full authority, who is destined to suffer, die, and be raised, and who will finally execute universal judgment at the end of time. It is only when we see Luke's careful interweaving of these several messianic titles and roles that we can appreciate both the richness and complexity of his portrait of Jesus.

Apart from these titles and images, we should note how openly Luke presents the identity of Jesus. In Luke, we find nothing comparable to Mark's messianic secret. From the start, we hear bold, confessional claims in the birth narrative. The announcements, the prayers and hymns, and the narrative itself all overflow with the language of Christian confession (e.g., 1:32–35, 43; 2:11, 26, 38). Several times Jesus enjoins people to silence (4:41; 5:14; 8:56; 9:21; cf. 9:36), but his messianic identity is not a mystery. The demonic order recognizes and confesses Jesus as Son of God (4:41; 8:28) and Jesus' disciples recognize him as something more than a teacher, as their master and Lord. Perhaps most remarkable of all is Peter's unequivocal confession that Jesus is "the Messiah of God" (9:20). Since Peter does not question Jesus' passion prediction, he receives no censure from Jesus that cancels out his confession.

The Kingdom of God

Luke follows Mark in having Jesus initiate the proclamation of the kingdom of God. Matthew, by contrast, reports that its proclamation already began with John (Matt 3:2). Luke goes beyond Mark in emphasizing John's role as a precursor rather than participant in the kingdom of God. In Luke, John belongs to the age of the law and the prophets, even if he is the last in a long succession of prophets from that period. This is why the most insignificant person in the kingdom of God could be counted greater than John (Luke 7:28). Such a person participates in a new era John never lived to see. Once John was off the scene, the preaching of the kingdom of God began, and it was so successful that people even tried to force their way in (Luke 16:16).

For Luke, the heart of Jesus' message could be put quite simply: the kingdom of God. When he summarizes Jesus' activity as "proclaiming the good news of the kingdom of God," he actually employs the Greek verb *euangelizesthai*, literally "to gospel" or "announce the good news" (Luke 4:43). It may seem redundant to us, but Luke can even report Jesus going through villages "preaching and gospeling [*kērussein kai euangelesthai*] the kingdom of God" (8:1). Typically Jesus' proclamation of the kingdom of God is linked with his healing (9:11). When Jesus sends the Twelve on their mission of preaching and healing, they too are to "proclaim the kingdom of God" (9:2). So too does the kingdom of God constitute the heart of the message of a wider circle of disciples, including the specially commissioned seventy (9:60; 10:9). It also continues in the apostolic proclamation of the early church (Acts 8:12; 14:22; 19:8; 20:25; 28:23, 31).

What does "the kingdom of God" signify in Luke? When Luke summarizes the preaching of Jesus or that of the Twelve, the other disciples, or the seventy as "announcing the good news of the kingdom of God," he does not elaborate further on the content of this preaching because he has already done so in chapters 1–2. In Gabriel's announcement to Mary we are told that Jesus, as "Son of the Most High," would receive from God "the throne of his ancestor David" from which he would "reign over the house of Jacob forever" in a "kingdom" of which there would "be no end" (1:32–33). In the Magnificat (1:46–55), Mary praises God as One who always acts mercifully toward those "who fear him" and who exercises power in the service of mercy, as One who has always sided with the powerless and poor by dashing the hopes of the proud and powerful. In recalling God's promise to "our ancestors, to Abraham and to his descendants forever," she envisions a time when Israel would again experience God's merciful remembrances, when power arrangements would be reconfigured.

The picture is expanded when Zechariah praises God for raising up "a mighty savior for us in the house of his servant David" (1:69). Here again Jesus is God's duly appointed successor to David's throne, the one whom the prophets of old had foreseen, and the one through whom God's "holy covenant" and the "oath that [God] swore to our ancestor Abraham" (1:72–73) would be fulfilled. And what would characterize this new Davidic kingdom over which Jesus would preside as God's Anointed One? It would offer deliverance from oppressors whose intimidating presence suffocates free and unfettered worship of God; the prospect of peace; the opportunity to pursue holiness and righteousness as a way of life and to experience salvation when sins are forgiven; and the hope of liberation from bondage and the sentence of death (1:74–79). These are the promised blessings for which John's preaching would prepare the way (1:76).

Once Jesus is born "in the city of David" and heralded as "Savior, who is the Messiah, the Lord" (2:11), he is recognized by Simeon as the one who would bring about the "consolation of Israel" (2:25) and enable God's salvation to be experienced by "all peoples," both Gentiles and the people of Israel (2:29–32). When Anna recognizes Jesus as the one who would bring about "the redemption of Jerusalem" (2:38), she is also expressing the hope that "the Lord's Messiah" would usher in a new reign in which God's earlier promises could be realized.

As John begins his ministry preparing "the way of the Lord," he sounds the notes of salvation and forgiveness, calls for moral reform as appropriate preparation, and envisions that "all flesh" would experience God's salvation (3:1–20). In his inaugural address at Nazareth, Jesus expands John's vision by declaring "the year of the Lord's favor," a time of Jubilee when debts are forgiven and wrongs are righted. By promising hope to the poor, the sick, and those oppressed and imprisoned, Jesus adopts Zechariah's vision as his own. By emphatically declaring that Isaiah's prophetic vision was being realized then and there, Jesus launches this new era of God's dominion. When Luke describes him as proclaiming "the good news of the kingdom of God" (4:43), there is no need to amplify what this phrase means because Mary, Zechariah, Simeon, Anna, and John the Baptist have already done so.

When Jesus goes about "gospeling the kingdom of God" and instructs the Twelve, his other disciples, and the seventy to do the same, he does so as "the Lord's Messiah" who takes up the mantle of David and who, in so doing, becomes the one through whom God's original promise to Abraham and the renewed promise of a "holy covenant" would be brought to fulfillment. We are invited to envision a time when God's saving power would be experienced universally by Gentiles and Jews alike, when the powerless and oppressed would find a new ally in their plight against powerful oppressors, when those who are poor, sick, hungry, and imprisoned would find an advocate who enriches, heals, feeds, and frees them. And what are the blessings that accompany God's dominion? Redemption, consolation, salvation, forgiveness, mercy, liberation, and healing. Taken singly or together, they are "good news."

Given this set of expectations, we are not surprised when Jesus' opening words in the Sermon on the Plain (6:20–49) sketch a vision of the kingdom of God that dramatically reverses life as it is usually experienced. "The kingdom of God is yours," Jesus tells the poor and, by extension, the hungry, the grieved, and the reviled. Their counterparts in society—those who are rich, filled, happy, and well regarded—are duly warned that everything can come tumbling down quickly. Rather than easing entry into the kingdom, wealth is a real obstacle (18:24–25). Children can teach us a lot about life in the kingdom, about getting in as well as staying in (18:16–17). The "mysteries of the kingdom of God" are best understood by those who "hear the word of God and do it" (8:21). The kingdom of God is a place where God's word and will reign supreme.

Those who have an ear for God constitute Jesus' true family. Being part of God's kingdom is more about obedience than bloodline. Life in the kingdom of God is closely associated with wellness; curing diseases and preaching the good news go hand-in-hand (10:9). Simple things of nature, like the mustard seed and yeast, help us understand the dynamic quality of life in the kingdom where truly phenomenal change can occur (13:18–21). We receive God's kingdom as a gracious gift, as something bestowed at the "Father's good pleasure" (12:32). Our one obsession should be God's kingdom, not food and clothing (12:31). Sacrifice for the kingdom will be amply repaid, both now and later (18:28–30). People who have second thoughts about pursuing life in the kingdom thereby disqualify themselves (9:62). Disciples must learn to pray fervently for God's dominion to be realized (11:2).

Life so radically reconfigured attracted people, and they were prompted to ask when it would occur. They wondered whether the kingdom of God is a present reality or future hope. The short answer is both.

Jesus himself symbolizes God's presence among the people because he is so closely identified with the Father (10:21–22). On several occasions he assures people that the kingdom of God "has come near" (10:9, 11; 11:20). Asked by the Pharisees when the kingdom of God would come, Jesus answers that easily observable signs do not mark its coming. "In fact," he assures them, "the kingdom of God is among you" (17:20–21).

The kingdom also has a future aspect. When Jesus assures his disciples that "there are some standing here who will not taste death before they see the kingdom of God," he envisions the kingdom as arriving in the near future, within the lifetime of his hearers (9:27). Several times Jesus speaks of the future blessings his disciples would experience in the kingdom. Eventually the scattered people of God will gather for the messianic feast in God's kingdom (13:28). A future messianic banquet is envisioned elsewhere (14:15). At the Last Supper when Jesus shares the Passover meal with his disciples, he vows not to eat it (again) "until the kingdom of God comes" (22:16–18). He also promises his faithful disciples the kingdom that he had received from his Father. In the future they would eat the messianic banquet and share in his kingly reign (22:28–30).

Likewise, one of the criminals crucified with Jesus asks to be remembered when "you come into your kingdom" (23:42), and Joseph of Arimathea, who takes care of Jesus' burial, is described as someone "waiting expectantly for the kingdom of God" (23:51). In the context of Jesus' discussion of the temple's destruction, he warns that "the kingdom of God is near." Its coming would be preceded by easily recognized cosmic signs (21:25–33). He tells the parable of the pounds in response to those who "supposed that the kingdom of God was to appear immediately" (19:11).

After the resurrection and prior to Jesus' ascension, we find the risen Lord speaking to the disciples about the kingdom of God (Acts 1:3). The disciples wonder whether he would "restore the kingdom to Israel" (Acts 1:6). Though he does not employ the explicit language of the kingdom of God in his description of Pentecost in

Acts 2, Luke envisions this inaugural event as the time when a new stage of the promise of God breaks in. The coming of the Holy Spirit is seen as the fulfillment of Joel's eschatological promise, and subsequent messengers, such as Philip (8:12) and especially Paul, proclaim the kingdom (Acts 14:22; 19:8; 20:25; 28:23, 31). Even so, as Luke 21:25–33 suggests, the final consummation of the kingdom does not occur until the end time when the Son of Man comes "in a cloud" to execute universal judgment. [See Expanded CD Version p. 255: *The Kingdom of God in Luke*]

Jesus' Vision of Life before God: Blessings and Woes

Even though Luke draws heavily on earlier tradition for his understanding of Jesus' mission, he sketches his own distinctive profile of this mission. We are introduced to it in the Nazareth inaugural (4:16–30) when Jesus, drawing on Isa 61:1–2, directs his ministry toward those who are poor, imprisoned, sick, and oppressed. By citing the examples of Elijah and Elisha, he further signals that, like them, he will have to go to outsiders to get a hearing. Shortly thereafter, in Jesus' first major address—the Sermon on the Plain—we find the profile more fully elaborated.

With the opening set of highly stylized blessings and woes (6:20–26), Jesus offers hope to those who suffer and issues warnings to those who are secure. He sets forth "two ways" that will be sharply contrasted throughout his ministry. Time and again, he will side with those who are poor, hungry, joyless, and ill spoken of, and just as often will he castigate their counterparts: those who are rich, full, happy, and well spoken of. With these "blessings and woes" Luke signals the sharp double edge Jesus' preaching will exhibit as the narrative unfolds. It is a mistake to think of these two edges as soft and hard, as though pronouncing blessings comes easily and issuing warnings does not. Mercy is not a "soft" virtue any more than justice is a "hard" one; properly practiced, both are sharp-edged and require uncommon strength and fortitude.

In the remainder of the Sermon on the Plain, Jesus sounds several notes that will be heard again. Much of this teaching we also find in Matthew's Sermon on the Mount, but Luke's sermon is much tighter and slimmer—a case of less is more. While it is difficult to reduce the sermon to specific themes, one overarching value is *generosity of spirit*. In dealing with our enemies, we are asked to respond in surprising ways—to love, do good, bless, pray, turn the other cheek, let go—all requiring us to reverse primal human instincts. In learning to extend ourselves to our enemies rather than only our friends, we are asked to do good for its own sake, "expecting nothing in return" (Luke 6:35). By practicing uncalculating mercy, we imitate God and earn the right to be God's children. Cultivating a generous spirit makes us slow to condemn others and eager to forgive, once again reversing the ways we ordinarily behave. This enables us to develop an honest sense of ourselves that makes us loath to spot minor flaws in others.

We are also told how to learn this: by attaching ourselves to a teacher worth imitating rather than following blind guides (Luke 6:39–40). We can learn much about moral laws from nature's laws: Just as bad trees do not produce good fruit, evil hearts cannot produce good people. At one level, faithful discipleship can be simply put: hearing the Lord's words and acting on them (6:46–49).

Rather than providing a full table of contents for Jesus' messianic program, Luke's Sermon on the Plain introduces themes that he develops incrementally. As the narrative unfolds, Jesus exemplifies a spirit of generosity by practicing uncalculating mercy. In numerous miracle stories, he enacts the messianic ministry outlined in the Nazareth inaugural by extending mercy to the blind, lame, lepers, deaf, dead, and the poor (7:22–23). He does so with no strings attached. When Jesus' opponents charge that he "welcomes sinners and eats with them" (15:2), they aptly express Luke's view of Jesus as one who embraces "the other." It is an image of Jesus that Luke repeatedly presents. When James and John want lightning to strike unresponsive Samaritans, Jesus rebukes them (9:51–55).

The behavior Jesus exemplifies is also commended in his teaching. Luke gives greater precision to Jesus' teaching about love of God and neighbor by presenting the story of the good Samaritan as a commentary on the meaning of "neighbor" and "showing mercy" (10:25–37). He gives concrete examples of behavior that "expects nothing in return" (6:35). The disciples should issue dinner invitations not to those who can reciprocate, such as friends and rich neighbors, but to those who cannot possibly repay—the poor, crippled, lame, and blind (14:12–14). The story of the rich man and Lazarus is a stinging critique of the inability to extend mercy to beggars at our doorstep (16:19–31). Jesus' denunciation of the Pharisees for neglecting justice and the love of God should probably be read in the same light. In a similar way, he condemns lawyers—Scripture specialists—who refuse to lift a finger to ease other people's burdens (11:46).

Another side of Jesus' messianic preaching in Luke is frequently overlooked. Along with blessings he also speaks woes. It is only by suppressing this harsh side of Jesus' message that the nineteenth century romantic philosopher-historian Ernest Renan was able to describe the Gospel of Luke as "the most beautiful book ever written." Such characterizations of Luke's Gospel, which tend to portray Luke's Jesus as an eminently humane idealist given to good deeds and positive thinking, all too easily tune out the raging Jesus whose voice is heard throughout Luke's Gospel. After the Sermon on the Plain, severe warnings are sounded in the two sets of fourfold woes uttered against the Pharisees (11:42–44) and the lawyers (11:45–52). They are heard elsewhere as well (10:13; 17:1; 21:23; 22:22). We might have expected Jesus' message to have some strident tones, given Simeon's ominous prediction that he would be "destined for the falling and the rising of many in Israel" and "a sign that will be opposed" (Luke 2:34).

Already in the Nazareth inaugural, Jesus' prickly remarks rankle an otherwise friendly audience; their hostile response is not surprising (4:16–30). Nor are we surprised at the barbs he tosses at his ever-present critics, the scribes and Pharisees (e.g., 5:21–23, 30; 12:1). But we may be surprised by the critical tone he adopts toward others. He is quite happy to relegate his cousin John the Baptist to a status lower than "the least in the kingdom of God" (7:28). He is not quite as critical of his own disciples as Mark's Jesus, but he can critique their lack of faith (8:25) and rebuke them for their narrow attitudes (9:49–55). He seems to lose patience with a well-meaning crowd, whom he calls a "faithless and perverse generation" (9:41). He displays similar impatience with unrepentant cities (10:13–15), and he seems less than generous toward innocent victims who provide incentives to repent (13:1–5). He chastises Martha for attending to housekeeping duties (10:38–42) and counters a woman's well-meant benediction with a curt response (11:28).

John sounds an early warning that fiery judgment will be a part of Jesus' ministry (3:16–17), and this theme is picked up by Jesus himself when he says, "I came to bring fire to the earth" (12:49). His role as one who brings division rather than peace continues this theme, although it is not unique to Luke (see Matt 10:34–36). Jesus often speaks the language of judgment. He can be quite emphatic that those who do not make it through the narrow door will weep and gnash their teeth when they are "thrown out" of the kingdom of God only to see themselves replaced by foreigners who participate in the messianic banquet (13:22–30). In the parable of the great dinner, he is equally emphatic that "none of those who were [initially] invited will taste my dinner" (14:24). An even harsher image is used in the parable of the pounds when the king orders his enemies to be brought before him and slaughtered (19:27). Jesus also interprets the destruction of Jerusalem as punishment for its failure to recognize the "time of God's visitation," probably in the arrival of Jesus as God's Messiah (19:41–44).

In keeping with these severe words of prophetic judgment, we find stringent demands made upon the disciples. The competing demands of family and discipleship are put quite harshly when Jesus calls for his disciples to "hate" their family, "and even life itself" (14:26). By comparison, the parallel account in Matt 10:37–38 looks gentle. Insisting that disciples "carry the cross" (14:27) makes it more difficult to spiritualize the "way of the cross." Refusal to "give up all your possessions" disqualifies aspiring disciples (14:33). No wiggle room is envisioned here. We see the same Lukan emphasis when he reports that disciples, when called, "left everything" and followed Jesus (5:11, 28; 18:22–23; cf. 9:57–62).

By sharply distinguishing those whom he blesses from those whom he warns, Jesus provides his disciples with two alternate visions of life before God. To the one group—those who suffer—he offers hope and salvation, and he consistently takes the side of people in this group. To the other group—those who are secure in life—he offers words of warning, and he is unrelenting in his criticism of those in this group. It is within this broader framework that Luke's teachings about riches should be seen. Jesus offers good news to the poor and warnings to the rich, but these two groups are part of a much larger tapestry that depicts two competing visions of life: those who recognize their need for God because they have nothing versus those who do not because they have everything.

Leaving Everything: Discipleship and Wealth in Luke

Luke is not the first to record Jesus' warnings against wealth. Already in Mark's version of the parable of the sower Jesus tells of those who are "choked by the cares and riches and pleasures of life" (Mark 4:19; also Luke 8:14 and Matt 13:22). We also find in Mark the story of Jesus' encounter with the "rich young man" followed by sayings about wealth as an obstacle to entering the kingdom (Mark 10:17–31; also in Luke 18:18–30 and Matt 19:16–30). Firmly embedded in the Passion Narrative is the story of the poor widow whose generosity is contrasted with the rich people making gifts at the temple (Mark 12:41–44; repeated in Luke 21:1–4; omitted by Matthew).

Yet what is a relatively minor theme of the earlier Jesus tradition becomes much more prominent in Luke. This becomes especially clear from the number of sayings and stories about wealth found only in Luke. The first set of antitheses in the Sermon on the Plain, "Blessed are the poor; Woe to the rich" (6:20, 24), defines the Lukan perspective. This antithesis could easily serve as the subtitle for the story of the rich man and Lazarus, in which its truth comes to life in an unforgettable way (16:19–31). We find this theme hammered home elsewhere in Luke's narrative.

It occurs early on when Luke renders John the Baptist's preaching of repentance as a call to abandon greed and embrace generosity and honesty (3:10–14). Later on, Jesus, after warning his disciples, "Be on your guard against all kinds of greed; for one's life does not consist in the abundance of possessions," tells the parable of the rich fool to show how "it is with those who store up treasures for themselves but are not rich toward God" (12:13–21). We are rightly puzzled by the story of the dishonest manager and Jesus' advice "to make friends for yourselves by means of dishonest wealth" (16:9), yet Luke seems to salvage it by suggesting that what we do with a dime says a lot about what we will do with a dollar (16:10–12). From Q he gets his final admonition, "You cannot serve God and wealth" (16:13; cf. Matt 6:24).

To sharpen his critique of the Pharisees, Luke characterizes them as "lovers of money" (16:14). Also unique to Luke is Jesus' encounter with Zacchaeus, a "chief tax collector" who is also "rich" (19:2), but unlike his counterparts, Zacchaeus shows there is hope for the rich. His is a story of true conversion: a sinner who receives salvation by being generous toward the poor and making fourfold restitution to those whom he has defrauded (19:3–10). Luke shares with Matthew the story of the centurion whose servant is healed, but by noting his generosity Luke includes yet another positive role model in his narrative (Luke 7:5; cf. Matt 8:5–13). Also among the blessed belongs the good Samaritan, whose compassionate care on the road is matched by his willingness to open his wallet (10:35). We also find the women who accompanied Jesus in Galilee displaying the mark of true discipleship: they give generously of their resources (8:3). Their loyalty resurfaces at Jesus' burial and resurrection (23:49, 55–56; 24:10).

It is hardly surprising that "leaving everything" becomes a fixed condition of discipleship in Luke (Luke 5:11; cf. Mark 1:16–20 and Matt 4:18–22; Luke 5:28; cf. Mark 2:14 and Matt 9:9). Jesus' command to the "rich young ruler" to "sell all that you own and distribute the money to the poor" (Luke 18:22) becomes a general requirement for all disciples. This is stated quite radically in a passage unique to Luke: "none of you can become my disciple if you do not give up all your possessions" (14:33). As Jesus' earlier remarks show, one's "possessions" encompass one's family (14:26; cf. 9:57–62 and Matt 8:19–22). From Q, Luke also knows Jesus' teachings about anxiety, including his reminders that "life is more than food, and the body more than clothing" (12:23; Matt 6:25) and "where your treasure is, there your heart will be also" (12:34; cf. Matt 6:21), but he intensifies Jesus' demands by adding, "Sell your possessions, and give alms" (Luke 12:33).

We may easily miss the radical edge Luke gives to Jesus' teaching about discipleship if we try to find a consistent pattern in Luke's teaching. On the one hand, Jesus demands disciples to sell all of their possessions as a condition of discipleship; yet on the other hand, he teaches the value of almsgiving, which presupposes that people have possessions to give. Which is it? Selling everything or giving alms? For Luke, it is both. He is advocating neither a rigorous asceticism nor a robust capitalism. He is calling instead for a way of life, a form of discipleship, that understands the addictive power of possessions, their capacity to create distorted views of ourselves and the world that turn us into fools, and, even more so, the base human desires that cause us to want more than we need and cling selfishly to what we have.

By presenting us with a parade of characters who display different attitudes in quite different but very real human situations, Luke gives us enough examples of noble generosity and tragic greed to help us chart our own way. We can spot the heroines and heroes—those who are blessed—and the villains—those who are cursed—easily enough. We also know by the end of the narrative what Luke's Jesus means when he calls disciples to "leave everything" and follow him. Whatever stands in the way of true, authentic discipleship—family and friends or enemies, but especially wealth and possessions—must be left behind.

The women at Jesus' tomb on Easter morning. This woodcut illustrates Martin Luther's sermon on Mark 16. It is dated 1562 and has the engraver's symbol. It is taken from *Kercken Postilla*, a work published in the vicinity of Wittenberg, Germany, in 1563. From the Digital Image Archive of The Richard C. Kessler Reformation Collection, Pitts Theology Library, Candler School of Theology, Emory University, Atlanta, Georgia.

1	2	3	4	5
Jerusalem & Nazareth		Judea		
Preface (1-4) John the Baptist's birth announced (5-25) Jesus' birth announced (26-38) Mary visits Elizabeth (39-56) - The visit (39-45) - Magnificat (46-55) - Conclusion (56) Birth & presentation of John the Baptist (57-80) - Birth, circumcision, naming (57-66) -Benedictus (67-79)	Birth of Jesus (1-20) - Census (1-3) - Birth (4-7) - Shepherds & angels (8-20) Jesus is named and presented in Temple (21-39) - Circumcision (21) - Presentation (22-24) - Simeon (25-35) - Anna (36-38) Return to Nazareth (39-40) Boy Jesus in Temple (41-52)	John the Baptist (1-20) - Rulers (1-2) - John the Baptist's preaching (3-6) - Call to repent (7-9) - Groups (10-14) - Coming one (15-18) - John the Baptist's imprisonment (19-20) Baptism of Jesus (21-22) Genealogy: "son of Adam, son of God" (23-38) Temptation (4:1-13)	**Galilean Ministry (4:14-9:50)** Rejection at Nazareth (14-30) - Preaching starts (14-15) - Synagogue sermon (16-21) - Response (22-24) - Elijah & Elisha (25-27) - Escape (28-30) Healing man with unclean spirit (31-37) **M** Healing Peter's mother-in-law (38-39) **M** Healing sick at evening (40-41) **M** Jesus retreats, preaches Judea? (42-44)	Jesus calls Peter, James, & John; miraculous catch of fish – Sea of Galilee (1-11) Healing the leper (12-16) **M** Healing the paralytic (17-26) **M** Call of Levi (27-28) Eating w/ tax collectors & sinners (29-32) **C/P** Question about fasting (33-39) **T**

9:51-10:42	11	12	13	14
9:51-19:27 Travel Narrative—Journey to Jerusalem				
9:51-19:27 Journey to Jerusalem Samaritan villagers' refusal (9:51-56) Would-be followers of Jesus (9:57-62) **T** Sending of the Seventy (10:1-12) **T** Woes to unrepentant cities (13-16) **T** Return of the Seventy (17-20) **T** Jesus' prayer to Father (21-22) Jesus blesses disciples (23-24) **T** Lawyer's question (25-28) **C** Good Samaritan (29-37) **T** Martha & Mary (38-42) **T**	Lord's prayer (1-4) **T** Friend at midnight (5-8) **T** Answer to prayer (9-13) **T** Beelzebul controversy (14-23) **T** Return of unclean spirit (24-26) **T** True blessedness (27-28) **P** Sign of Jonah (29-32) **T** Light of body (33-36) **T** Discourse against Pharisees (37-54) **T**	Warning against hypocrisy (1-3) **T** Exhortation to fearless confession (4-12) **T** Parable of rich fool (13-21) **T** Not to worry (22-34) **T** Watchfulness & faithfulness (35-48) **T** Jesus brings division: judgment (49-56) **T** Settling with one's accuser (57-59) **T**	Repentance or destruction (1-5) **T** Parable of fig tree (6-9) **T** Healing crippled woman (10-17) **M** Parable of mustard seed (18-19) **T** Parable of yeast (20-21) **T** En route to Jerusalem – narrow door (22-30) **T** Departure from Galilee (31-33) Lament over Jerusalem (34-35)	Healing man w/ dropsy (1-6) **M/P** Parable of banquet seating - teaching on humility (7-14) **T** Parable of great dinner (15-24) **T** Cost of discipleship (25-35) **T**

19:28-48	20	21	22	22
			Jerusalem	
19:28-21:38 Days in Jerusalem Entry into Jerusalem (28-38) Jesus predicts destruction of Jerusalem (39-44) Jesus cleanses the temple (45-46) Conspiracy of the leaders (47-48)	Question about Jesus' authority (1-8) **C** Parable of wicked tenants (9-19) **T** Question about paying taxes (20-26) **C** Question about resurrection (27-40) **C** Question about David's son (41-44) **C** Jesus denounces scribes (45-47) **T** Widow's gift (21:1-4)	**Apocalyptic discourse (21:5-38) T** Prediction of Temple destruction (5-6) Signs of end of age (7-11) Coming of persecution (12-19) Desolating sacrilege (20-24) Coming of Son of Man (25-28) Lesson of fig tree (29-31) Day and hour known only to God (32-33) Watch! (34-36) Conclusion (37-38)	**Passion Narrative (chs. 22-23)** Plot to kill Jesus (1-2) Judas (3-6) Preparation of the Passover (7-13) Institution of Lord's Supper (14-23) Dispute about greatness (24-27) **T** Prediction re sitting on 12 thrones (28-30) Jesus predicts Peter's denial (31-34) Purse, bag, sword (35-38)	Prayer & agony on Mt. Olives [Gethsemane] (39-46) Betrayal & arrest of Jesus (47-53) Peter's denial (54-62) Mocking Jesus (63-65) Jesus' appearance before council in a.m. (66-71)

186

6	7	8	9
Galilee			

Sabbath conflicts (1-11)
- Plucking grain on
  Sabbath (1-5) **P**
- Healing man with
  withered hand (6-11)
  P/M
Call of the Twelve
  (12-16)
Gathering crowds (17-19)
Sermon on the Plain
  (20-49) **T**
- Blessings (20-23)
- Woes (24-26)
- Love of enemies (27-36)
- Judging (37-42)
- Being good (43-45)
- Hearing and doing
  (46-49)
	Healing centurion's slave
	  at Capernaum (1-10) **M**
	Raising widow's son at
	  Nain (11-17) **M**
	John the Baptist's
	  question to Jesus (18-23)
	Jesus' words about John
	  the Baptist (24-35) **T**
	Woman with ointment
	  (36-50)
	- Anointing (36-38)
	- Criticism (39-40)
	- Two debtors (41-43)
	- Forgiveness (44-50)
		Jesus preaches, heals –
		  ministering women (1-3)
		Parable of sower (4-8) **T**
		Reason for speaking in
		  parables (9-10) **T**
		Parable of sower
		  explained (11-15) **T**
		Purpose of parables:
		  lighting lamp (16-18) **T**
		Jesus' true family
		  (19-21) **P**
		Stilling the storm
		  (22-25) **M**
		Healing Gerasene
		  demoniac (26-39) **M**
		Healing Jairus' daughter
		  and woman with
		  hemorrhage (40-56) **M**
			Sending the Twelve (1-6)
			Herod's Question (7-9)
			Feeding the 5000
			  (10-17) **M**
			Peter's confession (18-20)
			First passion prediction
			  (21-22)
			Teaching about
			  discipleship (23-27) **T**
			Transfiguration (28-36)
			Healing boy with demon
			  (37-43a) **M**
			Second passion prediction
			  (43b-45)
			True greatness (46-48) **T**
			Another exorcist
			  (49-50) **T**

15	16	17	18:1-19:27
9:51-19:27 Travel Narrative—Journey to Jerusalem			

Parable of lost sheep
  (1-7) **T**
Parable of lost coin
  (8-10) **T**
Parable of lost son and his
  brother (11-32) **T**
	Parable of dishonest
	  manager (1-9) **T**
	Sayings about faithfulness
	  (10-13) **T**
	Hypocrisy of Pharisees
	  (14-15) **T**
	Law & prophets until
	  John the Baptist
	  (16-17) **T**
	Teaching about divorce
	  (18) **T**
	Parable of rich man and
	  Lazarus (19-31) **T**
		Sayings of Jesus (1-10) **T**
		- On causing sin (1-2)
		- On forgiveness (3-4)
		- On faith (5-6)
		- The slave's wages
		  (7-10)
		
		En route to Jerusalem (11)
		Healing ten lepers (12-19)
		M
		On kingdom of God
		  (20-21) **T**
		The day of the Son of
		  Man (22-37) **T**
		
		Note: Passion prediction:
		  (17:25)
			Parable of widow &
			  unjust judge (1-8) **T**
			Parable of Pharisee & tax
			  collector (9-14) **T**
			
			--**Judea**--
			
			Jesus blesses little
			  children (15-17)
			Rich ruler (18-27)
			Leaving all (28-30) **T**
			Third passion prediction
			  (31-34)
			Healing blind beggar at
			  Jericho (35-43) **M**
			Zacchaeus (19:1-10) **P**
			Parable of the ten pounds
			  (19:11-27) **T**

23	24

Jesus before Pilate (1-5)
Jesus before Herod
  (6-[17])
Sentence of death (18-25)
Simon of Cyrene carries
  Jesus' cross – wailing
  procession (26-31)
Crucifixion (32-43)
Death on the cross
  (44-49)
Burial of Jesus (50-56)
	Empty tomb (1-12)
	Road to Emmaus (13-35)
	Jesus appears to the
	  disciples (36-49)
	Ascension (50-53)

> **Legend:**
>
> C – Controversy Story
> P – Pronouncement Story
> M – Miracle Story
> T – Teaching

Note

1. Daniel J. Theron, *Evidence of Tradition* (Grand Rapids: Baker, 1957), 61.

Bibliography

Commentaries

Caird, George B. *The Gospel of St Luke*. The Pelican New Testament Commentaries. Harmondsworth: Penguin, 1963; republished New York: Seabury, 1968; later republished in Westminster Pelican Commentaries; Philadelphia: Westminster, 1978.

Craddock, Fred B. *Luke*. Interpretation: A Bible Commentary for Teaching and Preaching. Louisville: John Knox, 1990.

Culpepper, R. Alan. "The Gospel of Luke: Introduction, Commentary, and Reflections." Pages 1–490 in vol. 9 of *The New Interpreter's Bible*. Edited by Leander E. Keck. 12 vols. Nashville: Abingdon, 1995.

Evans, Christopher F. *Saint Luke*. Trinity Press International New Testament Commentaries. London/Philadelphia: SCM /Trinity, 1990.

Fitzmyer, Joseph A. *The Gospel According to Luke: Introduction, Translation, and Notes*. Anchor Bible 28. 2 vols. Garden City: Doubleday, 1981–1985.

Johnson, Luke T. *The Gospel of Luke*. Sacra Pagina 3. Collegeville: Liturgical, 1991.

Schweizer, Eduard. *The Good News According to Luke*. Translated by David E. Green. Atlanta: John Knox, 1984.

Tiede, David L. *Luke*. Augsburg Commentaries on the New Testament. Minneapolis: Augsburg, 1988.

Other Resources

Cadbury, Henry J. *The Making of Luke-Acts*. New York: Macmillan, 1927; republished London: SPCK, 1968; Peabody: Hendrickson, 1999.

Conzelmann, Hans. *The Theology of St. Luke*. Translated by Geoffrey Buswell. First published in English: New York: Harper, 1961; Philadelphia: Fortress, 1982.

Fitzmyer, Joseph A. *Luke the Theologian: Aspects of His Teaching*. New York: Paulist, 1989.

Jervell, Jacob. *Luke and the People of God: A New Look at Luke-Acts*. Minneapolis: Augsburg, 1972.

Johnson, Luke T. *Luke-Acts: A Story of Prophet and People*. Herald Biblical Booklets. Chicago: Franciscan Herald, 1981.

———. *Sharing Possessions: Mandate and Symbol of Faith*. Overtures to Biblical Theology. Philadelphia: Fortress, 1981.

Juel, Donald. *Luke-Acts: The Promise of History*. Atlanta: John Knox, 1983.

Kingsbury, Jack D. *Conflict in Luke: Jesus, Authorities, Disciples*. Minneapolis: Fortress, 1991.

Kurz, William S. *Reading Luke-Acts: Dynamics of Biblical Narrative*. Louisville: Westminster/John Knox, 1993.

Marshall, I. Howard. *Luke: Historian and Theologian*. Exeter: Paternoster, 1970; Grand Rapids: Zondervan, 1971.

Powell, Mark A. *What Are They Saying About Luke?* New York: Paulist, 1989.

Tannehill, Robert C. *The Narrative Unity of Luke-Acts: A Literary Interpretation*. Foundations and Facets. 2 vols. Philadelphia: Fortress, 1986–1990.

Tuckett, Christopher M. *Luke*. New Testament Study Guides. Sheffield: Sheffield, 1996.

———, ed. *Luke's Literary Achievement: Collected Essays*. Journal for the Study of the New Testament Supplement Series 116. Sheffield: Sheffield, 1995.

Chapter 9

The Gospel of John

"John, noticing that the physical things had been set forth in the [other] Gospels, wrote a spiritual Gospel."

Clement of Alexandria

" . . . count John as fourth in time, but first in height of teachings."

Amphilochius of Iconium

"It is not so much a picture of Christ that John sets forth, as a conception of Christ; his Christ does not speak in his own person, but of his own person."

Christian Hermann Weisse

John was perceived as the Fourth Gospel from quite an early date. Initially this meant that it was written fourth. So says Irenaeus (ca. 130–200 C.E.), who, after mentioning Matthew, Mark, and Luke, reports that "afterwards John, the disciple of the Lord who also leaned upon his breast . . . published a Gospel while residing in Ephesus [in] Asia."[1] Echoing the same sentiments in the East, Origen (ca. 185–254 C.E.) rehearses the same canonical order, concluding, "last of all, the [Gospel] according to John [was written]."[2] This is the order found in many of the early canonical lists. By putting John in the fourth position, the early fathers were acknowledging its late composition as well as its distinctive content.

Yet something about John caused people to elevate it from the fourth position. In some canonical lists, we find the so-called apostolic order—Matthew, John, Mark, and Luke.[3] The two Gospels thought to have been composed by apostles were listed first, followed by those written by disciples or associates of the apostles. Writing against Marcion in the early third century, Tertullian (ca. 160–225 C.E.) distinguishes between "apostles" and "apostolic men" who composed the Gospels, the former including John and Matthew (Tertullian's order) who "instill us with faith," the latter including Luke and Mark who "renew [faith]."[4] As we saw earlier in our discussion of the Gospel of Luke, a lot was at stake for Tertullian. Arguing against Marcion, he needed reliable, authoritative sources, and gospels that could be attributed to apostles aided him in establishing and defending the priority of the orthodox faith against its later distortions. In this way John became linked with Matthew as an "eyewitness" Gospel.

But something else lifted John from fourth position—its sheer capacity to engage readers. One of its most passionate enthusiasts was Origen, who rated the Gospels as the "firstfruits of all Scripture" and John as the "firstfruits of the Gospels."[5] One indication of his fervor for John is that he composed thirty-two books of commentary on John, but only got as far as John 13:33; it took him over 300 pages to get through the first twenty-nine verses of chapter 1! In an earlier generation, John's Gospel created similar excitement in Gnostic circles, prompting Heracleon, a disciple of Valentinus, to write the earliest known commentary on John (ca. 170 C.E.).[6] It was among Gnostic readers, perhaps early in the second century, that the Fourth Gospel first worked its magic, for we find Irenaeus in the 170s making a valiant (and ultimately successful) effort to wrest John from Gnostic control. For Gnostics, John was read as a source of esoteric wisdom, and its portrait of the divine Jesus who barely skated on the surface of humanity naturally appealed to them. Irenaeus, however, found much in John to support his construal of orthodox Christianity. He made frequent use of its opening verses to insist on one Creator God, and he became a passionate defender of the Fourth Gospel in this early tug-of-war with the Gnostics. [See Expanded CD Version pp. 270–71: *The Church's Use of John from the Ancient to the Modern Periods*]

However we explain John's enduring capacity to engage the church's attention and to do so from every quarter, we must acknowledge its impact on the church's life and thought. Luke's Gospel may be most fully represented in the Apostles' Creed, but John's influence is also felt in its confession of Jesus as God's "only begotten Son" (*ton huion ton monogenē*). We especially see John's power to shape belief in the Nicene Creed's confession of Jesus as the one "begotten of the Father, only-begotten . . . begotten not made . . . through whom all things were made . . . who . . . was made flesh."

Perhaps one of the most vivid testimonies of John's power to seize center stage is its truly pervasive influence in the church's lectionary. At no time during the liturgical year is the church very far from the Fourth Gospel, and at certain times Origen's praise of John as the "firstfruits of the Gospels" is simply confirmed. Especially during Holy Week and Easter does the church submit to the Fourth Evangelist's voice, but it also hears the Word of God through John at Christmas and during Lent, as well as at Pentecost, on Trinity Sunday, in the season of Pentecost, and on such special days as Thanksgiving Day and Holy Cross.[7]

The Maverick Gospel

Reading John's Gospel after the Synoptics, we sense that the song of the synoptic Jesus has been rendered in a new key, even raised an octave or two. Early readers of John also sensed how different its story of Jesus was. Clement of Alexandria (ca.

150–215 C.E.) expressed it this way: "John, noticing that the physical things [*ta sōmatika*] had been set forth in the [other] Gospels . . . wrote a spiritual Gospel" [*pneumatikon euangelion*].[8] Origen makes a similar distinction when he explains his work as a commentator: "The task before us now is to translate the gospel perceptible to the senses into the spiritual gospel."[9] Augustine's way of putting it was that whereas Matthew was the "gospel of the flesh," John was the "gospel of the Spirit."[10] John Calvin (1509–1564) reflects this same perspective when he observes that the Synoptic Gospels allow us to see the "body of Jesus," whereas John reveals the "soul of Jesus." More recently, John has been called the "maverick Gospel," still another way of underscoring its thoroughly idiosyncratic character.[11]

Before highlighting the main differences between John and the Synoptics, we should note some of their similarities. They reflect the same broad outline. The beginning of Jesus' ministry is linked with John the Baptist, and it begins in Galilee. The story moves toward Jerusalem, with Jesus meeting early resistance from Jewish leaders that eventually becomes outright rejection and results in his death. Jesus' last days in Jerusalem include the Last Supper, which is followed by a series of events that culminates in Jesus' crucifixion: his betrayal by Judas, his arrest, a trial before Pilate, his crucifixion, his burial by Joseph of Arimathea, his resurrection and appearances to disciples both in Jerusalem and Galilee. We also find in John several stories found in the Synoptic Gospels: cleansing the temple, healing the official's son, and feeding the 5,000 followed by Jesus' walking on the water, to mention the most obvious cases.

Broadly speaking, the differences between John and the Synoptic Gospels are of two types: formal and material. By formal, we mean the differences in the way their stories are structured—their architecture, if you will. By material, we mean their different content—what is actually reported in their respective accounts.

Formal Differences

One way of thinking about the underlying structure of John's Gospel is to ask about its geography and chronology. How does it map Jesus' movements? How does it understand the timeline of the Jesus story? We can also ask about the literary shape of the stories that it reports about Jesus and the words attributed to him.

Geography. The Synoptic Gospels tend to report Jesus' ministry in two stages: a period of ministry in Galilee followed by a brief period of ministry in Jerusalem. Even Luke's inclusion of an extended Travel Narrative does not alter but presupposes this Galilee-Jerusalem geographical framework. John, by contrast, depicts Jesus' ministry oscillating between Jerusalem and Galilee. Three times, early in the narrative, Jesus travels from Galilee to Jerusalem (2:13; 5:1; 7:10). Jerusalem may be regarded as the pivotal center of John's Gospel (1:19, 28, 29, 43, et al.) since it reports only a handful of events outside Jerusalem and Judea: the wedding at Cana of Galilee (2:1–12); Jesus' encounter with the Samaritan woman (4:1–42); healing the official's son (4:46–54); feeding the 5,000 (6:1–15); walking on the water (6:16–21); the bread from heaven discourse in Capernaum (6:22–59); Jesus' temporary stay in Galilee (7:1–9); and the resurrection appearances reported in chapter 21.

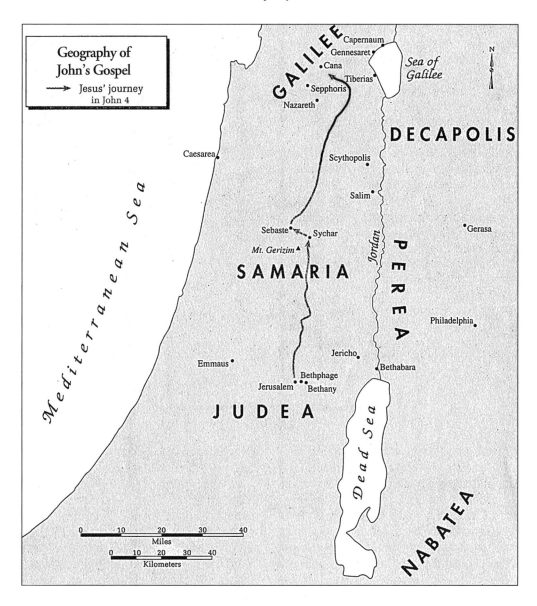

Chronology. As a rule, the Synoptics express relatively little interest in chronology, but given their chronology, Jesus' ministry can be compressed into a single year. His ministry concludes with a final week in Jerusalem in the spring, when Passover is observed (see Mark 11–15). John's chronological framework is quite different. Three Passovers are mentioned (2:13; 6:4; and a third in 11:55; 12:1; 13:1; 18:28); another unnamed festival (5:1) is possibly a fourth Passover. If these are separate Passovers, they suggest a period of ministry at least two, possibly three, years in duration.

Even more remarkable is how John reports Jesus' final period of ministry in Jerusalem, which begins in 7:10. The festival that brings Jesus to Jerusalem is Booths or Tabernacles (Hebrew *Sukkoth*), a week-long celebration observed in October (John 7:2; see Lev 23:33–43; Deut 16:13–17; Neh 8:13–18). He is also in Jerusalem for the

THE GOSPEL OF JOHN: THE LENGTH OF JESUS' MINISTRY

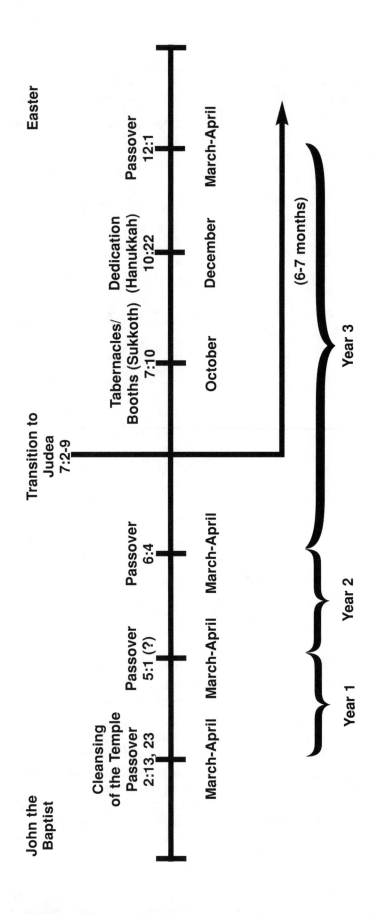

festival of the Dedication (Hebrew *Hanukkah*, 10:22–23), a December observance cel-ebrating the Maccabeans' victory over the Seleucids and Judas Maccabeus's rededica-tion of the temple in 164 B.C.E. (1 Macc 4:36–59). He remains there through Passover (Hebrew *Pascha*), a spring festival occurring in March or April celebrating Israel's exo-dus from Egypt (John 11:55; 12:1; 13:1; 18:28; see Exod 12:1–13:10; Deut 16:1–8). If these chronological markers reflect a continuous stay by Jesus in Jerusalem, they sug-gest a period of ministry in Jerusalem lasting approximately six months.

Literary Structure. The Synoptic Gospels are typically composed of short literary units. These may be brief episodes in Jesus' ministry, such as miracle stories or stories of confrontation. Even when these are joined together to form cycles of stories, such as the cycle of miracle stories in Mark 1–2 or the cycle of confrontation stories in Mark 12, the smaller building blocks that constitute them are quite evident. Or, when the Synoptics report discourses of Jesus, such as Matthew's Sermon on the Mount (Matt 5–7), Luke's Sermon on the Plain (Luke 6), or the "little apocalypse" (Mark 13; Matt 24; Luke 21), we can easily detect the smaller literary units that make up these larger discourses. Often they deal with quite different topics rather than developing a single theme. The longest connected narrative shared by the Synoptics is the Passion Narrative, but even it consists of smaller units of material.

The building blocks used in the Fourth Gospel look quite different. While we do encounter some short episodes similar to what we find in the Synoptics (2:1–12, 13–25; 4:46–54; 12:1–8), we find a much different literary pattern in John. More often we find John reporting an episode that introduces a question or theme, which is then developed by Jesus in a rather lengthy discourse. In chapter 3, his conversation with Nicodemus introduces the new birth metaphor, which sets up the subsequent remarks about eternal life in the remainder of the chapter. Similarly, the bread motif in the feeding of the 5,000 (6:1–14) is developed in the "bread from heaven" discourse later in chapter 6.

In other instances, Jesus' discourse may take the form of an extended conversa-tion in which he engages in dialogue with other characters in the story. His encounter with the Samaritan woman in chapter 4, when the image of water figures centrally in their conversation, is presented as a carefully structured dialogue that allows Jesus to speak about living water (see 4:13–14). Similarly, the raising of Lazarus in chapter 11 does not prompt a long discourse by Jesus about resurrection, but a much shorter dec-laration (11:25–26) that is no less theologically significant simply because it occurs as part of an extended dialogue between Jesus and Mary and Martha. A slightly different pattern is seen in chapters 9–10. The healing of the blind man primarily triggers lively dialogue between Jesus and the characters in the story, but the entire episode is then followed by Jesus' monologue about the good shepherd (10:1–18). The thematic con-nection, if any, between the good shepherd discourse and the previous healing story has always puzzled interpreters. Even so, it still illustrates John's method of literary composition: reporting an episode that is followed by a rather lengthy discourse. The most dramatic example is the extended Farewell Discourse, which constitutes almost one-fifth of the Johannine narrative (chs. 13–17), all set within the context of the farewell meal (13:1–30). It too contains dialogue between Jesus and his disciples (see 13:31–14:14), but from 14:15 onward it is mainly Jesus who speaks.

Along with this Johannine pattern of linking episodes with Jesus' dialogues and monologues, we should note the highly stylized "I am" sayings or discourses, another distinctive feature of John's Gospel:

- living water (4:14);
- bread of life (6:35);
- the light of the world (8:12);
- the gate for the sheep & the good shepherd (10:7, 11);
- the resurrection and the life (11:25);
- the way, truth, and life (14:6); and
- the true vine (15:1).

These are as distinctive of the Fourth Gospel as Jesus' parables are of the Synoptic Gospels, which are conspicuously absent in John. Not a single parable reported in the Synoptic Gospels is reported in John, nor does the book even describe Jesus as a teacher of parables. John does report Jesus' using "figures of speech" (*paroimia*, 10:6; 16:25, 29), and some of his teachings resemble the synoptic parables (12:24), but John's portrait of Jesus' teaching is a long way from the synoptic report that Jesus "did not speak to them except in parables" (Mark 4:34). Although the word "parable" (Greek *parabolē*) does not occur in John, it has been proposed that seven of the sayings (12:24; 16:21; 11:9–10; 8:35; 10:1–5; 3:29; 5:19–20a) are parabolic in form.[12]

Material Differences

If formal differences refer to the shape of the story, material differences refer to what is contained in the story. These include the events that John reports and the characters in the story, but we will also treat here the role the Fourth Evangelist plays in telling the story as well as some of the features of the Johannine portrait of Jesus.

Events. Certain events that are pivotal in the Synoptics go unmentioned in John. Some of the most notable examples are Jesus' baptism (although it is implied in 1:32–34; see 1:24–28); the temptations; the transfiguration (is 12:28–30 a reminiscence?); the prayer in Gethsemane; and the institution of the Lord's Supper (though perhaps 6:51–58 reflects an early Eucharistic setting; chapter 13 reports a farewell meal, but no account of Jesus' instituting the Eucharist).

Besides these rather striking omissions are events found in both John and the Synoptics that have different significance in John. The most obvious instance is the cleansing of the temple (2:13–22), which John reports at the beginning of Jesus' ministry, right after the wedding at Cana (2:1–12), but which the Synoptics report at the end of Jesus' ministry as part of the Passion Narrative (see Mark 11:15–18 and parallels). For Mark, this event is bracketed by the story of the cursing of the fig tree, suggesting that it anticipates the temple's destruction. In John, by contrast, the charge reported by the Synoptics at Jesus' trial that he would destroy the temple and rebuild it in three days (Mark 14:55–59; Matt 26:59–61) occurs on Jesus' lips at the cleansing of the temple (2:19). This prompts an editorial explanation by the Fourth Evangelist: By cleansing the temple Jesus signals its destruction but also anticipates its replacement by his resurrected body (2:21). The feeding of the 5,000, the only miracle story reported by all four Gospels, also takes on a different meaning in John: It serves as a "sign" that creates faith (6:14) and also prompts the "bread from heaven" discourse. In sharp contrast, especially in Mark, the feeding of the 5,000 and its doublet, the feeding of the 4,000, become occasions of disbelief by the disciples (see Mark 8:14–21).

Characters. In John we meet a different cast of characters. Several persons unmentioned in the Synoptics appear in John: Nathanael (1:45–49; 21:2); Nicodemus (3:1, 4, 9; 7:50; 19:39); the Samaritan woman (ch. 4); the paralytic man (ch. 5); the man born blind (ch. 9); and Lazarus (11:1–44; 12:1–8). Some of John's characters overlap with the Synoptics, but they tend to play different roles: Andrew (1:40–44; 6:8; 12:22); Philip (1:43–51; 6:5, 7; 12:21–22; 14:8–9); Thomas (11:16; 14:5; 20:24–29; 21:2); and Peter (1:40–42; 6:66–71; 13:6–9; 18:10–11, 15–18, 25–27; 20:3–10; 21:1–19). The Twelve are mentioned only briefly (6:67, 70–71; 20:24), and John gives no formal listing of their names (see Mark 3:13–19; Matt 10:1–4; Luke 6:12–16). Rather than the synoptic hierarchy of Peter, Andrew, James, and John, we meet a different hierarchy in the Fourth Gospel. Peter remains a central figure, but John's hierarchy includes especially Thomas and Philip (see 21:1–3). Naturally, the "beloved disciple" must be included here (13:23–26; 19:26–27; 20:1–10; 21:7, 20–24; cf. 18:15–16; 21:2–14). The "sons of Zebedee" are mentioned only once (21:2), and they are never identified as James and John. Demons, who are prominent in the Synoptic Gospels as participants in the story, play no such role in John. Several times Jesus is accused of being possessed by demons (7:20; 8:48, 49, 52; 10:20–21), but no talking demons such as we find in the story of the Gadarene demoniac are found in John (see Mark 5:1–20).

The Role of the Fourth Evangelist in the Narrative. With rare exceptions, the Synoptic Gospels exhibit reserve in providing explanatory comments. In the Synoptics, there are occasional translations of words or expressions that might be unfamiliar to the reader, but not much more than that. These too we find in John (e.g., 1:38, 41–42), but in addition we find the Fourth Evangelist including explanatory comments as he tells the story (2:21–22; 12:16–19; 20:9–10). More than this, the Fourth Evangelist sometimes blends his own voice with that of Jesus, or someone else in the narrative, so that it becomes difficult to tell who is actually speaking: the author or the character within the story. **[See Expanded CD Version pp. 277–78: The Fourth Evangelist's "Voice" in Ch. 3]**

Jesus' Speech. Not only is the form of Jesus' speech distinctive in the Fourth Gospel, so also is its content. Jesus' proclamation of the kingdom of God is a central feature of the Synoptic Gospels. It may be referred to in different ways, for example, the "kingdom of heaven" (Matthew), and its profile may be sketched somewhat differently in each of the Synoptics, but in many ways it constitutes their thematic thread. By contrast, the kingdom of God is virtually absent in the Fourth Gospel (3:3, 5; 18:36). In its place emerge new images and metaphors that constitute Jesus' theological vocabulary: life, light, glory, truth, and several other distinctive phrases such as "the Son" and "the Spirit of truth." Also worth noting is the absence of the usual language of repentance (*metanoeō/metanoia*) in the teaching of Jesus, a prominent feature of his proclamation in the Synoptic Gospels.

Even allowing for different emphases in the Synoptics, typically the identity of Christ develops from relative obscurity to full revelation. Especially in Mark, Jesus shows extreme reserve in speaking about his messianic identity. The birth and infancy stories in Matthew and Luke alter this pattern somewhat, but even then, Mark's basic pattern remains intact. John's Gospel, by contrast, begins with full revelation. From the opening prologue (1:1–18) through John the Baptist's testimony and Jesus' interchanges with Andrew, Peter, Nathanael, and Philip in chapter 1, we experience a full messianic revelation rather than a messianic secret. This pattern continues with the emphatic sign at the wedding in Cana (2:1–12) and is simply repeated as the Gospel unfolds. John's imagery of light and darkness should be taken seriously: In the Synoptics Jesus often moves about in the shadows, but in John he moves about under the noonday sun.

Along with the "I am" sayings of Jesus, the *seven signs* reported in John's Gospel reinforce this openly revealed portrait of Jesus:

- turning water into wine (2:1–12);
- healing the official's son (4:46–54);
- healing the lame man on the Sabbath (5:1–18);
- feeding the 5,000 (6:1–15);
- walking on the water (6:16–21);
- healing the man born blind (ch. 9); and
- raising Lazarus (11:1–44).

By providing literary markers, the Fourth Evangelist calls attention to these signs (2:11; 4:54; 6:14; 9:37; 11:27), and they typically bring about faith. Readers are not left wondering about their significance.

Combined with these open declarations of Jesus' identity and the seven repeated manifestations of his power are those places in which the Fourth Gospel underscores Jesus' omniscience or prescience (2:23–25; 4:18; 6:15, 70; 11:41; 13:11) and reports him speaking audaciously, if not impertinently, to those in authority during his trial (18:19–24, 36–38; 19:10–11).

Why John Is Different

When we move from the Synoptics to the Fourth Gospel, we have an experience comparable to returning home after a long trip, only to find that our house has been renovated and the furniture moved around. How do we account for these changes?

In the history of interpretation of John's Gospel, several options have emerged to explain the differences between John and the Synoptics.

1. *Late or Early?* Especially from the eighteenth century onward, John's apostolic authorship began to be questioned, which enabled some scholars to push the composition of the Fourth Gospel into the second century C.E. Because of its "high Christology," it was thought that a considerable length of time was needed for such theological development to occur. Its unusual shape could be explained as the culmination of lengthy evolutionary development. According to this view, the Fourth Gospel was to the Synoptic Gospels what a frog is to a tadpole.

The discovery of $\mathfrak{P}^{52}$ (the Roberts Papyrus dated 125–140 C.E.), possibly the oldest extant fragment of any NT writing, contains portions of John 18. This confirmed that John was in circulation in Egypt in the early second century. Other early papyri ($\mathfrak{P}^{66}$ dated in the mid-second century and $\mathfrak{P}^{75}$ dated in the late second or early third century C.E.) also contain portions of the Fourth Gospel. If we allow time for the Gospel to be written and to reach Egypt, we should think of a time of composition no later than the early part of the second century. Moreover, the discovery of the writings of Qumran in 1947 revealed patterns of thought quite similar to the Fourth Gospel. Since many of these writings predate Jesus and the Christian movement by several decades, it is no longer necessary to use late composition to explain the unusual thought world of John. While most scholars tend to date the composition of the Fourth Gospel around 100 C.E., some scholars have plausibly argued for a pre-70 dating. It is worth noting, however, that the earliest patristic witnesses, such as Irenaeus, Clement, and Origen, thought it was the latest Gospel written.

2. *Palestine or the Diaspora?* Many things about the Fourth Gospel have suggested a connection with Greek modes of thought. Its use of the *Logos* metaphor along with its seemingly Platonic view of the world have caused many scholars to posit strong Hellenistic influence. Still other scholars have looked to other locations, including Iran, Syria, and Egypt, to account for the presence of some of its distinctive features.

An early tradition, reported by Irenaeus, located the Fourth Gospel in Ephesus. These efforts to look outside Palestine for John's provenance tended to assume that John's worldview could not have arisen in a Palestinian setting. Yet the discoveries at Qumran have yielded enough similarities with the outlook of the Fourth Gospel to make a Palestinian setting conceivable. A Palestinian provenance has also been rendered more probable by the increasing scholarly awareness of strong Hellenistic influence within Palestine from the second century B.C.E. onward. This would more easily account for the presence of such seemingly "foreign" elements as the *Logos* Christology.

3. *Dependent or Independent?* One way of explaining the idiosyncratic character of the Fourth Gospel is to see it as virtually, or even completely, unrelated to the synoptic tradition. If we could assume that its author or the community in which it arose had no knowledge of the synoptic traditions about Jesus, then it would be easier to account for its unusual shape—at least, according to some scholars. If the Fourth Gospel knew the synoptic tradition, or part of it, such as Mark or Luke, how can we account for its radical departure from that tradition? Would its differences best be explained as a thorough reinterpretation of that tradition? If so, would this suggest serious dissatisfaction with earlier Jesus traditions? Or were Clement and others right to explain the Fourth Gospel as an effort to move beyond the "bodily" presentations of the Synoptic Gospels in order to get at the "spirit" of Jesus?

Scholarly debate has moved back and forth on this question, with some scholars seeing no conceivable connection between John and the Synoptics, and others arguing that John both knew and used the synoptic tradition. Recent efforts, especially among Continental scholars, have renewed the call for seeing the Fourth Gospel as dependent on the synoptic tradition.

4. *The Work of One Person or Several?* Early tradition held that the Fourth Gospel was written by one person, either John the apostle or John the presbyter. Single authorship of the Gospel was questioned, however, as readers began to notice its literary

𝔓⁷⁵, an early third-century papyrus with most of Luke and most of John 1–15, contains a text remarkably similar to that of Codex Vaticanus (B) of the mid-fourth century. The portion reproduced here (folio 44 recto) preserves the end of Luke (24:51–53) and the beginning of John (1:1–16).

Reproduced by courtesy of the Bibliotheque Bodmer, Cologny-Geneve, Switzerland.

𝔓⁵², a papyrus fragment containing (on its two sides) vv. 31–33 and 37–38 of John 18, is the oldest manuscript of the NT, dating around 125 C.E., or perhaps even earlier.

Reproduced by courtesy of the University Librarian and Director, The John Rylands University Library, The University of Manchester.

unevenness. The concluding paragraph of chapter 20, which states the purpose of the Gospel, looks like the conclusion of the book. This suggests that chapter 21 is a later addition, and thus a second ending, perhaps included to rehabilitate Peter's tarnished reputation and to legitimate the role of the beloved disciple within the Johannine community.

Some of the chapters also appear to be out of sequence. Chapter 6 begins with Jesus going to the other side of the Sea of Galilee, but the previous chapter has him in Jerusalem, with no indication of his making a trip from Judea to Galilee. If chapter 5 were placed after chapter 6, the movement of the story would be much more logical. The prologue has also been considered by some as a later editorial addition; the Gospel could conceivably have begun at 1:19 and the prologue added later in order to emphasize the humanity of Jesus (1:14).

Probably the most well-known case suggesting a fluid tradition is the story of the woman caught in adultery (7:53–8:11), which is absent in the earliest and most reliable manuscripts. For this reason, it is printed in double brackets in many translations to indicate that it was a later addition to the Gospel. Because of these and other considerations, some scholars have envisioned a long, complicated editorial process that finally culminated in our canonical version of the Fourth Gospel. One way of accounting for the current shape of the Fourth Gospel is to think of a single figure, perhaps the apostle John, a highly influential leader in the early church, as being responsible for the core story and his followers, or the community of believers who gathered around him, as those responsible for the later stages of editing.

5. *History or Theology?* For a long time, it was assumed that John was the most explicitly theological Gospel, and thus virtually devoid of any historically reliable content. The discourses that were attributed to Jesus and many of his conversations with different characters were read as highly impressionistic, literary creations, even homilies, that were never intended to be read with photographic realism. Compared with the Synoptic Gospels' portrait of Jesus, John's account was read as much more theologically creative and much less historically realistic.

But the last two centuries have shown how theologically weighted the Synoptic Gospels are. No longer can we read any of the Synoptics, including Mark, as straightforward, realistic history. They are all written "on the slant." Nor can we assume that John's Gospel, merely because it departs so radically from the Synoptics, is less reliable historically. In some respects, John's Passion Narrative presents a more probable account than what we find in the Synoptic Gospels. It is not at all certain that the synoptic presentation of a year-long Galilean ministry followed by a final week in Jerusalem is inherently more probable than John's picture of a longer ministry that oscillated between Judea and Galilee and culminated in a six-month ministry in Jerusalem.

The presence or absence of miraculous or mythological elements does not necessarily provide a reliable gauge for determining historicity. Many scholars once assumed that the account of the Maccabean revolt in 1 Maccabees was more historically reliable than 2 Maccabees because the latter employed so many mythological and legendary elements. By contrast, 1 Maccabees looked as though it was much more straightforward and unembellished. Recent scholarship, however, tends to view the

A woodcut depiction of the evangelist John, receiving inspiration from the Trinity. John is shown with his attribute, the eagle (Rev 4:7); taken from a 1541 printing of Martin Luther's German translation of the New Testament. From the Digital Image Archive of The Richard C. Kessler Reformation Collection, Pitts Theology Library, Candler School of Theology, Emory University, Atlanta, Georgia.

sequence of events reported in 2 Maccabees as more probable in spite of its highly embellished features. Similarly, John's Gospel should not be dismissed as historically unreliable because of its ostensibly mythological character. If anything, the Fourth Gospel illustrates the difficulty in using history and theology as though they were tightly conceived, mutually exclusive categories. It contains more and less of both than is often imagined. [See Expanded CD Version pp. 283–85: *Expressing Truth through Story*]

John's Conversation with Scripture

The Jesus traditions that John received had already been heavily shaped by the OT. When he used these traditions, he was already in conversation with Scripture, however indirectly. Yet like the other evangelists, especially Matthew and Luke, John carried on a separate conversation with Scripture. Or to put it more accurately, he continued the conversation with Scripture that had already begun in the earlier stages of the Jesus tradition. In a number of places we find him correlating an OT passage with some aspect of Jesus' life or teaching, similar to Matthew's formula quotations. Even so, John is eager to press the theological significance of these correlations in new directions.

When crowds were unresponsive to the "many signs" that Jesus did in their presence, the Fourth Evangelist interprets their behavior as a fulfillment of "the word spoken by the prophet Isaiah," then quotes Isa 53:1 (John 12:36b–43). He is the only evangelist to cite this passage (cf. Rom 10:16). Strikingly, he follows this with a quotation of Isa 6:10 and makes the same point Mark made when he quoted it: Jesus' hearers "could not believe" (see Mark 4:12; Matt 13:14–15). In a further editorial comment, John reports that "Isaiah said this because he saw his glory and spoke about him" (v. 41). This may suggest that John understood Isaiah's vision in the temple as an occasion on which Isaiah saw the "glory" of Jesus the Messiah and even back then anticipated the people's negative response (see Isa 6:1–4). Here John may be drawing on an extrabiblical Jewish interpretation of Isaiah's vision; if so, he was extending his conversation with Scripture to include other interpretive traditions, such as the Jewish Targums. This case is instructive in illuminating John's conversation with Scripture. Taking a passage that had already been used in the synoptic tradition to make sense of people's unresponsiveness to Jesus (Isa 6:9–10), John adds to it yet another (Isa 53:1). He also pushes beyond the church's earlier readings of Isa 6 to find within it an allusion to Christ's glory, a prominent Johannine theme.

We see similar efforts to push for a deeper understanding of Scripture in other places as well. In the synoptic accounts of the cleansing of the temple, Isa 56:7 and Jer 7:11 figure centrally: "My house shall be called a house of prayer, but you have made it a den of robbers" (Mark 11:17; Matt 21:13; Luke 19:46). In John's account, however, these OT passages are replaced by Ps 69:9, "Zeal for your house will consume me." In the synoptic account of Jesus' crucifixion, the narrative description employs imagery from Ps 22:18, "They divide my clothes among themselves, and for my clothing they cast lots" (Mark 15:24; Matt 27:35; Luke 23:34). The synoptic evangelists, however, do not cite Ps 22 as the source of this imagery. John's Gospel, by contrast, cites Ps 22:18, but he understands the passage as envisioning two separate actions. Accordingly, he reports two actions by the soldiers: dividing Jesus' clothes among the four soldiers and casting lots for his seamless tunic (John 19:23–25). By pushing for greater precision and clarity, John tells his story so that it becomes an exact fulfillment of the passage he cites. He makes a similar move (though not as detailed) in reporting Jesus' words on the cross, "I am thirsty" (John 19:28). Like the Synoptic Gospels, John reports the offer of sour wine (John 19:29; Mark 15:36; Matt 27:48), but he adds the editorial comment that this was "in order to fulfill the scripture," doubtless referring to Ps 69:21, though not citing it.

Perhaps even more illustrative of John's use of Scripture is his report of the piercing of Jesus' side, an episode unique to his Gospel (19:31–37). Two motifs stand out: Jesus' legs were not broken and his side was pierced. Once again, the Fourth Evangelist reports that "these things occurred so that the scripture might be fulfilled" (19:36). Citing the passage, "None of his bones shall be broken" (Exod 12:46; Num 9:12; Ps 34:20), reinforces John's theological interpretation of Jesus as the slain Passover Lamb. This helps explain why he reports Jesus' death on Passover eve, when the lambs were being slain in preparation for Passover, rather than on Passover, as in the Synoptic Gospels. Citing yet a second passage, "They will look on the one whom they have pierced" (Zech 12:10), brings the event even further in line with Scripture (19:37).

In keeping with his tendency throughout the Gospel, John also shows Jesus applying other OT passages to himself (13:18 [Ps 41:9]; 15:25 [Ps 35:19; 69:4]; 17:12; 19:28). This becomes especially prominent in Jesus' appropriation of certain OT images or themes. Here John is moving well beyond "fulfillment quotations," in which OT passages are correlated with certain events in Jesus' life. The trend was already set within the Synoptic Gospels when Jesus was seen as the "new Moses" or the "son of David," or interpreted in light of other prominent OT figures. This too we find in John, but we find these correlations between Jesus and OT figures such as Moses pushed in a new direction. One of the most vivid examples occurs in chapter 6, in which John sees the feeding of the 5,000 as an event analogous to God's providing Israel manna in the wilderness. In the discourse that follows (6:22–59) Jesus draws on the Moses story, but rather than developing an interpretation of himself as the "new Moses," he claims instead that he is the "bread from heaven" (6:35, 41). His exposition is triggered by a single OT passage, "He gave them bread from heaven to eat" (6:31; see Exod 16:4, 15; Ps 78:23–25). As Jesus develops his interpretation, he contrasts himself with Moses (6:32). Just as the Father gave life to Israel by feeding them manna in the wilderness, so has the Father now given Jesus as the "bread of life" (6:35). Those who "feed on him" are promised to "live forever" (6:58). Nothing comparable to this bold appropriation of the "bread/manna" motif from the Exodus account is found in the synoptic tradition. John's appropriation of Scripture in chapter 6 more closely resembles a "midrashic" form of exposition in which an interpreter takes a biblical theme or motif and develops it in a new way to make its "past meaning" even more meaningful in the interpreter's present. [See **Expanded CD Version p. 287:** *Other Examples of Jesus' Appropriation of the OT in John*]

Like the Synoptic Gospels, John wants to make sense of Jesus in light of Scripture, but he does not merely repeat what is known from the synoptic tradition. In some cases, he retains those traditions. Like the Synoptics, John uses Isa 40:3 to interpret John the Baptist (1:17; see Mark 1:2–3). In his account of Jesus' entry into Jerusalem (John 12:12–19), the crowds' acclamation is drawn from Ps 118:25–26 (see Mark 11:9–10; Matt 21:9; Luke 19:38; also cf. Matt 21:5 and Zech 9:9). Yet OT passages of prime importance to the synoptic evangelists are conspicuously absent in John: Ps 110:1, David's recognizing the exalted Lord (Mark 12:36; Matt 22:44; Luke 20:42–43), and Ps 118:22–23, the rejected stone (Mark 12:10–11; Matt 21:42).

John's attitude toward Scripture is aptly summarized in Jesus' remark to the Jews concerning Scripture, "it is they that testify on my behalf" (5:39), or in his further insistence that Moses "wrote about me" (5:46; also cf. 1:45). As the narrative unfolds, the Fourth Evangelist observes that much later, well after the time of Jesus' ministry, his disciples remembered that "these things had been written of him" (12:16; cf. 2:22). This implies a community of believers in which the study and interpretation of Scripture played a prominent role in making sense of the Jesus they remembered, believed, and proclaimed. There is ample evidence to suggest that John's conversation with Scripture was ongoing, probing, imaginative, and anything but simple. Like John's Gospel itself, his conversation with Scripture reveals a passion for finding deeper meaning within texts and traditions from the past to make sense of the present. His creative use of Scripture, far from reflecting a casual attitude toward the sacred text, reveals just the opposite: the conviction that searching the Scriptures for their true meaning and finding eternal life are closely related pursuits (5:39).

John's Context

Like the other Gospels, John displays little evidence of the circumstances that led to its composition. Its primary concern is to unfold an account of Jesus, and interpreters can only make educated guesses about its context by reading between the lines.

One clue is provided by its purpose statement in 20:31: "these are written so that you may come to believe that Jesus is the Messiah, the Son of God." Whether *believe* means "begin to believe" (*pisteusēte*) as some manuscripts read, or "go on believing" (*pisteuēte*) as is read in other manuscripts, is an open question. The former might suggest an evangelistic purpose and point to a setting in which John or his church was trying actively to convert outsiders. The latter, by contrast, would suggest a setting in which the author is trying to strengthen his readers' faith.

Over the centuries, several different settings have been proposed for the Fourth Gospel. Scholars have debated whether it is best understood as deriving from a Palestinian setting or from a setting outside Palestine, such as Asia Minor (Ephesus) or Syria. It is difficult to decide on a specific geographical setting because each proposal is plausible to some degree.

Apart from locating the Gospel geographically, recent efforts have been made to imagine the circumstances that produced it. Three times John refers to "being expelled from the synagogue" (*aposynagōgos*, 9:22; 12:42; 16:2). The first instance, which occurs in the dispute created by Jesus' healing of the man born blind, occurs in an editorial statement by the Fourth Evangelist himself, when he reports that "the Jews had already agreed that anyone who confessed Jesus to be the Messiah would be put out of the synagogue." Expulsion from synagogues as an official punishment for those who believed in Jesus as Messiah appears not to have been practiced during Jesus' ministry but rather occurred several decades later, especially after the destruction of Jerusalem in 70 C.E. when Jesus' followers were more easily differentiated from other groups of Jews in Palestine. There are good grounds for thinking that the statement in 9:22 reflects John's own situation.

Combined with this is evidence suggesting that some Palestinian synagogues toward the end of the first century C.E. included a "ban against heretics" (*Birkath ha-Minim*) in their prayer liturgy as a way of excluding Jesus' followers and others from the Jewish community. This is possibly alluded to in John 16:2: "those who kill you will think that by doing so they are offering worship to God" (also see 16:33). If this was the case, John's Gospel might well have arisen from a context in which relations between Jesus' followers and their fellow Jews had become severely strained over the question of belief in Jesus as the Messiah, to the point that a formal breach between their two communities had occurred. This would help account for the negative portrayal of "the Jews" in the Fourth Gospel (see discussion below).

Such a context would help explain why the OT figures so prominently within the Gospel. John has probed deeply into the Scriptures to establish even more correlations between Jesus and Scripture than those found in the synoptic tradition. His response to the synagogue is quite different from what we found in Matthew. Rather than presenting Jesus as a "new Moses" or even as a rabbi superior to Moses, John presents Jesus in even bolder terms: as God's own Son, uniquely qualified as the Revealer of God's will since he, like Wisdom, was God's collaborator at creation. These christological claims, along with many other features of the Gospel, would be seen by readers of this Gospel as efforts to strengthen the faith of a community shattered by the crisis of separating—or even worse, of being banished—from its root tradition.

John's Theological Vision

John's theological vision is captured especially well in the concluding paragraph of chapter 3:

> The one who comes from above is above all; the one who is of the earth belongs to the earth and speaks about earthly things. The one who comes from heaven is above all. He testifies to what he has seen and heard, yet no one accepts his testimony. Whoever has accepted his testimony has certified this, that God is true. He whom God has sent speaks the words of God, for he gives the Spirit without measure. The Father loves the Son and has placed all things in his hands. Whoever believes in the Son has eternal life; whoever disobeys the Son will not see life, but must endure God's wrath. (3:31–36)

This passage illustrates a typical feature of John: It is difficult to know whether these are the words of John the Baptist (NIV) or of the Fourth Evangelist (NRSV). Several elements of John's theological vision are expressed in this passage.

First is its spatial imagery. John envisions two worlds: the world above and the world below, or, quite simply, heaven and earth. These are more than spaces, however; they represent ways of thinking and being. Since John's entire universe is viewed this way, we can refer to it as cosmological dualism—a universe with two (and only two) realms: heaven above, earth beneath.

Second is Jesus as cosmic redeemer. Jesus is variously called "the one who comes from above [heaven]," the "one whom God sent," the Son whom the Father loves, and the one who "testifies to what he has seen and heard." In different ways these phrases depict Jesus as a figure who lives with God in heaven, and thus as a divine figure whom God sends as an envoy to the earth below to bring eternal life and redeem the world.

Third are polarities of response. Only two ways of responding to God's Envoy are envisioned: acceptance or rejection, believing or disobeying. Fence straddling is not an option in John's world.

Fourth is receiving "the Spirit without measure." In John's theological vision, Jesus not only possesses the Spirit but also confers the Spirit on his disciples after his resurrection. After Jesus is gone, the Spirit carries on his work within the community of believers. **[See Expanded CD Version pp. 290–91:** *"Heaven" and "Earth" in John***]**

Heaven and earth are spatial realities for John, but they are more than that. They also symbolize ways of thinking: "the one who is of the earth belongs to the earth and speaks about earthly things" (3:31). Jesus says to Nicodemus: "If I have told you about earthly things and you do not believe, how can you believe if I tell you about heavenly things?" (3:12). Being born "from above" (or "again," 3:3, 7) implies a change in the human personality that has a psychological and moral dimension. To order one's life according "to heavenly things" creates the equivalent of a newborn child—a new person. Conversely, to be an earthling means more than living on the earth; it is to live and think a certain way, oblivious to a whole other dimension of reality. When Jesus tells Pilate, "My kingdom is not from this world" (18:36), he is talking about more than spatial location; he is speaking of ideological distance.

The Cosmic Redeemer

No single image or phrase adequately captures the Johannine Jesus. Since "cosmic" derives from *kosmos*, the Greek word for world, it signals the arena of Jesus' activity: "God so loved the world . . ." (3:16). But it is also intended to capture the image of Jesus as one who bridges both heaven and earth, who was with God "at the beginning." Jesus does many things in John's Gospel, but the essence of his work is redemptive. He brings eternal life. He comes not to condemn but to save. There may be some doubt whether Luke's Gospel portrays Jesus' death as a redemptive act; in John's Gospel, there is no doubt.

In the Fourth Gospel we find language used of Jesus that is familiar to us from the Synoptic Gospels. **[See Expanded CD Version pp. 291–93:** *John's Use of Christological Images Found in the Synoptic Gospels***]**

Three christological images used in John deserve special attention: (1) Son of God; (2) *Logos*; and (3) heavenly Savior.

Son of God. Even the casual reader of the Fourth Gospel is struck by how much Jesus' divine sonship dominates the narrative. It surfaces not only in the expression "Son of God," which is used fairly infrequently, but also in the distinctively Johannine expressions "the Son" and "the only Son" (*monogenēs huios*). Since Jesus is without peer, he needs no further identification. Being one of a kind, he is simply "*the* Son." While this absolute use of "the Son" is not unique to the Fourth Gospel (cf. Matt 11:25–27; Luke 10:21–22), it is distinctive. Closely related are the numerous references to "the Father" or "my Father," which merely extend the net more widely.

It is not just the frequency of "Son" language that is significant, but also how it is distributed throughout the narrative. It is difficult to find a single episode or discourse in the Fourth Gospel prior to the Passion Narrative in which Jesus' divine sonship does not figure in some way. If we look at who uses the expression, we find a striking pattern. Unlike Mark, for example, in which acknowledgements of Jesus' divine sonship are limited to God, the demonic order, and the Roman centurion at his death, or Matthew, who reports Peter confessing Jesus as the "Son of the living God," the Fourth Evangelist scatters these claims all over his narrative.

Belief in Jesus' divine sonship is frequently expressed by the Fourth Evangelist in his narrative comments (1:18; 3:18, 35–36; 20:31). His voice is joined by that of John the Baptist (1:34), Nathanael (1:49), and Martha (11:27), but most significantly by that of Jesus himself, who repeatedly speaks of himself as "the Son" (3:16–17; 5:19–26; 6:40; 8:36; 11:4; 14:13; 17:1) or who can even be said to have proclaimed, "I am God's Son" (10:36; 19:7). In the Fourth Gospel we hear a chorus of voices backing up the soloist Jesus, who unabashedly lays claim to this unique status.

Rather than just asserting Jesus' divine sonship, the Fourth Evangelist fills out its content. Unlike Matthew and Luke, in John's Gospel Jesus does not become Son of God through miraculous conception; no such traditions are reported by him. Rather, he has always held this status—from the beginning. As the pre-existent *Logos*, he is the eternal Son of God, which enables him to be the bringer of eternal life (3:16, 36). John's four uses of *monogene⁻s* as an attribute of "the Son" (1:14, 18; 3:16, 18) have figured prominently in the church's debates about Jesus' pre-existent status. Translated "only begotten" it would imply a moment of conception, and thus a "time when he was not," but rendered as "only," in the sense "the only one of his kind," it is less amenable to such claims. Either way, the term connotes his uniqueness.

In Jesus' preincarnate state, he occupies a unique position in which he is equal to the Father (5:18), even to the point of being God (1:1). Their relationship is sealed by love, making it personal rather than abstract and distant (3:35; 5:20; 10:17). It is also a relationship of intimate, complete, and mutual knowledge. Out of this knowledge, the incarnate Son testifies to "what he sees and knows." His role as Revealer derives from his status as Son (1:18; 5:19).

Since Jesus alone has seen God, he can reveal the interior of God's being and interpret God's will. So closely are the wills of the Son and the Father united that the Father "works" through the Son (5:20). Their identity becomes virtually collapsed. To honor one is to honor the other (5:23), and to glorify one is to glorify the other (14:13; 17:1). As the Father's alter ego, the Son operates with his full authority, having received "all things" (3:35), and from this position of authority he can exercise judgment (5:22). It is from this uniquely conceived, heavenly position that the Father sends the Son, thus making him God's Envoy to the earth. But his mission is redemptive rather than punitive (3:17). He executes judgment both as the incarnate Son and the eschatological judge (5:25). His ultimate purpose is to give life (5:21, 26), since this is the essence of his relationship with the Father. The Father's capacity to give life—to raise the dead—is extended to the Son (5:21). At no time does the incarnate Son relinquish the role of life giver. It might be seen as the role that defines all of his other roles.

The Logos.[13] From Jesus' divine sonship emerges his role as Revealer. Our illustrative passage highlights the Revealer's role: "He testifies to what he has seen and heard . . . he whom God has sent speaks the words of God" (3:32, 34). To express Jesus' unique role as the one who brings the Living Voice of God to life, the Fourth Evangelist employs the metaphor of the *Logos* (1:1–18). In doing so, he makes one of the most innovative theological moves found anywhere in the NT.

Where John derives his understanding of the *Logos* has puzzled readers for centuries. **[See Expanded CD Version pp. 294–95: *Possible Sources of John's* Logos Christology]**

Regardless of the sources informing the Fourth Evangelist's *Logos* Christology, he crafts what many scholars regard as a poetic, even hymnic, prologue into a profoundly moving theological interpretation of the figure Jesus. Not content with what he finds in the Jesus tradition at his disposal, John draws on the creation account in Genesis and on other images and traditions familiar to both Jewish and non-Jewish readers. From this rich set of resources, he engages in his own distinctive form of theological sense-making to shape what has become one of the most memorable interpretations of Christ ever written.

With the opening line, the Fourth Evangelist recalls the opening verses of Genesis to introduce his Christianized account of creation. Earlier interpreters had wondered who was included in the "us" of Gen 1:26: "Let us make humankind in our own image." John supplies an answer by placing the preincarnate Jesus with God "in the beginning." Also striking is the unequivocal identification of the *Logos* as God: "and the Word was God" (1:1). As God's creative agent, the Word becomes the one through whom everything came into being (1:3). Since life emerged and light dawned at creation, the *Logos* is both the embodiment and bringer of life and the bearer of light. Like divine *Sophia*, the *Logos* had to endure people's blindness and ignorance and be present among those who could neither discern nor appreciate the presence of God's Envoy among them. Given the close association of "light" and "glory," the *Logos* also exudes brilliant radiance that comes with a full measure of "grace and truth."

Relating the human figure Jesus of Nazareth to the divine *Logos*, or conversely, claiming that the divine *Logos* took concrete form in a single human being, is possibly the Fourth Evangelist's most daring—certainly an enduring—theological claim. Moving well beyond the birth and infancy stories of Matthew and Luke, who placed the miracle of Christ's appearance at a particular time and place, John pushes the miracle much further back, beyond time and space as we know it. By moving the origin of Christ back to the time of creation and to the "world above," to the realm of the transcendent God, John enlarges the miracle by bringing the pre-existent Christ forward in time and by bringing him "down" from such lofty heights.

How does Jesus close such a vast chronological and spatial gap? By emerging as the incarnate *Logos*, who brings the Living Voice of God to full expression. Realizing this enables us to understand why the voice of Jesus in the Fourth Gospel is such an unequivocally powerful voice. It carries with it the full force of God's creative Word so vividly displayed in creation. It is also a voice spoken with the conviction of an eyewitness who has seen and heard firsthand what he now reveals in his preaching, his teaching, his conversations with friends and opponents, and even in the signs he performs.

Even though Jesus is identified as God's *Logos* only in the prologue, this image sets the stage for the rest of the Gospel. For this reason, Jesus' voice is heard frequently and loudly in the Fourth Gospel. With a stunning display of extended discourses, lengthy conversations, and a series of highly stylized "I am" sayings and discourses, the Fourth Evangelist gives voice to the Word of God. The reader hears Jesus the incarnate Word speaking but soon recognizes that not only is he speaking for God, but God is speaking through him. This is the duly appointed Son of God, the one sent by the Father to speak his words and perform his work. So closely are they identified—"The Father and I are one" (10:30)—that the words of Jesus are heard as the Word of God.

Since many of the images and metaphors that figure prominently in Jesus' discourses are drawn from the OT, Jesus' words have the effect of bringing the Living Voice of God to expression in another sense. By identifying himself, for example, with the bread in the wilderness (John 6) or the good shepherd (John 10), Jesus is bringing forward these images from the Jewish Scriptures and laying claim to these himself. It is a different form of promise fulfillment than we find in the Synoptic Gospels, but it is no less powerful a means of making Scripture contemporary. By claiming to be living water, living bread, or the true vine, Jesus is also enacting his role as Revealer. Through these claims, he is unveiling Scripture's true meaning through his own speech and action. Through Jesus, the Word of God—Scripture—is being revealed as the word of life.

The more we read John's Gospel, the more we see the many dimensions of Jesus the Revealer. As one who was with the Father, who had seen and heard the Father, the Son reveals the Father's will. He speaks *for* the Father and *about* the Father. To see the Son is to see the Father (14:9); to hear the Son is to hear the Father; to know the Son is to know the Father (14:7). Not only his words but also his actions are revelatory. At the cleansing of the temple (2:13–22), the Jews ask him for a sign (v. 18) and he responds, "Destroy this temple, and in three days I will raise it up" (v. 19). Through his death and resurrection he replaces the temple. John shapes his narrative to give prominent billing to the seven signs Jesus performs. Unlike the Gospel of Mark, in which faith tended to precede miracles, in John's Gospel Jesus' signs create faith (e.g., 2:11).

John goes further than this: even Jesus' person is revelatory. Not only does Jesus perform signs, he is a sign. Like the bronze serpent in the wilderness, Jesus is "lifted up." He is held high where he can be seen by everyone and where his magnetic drawing power can be felt universally. It is almost as though Jesus' crucifixion blends easily into his resurrection and ascension, and as it does so Jesus gradually rises to become a universally recognized symbol of life (3:14–15; 12:32). In the same way, washing the disciples' feet (13:1–20) is a revelatory symbol: "I have set you an example," he says to his disciples, "that you also should do as I have done to you" (13:15).

The Heavenly Savior. Only once does the expression "Savior of the world" occur in the Fourth Gospel (4:42), but it captures an important dimension of the Johannine Jesus. Its one occurrence is a strong confessional use, expressing the Samaritans' full-fledged faith in Christ. By making this confession, they recognize the human being in their midst. As one who engages the Samaritan woman in conversation and thirsts (4:7), Jesus is presented as someone who experiences human emotions. He expresses rage by cleansing the temple (2:13–22), weeps when Lazarus dies (11:35), experiences anxiety at the prospect of death (12:27), and loves his disciples (13:1), to mention just a few examples. But as our illustrative passage states, he is the "one who comes from heaven" (3:31). He displays unusual levels of knowledge, both prescience and omniscience (e.g., John 2:24–25; 16:30).

As an alien presence in the world, Jesus constantly refers to where he came from and where he is going, and even insists before Pilate, "My kingdom is not from this world" (18:36). We can readily see why John's Gospel has been criticized as "naïve docetism." Looked at one way, Jesus only "seems" (Greek *dokeō*) to be fully human. As in the Synoptic Gospels, he performs suprahuman feats, such as walking on the water (6:16–21), and does miracles, such as turning water into wine and raising Lazarus from the dead. After Easter he appears in places where the "doors were shut" (20:26). Both dimensions—the heavenly and the earthly, the divine and the human—are brought together in John's Gospel. This is why the Johannine Jesus is so aptly characterized as the "man from heaven." He is a man—he became flesh (1:14), which suggests that he experienced an ordinary human birth. He experienced the whole range of human emotions and behaved like a human being. Yet he is "from heaven"—a stranger on earth, never unaware of where he is from and where he is going. He is "above" the fray, always in control, even in times of severe crisis.

We miss the point if we try to balance the seesaw between Jesus' humanity and divinity in John. The purpose of the Son of God's descent to the earth was redemptive: to those who believed him, he gave the power to become children of God (1:12). John often uses the explicit language of "saving" to describe Jesus' work (10:9; 12:47). Frequently the metaphor of "bringing [eternal] life" is used. We may think of eternal life as unending future life after we die, but John's conception of eternal life includes more than this.

Eternal life is a future possession (3:15–16; 6:40, 54), but believers can already experience it during their lifetimes. "Anyone who hears my word and believes him who sent me *has* eternal life, and does not come under judgment, but has passed from death to life" (5:24; emphasis added; also see 3:36; 4:14; 6:47, 54; 12:50; 17:2–3). Eternal life is not merely a quantitative extension of this life but life qualitatively transformed by faith here and now. By bearing witness to the relationship he enjoys with God, Jesus exemplifies the eternal life already available to those who believe in him as God's Son. This begins even as the life of faith begins, even though it is not finally consummated until death marks the transition to a new form of life with God.

Jesus' saving work receives special emphasis in John through the image of the "Lamb of God who takes away the sin of the world" (1:29, 36). This is a remarkable image not only because it is distinctively Johannine but also because we are not sure where the Fourth Evangelist gets it or how he understands it. In the Jewish sacrificial system animals could be offered as sacrifices (Lev 4–5), but lambs were not one of the prescribed animals. In John's Passion Narrative, Jesus' death occurs at the time the Passover lamb is being slaughtered on the day before Passover (John 19:14; cf. 19:36 and Exod 12:46; Num 9:12). This suggests that John interprets Jesus' death as the death of the Passover lamb, but the Passover lamb was not slaughtered in order to take away sin. The imagery of the innocent lamb being taken away to be slaughtered (Isa 53) may inform John's image here. In spite of this lack of clarity, John understands Jesus' mission as redemptive—that it was meant somehow to deal with, even remove, "the sin of the world." This is what the image of Jesus as Cosmic Redeemer signifies in John's theological vision.

Polarities of Response

As our illustrative passage suggests, there are only two ways to respond to Jesus: acceptance or rejection. To accept is to believe, to reject is to disobey (3:36). John envisions only two levels of reality, and his construal of human behavior is equally dualistic. For this reason, John is sometimes said to operate with an ethical dualism in which there are only two categories of behavior: good and evil. As we find in other religious communities during the Hellenistic-Roman period, most notably the Jewish separatist community of Qumran, these two ways can be thought of metaphorically as light and darkness. As the prologue asserts, Jesus' coming into the world is seen as light shining in darkness (1:5). "The light [Jesus] has come into the world," we are told, "and people loved darkness rather than light because their deeds were evil" (3:19; similarly 12:35, 46).

John also presents God and Satan as polar opposites. This becomes clear in Jesus' discussion with the Jews concerning the true descendants of Abraham (8:31–47), in which the question is, "For whom is God rightfully said to be 'Father'?" Is God Jesus' Father, or has God fathered the Jews through Abraham? Claiming sole title to be God's Son, Jesus chastises the Jews as illegitimate children whose real father is not God but Satan: "You are from your father the devil" (8:44). Jesus associates the devil with undiluted evil—"he is a liar and the father of lies" (8:44)—and in his discussion yet another polarity emerges: lying and telling the truth (8:44–45).

Still another set of opposites is implied in Jesus' claim that "all who do evil hate the light and do not come to the light" (3:20). Responses to Jesus can be framed as expressions of hate. The world hates Jesus because he castigates its works as evil (7:7); when the world expresses hatred for Jesus' disciples, it only mirrors its hatred for Jesus himself (15:18). Disciples who conform to the world's expectations experience the world's love, but by standing apart from the world they experience the world's hatred (15:19; see 17:14). The two primary emotions through which responses to Jesus can be calibrated are love and hatred. These may be equated with believing and disbelieving respectively. Also surfacing within this discussion are two other opposites: belonging to the world and not belonging to the world (15:19; 17:14, 16). Similarly, living the moral life requires one to choose between two options: slavery and freedom (8:34–38).

John's categories line up neatly: heaven and earth, God and Satan, light and darkness, good and evil, love and hate, believing and disbelieving, freedom and slavery. This provides a larger framework for understanding two distinctive features of John's theological vision: his sectarian understanding of Christianity and his negative portrait of Jews.

A Community Apart. With such a sharp distinction drawn between good and evil and everything associated with each, we are not surprised when scholars characterize Johannine Christianity as sectarian. John's followers would draw firm boundaries between themselves and outsiders, or as John would put it, between themselves and "the world." They probably formed enclaves of believers that closely resembled the Jewish community at Qumran, whose geographical distance—some twelve miles east of Jerusalem—symbolized their ideological distance from the Jewish leadership associated with the temple. As a community set apart from official forms of Judaism, the Qumran community established a way of life that enabled them to prepare for the end of the world. While the Johannine community may not have been equally sectarian in outlook or organization, it seems to have viewed itself as an island of loving friends in a sea of hateful enemies. One prominent metaphor Jesus uses to characterize his disciples is "friends" (15:12–17). He measures "greater love" by one's willingness to die for one's friends (15:13). When he promotes love as the primary ethic to be cultivated among the disciples, he especially commends love among the disciples—love directed inwardly within the community rather than outwardly toward those not in the community (13:34–35).

The Jews. One of the most distinctive—and one of the most problematic—features of the Fourth Gospel is its characterization of Jews. Occasional reference is made to distinct Jewish groups, such as priests and Levites (1:19), scribes (8:3), and, more often, Pharisees (7:47–48; 8:3, 13; 9:13, 15–16, 40; 11:46, 57; 12:19, 42), especially when linked with the chief priests (7:32, 45; 11:47, 57; 18:3), or to the chief priests alone (12:10; 18:35; 19:6, 15, 21; see 18:10). The Fourth Gospel makes no reference to Sadducees as do the Synoptic Gospels, especially Matthew, or to Herodians (Mark 3:6; 12:13; Matt 22:16).

In sharp contrast to the Synoptic Gospels, John's Gospel displays unusual interest in "the Jews" as a group. Here is a case in which the statistics are truly revealing. The term "Jew" (*Ioudaios*) or "Jews" (*Ioudaioi*) occurs five times in Matthew, six times in Mark, and five times in Luke; in the Fourth Gospel it occurs seventy-one times! The Fourth Evangelist acknowledges that Jesus himself was a Jew (4:9; 18:35), and he reports Jesus' teaching in the synagogue (6:59), though not as often as do the Synoptics. Several times Jesus goes to Jerusalem to participate in separate Jewish feasts, including Booths, Dedication, and Passover. On three separate occasions Jews believe in Jesus (8:31; 11:45; 12:11). The Samaritan woman acknowledged that "salvation is from the Jews" (4:22). A sympathetic treatment of the Jews also occurs in the story of the raising of Lazarus, in which they console Mary (11:19, 31, 33). Although

Nicodemus is not presented as one who became a full-fledged disciple, he is identified as a "leader of the Jews." He strikes a sympathetic pose as a genuine learner (3:1).

Set against these positive references to Jews are numerous other references in which they are portrayed in various levels of opposition, ranging from general adversarial responses (1:19; 2:18–20; 3:25; 5:10; 6:41, 52; 7:15, 35; 8:22, 48, 52; 9:18; 10:19, 24; cf. 13:33) to more hostile reactions, from plots to resist to outright efforts to kill Jesus (5:16, 18; 7:1, 11; 10:31, 33; 11:8, 54; 18:36; 19:7, 12; also see 19:3). Several times the Jews are mentioned as an intimidating presence that inhibits people from speaking or acting openly (7:13; 9:22; 19:38; 20:19). They play a key role in the Passion Narrative, although references to them often have a neutral quality. They may be in an adversarial position, but the narrator can refer to them without doing so pejoratively (18:14, 20, 31, 33, 38–39; 19:14, 19–21, 31). In a number of instances the Fourth Evangelist describes certain customs or observances as "Jewish" or as being a practice "of the Jews," and he does so as though he is speaking as an outsider, although this is not necessarily the case (2:6, 13; 5:1; 6:4; 7:2; 11:55; 19:40, 42).

Perhaps the severest denunciation of "the Jews" occurs in chapter 8, in which Jesus calls them children of the devil (8:44) and they in turn accuse him of being demon possessed (8:48–52). The encounter concludes with their trying to stone him (8:59).

In many respects John's characterization of "the Jews" corresponds to Matthew's characterization of the "scribes and Pharisees." Matthew's polemical rhetoric can be explained by the Matthean church's tension with the synagogue, although it is difficult to tell whether a break between the church and synagogue had already occurred. The critical issue in Matthew is deciding who qualifies as the legitimate interpreter of Torah—the Pharisees and their rabbis or Jesus, the church's "rabbi." The language used in the Fourth Gospel, by contrast, is more revealing because it actually envisions expulsion from the synagogue. If those who believed in Jesus' messiahship and were still attending synagogue had been forced to choose whether to remain as members of the synagogue or sever their ties and begin attending Christian worship exclusively, this must have created a severe crisis among families and friends. With such strong barriers already erected between church and synagogue and with a corresponding level of alienation between the two communities, the Fourth Gospel would understandably characterize "the Jews" in the most unflattering terms imaginable. In religious controversies that deeply divide communities, as the level of rhetoric rises the distance between communities of faith increases, and mutual hostility results.

John's tendency to think in exclusively dualistic terms may be both a contributing cause as well as an effect of this controversy. Allowing no option other than believing or disbelieving and being unable to concede the legitimacy of Jewish belief apart from Jesus the Messiah, the Fourth Evangelist found it natural to align his opponents—any opponents—with the world below and its associated metaphors: darkness, lies, slavery, Satan, evil, and sin. Yet just as surely as his two-category disposition contributed to the problem, so was it intensified by the split. Once Christians were excluded from the synagogue, the two worlds of Johannine thought became reinforced, providing the newly emerging Christian community boundaries broad enough to keep them separated from the world. John's negative portrait of "the Jews" reflects this sectarian spirit.

It is better to account for this dimension of John' Gospel by looking to the historical-social situation out of which it emerged rather than resorting to explanations in which the Jews are stick figures or foils against which the Fourth Evangelist can tell his story. Highly polemical rhetoric tends to lose historical precision the more it heats up. This is all the more reason why responsible interpreters of John's Gospel should not equate its portrait of "the Jews" with actual persons and groups, either ancient or modern. Such naïve equations have always had disastrous results both for Jews so labeled and Christians who did the labeling.

One strength of John's dualistic tendency is its capacity for establishing clear boundaries that create identity and solidarity within the community of believers. To the extent that this helps the community understand itself and strengthen its own belief system, it is a beneficial exercise. Its weakness is the mentality it creates: the inability to see complexities that do not easily fall into one of two categories. With such tightly constructed categories that neatly align with moral categories, the community divides and both sides begin using the same rhetoric in characterizing each other. Those who are taught to love and hate with such zeal find it easy to hate their fellow believers when they too must part ways. We will see how this happens when we look at the Johannine letters.

Life after Jesus: Living by the Spirit in the World

A fourth aspect of the Johannine theological vision relates to the time when Jesus is no longer among the community. In John's Gospel, the Cosmic Redeemer's work is accomplished with his death. "I glorified you on earth," Jesus says to the Father, "by finishing the work that you gave me to do" (17:4). When he says from the cross, "It is finished" (19:30), he is referring to the work for which he was sent by the Father. His time "in this world" has been a time of revealing the Father's will. His signs have borne witness to the Father's authority. He has created a confrontation that has exposed the sharp division among the Jews. Consequently, Jesus' Farewell Discourse (chs. 13–17) occupies a prominent place in the Fourth Gospel. Here Jesus prepares for his "departure," in other words, his death and planned return to the Father. As the longest sustained speech in the Gospel, the Farewell Discourse compares with the Sermon on the Mount in Matthew's Gospel. Reflecting all the literary characteristics of a testament, Jesus' Farewell Discourse summarizes his legacy even as it prepares for the passing of the torch to the disciples after his death. Here John sketches what life will be "after Jesus." It contains hints throughout of his eventual return (13:36; 14:3, 19–20, 28; 16:16–24) and creates the expectation that his disciples will eventually join him "above" with the Father.

Here the Fourth Evangelist expresses how the Johannine community sees itself or, at least, how it should see itself. In either case, the Farewell Discourse sketches the Johannine view of the church, even though the term "church" (*ekklēsia*) does not occur in it. The Farewell Discourse shows how the Fourth Evangelist envisions authentic faith being lived out in response to the Johannine Christ. Several things distinguish this vision: (1) it is a community guided by the Spirit; (2) its community ethic is mutual love; (3) its posture is one of standing against the world; and (4) it faces the future with hope.

1. *Guided by the Spirit.* Jesus reassures his disciples that he will not leave them orphaned (14:18). He promises that once he is raised from the dead, he will confer the Spirit on them (14:26; see 20:22). He also promises that the Spirit will continue the work he did while he was among them. Especially will he continue Jesus' role as Revealer. Like Jesus he will speak what he has heard (16:13), teach the disciples everything by reminding them of Jesus' own teaching (14:26), and assist them in pursuing the truth (16:13). The Spirit will also continue Jesus' role as witness in the world, testifying on Jesus' behalf (15:26) but actively confronting "the world" in speaking about sin, righteousness, and judgment (16:8–11). As Jesus glorified the Father, so will the Spirit bring glory to Jesus (16:14). In this way the Spirit's presence among the disciples will keep them from becoming abandoned children.

John's language for the Spirit in these chapters is distinctive. As Advocate or Helper (*parakletos*, 14:16, 26; 15:26; 16:7), the Spirit reassures the disciples even as they grieve the loss of Jesus and find their own strength to carry on. As the "Spirit of truth" he will bear true witness to Jesus and extend the truth of God's revelation into the world. In Acts the risen Jesus is still active within the church, sharing the stage with the Spirit poured out at Pentecost and continuing to make his presence felt. Although it is conceptualized differently, this vision is also present in the Fourth Gospel, in which the living Jesus is present and the Spirit carries on Jesus' work within the community of believers. Ask the Johannine community how it experiences Jesus' presence within their midst, and it will answer, "Through the Spirit that he conferred on us."

2. *Loving Each Other.* In the Synoptic Gospels, Jesus teaches his disciples to love God and to love their neighbor as themselves. That their love is to reach beyond their own community is exemplified by such stories as that of the good Samaritan. The Fourth Gospel, by contrast, stresses the importance of love among the disciples themselves. The Fourth Evangelist's emphasis on the "new commandment" that Jesus gives to his disciples acknowledges the novelty of this dimension of its ethical teaching. Jesus' disciples are expected to replicate among themselves the mutual love that exists between the Father and the Son (15:9), as well as the love that Jesus has shown for them (13:34; 15:12). To love Jesus is to share in his love with the Father (14:21), and this gives access to Jesus' revelation of the Father. Love becomes an entrée to divine knowledge. One loves in order to know God; one also loves as a way of knowing God. Love and obedience are also mutually expressive. To hear Jesus' commandments and keep them is an expression of love (14:21, 23; 15:10). By loving in this way, the disciples will reflect on earth the unity and harmony that exists in heaven. They are to relate to each other as "friends" (15:12–17), exhibiting love that is measured by willingness to sacrifice for each other.

Especially significant in chapters 13–17 is how the Fourth Evangelist reports Jesus' farewell meal with his disciples (13:1–11). Instead of the Passover meal that serves as an occasion for instituting the Eucharist, as is the case in the Synoptic Gospels, John's Gospel has a meal in which the dominant symbolic act is Jesus' washing the disciples' feet. The Fourth Evangelist wants his community to remember Jesus on his knees before the disciples washing their feet rather than his celebrating the Eucharist with them. He intends this action to be symbolic (13:15): it becomes a gauge by which their love for each other can be measured. Another image is that of the vine and branches (15:1–11). The disciples' relationship to each other is to exhibit the dynamic and unified life of a growing, vibrant vine. Their communal relationship is to be an extension of their relationship with Jesus himself, the true vine.

3. *Standing against the World.* The Fourth Evangelist's universe contains no shades of gray. The world is seen as a hostile place, a necessary evil. Recognizing this, the disciples must learn to be "in the world" but not "of the world." The world provides a space in which to live, but the disciples are expected to erect walls to separate their enclave of friends from the world's hostile forces. When it faces persecution or attack from outsiders, the church is to remember Jesus' own experience (15:18–20). After all, he was an alien presence within an unfriendly world and the disciples will be expected to take their cue from him and his behavior. As the world hated him, so will it hate the church. As the world was unable to recognize this "man from heaven," so will it fail to recognize the heavenly community he left behind.

The Johannine church has been seen as sectarian in its outlook for good reason—hunkered down, set against the world, and drawing sustenance from a Christ whom it remembers as a stranger on the earth, rejected by his people. Exhibiting a "Christ against culture" mentality, it is a community in solidarity, which can easily turn inward to breed its own form of communal self-love.

4. *Facing the Future.* Several times in Jesus' Farewell Discourse, he promises his disciples that he will "come again" (14:3; cf. 14:19–20, 28). In language much more allusive than the synoptic Jesus' promise to return as the Son of Man coming in the clouds of heaven (Mark 13:26), the Johannine Jesus speaks of being seen in a little while: "A little while, and you will no longer see me, and again a little while, and you will see me" (16:16). This is typical of the cryptic way John refers to Jesus' second coming. Several times in the Fourth Gospel Jesus speaks of the future in ways reminiscent of the synoptic tradition: of a "last day" when Jesus would "raise up" those who believe in him (6:39–40; cf. 6:54), or when people will be judged (12:48), or when people will receive eternal life (12:25; see 11:25–26).

Several other times we encounter language suggesting that experiences normally reserved until the "last day" have already begun to occur during Jesus' encounters with his disciples. To believe in Jesus is to undergo a transition from death to life so that believers experience eternal life as a present possession (5:24; 6:47, 54). Whether the passages that have a strong eschatological dimension are carry-overs from the earlier Jesus tradition and the passages that see resurrection and eternal life as a present gift represent John's modified point of view is much debated. Since both viewpoints stand side by side in the Fourth Gospel, they are in some tension with each other.

Taken as a whole, the Fourth Gospel presents a modified view of the Christian future. It resembles Luke-Acts by diminishing the note of urgency that was often associated with Jesus' coming. But rather than postponing Jesus' coming to a distant future and urging his disciples to be concerned with how they live during the interim, as Luke-Acts does, John proposes an alternative: bring the future into the present. The Johannine community is urged to see its faith in Christ as God's gift from the future and also as a work that God does among them (6:29). Through their faith, Jesus' disciples already experience what the Son and the Father mutually share: love, knowledge, and life. Since these are unbounded by time and space, believers experience eternal life as a present gift as well as a future hope.

1:1-18	1:19-1:51	2:1-12	2:13-3:36
Prologue	**Jerusalem/Bethany**	**Galilee**	**Jerusalem**
Word, life, light (1-5) JnB as witness (6-9) Children of God (9-13) Word – flesh (14) JnB & Jesus (15) Grace & truth (16-18)	**BOOK OF SIGNS: CHS. 1-12** JESUS' MINISTRY: THE MAN FROM HEAVEN REVEALED (1:19-7:9) → Jerusalem (1:19) → Bethany (1:28) Witness of JnB (19-34) Andrew & Peter (35-42) Philip & Nathanael (43-51) → Galilee (1:43)	Wedding at Cana of Galilee (1-12) **M – Sign # 1** (v. 11) → Cana (1) → Capernaum (12)	Cleansing the Temple (2:13-25) **- Passover** (13, 23) →Jerusalem (13, 23) Jesus & Nicodemus (3:1-21) -J & N Dialogue (1-10) **-DISCOURSE: Eternal life** (3:11-21) Jesus & JnB (3:22-30) → Judea, Aenon near Salim (22-23) JnB's witness (24-30) **-DISCOURSE: The one from heaven** (3:31-36)

7:10-8:59	9-10	11-12	13-14
Jerusalem	**Jerusalem**	**Jerusalem**	**Jerusalem**
CONFLICT IN JERUSALEM (7:10-10:42) Jesus to Jerusalem secretly (7:10-13) → Jerusalem (10) **– Festival of Booths (October)** (7:2-10) **DISCOURSE: Law & Circum.** (7:14-24) Jews resist (7:25-31) Pharisees send officers, arrest Jesus (7:32-36) Disputes in Temple (7:37-52) [[Woman caught in adultery (7:53-8:11)]] **DISCOURSE:** **- Disputes with Pharisees in Temple: light of world, the Father** (8:12-20) **- Jesus from above** (8:21-30) **- Jesus & Abraham** (8:31-59)	Healing of blind man at Pool of Siloam (9:1-12) **M – Sign # 6** Dialogue and interrogation (9:13-41) **DISCOURSE: Good Shepherd** (10:1-21) Jesus rejected at **Feast of Dedication (December)** – Temple (10:22-42) → crosses Jordan (40)	PRELUDE TO JESUS' HOUR (11:1-12:50) Raises Lazarus (11:1-44) **M - Sign # 7** Plot to kill Jesus – Pharisees & Caiaphas (11:45-57) → Ephraim (54) **– Passover (March-April)** (55-57) Mary anoints Jesus at Bethany (12:1-8) **- Passover** (1) Plot to kill Lazarus (12:9-11) Jesus' entry into Jerusalem (12:12-19) Jesus interprets his death (12:20-36) Response to Jesus (12:36b-43) **DISCOURSE: Summary of Jesus' teaching** (12:44-50)	**BOOK OF GLORY CHS. 13-20** FAREWELL MEAL AND FAREWELL DISCOURSE (13:1-17:26) Farewell Meal (13:1-38) **– Passover** (1) Foot washing (1-11) **DISCOURSE: Communal service** (12-20) Jesus prophesies betrayal (21-30) **DISCOURSE: Love one another** (31-35) Jesus foretells Peter's denial (36-38) **FAREWELL DISCOURSE:** (14:1-16:33) **Jesus-way to Father** (14:1-14) **Promise of Spirit – peace** (14:15-31)

4:1-42	4:43-54	5	6-7
Samaria	**Galilee**	**Jerusalem**	**Galilee**
Samaritan woman – Sychar (1-42) → Judea to Galilee (3) → Samaria – Sychar **- DISCOURSE:** **Living water, true** **worship** Jesus & woman dialogue: water (4-15) Dialogue cont. – worship (16-26) Woman gets Sam. Friends (27-30) Jesus' food (31-38) Samaritans' faith (39-42)	→ Galilee (4:43-45, 54) Healing an official's son (4:46-54) **M –** **Sign # 2** (54) →Cana of Galilee (46)	Healing man at Bethzatha pool (1-9) **M – Sign # 3** - **"festival of the** **Jews"** (1) – **Passover ?** →Jerus. (Temple) (2) Controversy with Jews re Sabbath (9b-18) Resistance: Jews persecute Jesus, seek to kill him (16-18) **DISCOURSE: Son's** **authority, resurrec-** **tion, witness of JnB &** **Scripture to Jesus,** **Moses** (19-47)	Feeding 5000 (6:1-15) **M – Sign # 4** → Sea of Galilee (1) – **Passover** (4) Walking on water (6:16-21) **M – Sign # 5** Crowds → Capernaum (6:22-24) **DISCOURSE: Bread** **from heaven** (6:25-59) →Capernaum syn. (59) Disciples' response (6:60-71) Unbelief of Jesus' brothers (7:1-9) → Galilee (1, 9)

15-17	18-19	20	21
Jerusalem	**Jerusalem**	**Jerusalem**	**Galilee**
FAREWELL **DISCOURSE** **(cont.)** **True vine** (15:1-11) **Love & friends** (15:12-17) **World's hatred** (15:18-25) **Advocate promised** 15:25-27) **Expulsion from** **synagogues** (16:1-4) **Work of the Spirit** (16:5-15) **Jesus promises to go** **away but return** (16:16-24) **Predicting the future** (16:25-33) **Farewell prayer** (17:1-26)	PASSION NARRATIVE (18:1-19:42) Betrayal and arrest (18:1-12) Jesus before high priest Annas (18:12-14) Peter's 1st denial (18:15-18) Annas questions Jesus (18:19-24) Peter's 2nd & 3rd denials (18:25-27) Jesus before Pilate (18:28-38a) – **Passover** (28) Pilate and the Jews (18:28b-40) Jesus flogged, mocked (19:1-7) Jesus &Pilate (19:8-12) Pilate before the Jews (19:13-16) Crucifixion(19:16b-30) Jesus' side pierced (19:31-37) Jesus' burial (19:38-42)	FIRST RESURRECTION APPEARANCES (20:1-31) Empty tomb: Mary Magdalene; Peter and beloved disciple go to tomb (1-10) Appearance to Mary Magdalene (11-18) Jesus' 1st appearance to the gathered disciples; transfers Spirit (19-23) Disciples report Jesus' appearance to Thomas (24-25) Jesus' appearance to Thomas (26-29) Purpose of gospel (30-31)	RESURRECTION APPEARANCE AT SEA OF TIBERIAS (21:1-25) Appearance to gathered disciples – Peter, Thomas, Nathanael, sons of Zebedee, two other disciples (1-14) →Sea of Tiberias (1) Jesus and Peter (15-19) Jesus, Peter and the beloved disciple (20-23) Beloved disciple's testimony (24-25) **M** – Miracle Story → - Geography marker

Notes

1. *Haer.* 3.1.1–2; Eusebius, *Hist. eccl.* 5.8.4.

2. Cited in Eusebius, *Hist. eccl.* 6.25.3–10.

3. This is the order in the Monarchian Prologues, brief paragraphs introducing each Gospel found in some early manuscripts of the Vulgate. They were once thought to be dated as early as the second or third century, but are now more probably dated in the late fourth or early fifth century. It is also the order found in the late third century list of NT writings found in Codex Claromontanus, dated about the sixth century.

4. *Marc.* 4.2; also cf. 4.5.

5. *Comm. Jo.* 1.23.

6. Many fragments of Heracleon's commentary are preserved in Origen's *Commentary on John*.

7. The voice of the Fourth Evangelist dominates Holy Week, supplying the Gospel Reading for each day of Holy Week. Its influence continues through Easter, supplying one of the two Gospel Readings for Easter Day and the Gospel Readings for the Fourth through Seventh Sundays of Easter in all three years (also for the Third Sunday of Easter in Year C). Also, for Pentecost in all three years, the Gospel Readings come from John.

Other parts of the liturgical year also feel the impact of the Fourth Gospel. The Johannine prologue supplies the Gospel Reading for the Third Proper of Christmas and the Second Sunday After Christmas in all three years, and the Gospel Reading for the Second Sunday After the Epiphany in all three years comes from John. In the Second through Fifth Sundays of Lent, the majority of Gospel Readings are taken from John. For Trinity Sunday, in two of the three years, the Gospel Readings are from John. Also in the Sunday after Pentecost in Year B, Gospel Readings are taken from John in Propers 12 [17] – 16 [21] and 29 [34]. It also supplies the Gospel Reading for Holy Cross in all three years and for Thanksgiving Day in Year C.

8. Cited in Eusebius, *Hist. eccl.* 6.14.7.

9. *Comm. Jo.* 1.45.

10. *Cons.* 1.4.7.

11. Robert Kysar, *John: The Maverick Gospel* (rev. ed.; Louisville: Westminster John Knox, 1993).

12. C. H. Dodd, *Historical Tradition in the Fourth Gospel* (Cambridge: Cambridge University Press, 1963), 366–87.

13. For the following treatment, I am indebted to Thomas H. Tobin, "Logos," ABD 4:348–56.

Bibliography

Commentaries

Barrett, C. K. *The Gospel According to St. John: An Introduction with Commentary and Notes on the Greek Text.* 2d ed. Philadelphia: Westminster, 1955; London: SPCK, 1978.

Brown, Raymond E. *The Gospel According to John.* Anchor Bible 29. 2 vols. New York: Doubleday, 1966–1970.

———. *The Gospel and Epistles of John: A Concise Commentary.* Collegeville: Liturgical, 1988.

Bultmann, Rudolf. *The Gospel of John: A Commentary.* Philadelphia/Oxford: Westminster/Blackwell, 1971 (Göttingen, 1941).

Dodd, C. H. *The Interpretation of the Fourth Gospel.* Cambridge: Cambridge University Press, 1998 (1953).

Hoskyns, Edwyn C., and Francis N. Davey. *The Fourth Gospel.* 2d ed. London: Faber & Faber 1972 (1940; 2d ed. 1947; 2d rev. ed. 1961).

Kysar, Robert. *John.* Augsburg Commentaries on the New Testament. Minneapolis: Augsburg, 1986.

Lindars, Barnabas. *The Gospel of John.* New Century Bible. London/Grand Rapids: Marshall, Morgan, & Scott/Eerdmans, 1972.

O'Day, Gail R. "The Gospel of John: Introduction, Commentary, and Reflections." Pages 491–865 in vol. 9 of *The New Interpreter's Bible.* Edited by Leander E. Keck. 12 vols. Nashville: Abingdon, 1995.

Schnackenburg, Rudolf. *The Gospel According to St. John.* Translated by Kevin Smyth, Cecily Hastings, Francis McDonagh, David Smith, Richard Foley, and G. A. Kon. 3 vols. 1968–1982. New York: Crossroad, 1990 (Freiburg, 1965–1975).

Other Resources

Ashton, John. *The Interpretation of John.* Issues in Religion and Theology 9. Philadelphia: Fortress, 1986.

———. *Understanding the Fourth Gospel.* New York: Clarendon, 1991.

Culpepper, R. Alan. *Anatomy of the Fourth Gospel: A Study in Literary Design.* Philadelphia: Fortress, 1983.

———. *The Gospel and Letters of John.* Interpreting Biblical Texts. Nashville: Abingdon, 1998.

Dodd, C. H. *Historical Tradition in the Fourth Gospel.* Cambridge: Cambridge University Press, 1963; repr. 1999.

Koester, Craig R. *Symbolism in the Fourth Gospel: Meaning, Mystery, Community.* 2d ed. Minneapolis: Fortress, 2003 (1995).

Kysar, Robert. "John, Gospel of." Pages 609–19 in vol. 1 of *Dictionary of Biblical Interpretation.* Edited by John H. Hayes. 2 vols. Nashville: Abingdon, 1999.

———. "John, The Gospel of." Pages 912–31 in vol. 3 of *The Anchor Bible Dictionary.* Edited by David N. Freedman. 6 vols. Garden City: Doubleday, 1992.

———. *John: The Maverick Gospel.* Rev. ed. Louisville: Westminster/John Knox, 1993.

Martyn, J. Louis. *History and Theology in the Fourth Gospel.* 3d ed. Louisville: Westminster John Knox, 2003 (1968).

Neyrey, Jerome H. *An Ideology of Revolt: John's Christology in Social-Science Perspective.* Philadelphia: Fortress, 1988.

O'Day, Gail R. *Revelation in the Fourth Gospel: Narrative Mode and Theological Claim.* Philadelphia: Fortress, 1986.

Rensberger, David K. *Johannine Faith and Liberating Community.* Philadelphia: Westminster, 1988.

Sloyan, Gerard S. *What Are They Saying About John?* New York: Paulist, 1991.

Smith, D. Moody. *Johannine Christianity: Essays on Its Setting, Sources and Theology.* Columbia: University of South Carolina Press, 1984.

————. *John Among the Gospels: The Relationship in Twentieth-Century Research*. Minneapolis: Fortress, 1992.

————. *The Theology of the Gospel of John*. New Testament Theology. Cambridge: Cambridge University Press, 1995; repr. 1996.

Thompson, Marianne Meye. *The God of the Gospel of John*. Grand Rapids: Eerdmans, 2001.

————. *The Humanity of Jesus in the Fourth Gospel*. Philadelphia: Fortress, 1988.

Wiles, Maurice F. *The Spiritual Gospel: The Interpretation of the Fourth Gospel in the Early Church*. Cambridge: Cambridge University Press, 1960.

Part 3

THE STORY OF JESUS CONTINUED: THE CHURCH'S ORIGIN AND EXPANSION

Chapter 10

The Acts of the Apostles

"Luke tells a story, but, while doing so, he is also preaching."

Martin Dibelius

Even though Luke and Acts are now regarded as a single, continuous two-volume work, Acts does not follow Luke in early lists of NT writings. As early as the second century both works were attributed to Luke the physician, companion of Paul. The earliest use of Acts occurs in the mid-second century, with probable citations by Justin Martyr (ca. 100–165 C.E.).[1] Toward the end of the second century, Acts, with its numerous sermons by Peter and Paul often reflecting common themes, proved useful to Irenaeus (ca. 130–200 C.E.) in demonstrating a single apostolic faith in his refutation of Gnostics. Irenaeus appears to have been the first Christian writer to quote Acts explicitly.[2]

It is difficult to know why Acts was cited infrequently during the second century. Was it truly neglected before Justin made use of it, or are we simply unaware of its earlier use? Does its first clear appearance in the mid-second century suggest late composition, perhaps in the first quarter of the second century, or even later, as some have thought? About the year 400 in Constantinople, John Chrysostom (ca. 347–407 C.E.) complained of its neglect: "To many persons this Book [of Acts] is so little known, both it and its author, that they are not even aware that there is such a book in existence."[3] To fill the void, Chrysostom devoted fifty-five sermons to Acts, insisting on its value for providing reliable historical information about the early church. Was his complaint homiletical hyperbole? Eusebius of Caesarea (ca. 260–340 C.E.) had certainly made ample use of Acts in the early sections of his *Ecclesiastical History*, composed about 300.[4] **[See Expanded CD Version pp. 317–18: *The Church's Use of Acts in the Medieval and Reformation Periods*]**

Well into the period following the Reformation, Acts was read as a relatively complete, reliable account of the origin and development of the early church. Eventually questions were raised about the harmonious picture of the early church in Acts, most notably by the English Deists John Toland (1670–1722) and Thomas Morgan (ca. 1680–1743). Anticipating the highly influential views of the nineteenth-century German theologian Ferdinand Christian Baur (1792–1860), Morgan saw two competing streams within early Christianity: a free-spirited, anti-Jewish viewpoint championed by Paul and a more conservative, pro-Jewish viewpoint represented by Peter. In his work on Paul, Peter Annet (1693–1769) noted discrepancies between the way Paul is presented in his own letters and in Acts.

During the eighteenth century, Acts received more attention and thus more scrutiny. Scholars wondered why its account of the early church was incomplete and tendentious. Was it because Luke did not wish to say more, or that he could not say more? Was he limited by his purpose or by his sources? Recognizing Luke's highly selective treatment of persons and events, scholars began proposing alternative purposes for Acts. Perhaps it was an apology designed to answer charges brought against early Christianity and its leaders, such as Paul. Or perhaps its aim was theological rather than historical—an effort to treat the Holy Spirit and miracles more than the development of events and the movement of persons. Or perhaps it was meant to provide a history of Christian missions.

In the mid-nineteenth century, Acts figured centrally in Ferdinand Christian Baur's historical reconstruction of early Christianity. Like Morgan, Baur saw two competing streams at the earliest stages of Christianity. Acts, he argued, must have come much later, in the early to mid-second century C.E., as an effort to synthesize these two divergent points of view. Instead of reflecting the controversial, polemical spirit of Paul, Acts presented a moderating position, even exuded a spirit of compromise. According to Baur, Luke rewrote history to demonstrate solidarity between Peter and Paul and create a single orthodoxy to undergird the church that emerged in the second century.

Baur exercised enormous influence in the nineteenth century and continues to do so. His controversial views prompted scholars to debate the reliability of Acts. This generated a debate about the sources of Acts that continued well into the twentieth century. Much attention was given to the "we" sections in Acts 16–28, which many considered eyewitness sources. Still others, noticing stylistic differences between chapters 1–12 and 13–28, posited sources connected with individual persons, such as Peter, Stephen, and Philip, or with locations, such as Jerusalem, Antioch of Syria, Ephesus, and Rome. The many proposals about sources in Acts sought to explain why Luke omitted certain things, for example, the deaths of Peter and Paul. These critics also wanted to determine whether Luke had a firm basis for what he included.

By the end of the nineteenth century, confidence in establishing sources in Acts began to wane. Attention shifted to the literary shape of the narrative and the individual stories and smaller literary units in Acts. With this transition from questions of historical reliability to interest in literary history, the study of Acts entered a new period. Less concerned to confirm the accuracy of what Luke reported in Acts than to understand how his literary arrangement reflected his overall purpose, many scholars focused on Luke's literary artistry. While never completely detached from historical concerns, these efforts nevertheless redirected the study of Acts.

Interest in Luke's literary purpose assisted in determining his theological purpose. Once it was seen that Luke's selectivity was intentional, that his style and use of literary traditions were revealing, he could be judged as a theologian in his own right. Naturally this had to be done in close conjunction with exegetical analysis of Luke's Gospel. By doing so, however, scholars could ascertain Luke's theology as it was reflected in his two-volume work. This too remains a lively area of interest in Lukan studies.

From this brief survey, we get a glimpse of how the different images of Luke as the author of Acts complement and compete with each other. One consistent stream of interpretation has read Acts as history, either as solid, reliable history or as incomplete, tendentious history. Still another emphasis has been on Acts as literature, in which scholars are less concerned with its relative historical reliability than with how the overall shape of the story reflects the author's literary purpose. Never completely divorced from either of these perspectives is an approach that reads Acts as theology and takes seriously its passion for proclaiming the gospel and edifying its readers. As interpreters, we should think of these as distinct emphases with blurred edges rather than as mutually exclusive interests. *Luke is the one NT writer who possesses genuine historical instincts and refined literary sensibilities and uses both to advance his theological purpose.* [See **Expanded CD Version pp. 319–20: *The Church's Use of Acts: (1) Two Textual Traditions in Antiquity; (2) Acts in the Church's Lectionary; and (3) Acts and the Apostles' Creed*]**

Luke's Motivations for Writing Acts

By the time Acts was written, probably toward the end of the first century, the Jesus movement had spread far beyond Palestine. In the aftermath of Jesus' death in Jerusalem, his followers had traveled in many directions, taking with them memories of his life and teachings along with reports of his death and resurrection. By the beginning of the second century, clusters of Jesus' followers had formed in Egypt, in regions east of Palestine, and in areas north and west of Palestine reaching from Syria all the way to Rome. Within the space of fifty to seventy-five years, what had begun as a reform movement within Palestinian Judaism had gained many adherents among both Jews and non-Jews, especially outside of Palestine. Acts is the one NT writing that offers a detailed narrative account of how the "sect of the Nazarenes" (Acts 24:5) spread from Jerusalem to Rome.

Luke's interest in providing an "orderly account" (Luke 1:1–4) of events that happened after Easter distinguishes him from the other canonical evangelists. None of them, as far as we know, sought to write anything comparable to his second volume. It is not as if Luke had any special claim to write about the period following Jesus' death and resurrection. Presumably the other evangelists knew the circumstances that brought the Christian church into being, which events were pivotal, and who the major players were. Yet Luke alone saw the need to connect the church's beginning with the events that transpired after Jesus' death and resurrection; indeed, he alone of the NT writers located the church's beginning at a particular time and place. Luke's unique contribution is in recognizing the need to tell the story in the first place. While we should appreciate his ability to see the gaps that needed to be filled, we should also be impressed with how he filled them.

How to fill the gap between the time of Jesus and Luke's own time was not self-evident. Since the Jesus movement emerged as a public phenomenon, Luke gives us a generous supply of terms to describe it: "church," "disciples," "brothers," "the Way," "sect of the Nazarenes," and "Christians," to mention the most prominent ones. He also identifies the leading groups (the Twelve, the Seven, and elders) and individuals

(Peter, John, Philip, Stephen, James, and Paul) and has a clear sense of the roles each played in the overall story.

Also evident are Luke's convictions about the persons, groups, and institutions that have defining roles within Jewish and Greco-Roman society. Luke shows how the church relates to Jewish institutions (the temple and synagogues in Palestine and synagogues outside Palestine), various Jewish groups and leaders (e.g., Pharisees), and Jewish religious practices (Sabbath observance and circumcision). Luke is equally concerned with the church's relationship to Roman institutions, officials, and practices. Throughout the narrative, especially in the latter half, various Roman officials, ranging from local magistrates to Caesar himself, figure prominently in the story. This is Luke's way of placing the church on the stage of world history.

The story of Acts is more than a human drama played out on the Mediterranean stage. It may be the story of impassioned religious persons driven by their beliefs in a messianic Savior to challenge traditional Jewish assumptions and confront Jewish leaders and institutions. Acts may also be a story of Christians appearing before public officials to defend the legitimacy of their message and to present themselves as a beneficial force within Roman society. But it is more. It is a divine drama with God as one of the lead actors, with the Holy Spirit making repeated appearances and the risen Lord far from being absent or silent. Even the "word of God" comes to life in the Acts narrative; it is not merely heard but grows (6:7; 12:24; 19:20).

The gap between Jesus' time and Luke's time may be filled with human drama and adventure, with moments of controversy, tragedy, and triumph, but from the point of view of Acts, Luke's real challenge is to find God's tracks through it all. He expresses his purpose through Gamaliel, who wishes to discern whether "this plan or this undertaking is of human origin . . . or of God" (5:38–39). As Luke puts it in his preface to the Gospel, Acts provides an "orderly account" of "the events that have been fulfilled among us" (Luke 1:1). Just as the Gospel demonstrates that Scripture's expectations have been fulfilled in Jesus, Acts too is a theological narrative showing how God's purposes are fulfilled in the church.

Luke's Sources

By the time Luke wrote his Gospel, the Jesus tradition had already been shaped into a coherent story by Mark. No comparable narrative of events following Jesus' death existed when Luke set out to write Acts. Here he was sailing into uncharted waters. His willingness to go where no Christian writer had previously gone reflects the independent spirit we saw in his handling of Mark.

Writing some fifty to seventy-five years after the death of Jesus, Luke knows of the church's spread from Jerusalem to other parts of the world. He knows something of the church's successes and failures, its tensions with Jewish authorities and communities in Palestine and throughout the Mediterranean region, and its favorable reception among Gentiles, many of whom had been attached in some way to Jewish communities. He knows of the destruction of Jerusalem in 70 C.E. and sees it as a significant event in both Jewish and Christian history.

This much we can say with relative confidence. But what sources and traditions Luke had at his disposal when he wrote Acts is much harder to determine. The "orderly accounts" of "events that have been fulfilled among us" undertaken by his predecessors (Luke 1:1) possibly took the story beyond Jesus' death, but, if so, we have no record of them. In addition to the earlier collections of stories and sayings of Jesus that included the synoptic sayings source (Q), Luke's special material (L), and expanded narrative accounts such as the Gospel of Mark, there were doubtless similar traditions about persons and events from the period following Jesus' death. They were probably associated with places where there were sizable Christian communities, such as Jerusalem, Antioch of Syria, Alexandria, Ephesus, and Rome.

Given the nature of such traditions, they would also have included stories about leading figures in the Jesus movement, such as Peter and Paul, but others as well. By this time we can also well imagine a fairly coherent outline of early Christian preaching and a collection of OT texts and their interpretations that were used to support Christian claims about Jesus. Much of this material must have been circulating in oral form, although some of it, even much of it, could just as easily have been written down. If the Jesus tradition had already reached written form, there is no reason the "church tradition" could not have begun to be written down as well. How much and in what form, we can only speculate. [See Expanded CD Version pp. 322–25: *Further Examination of Luke's Sources in Acts*]

Luke's Strategy

Even if our knowledge of the sources and traditions available to Luke when he wrote Acts is quite limited, several aspects of his literary strategy deserve mention.

Opting for History

In his treatment of Jesus, Luke had no choice about genre. This had already been decided by Mark, who chose to call his narrative about Jesus a "gospel"—the word used by his predecessors, such as Paul, for the content of the church's preaching (cf. 1 Cor 15:1–2). For Luke's sequel, the choice of genre was open. Given the literary shape of his Gospel, his sequel naturally had to be a narrative, but what kind of narrative? Several options lay before him. Since biography was a well-established genre by his time, he might have produced "lives" of Peter and Paul as a way of recording their words and deeds. The tradition of Greek novels was probably well enough established to provide yet another option; if so, he could have shaped a story rehearsing the travels and exploits of early Christian leaders even more adventurous and entertaining than the delightful tale we already have in Acts. Instead of these, Luke chose to write a history.

But history in what sense? Nowhere does Luke call his narrative *historia*, which technically means "inquiry" but came to mean a historical narrative—or, as Aristotle says, "the investigations [*hai historiai*] of those who write about human actions."[5] Luke recognized the need for a continuous account of "historic" events that had occurred over several decades. In trying *to discern the meaning of those events,* Luke displayed unmistakable historical instincts that distinguish him from every other NT writer, even from his previous work in the Third Gospel, in which he faced a different task.

By deciding to write a narrative that filled the gap between the death and resurrection of Jesus and his own time, Luke is responding to the same impulse that motivated Thucydides (ca. 460–400 B.C.E.) to produce an account of the Peloponnesian War. The church's origin and growth were events of momentous significance that begged for treatment and were events in which he had participated. But Luke is no Thucydides, even if he employs many elements of this eminent historian's craft, most notably the practice of reporting speeches by major figures as a means of enlivening the narrative and expressing his own point of view.

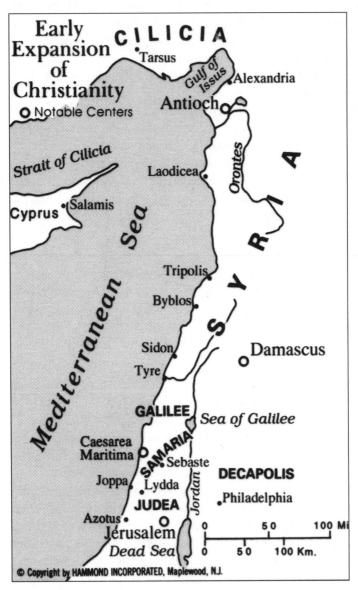

There can be little doubt that Luke knew the tradition of Greek and Roman history writing that went back as far as Herodotus, the fifth-century B.C.E. "father of history," and that became refined through a succession of eminent Greek historians from Thucydides forward, including Xenophon (ca. 431–352 B.C.E.), Polybius (ca. 200–118 B.C.E.), and Dionysius of Halicarnassus (fl. ca. 20 B.C.E.), and their Roman successors Sallust (ca. 86–35 B.C.E.), Livy (ca. 59 B.C.E.–17 C.E.), and

The early chapters of Acts report the origin of Christianity in Jerusalem (ch. 2), its gradual spread throughout Judea and Samaria (chs. 3–8), regions north, including Damascus (ch. 9), the coastal towns of Joppa and Caesarea Maritima (chs. 10–11), and northward to Antioch of Syria (ch. 11).

Luke's own contemporary, Tacitus (ca. 56–118 C.E.). But this tradition of "scientific history" was not the only pond in which Luke fished and may not even have been the main one.

There were other representatives of the historical tradition, especially on the Jewish side, beginning with the Deuteronomistic History (Deuteronomy–2 Kings). From the Hellenistic and Roman periods there were 1–2 Maccabees and a string of Greek-speaking Jewish historians whose works survive only in short extracts. There was also Luke's contemporary, Flavius Josephus, who wrote an account of the Jewish war that resulted in the destruction of the temple in 70 C.E. and an extensive historical work, *The Antiquity of the Jews*, which traced Jewish history from its beginnings until Josephus's own time.

Acts shows affinities with these Jewish histories in various ways. Luke's view of God as an active participant in history—indeed as the One who exercises providential control over history, never far away, intervening when necessary to ensure that the divine will is carried out—reflects the theological outlook of the Deuteronomistic History. Josephus shares this viewpoint, even though he does not develop it in the same way as Luke. Josephus also provides a generous supply of speeches that provide illuminating parallels for Acts. Enough fascinating similarities between Acts and

A woodcut depicting the coming of the Spirit on Pentecost (Acts 2). It is taken from *Kirche(n) Gesäng*, a hymnal by Johann Wolff published in 1569. From the Digital Image Archive of The Richard C. Kessler Reformation Collection, Pitts Theology Library, Candler School of Theology, Emory University, Atlanta, Georgia.

Greek novels have been noted to make a plausible argument for Luke's indebtedness to the historical novel for some of his literary technique.

To place Luke within any one of these traditions or to classify Acts as history in some narrow, much less modern, sense does injustice to Luke and to what he achieved in Acts. Quite often Acts has been classified as history to certify its reliability. Since history dealt with the factual, and since Acts is history, some argue, it gives us a factual—reliable—account of the events it reports. Assigning Acts to the genre "history" usually leads to evaluations of Luke's accuracy: "Did he get it right?" the interpreter tends to ask, and if not, why not? But the line between fact and fiction, even among ancient historians, was often blurred. Equating history with fact and novels with fiction, however much it may suit our own disposition, causes us to ask the wrong questions when reading Acts.

It is far more important to recognize what it meant for Luke, in writing Acts, to opt for history. In making this decision, he accepted the responsibility of (1) collecting those stories and traditions that were remembered by the church; (2) fashioning them into a continuous narrative that was both coherent and credible; and (3) perhaps most important of all, conveying what they meant—*discerning their truth*. It was this double concern for *narrating and interpreting events* that made Luke more than a collector of stories. While not a historian in many senses, Luke still deserves to be called the first Christian historian. Acts may be popular history with a fondness for the miraculous and a flair for the heroic, but its sustained unifying purpose, its coherent structure, and its consistent interest in tracing the meaning of the events it records make it more than an "edifying narrative of apostolic times."[6]

To call Acts history or to speak of the historical instincts that drove Luke to compose Acts is neither to dignify nor to denigrate his achievement. It is rather an attempt to be descriptive. Nor does this characterization intend to place Luke in the company of Herodotus or Thucydides. He might be flattered, but he would also be embarrassed. Luke could tell a hill from a mountain. His aims in Acts are much more explicitly theological than his Greek and Roman counterparts, even when they express belief in the gods and report miraculous events. Acts breathes the air of the Deuteronomistic History and later Jewish historians who saw God actively at work in human events. Even the first-time reader of Acts recognizes that it is "written on the slant." This did not necessarily distinguish it from its Greek and Roman counterparts, which were often blatantly moralistic and expressed optimistic or pessimistic outlooks, depending on the author.

The peculiar slant of Acts is evangelistic. Luke may be a historian but he also has a preacher's instincts. From start to finish he is interested in the proclamation of the word of God—reporting the sermons that express it, demonstrating its effects in the lives of people, marking its growth, all the while showing its irrepressibility. Those who speak the word of God in Acts speak to their audiences but they also speak to the reader(s), and in doing so, they speak for Luke.

Selective Treatment

Considering the period of time—some thirty years or more—and the extent of territory—the entire Mediterranean basin—covered by the narrative, we can understand why Luke reports less than he knows. From the narrative itself, we know that Christianity had reached Rome before Paul arrived (28:14–15), but Luke provides no account of how or when this happened (see 18:2). He reports relatively long stays by Paul in Corinth (18:11) and Ephesus (19:8, 10), but his accounts of Paul's ministry in both cities are comparatively brief. By contrast, Paul's stay in Philippi appears to have been much shorter, but Luke's account is fairly lengthy (16:11–40). Luke can telescope extensive journeys into a few short verses (14:21–26). That Peter and John's healing of the lame man at the temple gate was only one of many such incidents is clear from Luke's summary statement that "many signs and wonders were done among the people through the apostles" (5:12). Equally puzzling is Luke's failure to report Peter's fate: where did he go after the Jerusalem Council? How did he die? Where? The same can be said for Paul, especially since Luke knows of his death (20:25). Although it is not explicitly stated in the narrative, Luke probably knows that Christianity has spread into regions of the world other than those he reports, such as Egypt, Parthia, and the eastern regions of Syria (see 2:9–11; 8:26–27).

From the wealth of traditions at his disposal, Luke constructs a narrative that traces the church's development north and westward, or, as he puts it, using the risen Lord's words, his story will move from Jerusalem to "all Judea and Samaria, and to the ends of the earth" (1:8). As the narrative shows, the development is not strictly linear. In the first twelve chapters, the story begins in Jerusalem and gradually extends to Samaria (ch. 8), Damascus (ch. 9), regions northwest of Jerusalem extending to the coastal city of Caesarea (9:32–10:48), and even to Cyprus and points as far north as Antioch of Syria (11:19–30). Jerusalem, however, remains the center to which people return (8:25; 9:26; 11:2, 29; possibly 12:25).

Even in chapters 13–28, in which Paul is the leading figure, the pattern is repeated. The storyline first moves west into eastern Asia Minor (chs. 13–14) but returns to Jerusalem for the Council (ch. 15). The story then moves farther west to western Asia Minor and the area around the Aegean, most notably Greece (chs. 16–20). Paul again returns to Jerusalem (most likely 18:22; certainly 19:21; 21:15–26), where his arrest and first trial occur (21:27–23:30) before he is taken to Caesarea (23:31–26:32). Even when he reaches Rome, the magnetic force of Jerusalem is still felt (28:17, 21). By constructing the narrative this way, with major figures repeatedly circling back to Jerusalem, Luke signals the symbolic importance of Jerusalem even as he shows it gradually giving way to Rome. In Acts we see the transition from a circle to an ellipse— from a church whose central defining point is Jerusalem to a church with two centers, Jerusalem and Rome.

Also worth noting is the way Luke positions characters in the story. Like the direction of the storyline he traces, his choice of characters is also selective. He probably knows of many stories about the apostles, but the one apostle whose activity he chooses to highlight is Peter (Paul's apostleship is discussed later in this chapter). Other characters figure prominently in the first half of the narrative, but they stand in Peter's shadow. He is the main speaker, even when he is paired with the apostle John. To Peter falls the responsibility of giving the church's inaugural speech at Pentecost (ch. 2), but he also undergoes his own form of conversion in becoming God's messenger to the Gentiles (chs. 10–11). Because of this transforming experience, he gets the podium first at the Jerusalem Council (15:6–11). While that is his last appearance in the narrative, the reader knows who Luke thinks played the leading role in the Jerusalem church during its earliest years.

Paul plays an equally central role in the second half of the narrative. Luke is well aware that Paul is not responsible for planting Christianity in Rome (28:15). Neither is Paul the first to break the ethnic barrier and proclaim the gospel to non-Jews. This began with Philip (ch. 8) but occurred most dramatically with Peter (chs. 10–11). Yet Luke knows the dramatic impact of Paul's mission work among Gentiles, especially outside Palestine, and the controversy Paul's outreach created within the Jewish community there and in Palestine. He also knows of Paul's uniquely understood sense of vocation, stemming from his encounter with the risen Lord, and the way he fulfilled his role as the risen Lord's "chosen instrument" to bear his name before Jews and Gentiles (9:15). From the way Luke tells the story of Paul, going back to the dramatic conversion of the church's archenemy and extending all the way to his arrival in Rome, we can easily see the heroic qualities Luke attributes to Paul. Luke is such an admirer of Paul that later church tradition saw him as Paul's disciple.

But if Paul was not responsible for planting the church in Rome or for being the first to preach the gospel to Gentiles, wherein does Luke see his achievement? Why does he loom so large in Luke's conception of early Christianity and figure so prominently as one of its two leading figures? The short answer is that Paul did for the church in regions along the northern edge of the Mediterranean what Peter did for it in Palestine. Whether the extent of Paul's accomplishment was greater numerically than Peter's is hard to say, although, given the numbers reported in the early chapters of Acts, this does not appear to have been the case. But the geographical extent of Paul's accomplishment was much greater.

What may have impressed Luke more than anything else was Paul's role in bringing the gospel to the world's attention. With him the name of Jesus achieved a level of visibility in the Roman world far beyond what it experienced in Palestine under Peter's leadership. By methodically reporting Paul's activities in Asia and Europe and his appearance before one Roman official after another, and by giving an extensive account of the circumstances that led to his arrest and his court appearances before Jewish and Roman officials, reaching even to Caesar himself, Luke singles out Paul as the one who truly brought about the "universal people" that was envisioned in God's original promise to Abraham. To Paul, more than anyone else in Luke's view, belongs the credit for "turning the world upside down" (17:6) with the gospel.

As with Peter, Luke's sketch of Paul's missionary activity is highly selective. Some things are important for Luke to emphasize, while others are not. His decision to rehearse Paul's conversion three times, once as part of his own narrative (ch. 9) and twice through Paul's defense speeches (chs. 22 & 26), shows how centrally this event figures in Luke's understanding of Paul. For one thing, it underscores the exceptional nature of Paul's call and validates Luke's conviction that Paul's role in the church's expansion matches and perhaps even surpasses that of Peter.

Similarly, the extensive attention given to Paul's arrest and trial, especially the threefold repetition of Paul's defense speech (22:1–21; 24:10–21; 26:2–23), strikes an

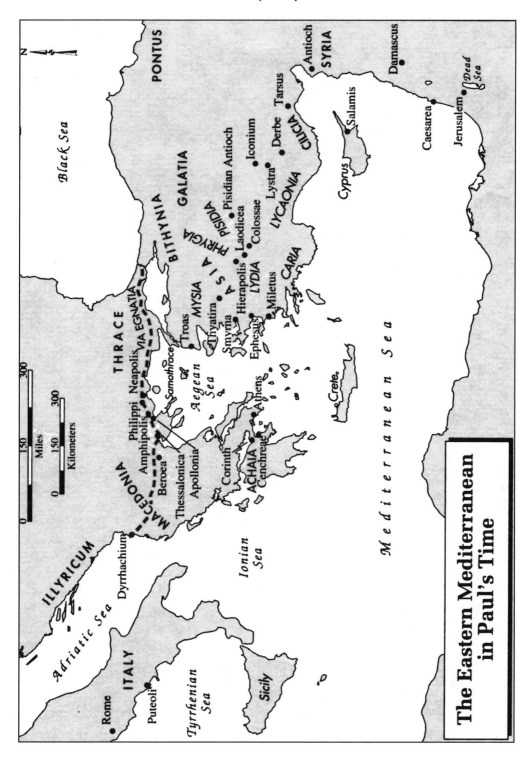

The Eastern Mediterranean in Paul's Time

apologetic note: not only is Paul defending himself, but Luke, by giving so much attention to it, is doing so as well. He is keen to counter a negative image of Paul whose features surface several times in the narrative (21:21, 28; 24:5–9). Considering how much of the Acts narrative Luke devotes to Paul's arrest and trials (chs. 21–28), Luke's selection of material appears to be influenced by a concern to defend his hero as much as anything else. We detect no comparable interest on Luke's part to defend Peter, which suggests that it was Paul's image that was tarnished rather than Peter's.

As often noted, this is not so much an account of "the acts of the apostles" as it is "some of the acts of some of the apostles," or more correctly, "some of the acts of Peter and Paul." It has even been suggested that Luke's preoccupation with Peter and Paul reflects an early second-century viewpoint that saw them as the two chief figures around whom the church's tradition had crystallized. Whether this is the case or not, Luke saw the significance of linking them as the persons mainly responsible for the church's dramatic outreach during its earliest stages of development—and he appears to have been the first to do so.

Speeches

A third key element in Luke's strategy is his use of speeches in constructing the Acts narrative. Depending on how a "speech" is defined, Luke devotes 20 to 30 percent of Acts to speeches (see chart). In doing so, he reflects a concern for right proportion seen in other ancient writers, such as Thucydides, who sought to balance otherwise unwieldy narratives with an appropriate amount of speech and dialogue. Varying considerably in type and length, the speeches include evangelistic sermons, forensic speeches, at least one sermon addressed to the church, and prayers, to mention the most obvious types. Even the several letters reported in Acts function like speeches.

THE SPEECHES IN ACTS

PETER

Advising the 120 in Jerusalem about Judas's replacement (1:16–17, 20–22)
Missionary sermon before the Jerusalem crowd at Pentecost (2:14–36, 38–40)
Sermon in the temple after healing the crippled beggar (3:12–26)
Defense before the Sanhedrin in Jerusalem about the healed beggar (4:8–12, 19–20)
Defense (with the apostles) before the Sanhedrin in Jerusalem (5:29–32)
Missionary sermon to Cornelius and his household at Caesarea (10:34–43)
Explaining to the Jerusalem church why he preached to Cornelius (11:5–17)
Giving advice at the Jerusalem Council (15:7–11)

STEPHEN

Defense before the Sanhedrin in Jerusalem (7:2–53)

JAMES (THE BROTHER OF JESUS)

Giving advice at the Jerusalem Council justifying the Gentile mission (15:13–21)

With the elders in Jerusalem advising Paul how to respond to charges (21:20–25)

PAUL

Missionary sermon in the synagogue at Pisidian Antioch (13:16–41)

Missionary sermon to the crowds at Lystra (14:15–17)

Missionary sermon before the Areopagus in Athens (17:22–31)

Pastoral sermon bidding farewell to the Ephesian elders at Miletus (20:18–35)

Defense before the crowds near the Temple in Jerusalem (22:1, 3–21)

Defense before the Sanhedrin in Jerusalem (23:1, 6)

Defense before the Roman governor Felix in Caesarea (24:10–21)

Appeal to Caesar before the Roman governor Festus in Caesarea (25:10–11)

Defense before King Herod Agrippa II in Caesarea (26:2–23, 25–27, 29)

Reassuring speech on the ship en route to Rome (27:21–26)

Addressing the Jewish leaders in Rome (28:17-20, 25–28)

OUTSIDERS

Gamaliel advising the Sanhedrin in Jerusalem (5:35–39)

Demetrius the silversmith's speech before his fellow artisans at Ephesus (19:25–27)

The town clerk's speech in the theater at Ephesus (19:35–40)

The letter of the Roman tribune Claudius Lysias to Felix concerning Paul (23:26–30)

Tertullus's summary of charges against Paul before Felix at Caesarea (24:2–8)

Festus's summary of charges against Paul before Agrippa at Caesarea (25:14–21, 24–27)

OTHERS, INCLUDING PRAYERS, LETTERS, AND SHORTER SPEECHES

The disciples' prayer for Judas's replacement (1:24–25)

The church's prayer after Peter and John's release in Jerusalem (4:24–30)

Peter rebuking Ananias (5:3–4)

The Twelve calling for the selection of the Seven (6:2–4)

Peter rebuking Simon Magus (8:20–23)

Paul rebuking Elymas (13:10–11)

Paul and Barnabas defending the Gentile mission (13:46–47)

The Jerusalem Council's letter to Gentile Christians (15:23–29)

Proposal by the forty men to kill Paul (23:14–15)

Nephew's report to the Roman tribune of the plot against Paul (23:20–21)

The response of the Jewish leaders in Rome to Paul (28:21–22)

Including such a variety of speeches as part of a narrative conforms to the well-established ancient rhetorical practice of *prosōpopoeia* (lit., "to create a face or person"), in which authors dramatized their narratives by putting speeches on the lips of characters. Without rehearsing the long debate about Luke's sources for the speeches—whether they are based on notes of speeches actually delivered by the persons to whom they are attributed or whether, as is more likely, they are Luke's free creations crafted for the characters as he understood them and the settings in which he placed them—we can observe how they function. Besides enlivening the narrative, they give voice to the apostles and ministers of the word who are responsible for the proclamation of the gospel. The speeches allow us to hear Jesus' followers bearing testimony to his life, death, and resurrection as well as defending themselves in a variety of settings. Through the speeches we also hear outsiders expressing their views both positively and negatively about "the sect of the Nazarenes."

In terms of sheer stage time, Peter and Paul are given the most lines, but the other speeches are not for that reason inconsequential. Each speech plays a special role, depending on where it occurs in the narrative. For this reason each speech should be read within the context of the entire narrative. Rather than reading the speeches separately, we should read them in light of each other. Twice Paul addresses Gentiles, briefly at Lystra and more fully at Athens, but the Lystra speech supplies the presupposition for the Athens speech—that the "unknown God" is "known" through "doing good" to humanity. In three of the speeches—Peter in the temple (3:12–26), Stephen (7:2–53), and Paul in Pisidian Antioch (13:16–41)—rehearsals of Israel's history figure prominently, but they tend to complement rather than repeat each other. Read together, they reveal Luke's understanding of Israel's story from God's original promise to Abraham until the period of the monarchy.

We should also note where and in what settings Luke includes speeches. Following the practice of other Greek and Roman writers, Luke carefully places the speeches at pivotal moments in the story and before a significant group of hearers. In the first part of Acts, speeches occur at the church's inauguration (ch. 2), the first martyrdom (ch. 7), the first Gentile conversion (ch. 10), and the first church council (ch. 15); or, within Paul's ministry, before Jews (ch. 13), Gentiles (ch. 17), and Christians (ch. 20), the last speech serving as a farewell address closing out his Aegean ministry. Paul defends himself before audiences of ascending importance: crowds (ch. 22), the Sanhedrin (ch. 23), the Roman governor Felix (ch. 24), and finally King Herod Agrippa II (ch. 26).

The speeches should be read as Lukan compositions; we may hear Peter, Stephen, and Paul speaking, but they are speaking in Luke's voice. There is enough similarity in wording and style throughout the speeches to suggest a single viewpoint, and this is reinforced when we compare the sentiments of the speeches with the surrounding narrative. The speeches enable Luke to do three things: (1) rehearse the contents of the early Christian preaching (*kerygma*); (2) expound the OT; and (3) defend against charges brought against the church, especially Paul.

The Kerygma. In the evangelistic speeches, but in some of the other speeches as well, there emerges a set of themes that, taken together, represent the heart of early apostolic preaching. It is nowhere stated fully but can be summarized as follows: the

OT promises have been fulfilled in Jesus; God's messenger John the Baptist prepared the way for Jesus; God empowered Jesus by anointing him with the Holy Spirit to teach and heal; as the OT predicted, Jesus was rejected, suffered, died, and was raised from the dead, thereby confirming his status as Lord and Messiah; after his resurrection, he appeared to his disciples, then ascended to heaven; and he will come again as judge of the world. This is the common message proclaimed by everyone in Acts, especially Peter and Paul.

The Old Testament. Most of Luke's exposition of Scripture in Acts takes place in the speeches, usually in Jewish settings before Jewish audiences. That these are OT passages of great importance to Luke is seen by the way he uses different sermons or speakers to interpret the same passage. Psalm 16:10 is cited by Peter (Acts 2:27, 31) and Paul (13:35); Deut 18:15–19 by Peter (3:22–23) and Stephen (7:37); Exod 20:11 and Ps 146:6 by the disciples (4:24) and Paul (14:15). If we gather the OT passages from the various speeches, we get a sense of the pool of texts that were formative for Luke's theology: Ps 69:25 and 109:8 (Acts 1:20); Joel 2:28–32 (Acts 2:17–21); Ps 16:8–11 and Ps 110:1 (Acts 2:25–35); Deut 18:15–19 (3:22–23; 7:37); Ps 118:22 (Acts 4:11); Ps 2:1–2 (Acts 4:25–26); Amos 5:25–27 (Acts 7:42–43); Isa 66:1–2 (Acts 7:49–50); Ps 2:7 (Acts 13:33); Isa 55:3 (Acts 13:34); Ps 16:10 (Acts 13:35); Hab 1:5 (Acts 13:41); and Amos 9:11–12 (Acts 15:16–17).

Taken together, these texts enable us to see inside Luke's world of Scripture and also to see how he read Scripture. Typically, his form of reasoning is as follows: (a) an OT text refers to someone or some event; (b) this person or event must be someone or something other than the author or in the author's time and situation; (c) since it cannot be the author or an event in the author's time, it must refer to someone or some event in the future; (d) the most obvious referent is Jesus or some event related to the Jesus movement. What is significant about the concentration of Scripture interpretation in the speeches is that the speakers do what Jesus had done, both during his ministry and after his resurrection. The Scripture interpretation that occurs in the speeches continues Jesus' insistence that what happened to him in his suffering, death, and resurrection, as well as the events that followed, were required to happen because of what Scripture had said.

Answering Charges. Several of the speeches are forensic speeches in which Peter and Paul, but others such as Stephen, respond to charges brought against them. Usually these charges relate to the temple, the Mosaic law, or observances of the law, especially circumcision, table fellowship, or other social practices involving Jews' associating with Gentiles. The charges may also include behavior that creates disturbances or upsets the peace. Paul's defense speeches, in particular, refute charges that he is a "pestilent fellow," a menace to Roman society, and a threat to Jewish religion, life, and customs throughout the Empire. In the evangelistic sermons we hear early Christians proclaiming the gospel; in the forensic speeches we hear them defending themselves. In this way Luke is offering his own defense for the church, explaining to his readers how the church relates to venerable Jewish institutions and practices. He offers reassurance that the church, rather than posing a threat to civil order, is a positive force within Roman society.

When read together, the speeches reveal Luke's concerns at the end of the first century. Yet just as they reflect common themes, so do they display his ability as a writer, for they show him fitting speeches to their occasion. Before Jewish audiences, speakers quote Scripture; before Gentile audiences, Greek poets; and before the church, the words of Jesus.

Luke's Theological Vision in Acts

Given the traditions Luke inherited, the situation he faced in writing a sequel to the Gospel, and his literary strategy, what theological vision does he create? It is a narrative vision through which Luke expresses a coherent, consistent theological argument, which can be summarized briefly:

(1) Rightly understood, Scripture envisioned the story of Jesus and the church that is unfolded in Luke-Acts. Like Jesus the Messiah, the church is a "divine necessity."

(2) Jesus is the necessary cause for the church, just as the church is the necessary effect of Jesus. The church is the story of Jesus continued.

(3) As the people of the Spirit, the church both justifies the Spirit's existence and exercises its mission in the world.

Luke's Three Stories

When reading Acts, we must keep three stories in mind: the story of the church that unfolds in the narrative, but also the stories of Israel and Jesus that preceded it. Luke assumes that the reader knows the story of Jesus from his first book, or as he puts it, "all that Jesus did and taught" (Acts 1:1–2). There he touched on the story of Israel but did not devote much attention to it. Apart from Jesus' genealogy (Luke 3:23–38) and scattered references to the period of the "law and the prophets" that preceded Jesus (Luke 16:16–17), Luke presupposes the story of Israel rather than elaborating on it. Since the story of Israel had been told adequately in the OT, Luke devoted one volume to the story of Jesus and a second volume to the story of the church.

As Luke unfolded the story of the church, he used the numerous speeches in Acts to keep before the reader's mind the stories of Jesus and Israel. One of the speeches— Peter's sermon before Cornelius's household—serves as a virtual summary of the Jesus story in Luke's Gospel (Acts 10:34–43). The Jesus story also figures prominently in some of the other speeches. The story of Israel receives its fullest treatment in two other speeches, Stephen's defense before the Sanhedrin (7:1–53) and Paul's sermon in the synagogue at Antioch of Pisidia (13:16–41). Readers of Acts must be attentive to the story of the church that unfolds in the Acts narrative itself, but also to the ways Luke links this story to the previous stories of Israel and Jesus.

Rather than seeing each of these stories as three clearly demarcated periods of salvation history—the larger story of God's dealings with humanity—Luke understands them as three parts of a single, continuous story. When Jesus asserts that "the law and the prophets were in effect until John came" (Luke 16:16), he does not imply that they went out of effect once John arrived. On the contrary, he thinks the law will always be in effect (Luke 16:17), as indeed it is both for Jesus and the church. In Luke's Gospel Jesus is a fully observant Jew (see Luke 4:16), and in Acts the church's leading figures, especially Paul, are loyally devoted to the law (Acts 21:26). Just as the "law and the prophets" expressed God's intentions for Israel, so do they remain in effect for Jesus and the church. They are the authoritative text for Jesus throughout his ministry as well as for the period following Easter.

"Thus it is written": Scripture's Promises Fulfilled

To understand how Luke construes the stories of Israel, Jesus, and the church as a continuous story—God's story—we must look at how he reads Scripture. For Luke, everything written in the OT ultimately pointed forward to Jesus. He reads the OT as a forward-looking book with numerous unfulfilled, open-ended promises, many of which envisioned a future "time of salvation" or "period of consolation" when God would bring Israel's highest hopes to realization. Luke's reading of the OT is especially informed by Isa 40–66, in which these hopes are spelled out as part of God's promise to return Israel from Babylonian exile.

Luke looks beyond Israel's return from exile to a time when the "house of David" would be restored not as a military dynasty but as a newly constituted people who embody God's earlier promise to Abraham that through his descendants "all the families of the earth shall be blessed" (Gen 22:18; 26:4; see Acts 3:25). Luke understands this promise to mean a truly universal people of God comprising Jews and Gentiles. Hints of this vision are already given in the Gospel of Luke (1:79; 2:32; 3:6: 24:47), but it is more fully amplified in Acts, in which Luke's reading of the OT becomes more evident. At Pentecost, Peter interprets Joel 2 as envisioning a time when "all flesh" would receive God's Spirit and when salvation would be available universally (2:17, 21). At the Jerusalem Council, James takes Amos 9:11–12 to refer to a rebuilding of the house of David that would enable "all other peoples" to "seek the Lord—even all the Gentiles over whom [God's] name has been called" (Acts 15:16–17).At Pisidian Antioch, as a warrant for directing his missionary efforts toward Gentiles, Paul cites Isa 49:6, which speaks of God's commissioning emissaries "to be a light for the Gentiles, so that [they] may bring salvation to the ends of the earth" (Acts 13:47).

For Luke, the story of Israel pointed to the story of the church as the time when Scripture's vision of a truly universal people of God would be realized. But the crucial middle stage was the story of Jesus, and it is important to see how it functions within Luke's overall reading of Scripture. To state Luke's understanding briefly, Scripture envisions two future, unfulfilled events, both of which are directly related: (1) the appearance of God's Messiah, and (2) the formation of "a people for [God's] name" (15:14). Or as the risen Lord himself formulated these two scriptural mandates: "the Messiah is to suffer and to rise from the dead on the third day" and "repentance and forgiveness of sins is to be proclaimed in his name to all nations, beginning from Jerusalem" (Luke 24:46–47). We now consider these in turn.

(1) God's Messiah. Luke sees three places in Scripture that envision the appearance of a future Messiah.

(a) First is Moses' prediction in Deut 18:15 that God would "raise up for you a prophet like me from among your own people." That Jesus is the "new Moses" envisioned in this Deuteronomic promise is clear in the speeches by Peter and Stephen in which this passage is cited (Acts 3:22; 7:37). As Moses' successor, Jesus would be expected to assume his roles of prophet, savior, and deliverer.

(b) Second is David's testimony in Ps 16:8–11 and 110:1 (Acts 2:22–36; 13:32–37). As Luke reads these psalms, he sees David envisioning someone other than himself as "Lord" or as God's "Holy One," someone whose soul would not be "abandoned to Hades" or whose flesh would not "experience corruption"—someone, in other words, whose body would not decompose in its tomb as David's did. Since David appeared to be thinking of a future figure, someone he addresses as "my Lord" who would be exalted to God's "right hand," Luke calls David a prophet (2:30). Thus, like Moses, David predicted a future Messiah, but it would be someone who would ascend the Davidic throne (2:30), a "new David."

(c) Third are the Servant Songs of Isaiah. That Luke thinks Isaiah's Servant prefigures Jesus is seen in Luke 22:37, in which Jesus claims that his passion is a fulfillment of Isa 53:12, a passage he quotes directly. This is reinforced by the story of the Ethiopian eunuch's conversion in Acts 8, in which Isa 53:7–8 is quoted. The eunuch's question reflects Luke's view: the prophet Isaiah is speaking about someone else, a future innocent sufferer (8:34), and Philip ties the knot that links the Isaiah passage to "the good news about Jesus" (8:35).

(2) A people for God's name. As early as the birth narratives in Luke, we hear references to "the promise [God] made to our ancestors, to Abraham and to his descendants forever" (Luke 1:54–55; see 1:72–75). This is given further precision in Peter's speech in the temple, in which he reminds his hearers that they are the "descendants of the prophets and of the covenant that God gave to your ancestors," and then quotes Gen 22:18: "And in your descendants all the families of the earth shall be blessed" (Acts 3:25). For Luke, the operative phrase is "*all* the families of the earth," which he takes to mean both Jews and Gentiles. Understood this way, God's promise to Abraham envisioned a time when everyone, regardless of bloodline, would have access to the fullness of God's blessings.

Luke understands this *universal people of God* at several levels. It is universal geographically, extending throughout the Mediterranean from Jerusalem to Rome; ethnically, comprising Jews, Samaritans, and Gentiles; and socially, including old and young, rich and poor, men and women, people of both low and high estate. This much is clear from the programmatic role Joel 2 plays in Peter's Pentecost sermon. As Luke reads Joel's prophecy, it remains an unfulfilled promise—that is, until the events of Pentecost, which he interprets as the time when God's Spirit begins to be poured out "upon all flesh" (2:17). With the gathering of the Twelve and the other disciples in Jerusalem, along with people representing "every nation under heaven" (2:5), everything is in place for Joel's vision to become a reality. As Peter reminds the Jewish crowds in his concluding remarks, God's promise is for them and their children, but also for "all who are far away, everyone whom the Lord our God calls to him" (2:39).

In one sense, Acts tells the story of how this "people for God's name" takes shape—or, to put it in Luke's terms, how God calls this people into existence (2:39). A lot hinges on how Luke understands this to have taken place. How we understand

Luke has important theological implications for us. In what sense does he think of the church as Israel's successor? In what sense, if any, should the emergence of a "people for God's name," which begins at Pentecost, be thought of as the emergence of a new people? Does Luke think of the church as "new Israel"?

Luke does not draw a sharp distinction between Israel and the church. Neither does he think of the church as the "new Israel" that somehow replaces the "old Israel." When he thinks of the church's relation to Israel, he thinks in terms of continuity rather than discontinuity. **[See Expanded CD Version pp. 338–41:** *Further Examination of Luke's View of the Church and Israel***]**

What emerges in Acts is not a people who succeed Israel, much less supersede Israel, but a people in whom God's promise to Israel comes true. As Luke reads Scripture, the story of Israel flows naturally into the story of Jesus, which flows just as naturally into the story of the church. These three stories constitute one continuous story whose narrative framework is provided by Scripture itself. As Luke sees it, Abraham, Moses, and David would have been delighted to see their dreams come true in the person of Jesus. They would not have been surprised at the resistance Jesus encountered. Moses especially would have sympathized with the rejection and ultimately the death Jesus experienced at the hands of his own kinsmen. Isaiah may have had one eye on the return of Israel from Babylonian exile, but, according to Luke, he had the other eye directed toward a much more distant future—toward a time when a "way of the Lord" would be carved in Israel's landscape to enable "all flesh [to] see the salvation of God" (Luke 3:4–6). The "Righteous One" who stood among the lawless and finally died as an innocent man would, in Luke's view, meet Isaiah's expectation of the Suffering Servant.

The Church: The Story of Jesus Continued

By deciding to write a sequel that continued the story of Jesus into the life of the church, Luke surfaced several questions: How does Jesus relate to the church? Is Jesus the church's founder? Is his relationship to the church one of cause and effect? Is Jesus best understood as the Primal Cause of the church? Is he a figure of the past whose memory the church celebrates, for example, when it observes the Eucharist? As the risen Lord, is he an absent figure, exalted to God's right hand, where he will remain until he comes again? Or is he present within the church, and if so, how? How does Jesus inform the church's preaching? Do his life, teachings, and deeds merely supply the church material for sermons or curriculum for catechesis? Or do they operate more dynamically in the church's preaching and teaching? Does the church's story somehow embody and continue Jesus' story, and if so, how?

Luke's construction of the story of the church in Acts shows that he had thought seriously about these and a range of other questions relating to Jesus and the church. Or to express it more technically, by writing his second volume Luke had to explore more deeply the relationship between ecclesiology and Christology. Acts explicitly raises the question: How does the church's understanding of itself—its identity, mission, behavior, and structure—relate to its understanding of Jesus?

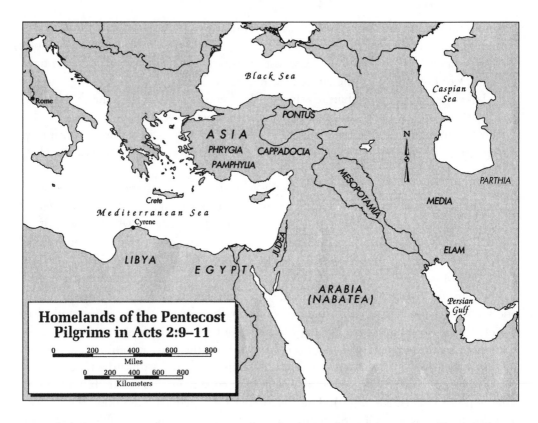

Homelands of the Pentecost Pilgrims in Acts 2:9–11

Luke's answer to these questions takes the form of a narrative—itself a significant theological decision, since it implies that an informed understanding comes best by hearing and experiencing the church's story. Luke expects his readers to see themselves as part of that story. He also expects them to pick up the story where it leaves off and, through their own discipleship and ministries of preaching and teaching, extend it even further. From Luke's story of the church, we can discern several elements in his own theological vision that help us understand how he construed the relationship between Jesus and the church.

The Risen Lord Is an Active Presence within the Church. Read one way, Luke-Acts seems to present Jesus as an "absent presence" within the church. After all, Luke is the only NT author to present a narrative account of Jesus' ascension (Luke 24:50–53; Acts 1:1–11; cf. Luke 9:51). Elsewhere, references to the ascension are brief and allusive (see Mark 16:19; John 3:13; 6:62; 20:17; also Eph 4:8–11; 1 Tim 3:16). When the "two men in white robes" respond to the disciples' query, they only mention Jesus' ascent and future coming and do not appear to envision much activity in between (Acts 1:11). A similar interim of exalted inactivity seems to be implied by Peter's remark that the risen Lord "must remain in heaven until the time of universal restoration" (3:21).

What Luke actually reports in the Acts narrative belies this. Jesus may be "offstage" from his ascension forward, but he is not excluded from the drama that unfolds in Acts. The risen Lord "pours forth his Spirit" on the disciples at Pentecost (2:33), and the story of Peter and John's healing the lame man at the temple gate in Acts 3–4

244

reveals the power released by Jesus' name (3:16; 4:10; also 16:18). When Stephen gazes "into heaven" and sees the exalted Son of Man, he is comforted and emboldened (7:54–56)—unforgettable testimony that Jesus may be absent physically but is not invisible or inaccessible in times of genuine distress.

One of the most dramatic appearances occurs in Saul's conversion, when the risen Lord confronts Saul in a vision, identifying himself as "Jesus, whom you are persecuting" (9:4; also 22:8; 26:15). Later, Paul confirms that he had received his ministry from the Lord Jesus (20:24) and expresses in his defense before the Jerusalem crowds that he received his commission from Jesus while experiencing a trance in the temple (22:17–21). And it is the risen Lord who appears to Ananias in a vision, converses with him, directs his movements, and through him issues Paul's apostolic call (9:10–19). When Peter heals Aeneas, he declares, "Jesus Christ heals you" (9:34). This rather bold declaration implies considerably more than healing accomplished through the power of Jesus' name, and may even suggest that the risen Jesus continues to do through his apostles what he repeatedly did during his ministry. Depending on how Acts 13:39 is interpreted, Jesus appears to set people free from their sins; if so, the risen Lord is enacting his role as Savior and Liberator. The striking reference to the "Spirit of Jesus" who actively intervenes in Paul's travel plans in Asia Minor (16:7) suggests a more proactive risen Lord who directs the church's mission than is sometimes imagined. It is probably the risen Lord Jesus who opens Lydia's heart to be receptive to Paul's preaching (16:14). It is equally probable that the "Lord" who reassures Paul in a vision at Corinth is the Lord Jesus (Acts 18:9–10; also 23:11). There is also the intriguing reference in Paul's defense before Agrippa, in which he proclaims that "by being the first to rise from the dead, [Christ] would proclaim light both to our people and to the Gentiles" (Acts 26:23). No doubt this proclamation is done through the apostles and ministers of the word, but the language clearly suggests that the actual proclaimer is Christ himself.

The risen Lord does not appear in every episode in Acts, nor even often enough to be called the leading actor, but he is by no means offstage. Especially at critical moments in the lives of his key witnesses his presence is felt and his voice is heard. Granted that he makes an exceptional appearance to Paul, which Luke might well have portrayed as a moment of silent revelation rather than a dramatic encounter between the heavenly Christ and the earthly Paul. But he did not.

Nowhere does Luke indicate that such experiences will cease; if anything, his narrative leaves the impression that they typify the church's life and are likely to continue to do so. His readers might easily conclude that the risen Lord's outpouring of his Spirit at Pentecost, given its status as an inaugural event, is a one-time occurrence, or even that Saul's conversion and call occupied a unique place in the church's story. But they could just as easily conclude that the risen Lord would continue to extend his healing power to the sick, open the hearts of receptive hearers, reassure his anxious witnesses, and direct the church's mission.

The church depicted in Acts is not an orphaned church that has come to terms with their Messiah's departure, that neither hears from him nor experiences his living presence, or that waits anxiously for his return. It is instead a church empowered by Jesus as an active presence, risen and exalted but neither absent from their midst nor silent in responding to their needs.

The Proclaimer Becomes the Proclaimed. The speeches in Acts, especially the evangelistic sermons, have one thing in common: they proclaim Christ. The rare exception is Paul and Barnabas's preaching at Lystra in Acts 14:15–17; even the Areopagus speech in Acts 17 concludes with a reference to Christ's resurrection and his role as the man whom God appointed to judge the world in righteousness (17:31). This is Luke's way of emphasizing yet another connection between Jesus and the church: Christ stands at the center of the church's preaching.

If we look at how Christ is presented in the sermons in Acts, we notice considerable overlap with Luke's portrait of Jesus in the Gospel. The titles used by and of Jesus in the Gospel tend to figure prominently in the sermons, though not always. Jesus as Son of Man is mentioned only once in Acts, when Stephen sees him standing in heaven beside God (7:56). But even this may be illuminating. Perhaps Luke is preserving an authentic memory that "Son of Man" was a term exclusively used by Jesus and thus associated with his own preaching, and that it was not a term used by the church in its proclamation of the gospel, either to Jews, who would have presumably understood it, or to Gentiles, who would have found it puzzling.

Other terms of prime importance in the Gospel, such as Messiah, Son of God, Lord, and prophet, also loom large in the church's preaching (Messiah: 2:31, 36; 3:20; 8:5; 9:22; Lord and Messiah: 2:36; Lord: 10:36; Son of God: 9:20; Savior: 13:23; prophet: 3:22; 7:37). It is not necessary to provide a comprehensive list to see what is happening here: the Jesus who is recognized and experienced as Messiah, Lord, and Son of God during his lifetime is now being proclaimed in the same way after his death and resurrection. To put it briefly: *The Jesus story has become the church's story.* The sermons provide occasions to amplify the meaning and significance of these terms.

This helps explain the "midrashic" character of some of the sermons, especially Peter's Pentecost sermon (ch. 2) and Paul's Pisidian Antioch sermon (ch. 13). In both instances the basic Christian proclamation is rehearsed and then supported by appeal to OT texts, especially from the Psalter. The relevant texts are cited and then explained by Peter and Paul to show how they support the church's claim that Jesus is the Messiah. Some of this occurred in the Gospel, but it occurs in greater detail in the sermons in Acts, in which we are allowed to hear how early Christian preachers actually made these connections between Christ and Scripture and to see how their belief and experience of Jesus simultaneously derived from and informed their reading of the OT.

What the risen Lord left unsaid when he insisted that his death and resurrection had conformed to Scripture (Luke 24:27, 44–47) gets said by his duly appointed interpreters in Acts. Luke knows from Mark the use of the "rejected stone" passage from Ps 118:22–23 to explain Jesus' death and exaltation, and he retains it within the context of the parable of the wicked tenants (Luke 20:17; cf. Mark 12:10–11; Matt 21:42). By repeating it in Peter's remarks before the Sanhedrin, Luke shows it being used in early Christian preaching to illustrate the paradox of the rejected Messiah who became exalted (Acts 4:11).

The sermons in Acts repeat and amplify the Gospel's claims about Jesus, but they also move beyond them. We hear the church's preachers using titles for Jesus not found in the Gospel or making explicit claims that remained implicit in the Gospel: they call him "servant" (*pais*, perhaps "child," 3:13, 26), "holy servant" (4:27), "Holy and Righteous One" (3:14; see Luke 4:34), "Author of life" (*ton archēgon tēs zōēs*, perhaps "pioneer of life," 3:15), the "Righteous One" (7:52; 22:14), "Leader and Savior" (*archēgon kai sōtēra*, 5:31), and "Lord of all" (10:36). The sermons also expand on certain roles attributed to Jesus in the Gospel, for example, his role as eschatological judge (3:20–21; 10:42).

Some of these christological claims may reflect early stages of Christian preaching, but they also show the church actively engaged in making sense of Jesus and deepening its understanding of him. Not content with the titles and categories they derived from the Jesus tradition, Jesus' followers strive to find new ways to express more fully the significance of his death and resurrection. Their explicit use of "servant" for Jesus, along with their designation of him as the "Righteous One," for example, reflects their fuller confidence that he is rightly seen as the one prefigured in Isaiah's Servant Songs.

Looking at the way Jesus is described in the speeches also reveals other Lukan concerns. Realizing the exceptional manner of Paul's call and his distance from the formative events of Jesus' ministry, Luke shows Paul preaching Jesus in ways that conform to his portrait of the pre-Easter Jesus. Like Jesus, Paul preaches the kingdom of God (19:8; 20:25; 28:23) and can be heard proclaiming Jesus as Messiah (17:3; 18:5; 26:23). Like Jesus himself and his predecessor Peter (3:18), Paul insists on the necessity of the Messiah's suffering (17:3; 26:23). He also voices other traditional claims about Jesus, proclaiming him as Son of God (9:20), Savior (13:23), Lord (22:8–10), and the Righteous One (22:14). Also revealing is the way Luke shows Paul using John the Baptist in his preaching, suggesting that Paul has intimate knowledge of traditions about John that Luke had already reported in his Gospel (Acts 13:24–25). In these and other ways, Luke places Paul's preaching squarely within the mainstream of the earliest apostolic preaching.

The Church Embodies Jesus' Messianic Vision of the Kingdom of God. In Acts the proclamation of the kingdom of God and Jesus' messiahship are closely linked (8:12; 28:23, 31). The risen Lord instructs the disciples in matters pertaining to the kingdom of God (1:3) and it remains a theme in the church's preaching, especially that of Paul (14:22; 19:8; 20:25). Apart from these explicit references to the church's proclamation of the kingdom of God are numerous echoes in Acts of Jesus' teaching in the Gospel, enough to see how Luke portrays the church exemplifying the authentic discipleship about which Jesus taught in the Gospel.

The several vignettes depicting the church selling possessions, sharing their goods, and collecting relief funds for the Jerusalem famine (2:44; 4:32–37; 11:27–30) show how seriously the disciples take this aspect of Jesus' teaching, so prominently treated in Luke's Gospel. The church displays forms of authentic discipleship deriving from Jesus' teaching. Paul's generosity serves as an example for the church and is grounded directly in the "words of the Lord Jesus" himself, who said, "It is more blessed to give than to receive" (20:35). What Jesus teaches, the church does.

That the church follows Jesus' teachings about the "way of the cross" (Luke 9:3–27) is unforgettably depicted in the deaths of Stephen (ch. 7) and James (ch. 12), not to mention the numerous threats, imprisonments, and repeated harassments the church encounters as it preaches the gospel. Paul's reminder to his young churches that "it is through many persecutions that we must enter the kingdom of God" (14:22) encapsulates Luke's overall perspective in Acts. Yet for all the resistance the church encounters, it manages to live up to Jesus' expectations of disciples as bold witnesses who, when threatened or intimidated, will remain unfazed. Jesus' call for his disciples to be fearless before oppressive authorities (Luke 12:4–12) is heeded repeatedly by those same disciples in Acts. Luke directly connects their bold behavior with public perceptions of their experience with Jesus himself (4:13; see 5:17–42).

Also revealing is the close similarity between Stephen's final words and those of Jesus as he confronted death—yet another way Luke portrays the close correlation between Jesus' exemplary behavior and that of leading figures in the church (7:54–60; cf. Luke 23:34, 46). Disciples in the church not only live up to Jesus' expectations but also follow his example of confident, steadfast faith even in the face of death.

The church also lives out Jesus' expectations of the kingdom of God by reenacting the two major activities that characterized his ministry: preaching and healing. With impressive detail Luke graphically depicts the major figures in the church replicating these activities. Like Jesus, Peter heals and proclaims (Acts 3:1–26); not only can he heal the sick, but he can also raise the dead (9:32–43). So can Paul, who exorcises demons (16:16–18), heals (14:8–10; 19:11–12; 28:7–10), and raises the dead (20:7–12).

Performing wonders and signs, which include impressive forms of healing, is a typical activity of the apostles and other ministers of the word in Acts (2:43; 5:12–16; 6:8; 8:6–8). By repeatedly connecting these healings with the power of Jesus' name, Luke links the church's therapeutic powers directly to Jesus himself.

Summary. Luke knits an intricate tapestry showing how the church's story continues Jesus' story by reenacting it. The risen Jesus is portrayed as an active presence in both the ordinary and extraordinary moments of the church's life. Convinced that the Jesus who proclaimed the kingdom of God continued to do so through his apostles and disciples, Luke closely correlates the church's life and behavior with that of Jesus.

As the central topic of the church's preaching, Jesus is *what is preached*; as the energizing force behind the preaching, he is also *the One who is preaching*. By heeding the risen Lord's instructions, the church through its preaching and teaching extends Jesus' mission that began in Galilee and Judea. Like Jesus, the church boldly crosses geographical, ethnic, and social boundaries, even when facing stout resistance and death. In its behavior, the church exhibits the profile of discipleship that Jesus sketched in his preaching. The disciples' bold witness is so visible that they are identified in the public mind with Jesus himself. Their generosity overflows as they remember Jesus' insisting that it is better to give than to receive.

Through it all, we see the visible outlines of Jesus' vision of the kingdom of God gradually taking shape in the form of a people who embody Israel's oldest and fondest hopes. By connecting Jesus and the church with such methodical artistry, Luke boldly asserts his own theological vision: what the soul is to the body, Jesus is to the church.

The Church as the People of the Spirit

Luke-Acts is well known for the prominent role the Holy Spirit plays in the narrative. In one sense, the Holy Spirit is a major character in Luke's unfolding drama.

Luke already knows from Mark of Jesus' reception of the Holy Spirit at his baptism (Mark 1:9–11; Luke 3:21–22) and how the Spirit served as a catalyst for Jesus' behavior (Mark 1:12) and a topic for his teaching (Mark 3:29; 12:36; 13:11). Luke considerably expands the Holy Spirit's role in Jesus' ministry, insisting that the Spirit was at work long before Jesus arrived and long after he departed.

Taking into account the entire scope of Luke-Acts and the many times and different ways the Holy Spirit is referred to, we can formulate Luke's understanding as follows: the Holy Spirit, who was present long ago in Israel (Acts 7:51) and who inspired the writers of Scripture (1:16; 4:25; 28:25), uniquely empowered the messianic ministry of Jesus. This same Spirit remained alive in the risen Jesus and was bestowed by him upon the community of believers that formed in his name, where it became an abiding presence and an energizing force. As its name suggests, the Holy Spirit served as the divine breath that enlivened God's Word as it addressed Israel, became written in Scripture, and came to life in God's Messiah, Jesus, and his church. To track God's Spirit, Luke would insist, is to follow its path through the stories of Israel, Jesus, and the church. The Holy Spirit is the one visible thread that connects them. To say that the church is the people of the Spirit lays claim to the heritage of Israel through the one who enabled God's promise to Abraham to be fulfilled: Jesus the Messiah.

Jesus is remembered in the church's preaching as the one whom "God anointed . . . with the Holy Spirit and with power" (10:38). Spelled out further, this phrase would prompt memories of Jesus' baptism, when the Spirit "in bodily form like a dove" descended on him (Luke 3:22); his temptations, which he experienced "full of the Holy Spirit" (Luke 4:1, 14); and the Nazareth inaugural, where he laid claim to the Spirit's anointing mentioned in Isa 61 (Luke 4:16–21). While the Holy Spirit had been active earlier by impregnating Mary (Luke 1:35) and prompting Elizabeth's praise of Mary (Luke 1:41) and the prophecies of Zechariah (Luke 1:67) and Simeon (Luke 2:25–26), it became Jesus' singular possession during his ministry. In sharp contrast to the Gospel of John, in which Jesus repeatedly promises to send the Holy Spirit to the disciples (John 14:15–17, 25–26; 15:26; 16:7–15) and in which the risen Lord actually confers the Spirit on them (John 20:22), Luke's Jesus shows little interest in imparting the Spirit until after Easter (cf. Luke 11:13). Prior to that, he is the sole bearer of God's Spirit, even though he anticipates a time when the disciples will have it (Luke 12:10–12).

The Spirit's presence is not actively displayed in Jesus' passion, although Peter later claims that the Spirit witnessed those events (Acts 5:32). Even as Jesus escaped the jaws of death (Acts 2:24), so did the Spirit remain alive, actively assisting the risen Lord in instructing the disciples (Acts 1:2). It was during this time that the risen Lord promised to confer the Holy Spirit on the disciples (Acts 1:8), thereby fulfilling John's prediction that he would eventually baptize people with the Holy Spirit (Acts 1:4–5; cf. Luke 3:16).

Luke breaks new ground by locating the fulfillment of Jesus' promise in the events of Pentecost and showing the effect of its distribution among Jesus' followers. Just as Isa 61 figured as the programmatic text for Jesus' receiving the Spirit, Joel 2 serves as the scriptural basis for the church's anointing with the Spirit. What had until then been the exclusive possession of Jesus is now poured out by the risen Jesus on those gathered in Jerusalem, and their full immersion with the Spirit is marked by signs both visible and audible (Acts 2:1–4). Thanks to his editorial modification of Joel's prophecy, Luke interprets the events of Pentecost as the arrival of the "last days," the final period of salvation history that would see God's Spirit generously distributed among all people.

From this point onward, the Holy Spirit moves freely among the people of God, marking them as disciples of the Messiah Jesus. Just as the Spirit had energized Jesus to preach (Luke 4:14), so also does it enable the church's witnesses to preach the gospel about Jesus complete with authoritative Scripture interpretation (Acts 4:8–12). Their testimony is marked by a boldness that confirms Jesus' earlier prediction of the Holy Spirit's reassuring presence among them. The result of their boldness is that people perceive the connection between the disciples' behavior and that of Jesus himself (Acts 4:13; cf. Luke 12:10–12).

Those who emerge as leading figures in the church characteristically possess the Spirit: Peter (Acts 4:8; 8:17; 10:19, 44), John (8:17), the seven apostolic assistants (6:3), Stephen (6:3, 5, 10; 7:55), Philip (8:29, 39), Barnabas (11:24), and especially Paul (9:17; 13:2, 4, 9; 16:6, 7; 19:6, 21; 20:22–23). But the Spirit is by no means limited to the church's leaders. Since it is the possession of every believer (2:38; 5:32; 13:52), young, flourishing churches enjoy the "comfort of the Holy Spirit" (9:31). The Spirit can accompany baptism (2:38) or it can be received afterward through special conferral by those, usually apostles, who already have it (8:15–19; 19:6).

Dramatic outpourings of the Spirit occur when the church experiences landmark moments, such as its inauguration at Pentecost (2:1–4) and its initial inclusion of Gentiles (10:45; 11:15; 15:8). In both cases, the Spirit's arrival is accompanied by signs and wonders, most notably speaking in tongues (2:4; 10:46; cf. 19:6). Its presence within the community is seen in the episode involving Ananias and Sapphira, a reminder to the church that lying to, or testing, the Spirit can have tragic consequences (5:3, 9). Equally emphatic is Simon the sorcerer's ill-motivated quest to purchase the Spirit (8:18–24). The community also experiences the Spirit's presence in other crises, most notably when it crosses ethnic boundaries to embrace Gentiles. It is the Spirit, after all, who moves Peter into place in preparation for his visit to Cornelius (10:19); the Spirit who convinces the Jewish Christian gradualists by its undeniable presence among the Gentiles (10:45–47; 11:15–17; 15:8); and the Spirit who stands behind the agreement worked out at the Jerusalem Council (15:28). In the impending crisis created by Paul's approach to Jerusalem, the Spirit prompts ominous warnings about what lies ahead for Paul (21:4, 11), even though Paul himself feels "captive to the Spirit" (20:22–23).

Wherever it goes, the church experiences the Spirit's guidance and protection, much like the cloud guiding the Israelites in the wilderness. Just as the Spirit prompted the church to embrace Gentiles, so also does it direct the church's mission. The Spirit moves God's messengers around for their mission assignments, as if they were chess pieces being strategically positioned for attack (8:29, 39; 10:19; 11:12; 20:22). Paul and Barnabas are commissioned by the Spirit through the prophets at Antioch (13:2, 4). The Spirit also serves as the compass guiding the Pauline mission through Asia Minor

(16:6, 7). As Paul makes decisions about mission strategy, he makes his resolutions "in the Spirit" (19:21). The Spirit also appoints presbyters as overseers of the church (20:28) and activates the prophetic voice of Agabus (11:28) and the prophetic speech of the newly baptized twelve at Ephesus (19:6).

The Holy Spirit and the risen Lord work in tandem as God's surrogate Presence within the church. While their respective roles should not be fused, they sometimes converge, as when the "Spirit of Jesus" guides the Pauline mission (16:7). Luke cannot envision the church apart from God's Spirit because the Spirit is the sure sign marking the direction God's promise has taken from Israel's past into the church's present. Since the Spirit is so clearly understood as the risen Messiah's gift to the church, it marks the church as the place where the "hope of Israel"—belief in the resurrection—remains alive. Not only in its proclamation but also in its ongoing mission of teaching, healing, and doing good does the church exhibit the Spirit's life-giving energy. This is Luke's theological vision of the church in Acts.

The Lukan Paul

Even though Paul shares the stage with other Christian leaders in Acts, he is a heroic figure for Luke. Whatever else Luke's treatment of Paul does, it reflects Paul's emergence as a force to be contended with in early Christianity. Since Acts precedes the Pauline letters in our canon, it invariably affects the mental image we form of Paul as we read the letters. Because Luke's portrait of Paul in Acts differs in some important respects from the one that emerges in the Pauline letters, we treat some of those differences here.

Paul's Relationship to Jerusalem

For Luke, Jerusalem is the center of Paul's universe: he was raised there (22:3), persecuted the church there (7:58; 8:1, 3), returned there from his Damascus conversion (9:26), experienced there a prophetic call from the risen Lord in the temple (22:17–21), and returned there on four subsequent occasions (11:27–30; 15:2–5, 12; 18:22 [?]; 21:17) before he finally left for Rome.

In the Pauline letters, we get a somewhat different picture. When Paul discusses his "earlier life in Judaism" (Gal 1:13), he does not refer to a "Jerusalem stage" of his upbringing. He emphatically denies having gone to Jerusalem after his encounter with the risen Lord (Gal 1:17), claiming instead that he went to Arabia, after which he "returned" not to Jerusalem but to Damascus (Gal 1:17). By his own account, his first trip to Jerusalem occurred three years later (Gal 1:18), a fifteen-day visit with Peter (Cephas) and James the Lord's brother (Gal 1:18–19). Thereafter he went to Syria and Cilicia, still "unknown by sight to the churches of Judea" (Gal 1:22). He reports making a second trip to Jerusalem fourteen years later (Gal 2:1), when he was accompanied by Barnabas and Titus. It was "a private meeting with the acknowledged leaders" (Gal 2:2) that included James the Lord's brother, Peter (Cephas), and John (Gal 2:9). The result was that they approved Paul's mission to the Gentiles (Gal 2:9–10). A third trip is envisioned by Paul when he discusses his plans to deliver to the Jerusalem church the funds collected from his Gentile churches in the Aegean (Rom 15:25–33; also 1 Cor 16:3; 2 Cor 1:16). In this same context Paul describes the scope of his preaching as extending "from Jerusalem and as far around as Illyricum" (Rom 15:19), but it remains unclear from his letters when, apart from the two trips mentioned in Galatians, he might have preached in Jerusalem.

Whereas Acts emphasizes Paul's connection with Jerusalem, in his own letters Paul distances himself from Jerusalem. It is neither the city of his youth to which he constantly returns nor the defining center of his spiritual universe. Acts presents Paul in solidarity with Jerusalem's church leaders, especially at the Apostolic Council (ch. 15) and at his final return (ch. 21), which sharply contrasts with his stormy relationship with them in the letters (esp. Gal 2).

How are we to account for these discrepancies? Even though Paul's report in Gal 1–2 is polemical, it is given under oath (1:20). This, combined with the fact that it is primary evidence from a participant in the events, whereas Acts is secondary evidence from a nonparticipant writing much later, requires us to give priority to Paul's account. Accordingly, Paul's two prior visits to Jerusalem reported by Luke (Acts 9:26;

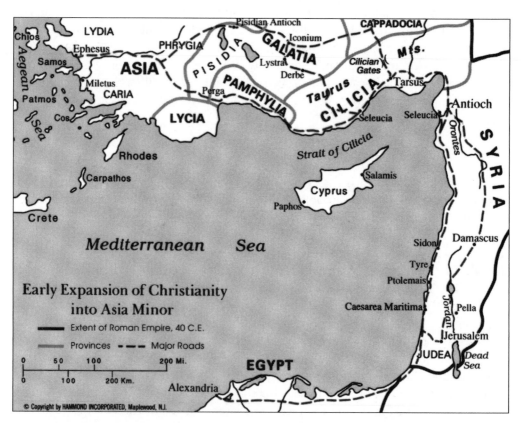

Acts reports the expansion of early Christianity along major highways in the Roman province of Syria and in the provinces of Asia Minor. Paul's mission westward originated in Antioch of Syria, located on the Orontes River (Acts 11:19–30).

11:30) must either be out of sequence or factually incorrect, or both. Even though Paul's description of his "private" meeting with the "acknowledged leaders" in Jerusalem differs markedly from Luke's account of the Apostolic Council as a much more public, formal gathering (Acts 15), they appear to be describing the same event. But we must recognize their clear differences. The main issue at the meeting reported by Paul in Gal 2 is the legitimacy of his (and Barnabas's) mission to the Gentiles, whereas the Apostolic Council primarily addresses the terms of admission for Gentiles who wish to become Christians—whether they must be circumcised. One possibility is that Luke knows of this watershed meeting at Jerusalem between Paul and Barnabas and the leaders of the church, but in Acts 15 interprets it differently. Rather than seeing it as the moment when the Jerusalem church confirmed the legitimacy of the Gentile mission (for Luke, this occurred after Peter's conversion of Cornelius in Acts 10), he sees it as the occasion when the church at a momentous meeting resolved the question of circumcision as a requirement for male Gentile Christians. [See Expanded CD Version p. 349: *How Paul Relates to Jerusalem in Acts: A Detailed Discussion*]

Paul's Jewishness

Like Luke's other characters, especially Jesus, Paul is an observant Jew, which means that he not only respects Torah, speaks approvingly of it, and constantly appeals to it, but also lives by it. Besides his regular visits to synagogues, we find him honoring the rite of circumcision (16:3), observing the Nazirite vow (18:18; cf. Num 6:1–21), making travel plans around Jewish feast days (20:16), and engaging in purification rites in the temple (21:17–26). He speaks Hebrew (21:40), stresses his commitment to "our ancestral law" (22:3), declares himself to be a practicing Pharisee (23:6; 26:5), and presents himself to the leaders of the Roman Jewish community as someone imprisoned "for the sake of the hope of Israel" (28:20). Nowhere in Acts does Paul polemicize against Torah or even reflect ambivalence about it, although his synagogue sermon at Pisidian Antioch refers to the law's inability to forgive sins (13:39). By no means do the Pauline letters reveal Paul as someone cut off from his Jewish roots. He calls Israelites "my own people, my kindred according to the flesh" (Rom 9:3), even insisting that "I myself am an Israelite, a descendant of Abraham, a member of the tribe of Benjamin" (Rom 11:1). Yet he can speak of his Jewish pedigree as a thing of the past (Phil 3:4–7), and his attitude toward Torah is, at the very least, ambivalent (Rom 7:14; Gal 3:19–22), and, at most, critical (Rom 3:21–31; Gal 3:10–14).

Paul's Apostleship

Perhaps no single title captures Paul's self-understanding better than "apostle," the word he typically uses of himself in the greeting that opens each letter (e.g., Rom 1:1; 1 Cor 1:1). Asked to choose an epitaph for himself, Paul would probably have said, "apostle to the Gentiles" (Rom 11:13). The sheer frequency of his use of the term "apostle" in describing his own work, to say nothing of the way his own sense of vocation as one "sent by God" informs every one of his letters, attests how central this category was to his identity. Yet Acts calls Paul an apostle only twice (14:4, 14), each time in company with Barnabas. The apostles constitute a distinct group in Acts; they are "the Twelve" (1:26) who, along with the "elders," form the core leadership in the Jerusalem church (see 15:2, 4, 6, 22–23). But Paul is not among them, nor is he seen by Luke as an "exceptional apostle" (see 1 Cor 15:7–10). He receives a divine call in Acts, but in none of the several reports of this event is he called "apostle" either by God, by the risen Lord who summons him, by Ananias who baptizes him, or by himself. The two times Luke refers to Paul as an apostle seem quite incidental. Asked to choose an epitaph for Paul, Luke would have probably said, "God's chosen instrument" (Acts 9:15). [See Expanded CD Version pp. 352–53: *Other Differences between the Paul of Acts and the Paul of the Letters*]

An image of Saul's conversion (Acts 9), taken from *Biblia ectypa*, a book of biblical images by Christoph Weigel published in Germany (1695). From the Digital Image Archive of The Richard C. Kessler Reformation Collection, Pitts Theology Library, Candler School of Theology, Emory University, Atlanta, Georgia.

1	2	3	4	5	6	7
			Jerusalem			
Introduction (1-5)	Pentecost	Peter & John in Temple	Peter & John in Temple	Witness in Temple cont.	Beyond Temple	Stephen's Sermon (1-53)
Risen Lord appears to disciples over 40 days	Holy Spirit comes (1-4)	-Lame man healed (1-10)	- P&J arrested (1-4) - P&J before Sanhedrin (5-22)	- Hoarding possessions: Ananias and Sapphira (1-11)	Choosing of Seven (1-7)	- Abraham (2-8) - Joseph (9-16)
Ascension (6-11)	Worldwide audience (5-13)	Peter's sermon in Temple (12-26)	-Peter's Sermon to Jewish rulers (8-12)	- Summary: apostolic signs & wonders (12-16)	Arrest of Stephen (8-15)	- Moses (17-43) - Dt 18:New Moses
Selection of Matthias (12-26) - Pss 69 & 109	Peter's sermon (14-36) - Joel 3:1-5 fulfilled (14-21) - Jesus & Ps 16:10; 110:1 (22-36) - Response (37-41) - Profile of early church (42-47)	- Jesus (12-16) - Call to repent (17-21) - Dt 18: New Moses (22-23) - Prophetic legacy (23-26)	Ps 118:22 - Prayer meeting (23-31) - Ps 2:1-2 - Sharing Possessions: Barnabas (32-37)	- Arrest of apostles (17-26) - Apostles' defense (29-32) -Vindication Gamaliel (33-42)		- Am 5:25-27 - Tabernacle / Temple (44-50) - Is 66:1-2 - Heritage of resistance (51-53) Stephen's Death (7:54-8:3)

15	16	17	18	19	20	21
Jerusalem	Mission in Aegean: Macedonia, Achaia, and Asia					Jerusalem
Jerusalem Council Causes (1-5) - Peter (6-11) - B & P (12) - James, bro. of Jesus (13-21) - Amos 9:11-12 - 4 requirements -Jeru. decree (22-29) Joy in Antioch (30-35) P&B separate (36-41)	To Europe - Lystra – Timothy circ. (1-5) - Troas: Macedonian call (6-10) Philippi (11-40) - Lydia (11-15) - Slave girl (16-18) - P & Silas imprisoned; conversion of jailer (19-34) -Vindication (35-40)	Thessalonica (1-9) Beroea (10-15) Athens (16-34) - Arrival & preaching (16-21) Areopagus Sermon (22-31) - "unknown god" (23) - Creator - Greek poets - Repentance Response: (32-34)	Corinth (1-17) 1.5 yrs - Aq. & Priscilla (1-3) - Jewish resistance - house of Titius Justus - Crispus - Proconsul Gallio: Vindication (12-17) - Transition (18-23) - Ephesus (18:24-19:41) - Apollos (24-28)	Ephesus 3 yrs 12 JnB disciples (1-7) Eph. work begins (8-10) Miracles, Jewish exorcists, magic (11-20) P. decides to leave (21-22) Demetrius, silversmiths Theater riot (23-41)	Paul's final approach to Jeru. (1-16) - travel - P's circle (4-6) - Troas: Christian meeting (7-12) Miletus: Farewell sermon to Ephesian Elders (17-38) - reviews ministry - warnings - saying of Jesus	Journey to Jerusalem (1-14) - travel diary - Churches: Tyre Ptolemais Caesarea Summary (14) Paul in Jerusalem (15-26) - reception - change of leadership - resistance - elders' speech (20-25) Paul's arrest (27-40)

Second and Third Journeys

8	9	10	11	12	13	14
Samaria	Damascus/Coast/Caesarea/Antioch			Jerusalem	Eastern Asia Minor	
Philip's Ministry in **Samaria**	**Beyond Jerusalem**	**Coastland: Caesarea**	Cornelius & **Antioch**	**Return to Jerusalem**	**Antioch of Syria** (1-3)	
- Philip preaches in Samaria (4-8)	- Saul's Call (1-19a)	- Cornelius's vision (1-8) - Peter's vision (9-16)	- Resistance from Jerusalem & Peter's report (1-18)	- Resistance intensified (1-5) - Death of Jas. apostle	**Cyprus** (4-12) BarJesus Serg. Paul.	**Iconium** (1-7)
- Simon the Magician converted (9-13)	- Saul in Damascus & Jerusalem (19b-30)	- P. receives messengers (17-23a) - P&C meet (23b-33)	- Expanding mission north: **Antioch of Syria** (19-30)	- Peter imprisoned - Peter's deliverance (6-11)	**Antioch of Pisidia**; syn. sermon (13-41) - Israel's past (17-22)	**Lystra & Derbe** (8-20) P & B's sermon at Lystra (15-17)
- Apostles confirm Samaritan mission (14-25)	- Summary (31) - Peter in coastal region (32-43)	- Sermon to Cornelius (34-43) - universal Lord (34-36)	- Christians (26)	- Prayer mtg (12-17) Response (18-19)	- Jesus, David's seed (23-25) -OT: *Ps 2, Isa 55, Ps 16; Hab 1:5*	- Return to **Antioch** (21-28)
- Ethiopian official converted – *Is 53* (26-40)	- healing Aeneas - raising Dorcas	- X ministry (37-38) - J's death (39-41) - Invitation (42-43)	- Proof of discipleship: relief effort (27-30)	Death of Herod (20-23) Summary (24-25)	Response (42-52) *Is 49:6*	
					First Journey	

22	23	24	25	26	27	28
Jerusalem	Jeru/Caes.	Caesarea			Rome	
P's defense to Jewish crowd (1-21)	Paul speaks to Jewish Council (1-10)	P's defense before procurator Felix (1-21)	Paul before procurator Festus and Agrippa (1-27)	Paul's defense before King Agrippa (1-23)	**Journey to Rome** - Preparation (1-8)	**Malta** (1-10) - snake bite - healing of Publius (8)
- credentials (3) - Damas. rd. experience (4-11)	- high priest episode (2-5) *Ex 22:28* - Phar. vs. Sadd. (6-10)	- Formal accusation: Tertullus (2-8)	- Festus goes to Jeru (1-5) - Jeru. Jews charge Paul; P appeals to Caesar (6-12)	- gracious opening (2-3) - early life (4-8) - actions vs. Xns (9-11)	Paul's Prediction (9-12) Getting off course in storm (13-20)	**Arriving in Italy** (11-16) **Rome:** Paul with Jewish leaders (17-28)
- Ananias (12-16) - vision in Jeru. Temple (17-21) - cf. *Is 6*	Divine reassurance (11) Plot vs. Paul (12-22)	- Paul's response (10-21) - Felix's response (22-23)	- Festus' speech # 1 (14-21)	- Damascus experience (12-18) - Obedience to God's Will (19-23)	Paul's 2nd Speech (21-26) Approaching land (27-32)	- Paul's defense (17-20) -Jews (21-22) - P's last word: *Isa 6:9-10* (25-28)
P & tribune (22-29) P before Sanhedrin (22:30-23:11) P in prison	- **Move to Caesarea** (23-35) - Tribune's Letter (26-30)	- Felix & P meet (24-26) -P in prison 2 years (27)	- Festus' speech # 2 (24-27)	Response: Festus & Agrippa (24-32)	Paul's 3rd speech (33-38) To shore (39-44)	Vindication: (30-31)
					Journey to Rome	

Speeches

Notes

1. *1 Apol* 39.3; 40.6, 11; 49.5; 50.12; *2 Apol* 10.6; *Dial.* 20.3–4; 60.1; 68.5; 80.3; 108.2; 118.1; 131.3.

2. Irenaeus quotes Acts fifty-four times, according to Bruce M. Metzger, *The Canon of the New Testament* (Oxford: Clarendon Press, 1997), 154. See *Haer.*1.6.3; 1.23.1, 2; 1.26.3; 2.32.3; 3.1.1; 3.12.1; 3.12.5; 3.13.3; 3.14.1; 3.15.1; 4.23.2.

3. *Hom. Act.* 1 (*NPNF*[1] 11:1).

4. See *Hist. eccl.* 2.1.1–2, 8–14; 2.3.1–4; passim. According to Edgar J. Goodspeed (*The Formation of the New Testament* [Chicago: University of Chicago Press, 1926]), Clement of Alexandria "quotes [Acts] very much as he does the Catholic letters, with no especial mark of reverence but with familiarity and confidence, as though it were as well known to his readers as to himself" (87).

5. *Rhet.* 1360[a]37.

6. W. G. Kümmel, *Introduction to the New Testament* (Nashville: Abingdon, 1975), 163–64.

Bibliography

Commentaries

Barrett, C. K. *The Acts of the Apostles. A Shorter Commentary*. London: T&T Clark, 2002.

Bruce, F. F. *Commentary on the Book of the Acts*. New International Commentary on the New Testament. Grand Rapids: Eerdmans, 1960.

Dunn, James D. G. *The Acts of the Apostles*. Narrative Commentaries. Valley Forge: Trinity, 1996.

Fitzmyer, Joseph A. *The Acts of the Apostles*. Anchor Bible 31. New York: Doubleday, 1998.

Gaventa, Beverly Roberts. *The Acts of the Apostles*. Abingdon New Testament Commentaries. Nashville: Abingdon, 2003.

Haenchen, Ernst. *The Acts of the Apostles: A Commentary*. Translated by Bernard Noble and Gerald Shinn, with Hugh Anderson; revised and updated by R. McL. Wilson. Oxford/Philadelphia: Blackwell/Westminster, 1971.

Johnson, Luke T. *The Acts of the Apostles*. Sacra Pagina 5. Collegeville: Liturgical Press, 1992.

Kee, Howard C. *To Every Nation Under Heaven: The Acts of the Apostles*. The New Testament in Context. Harrisburg: Trinity, 1997.

Marshall, I. Howard. *The Acts of the Apostles: An Introduction and Commentary*. Grand Rapids: Eerdmans, 1980.

Other Resources

Brawley, Robert L. *Luke-Acts and the Jews: Conflict, Apology, and Conciliation*. Society of Biblical Literature Monograph Series 33. Atlanta: Society of Biblical Literature (Scholars Press), 1987.

Cadbury, Henry J. *The Making of Luke-Acts*. London: Macmillan, 1927; repr. Peabody: Hendrickson, 1999.

Conzelmann, Hans. *The Theology of St. Luke.* Translated by Geoffrey Buswell. Philadelphia: Fortress, 1982 (1961).

Dibelius, Martin. *Studies in the Acts of the Apostles.* London/New York: SCM/Scribner, 1956.

Dupont, Jacques. *The Salvation of the Gentiles: Essays on the Acts of the Apostles.* New York: Paulist, 1979.

————. *The Sources of the Acts.* New York: Herder & Herder, 1964.

Esler, Philip F. *Community and Gospel in Luke-Acts: The Social and Political Motivations of Lucan Theology.* Society for New Testament Studies Monograph Series 57. Cambridge: Cambridge University Press, 1987; repr. 1996.

Fitzmyer, Joseph A. *Luke the Theologian: Aspects of his Teaching.* New York: Paulist, 1989.

Gasque, W. Ward. *History of the Interpretation of the Acts of the Apostles.* 2d ed. Peabody: Hendrickson, 1989 (1975).

Hemer, Colin J. *The Book of Acts in the Setting of Hellenistic History.* Wissenschaftliche Untersuchungen zum Neuen Testament 49. Tübingen: Mohr (Siebeck), 1989.

Hengel, Martin. *Acts and the History of Earliest Christianity.* Translated by John Bowden. London: SCM, 1979; Philadelphia: Fortress, 1980.

Jervell, Jacob. *Luke and the People of God: A New Look at Luke-Acts.* Minneapolis: Augsburg, 1972.

————. *The Theology of the Acts of the Apostles.* New Testament Theology. Cambridge: Cambridge University Press, 1996; repr. 2000.

Keck, Leander E., and J. Louis Martyn. *Studies in Luke-Acts: Essays Presented in Honor of Paul Schubert.* Philadelphia: Fortress, 1980 (1966).

Kee, Howard C. *Good News to the Ends of the Earth: The Theology of Acts.* London/Philadelphia: SCM/Trinity, 1990.

Kurz, William S. *Reading Luke-Acts: Dynamics of Biblical Narrative.* Louisville: Westminster John Knox, 1993.

Lentz, John Clayton, Jr. *Luke's Portrait of Paul.* Society for New Testament Studies Monograph Series 77. Cambridge: Cambridge University Press, 1993.

Maddox, Robert L. *The Purpose of Luke-Acts.* Forschungen zur Religion und Literatur des Alten und Neuen Testaments 126. Göttingen: Vandenhoeck & Ruprecht, 1982.

Marguerat, Daniel. *The First Christian Historian: Writing the 'Acts of the Apostles.'* Society for New Testament Studies Monograph Series 121. Cambridge: Cambridge University Press, 2002.

Marshall, I. Howard. *Luke: Historian and Theologian.* Exeter: Paternoster, 1970; Grand Rapids: Zondervan, 1971.

Mount, Christopher. *Pauline Christianity: Luke-Acts and the Legacy of Paul.* Supplements to Novum Testamentum 104. Leiden: Brill, 2002.

Neyrey, Jerome H., ed. *The Social World of Luke-Acts: Models for Interpretation.* Peabody: Hendrickson, 1991.

Pervo, Richard I. *Luke's Story of Paul.* Minneapolis: Fortress, 1990.

————. *Profit with Delight: The Literary Genre of the Acts of the Apostles.* Philadelphia: Fortress, 1987.

Powell, Mark A. *What Are They Saying About Acts?* New York: Paulist, 1991.

259

Reimer, Ivoni R. *Women in the Acts of Apostles: A Feminist Liberation Perspective*. Minneapolis: Fortress, 1995.

Smith, David E. *The Canonical Function of Acts: A Comparative Analysis*. Collegeville: Liturgical (Michael Glazier), 2002.

Sterling, Gregory E. *Historiography and Self-definition: Josephos, Luke-Acts, and Apologetic Historiography*. Supplements to Novum Testamentum 64. Leiden: Brill, 1992.

Talbert, Charles H. *Literary Patterns, Theological Themes, and the Genre of Luke-Acts*. Missoula: Society of Biblical Literature (Scholars Press), 1974.

Tannehill, Robert C. *The Narrative Unity of Luke-Acts: A Literary Interpretation*. Foundations and Facets. 2 vols. Philadelphia: Fortress, 1986–1990.

Tiede, David L. *Prophecy and History in Luke-Acts*. Philadelphia: Fortress, 1980.

Tyson, Joseph B. *Images of Judaism in Luke-Acts*. Columbia: University of South Carolina Press, 1992.

Winter, Bruce W., ed. *The Book of Acts in Its First Century Setting*. 5 vols. Grand Rapids/Carlisle: Eerdmans/Paternoster, 1993–1996.

Witherington, Ben. *History, Literature and Society in the Book of Acts*. Cambridge: Cambridge University Press, 1996.

Part 4

THE
PAULINE LETTERS
AND HEBREWS

Chapter 11

Reading the Pauline Letters

"I thank you for writing to me so often; for you are revealing your real self to me in the only way you can. I never receive a letter from you without being in your company forthwith."

Seneca, *Writing to Lucilius*

"In every other form of composition it is possible to discern the writer's character, but in none so clearly as in the letter."

Demetrius, *On Style*

"One might write a history of dogma as a history of the Pauline reactions in the Church, and in doing so would touch on all the turning points of the history."

Adolf von Harnack

It may seem strange that the theological legacy of the most influential figure in early Christianity, apart from Jesus himself, is preserved in thirteen letters. Yet considering the unique web of circumstances that produced them, it is not that surprising. As a flexible literary form for conveying a sense of immediacy, even serving as a person's surrogate presence, letters were the perfect medium through which Paul could communicate with the network of churches and individuals who came under his influence. Letters were ideally suited for people on the move, such as the itinerant apostle to the Gentiles. Although Paul's letters do not supply detailed itineraries of his travels comparable to what we find in Acts, they allow us to track his journeys from the early days of his ministry in the eastern Mediterranean until the closing days of his ministry in the West. Paul's letters are peppered with place names throughout the Mediterranean where he traveled and started churches. Paul's theology was cast in the form of letters because they enabled him to conduct his apostolic ministry by being in several places at once. More than that, letters made it possible for Paul to spread his teachings throughout the Mediterranean, so that even after he was gone his ideas remained behind to work their magic among his devotees and irritate his critics.

Recognizing that Paul's apostolic presence was mediated to his churches through his letters helps us appreciate their occasional nature. As we would expect, each letter is prompted by different circumstances. In some cases, for example, Galatians and 2 Corinthians, Paul is addressing a pressing crisis, and we often detect a tone of desperation. Other letters, such as Romans, are more reflective in outlook and their content is not as tied to a specific set of issues in a single location. The occasion for Philemon is quite concrete—the return of Onesimus to his master—and Paul's strong personal bond with the addressee is evident. Several letters are written while Paul is imprisoned, yet the circumstances of those he addresses from prison are quite different. To the Philippians, a church with whom he had a long-standing relationship, he sends thanks for their financial support of his ministry and also addresses some tensions within the church.

Because of their strong occasional quality, the Pauline letters display *situational theology*. The letters typically show Paul developing his theological position in response to questions that have arisen from specific situations. This is especially evident in the latter part of 1 Corinthians when Paul takes up questions sent to him by the church at Corinth. His responses are situation specific. His primary audience is the church at Corinth, and his instructions are intended for them. This helps explain the stopgap quality of some of his instructions. After addressing the tensions surrounding their observance of the Eucharist, Paul concludes, "About the other things I will give instructions when I come" (1 Cor 11:34).

Had Paul been in a context such as that of Philo of Alexandria (ca. 20 B.C.E.–50 C.E.), located in one place and working as a "resident theologian," his teaching about the Eucharist might have looked different. It could easily have taken the form of a lengthy treatise in which he gave detailed attention to how he had received the tradition of the Last Supper "from the Lord" (1 Cor 11:23). It might even have dealt more fully with eucharistic protocol—what OT texts should be read, how the elements were to be distributed, or what prayers and hymns were appropriate. He might have given more extended theological reflection to the symbolic significance of the Lord's Supper and how it related to Jewish Passover observance. Instead of such leisurely, reflective theology we get a succinct yet substantive response in 1 Cor 11:23–34, written on the run, as it were.

Paul's letters have been aptly characterized as "conversations in context,"[1] which suggests that they also yield *dialogical theology*. Often the letters reflect a larger, more extended conversation between Paul and his churches. Reading the Corinthian correspondence, we quickly sense that we have joined a conversation that has been going on for some time. We see evidence of this in the editorial decisions of modern translators to use quotation marks in identifying the voice of Paul's addressees. In 1 Cor 6, for example, we can hear the dialogue between Paul and the church. "All things are lawful for me" (v. 12*a*), some of them are saying. Paul answers, "but not all things are beneficial" (v. 12*b*). "Food," they say, "is meant for the stomach and the stomach for food" (v. 13*a*), expressing their view of the body as a physical machine. Paul responds that "God will destroy both one and the other" (v. 13*b*), thereby defining the body within a larger theological framework. A similar conversation is reflected in 1 Cor 7 when, in the opening verse, we hear the voice of the spiritually minded ascetics saying, "It is well for a man not to touch a woman" (v. 1). Verse 2 begins Paul's theological response, which continues for the rest of the chapter. The dialogue is resumed in chapter 8: "All of us possess knowledge," to which Paul responds, "Knowledge puffs up, but love builds up" (v. 1). And so on.

Close attention to this dialogical element reveals a critically important aspect of Paul's theology. Not only does he bring clearly formulated theological convictions *to the conversation*, but he also works out his theological position *in the conversation*. By giving us a glimpse of these "conversations in context," the letters take us inside Paul's mind as he engages in theological reflection. The conversations with his churches—his letters—actually become the medium through which Paul does theology.

When Paul carries on conversation with his churches, it is not as though his theological positions are infinitely variable, subject to change depending on the circumstance. Instead the letters show Paul bringing to the conversation certain theological convictions, some of which he has received as part of the church's tradition, for example, as creedal formulations or OT testimonies about Jesus Christ. These occur in different locations throughout the letters, sometimes as part of an opening greeting (Rom 1:1–6), as a benediction (2 Cor 13:13), or within a specific discussion (1 Cor 8:6). In 1 Cor 15, Paul gives a formal statement of creedal belief at the outset—a statement that he fully embraces. After placing himself squarely within the legacy of those who witnessed the risen Christ (1 Cor 15:7–11), he then addresses the theological issues raised by those who say "there is no resurrection of the dead" (v. 12). In this instance, basic theological convictions shared by the larger church undergird Paul's extended theological argument for the resurrection in chapter 15. Even here his argumentation acquires a dialogical tone, although this time he uses the Greco-Roman diatribe as a literary strategy for structuring the argument. In verse 35, we hear the dissenting questions of the interlocutor: "How are the dead raised? With what kind of body do they come?" In typical diatribal form, Paul addresses his imaginary opponent—"Fool!"—then proceeds to develop his argument.

Letters were perfectly suited for such theological give-and-take. There was a long tradition within the Greco-Roman world in which letters functioned as the means by which kings, politicians, government officials, philosophers, and literary figures remained in contact and conducted business with their constituents and friends, both near and far. Equally well established was the tradition of collecting the letters of eminent figures so that their admirers in succeeding generations could have access to their thoughts.[2] Thirteen letters attributed to Plato (ca. 429–347 B.C.E.)—most of them pseudonymous, with the possible exception of the seventh and eighth letters—were often quoted by later writers such as Cicero (106–43 B.C.E.) and Plutarch (ca. 50–120 C.E.). The letters of the philosopher Epicurus (341–270 B.C.E.) became valuable resources for his later followers such as Philodemus (ca. 110–40/35 B.C.E.) in the first century B.C.E. Letters attributed to the colorful Neopythagorean philosopher Apollonius of Tyana, born in the early part of the first century C.E., circulated during the reign of Hadrian (117–138 C.E.) and were reportedly deposited in the latter's palace at Antium.[3]

While Paul's letters should be seen as part of this much older tradition, they also bear his distinctive stamp. They were not only the ideal medium through which to express his theology, but they also reveal his personality. Far from showing us a two-dimensional figure with a limited emotional range, Paul's letters display an extraordinarily complex personality. They allow us to see him at his best and worst, at his most memorable and most forgettable. It is precisely because Paul's letters show him speaking on the record that he has been both warmly embraced and hated.

The Study of Ancient Letters

Over the last century or more, scholars have devoted considerable attention to ancient epistolography, the study of ancient letters. Many biblical scholars have contributed to this research to gain a better appreciation of NT letters, especially the letters of Paul. These investigations have benefited from the discovery of Egyptian papyri in the late nineteenth and early twentieth centuries, which yielded a fascinating variety of letters from the ancient world. Alongside diplomatic correspondence and other formal letters from government officials were found personal letters through which the voices of ordinary people could be heard. [See Expanded CD Version pp. 368–69: *Three Letters from Ancient Egypt*]

Before such letters surfaced and began to be examined closely by biblical scholars, there was a tendency to read NT letters as theological treatises. Not that earlier readers were unaware of their epistolary features, since these were too obvious to be overlooked. But Paul's letters were often read as doctrinal writings—as part of a holy book—rather than as occasional letters that addressed theological issues. The work from which the previous examples were taken, Adolf Deissmann's *Light from the Ancient East*, represents an effort in the early twentieth century to set the Pauline letters within their proper social context. Deissmann drew a distinction between epistles, which he understood as formal writings or essays cast in epistolary form, and actual letters that reflected the circumstances of everyday life. The examples just mentioned belong to the latter category, but Deissmann was interested in determining the category to which the Pauline letters belonged.

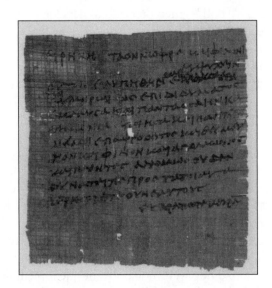

Oxyrhynchus Papyrus No. 115, a letter of consolation from Egypt, dated in the second century C.E., in which Irene offers condolences to Taonnophris and Philo, whose child, Eumoerus, had died. The photograph was provided by the Beinecke Rare Book and Manuscript Library, Yale University, where the papyrus is located and catalogued as Papyrus No. 32. Reprinted with permission.

Papyrus letter from Theon to his father from Egypt, second or third century C.E. The photograph was provided by The Bodleian Library, Oxford University, where the papyrus is catalogued as MS. Gr. Class. f. 66 (P). Reproduced with permission.

Deissmann's research prompted a number of twentieth-century NT scholars to examine the Pauline letters in light of the ancient practices of letter writing. To some extent, these scholarly efforts sought to move away from reading Paul's letters as formal theological treatises and to see them instead as "real letters"—lively exchanges with his churches and followers. By calling attention to a personal dimension of the letters that had largely been ignored, scholars sought to humanize Paul. This shift also enriched their understanding of the social settings in which the letters were written. As a result, the letters could be interpreted in the concrete circumstances of his apostolic mission to the Gentiles.

There was another benefit: The Egyptian papyri introduced scholars to the everyday (Koine) Greek that was widely used in the Mediterranean world. Scholars had often been struck by the peculiar Greek of NT writings. This was also true of the Pauline letters, which seemed to offer a mixture of OT Greek, literary Greek, and vernacular Greek. By studying other ancient letters, scholars were able to gain a better understanding of Paul's language. This in turn provided valuable clues for understanding problematic or difficult features of his theology.

The Structure of Paul's Letters

As scholars looked at the many letters preserved among the Egyptian papyri, they were struck by the structural similarities between these everyday letters and the Pauline letters. The Egyptian letters often began with a greeting and concluded with a benediction that were similar to what we find in Paul's letters. Even within the body of some of the longer letters, other structural similarities surfaced. By comparing Paul's letters with these "real letters," as well as the many other letters from antiquity preserved in the writings of more well-known figures such as Cicero or Seneca (ca. 4 B.C.E.–65 C.E.), scholars have been able to identify several structural components of Pauline letters.

Greeting

Ancient letters typically began with a greeting in the form, "Sender to Addressee(s), Greeting." Ancient letter greetings were formulated using a standard set of Greek terms, many of which appear in NT letters. Comparisons between the Pauline form of greeting and those of ancient letters show that Paul not only employed conventional language but that he could also adapt these conventions for his own purposes. Some of the Pauline greetings are relatively simple and straightforward (e.g., 1 Thess 1:1), whereas others are more elaborate. Typically, though not always, Paul identifies himself as an apostle, which illuminates how he defined the relationship between himself and his readers. Sharply contrasted to the brief greeting in several letters is the greeting in Rom 1:1–7, which is not only elaborate but filled with creedal language. Since Romans was addressed to a church that Paul had never visited, he needed to align himself at the outset with the church's faith. Since his reputation as a controversial apostle probably preceded him in Rome, adapting the standard literary convention to his own purpose was all the more urgent. These opening verses of Romans illustrate that something as simple as the opening greeting of a letter can provide the reader clues about the circumstances and overall mood of the letter.

Opening Prayer

After the initial greeting, Pauline letters typically include a prayer. Most often the prayer is in the form of a thanksgiving that Paul offers on behalf of his readers, although in at least one instance the prayer is in the form of a blessing (2 Cor 1:3–7; see Eph 1:3–14). One of the most influential studies on Pauline letters was done by Paul Schubert, titled *The Form and Function of Pauline Thanksgivings*.[4] Concentrating on this section of the Pauline letters, Schubert carefully analyzed the language patterns within the thanksgiving prayers as well as their thematic connections with other parts of the letters. He discovered that Pauline thanksgivings typically do two things: (1) they set the tone for the rest of the letter, and (2) they signal important themes or motifs that are addressed later in the letter. In the latter respect, they function loosely as a "table of contents" for the letter.

When we recall that Paul's letters were read aloud in the churches to which they were sent, we can understand why the opening prayers would be constructed this way. In a certain sense they function as pastoral prayers in which the congregation's concerns are mentioned by the minister. By establishing a certain mood the opening prayer connects Paul, the sender, with the readers who were more than just readers—they were his churches and friends with whom he had close personal and spiritual ties.

One example will suffice. Paul's prayer of thanksgiving in his Letter to the Philippians (1:3–11) is a tightly structured composition that illustrates Schubert's thesis. Paul uses highly personal, endearing language throughout the prayer: "constantly praying with joy . . . you hold me in your heart . . . I long for all of you . . . ." He also strikes a note of confidence (v. 6) to reassure readers who may be anxious about his imprisonment (v. 7). The letter was prompted by the receipt of a financial gift from the Philippian church, yet another in a series of such generous contributions (cf. 4:10–20).

Paul's prayer of thanksgiving touches on this theme several times, sometimes explicitly, sometimes indirectly. He mentions their "sharing in the gospel from the first day until now" (v. 5) and also how they "share in God's grace with [him]" (v. 7). Like his other prayers of thanksgiving, this one also looks to the culmination of Christian hope— "the day of Christ" (v. 10).

Readers who are sensitive to the *form and function* of Pauline thanksgivings are alerted to concerns that will receive further attention. They are also oriented emotionally, along with the original addressees, toward Paul's instructions. Opening prayers may create confidence, provide encouragement, allay fears and anxieties, or even give subtle warnings. When the opening prayer is omitted altogether, as in Galatians, readers are also alerted negatively. Paul's withdrawal of a pastoral blessing leaves a yawning gap at the beginning of the letter, preparing readers for the rather unpleasant rhetoric to follow.

Paul's opening prayers are not invariably cast in the same mold. First Thessalonians, for example, displays a distinct variation in a threefold form of thanksgiving that extends through the first three chapters. In some cases it is difficult to determine when the thanksgiving actually ends. The beginning is always clear, but not the ending. This suggests that Paul, rather than being captive to the epistolary form, can adapt it to suit his purpose.

Body of the Letter

By this designation we mean everything contained in the letter between the opening greeting and prayer and the concluding sections. No uniform way of structuring the body of the letter surfaces in the Pauline letters. Here again Paul adapts the epistolary form to suit his purposes. In 1 Corinthians, for example, the prayer of thanksgiving (1:4–9) is followed by a unified section (1:10–4:21) that is bracketed by language typically used by Paul in paraenetic, or hortatory, instruction: "I appeal to you" (1:10; 4:16). This fairly extended section is then followed by chapters 5–6, which address issues not raised by the Corinthians but which Paul thinks need urgent attention. Chapters 7–16 address a series of questions, several of which the Corinthians had inquired about in a letter sent to Paul (cf. 1 Cor 7:1).

Other Pauline letters exhibit different structures within the body of the letter. Romans, for example, comprises three identifiable sections. First is an opening section that begins after the thanksgiving (1:8–15, possibly to v. 17) and extends through chapter 8. This section consists of an extended theological exposition that develops the thesis of 1:16–17. Chapters 9–11 form a self-contained section, though integral to the overall argument, in which Paul addresses the role of the Gentiles in God's overall scheme of redemption. The final section, which consists of chapters 12–15, differs in texture and content from the other parts of the letter since it provides moral instructions on different topics. Chapter 16 concludes the letter with an extended series of personal greetings and a benediction (16:25–27).

Romans thus illustrates an epistolary structure in which moral instruction is gathered at the conclusion of the letter. A somewhat similar structure is found in Galatians, which contains miscellaneous admonitions at the end of the letter (cf. Gal 5:13–6:10).

Yet another variation is found in Ephesians (from the Pauline school), whose first half is theological exposition (chs. 1–3) and the second half moral exhortation (chs. 4–6).

Remembering the occasional nature of Pauline letters will assist readers in making sense of the body of the letter. In Romans Paul adopts the literary strategy of the Greco-Roman diatribe as a way of unfolding the argument. The brief Letter to Philemon, by contrast, resembles ancient letters of recommendation, although Paul has adapted the form for his own purposes. The body of the letter is structured to fit the occasion, and it can display as much variation as the occasion requires.

Concluding Greetings

Once the formal instruction of the letter is concluded, Paul will typically (though not always) turn to personal concerns. These may relate to his immediate travel plans and how these will affect his readers (e.g., Rom 15:22–33; 1 Cor 16:5–9). Matters relating to his co-workers are also treated (e.g., 1 Cor 16:10–12). Since Paul is often surrounded by co-workers or other acquaintances when he writes, at this point in the letter he may rehearse their circumstances and send greetings on behalf of them (e.g., Col 4:7–17). The most conspicuous example of this occurs in Rom 16, in which Paul enumerates a long list of co-workers and acquaintances, some of whom are with Paul (in Corinth) at the time of writing and who send greetings to Rome. He mentions others who are in Rome, to whom he sends greetings.

When readers are interested primarily in the Pauline letters for their theological argument and doctrinal content, they may easily ignore these richly personal sections, which reveal the role that Paul's extensive network of co-workers played in his overall mission. New Testament scholars interested in the social dimensions of Pauline Christianity have found in these sections a treasure trove of information. Though often overlooked, these sections of Paul's letters yield valuable information about the social status of Paul's circle of followers and some of the personal dynamics of their relationship to him and with each other. They also give clues about his ministerial practices.

These sections of the letters also anchor Paul's ministry in the realities of the ancient world and give his theological instructions even greater concreteness. They remind us that the Pauline mission forged ahead through the collective efforts of named individuals—women and men—many of whom are now forgotten, but who played a vital role in establishing and spreading Pauline Christianity. Among them were the devoted followers of Paul who treasured his letters, eventually collected them, and preserved them for posterity. Whether we think of this group of followers as "the Pauline school" or "the Pauline circle," their memory is forever etched within the Pauline letters.

Doxology/Benediction

Although Paul's letters conclude with different formulations, they typically include some form of prayer or benediction. The doxology in Rom 16:25–27 represents one of the longer conclusions. As the textual tradition indicates, it seems to have been a floating doxology, sometimes found at the end of chapters 14, 15, or 16. Benedictory prayers typically sound a positive note, for example, 1 Cor 16:23–24: "The grace of the Lord Jesus be with you. My love be with all of you in Christ Jesus." Somewhat unexpected is the stern imprecation that precedes it: "Let anyone be accursed who has no love for the Lord. Our Lord, come!" (1 Cor 16:22). Even in Galatians Paul manages an upbeat benediction (Gal 6:18).

The Apostle Paul. A woodcut from a German translation of the Latin Vulgate, printed in 1477 in Augsburg. From the Digital Image Archive, The Richard C. Kessler Reformation Collection, Pitts Theology Library, Candler School of Theology, Emory University, Atlanta, Georgia.

Types of Pauline Letters

Another valuable benefit of research into ancient letter writing is a broader understanding of the types of letters that circulated in antiquity. Ancient rhetorical handbooks provide instructions concerning the composition of letters, with due attention given to matters of style and substance. School children were taught to write letters according to these instructions. They learned the difference between writing a thank-you letter and a more formal letter designed to make a special request. In addition to rhetorical handbooks and other treatises giving instruction about letter writing, we also have many examples of actual letters. These too provide ample evidence of the variety of letter types in the ancient world. Some well-defined types are easily identified, such as the letter of recommendation in which the sender wrote on someone else's behalf, perhaps recommending the person for a job, a government appointment, or military promotion. Letters of consolation were a distinguishable type, as were paraenetic letters that were written to give moral instruction or encouragement.

Pauline letters do not always fall into distinct categories; instead, they sometimes combine several genres. First Thessalonians is now widely recognized as a paraenetic letter, even though it contains some elements of consolation (1 Thess 4). Philemon easily fits the form of a letter of recommendation, as do other parts of Pauline letters (e.g., Rom 16:1–2; 2 Cor 3:1–3). Parts of Philippians conform to the letter of thanksgiving (Phil 4:10–20), but it also contains elements of the ancient letter of friendship. Some scholars argue that the entire letter should be classified as a friendship letter. Letters of instruction, which have a specifically didactic purpose, are represented in parts of 1 Corinthians (chs. 7–15) and perhaps Romans (chs. 1–11). The apologetic letter, designed to defend the letter writer, also surfaces, for example, in Gal 1–2, and especially in 2 Cor 10–13.

Knowing the different types of ancient letters and being able to correlate them with the Pauline letters can benefit interpreters in several ways. If we know what expectations were associated with certain letters and the literary markers with which we can identify them, this gives us some leverage in interpreting the letter. Reading 1 Thessalonians as a paraenetic letter enables us to identify its rhetoric of reassurance and to understand better Paul's strategy for reinforcing the faith of the young Thessalonian church. Reading it alongside other ancient letters that feature moral instruction also exposes certain features of the letter that are not as visible otherwise.

Just as Schubert's analysis of the form and function of Pauline thanksgivings made it possible to read those sections of Pauline letters differently, so are we better positioned to see the connection between the form and function of an entire letter. How one illuminates the other may vary. It may be easier, for example, to see that 1 Thessalonians is functioning paraenetically, which in turn enables us to recognize its form as a paraenetic letter, rather than vice versa. In other cases, identifying the form first may assist us in determining the letter's function. Philemon, for example, is easily recognizable as a letter of recommendation. It bears all of the standard characteristics of such letters. Having recognized the form, we are then in a position to ask about its function. The letter recommends Onesimus, but how does it function precisely? As a commendation of a runaway slave to Philemon—the standard interpretation—or as a technical, legal mechanism in which Paul, as a mutual friend of both parties, makes a formal appeal for reconciliation to Philemon on behalf of Onesimus? (See the fuller discussion in the chapter on Philemon.)

Rather than seeing all of the Pauline letters as belonging, more or less, to the same literary genre—a theological treatise—we are now in a better position to recognize the several genres that they represent. This makes it possible to interpret each letter with greater attention to the special situation that it addresses and with an appreciation for the particular dynamic created in the interplay between form and function that we find in each letter.

The Use of Earlier Christian Materials

Although form criticism initially focused on the Gospels, it was applied eventually to the Pauline letters. The Pauline letters posed a different challenge since they were not connected literarily in the same way the Gospels were. But scholars sought to arrange them chronologically and identify sections that might represent earlier and later treatments of the same topic. More significant were the literary clues in the Pauline letters that made it possible to identify earlier materials on which Paul drew—pre-Pauline traditions. Formulae for introducing traditional material were identified. In 1 Cor 11:23 Paul introduces the tradition of Jesus' institution of the Lord's Supper with the words, "I received from the Lord what I also handed on to you." Similar wording occurs in the Jewish rabbinic tractate *Pirke Aboth*, the "Chapters of the Fathers," which is introduced with the words, "Moses received Torah at Sinai and handed it on to Joshua, Joshua to elders, and elders to prophets. And prophets handed it on to the men of the great assembly" (1.1).[5] The notion of receiving and transmitting sacred traditions is not uniquely Jewish, since we find comparable descriptions among Greek and Roman authors. In 1 Cor 15:1–11, Paul employs the technical language of "receiving and handing on" when speaking of the gospel: "For I handed on to you . . . what I in turn had received" (v. 3). This suggests that the following creedal summary (vv. 3–4) constitutes a pre-Pauline kerygmatic tradition that encapsulates the essential elements of the early Christian gospel: Christ's death, burial, resurrection, and appearances.

The material introduced by such formulae typically displays a literary structure sharpened and refined by repetition and liturgical usage. Elsewhere, Paul cites similar material, although it is not introduced with such readily identifiable formulae. Form critical analysis of the Pauline letters has identified a number of places in which he cites early Christian hymns (Phil 2:5–11; Col 1:15–20), creedal or kerygmatic summaries (Rom 1:1–7; 1 Cor 8:6; 1 Thess 1:9–10), or other traditions that originated in an earlier period. In the latter category belong certain OT passages that were identified as testimonies relating to Christ, for example, the "rejected stone" passages (Isa 28:16; 8:14; see Matt 21:42; Acts 4:11; 1 Pet 2:6–8).

The abundance of such passages throughout the Pauline and post-Pauline letters places Paul within the mainstream of early Christian tradition. This by no means detracts from his originality. Paul's letters give ample evidence of his capacity for stunningly creative christological formulations and OT interpretations. His use of earlier Christian material makes it more difficult to think of Paul as the "second founder of Christianity" in the sense that he was once thought to be. His individuality is undisputed but so is his continuity with earlier Christian tradition.

Paul's letters reveal a layered texture. If we can use the image of excavation, we find that Paul's letters often contain passages consisting of different strata of material. At a lower or earlier level we may find creedal formulations that derive from the earliest stages of Christian belief or even words that ultimately derived from Jesus himself (1 Cor 7:10; 9:14; 11:23–26; 1 Thess 4:15). At higher or later levels, we detect Paul's own interpretation or application of these earlier Christian traditions. In 1 Cor 15:8–11, when Paul adds to the earlier tradition that he had received, his remarks can be considered a second stage of the tradition.

The Pauline letters reveal the traditioning process that we find elsewhere in the NT. Rather than reading his letters as the accumulation of his original thoughts, we should read them as his own highly original exposition of earlier Christian tradition. Practically, this means that Paul had predecessors who had already begun to shape the early Christian tradition and that he stands on their shoulders. Recognizing this enables us to appreciate Paul's continuity with his Christian predecessors but still allow for the highly individual way in which he extended the early Christian tradition.

A woodcut depicting Paul at his writing desk dictating to another man at a writing desk with pen and book before him; taken from a German translation of the Bible printed in 1536 in Zurich. From the Digital Image Archive of The Richard C. Kessler Reformation Collection, Pitts Theology Library, Candler School of Theology, Emory University, Atlanta, Georgia.

An Edited Collection

When we read Paul's letters we experience them as carefully written, unified compositions. We may read them from start to finish as though they were composed in precisely that way by Paul himself. But there is good reason to believe that the Pauline letters in our NT constitute an edited collection. We read them, in other words, not necessarily as Paul might have wanted them read but as his successors wanted us to read them.

Paul's letters are not arranged in chronological order. They are not even arranged in a clearly defined topical order. Instead, they are arranged in two groups: letters addressed to churches and those written to individuals. Letters in each category are arranged roughly according to descending length. Placing Romans in the first position might well have suited Paul since it appears to represent the culmination of his thinking concerning his mission to the Gentiles. But Romans is by no means a comprehensive treatment of his thought. Because of its wide-angle vision and its having been written at the end of his Aegean mission, it was judged worthy to stand at the head of the Pauline collection. This was not the case in every ancient collection of Paul's letters, but it is the case in our Pauline "table of contents."

Apart from the overall arrangement of Paul's letters, there are signs of internal editing. As noted earlier, the doxology at the end of Romans sometimes occurred at the end of chapters 14, 15, and 16 respectively. It is conceivable that Rom 16 circulated as an independent letter and was later joined to Rom 1–15 to form a single letter. Evidence of possible editing is also seen in the Corinthian letters, which display literary seams in several places, for example, 2 Cor 6:14–7:1. The passage enjoining women to silence in 1 Cor 14:33*b*–36 may be another instance of later editing. Because the passage has figured prominently in shaping the church's attitude toward the role of women, determining whether it is a later interpolation becomes more than a theoretical question. The status of Ephesians in the Pauline corpus is highly debated, but what is undisputed is the absence in the earliest manuscripts of the name of the addressee, "in Ephesus," in the opening greeting. At some point, the phrase became lodged in the letter and yielded the name "The Letter of Paul to the Ephesians."

When we read the Pauline letters, we are reading an edited Paul, not necessarily the letters in the actual form that Paul produced them, much less in the order that he might have wished them to be read. The canonical arrangement clearly privileges Romans, giving it pride of place within the Pauline collection. Its influence on the church's thinking has been proportionately significant. Shorter letters such as 1–2 Thessalonians might easily be overshadowed by the longer letters or the more controversial letters such as Galatians. Once we allow for the fact that we are reading Paul as later editors—probably his own followers—wanted him to be read, we are then in a position to incorporate this in our interpretation.

A Chronological Framework for the Pauline Letters

There is broad scholarly agreement that the Pauline letters were not written in the order in which they appear within the NT canon. While the letters often contain information relating to their composition, they seldom do so in relationship to each other. And it is often difficult to correlate historical references in the letters with other firm chronological markers, such as the dates of Roman officials, or memorable events, such as battles, censuses, earthquakes, or famines. For this reason readers have typically used Acts to establish the broad chronological framework for the life of Paul. Since the Pauline letters have traditionally followed Acts in canonical lists, including our modern canonical arrangement, this is a fully understandable move. It has been commonplace for scholars to date the Pauline letters by fitting them into the storyline of Acts.

Synchronizing the chronology of Acts with whatever chronology we are able to reconstruct from the Pauline letters presents serious difficulties. In particular, the chronological framework outlined by Paul himself in Gal 1–2 is difficult to square with Acts. In these chapters Paul responds to critics who have challenged the legitimacy of his apostleship by rehearsing the course of his life, beginning with his prophetic call or conversion. As Paul defends himself, he insists that he is speaking under oath (Gal 1:20). Because this is Paul's own testimony, given some twenty years after his conversion, scholars understandably weight it more heavily than the account in Acts, which is secondhand testimony written several decades later. It is now a widely accepted scholarly principle to privilege chronological information in the Pauline letters over what we find in Acts—or, at least, when the Pauline evidence conflicts with Acts, to weight it more heavily. [**See Expanded CD Version pp. 378–82:** *Developing a Chronology of Paul's Life and Letters: Some Specific Issues*]

The following chronology of Paul's life can be proposed:

Suggested Pauline Chronology

**Approximate
Dates**

30–33	Jesus' crucifixion
33–34	Paul's call/conversion (Gal 1:15)
	THREE-YEAR MISSION IN DAMASCUS/ARABIA (Gal 1:18)
36–37	Escape from Aretas in Damascus (2 Cor 11:32–33; Acts 9:23–25) and the first trip to Jerusalem "after three years," lasting fifteen days, meeting with Peter and James (Gal 1:18)
	MISSION IN SYRIA & CILICIA - TARSUS (Gal 1:21), which includes the mission originating from Antioch of Syria conducted in Cyprus, eastern Asia Minor (Pamphylia, South Galatia), i.e., the "first missionary journey" (Acts 13–14)
46–47	Second trip to Jerusalem "after fourteen years" (probably from the time of his call/conversion) accompanied by Barnabas and Titus (Gal 2:1); = the Jerusalem Conference (Acts 15)
47	Beginning of the "second missionary journey," from Antioch of Syria through North Galatia to Troas (Acts 15:36–16:10)
47–52	MISSION IN MACEDONIA & ACHAIA (Acts 16–18)
48	Ministry in Philippi (Acts 16:11–40)
49	Ministry in Thessalonica, Beroea, Athens (Acts 17:1–33)
49	Expulsion of Jews from Rome by the emperor Claudius
50/51–52	Ministry in Corinth (Acts 18:1–17), lasting eighteen months (Acts 18:11)
	1 & 2 Thessalonians
52	Hearing before Gallio, the proconsul (Acts 18:12–17)
52/53	Paul's return to Syria and his "going up," probably to Jerusalem (Acts 18:22)
53	Beginning of the "third missionary journey," through North Galatia (Acts 18:23)
54–57	MISSION IN WESTERN ASIA MINOR - EPHESUS, lasting three years (Acts 20:31; cf. Acts 19:8, 10); includes probably "Ephesian imprisonment," dealings with Corinth
54–55	*Galatians, 1 Corinthians, Philippians* (from Ephesian prison)
56–57	Activity in Asia (2 Cor 1:8), painful visit to Corinth (2 Cor 2:1), return to Macedonia (2 Cor 2:12–13; 7:5–16; Acts 20:1–6), possibly a trip to Illyricum (Rom 15:19)
	2 Corinthians (probably from Philippi, 2 Cor 2:13)
57/58	Corinth (Rom 16:1–2), Paul completes the collection (Rom 15:23–26), then departs from Philippi (Acts 20:6)
	Romans

58	Third trip to Jerusalem, bringing the collection (Rom 15:25–33; cf. 1 Cor 16:3; 2 Cor 1:16; Acts 21:17–26); arrest in Jerusalem (Acts 21:27–22:29), defenses before the Sanhedrin (Acts 22:30–23:10), plot against Paul (Acts 23:12–30); transfer to Caesarea (Acts 23:31–35)
58–59	Defense before Felix in Caesarea (Acts 24:1–16); two-year imprisonment in Caesarea (Acts 24:27); Festus (Acts 25:1–12); defense before Agrippa (Acts 25:13–26:32)
60–61	Voyage to Rome (Acts 27:1–28:10); arrival in Rome, appearance before Jews (Acts 28:11–28)
61–63	Two-year imprisonment in Rome (Acts 28:30) *Philemon, Colossians*
64–67	Execution in Rome by Nero
ca. 70–90	*Ephesians, 1 Timothy, Titus, 2 Timothy*

Implications of Chronology for Reading Paul's Letters

Solving such chronological jigsaw puzzles presents a challenge in its own right, but developing a workable chronological framework for Paul's life is not done merely to satisfy our intellectual curiosity. It directly affects the way we read Paul and how we understand his theology. Several observations are in order:

(1) The undisputed Pauline letters were composed within a relatively short time span. At the maximum, Paul's composition of the letters would have occurred over a ten-to-twelve-year period, extending from around 50 until the early 60s. If, as some scholars argue, Philemon and Colossians should be dated earlier and were perhaps written during the Ephesian imprisonment, the time span would be reduced to a period of from eight to ten years.

(2) The Pauline letters were written in the latter part of Paul's twenty-to-thirty-year period of ministry. To the best of our knowledge no letters survive from the first two-thirds of Paul's ministry—from the time of his conversion through his "desert stay" in Arabia (Nabataea), his early mission around Damascus, and his travels in Syria and Cilicia, until the Jerusalem Council. Only after the "second missionary journey" commenced did his letter writing begin.

(3) Both of these first two considerations relate to the question of whether Paul's theology developed and possibly even changed substantially. First-time readers might easily assume that the thirteen letters attributed to Paul were composed over two-to-three decades of ministry. In this case we might look for patterns of development in his thought or even try to locate significant points at which his theology changed. But the letters do not cover his entire period of ministry; instead, they come from the latter third of his ministry. This leaves us wondering how his theological outlook was shaped during the first two-thirds of his ministry.

Paul occasionally mentions having received certain "traditions" from the Lord (e.g., 1 Cor 11:23). In what sense? Did he receive instructions directly from the risen Christ in some form of ecstatic revelation? Or did he learn from other disciples or teachers sayings and traditions that were ultimately traceable to Christ? Did he, in other words, receive traditions "from the Lord" in the sense that they originally derived from the Lord himself? Further, if Paul's encounter with the risen Lord was not only a conversion but also a prophetic call in which he received his commission to preach to the Gentiles (Gal 1:16), how did he discharge that responsibility during the early years of his ministry? How clearly formulated was his self-consciousness as God's apostle to the Gentiles? How did this develop over time? Acts relates how Paul's misson was carried out under the auspices of the church at Antioch (Acts 13–14). But what about before that time? The fourteen- (or perhaps seventeen-) year period prior to the Jerusalem Council, apart from the mission in eastern Asia Minor (Acts 13–14), for the most part remains a blank in our understanding of Paul.

But if we take seriously the fact that his undisputed letters derive from the last third of his ministry, we should probably conclude that they reveal a mature Paul, not someone who is still working out his theological positions. We should nevertheless allow for the possibility that he changed his mind and refined his theological views over the course of a decade or more of ministry. His letters reveal the intensity with which he engaged issues within his churches. There is good reason to believe that between the writing of 1 Thessalonians in the early 50s and the composition of 2 Corinthians several years later, he concluded that he would not be alive at Christ's Parousia.

(4) Throughout the preceding discussion, I have used quotation marks or "so-called" in speaking of Paul's "missionary journeys." This is a reminder that "missionary journey" is a modern construct, not one that derives from either Paul or Acts. It is virtually impossible to tell from Acts when the "second missionary journey" ends and the "third missionary journey" begins. This transition occurs within the space of two verses (Acts 18:22–23). Luke is quite capable of depicting a dramatic new beginning, but he does not do so here. For the sake of convenience, people have tended to organize the Lukan account in Acts by using the "missionary journey" scheme—the first coming in Acts 13–14; the second in Acts 16–18; and the third in Acts 19–20. Such a schematization suggests that Paul operated with a well-thought-out missionary strategy, moving as it were in concentric circles from Antioch of Syria, or at least in well-defined stages from eastern Asia Minor to the Aegean, first in Macedonia and Achaia and then in Ephesus. But a close reading of Acts suggests that Paul was guided by the Spirit (Acts 16:6–10) rather than working with a well-formulated mission plan that had been developed in advance. A "missionary journey" scheme can easily imply more preplanning and organization than the Acts narrative (and the Pauline letters) actually indicate.

In the diagram of Pauline chronology on pages 276–77 (also see the diagram on p. 279), I have highlighted in capital letters the mission areas in which Paul worked. It makes more sense to think of Paul's ministry as having focused on certain regions or centers: Damascus and Arabia (Gal 1:17); Syria and Cilicia (Acts 13–14); Macedonia and Achaia, especially Philippi, Thessalonica, and Corinth (Acts 16–18); and western Asia Minor, especially Ephesus (Acts 19–20).

(5) We have placed the letters at points in his ministry that seem to be supported by his own testimony as well as Acts. Whether this is the most plausible order or not, it reminds us that how we conceive the chronological order of the letters can affect the

CHRONOLOGY OF PAUL'S LIFE (BASED ON PAUL'S LETTERS)

Paul's Death (70–90)

Ephesians, 1 Timothy, Titus, 2 Timothy 64–67

Paul in Rome 60–61

Philemon, Colossians 58

Paul's Third Trip to Jerusalem / Jerusalem Collection (Rom 15:22-33)

Romans 56

2 Corinthians

Philippians (from Ephesian prison) 52

Galatians; 1 Corinthians; 51

Gallio Inscription (Acts 18:12-17)

Mission in Asia Minor (Ephesus)

Mission in Macedonia and Achaia (Corinth)

1&2 Thessalonians

Paul's Second Trip to Jerusalem (Gal 2:1) 46–47

14-yr. period

Mission in Syria & Cilicia (Tarsus)

Paul's First Trip to Jerusalem (Gal 1:18) 36–37

3 yrs

Three-year Mission in Damascus / Arabia

Paul's Call (Gal 1:15) 33–34

Jesus' Death 30–33

way we read each letter individually and the collection as a whole. Since Galatians, for example, is such a polemical letter that addresses the issue of Gentile circumcision and the efforts of opponents who were insisting on complete observance of the Mosaic law by Gentiles, it must be placed at a point where this controversy was raging within the Galatian churches. We must allow time for Paul to have founded the Galatian churches and moved on, and then for opposing teachers to have infiltrated the Galatian churches to pose a threat. Similarly, 2 Corinthians must be placed at a point that allows for a similar threat to have developed in the church at Corinth—that is, for "false apostles" to have entered and begun to oppose Paul.

The placement of the letters allows us to interpret certain sections of the letters that are similar in tone and content. In 1 Cor 12, for example, Paul's discussion of ministerial gifts is formulated in terms of the Holy Spirit; in Rom 12, by contrast, a similar list is given but without any reference to the Holy Spirit. Recognizing the different points in Paul's ministry at which each letter is written helps us understand the difference. In the church at Corinth the presence of the Spirit was an issue in a way that it was not for the Roman church; when Paul writes Romans from Corinth, he generalizes the discussion, as compared with the more Spirit-specific form that we find in 1 Cor 12.

(6) Whether we understand Paul's theology based on his undisputed letters or whether we also include his disputed letters becomes a major issue. In my reconstruction I have anticipated the positions that I shall develop in the following chapters on each letter or group of letters. Whether one is inclined or disinclined to accept the Pauline authorship of all the letters, we can classify the thirteen letters attributed to Paul into two categories:

The undisputed letters	The disputed letters
1 Thessalonians	2 Thessalonians
Galatians	Colossians
1–2 Corinthians	Ephesians
Philippians	1–2 Timothy
Romans	Titus
Philemon	

In the following chapters I accept the scholarly consensus relating to the Pauline authorship of the undisputed letters, but also argue that 2 Thessalonians and possibly Colossians were written by Paul himself. I am less confident about the Pauline authorship of Ephesians and remain unconvinced of the direct Pauline authorship of 1–2 Timothy and Titus.

In terms of Pauline chronology, those who argue for the Pauline authorship of all thirteen letters would construct a somewhat different timeline for Paul's ministry. It is sometimes proposed, based on information in the Pastoral Letters, that Paul was released from prison in Rome, conducted a mission in the eastern Mediterranean (including Crete), was imprisoned a second time, and from that imprisonment wrote 2 Timothy. Others have tried to fit the Pastoral Letters into an earlier period of Paul's ministry in the mid-fifties. In my treatment of the Pastoral Letters in a later chapter, I offer reasons why I do not find this reconstruction convincing.

For the purposes of constructing Paul's theology, the decision one makes concerning authentic and inauthentic letters or undisputed and disputed letters is consequential. The more minimalist position, which is adopted by a large number of scholars, is to accept the seven undisputed letters as the indisputable core from which we can construct Paul's theology. Naturally this yields a theological reconstruction that no one can seriously contest; the only question is whether by narrowing the database, Paul's thought is unduly constricted. Whether the theological viewpoints articulated in the six disputed letters can be attributed to Paul directly or reflect later stages of development among Paul's followers, especially within the "Pauline school," remains a hotly contested issue within NT scholarship. Since it has not been done in recent scholarship, it would be intriguing to construct a picture of Pauline theology based on all thirteen letters. Regardless of individual scholarly judgments concerning the authenticity of various disputed letters, the thirteen letters constitute the "canonical Paul"—the Paul many people experience in reading the NT. It would be interesting, at the very least, to construct Paul's theological vision based on this "canonical Paul."

Paul's Influence on the Church

If the history of Pauline interpretation teaches us anything, it is the persistently contested legacy of Paul and his enduring status as a truly seminal thinker whose imprint on the church's life and practice, while by no means uniform, is nevertheless deep and lasting. When contemporary readers of Paul find him both baffling and inspiring, both liberating and oppressive, or challenging yet deeply troubling, they are mirroring the way people have experienced Paul in every age. Just as Paul's letters breathe the spirit of controversy, offering glimpses of the furor he often created, so also is the story of the church's reading of his letters often a story of turbulence and controversy. **[See Expanded CD Version pp. 387–88: *The Collection and Circulation of Paul's Letters in the Early Church*]**

If there is any doubt about the extent of Paul's influence on catholic Christianity during the first few centuries, such doubt vanishes with Augustine (354–430 C.E.), for whom Paul was, to paraphrase Karl Barth (1886–1968), not so much the door as the hinge for much of his thought. This was clear when Augustine read Rom 13:13–14 in his celebrated conversion experience, and even clearer in his penetrating analysis of the entire Letter of Romans, especially chapters 3–7 and 9, as he developed a response to Pelagius (late fourth–early fifth centuries). In the Pelagian controversy, one of the central issues was whether human beings possess an inherently sinful nature that is transmitted to us at birth or whether sin results from choices we make freely when faced with right and wrong options. Augustine drew heavily on Paul in working out his views on original sin, predestination, free will, and God's saving grace—views destined to have far-reaching influence on the way Christians would understand themselves and God's saving work.

Reflecting his own experience, Augustine's highly individualized reading of Paul that saw God's gracious action toward the guilt-ridden sinner as the focal center of his thought was to receive even further refinement with Martin Luther (1483–1546), the former Augustinian monk who elevated the Pauline emphasis on justification by faith to programmatic status. While Luther's was only one voice among the Reformers, it was a booming voice that helped define a Protestant way of reading Paul that still sees Romans and Galatians as the canon within the canon and justification by faith as the crowning achievement of Pauline thought. Even with their differences, many of Paul's major interpreters stand directly within the Augustine-Luther tradition in which the needs of the individual sinner, understood either as the one who is utterly dependent on God (Barth), caught in a web of despair (Kierkegaard, 1812–1855), or in search of authentic existence (Bultmann, 1884–1976), are seen as the "sickness unto death" for which Paul's gospel of grace and freedom offers a remedy.

For all the compelling power of this deeply entrenched way of reading Paul, it is only one of several construals of the Pauline gospel. Even within the ancient church Paul could be read differently. While Western interpreters such as Irenaeus, Tertullian, and Hippolytus (ca. 170–236 C.E.) made great strides in bringing Paul into the mainstream of catholic Christianity, the Alexandrians Clement (ca. 150–215 C.E.) and Origen (ca. 185–254 C.E.) read Paul through a Platonic lens. Their Paul is less critical of the Mosaic law and presents a God who foreknows rather than predestines. Accenting Rom 8 more heavily than Rom 5–7, Origen presents Paul as a prototype of spirituality. Origen sees no difficulty in understanding "faith only" in Rom 3:28 to include responsible moral practice.

In the Eastern church, still other aspects of Paul's thought received emphasis. Since Romans was largely neglected by Eastern commentators, justification by faith received little attention among Greek-speaking churches. Given the Eastern church's strongly meditative, even mystical perspective, it is not surprising that it mined Paul differently. Distinctive Pauline metaphors such as the church as the body of Christ and Christ as the image of God received emphasis, along with Paul's teachings on mystical union with Christ and the sacraments as the focus of that union.

When scholars raise serious questions about the legacy of an "introspective conscience" that Augustine bequeathed to the West and that was mediated through the centuries by some of the most towering interpreters of Paul, they do so not as dissonant voices contesting a single line of interpretation but as part of a chorus of dissenting voices. Even if Augustine and Luther struggled to free themselves from deeply troubled consciences, was this necessarily the case with Paul himself? Many scholars think not, insisting instead that such a highly individualized way of reading Paul obscures other dimensions of his thought that are also central.

Pointing to Paul's overarching concern with his apostolic mission to the Gentiles and his compelling need both to justify this mission in terms of God's larger purpose and to explain Israel's role within that purpose, some scholars have emphasized Paul's cosmic view of God's saving work and its corporate dimension. Was Paul concerned primarily with the individual sinner's needs? Or was he more concerned with how one people—the church—might be formed out of two peoples—Jews and Gentiles? If Paul's thought was more preoccupied with "one people" than with "one person," this changes appreciably how passages such as Rom 7 and Rom 9–11 are read.

Recognizing how major lines of interpreting Paul that run from the ancient to the modern period emphasize now one, now the other, dimension of Pauline thought serves as a useful reminder of the many different versions of Paul's thought and the various claims made to his legacy. Being aware of the difference between Paul the interpreter and the interpreted Paul, we are invited always to listen to Paul on his own terms.

Some appreciation of how Paul has been read by the church through the centuries helps establish perspective for our own reading of Paul. It helps position us over against the tradition of Pauline interpretation, thereby enabling us to learn from its enduring insights as well as to avoid some recurring pitfalls. Among the things we learn from surveying the history of Pauline interpretation are the following:

1. *Paul's Formative Influence in Shaping Christian Belief and Practice.* Whether we think of the history of Christian theology as a series of footnotes to Paul or whether we identify Paul as a major catalyst for some of the church's most dramatic reforms, the extent of his influence on the church is truly extraordinary.

One way of capturing Paul's seminal role in the church's development is to think of him as the "second founder of Christianity" (William Wrede, 1859–1906), as a truly originative figure who almost single-handedly transformed the religion of Jesus, with its particular Jewish identity, into a universal Hellenistic religion. This way of putting it underscores Paul's highly creative role in setting the church on a new course, but it does so by driving a wedge between Jesus and Paul. It also fails to recognize the extent to which Paul was indebted to his predecessors who preserved and transmitted many of the traditions on which he drew. Even so, the notion of "second founder" contains an element of truth: with Paul, the early church turned a corner, and in him it found its single most influential thinker.

Paul's lasting influence partly derives from his capacity for developing, perhaps even coining, root metaphors that would eventually be developed into major Christian doctrines—the church (congregation) as the body of Christ, the body (both the individual and the church) as the temple of God, and Christ as the second Adam, to name just a few. Or we might think of the cluster of metaphors that he used of God's saving action, some of which were freshly minted, while others were inherited but newly accented: redemption or deliverance, recalling Israel's deliverance from Egyptian bondage; justification or being declared righteous, probably a forensic metaphor drawn from the courts; adoption or being made God's true child, a commonly known social practice; and sanctification or being made holy (separate), a cultic image.

One of Paul's most influential metaphors was Christ as the second Adam (Rom 5; 1 Cor 15). In combating Gnostic dualism, with its tendency to distinguish sharply between the two Testaments as well as the God of each Testament, Irenaeus found Paul's Adam-Christ typology immensely useful in sketching his theological vision of a single story of salvation history stretching from creation to resurrection. Or in developing his doctrine of original sin, Augustine, drawing on the enigmatic "Ambrosiaster,"[6] could take Rom 5:12, "[in whom] all have sinned," to mean that Adam's sin was not merely a representative act that other humans could replicate but one in which "all" had participated. Thus through Adam sin was transmitted genetically to all of his descendants.

It is difficult to think of a major doctrine, a major movement, or a major figure in Christian history that does not bear Paul's imprint. Early Christian asceticism owed much to what were understood as deeply ascetic sentiments in his letters. His brief remarks on Christian attitudes toward the state (Rom 13:1–7) proved enormously influential as later thinkers developed political theories clarifying how the church and state should relate to each other. Further, this passage has been a restraining force in quelling active Christian resistance to political powers. When resistance seemed the only moral course of action, the force of Paul's remarks had to be dealt with.

2. *The Dialectical Dimension of Paul's Thought.* One recurrent feature of Paul's letters is his use of antithesis—framing issues as contrasting pairs: spirit and flesh, faith and works, life and death, etc. Part of this same cast of mind is his penchant for holding what appear to be contradictory, inconsistent elements together in dynamic tension. His dialectical outlook is reflected in his many statements about the Mosaic law. Some of them are critical, others appreciative, none of them neutral. On any showing Paul's views about the Mosaic law are full of qualifications, which in some instances mute his critique. And yet his views of the Mosaic law, taken as a whole, constitute a genuine critique.

In the history of Pauline interpretation we often find interpreters collapsing the tension between two seemingly opposite positions by stressing one to the exclusion of the other. Marcion and Jewish Christian groups rightly see Paul's statements about the Mosaic law as a critique, both bending the critique in their own direction. Marcion refuses to see Paul's strongly held sense of continuity between Jewish past and Christian present, while Jewish Christian groups fail to see how Paul's critique relativizes all forms of submission to Torah, even for Jews like himself.

On issue after issue Paul's interpreters can be found flattening, even domesticating, his highly nuanced positions. Not content with his critique of the Mosaic law, later interpreters would distinguish between the moral law and the ceremonial law, insisting that Paul affirmed the former while rejecting the latter. Yet Paul himself introduced no such distinction. Or in arguing for justification by faith, Paul could be seen as wholeheartedly disparaging the value of doing good, as the position opposed in the Letter of James seems to imply. Yet at some fundamental level Paul holds faith and works together in a dynamic tension, Luther notwithstanding.

With such seemingly inconsistent elements running throughout his letters, interpreters have often sought to resolve the tension by forcing a consistency on Paul's thought or explaining the inconsistencies as different stages in Paul's development. How to deal with these antinomies in Paul's thought remains one of the most persistent challenges in Pauline interpretation.

3. *The Difficulty of Finding a Single Center in Paul's Thought.* Whether we try to organize Paul's thought around a single doctrine or theological perspective—for example, justification by faith (Luther) or his Christ-mysticism (Albert Schweitzer, 1875–1965)—or whether we see certain letters, for example, Galatians and Romans, as the center of Paul's theological thought, in both instances we are seeking some single principle or perspective around which the rest of Paul's thought can be organized. While such interpretive moves usually succeed in taking a distinctive Pauline insight and elevating it to a norm, they do so at the expense of other equally important dimensions of Paul's thought. Highly individualized readings of Paul tend to blur or diminish his corporate understanding of Christ or his overarching concern for sacred history, especially as it relates to the roles of Israel and the Gentiles in God's overall plan.

A better way forward is to recognize the multifaceted nature of Paul's thought and the interconnectedness of its many dimensions. Some scholars see Paul's thought primarily as a theology of salvation, which is consistently worked out in his letters that focus on God's saving action in Christ. Such a perspective encompasses a broad range of Paul's ideas, including elements of his soteriology, Christology, and even eschatology. And yet certain dimensions of his thought, such as his attitudes toward the state (Rom 13), may not easily fit into such a scheme.

Pauline thought should rather be viewed as a set of theological reflections that brilliantly illuminate different aspects of the Christ event and its implications for Christian life and practice, but that are much too rich and varied to be organized around a single focus.

Notes

1. Calvin J. Roetzel, *The Letters of Paul: Conversations in Context*. (4th ed.; Louisville: Westminster John Knox, 1998).

2. For the following, see Edgar J. Goodspeed, *The Formation of the New Testament* (Chicago: University of Chicago Press, 1926), 25–26.

3. Philostratus, *Apollonius of Tyana* 1.7; 4.27; 5.39–41; 7.35.

4. Paul Schubert, *The Form and Function of Pauline Thanksgivings* (Berlin: Töpelmann, 1939).

5. Jacob Neusner, ed. and trans., *The Mishnah: A New Translation* (New Haven: Yale University Press, 1988), 672.

6. This name describes the author of a set of Latin commentaries on the thirteen letters of Paul, originally attributed to Ambrose (ca. 339–397) but later recognized as written by someone else.

Bibliography

The Pauline Letters

Cousar, Charles B. *The Letters of Paul*. Interpreting Biblical Texts. Nashville: Abingdon, 1996.

Deissmann, Adolf. *Light From the Ancient East: The New Testament Illustrated by Recently Discovered Texts of the Graeco-Roman World*. Translated by Lionel R. M. Strachan, taking into account the 4th German edition, 1923. Grand Rapids: Baker, 1965 (1908).

Francis, Fred O., and J. Paul Sampley, eds. *Pauline Parallels*. Foundations and Facets: New Testament. 2d ed. Philadelphia: Fortress, 1984.

Keck, Leander E. *Paul and His Letters*. Proclamation Commentaries. 2d ed. Philadelphia: Fortress, 1988.

Murphy-O'Connor, Jerome. *Paul the Letter-Writer: His World, His Options, His Skills*. Good News Studies 41.Collegeville: Michael Glazier (Liturgical), 1995.

Rigaux, Beda. *The Letters of Paul: Modern Studies*. Translated by Stephen Yonick and Malachy J. Carroll from the 1962 French edition. Chicago: Franciscan Herald, 1968.

Roetzel, Calvin J. *The Letters of Paul: Conversations in Context*. 4th ed. Westminster John Knox, 1998.

Stirewalt, M. Luther. *Paul, the Letter Writer*. Grand Rapids: Eerdmans, 2003.

Stowers, Stanley K. *Letter Writing in Greco-Roman Antiquity*. Library of Early Christianity. Philadelphia: Westminster, 1986.

Trobisch, David. *Paul's Letter Collection: Tracing the Origins*. Minneapolis: Fortress, 1994.

Paul's Life and Thought

Barrett, C. K. *Paul: An Introduction to His Thought*. Outstanding Christian Thinkers. Louisville: Westminster, 1994.

Beker, J. Christiaan. *Paul the Apostle: The Triumph of God in Life and Thought*. 2d ed. Philadelphia: Fortress, 1984.

Bornkamm, Günther. *Paul*. Translated by D. M. G. Stalker from the 1969 German ed. London: Hodder & Stoughton, 1971.

Bruce, F. F. *Paul: Apostle of the Heart Set Free*. Grand Rapids: Eerdmans, 1980 (1977).

Bultmann, Rudolf. "The Theology of Paul." Pages 185–352 in vol. 1 of his *Theology of the New Testament*. Translated by Kendrick Grobel. 2 vols. New York: Scribner's, 1951–1955.

Dahl, Nils A., assisted by Paul Donahue. *Studies in Paul: Theology for the Early Christian Mission*. Minneapolis: Augsburg, 1977.

Davies, W. D. *Paul and Rabbinic Judaism: Some Rabbinic Elements in Pauline Theology*. Harper Torchbooks. 4th ed. London: SPCK, 1980 (1948).

Deissmann, Adolf. *Paul: A Study in Social and Religious History*. Translated by William E. Wilson. 1st ed., 1912; 2d rev. ed., 1927. Gloucester: Peter Smith, 1972 (1912).

Dibelius, Martin. *Paul*. Edited and completed by Werner Georg Kümmel. Translated by Frank Clarke. Philadelphia: Westminster, 1953.

Dodd, C. H. *The Meaning of Paul for Today*. London: Swarthmore, 1920; repr. London: Collins (Fontana Books), 1971.

Dunn, James D. G. *The Theology of Paul the Apostle*. Grand Rapids: Eerdmans, 1998.

———, ed. *The Cambridge Companion to St. Paul*. Cambridge: Cambridge University Press, 2003.

Engberg-Pedersen, Troels. *Paul and the Stoics*. Louisville/Edinburgh: Westminster John Knox/T&T Clark, 2000.

———. *Paul in His Hellenistic Context*. Minneapolis/London: Fortress/Routledge, 1994.

Fitzmyer, Joseph A. *According to Paul: Studies in the Theology of the Apostle*. New York: Paulist, 1993.

———. *Pauline Theology: A Brief Sketch*. 2d ed. Englewood Cliffs: Prentice-Hall, 1989 (1967).

Furnish, Victor P. *Theology and Ethics in Paul*. Nashville: Abingdon, 1982.

Hays, Richard B. *Echoes of Scripture in the Letters of Paul*. New Haven: Yale University Press, 1989.

Hengel, Martin, and Anna Maria Schwemer. *Paul Between Damascus and Antioch: The Unknown Years*. Translated by John M. Bowden. Louisville: Westminster John Knox, 1997.

————, and Roland Deines. *The Pre-Christian Paul*. London/Philadelphia: SCM/Trinity Press International, 1991.

Hock, Ronald F. *The Social Context of Paul's Ministry: Tentmaking and Apostleship*. Philadelphia: Fortress, 1980.

Hooker, Morna D. *Paul: A Short Introduction*. Oxford: Oneworld, 2003.

Horrell, David. *An Introduction to the Study of Paul*. Continuum Biblical Studies Series. London: Continuum, 2000.

Käsemann, Ernst. *Perspectives on Paul*. Translated by Margaret Kohl. New Testament Library. London: SCM, 1971.

Kim, Seyoon. *The Origin of Paul's Gospel*. 2d ed. Wissenschaftliche Untersuchungen zum Neuen Testament 2, 4. Tübingen: Mohr (Siebeck), 1984.

————. *Paul and the New Perspective: Second Thoughts on the Origin of Paul's Gospel*. Wissenschaftliche Untersuchungen zum Neuen Testament 140. Tübingen: Mohr Siebeck, 2002.

Malherbe, Abraham J. *Paul and the Popular Philosophers*. Minneapolis: Fortress, 1989.

Meeks, Wayne. *The First Urban Christians: The Social World of the Apostle Paul*. New Haven: Yale University Press, 1983.

————, ed. *The Writings of St. Paul*. Norton Critical Edition. New York: W. W. Norton, 1972.

Munck, Johannes. *Paul and the Salvation of Mankind*. Richmond: John Knox, 1959.

Murphy-O'Connor, Jerome. *Paul: A Critical Life*. Oxford: Oxford University Press, 1996.

Neyrey, Jerome H. *Paul, in Other Words: A Cultural Reading of His Letters*. Louisville: Westminster John Knox, 1990.

Nock, Arthur Darby. *St. Paul*. Harper Torchbooks. New York: Harper, 1963.

Pagels, Elaine. *The Gnostic Paul: Gnostic Exegesis of the Pauline Letters*. Harrisburg: Trinity, 1992 (1975).

Roetzel, Calvin J. *Paul: The Man and the Myth*. Studies on Personalities of the New Testament. Minneapolis: Fortress, 1999. Excellent introduction to Paul.

Sampley, J. Paul, ed. *Paul in the Greco-Roman World: A Handbook*. Harrisburg: Trinity (Continuum), 2003.

Sanders, E. P. *Paul and Palestinian Judaism: A Comparison of Patterns of Religion*. Philadelphia/London: Fortress/SCM, 1977.

Scroggs, Robin. *Paul for a New Day*. Philadelphia: Fortress, 1977.

Segal, Alan. *Paul the Convert: The Apostolate and Apostasy of Saul the Pharisee*. New Haven: Yale University Press, 1990.

Stendahl, Krister. *Paul Among Jews and Gentiles*. Philadelphia: Fortress, 1976.

Watson, Francis. *Paul, Judaism, and the Gentiles: A Sociological Approach*. Society for New Testament Studies Monograph Series 56. Cambridge: Cambridge University Press, 1986.

Ziesler, J. A. *Pauline Christianity*. Rev. ed. Oxford Bible Series. Oxford: Oxford University Press, 1990.

Pauline Chronology

Buck, Charles Henry, Jr., and Greer Taylor. *Saint Paul: A Study of the Development of His Thought*. New York: Scribner's, 1969.

Jewett, Robert. *A Chronology of Paul's Life*. Philadelphia: Fortress, 1979.

Knox, John. *Chapters in a Life of Paul*. Rev. ed. Macon: Mercer University Press, 1987 (1950).

Lüdemann, Gerd. *Paul, Apostle to the Gentiles: Studies in Chronology*. Translated by F. Stanley Jones. Philadelphia: Fortress Press, 1984.

Ogg, George. *The Chronology of the Life of Paul*. London: Epworth, 1968.

Chapter 12

The Thessalonian Letters

"The Thessalonian letters give us a notable picture of the human failings of a new community."

A. D. Nock

"Paul's two letters to the Thessalonians, the earliest extant Christian writings . . . open windows onto newly founded Christian communities as no other documents do . . . [they show that] Paul was as much concerned with the moral, emotional, and spiritual nurture of his converts as he was with their theological development."

Abraham J. Malherbe

"E ven in brief works there is much pungency." So wrote Tertullian (ca. 160–225 C.E.) as he began his critique of Marcion's (died ca. 160 C.E.) condensed version of the Thessalonian letters.[1] We can well understand Tertullian's impatience with the "shipmaster of Pontus."[2] Why take the carving knife to 1 Thessalonians, one of Paul's shortest letters, and to 2 Thessalonians, only half as long? The first letter, which has only faint echoes of the OT and nowhere quotes it outright, was one of the least Jewish-sounding Pauline letters. Its one reference to Jews (1 Thess 2:14), which is less than complimentary, should have appealed to Marcion. Second Thessalonians was another story, however, with its strongly Jewish apocalyptic cast.

Perhaps the brevity of the Thessalonian letters commended them to early readers, but surely it was their compelling content that explains their early popularity. "Pray without ceasing" (1 Thess 5:17) caught the attention of Ignatius (ca. 35–107 C.E.),[3] as it has the attention of readers ever since. The frequent use of the letters from the second century forward is amply attested.[4] Naturally their eschatological sections piqued the interest of early readers and have continued to do so.[5] But so did their moral instruction and their capacity to encourage, console, and uplift readers.[6] Considering their perennial popularity from the patristic period forward, the Thessalonian letters influenced the church's thinking far out of proportion to their length.[7]

Early canonical lists typically mention two letters written by Paul to the Thessalonians.[8] The early church attributed both letters to Paul and tended to read them in tandem,[9] but since the eighteenth century serious doubts have been raised about whether Paul wrote 2 Thessalonians. One consideration was the distinct scenarios of the end time sketched in 1 Thess 4:13–5:11 and 2 Thess 2:1–12. Some found them too divergent for both to have been written by Paul. Compared with 1 Cor 15, the latter was even more suspect. The pervasive similarity of certain literary features and phraseology was also taken to be evidence that 2 Thessalonians was written by someone else who had drawn heavily on the first letter. The mention in 2 Thess 2:1–2 of a letter forged under Paul's name simply confirmed that the practice occurred in Paul's time. This made the pseudonymity of 2 Thessalonians a more plausible suggestion. To account for the literary similarity of the two letters, it was even suggested that 2 Thessalonians was written first, then became the basis for the longer letter.

Of these considerations, the most serious difficulty is posed by the sharply contrasted eschatologies of the two letters. Rather than harmonizing them by downplaying the tensions between them, we should acknowledge the sharp profile of each, even if they cannot be correlated happily. The literary echoes of the letters are plausible because they were composed so close together. Even the most skilled wordsmith need not be entirely original, even when writing repeatedly to the same person. To suggest that the order of the letters should be reversed, while creative, is a real stretch. Maintaining the authenticity of 2 Thessalonians creates difficulties for interpreters who long for a more consistent and less radically apocalyptic Paul, but it is the most compelling view.

While the debate about the pseudonymity of 2 Thessalonians is important, it should not obscure how valuable both letters are to the church and contemporary Pauline scholarship. As the earliest extant letter of Paul—and thus the earliest surviving Christian writing—1 Thessalonians marks the beginning of his literary legacy.[10] This makes it an invaluable source for deciding such questions as the origin and development of Paul's thought, to say nothing of reconstructing a chronology of his life. It renders all the more remarkable his reference to the "word of the Lord" (1 Thess 4:15), which, if it is properly understood as a saying attributable to Jesus himself, makes the instructions about the Parousia (1 Thess 4:15–17) the earliest isolated saying of the Lord (agraphon) found in the NT and this "little apocalypse" the earliest apocalyptic text in the NT. Also remarkable is the scenario of the end time sketched in 2 Thess 2:3–12, its disputed Pauline authorship notwithstanding. Because it is an early apocalyptic text, with images, motifs, and themes resonant with other strata of the NT (e.g., the "little apocalypses" of the Synoptic Gospels: Mark 13; Matt 24; Luke 21; also Rev 13), it is an invaluable piece of evidence in reconstructing the origin and development of early Christian apocalyptic.

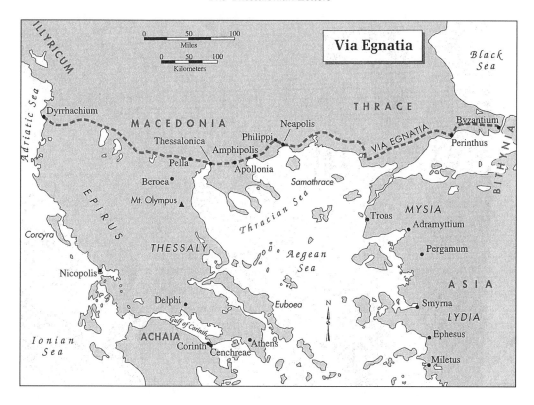

Paul and the Thessalonian Church

When Paul wrote 1 Thessalonians, he had been gone only "a short time" (1 Thess 2:17). Since his founding visit was still a fresh memory, the letter abounds with details of that visit: Paul, Timothy, and probably Silvanus (though he is not mentioned after the opening verse) as the "apostles of Christ" who started the church (1 Thess 1:1; 2:7; 3:1–2, 6); Paul's Spirit-empowered preaching (1 Thess 1:5) and its two-pronged message of the one God and his raised, exalted Son, who was expected to return as eschatological deliverer (1 Thess 1:9–10); Paul's preaching in the face of "great opposition" reminiscent of his earlier experience in Philippi (1 Thess 2:2); the "persecution" (1 Thess 1:6) and "suffer[ing] . . . from [their] own countrymen" (1 Thess 2:14 NJB; cf. 3:3) marking the Thessalonians' reception of his preaching; his further instructions about how "to live and to please God" (1 Thess 4:1–2), God the avenger (1 Thess 4:6), and behavior outsiders would admire (1 Thess 4:11–12); the certain yet sudden Day of the Lord (1 Thess 5:2); and Paul's exemplary ministerial behavior among them—nobly motivated, unpretentious, aboveboard, tenderly affectionate, marked by hard work and financial self-support (1 Thess 2:3–12). Word of the Thessalonians' valiant faith had already spread throughout Macedonia and Achaia (1 Thess 1:7–8; 4:10).

How long this initial visit lasted Paul does not say, but it was probably three to four months. After Paul's departure, his efforts to return were thwarted (1 Thess 2:17–18), and from Athens he sent Timothy back to Thessalonica to encourage and strengthen the church (1 Thess 3:1–2). Whether he is still in Athens when Timothy returns with his reassuring report is not clear (1 Thess 3:6–7). The letter gives no further details of Paul's location when he wrote it, though Corinth or even Ephesus is a possibility. (Corinth as the place of composition is supported by the sequence of events in Acts.) Apart from Timothy's report, no letters or other communications between Paul and the church are mentioned. But there is good reason to think that Paul had received a letter from the Thessalonians that was delivered to him by Timothy along with his oral report. Who delivered and read Paul's letter to the church is not stated (1 Thess 5:27); possibly it was Timothy or Silvanus.

Second Thessalonians provides no firm clues about where it was written; probably it was the same place as 1 Thessalonians. But 2 Thessalonians sheds some light on the circumstances in which it was written. As in 1 Thessalonians, its co-senders are Paul, Silvanus, and Timothy (2 Thess 1:1), but no indication of their location is given. As in 1 Thessalonians, there are references to Paul's founding visit when they believed "the truth" and experienced God's call "through our proclamation of the good news" to receive God's Spirit-given sanctification (2 Thess 2:13–14). His initial visit is also remembered as a time of oral instructions about eschatology (2 Thess 2:5, 15) and the need to work (2 Thess 3:10). Such instructions he designates as "traditions" they had received from him (2 Thess 2:15; 3:6). As in 1 Thessalonians, Paul also recalls his exemplary behavior on his founding visit (2 Thess 3:7–10). This account is more abbreviated but it accents similar themes: orderly conduct and working night and day to keep from being a financial burden on anyone (2 Thess 3:7–10; cf. 1 Thess 2:1–12). The readers' situation is also one in which they endure persecutions and afflictions (2 Thess 1:4; cf. 1:6–7).

Also envisioned in 2 Thessalonians are contacts between Paul and the church subsequent to his founding visit, most notably "our letter" in which he had given eschatological instructions (2 Thess 2:15). The intended referent is 1 Thessalonians. Paul has also received reports ("we hear") of disorderly conduct within the church (2 Thess 3:11). They are presumably oral, but no names are attached to them. The situation envisioned in 2 Thessalonians is ominous ("Let no one deceive you in any way," 2 Thess 2:3). Paul is worried about the potentially unsettling effects of a "spirit or . . . word or . . . letter, as though from us" reporting the arrival of the Day of the Lord (2 Thess 2:2). No outside teachers are mentioned, though Paul himself is threatened by "wicked and evil people" (2 Thess 3:2). The reported disorderly conduct is internal to the congregation (2 Thess 3:11).

The report of Paul's founding visit to Thessalonica in Acts 17:1–9 confirms some of the essential details from the letters: Silas as Paul's accompanying co-worker and probably Timothy as well, though he is not named (cf. Acts 16:1–4; 17:14–15); positive responses by some Thessalonians; stout resistance to Paul's preaching; being "driven out" by the Jews; and Paul's subsequent presence in Athens. Acts 16:11–40 confirms Paul's earlier difficult experience in Philippi (1 Thess 2:2). Some aspects of the Acts report are more difficult to harmonize with what the letters report. In Acts the thrust of Paul's preaching is Scripture-based demonstration of the necessity of the suffering and resurrection of the Messiah, who is identified with Jesus. The two-part summary in 1 Thess 1:9–10 suggests a different focus. Acts emphasizes the Jewish synagogue as the primary context for Paul's preaching and the positive response by some Thessalonian Jews as well as other Gentiles. In 1 Thessalonians, converted Gentile addressees are in the forefront (1 Thess 1:9–10; cf. 2:16), which is confirmed by the letter's overall Hellenistic complexion and its conspicuous lack of OT citations and allusions.[11] The more explicit apocalyptic cast of 2 Thessalonians and its more frequent OT allusions,[12] however, presuppose readers of Jewish background. Another difference is the length of Paul's initial visit. Acts 17:2 ("three sabbath days") suggests a short stay, while the letters imply a longer stay (1 Thess 2:1–12; cf. Phil 4:16).

Even with its different accent and distinctly Lukan agenda, Acts still confirms some of the overarching impressions gained from the letters: that the Thessalonian church came into existence in response to the preaching of Paul and his co-workers and did so in the face of stiff resistance, harassment, and even persecution; that such resistance would probably continue, and even intensify; that persons converted from Gentile backgrounds constituted a central core of the church; and that there was enough of a Jewish presence within the church to warrant Paul's use of an identifiably Jewish apocalyptic timetable, initially in the first letter and more fully in the second letter.

Anxieties, Exhortations, and Continuing Instruction: The Rhetoric of Reassurance in 1 Thessalonians

First Thessalonians is best read as a paraenetic letter whose overall goal is to encourage and strengthen its readers. Sometimes referred to as a letter of exhortation or even as a pastoral letter, this type of letter could have multiple purposes. It could console, edify, and even admonish. The writer could give various instructions to achieve these aims. Ancient rhetorical handbooks and other guides for composing letters emphasized several features of such letters that figure prominently in 1 Thessalonians: (1) recalling what was learned earlier and an emphasis on the familiar—what one already knows; (2) the use of personal examples as models worthy of imitation; and (3) language carefully crafted to reassure and encourage the readers.

Understanding the overall genre of 1 Thessalonians helps us appreciate its distinctive structure. It exhibits typical epistolary features of Pauline letters: initial greeting (1:1) followed by an opening prayer of thanksgiving that sets the overall tone of the letter and signals major thematic concerns (1:2–10); explicit exhortation in the latter part of the letter (4:1–5:22); benediction (5:23–24); and conclusion (5:25–28).

The letter is remarkable for the way Paul adapts the epistolary structure to serve his own purpose. Rather than a single opening prayer of thanksgiving, which is more typical of his other letters, here he extends the thanksgiving section well beyond its usual limits to 3:13—roughly half the letter! By no means one continuous prayer, this section includes a variety of material: Paul's rehearsal of his conduct during his founding visit (1 Thess 2:1–12); the Thessalonians' exemplary conversion (1 Thess 2:13–16); and details of Paul's separation from the church and his sending of Timothy (1 Thess 2:17–3:10). It is moved along by two additional thanksgivings (1 Thess 2:13; 3:9) and is concluded by a pastoral prayer (1 Thess 3:11–13).

This first major section of the letter (1 Thess 1:2–3:13) is carefully crafted by Paul to achieve its paraenetic purpose, even if it means altering his usual epistolary practice. Anxieties are writ large throughout this part of the letter. The difficult circumstances of the Thessalonians' reception of the gospel are repeatedly mentioned (1 Thess 1:3, 6; 2:2, 13–16; 3:3–4), but their distress has its counterpoint in Paul's own anxieties, also repeatedly mentioned (1 Thess 2:2, 17–20; 3:1, 5–7). Paul's need to allay their anxieties accounts for the *rhetoric of reassurance* that characterizes this section.

His appeal is anchored in repeated references to what they already know (1 Thess 2:1, 2, 5, 11; 3:3). Exemplary behaviors are singled out as worthy of imitation: Paul and his co-workers (1 Thess 1:6; 2:1–12); Christ himself (1 Thess 1:6); and the Judean churches (1 Thess 2:14). The Thessalonians in turn became examples for other churches (1 Thess 1:7–8). Apt images, such as gentle nurse (1 Thess 2:7), attentive father (1 Thess 2:11–12), and orphaned child (1 Thess 2:17), combined with deliberately formulated, affective language throughout the section, reinforce the intimacy and integrity of Paul's relationship with his readers. The intermittent expressions of thanksgiving and the final prayer place their anxieties and his reassuring appeal within the larger context of God's active love. They will be reminded later of God's absolute faithfulness (1 Thess 5:24). The combined rhetorical effect of these well-chosen words and this deftly executed strategy is ultimately reassuring.

Although the formal hortatory remarks do not begin until 4:1, the exhortation does not begin there. Rather, the thoroughly hortatory previous section, with its carefully devised rhetoric of reassurance, undergirds 4:1–5:22. Here Paul provides fresh instruction, but even it is grounded in familiar precepts he has already taught them (1 Thess 4:1–2, 6, 9, 11; 5:1). In his instructions about sexual purity (1 Thess 4:3–8), mutual love and responsible conduct admired by outsiders (1 Thess 4:9–12), the destiny of those who die before the Parousia (1 Thess 4:13–18), the certainty and suddenness of the Day of the Lord (1 Thess 5:1–11), and constructive internal conduct (1 Thess 5:12–22), he is amplifying earlier teaching as much as introducing new teaching. Woven throughout the teaching are periodic calls to mutual exhortation (1 Thess 4:18; 5:11).

Understood this way, 1 Thessalonians would have been heard by its first audience as a rhetorical performance in exhortation. From the opening thanksgiving (1:2–10) until the concluding exhortations and prayer of benediction (5:12–28), Paul speaks in a pastoral voice, now praying, now recalling his ministry among them, now recalling their experiences in coming to faith in Christ, now remembering earlier teaching, and now elaborating that teaching and broadening its boundaries, but through it all, exhorting. It is the voice of reassurance, consolation, and edification that constantly echoes throughout the letter. What unfolds, finally, is Paul's pastoral letter to the young Thessalonian church.

Resisting Resistance:
The Hard-Edged Exhortation of 2 Thessalonians

Compared with the first letter, 2 Thessalonians is a paraenetic letter with a sharper edge. It develops the dual purpose expressed in 1 Thess 5:14—to comfort

(2 Thess 1:3–3:5) and to admonish (2 Thess 3:6–12, 15)—but does so with more muscle. The church continues to suffer because of active resistance and persecution (2 Thess 1:4–7); its psychological equilibrium is being threatened (2 Thess 2:1–2), as is Paul's (2 Thess 3:2). Bedeviled by loafers and busybodies, it is experiencing internal turbulence (2 Thess 3:6–12). These changed circumstances prompt Paul to adjust his rhetoric accordingly, which accounts for the letter's overall sterner, more admonitory tone.

Even so, the letter exhibits the standard marks of paraenesis: recalling the familiar and appealing to traditional teaching (2 Thess 2:5, 6, 15; 3:6–7); setting Paul as an example to be imitated (2 Thess 3:7–9); and using the language of reassurance (2 Thess 1:3–4; 2:13–14, 16–17; 3:4, 16). Prayers of thanksgiving (2 Thess 1:3; 2:13) and intermittent petitionary prayers (2 Thess 1:11–12; 2:16–17; 3:5, 16) serve to bolster confidence, deepen faith, and exemplify to the Thessalonians the faithful life before God being commended. The letter's structure is straightforward: opening greeting (1:1–2); prayer of thanksgiving (1:3–12); hortatory instruction about the Day of the Lord (2:1–3:5); commands and instructions about congregational behavior and church discipline (3:6–15); and concluding prayer and benediction (3:16–18).

The letter's hard edge is reflected in three ways: (1) depicting, within the opening prayer of thanksgiving, the "righteous judgment of God" as vengeful action by God and Christ (2 Thess 1:5–10); (2) the strongly militant apocalyptic scenario of events preceding the Day of the Lord (2 Thess 2:3–11); and (3) the tough stance against disorderly conduct within the congregation (2 Thess 3:6–15). While the sharp edge of Paul's rhetoric here should not be minimized, in each case its hortatory purpose should be recognized.

Reminding the church that God and Christ can avenge wrongs is intended to strengthen the Thessalonians' endurance and translate their aspirations into actions (2 Thess 1:11–12). As much as the image of Divine Avenger may offend certain sensibilities, it was already introduced in the first letter (1 Thess 4:6), is elsewhere attested in Paul (Rom 12:19, probably quoting Deut 32:35; Prov 20:22; 24:29; cf. Heb 10:30–31; Rom 2:6–8; 2 Cor 5:10; Col 3:25), and has deep roots in the biblical (e.g., Ps 94; 99:8; Isa 63:4; 66:6; Mic 5:15; Nah 1:2; Sir 5:1–3, 7; 28:1) and broader Jewish tradition (*T. Reu.* 6.6; *T. Levi* 18.1; *T. Gad* 6.7). Located in the middle of an opening prayer, it is a steely reminder not to mess with God.

The eschatological battle sketched in 2 Thess 2:3–11 bears all the marks of an apocalyptic cosmic myth and resonates strongly with similar scenarios in the Johannine apocalypse (Rev 13; cf. 1 John 2:18, 22; 4:3; 2 John 7). Typical of such apocalyptically construed visions of the end time, the language is symbolic, allusive, and elusive. The identities of the lawless one (2 Thess 2:3, 8; KJV: "man of sin") and the one destined for destruction (2 Thess 2:3; KJV: "son of perdition") are unknown, as is the meaning of the restraining force and the "mystery of lawlessness" (2 Thess 2:6–7). Whatever the form of struggle taking place on earth, the real struggle is cosmic. The combatants are God and his designated Messiah, the Lord Jesus, on the one side, who are aligned against Satan and his agent, the man of lawlessness, on the other side. Typical of such apocalyptic scenarios, the rules of war apply, which means that God can resort to deceit in order to achieve final victory (2 Thess 2:11–12). The purpose of this rather fantastic rehearsal of end-time events is twofold: (1) to correct the mistaken notion that the Day of the Lord has already arrived (2 Thess 2:2), and (2) to encourage the church to "stand firm" and remain hopeful (2 Thess 2:13–17).

Instructing the Thessalonians to withdraw from members whose disorderly behavior upsets the equilibrium of the church may strike some as unnecessarily harsh, but such exclusionary practice is consonant with Paul's practice elsewhere (1 Cor 5). It also conforms to known practice of religious and philosophical communities in the first-century Mediterranean world, for example, the Essenes at Qumran (cf. 1QS 6:24–7:27; 8:21–26). As strong as Paul's language is—and his imperatives are strong and unequivocal—it is nevertheless tempered with softer language (2 Thess 3:13, 15–16). He recommends cauterization as a means of healing.

Elaborating Basic Beliefs

The conclusion of Paul's opening prayer of thanksgiving is widely recognized as a summary of his initial preaching to the Thessalonians (1 Thess 1:9–10). Two elements are prominent: (1) turning from idol worship to serve the "living and true God" (v. 9); and (2) awaiting God's Son, the risen Christ now exalted to heaven, who will come as the eschatological deliverer (v. 10). While these two foundational convictions are by no means developed systematically in the Thessalonian letters, they are nevertheless amplified and thus serve as two primary nodes of theological reflection.

Living in God's Space and Time

A relatively young Gentile church, which only recently shifted its loyalties from worshiping idols to believing in the one God, needed to be introduced to the world of the "living and true God." In the Thessalonian letters Paul does this by using language that brings them into God's space and orients them to God's time. As such, the letters are theological performances of the "gospel of God," in which both the good news about God and the good news God enacts come to life through the writing (and reading) of the letters themselves. The letters do what Paul would have done in person—they bring God into the midst of the Thessalonian church as the creative, formative Presence now reshaping the contours of its life, its temporal, spatial, and moral frame of reference. Since Paul and his co-workers Silvanus and Timothy have been "apostles of Christ" among the Thessalonians, it is equally important to show how their own ministerial conduct has also exemplified the "gospel of God," how their manner of life has conformed to God's expectations and, in doing so, has displayed a way of living in the world that the Thessalonian church should emulate. [See Expanded CD Version pp. 406–8: *Paul's Rhetorical Strategy for Bringing God to Life in the Thessalonian Church*]

Paul and his co-workers are bearers of "the word of God," which is fundamentally misconstrued if thought of as just so many human words about God; it is properly understood only when the preached message is seen as God's own actuating speech whose residual effects are visibly seen as faith comes to life within those who respond obediently (1 Thess 2:13). The "word of God" is not human speech about a divine sub-

The Apostle Paul. A woodcut from an apologetic work by Matthias Flacius (1520–1575), printed in Magdeburg, Germany, in 1549. From the Digital Image Archive of The Richard C. Kessler Reformation Collection, Pitts Theology Library, Candler School of Theology, Emory University, Atlanta, Georgia.

ject, but divinely effectual speech mediated through human words. When "the Jews" obstruct the progress of the gospel, they "displease God" (1 Thess 2:15). Paul understands his mission plans and movements as codirected by God and Jesus Christ (1 Thess 3:11).

Awaiting God's Son from Heaven

While Paul's original preaching to the Thessalonians began with an appeal to turn to God from idols, it also mentioned Christ (1 Thess 1:10). Since Christ is the natural complement of the one God, Paul can speak quite naturally of the "gospel of Christ" (1 Thess 3:2). Rather than accenting the crucified Christ in his initial preaching, Paul proclaimed Jesus as Son of God, a well-established image from early Christian tradition (cf. Mark 1:1, though chronologically later). Even so, Christ's suffering is far from peripheral (1 Thess 1:6; 2:15). Believing that "Jesus died and rose again" is a foundational conviction (1 Thess 4:14). Naturally, God's raising Christ from the dead figured centrally in Paul's missionary proclamation. Especially noteworthy is the forward thrust of Paul's message: the church awaits the risen Christ, now exalted to heaven, who will come as eschatological deliverer from "the wrath that is coming" (1 Thess 1:10). **[See Expanded CD Version pp. 409–10:** *Awaiting God's Son from Heaven: The Figure of Christ in Paul's Message***]**

As the dominating figure of this eschatological event, Christ is probably the referent in "the day of the Lord" (1 Thess 5:2; 2 Thess 2:2–3). In this case the OT prophetic Day of Yahweh has now been redefined with specific reference to Christ (cf. 2 Thess 1:9–10). In the final apocalyptic struggle, it is the Lord Jesus who slays the lawless one (2 Thess 2:8). Deliverance from the final wrath thus means salvation is understood fully and finally as life with the resurrected Christ (1 Thess 5:10).

The Holy Spirit

While the Holy Spirit may not have been part of the initial content of Paul's missionary preaching to the Thessalonians, it served as the source of empowerment that fully convicted them (1 Thess 1:5). When they encountered stiff resistance in responding to the gospel initially, it was the Holy Spirit who inspired them with joy (1 Thess 1:6). Their capacity for a distinctive moral life (sanctification) is seen as a function of the Holy Spirit God has given them (1 Thess 4:8): Holy Spirit produces holy living. Yet "sanctification by the Spirit" occurs not as a second stage of moral perfection but as an initial empowerment that comes when they have "belief in the truth" (2 Thess 2:13). So also does prophetic teaching within the church stem from the Spirit, whose pursuit should not be obstructed (1 Thess 5:19–20).

The Coming of the Lord and the Final Battle

When Paul first preached to the Thessalonians, he proclaimed Christ's resurrection and his expected return (1 Thess 1:10). He also probably stressed that Christ would return soon. How much he told them about their own resurrection is not certain. Given his understanding of baptism expressed elsewhere, we can imagine that they saw themselves as having "died with Christ" and, in some sense, "living with him," probably in the future (Rom 6). But precisely how Christ's imminent return and their future resurrection were connected appears not to have been clear. They are not *necessarily* connected conceptually. One might imagine Jesus' messianic deliverance as his returning to earth to establish his promised kingdom. The resurrection of the dead might occur at a much later date. How Paul had spoken to them about these three things—Christ's resurrection, Christ's Parousia, and the resurrection of believers—is not certain.

What is certain is that some of the Thessalonians developed questions about the end time to which Paul feels compelled to respond in his first letter. Their primary question appears to have been: If believers die prior to Christ's coming, will they miss out on "living with him"? Or if this is still a possibility for them, how might it occur?

To allay these anxieties Paul crafts his response in 1 Thess 4:13–18. At the core of his response is the foundational Christian conviction that "Jesus died and rose again" (v. 14). Its original wording suggests that this was not Paul's own formulation, but that he is citing a creedal confession probably traceable to the earliest stages of Christian belief in Palestine. While this particular formulation does not stress that God raised Jesus from the dead, Paul's original preaching to the Thessalonians did (1 Thess 1:10). From this core conviction, he offers this assurance to his readers: Just as God raised Christ, so will God "bring with him those who have died" (1 Thess 4:14). Just as God restored Jesus to life, God will do the same for those who have already died "in Christ"; what is more, God will accomplish this through Jesus himself.

How this will be accomplished has been revealed "by the word of the Lord" (1 Thess 4:15). The meaning of this cryptic phrase is uncertain, but it probably suggests that Paul attributes the scenario of events described in verses 15–17 to Christ himself. Whether this refers to an eschatological saying of Jesus that was not preserved in any of the four Gospels—as one of the agrapha (literally, "things unwritten") of

Jesus that somehow found its way through the tradition to Paul—or perhaps to a "prophetic word" or revelation received by a Christian prophet (maybe even Paul himself) under the impulse of the Spirit is uncertain. In either case, Paul transmits it as an authoritative description of end-time events.

The projected scenario has three stages: (1) Christ's descent from heaven, accompanied by apocalyptic signs usually associated with the arrival of the end time; (2) the resurrection of those who died "in Christ," in other words, as Christians; and (3) the "snatching up" of those who are still alive. From this results the eternal union of those "in Christ" with Christ: "so we will be with the Lord forever" (1 Thess 4:17).

Behind this sketch of events lies an early "descent/ascent" construal of the story of Christ. One form is preserved in Phil 2:6–11, in which the pre-existent Christ descends to the earth, becomes human "to the point of death," and is then exalted and ascends (back) to God. His ascent can be envisioned in different ways: in two stages, first as a resurrection, then an ascension into heaven at a later time (so Luke 24 and Acts 1); or in a single stage in which resurrection and exaltation are fused into a single "event" (so Hebrews). Either way, his exalted state is heavenly, and he "reigns with God."

The "descent/ascent" cycle is repeated in the end time, when the exalted Messiah again descends to the earth, this time as messianic deliverer to rescue the saints, and ascends once again into heaven. It is this later stage of the "descent/ascent" story that the "word of the Lord" amplifies for Paul. How it relates to apocalyptic sayings in the Synoptic Gospels that envision the return of the Son of Man (e.g., Mark 8:38–9:1) is not clear, but it may very well be the "narrative" working out of how the Son of Man's future return was actually envisioned.

Once expectations of the Messiah's return are raised, the inevitable question is, "When?" Paul responds to this question in 1 Thess 5:1–11. "Times and seasons" is a technical way of referring to such speculations about when the end would occur. That the Thessalonians (and Paul himself) were expecting the Parousia to occur soon is clear: they and he expected to be alive (1 Thess 4:15). His use of the thief metaphor underscores the suddenness and unpredictability of the Parousia: When it will occur, no one knows; that it will occur unexpectedly, everyone knows. His resulting advice: Be alert! (1 Thess 5:6). By appropriating the imagery of light and darkness as moral categories enabling the Thessalonians to shape an identity that best prepares them for the end time, Paul is employing a strategy found in other communities, for example, Qumran, who saw themselves as preparing for the end time.

The shape of Paul's response here is situation specific. Rather than developing an expanded, much less systematic, exposition of his eschatological views, he is instead responding to specific questions. They are questions pagans would ask. Questions that he deals with elsewhere, for example, the type of resurrection body Christians would receive (1 Cor 15), are not in view here. Nor is he primarily concerned with what happens to those who are not "in Christ" (cf. 1 Thess 4:13).

In 2 Thessalonians, prompted by the possibility that the Thessalonians might receive a letter purportedly from him claiming that the Day of the Lord is a present rather than a future reality, Paul sketches an elaborate scenario of end-time events (2 Thess 2:3–12). It is one of the most enigmatic such descriptions in the NT, not only because of its unusual language (unlike anything else in Paul) but also because it is so cryptic. It incorporates some standard features of eschatological timetables found in Jewish apocalyptic writings.

The "rebellion" or apostasy (*apostasia*, v. 3) that must precede the final day resonates with apocalyptic notions that a period of unprecedented evil, often characterized as rebellion against God, would usher in the last days (4 *Ezra* 4:26–28; 5:1–12; 1 *En.* 91:5–7; 2 *Bar.* 27; 1QpHab 2:1–10). That this evil would be embodied in a megalomaniacal usurper such as Antiochus IV Epiphanes (ca. 215–164 B.C.E.), who desecrated the Jerusalem temple (Dan 9:27; 11:31, 36–37; 12:11), or even in Pompey (106–48 B.C.E.) or Gaius Caligula (12–41 C.E.), was easy enough to conceive. That such a person would dare sit in God's seat might have been suggested by the OT (Ezek 28:2, 6, 9; Isa 14:13–14). Satan as the archetype of evil and the prime enemy to be dealt with in the ensuing cosmic struggle is also standard apocalyptic fare (*T. Dan* 5.10; *T. Jud.* 25.3; also cf. Rev 12:7–17).

More difficult to identify is the "lawless one" (2 Thess 2:3, 8, 9), a phrase possibly suggested by Ps 89:22, who is also identified as the "one destined for destruction" or the "son of perdition" (KJV). Whether he is envisioned as a human or supernatural figure is not clear, but since he sets himself against every form of conventional worship, he is usually seen as an antichrist figure, although the term is not used here (cf. 1 John 2:18). Especially difficult are the "mystery of lawlessness" that is at work at the time Paul writes and the restraining force that obstructs the work of the "lawless one" (2 Thess 2:6–7). The "restrainer" has been variously identified as the Roman Empire or emperor, in other words, the political instrument holding back the outbreak of chaos; some figure from the binding of Satan myth, in which perhaps an angel (as in Rev 20:1–2) or God holds back Satan until he is released at the end time; the mission to the Gentiles, thus perhaps even Paul himself, as that which delays the end; or some force hostile to God, perhaps a false prophet. Once the "restrainer" is removed and the "lawless one" surfaces, the role of the Lord Jesus at his coming is clear: to slay the "lawless one . . . with the breath of his mouth" (reflecting the language of Isa 11:4).

The differences between the eschatological scenarios of 1 Thess 4:13–18 and 2 Thess 2:1–12 are remarkable. No cosmic battle is envisioned in the former, whereas this is the central feature of the latter. The role of the saints, those "in Christ," is a central feature of the former, but absent in the latter. By contrast, "those who are perishing" and their fate is a central feature of the latter (2 Thess 2:10–12). These respective visions of the end time are so different that it challenges the imagination to correlate them. The perceived incompatibility between these respective eschatologies, coupled with the difficulty of finding close parallels to 2 Thess 2:1–12 in other Pauline letters, has been one of the major arguments against Pauline authorship of the second letter. While these difficulties should not be minimized, the two accounts are best left to stand on their own, to be read as different, even inconsistent, responses to different sets of concerns.

Notes

1. Tertullian, *Marc.* 5.15 (introducing his comments on 1 Thessalonians). *ANF* 3:461.
2. *Marc.* 5.1. *ANF* 3:430.
3. *Eph.* 10.1. He probably knew both letters (*Rom.* 2.1; cf. 1 Thess 2:4; *Rom.* 10.3; cf. 2 Thess 3:5).

4. Possible echoes in Herm. *Vis.* 3.9.10 (cf. 1 Thess 5:13–14); probable allusions in Pol. *Phil.* 11.3 (cf. 2 Thess 1:4); 11.4 (cf. 2 Thess 3:15). Possible echoes are also heard in the anti-Gnostic *Ep. Apos.* (third quarter of the second century) 22 (1 Thess 5:23); 26 (cf. 1 Thess 1:4); 38 (1 Thess 4:17); and 39 (1 Thess 5:5). The Christian addition to *4 Ezra* known as *5 Ezra* (ca. 200 C.E.) also reflects knowledge of 1 Thess 2:12 (cf. *5 Ezra* 2.37). Among the earliest explicit attributions of the letters to Paul is Hippolytus (ca. 170–236 C.E.), *Antichr.* 63 (2 Thess 2:1–12) and 66 (1 Thess 4:13–17).

5. Hippolytus quotes from 1–2 Thessalonians within his broader discussion of biblical prophecies and other apocalyptic texts.

6. The Antiochians Theodoret (ca. 393–466 C.E.) and John Chrysostom (347–407 C.E.), a trained rhetorician, noticed the strong pastoral thrust of 1 Thessalonians and even emulated Paul's strategy of "leading the soul by words" (psychagogy) in addressing their audiences.

7. Both letters receive extensive treatment in the patristic period. Origen (ca. 185–254 C.E.) appears to be the first to have written a commentary on the letters, though only a brief comment on 1 Thess 4:15–17 survives (Jerome, *Epist.* 119). From the numerous patristic commentaries, especially noteworthy are those of Theodore of Mopsuestia and Chrysostom, the latter of whom devoted eleven homilies to 1 Thessalonians and five to 2 Thessalonians. Among notable fourth-century Latin commentators on the letters are "Ambrosiaster" and Pelagius (late fourth–early fifth centuries). During the medieval period, both letters were frequently treated. Some of the more notable commentators were John of Damascus (ca. 655–750 C.E.), Theophylact (died after 1125), and Euthymius Zigabenus (early twelfth century). Latin commentaries on the letters were written by Thomas Aquinas (ca. 1225–1274) and Nicholas of Lyre (ca. 1270–1349). Other medieval treatments featured compilations from the earlier patristic and medieval sources. Among the Reformers, Calvin treated the letters (1539), as did Zwingli (1526), but neither Luther (1483–1546) nor Melanchthon (1497–1560) gave them commentary treatment. In the seventeenth century, Hugo Grotius (1583–1645) treated the letters in his *Annotations to the Old and New Testaments*, which began to appear in 1641. The letters received continuous extensive treatment in the eighteenth and nineteenth centuries and have continued to do so ever since.

8. The Muratorian Fragment (ca. 200 C.E.) includes among Paul's writings two letters written to the Thessalonians. So do Codex Sinaiticus (ca. 350), Canon of the Council of Laodicea (ca. 363), and Athanasius's *Thirty-Ninth Festal Letter* (367); they are absent, however, in the third-century list found in Codex Claromontanus (ca. sixth century). A brief introduction for each letter is included among the Marcionite Prologues (fourth century at the latest, possibly second century); the literary form of the prologue for 2 Thessalonians differs from that for 1 Thessalonians, suggesting a possible later composition. That Marcion included a shortened form of both letters in the "Apostle" section of his canon is clear from Tertullian's refutation of their use by Marcion (*Marc.* 5.15,16). $\mathfrak{P}^{46}$ (ca. 200 C.E.), which contains portions of the Pauline letters (including Hebrews, but excluding 2 Thessalonians, Philemon, and the Pastoral Letters), is defective at the end but includes portions of 1 Thessalonians. Since its heading reads *Pros Thessaloneikeis* A, we can assume that the complete manuscript also included *Pros Thessaloneikeis* B, in other words, 2 Thessalonians.

9. As noted above (n. 3), Ignatius appears to have known both letters.

10. I date 1–2 Thessalonians in the early 50s, during Paul's ministry at Corinth.

11. Cf. 1 Thess 2:4 (Jer 11:20), 16 (Gen 15:16; Dan 8:23; 2 Macc 6:14); 4:5 (Job 18:21; Ps 79:6; Jer 10:25), 6 (Ps 94:1), 8 (Ezek 36:27; 37:14); 5:8 (Isa 59:17; Wis 5:18), 22 (Job 1:1, 8; 2:3).

12. Cf. 2 Thess 1:9 (cf. Isa 2:10 LXX, 19, 21); 2:8 (cf. Isa 11:4); also 2:3 (Isa 57:3 LXX; Ps 89:23); 3:5 (cf. 1 Chr 29:18); 3:16 (cf. Num 6:26; Ruth 2:4).

Bibliography

Commentaries

Best, Ernest. *A Commentary on the First and Second Epistles to the Thessalonians*. Black's New Testament Commentaries. London: Black, 1972.

Malherbe, Abraham J. *The Letters to the Thessalonians*. Anchor Bible 32B. New York: Doubleday, 2000.

Richard, Earl. *First and Second Thessalonians*. Sacra Pagina 11. Collegeville: Liturgical Press, 1995.

Other Resources

Donfried, Karl P. "The Theology of 1 Thessalonians and 2 Thessalonians." Pages 1–113 in Karl P. Donfried and I. Howard Marshall, *The Theology of the Shorter Pauline Letters*. New Testament Theology. Cambridge: Cambridge University Press, 1993; repr. 1999.

Jewett, Robert. *The Thessalonian Correspondence: Pauline Rhetoric and Millenarian Piety*. Foundations and Facets. Philadelphia: Fortress, 1986.

Malherbe, Abraham J. *Paul and the Thessalonians: The Philosophical Tradition of Pastoral Care*. Philadelphia: Fortress, 1987.

Chapter 13

The Corinthian Letters

"We have always seen that those who were closest to Christ our Lord were those with the greatest trials."

Teresa of Avila

"First Corinthians represents the fundamental problem of practical ecclesiology . . . ."

Margaret M. Mitchell

I f ever proof were needed that congregational ministry is one of the most fertile fields for doing theology, the Corinthian letters provide it. In them, we see two primary players: Paul and the church he started at Corinth. The letters reveal much about both. Unlike some of the other Pauline letters in which the church addressed remains relatively faceless, in the Corinthian letters we get a remarkably detailed picture of a single Pauline church, or perhaps a cluster of house churches in the greater Corinth region that periodically met as a single congregation. We learn about their internal tensions, about cases of misconduct in the church, and especially about the questions they struggled with as they sought to make sense of the Christian gospel in a major urban center with a complex social, political, and religious makeup. We also see the church moving through different stages of development, first under the leadership of Paul, their founding apostle, then under his successor, Apollos, and then into a phase in which there was no single leader within the church. The latter appears to be the situation reflected in both Corinthian letters. This leadership vacuum is one of the contributing causes of the church's troubles.

Part of the difficulty is that Paul is no longer present within the church, yet he still considers himself their apostolic leader and continues to exert leadership within the church. As one of Paul's churches, Corinth was expected to participate in a major project that preoccupied him during this period of his Aegean ministry—the collection for the poor saints in Jerusalem. In these letters we are able to track the Corinthians' reluctant participation in this project. The letters also reveal a further stage in which Paul's relationship with the church deteriorated seriously, owing primarily to the arrival in the church of competing Jewish Christian missionaries who became Paul's rivals. We are thus able to witness a period of turbulence within the church in which Paul is fighting to keep the Corinthians within his fold, urging them to complete their part in the collection, and answering the charges of his opponents in the church. We are able to witness severely strained relations between the church and their founding apostle and at least one highly conflictual incident involving Paul, an unnamed individual, and the entire church.

It is impossible to talk about the church without talking about Paul, for as we describe how much the letters reveal about the Corinthian church, we also note how much they reveal about Paul himself. Since the letters were written by him, they reflect his point of view as well as his interpretation of the situation. They reveal much about his attitudes toward the church, his missionary practices, including what and how he preached when he started a church in a new location, his pastoral strategies for bringing a church to greater levels of maturity, and his theological views on a wide range of topics.

As the situation worsens and Paul himself becomes the center of controversy, we learn much about how he was perceived by others and how he responded when attacked. Since the nature and legitimacy of his apostolic ministry were directly questioned by his opponents, Paul's response to these attacks tells us much about how he understood his own apostolic ministry. The controversy provides an occasion for him to reflect extensively and systematically on his theology of ministry. Because the controversy became so personal, Paul's remarks take on a highly personal tone, and we find him revealing things about himself that he was otherwise reluctant to do. The controversy prompts him to open the curtain to his psyche, thereby revealing a broad spectrum of emotions.

Paul's interaction with the church at Corinth covers a period of roughly seven years, from the time he started the church in the early fifties until his final stop there en route to Jerusalem, probably in the spring of 57 C.E. The first eighteen months he spent as the church's founding missionary, and the rest of the time as its apostolic leader operating from other locations in the region, mainly Ephesus, some 200 miles east of Corinth across the Aegean, and cities northward in Macedonia where he had also started churches, including Philippi, Thessalonica, and Beroea. It was a time of intense missionary activity for Paul as he attended to the church he had started in Ephesus even while nurturing the other congregations he had founded in the region.

As he did with other churches he established, Paul remained in contact with Corinth by writing letters and making occasional visits. How many letters he wrote (and received from) the Corinthians during this period is not known, but there were enough to give the expression "Corinthian correspondence" genuine meaning. In 2 Cor 10:9 he mentions letters he had sent the Corinthian church. At least three separate letters are in view: (1) the "previous letter" (1 Cor 5:9), (2) our 1 Corinthians, and (3) probably the "tearful letter" (2 Cor 2:3–4, 9; 7:8, 12).

What we know as 1–2 Corinthians is either one part of that more extensive correspondence or its compilation. One of the chief difficulties in interpreting these letters is deciding which. In either case, when we read these letters we are joining a conversation between Paul and Corinth that had already gone on for quite a while, and the letters allow us to overhear a conversation that continued for several years.

How important Corinth became as a hub of Pauline missionary activity is seen not only by the number of letters Paul wrote *to* Corinth, but also by how much of his other correspondence originated *from Corinth*. While it is impossible to be certain in these matters, we are confident that 1 Thessalonians (and, if it is authentic, 2 Thessalonians) was written from Corinth shortly after he arrived there on his founding visit, and that Romans (and possibly Galatians) was written from there on his final visit, just before he headed to Jerusalem bearing the collection.

Since letters often reflect as much about the situation from which they are written as the one to which they are written, these other Pauline letters often provide illuminating insight into the Corinthian situation (see Rom 15–16). The Corinthian church's importance is further confirmed by Luke's treatment of Paul's founding visit in Acts 18:1–17, as well as by *1 Clement*, a letter from the church at Rome to the church at Corinth written toward the end of the first century. Taken together, Paul's letters written to and from Corinth, Luke's testimony in Acts, and *1 Clement* enable us to know more about this single Pauline congregation than any other first-century church.

Especially remarkable is how much detailed information we have about the persons who comprised the church, their comings and goings, their socio-economic status, their ethnic composition, and in many cases their names. For this reason the Corinthian church has lent itself to modern sociological analysis in a way no other first-century church has. **[See Expanded CD Version pp. 420–21:** *Selection or Compilation? The Literary Coherence of Paul's Letters to the Corinthians***]**

Relating the Letters to the Church's Story

Since the Corinthian letters reveal so much about the church's circumstances and its relationship to Paul, getting at the theology *in* the letters, or even the theology *of* the letters, requires some understanding, however hypothetical, of the Corinthian church's story. Our construal of that story, in turn, is inevitably shaped by decisions we make about the literary integrity of the letters. If we read 1–2 Corinthians as two single letters addressed to the church at different stages in Paul's interaction with them, we will read the church's situation one way. If, on the other hand, we see a series of several letters written over an extended period, we will read the situation of the Corinthians differently.

This is especially the case if we rearrange the chronological sequence of the sections. If we identify 2 Cor 10–13 with the "tearful letter" written shortly after the painful visit, and 2 Cor 1–9 as the "letter of reconciliation" written after the "tearful letter" had had its cauterizing effect on the church, the story has a happier ending. If, by contrast, we read 2 Cor 10–13 as a later letter, perhaps written just before Paul makes his "third visit," we are presented with a more difficult ending, perhaps but not necessarily resolved, in which Paul finally arrives in Corinth to finish the collection and stays for a short while before departing for Jerusalem.

For this reason, it is necessary to provide, however tentatively, some sketch of Paul's relationship to the church as reflected in these letters.

Paul's Founding Visit

Several times in the Corinthian letters Paul refers to his initial visit when he started the church at Corinth. Insisting that he had not overstepped his limits in coming to them but rather had full authority to make this visit, he claims to have been the "first to come all the way to [them] with the good news of Christ" (2 Cor 10:14). He insists that he, along with his co-workers Silvanus and Timothy, had proclaimed the Son of God to them (2 Cor 1:19), and elsewhere locates "Christ and him crucified" at the center of his missionary preaching (1 Cor 2:1–5). Along with the "good news" he transmitted to them (1 Cor 15:1–3), as would be expected on a founding visit, he also introduced early Christian traditions about worship (1 Cor 11:2), especially Jesus' institution of the Lord's Supper (1 Cor 11:23). All of this he regarded as elementary Christian teaching, food suitable for infants who were ready only for milk, not meat (1 Cor 3:1–2).

While among them, Paul had personally baptized some of the more prominent members of the church, including Crispus, Gaius, and the "first converts in Achaia," the household of Stephanas (1 Cor 1:14–16; 16:15). Paul uses several metaphors to describe his founding work: he is their "father through the gospel" (1 Cor 4:15), the one who "planted" the church (1 Cor 3:6–9), and the one who, by preaching Christ, had laid its sole foundation (1 Cor 3:10–11). He calls the church his "work in the Lord" and the "seal of [his] apostleship" (1 Cor 9:1–2). It was presumably during this founding visit that he performed among them the "signs of a true apostle . . . signs and wonders and mighty works" (2 Cor 12:12), which reinforce his earlier claim that his missionary preaching had been supported "with a demonstration of the Spirit and of power" (1 Cor 2:4). During this time, he proclaimed the gospel "free of charge," insisting that he "robbed other churches" by accepting financial support from them while he was ministering in Corinth. Specifically named are the "brothers [NRSV: "friends"] who came from Macedonia" to supply his needs (2 Cor 11:7–9; cf. 2 Cor 12:13).

Several of these details are confirmed by Luke's brief account of Paul's founding visit, written several decades later (Acts 18:1–17): the collaborative efforts of Paul's co-workers Silas and Timothy, Jesus the Messiah as the focus of Paul's preaching, and the mention of the synagogue officials Crispus and Sosthenes. Other details in the Acts account are new: the role of Aquila and Priscilla as founding members (cf. 1 Cor 16:19), opposition by the Jews, Paul's appearance before the proconsul Gallio, the mention of Titius Justus, and the length of Paul's stay as eighteen months.

Events Following Paul's Departure from Corinth

In the letters, Paul does not indicate why he decided to leave Corinth, but he recognizes Apollos as his successor responsible for the second stage of the church's growth (1 Cor 3:6). This is confirmed by the more detailed account in Acts, which reports Apollos's conversion by Aquila and Priscilla in Ephesus and his subsequent arrival in Corinth (Acts 18:24–28; 19:1). Clearly, Apollos was an important presence within the church (1 Cor 1:12; 3:4–5, 21–22; 4:6). At the time 1 Corinthians was written, Apollos was no longer at Corinth, but with Paul in Ephesus (1 Cor 16:12).

Whereas Acts traces Paul's movements from Corinth to Ephesus and reports an extended Ephesian ministry lasting three years (Acts 18:18–19; 20:31), in his letters Paul does not explain how he came to Ephesus. But he was there when he wrote 1 Corinthians (1 Cor 16:8) and possibly parts of 2 Corinthians.

While at Ephesus, Paul and the Corinthian church remained in contact with each other. He wrote a letter to the church—the "previous letter"—cautioning them against associating with sexually immoral people (1 Cor 5:9). Members of the Corinthian church, including Stephanas, Fortunatus, and Achaicus, visited Paul at Ephesus (1 Cor 16:17), perhaps bringing the letter from the church asking Paul to deal with several matters (1 Cor 7:1). He also received a report from "Chloe's people," presumably in person, of dissensions within the church (1 Cor 1:11). At least one other anonymous report, perhaps more, had reached him (1 Cor 5:1). At some point Paul had also sent Timothy as his emissary to remind the church of his "ways in Christ" (1 Cor 4:17; 16:10–11). We are not sure of the sequence of these various communications, but they suggest a period of ongoing contact between Paul and the church that must have lasted for several months.

The Writing and Reception of 1 Corinthians

What we know as 1 Corinthians may be read as a single composition, probably written over an extended period of time. In this letter Paul addressed the several concerns relayed to him in various reports and answered the questions about which the church had written. The letter presupposes a considerable level of tension within the church. There is some indication that the church as a whole does not recognize Paul's apostolic authority. The situation, while deeply troubling, appears remediable.

The sources of the tension are difficult to pinpoint. Socio-economic differences were a contributing factor, along with the church's mixed ethnic composition. Differences in attitude and theological beliefs also figured into the mix, but it is difficult to correlate particular sets of attitudes and beliefs with socio-economic and ethnic groupings. Even so, Paul's persistent critique of those who considered themselves spiritually enlightened suggests that a significant portion of the Corinthians were pursuing wisdom and knowledge in ways that closely resembled Hellenistic forms of religious and philosophical piety. While their enchantment with the "higher mysteries" does not deserve to be called Gnosticism as it came to be understood from the second century onward, this viewpoint represents the beginning of that trajectory. In this highly qualified sense, the Corinthian outlook reflected in 1 Corinthians is "proto-Gnostic."

Several times Paul mentions an intended visit when he will be able to give more detailed responses to their questions and when, if necessary, he will exert more direct force in trying to resolve the tensions within the church (1 Cor 4:19–20; 11:34; 16:2–3). His plans to send Timothy to Corinth also figure in his strategy to remain in contact with the church (1 Cor 4:17; 16:10–11). Toward the end of the letter, he lays out his travel plans: He will remain in Ephesus until Pentecost (in the spring); once he leaves, he will visit Macedonia first, then come to Corinth, possibly to spend the winter, but hoping to "spend some time" with them (1 Cor 16:5–12). When, how, and by whom 1 Corinthians was delivered to Corinth is not known, but it was received by the church and probably read aloud to the church by its courier. Having heard it read, the church would have felt instructed, encouraged, and warned, and they would now be expecting a visit from Paul shortly. They would also have been encouraged to proceed with their efforts to gather the collection for the saints in Jerusalem. [**See Expanded CD Version pp. 424–28: *Events after 1 Corinthians: Evidence from 2 Corinthians***]

A Proposed Reconstruction of Events after 1 Corinthians

The events referred to in 2 Cor 1–7 reflect the circumstances that followed the church's receipt of 1 Corinthians: a visit to the church by Paul that turned out badly, primarily owing to a confrontation with an unnamed individual; his trip via Corinth to Macedonia, where he decided not to return through Corinth; and his return to Ephesus, whereupon he writes the "tearful letter," which is now lost. Since Titus was its courier, he became the primary intermediary between Paul and the church at this point.

Upon leaving Ephesus and going to Troas, Paul is extremely worried about how the letter was received. Since he does not hear from Titus and therefore cannot even preach, he goes to Macedonia, where Titus finally arrives with a positive report: the "tearful letter" had done its work and the church had expressed appropriate regret. Paul then writes 2 Cor 1–7, and possibly even 2 Cor 8–9. Both parts, especially chapters 1–7, reflect the "consolation" Paul now enjoys, suggesting a mood of great relief. This too is delivered by Titus to the church while Paul remains in Macedonia for the winter.

Meanwhile, the Jewish Christian missionaries who had arrived earlier in Corinth from elsewhere, bringing with them letters of recommendation and asking for and receiving financial support from the church, intensify their efforts to gain the church's support. The timing could not have been worse: Paul is trying to complete the collection for the poor saints in Jerusalem; the Corinthian church had begun to collect their part a year earlier, and now their resources are being siphoned off by these unexpected interlopers. Paul finds their methods, which he characterizes as "peddling the gospel," contemptible, and their message even more reprehensible, the antithesis of how he understands the gospel message of Jesus and the Spirit.

Stung by Paul's exposition of his ministerial theology in 2 Cor 2:14–7:1, which directly challenged their theological basis for ministry, Paul's opponents naturally claim legitimacy for their presence in Corinth, a legitimacy he violently protests. While we see the opponents only through Paul's eyes, they appear to have been denigrating him personally as a strong letter writer but a weak speaker whose apostolic credentials were suspect in the first place.

Prompted by these ad hominem attacks, Paul responds with the severely polemical letter we know as 2 Cor 10–13. In this frontal assault on his opponents, Paul answers their charges, defends his apostleship, and even plays the fool by parading both the tribulations he has suffered for the sake of the gospel and his mystical experiences, all the while begging, like an anxious father, for the Corinthians to return to his fold. In the end, he is not optimistic, convinced that when he arrives for his third visit (2 Cor 12:14; 13:1), he may find an even sorrier state of affairs than when he wrote 1 Corinthians.

The Aegean Region

0   50   100
Miles

0   50   100
Kilometers

N

Black Sea

THRACE

MACEDONIA

Pella
Philippi
Neapolis

Thessalonica

Propontis

Beroea

Thasos

Samothrace

Thermaic Gulf

Troas
Assos

Pergamum

Aegean Sea

Lesbos

ASIA

Delphi

Euboea

Chios

Smyrna
Sardis

Gulf of Corinth

Patrae

ACHAIA

Ephesus

Laodicea

Corinth
Cenchreae
Athens

Miletus

Patmos

Myrtoan Sea

Cos

Rhodes

Crete

Mediterranean Sea

That he finally made the third trip to Corinth is almost certain. If Rom 15–16 is any indication (assuming that Romans was written in Corinth shortly after Paul's arrival there), the Corinthians did finally complete their part in the collection, since Paul is poised to travel to Jerusalem to deliver it. Worth noting is the probability that this intense controversy between Paul and his opponents in Corinth also informed his writing of Romans (and possibly Galatians).

1 Corinthians: What the Cross Means[1]

Paul's Opening Appeal: Understanding the Implications of the Cross (Chs. 1–4)

Paul begins the letter with a formal appeal in which he encourages the church to embody a form of fellowship that appropriately expresses their identity "in Christ." The first section of the letter opens with a call for unity (1:10) and concludes by inviting the church to imitate Paul (4:16). Convinced that some truly destructive attitudes and behaviors existed within the church, Paul adopts a carefully crafted strategy aimed directly at the offenders, but one designed to challenge them without alienating them.

While his strategy has practical implications, it is not merely an exercise in conflict management. It is rather built around an extended, thoughtfully conceived exposition of early Christian preaching, whose central focus was the crucified Christ (2:2). As a set of critical reflections on this basic element of Christian faith, these remarks deserve to be called *theologia crucis*, for here we find Paul not simply preaching the cross but elaborating his theology of the cross.

Since his remarks are prompted by a very specific set of circumstances—tension and strife within the Corinthian congregation—they are rightly viewed as situational theology or even as problem-based theology. The Corinthians' troubled situation provides the catalyst requiring Paul to reflect even more critically about the Christ event, but it also sets the terms within which he does so. The situation informs and shapes his theological reflections even as his theological reflections inform and shape the situation.

Rather than being torn asunder by deep ideological differences, the Christians at Corinth are experiencing internal strife arising from conflicting loyalties to different teachers. Tension exists at the level of "envy and jealousy" rather than doctrinal belief. It is the existence of a fractured community that prompts Paul's rhetorical question: "Has Christ been divided?" (1:13). If the congregation is the "body of Christ," once crucified but now living, how can it be dismembered? It either exists as a unified organism or it does not exist at all.

What determines whether the congregation is the body of Christ? How it understands and lives out the faith it confesses. More specifically, how the "message about the cross" is lived out. Since patterns of behavior reflect patterns of belief, Paul begins with the core proclamation: Christ crucified. The death of Christ may be experienced by those who respond to the gospel as a saving event (15:2), but Paul wants to move the Corinthians' understanding of Christ's death to another level.

Because the term "cross" (*stauros*) captures the inescapable scandal associated with Jesus' death, it symbolizes God's paradoxical character as one who subverts human construals of the world. The cross is not only about Christ; it tells us something about God as well. As a lens through which the character of God can be seen, the cross reveals a way of thinking about God and how God relates to humanity that, for Paul, constitutes a new way of knowing God—the ultimate human quest (1:21).

The cross poses an alternative to traditional ways of relating to God. When Paul says that "Jews demand signs and Greeks desire wisdom" (1:22), he is speaking not as an ethnographer but as a theologian. As he well knew, not every Jew whiled away the time waiting for a miracle to happen any more than every Greek awoke each morning looking for an argument, although there are plenty of miracles in the OT and a lot of attention given to rhetoric and logic by Greek philosophers.

"Signs" and "wisdom" instead symbolize two contrasting epistemologies, two fundamentally different ways of knowing God. In the one case, God stands at the end of a miracle, in the other, at the end of a syllogism. One places a high premium on shows of divine force, the other on human wisdom as an avenue to God. Yet both epistemologies are wrongly conceived, Paul insists, primarily because they see God through human construals of the world. The cross, by contrast, reveals a God who refuses to conform to human logic and human norms for measuring effectiveness. As the place where neither power nor reason reigned, the cross becomes an enacted symbol of God's paradoxical character. In terms that the world fails to grasp, Christ redefines how "power of God" and "wisdom of God" are understood (1:24). Since the cross inverts human values in the way it makes suffering redemptive and sees self-abnegation as a response to brute force, those who "belong to Christ" embody a set of values and a way of construing the world that radically challenge ordinary human expectations.

God's paradoxical character is seen no more vividly than in the Corinthians' own conversion and in Paul's own preaching. In the former case, God had very little to work with, humanly speaking, yet performed a miracle against all odds (1:26–31); in the latter, Paul's preaching and manner of life reflected neither confidence nor artful rhetorical skill, but found their sources of strength elsewhere: from the power of God's Spirit (2:1–5).

Just as the cross exposes a hidden side of God, so also does it open a window onto God's Spirit. Judged by ordinary human wisdom, the cross appears to be an act of folly. It seems neither logical nor compelling. But this is to view it within a limited scope. Seen against the broad sweep of God's eternal purpose, whose full scope and depth are hidden from human eyes, the cross reveals a higher mystery, "God's wisdom, secret and hidden," accessible not for those who *know* but for those who *love* God (2:7, 9).

At one level, the cross was an act of blind stupidity carried out by those in power—"rulers"—with narrow vision limited to "this age"; at another, much higher level, it exposed One with a broader view, who could achieve the divine purpose in spite of human ignorance masquerading as wisdom. Seeing the cross this way requires a special guide who, like no one else, knows the hidden paths that lead to God's eternal purpose—God's Spirit, given to lovers of God as interpreter, revealer, and teacher of God's ways. Not everyone sees this "other dimension" revealed by the cross. Operating with an outlook shaped by "the spirit of the world" (2:12), they are two-dimensional figures living in a three-dimensional world.

Where do such capacities for spiritual discernment originate? From the "mind of Christ" (2:16). In view is an outlook that *thinks like Christ* and *thinks through Christ*, that sees Christ as exemplifying a way of living faithfully before God but also as a medium of divine revelation. A mind thus configured sees the cross as an alternative epistemology to conventional ways of knowing God, as an event exposing God as one who acts paradoxically and surprisingly, and as a symbol through which the Spirit reveals the secrets of God's eternal purpose.

If the cross symbolizes a new way of knowing, how does this shape one's understanding of the Christian community? For one thing, it radically redefines how loyalty to Christian teachers and leaders is understood. To belong to someone like Paul or Apollos easily edges toward a form of idolatry in which a follower relates to a leader in terms of ultimate loyalty. Not only does this tend to idolize the leader and turn discipleship into a form of blind submission, but it also renders leaders as competing gods in a larger pantheon. A religious community so defined is an expression of human inclinations, and inevitably breeds jealousy and quarreling (3:3).

In a community where the cross establishes the angle of vision, the role of teachers and leaders is relativized, for they are seen not as competitors but as collaborators in a larger enterprise that belongs to God: They are God's servants working in God's field (3:9). As God's building, the congregation of believers is no ordinary structure; it is rather an inescapably sacred structure, God's temple, whose foundation is Jesus Christ (3:11) and whose energizing presence is God's own Spirit (3:16). As such, it is not a home for the world's wisdom. It is rather a place that creates a hierarchy in which Christian teachers and leaders like Paul, Apollos, and Cephas are at the disposal of the whole church and are seen as part of the great chain of being linked first with Christ, and ultimately with God.

The epistemology of the cross has another implication. It allows the congregation to see that what is needed is not absolute loyalty to a particular teacher or leader, but the ability to discern whether their teachers' and leaders' lives and ministries transparently reflect the way of the cross. Such an outlook enables believers to pose a different set of questions about their teachers and leaders: Are they faithful stewards of the divine mysteries with which they are entrusted? By which court do they live, the human court where the world's wisdom reigns, or the higher court of God, who stands at the end of history? Do they exemplify the world's values—the urge to dominate, to acquire, to prize honor, wealth, and strength? Or do they exemplify the values symbolized by the cross?

What emerges in the opening section of the letter is a carefully constructed exposition of Paul's theology of the cross that establishes the theological underpinnings of the rest of the letter. Convinced that the tensions and divisions within the church can be resolved only if some fundamental shifts in thinking occur, Paul sees the message of the cross as offering such a possibility. For him, it represents a radically new way of thinking about God that, if taken seriously, fundamentally alters the way his readers see the world.

What is this new epistemology? It recognizes God as truly sovereign, One whose character and actions are unique, in no way answerable to the court of human opinion. Correlatively, it recognizes the inherent limitations of human wisdom and power—human ways of thinking and human ways of ordering the world—and thus precludes attributing ultimate loyalty to them; it refuses to idolize them. It finds God emphatically yet mysteriously revealed through the death of the crucified Messiah, neither a sensible event nor a dramatic show of divine force, but one with its own ironic logic and magnetic power that can be understood properly only from God's angle of vision, thus as "God's power and God's wisdom."

Since "crucified Messiah" is itself a contradiction in terms, the cross inverts human expectations by challenging human construals of God's actions. It offers instead a violent death that is redemptive because love overcame brute force. An event with which others can identify, it is also one in which they can participate and thereby create a new order of humanity. Since God's ways are truly inscrutable, they can be revealed only by God's own Spirit, who interprets God's character and actions to believers. God, Christ, and the Spirit are the primary players in this new epistemology.

Behaving Responsibly as a Community of Faith (Chs. 5–6)

Once this epistemological vision is sketched, Paul can proceed to address concrete problems within the church. Before answering their questions, he first turns to some internal matters affecting their congregational life (chs. 5–6). Two topics are dealt with: sexual behavior (5:1–13; 6:12–20) and settling internal disputes before civil courts (6:1–11). Of greater concern to Paul than the specific persons involved in the problematic marriage or the civil dispute is the congregation's responses to both. For him, the cases raise deeply troubling questions about how the congregation understands itself. Rather than targeting the individuals involved, Paul addresses the congregation as a whole, inviting them to reflect on how their response (or their lack of response) to these situations reflects their shallow theological view of themselves. Their behaviors, in his view, are incompatible with the new epistemology sketched in chapters 1–4.

As Paul diagnoses their situation, he sees the congregation acting as an essentially secular community. He accuses them of adopting sexual standards even lower than those of their pagan neighbors and using pagan courts to settle internal civil disputes, presumably in a manner their pagan neighbors would employ. And if we take the slogans printed in quotation marks in English translations of 6:12–13 as expressions of attitudes within the Corinthian church, the members would appear to be justifying their behavior using the language of natural law and pragmatic ethics: individual rights and a functional view of the body. For them, sexual activity, like eating, is a bodily function, nothing more. Their words and actions betray their secular communal self-understanding. Thoroughly lacking, at least from Paul's portrayal of their attitudes and actions, is any transcendent view or any real understanding of the community as a sacred fellowship.

His correctives are sketched in light of the new epistemology. If Christ died as our "paschal lamb" (5:7), the community should see itself as an "unleavened community" free of defilement, like a community observing Passover. Its congregational conduct should reflect a more amplified understanding of Christ's death. Failure to recognize such an egregious case of misconduct within its own midst reflects the congregation's utter failure to grasp the significance of Christ's death.

Similarly, if the congregation is composed of people who fled the kingdom of the world to become members of the kingdom of God, thereby entering the realm of God, Christ, and the Spirit, how can it turn over its sensitive internal matters to outsiders who represent the very world they rejected and are ignorant of the dynamics operative in a community of the Spirit? And how can those who believe in a sovereign God, who breathe God's Spirit, and who are part of a community that sees itself as indissolubly linked with the risen Christ define their behavior in such naturalistic terms? Can they not see that the body has a transcendent dimension and that what one does with the body has implications beyond the sphere of the self?

Like the congregation itself, the Christian's body is a temple, a sacred space hallowed by the presence of God's Spirit. Rather than using the body thoughtlessly and indiscriminately, the Christian should operate with a sense of the self commensurate with its high purchase price. The Christian should value the body as a sacred trust.

Answering the Corinthians' Questions (Chs. 7–16)

In the latter part of the letter, beginning with 7:1, four questions submitted by the Corinthians are prominent: marital relations (ch. 7), eating food that had been offered as sacrifice (chs. 8–10), spiritual gifts (chs. 12–14), and the collection (16:1–4). In addition, questions pertaining to worship (ch. 11) and the resurrection (ch. 15) are also addressed. While these questions reflect different kinds of concerns—some dealing primarily with issues of behavior, others with matters of belief, and still others a combination of both—Paul's responses may be seen as working out the implications of his exposition of the cross in the opening chapter. The texture of his theological exposition varies because the nature of the issues varies, yet some common elements emerge. Two examples will suffice. [See **Expanded CD Version p. 434: *Marital Relations (1 Cor 7)*]**

1. *Eating Sacrificial Food (1 Cor 8–10)*. Within a religious community composed of converted Jews and Gentiles, different attitudes toward pagan worship were bound to exist. Those who had left paganism could still feel some affinity with older forms of worship they had left behind, while monotheistic Jews were inclined to sneer at idol worship. What should Christians do when faced with an opportunity to participate in a meal either in a pagan temple (8:10) or a private home (10:27) where meat from an animal that had been slaughtered for use in pagan sacrifice would be served? Was such meat tainted? Given the different backgrounds of the members of the church, different attitudes were inevitable. Since no clear guidelines appear to have been in force, a way forward needed to be found.

Finding that he must negotiate between two opposing positions, the spiritually mature, "enlightened" members and those with weaker consciences, Paul once again shapes a response informed by his theology of the cross. Human wisdom would see the primary issue as one of individual freedom, whereas the wisdom of the cross identifies the issue as the nature of Christian community.

Granting that there are certain things Christians know, Paul also insists that there are different levels of knowing and that some calculus for negotiating between various levels of spiritual maturity must be found. One solution would be for the spiritually enlightened to stake a claim on what's certain—belief in the one God that denies the existence of other gods—and pull the less enlightened in their direction, from a position of weakness to a position of strength. In this scenario, the strong would eat and the weak would not eat, but when the weak reached a higher level of spiritual maturity, they too would eat. But Paul recognizes other considerations, among them the genuine threat posed by the worship of idols not only to the weak but also to the strong. Also, for him, the freedom of the individual must be balanced with the corporate good.

What is striking throughout his discussion is the way he argues for a more enriched theological understanding of the Christian community. His remarks may be seen as the working out of the two elements of the Christian creed summarized in 8:6: "there is one God, the Father, from whom are all things and for whom we exist, and one Lord, Jesus Christ, through whom are all things and through whom we exist." What form of Christian community best expresses these twin beliefs? Above all, it must be a community in which clear boundaries are drawn between monotheistic and polytheistic belief (8:4–6; 10:1–22), but it must also be a community that exists through Jesus Christ.

The contours of the church's life together must reflect both of these convictions, and we find them woven together throughout Paul's argument in chapters 8–10. The death of Christ, understood properly, embraces everyone, strong and weak alike (8:11). For the strong to behave in ways that jeopardize the faith of the weaker members is to sin against them (8:12). Since the entire church exists "through Christ," and thereby shares jointly in its fellowship with Christ, such an action is a "sin against Christ" (8:12). So understood, the church is not a community of free agents with a "survival of the fittest" mentality, but a family in which the action of one affects the others and the actions of all relate to Christ.

The "wisdom of the world" also regards self-confidence and independent choice as marks of spiritual strength. It also sees pagan worship as no real threat, since the question of belief in one God has already been decided. But the "wisdom of the cross" recognizes that such self-confidence borders on arrogance and must be tempered with a collective consciousness that reaches back to Israel's past and remembers the seductive power of idol worship (10:1–13).

Even the strong should be warned to "flee from the worship of idols" (10:14), as should be evident from the experience of Christian worship. A sacred meal, properly understood, must be seen as an event in which the worshiper and the cult god become bonded together. To eat with someone, especially a deity, is more than a casual meal. Since believers through the death of Christ are linked with Christ and each other, they face a critical choice. Choosing between the Lord's meal and a pagan meal honoring a competing lord is an either-or choice (10:20–22). One cannot be blasé in negotiating the boundaries between competing visions of the world.

The urge to be free is rooted in knowing. Knowing the Christian confession and being experienced in the religious life breed a desire for individual independence. But knowing also breeds arrogance—"knowledge puffs up" (8:1)—and the countervailing impulse within a Christian community is loving—"love builds up" (8:1). The "wisdom of the world" values the former, the "wisdom of the cross" the latter, since it develops the capacity to embrace the weak and fuels the ability to seek the advantage of the other instead of one's own advantage (10:24). In cultivating this outlook, the community reflects the "mind of Christ."

What gives Paul's argument in chapters 8–10 special force is his own personal example. Insisting that he takes his cue from Christ (11:1), he pursues his apostolic ministry as one "under Christ's law" (9:21), and he exhibits the behavior that he is calling the strong to exemplify: willingness to relinquish his individual freedom for the sake of a greater good (ch. 9). **[See Expanded CD Version pp. 436–38: *Spiritual Gifts (1 Cor 12–14); The Collection (1 Cor 16:1–4); Worship (1 Cor 11:2–34)*]**

2. The Resurrection (1 Cor 15). Confronted with the report that some were saying "there is no resurrection of the dead" (15:12), Paul could hardly respond in a non-theological manner. A theological question demanded a theological answer. Whether the doubters were denying a future resurrection ("Having died and arisen with Christ, we are already experiencing resurrection"), the resurrection of the body ("Only the soul is immortal; the body decomposes"), or any form of afterlife ("There is no life of any kind after death") is not clear.

Quite clear, however, is Paul's theological strategy. He might have appealed to Pharisaic theology as a strong precedent for believing in a final resurrection of the dead, thus arguing that Christian belief by extension had good grounds for doing so. Yet as we have seen before, his instinct is to focus on the Christ event itself, and from there argue outward, as it were. Reciting a summary of the early Christian kerygma at the outset (15:1–11) has the same effect as reciting the Eucharistic tradition in chapter 11: the readers are reminded of the basis for their salvation. As a community of the risen Lord, they now embody what they had believed and confessed. Christ's resurrection is a given, and no one appears to have questioned whether or how it had occurred. If one denies resurrection in principle, Paul argues, this would eliminate belief in Christ's resurrection as a particular instance of resurrection. To do so would undermine the foundation of Christian belief.

Paul also appeals to nature: If a grain of wheat can "die" by being buried in the ground and shooting forth in another form, so can a human being (15:35–41). Their inconsistent practice is also introduced: Why baptize on behalf of the dead if there is no resurrection (15:29)? More compelling as a theological argument is his interpretation of Christ as the second Adam (15:42–49). Once again Paul returns to the Genesis story to make sense of the Christ event. If the first man, Adam, can be understood as a representative figure, someone who stands at the head of an order of humanity, why cannot Christ be so understood? The major difference is that the first Adam was a "living being," the second Adam a "life-giving spirit" (15:45). Whereas Adam symbolized death's entrance into the world, Christ became the symbol of life and hope. Modern readers may not find Paul's exegesis compelling, but no one can deny the thoroughly theological manner in which he argues. As before, Christ's resurrection is not merely an exaltation to God's right hand, but the prelude—or to use Paul's metaphor, the "firstfruits"—of a future resurrection. The Corinthians must reckon with a future defined by God's action in Christ.

Given Paul's theology of the church as the body of Christ (ch. 12) and his conviction that the church's destiny is inextricably connected with Christ's own destiny, it is hardly surprising that he calls the church to "stretch the kerygma" into its own communal life. The Corinthian believers are asked to hold beliefs and engage in practices that were consonant with the faith to which they were initially summoned when Paul preached the "word of the cross," a faith they continually celebrated in the ongoing preaching of the Word and observance of the Table. In short, he is calling them to exhibit a form of congregational life that befits the "word of the cross."

2 Corinthians: Doing Theology in the Context of Ministry

Getting at Paul's theology in 2 Corinthians presents a special challenge because his theological reflections are so closely intertwined with highly personal matters related to his ministry with the church. To some extent, this is the case in every Pauline letter, since his theological beliefs, practices, and behaviors are so deeply rooted in who he is and what he does as an apostle. In one sense, two conversations are going on simultaneously in 2 Corinthians: a conversation with the church about everyday matters—travel plans, daily pressures, congregational crises, battles with other ministers, working with associates, raising money—and a conversation with and about God. The second conversation so thoroughly informs the first that trying to extract Paul's "theology" from his richly textured conversation with the Corinthians does an injustice to both the theology *in* the letter and the theology *of* the letter.

In the first part of the letter, for example, Paul explains the reasons for his change in travel plans, which had prompted criticisms of his "vacillating" and seemingly indecisive ministerial style (1:17). He instinctively speaks in theological terms that emphasize God's fidelity: Christ Jesus, the Son of God, God's "Yes," the one who fulfills all of God's promises, in whom believers express confidence by saying "Amen" in prayer (1:18–20). Then comes one of the most revealing formulations in the letter: "The one who strengthens us with you in Christ and who has anointed us is God, who has also set his seal upon us and, as a pledge of what is to come, has given his Spirit to dwell in our hearts" (1:21–22 REB, adapted).

Here God is the One who joins minister(s) and church in an inseparable bond: through God's past action—anointing them with the Spirit in baptism—they have received a common identity. Through God's continuing empowerment in Christ, they are able to live as faithful disciples. By identifying God, Christ, and the Spirit as the shaping forces of their faith—the three nodes around which any Christian community is formed—Paul establishes the triadic character of their communal existence. Not surprisingly, his concluding benediction acknowledges these three girders of their common identity: "The grace of the Lord Jesus Christ, the love of God, and the communion of the Holy Spirit be with all of you" (13:13).

Paul's life as an apostolic minister and the church's experience as a community of faith show how the benediction actually comes to life. What began as an explanation of cancelled travel plans ends with a profoundly theological formulation of how Paul understands the living bond that exists between a church and its minister(s).

What characterizes 2 Corinthians is how the messiness of congregational ministry consistently serves as the catalyst for Paul's theological reflections. So closely is his theological discourse interwoven with his treatment of practical matters that it is virtually impossible to separate them. Whether we envision Paul as a missionary/pastor thinking out loud theologically as he nurtures a difficult church toward greater levels of Christian maturity, or as someone engaged in experimental theology developing ad hoc theological responses to a constantly changing congregational situation, we see something emerge besides systematic theology, in which theological beliefs and practices are conceived and presented in some well-ordered scheme. The only systematic feature of Paul's theologizing is how he does it. In the heat of ministerial practice, his basic theological convictions are tested even as he develops formulations that expand these convictions to address new questions and situations. [See Expanded CD Version p. 440: *Further Examination of How Congregational Life and Apostolic Ministry Are Intertwined*]

Because Paul stands so squarely within God's action in Christ, living by it and within it, he instinctively thinks out of it. However ordinary the question before him might seem to us, it consistently serves as a catalyst for theological reflection. To think theologically as he deals with the practical matters of ministry is second nature to Paul; indeed, it is these seemingly everyday problems that help give his theological insights their sharp edge. This is especially evident in 2:14–6:10, the section in which he reflects at some length on his theology of ministry. Because this section is bracketed by discussions of his travel plans and other personal matters (1:12–2:13 and 6:11–13; 7:2–16), it is often read as an independent section, perhaps composed separately and later inserted at this point in the letter. But if the close interweaving of personal and theological is such a pervasive pattern in 2 Corinthians, we should perhaps be more cautious in reading it as a separate, self-contained section. Even so, as a matter of convenience, we now turn to it.

Authentic Ministry (2 Cor 2:14–6:10)

What does it mean to be called into the service (*diakonia*) of the gospel? On behalf of himself and his larger circle of associates, Paul supplies an extended answer in 2 Cor 2:14–6:10. Since these remarks have a slightly polemical edge, he may have framed them in order to contrast his own understanding of ministry with other views of ministry that were circulating in the congregation. Even so, they are more in the spirit of thoughtful reflections on his theology of ministry than a response to charges that had been leveled against him. Writing in a highly compressed form that at times resembles shorthand, Paul explains why he does what he does. While many of the theological themes found here are elaborated more fully in his other letters, nowhere else does Paul reflect on ministry in such a detailed, thoughtful manner. Rather than reflecting a clear, logically ordered arrangement, his remarks explore some of the basic presuppositions and themes that informed his apostolic ministry.

If ancient manuscript chapter headings are any indication, the section should begin with 2:12, in which Paul mentions his inability to follow through on a mission opportunity at Troas because of his anxiety over Titus's failure to arrive with news from Corinth. If so, the remarks that follow would be prompted, once again, by "ordinary" ministerial concerns. And in any case, that is their canonical context.

Ministerial Sincerity (2 Cor 2:14–17). If ministers are captives in a triumphal procession who, as Christ's incense, make God known wherever they go—a fragrant smell to sympathetic listeners, a foul odor to sneering detractors—they can hardly take their role lightly, much less adulterate God's message by peddling it like cheap goods. A high sense of calling precludes a low sense of worth, and low motives as well.

As those who speak "from God before God in Christ" (2:17, literally rendered), ministers position themselves in the very space Christ occupied: as those sent "from God" they have God's full authority, and by doing their work "in the presence of God" they operate in full view of God. Paul stretches the metaphor of God's triumphal procession in some unusual directions. Probably drawing on the underlying metaphor of Christ's death as a sacrifice for sins, Paul portrays ministers as God's representatives who march with Christ at the end of the procession. As such, they are "handed over to death" and thereby share his destiny. This graphic image, drawn from everyday life in the Roman world, is crafted not to develop an elaborate Christology but to produce and reinforce an elevated view of ministry. One cannot function as "Christ's aroma," the smoke that arises before God from the sacrificial death of Jesus, an aroma salvific to some, lethal to others, without developing a profound sense of responsibility before God. To do otherwise, in Paul's view, is ministerial malpractice.

Ministerial Credentials: Moses and Christ, Old and New Covenant (2 Cor 3:1–18). The practical problem Paul addresses here is that of letters of recommendation used to introduce ministers to churches. Does authentic ministry turn on having strong letters, or are there better ways of deciding? Other teachers had come to Corinth bearing strong letters of introduction to certify their credentials, and to that extent they were challenging Paul's credentials. At one level it is an ordinary question, but one with potentially serious consequences. Rather than dealing with the question pragmatically—producing a letter written on his behalf that the church could compare with the other letters—Paul responds theologically. What finally authenticates ministry, Paul insists, are the ways God, Christ, and the Spirit are present (or absent) within the minister's church. More important than what is written "with ink" is what

The Apostle Paul. A woodcut by Lucas Cranach, the Elder (1472–1553), from *Hortulus animae*, a Lutheran prayer book (Wittenberg, 1550). From the Digital Image Archive of The Richard C. Kessler Reformation Collection, Pitts Theology Library, Candler School of Theology, Emory University, Atlanta, Georgia.

"the Spirit of the living God" has written in the church's heart(s). Divine action is what makes the church a "letter of Christ" (3:3)—a living, publicly accessible document, legible to everyone—delivered but not written by Paul.

God—not Paul or any other minister or teacher, certainly no written document—finally certifies authentic ministry. Why? Because God, through Christ, decided to relate to humanity no longer through the "letter" of the Mosaic law that was "chiseled in letters on stone tablets" but through the Spirit (3:7). What prompts Paul's midrashic exposition of Exod 34:29–35, the account of God's giving the law at Sinai, is an ordinary question: ministerial credentials and letters of introduction. Yet what results is a penetrating critique of the law that provides the rationale for his ministry in the service of Christ. The hard edge of his extended exposition should not be missed. Moses and Christ are seen as polar opposites, representing two different eras, two dispensations, contrasted in the sharpest possible terms:

Moses	Christ
Old covenant (3:14)	New covenant (3:6)
Letter (3:6)	Spirit (3:6)
Death (3:6-7)	Life (3:6)
Ministry of death (3:7)	Ministry of the Spirit (3:8)
Ministry of condemnation (3:9)	Ministry of justification (3:9)
Glory (3:10)	Greater glory (3:10)
Temporary (3:10)	Permanent (3:11)

For all of its splendor—and Paul readily concedes that the giving of the law at Sinai was a splendid moment in Israel's history—the Mosaic covenant was fatally flawed, and God brought it to an end through Christ. As the one who made the promise of Jer 31:31–34 come true, Christ, the Yes to all of God's promises, introduced God's "new covenant" and rendered the Mosaic system an "old covenant." Christ stands at the midpoint of history, marking the end of Moses' era and the beginning of a new era. Given this construal of God's story, the era of Moses is seen as "fading splendor," a temporary arrangement that eventually yielded to the "permanent splendor" of Christ's era.

What marks the essential difference between these two eras or covenants? Paul contrasts them succinctly: letter (*gramma*) and spirit (*pneuma*). What Paul signifies by this pair of opposites is much debated. Possibly "letter" is just another way of saying "law" (cf. Rom 2:27, 29; 7:6), but it has special force here because it points to an agreement that was written down (2 Cor 3:7). It was given by God to Moses, thus it assuredly came from God in a moment of splendid revelation. Yet the true meaning of this written code remained obscure. Just as the Israelites' vision of Moses' dazzling radiance was blocked by the veil that covered his face, so is their understanding of Moses' law "veiled" when they hear it read. Somehow, what was written—"the letter"—failed to yield an unobstructed vision of God. This was achieved only by Christ, God's life-giving Spirit, who gives unmediated access to God by creating the free, unrestricted space between God and God's people. The result is a living bond stronger than anything written on paper or stone because it is sustained by a splendidly revealed God with whom transformed human hearts connect. Since Christ enables the "one who turns to the Lord" to encounter God's Spirit directly, those who serve as "ministers of the new covenant" are engaged in the "ministry of the Spirit" (2 Cor 3:8).

Seen through Paul's eyes—the eyes of a strictly observant Pharisee who had been transformed by God's life-giving Spirit through his experience of the risen Lord—the law of Moses was severely flawed. Trying to live under it, Paul had only experienced frustration, which is why he speaks of the "ministry of death" and the "ministry of condemnation." Under the law he had experienced death, but in Christ he experienced life; where he had only felt condemned under the law, in Christ he experienced God's fidelity and integrity—God's justification.

Since the old order has been set aside (2 Cor 3:11, 14) and is now superseded by the new order, in no way can Paul have truck with ministers who are aligned with the old order, even if they are doing so in the name of Christ and producing strong letters of recommendation to back them up. Since ministry of the new covenant involves God and the people of God in a relationship of an utterly different texture, both its message and methods must be equally distinctive. Above all, they must be congruent with Christ, God's life-giving Spirit.

Much of Paul's tightly compressed argument remains obscure, but the upshot of his remarks is quite clear: for whatever reason, "Moses," the written law and therefore the source of true knowledge about God, remains "veiled" to those who read (or hear) Torah without seeing it as bearing witness to God's work in Christ. In Christ, by contrast, it is possible to have an unobstructed view of God, one so dazzling that it transforms the one who views God into a mirror-image reflection of God.

What is the point of this extended theological exposition of the old and new covenants? To show that authentic ministry occurs when God's Spirit, experienced through Christ, transforms the hearts of those who fix their gaze on God's splendor. Finally, authentic ministry is neither confirmed nor disconfirmed by letters of recommendation, however glowing.

Ministerial Methods (2 Cor 4:1–6). In a sharply apologetic tone, Paul eschews a wide range of tactics used by his opponents: secrecy, cunning, and distortion. He rebuts charges that his own gospel was "veiled"—hard to understand—by accusing his detractors of having vision obstructed by "the god of this passing age" (4:4 REB), perhaps the idolized values of "human thinking" rather than evil personified as Satan. But what is actually being blocked when people try to obstruct Paul's ministry? Not Paul himself, since he is not the content of his own preaching: "we do not proclaim ourselves" (4:5). Instead, as those who "proclaim Jesus Christ as Lord," he and his associates are "your slaves for Jesus' sake"—a highly unusual expression, since he ordinarily characterizes himself as a "slave of Christ."

In the proclamation of the gospel, more happens than words passing over lips. As God's authentic minister, Paul has experienced the transformation of which he spoke earlier—confronting the dazzling splendor of God by looking, not at the veiled face of Moses, but at the "face of Jesus Christ" (4:6). In a revelatory event comparable to creation itself, when God brought light out of darkness, the gospel reveals Christ as the very "image of God," as the primal human who represents God's imprint in a way no one else has, and therefore serves as the master mold by which every human being "created in the image of God" can be measured.

This highly compressed theological exposition of God's action in Christ draws heavily on OT imagery (Gen 1:3–4; Ps 112:4; Job 37:15; Isa 9:2). It mixes imagery of new creation with the metaphor of light, which is used frequently in antiquity of divine revelation and put to a different use in John's Gospel. This exposition is done not as an end in itself, but to establish the parameters within which all ministerial action must be viewed. Such dazzling illumination that comes from God exposes all secrets, all underhanded methods, and all forms of deceit and distortion, regardless of how successful they seem. Given this understanding of God's revelation in Christ, "declaring the truth openly" (4:2 REB) is the only form of speech appropriate to authentic ministry.

Ministry Shaped by Christ: Living the Gospel (2 Cor 4:7–15). "Clay jars" symbolize the fragility of ministerial existence, and any "treasure" they contain must have been put there by someone else. Whatever "transcendent power" passes through the minister's life cannot, therefore, be self-generated. Facing hardships, one can either yield to the pressures or stoutly resist, finding some deeper inner resources that allow one to say, "but not . . ." (2 Cor 4:8–9). How is this done? By understanding ministerial—and by extension Christian—existence as *living out of the gospel of Christ.*

The contours of ministerial life are shaped by the kerygma. Just as death and life comprise the complementary halves of Christ's existence, so do they form the interpretive axes of ministerial (and Christian) existence. Through experiences of "death"—suffering in all its forms, especially in the service of the gospel—ministers relive Christ's suffering and death. Paul expresses this in remarkably compact form in the blessing that opens the letter: "As Christ's cup of suffering overflows, and we suffer with him, so also through Christ our consolation overflows" (1:5 NEB).

The suffering of the physical Jesus ended with his death, but Paul seems to envision the risen Lord continuing to experience pain with those who suffer on his behalf. Yet pain is not Christ's only emotion; suffering is only half of the Christ story. The other half is the "life of Jesus," most likely, though not certainly, the resurrected life of Jesus. While not denying the "death of Jesus," the "life of Jesus" trumps it, thereby rendering hope as a defining emotion of ministerial existence. Despair and hope may live side by side, but the experience of Christ tilts the scales finally toward hope. As the one who exemplified death finally yielding to life, Christ engenders a pattern of living in which despair finally yields to hope.

This struggle between death and life, between despair and hope, is carried out in the human body, the one thing every person and Jesus have in common. Paul lives *from the gospel* by living *within the gospel.* Life so defined means that suffering experienced for the sake of the gospel is seen as an extension of Christ's suffering. Christ's death is relived as those in Christ "carry in the body the death of Jesus" and are "given up to death for Jesus' sake." But the other word of the gospel, the "life of Jesus," while not denying the first word, has the last word. Whether it is the fully free, yet fully obedient, life of the human Jesus exemplifying authentic existence before God that Paul has in view, or the resurrected Jesus who exemplifies life triumphing over death, the creative, irrepressible dimension of Jesus also finds a home "in our mortal flesh." As it does so in the minister, it enlivens the church: "death is at work in us, but life in you" (4:12). As the vicarious death of Jesus benefits the minister who replicates the Christ event by living the gospel, so does this cycle of death giving way to life within the minister give life to the church. By living out of the gospel, the minister experiences life. By seeing the creative power of the gospel exemplified in the minister's life, the church learns to appropriate and experience new life itself.

Confidence in proclaiming the gospel is grounded in confident faith; before one can speak with conviction, one must believe with conviction, Paul concludes from Ps 116:10 (Ps 115:1 LXX). The root conviction of authentic Christian ministry is faith in the One who raised Jesus from the dead (4:14). As something we know, this conviction serves as the authorizing warrant for all Christian proclamation and action. And it also has corporate implications. Ministers and their faithful churches, or, in this case, Paul, his associates, and the Corinthian church, all share in God's resurrection "with Jesus"; God "will raise us also with Jesus, and will bring us with you into his presence" (4:14). God's action in Christ extends to both minister and church, who together experience resurrection life "with Jesus." It is ultimately for communities of faith, "members of Christ," that the God of Life acts: "everything is for your sake" (4:15).

The Gospel Shapes the Present and Future (2 Cor 4:16–5:10). With seasonal changes come "decay" and "renewal," but this cycle takes on a different meaning when one's categories for living are drawn from the gospel rather than nature. Refracted through the lens of the gospel, human life has both an outer and inner dimension. By "outer nature" and "inner nature" Paul does not mean the soul/body distinction typical of much ancient thought, in which, in its Platonic form, the soul is understood as immortal—without beginning or ending—taking up residence in a human body, where it remains imprisoned until it is released at death and freed to repeat the cycle again in a future series of bodies. Seen this way, bodies decay while the eternal soul lives on. Paul concedes the fragility of bodily existence and the gradually deteriorating strength that comes with age, the pressures of living, and the battle for survival. The body, as his own experience confirmed, wastes away.

Yet to affirm the gospel is to affirm life and the possibility that a person can actually get stronger through the renewal of one's inner resources, a weakening body notwithstanding. Living out of the gospel means bucking the trend of deteriorating strength by refocusing one's understanding of strength. Looking through the lens of the gospel, Paul envisions a form of human existence that is appropriate to life with God. Whether it is seen as a new dwelling or as a new garment that one slips on over the (living) body, the outlook is one of hope, not despair. Having already tasted God's future by experiencing the Spirit, those in Christ can expect full payment eventually.

Living the gospel means acknowledging death—the fragility of human existence—yet affirming life—the capacity for experiencing inward renewal. Perspective is critical. How does one define reality? By what one sees with the eyes or by what one sees with the eyes of faith? By present reality that we experience with the senses, or by another eternal reality that is actually more real? Living the gospel points one to transcendent Reality, where God, Christ, and the Spirit are the Prime Realities.

Because God has already been experienced as decisively involved in human history, it is possible for those shaped by God's action in Christ to live in the present with an eye fixed, though not fixated, on the future, leaning into the future with hope, not despair. By extending the kerygma into ministerial (and Christian) existence, Paul provides interpretive categories that enable us to make sense of who we are and what we do "in Christ" and that also enable us to live not by what we see but by what we believe: "we walk by faith, not by sight" (5:7).

Motives for Mission: Christ's Compelling Love, New Creation, and the Ministry of Reconciliation (2 Cor 5:11–6:10). With all the abuses that come with persuasive speech, especially when spoken in the name of the gospel, a Lord to be feared and a God before whom our lives lie open serve as healthy antidotes. But Paul also hopes to have a place in the Corinthians' heart. Solicitous of their good will, he targets those who operate with a different understanding of ministry, who, as he characterizes them, fixate on outward behavior rather than inner dispositions and motives. To these opponents, Paul's behavior must have seemed bizarre. "Beside himself" probably expresses the opponents' view (5:13). His ministerial behavior, how the church views him, how he views the church and his critics, and how they all relate to each other—this set of issues prompts Paul to engage in further theological reflections in which he is forced once again to probe even more deeply the significance of God's action in Christ.

Throughout this section, the missionary impulse is evident. It opens with words about persuasion and concludes with a direct appeal to the Corinthians: "be reconciled to God" (5:20) and "[do not] accept the grace of God in vain" (6:1). Such overt appeals may not be addressed to non-Christians, but they are not for that reason any less strong as missionary appeals. They are appeals being made to the Corinthians on behalf of the gospel. As his concluding "hardship list" makes clear (6:4–10), Paul is operating in a defensive posture. He wishes to remove all obstacles coming between him and his church, hoping to convince them of his faultless ministry (6:3).

Once again, what is at stake is the credibility of Paul's own ministry with the Corinthian church and the viability of his relationship with them. A network of living, human relationships, forged over time and nurtured by sweat and tears, hangs in the balance. Perhaps this accounts for why some of his most profound theological probings of the Christ event occur within this context.

As before, we detect basic beliefs widely shared by other early Christians informing Paul's reflections: "one [Christ] has died for all" (5:14), Christ's compelling love (5:14), and Christ "who knew no sin" (5:21). In one sense, these creedal statements may seem ordinary, but Paul draws some extraordinary conclusions from them. Utterly unexpected is the conclusion he draws from Christ's vicarious death: not "therefore all might live," but "therefore all have died" (5:14)! What does he mean by this much disputed phrase? He probably means that Christ's death for all has enabled everyone *potentially* to experience a death to the self comparable to what Christ experienced when he died obediently, yielding his will to God. Christ's death somehow symbolized humanity's fate. Paul hopes that those who share the benefits of Christ's death "might live no longer for themselves" but for Christ (5:15). The effect is clear; properly understood, the death of Christ establishes new norms for human behavior that, when taken seriously, create different criteria for judging ministerial, especially Paul's, performance.

Equally practical in their implications are his remarks in 5:16–21, which is one Pauline passage that has heavily influenced Christian notions of Christ's atoning death—and justifiably so. At issue is what it means to think "from a human point of view," literally, "according to the flesh" (*kata sarka*). Paul apparently thinks this aptly characterizes the viewpoint of his critics. In his view, they utterly fail to grasp the nature of his apostolic calling and the relationship between his form of ministry and his understanding of the Christian kerygma.

Does *kata sarka* function as an adjective modifying Christ or as an adverb modifying the way Paul once knew Christ? If the former, he would appear to be disclaiming interest in the physical, human figure Jesus, which, in the view of some scholars, would account for his relatively infrequent references to Jesus' life and words. The latter would shift the emphasis somewhat, suggesting that he had indeed once known of, perhaps even seen, the figure Jesus, but that he had failed to see God at work in him—he had viewed him in essentially human terms, as Jesus, rather than Jesus Christ. Either way, Paul's perspective on Christ is now radically altered. What God did in Christ has its only counterpart in the act of creation, not in the giving of the law at Sinai or in God's covenant with Abraham.

God's action in Christ must be seen as an event in which history turned a corner, when the "turn of the ages" occurred, when God effectively started over again, creating a new universe of possibilities. The one who is incorporated into Christ steps into this new order, as it were, becoming part of its transformative, renewing process. Being "in Christ" is to experience the outburst of energy unleashed by the Creator God, thus becoming a "new creation." To be "in Christ" is to participate in a "new creation" and to become part of a reordered world as well as an active agent in the reordering of that world. This occurs at both the individual and corporate level—within the person so incorporated into Christ and within the community of faith who lives in Christ's "space." Had Paul known nuclear metaphors, he might have likened God's action in Christ to an atom-splitting event, one that forever changed both the universe and the human universe of meaning not only by the way it reconfigured human perceptions of life and death, but also by the sheer residual energy it released.

The particular form that the "new creation" takes is reconciliation. What God accomplished "in Christ" was the bringing together of God and the world—a cosmic reconciliation in which divine forgiveness was extended to sinful humanity. Christ becomes the person and event through whom God reaches out to humans in an embrace of reconciliation. Whether "in Christ" defines the sphere or the means of reconciliation, Christ is the prototypical sinless martyr whose death benefits sinful humanity—one shameful, innocent death—shameful in every way—enabling others to experience life in the goodness of God. Once again, Paul draws on a widely held Christian conviction: Christ "knew no sin" (5:21; cf. John 7:18; 8:46; Heb 4:15; 7:26; 1 Pet 1:19; 2:22; 3:18; 1 John 3:5). His own distinctive understanding is reflected in his insistence that "for our sake God made him to be sin." In what sense? That Christ identified with sinful humanity by becoming flesh (Rom 8:3)? Or that by being crucified, he took on the curse of transgressing the law (Gal 3:13)? Or perhaps in some other sense? Whichever it is, Paul is pushing traditional Christian belief in a new direction.

Through it all, God is the Prime Actor: "All this is from God" (5:18). Having accomplished this "macro-reconciliation," God brings about "micro-reconciliation" between individual human beings and within communities of faith through those who have been commissioned by God as ministers of reconciliation (5:18). The initiative is fully God's, yet God has embraced ministers as co-workers. The frame of reference here may be more cosmic, but it merely states in a different form the reality Paul expressed earlier in 1:21–22—a community of faith in solidarity with its minister(s), both seen as living in the presence of, and working under, a faithful God who sustains them as faithful disciples of Christ who have received God's Spirit.

What form of ministry derives from this theological perspective? Above all, ministers see themselves as "servants of God" (6:4) who, on the one hand, experience "death" by suffering hardships (6:5), but who exhibit "life" by living above reproach. They exemplify the paradoxical existence that comes with living the gospel—confronting false charges, harsh realities, and the skewed perceptions of others with confident counterassertions that derive from faith that has a firm center of gravity.

The Collection (2 Cor 8–9)

In Paul's firsthand account of the watershed meeting in Jerusalem at which church leaders finally recognized the legitimacy of his mission to the Gentiles, we learn where the idea of a collection originated. According to the "Jerusalem agreement," a division of labor was worked out that gave Peter, James, and John responsibility for the mission to Jews and that entrusted Paul and Barnabas with the mission to Gentiles. Recognizing the potential threat that two separate churches might emerge—a network of Gentile churches outside Palestine loyal to Paul and another group of churches composed mostly of Jewish Christians loyal to Jerusalem—those gathered stipulated one condition: that Paul and Barnabas "remember the poor" (Gal 2:10). Since Paul was firmly committed to a unified church, he eagerly complied and soon after began to encourage his Gentile churches to participate in the collection for the "poor among the saints at Jerusalem" (Rom 15:26).

Conceived as a one-time project that took place over time, the collection occupied much of Paul's attention during his ministry in the Aegean area in the 50s. The collection receives special attention in the Corinthian correspondence (1 Cor 16:1–4; 2 Cor 8–9), when it is still being gathered, and in the concluding section of Romans, in which Paul looks back on the collection as a completed project and anticipates its delivery to Jerusalem (Rom 15:22–33). Oddly enough, it does not receive comparable emphasis in Acts. It is not mentioned in Luke's account of the Pauline mission in the Aegean (Acts 16–20) and is only briefly alluded to in Paul's defense before Felix (Acts 24:17; cf. 24:26). [See Expanded CD Version pp. 449–52: *The Collection's Strategic Importance* and *Paul's Instructions Concerning the Collection in 2 Cor 8–9*]

Defending His Ministry (2 Cor 10–13)

At some point—and we do not know exactly when—some people claiming to be "ministers of Christ" arrived in Corinth and joined themselves to the church. We know about them only through Paul's highly polemical description. Even allowing for some rhetorical hyperbole generated in the heat of debate, we can deduce how they were describing themselves and what they were saying about Paul. That they were missionaries in some sense is suggested by Paul's sarcastic designation of them as "super-apostles" (11:5; 12:11) and his further characterization of them as "false apostles, deceitful workers, disguising themselves as apostles of Christ" (11:13). Since "apostle" could refer to a fairly broad spectrum of religious functionaries, this need not mean that they were members of Jesus' original apostolic circle or that they claimed some connection with that circle. It mainly suggests that they saw themselves as specially commissioned by God or designated for some specific task. The unnamed brothers, for example, who assisted Titus in gathering the collection are called "messengers [*apostoloi*] of the churches" (2 Cor 8:23).

That they claimed to be "ministers of Christ" (*diakonoi Christou*, 11:23) is clear, as is their claim to be of Jewish descent: Hebrews, Israelites, descendants of Abraham (11:22). At the very least, they were Jewish Christian missionaries. The best clue to what they were preaching comes from Paul's charge that the Corinthians were an easy target for "someone [who] comes and proclaims another Jesus . . . a different spirit . . . or a different gospel" (11:4). While this characterization provides only a faint outline of their theological differences with Paul, it is nevertheless quite revealing.

From Paul's viewpoint, they operated with an understanding of Christ and probably the Holy Spirit that differed fundamentally from his, which meant that their construal of God's action in Christ and everything entailed by that—the "gospel"—ran counter to Paul's construal of God's saving message. Even though Paul uses language of "another gospel" in Gal 1:6–9 to designate a Torah-centered form of the Christian gospel, that does not appear to be the case here. At no point does the role of Torah in Christian discipleship surface as an issue in the discussion. It is unwarranted to characterize these Jewish Christian missionaries as "Judaizers" who insisted that Gentiles were obligated to observe Torah in order to be full-fledged members of the people of God.

What prompted these outside teachers to come to Corinth is not stated, although Paul regards their arrival as an infringement on his territory. Insisting that he has kept "within the field that God has assigned to us" (10:13) and he does not "boast beyond limits" (10:15), Paul implies that these teachers have moved well beyond their limits in coming to Corinth. By moving into one of Paul's churches, they are benefiting from the "labors of others" (10:15).

They may have arrived with perfectly good motives, planning to build on the work Paul had already begun, but at some point, perhaps from the outset, they positioned themselves over against Paul and eventually became severe critics of his ministry. This is Paul's view, at least, and there is no reason to doubt it. From Paul's spirited defense of his apostolic ministry, we hear snippets of their derogatory characterizations of him: humble when present, bold when away (10:1); strong letter writer, weak personal presence (10:10); one who uses crafty, deceitful methods, especially regarding the collection (12:16). These are but variations of the charge that he was fickle, behaving one way in one setting, and just the opposite in another setting (1:17).

This may have been what was implied by the charge that he acted "according to human standards" (*kata sarka*, 10:2). Oddly enough, Paul's practice of refusing to accept pay from a congregation while actively working with it seems to have become a key issue. The newcomers, by contrast, appear to have been willing to receive money from the Corinthians and may have argued not only that this was a perfectly acceptable practice that had been authorized originally by Jesus himself (1 Cor 9:14) but also that it was a concrete way of expressing mutual love between the church and its teachers. Because the church loves and honors its teachers, it pays them; by accepting the pay, its teachers seal the bond of love and respect with the church. By refusing to accept pay, however, Paul could somehow be accused of not loving the church (11:11).

As much as personal behavior figured into the controversy, it was not simply a debate about ministerial style and matters of ministerial protocol. The very legitimacy of Paul's apostolic ministry was also an issue, and he even frames it in terms of "belonging to Christ" (10:7). For them to "desire proof that Christ is speaking in me" (13:3) suggests that somebody had convinced them to think otherwise. Was Paul a genuine representative of Christ? When he spoke, did he actually speak with legitimate authority from Christ? Was he, as his opponents claimed to be, a genuine "minister of Christ" (11:23)? Given his repeated emphasis on authority, there can be little doubt that his apostolic authority was being questioned at its core.

With such a frontal assault on the nature and authority of his apostolic ministry, Paul has no choice but to defend himself, and his remarks in chapters 10–13 constitute an apology that places it within a tradition of apologetic defense that goes back to Socrates' defense of his behavior before his Athenian critics. Unlike his defense in Gal 1–2, Paul does not rehearse here the circumstances of his apostolic calling and insist on his independence from Jerusalem church leaders.

Since the issues in 2 Corinthians centered around the nature of his ministry, he adopts a different approach. His response is a powerful counterattack, as seen by his opening remarks in which he employs strong military imagery to remind the Corinthians how forceful he can be (10:1–6). His defensive posture is strongly reminiscent of popular philosophers who also styled themselves as those who fought with their words and rhetorical strategies. Worth noting is Paul's insistence that he is defending not just himself but "the knowledge of God" (10:5). Standing at the forefront of battle, he sees himself fighting for appropriate ways of accessing God. It is not personal defense only, but theological defense as well.

One of Paul's strategies is to refute the scurrilous charges that his critics have lodged against him. Contrary to their accusations, he insists on the integrity of his behavior, which is not inconsistent (10:11). His refusal to accept pay from the Corinthians, far from being a symbol of disdain, should be seen as an expression of love (11:7–11). Added to these refutations are his countercharges. If his opponents can sling mud, so can he—and he does. The epithets he hurls at them are as insulting as those they hurl at him (11:12–15).

Within the heat of the battle—and it is a very heated battle—there emerges a fundamental theological stance. Insisting that "we are speaking in Christ before God," Paul recalls his earlier emphasis that ministers must define themselves "in Christ" as those sent from God and do their work in the presence of God (2 Cor 2:14). As Paul stated in his opening remarks in 1 Corinthians, in which he articulates his theology of the cross, at its heart the Christian gospel is a paradoxical message, and this paradox is aptly summarized in his claim, "whenever I am weak, then I am strong" (12:10).

This was an appropriate ministerial posture because it reflects the essential paradox of the gospel: "[Christ] was crucified in weakness, but lives by the power of God" (13:4). Given Paul's construal of the gospel, which took seriously the suffering and death of Jesus but also the triumph represented by God's resurrection of Christ, experiences in which he suffered on behalf of the gospel deserved to be in the forefront of his apostolic credentials. What truly commends him to the Corinthian church, in sharp contrast to his critics who commend themselves (10:18), is the form of his apostolic behavior, as it is etched unforgettably in the hardship list in 11:23–29. If he must take pride in any of his experiences and exploits, it must be those that connect him directly with the message of the crucified Christ—narrow escapes from death, for example (11:30–33).

What is remarkable about the rehearsal of his mystical experience (12:1–5) is how it is juxtaposed with the earthly experience of coping with recurrent suffering. To recall the former is to do so as though it were another person; it is that much of an "out of body" experience. To recall the latter is all too real, which is why his description is couched in the first person singular. Suffering was an experience that happened to him. Even though Paul was an apostle, Christ refused to grant his request. Indeed, it is Christ himself who asserts, "My grace is sufficient for you, for power is made perfect in weakness" (12:9). With this definitive interpretation of the gospel given by Christ himself, Paul can hardly live otherwise.

This may have been the fundamental difference between Paul's understanding of ministry and that of his critics. It has been plausibly suggested that the "other Jesus" whom they proclaimed was the triumphant Jesus, the powerful worker of miracles, and that the ministerial lifestyle they promoted was a proportionately powerful form of ministry—powerful in the use of words and in the use of authenticating miracles. Only when pressed does Paul insist that he too, like the "super-apostles," has the power to perform "signs and wonders and mighty works" (12:12), but, all things considered, this is not where he chose to place the accent of his ministry.

Well aware of the scandal of the cross and the ease with which one can move from Good Friday to Easter, Paul preferred instead to anchor his ministry in the experience of Good Friday and see his ministry as the arena where the power of God manifests itself and where the power of Christ is actually born. When defining himself in relation to Christ, Paul can insist that "we are weak in him," yet in dealing with the Corinthians he claims that "we will live with him by the power of God" (13:4). Given a choice of where to accent ministerial existence, Paul would much prefer to place it in the sphere of suffering and death, since this is where, paradoxically enough, genuine forms of strength are actually generated.

Worried that the Corinthians will lapse into self-destructive behaviors and that his ministry among them might eventually be for naught (12:19–21), Paul introduces Christ as the norm by which both his and their conduct should be measured. Christ speaks in him through his apostolic existence; both his message and his lifestyle are "in Christ." Consequently, he urges the Corinthians to consider whether they are "living in the faith" (13:5), reminding them that "Jesus Christ is in you" (13:5). Their behavior should be a reflection of what they believe and confess. The true test of their loyalty not only to God but also to Paul himself is whether they are "living out of the gospel."

Note

1. In this section I develop the seminal insight articulated by Charles Cousar, "The Theological Task of 1 Corinthians," in David M. Hay, ed., *Pauline Theology: Volume II: 1 & 2 Corinthians* (Minneapolis: Fortress, 1993), 90–102.

Bibliography

Commentaries

1 CORINTHIANS

Barrett, C. K. *A Commentary on the First Epistle to the Corinthians*. 2d ed. Black's/Harper's New Testament Commentaries. London: Black, 1971; repr. with additional preface, 1992; repr. 1994.

Beardslee, William A. *First Corinthians: A Commentary for Today*. St. Louis: Chalice, 1994.

Fee, Gordon D. *The First Epistle to the Corinthians*. New International Commentary on the New Testament. Grand Rapids: Eerdmans, 1987.

Hays, Richard B. *First Corinthians*. Interpretation: A Bible Commentary for Teaching and Preaching. Louisville: John Knox, 1997.

Héring, Jean. *The First Epistle of Saint Paul to the Corinthians*. Translated by A. W. Heathcote and P. J. Allcock from 2d French ed. London: Epworth, 1962.

Horsley, Richard A. *1 Corinthians*. Abingdon New Testament Commentaries. Nashville: Abingdon, 1998.

Sampley, J. Paul. "The First Letter to the Corinthians: Introduction, Commentary, and Reflections." Pages 771–1003 in vol. 10 of *The New Interpreter's Bible*. Edited by Leander E. Keck. 12 vols. Nashville: Abingdon, 2002.

Snyder, Graydon F. *First Corinthians: A Faith Commentary*. Macon: Mercer University Press, 1992.

2 CORINTHIANS

Barrett, C. K. *A Commentary on the Second Epistle to the Corinthians*. Harper's New Testament Commentaries. New York: Harper & Row, 1973.

Best, Ernest. *Second Corinthians*. Interpretation: A Bible Commentary for Teaching and Preaching. Louisville: John Knox, 1987.

Bultmann, Rudolf. *The Second Letter to the Corinthians*. Translated by Roy A. Harrisville from the 1976 German edition. Minneapolis: Augsburg, 1985.

Furnish, Victor P. *II Corinthians*. Anchor Bible 32A. Garden City: Doubleday, 1984.

Héring, Jean. *The Second Epistle of Saint Paul to the Corinthians*. Translated by A. W. Heathcote and P. J. Allcock. London: Epworth, 1967.

Sampley, J. Paul. "The Second Letter to the Corinthians: Introduction, Commentary, and Reflections." Pages 1–180 in vol. 11 of *The New Interpreter's Bible*. Edited by Leander E. Keck. 12 vols. Nashville: Abingdon, 2000.

Thrall, Margaret E. *A Critical and Exegetical Commentary on the Second Epistle to the Corinthians*. International Critical Commentary. 2 vols. Edinburgh: T&T Clark, 1994.

1–2 CORINTHIANS

Thrall, Margaret E. *The First and Second Letters of Paul to the Corinthians*. Cambridge Bible Commentary. Cambridge: Cambridge University Press, 1965; repr. 1990.

Witherington, Ben. *Conflict and Community in Corinth: A Socio-Rhetorical Commentary on 1 and 2 Corinthians*. Grand Rapids: Eerdmans, 1994.

Other Resources

Barrett, C. K. *Essays on Paul*. Philadelphia: Westminster, 1982.

Brown, Alexandra R. *The Cross and Human Transformation: Paul's Apocalyptic Word in 1 Corinthians*. Minneapolis: Fortress, 1995.

Dunn, James D. G. *1 Corinthians*. New Testament Guides. Sheffield: Sheffield, 1995.

Furnish, Victor P. *The Theology of the First Letter to the Corinthians*. New Testament Theology. Cambridge: Cambridge University Press, 1999; repr. 2003.

Georgi, Dieter. *Remembering the Poor: The History of Paul's Collection for Jerusalem*. Nashville: Abingdon, 1992.

Harvey, A. E. *Renewal Through Suffering: A Study of 2 Corinthians*. Studies of the New Testament and Its World. Edinburgh: T&T Clark, 1996.

Hay, David M., ed. *Pauline Theology. Volume II: 1 & 2 Corinthians*. Minneapolis: Fortress, 1993.

Hurd, John C. *The Origin of I Corinthians*. Macon: Mercer University Press, 1983. Corrected reprint of the 1965 edition.

Marshall, Peter. *Enmity in Corinth: Social Conventions in Paul's Relations with the Corinthians*. Wissenschaftliche Untersuchungen zum Neuen Testament 2.23. Tübingen: Mohr (Siebeck), 1987.

Martin, Dale B. *The Corinthian Body*. New Haven: Yale University Press, 1995.

———. *Slavery as Salvation: The Metaphor of Slavery in Pauline Christianity*. New Haven: Yale University Press, 1990.

Mitchell, Margaret M. *Paul and the Rhetoric of Reconciliation: An Exegetical Investigation of the Language and Composition of 1 Corinthians*. Hermeneutische Untersuchungen zur Theologie 28. Tübingen: Mohr (Siebeck), 1991.

Murphy-O'Connor, Jerome. *St. Paul's Corinth: Texts and Archaeology*. Good News Studies 6. 3d ed. Collegeville: Liturgical (Michael Glazier), 2002 (1983).

———. *The Theology of the Second Letter to the Corinthians*. New Testament Theology. Cambridge: Cambridge University Press, 1991; repr. 1996.

Theissen, Gerd. *The Social Setting of Pauline Christianity: Essays on Corinth.* Edited and translated by John H. Schütz. Philadelphia: Fortress, 1982.

Winter, Bruce W. *After Paul Left Corinth: The Influence of Secular Ethics and Social Change.* Grand Rapids: Eerdmans, 2001.

Wire, Antoinette C. *The Corinthian Women Prophets: A Reconstruction Through Paul's Rhetoric.* Minneapolis: Fortress, 1990.

Young, Frances M., and David Ford. *Meaning and Truth in 2 Corinthians.* Grand Rapids: Eerdmans, 1988.

Chapter 14

Galatians

"The whole epistle is full of a vehement and lofty spirit."

John Chrysostom

"Paul's theological horizon is given by the motif of God's warlike and liberating invasion of the cosmos in Christ's cross and in Christ's Spirit, coupled with the bold assertion of the new creation inaugurated by that invasion."

J. Louis Martyn

When Marcion put Galatians first among Paul's letters, he did so for a reason. Its strongly argued critique of the law reinforced his rejection of all things Jewish. Its sharply drawn polarities resonated with his own dualistic way of thinking. Its polemical tone also suited his argumentative spirit. When Adolf von Harnack wryly observed that "Marcion was the only Gentile Christian who understood Paul, and even he misunderstood him," he rightly saw Paul and Marcion as kindred spirits. Their spirits are nowhere closer than in Galatians.[1]

It comes as no surprise to find strong resistance to Galatians among early Jewish Christian groups for whom Peter was a heroic figure who faithfully conveyed Jesus' high regard for the Mosaic law. Their outlook is reflected in the Pseudo-Clementine literature (ca. third century C.E.) in which Peter calls Paul "that hostile man" and directly challenges Paul's unflattering portrait of him in Galatians.[2] But it may be a surprise to learn that Mani (ca. 216–276 C.E.), the founder of Manichaeism who was strongly influenced by Paul, drew heavily on Galatians to justify breaking with the tradition of his childhood, the Jewish Christian Elkesaite movement, before eventually embracing a radically dualistic Gnostic outlook.

Galatians' penchant for being at the center of controversy is confirmed by its pivotal role in the Reformation. Like Marcion, Luther held Galatians dear, lecturing on it while still an Augustinian monk (1516–1517) and well into his reforming movement (1531). Galatians was like a wife to him, he said, his "Katie von Bora." Later Protestantism's sharp contrast between law and gospel drew heavily on Luther's reading of Galatians, even though that was not Paul's precise way of formulating the issue.

And when the Reformers used Galatians' emphasis on justification by faith (*sola fide*) as heavy artillery against Catholic conceptions of the salvific value of accumulated good works, they too were tilting Paul in their direction. But, as has often been the case with Christian readers in every age trying to spring free from oppressive systems of belief and practice, both ecclesiastical and civil, the letter's call to freedom was too much for them to resist, and thus became dubbed the church's "Magna Charta."

The Crisis in Galatia

Whatever else it may be, Galatians is a letter prompted by a severe crisis within a group of Pauline churches located somewhere in Asia Minor. The letter is addressed to the "churches of Galatia" (1:2; cf. 3:1), whose precise location is uncertain. [**See Expanded CD Version p. 463**: *The Location of Galatia* and *Place and Time of Composition*]

The tone of the letter is polemical, its acid language often bombastic and sarcastic (5:12). Paul presents himself as an exasperated mother at her wits' end over an adolescent child she is trying to steer toward adulthood (4:19–20; cf. 4:11). Because of this parental relationship Paul can write tenderly emotive passages, as exaggerated in their rhetorical tone as the vitriolic passages are. Galatians runs the gamut of emotional expression.

The crisis in the Galatian churches accounts for some of the peculiar features of the letter: the opening greeting with its strong accent on Paul's divine apostleship (1:1–2); a doxology concluding the initial greeting (1:5); the absence of the usual prayer introducing the letter (ordinarily, between 1:5 and 1:6); the opening abrupt reference to the Galatians' defection (1:6–7); the double curse on the opponents (1:8–9); the lengthy autobiographical section (1:11–24); the reference to a physical infirmity that occasioned his initial visit (4:13–14); the Abraham-Hagar-Sarah allegory (4:21–5:1); and the concluding section written in Paul's own hand (6:11–18), indicating that he dictated the rest of the letter to a scribe. The distinctive literary form of the letter reflects the crisis that produced it.

The crisis in Galatia arose over a single issue: circumcision (see 2:3, 7–9, 12; 5:2–3, 6, 11; 6:12–13, 15). This was an instance in which disagreement over a seemingly straightforward religious practice exposed widely divergent attitudes on a set of interrelated larger issues: How does one access God's saving grace—or as Paul puts it, how is one justified by God (soteriology)? What are the actual effects of Christ's death (Christology)? On what terms do those "in Christ" relate to each other (ecclesiology)? [See Expanded CD Version pp. 464–66: *Paul's Opponents in Galatia*]

Paul's Response

Once we identify some of the issues that prompted the crisis, we can understand more clearly the shape of Paul's response—its overall logic as well as its content.

Paul's response takes the form of a letter, with most of the standard features of ancient letters. It contains the usual self-identification of the author (1:1–2); greeting

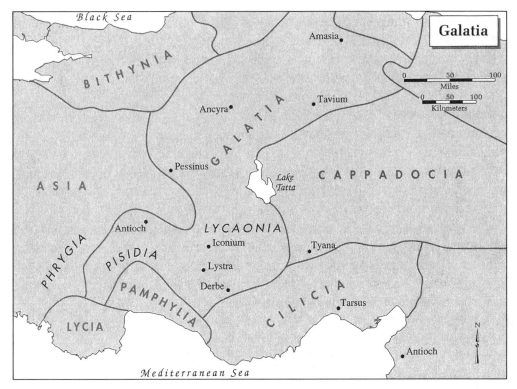

(1:3–5); and benediction (6:18). When the structure of the letter is analyzed using ancient rhetorical categories, the body of the letter consists of an opening introduction (*exordium*; 1:6–10); a statement of facts (*narratio*, 1:11–2:14); the proposition (*propositio*, 2:15–21); proofs (*probatio*, 3:1–4:31); the exhortation (*exhortatio*, 5:1–6:10); and a final peroration (*peroratio*, 6:11–18).

The shape of the letter is best explained by its threefold purpose: it is defensive (1:1–2:21); didactic (3:1–5:12); and hortatory (5:13–6:18).

Paul Defends Himself (1:1–2:21)

Given the opponents' assault on Paul's apostolic authority, the letter is necessarily defensive, and for this reason has been rightly characterized as an apologetic letter. This explains why the first two chapters, the *defensive section*, especially from 1:11 onward, are so heavily reactive in tone and autobiographical in content. Since Paul himself has become a central issue in the debate, he must begin with a personal apologia that rehearses his life from the point of his call/conversion forward (1:11–24)—the most complete such review anywhere in his letters.

He emphasizes several things: (1) the extraordinary nature of his call; (2) its reversing, transforming effects on his earlier life in Judaism; (3) its specific focus as an apostolic commissioning to "proclaim [Christ] among the Gentiles" (1:16); and (4) his autonomy and relative independence of church authorities in Jerusalem (esp. 1:16b–24).[3]

Two episodes from his extended period of missionary service are highlighted: first, his meeting with church leaders in Jerusalem (2:1–10),[4] and second, a pivotal episode in Antioch of Syria (2:11–14). The choice of these episodes is significant. The first underscores the controversy created by his (and Barnabas's) mission to the Gentiles and its resolution at this critically important meeting. The two results of the meeting were: (1) agreement on the division of labor for the church's mission—Peter is "entrusted with the gospel for the circumcised," Paul with "the gospel for the uncircumcised" (2:7), which meant that everyone there agreed on the full legitimacy of Paul's mission to the Gentiles; and (2) Paul's agreement to "remember the poor" (2:10), which led to the collection for the Jerusalem poor, a project of immense symbolic significance and practical benefit (see 1 Cor 16:1–4; 2 Cor 8–9; Rom 15:25–29).

Paul cited the Antioch episode because he thought it exposed the deep differences between himself and the very people who signed off on the Jerusalem agreement, most notably Peter. As Paul saw it, Peter's willingness to eat with Gentile Christians when they were alone, but his refusal to do so in the presence of "certain people [who] came from James" because he was worried about pressure from the "circumcision faction," sent conflicting signals about the status of Gentile Christians within the church. In Paul's view, either they were full-fledged members or they were not.

For a highly visible "pillar" like Peter to embrace Gentile Christians in one setting but exclude them in another raised not so much the question of whether Paul should have evangelized them, but the terms of admission under which he did so. At issue was the "truth of the gospel": whether Gentiles become believers by first becoming Jews or whether both Gentiles and Jews become believers in the same way, namely, by their faith in Christ.

For this reason Paul's tightly compressed summary expressing his theology of salvation for both Jews and Gentiles (2:15–21) belongs with the initial autobiographical review. (At least the first two verses, maybe more, may belong with verse 14 as a report of what Paul actually said to Peter.) Since this summary expresses not only his own view of how both Gentiles and Jews experience God's saving justification but also the view held by his fellow Christian Jews, it provides the rationale for his public condemnation of Peter's behavior at Antioch.

Paul Elaborates His Theology of Righteousness through Faith (3:1–5:12)

Once Paul completes the initial, highly personal review of (1) his apostolic call, (2) his discharge of that call through his preaching to the Gentiles, (3) the Jerusalem meeting that confirmed the legitimacy of his work, and (4) the Antioch episode in which the Jerusalem agreement became unraveled, he then moves to the *didactic section* of the letter (3:1–5:12).

Paul begins by addressing the "foolish Galatians" directly, asking them to reflect on their own experience in receiving the gospel. Since they were converted Gentiles, his question is rhetorical: Surely their initial reception of the gospel (the Spirit) had not occurred "by doing the works of the law" but rather by "believing what [they] heard" (3:2). If so, why move from a higher mode of experiencing God (Spirit) to a lower mode (law, i.e., flesh)?

What follows from 3:6 through 5:12 is an extended didactic section that fills out, and therefore undergirds, the theology of salvation compactly expressed in 2:15–21. It is a heavily, though not exclusively, midrashic argument, with many of the Scripture references and allusions drawn from the Pentateuch probably because Paul's opponents are basing their teachings on the Law.[5] Paul's critique of their Law-based position must itself be Law-based! In this section Paul not only unfolds another way of reading the Law, but also draws quite a different set of conclusions from this reading.

Without trying to summarize this intricate argument, we can observe the following points:

1. Paul sees the Abraham story as truly revelatory in several ways: (a) it reveals *how* we should relate to God—"in faith"; (b) it clarifies the *identity* of Abraham's true descendants—"those of faith"; (c) it anticipates the full reach of God's promised blessings—"to all the nations [Gentiles]"; and (d) it signals the eventual appearance of the "key" that would unlock the secrets of a, b, and c—"the seed of Abraham," Jesus Christ.

To summarize: Embedded within the Abraham story are clues revealing the means, the recipients, the scope, and the locus of God's saving activity.

2. Paul privileges the Abraham story over the Moses story. By insisting that God's covenant with Abraham and the terms in which it was conceived (i.e., that faith was established as the preferred mode in which God's people should relate to God) were never annulled and thus still operative, Paul redefines (at least from the standpoint of his opponents) the role of Moses and the era of the law that he initiated. It was an era that lasted until the arrival of Jesus Christ, who "in the fullness of time" (4:4) ushered in the era of faith.

Unable to deny how large the law looms within the Pentateuch, and within the OT generally, Paul must ask, "Why then the law?" (3:19). He answers by proposing that the law was an interim measure indirectly relating God's people to God. It was ordained through angels, but since it was given through a mediator (Moses, whom Paul nowhere mentions by name in Galatians), it provided only indirect access to God (3:20). God's promises were embedded within the law, but because it was inherently impotent to deal with the power of sin (3:21–22), it was practically ineffective as an ethical code. The era of the Mosaic law is best seen as a period when God's people were under the care of a *paidagōgos*, the person (usually a slave) responsible for getting a child to and from school and supervising the child's conduct. The metaphor was apt because the disciplinarian's role was temporary and restrictive (cf. 3:23).

3. Paul sketches two comprehensive frameworks—one apocalyptic, the other allegorical—within which his soteriology can be understood.

(a) An apocalyptic rehearsal of God's saving work (4:1–11). Picking up on the slave/child distinction in 3:23–29, Paul unfolds a story of salvation that sees the time before Christ as a time of guardianship, when humanity as a whole was still a minor. Whatever ownership rights humans possessed were potential rather than actual. Moreover, this time of being under trustees and guardians displayed all the pressures associated with adolescent life, including living under the tyranny of demonic forces beyond one's control, or what Paul calls the "elemental spirits of the world" (4:3). Humanity's rite of passage from childhood to adulthood occurred at a "date set by the father" (4:2), when "in the fullness of time" (4:4) "God sent his Son, born of a woman, born under the law, in order to redeem those who were under the law, so that we might receive adoption as children" (4:4–5). [See Expanded CD Version p. 469: *Humanity's Achieving Full Adulthood in Christ*]

(b) An allegorical rehearsal of God's redemptive story (4:21–5:1). Another strategy used by Paul to persuade his converts not to place themselves under the bondage of the law employs a reinterpretation of the story of Abraham, Hagar, and Sarah (Gen 16–21). This time, rather than emphasizing the permanence of God's original covenant with Abraham and the emergence of the Mosaic law as a temporary, interim measure, Paul delineates alternative ways of tracing one's lineage to Abraham. By Paul's own admission, his interpretation is an allegorical rendering of Gen 16–21, and a highly innovative one at that.

With an exegetical boldness that still astonishes modern readers, Paul constructs two lineages traceable to Abraham: one leading through the "slave woman" Hagar directly to Sinai (through the unnamed Ishmael) and finally to the "present Jerusalem," the Torah-loyal Judaism of Paul's own day; and the other leading through the "free woman" Sarah to Isaac, the child of promise, to the "Jerusalem above," who is "our mother" (4:26), the newly constituted messianic people that derives its life and identity from the risen Christ. Since the former lineage occurred through human conniving, Hagar's child was "born according to the flesh" (4:23). Isaac, by contrast, was the child "born through the promise" (4:23). It was "according to the Spirit" (4:29) and represented a different impulse—a willingness to trust in a promise and give way to God's gracious guidance of history rather than the need to insinuate ourselves into God's plan and to do God's own work ourselves.

Two ways lead back to Abraham, one characterized by slavery and human ingenuity—the way of law—and the other by freedom and trust—the way of faith in God's promise.

Given these two options for sketching a family tree, Paul draws two conclusions:

(1) The sets of heirs have always been bedeviled by sibling rivalry (4:29). This explains why the "children of promise" still have to contend with the "children of slavery," the proponents of Torah observance.

(2) One way of relating to Abraham is through promise and freedom, and within this line God's Spirit has been present (4:29). The other line has slavery as its defining feature. Rather than being the carrier of God's promise, this line began through human ingenuity. Since its outlook was "according to the flesh" (4:23, 29), it was initiated and sustained by a set of impulses antithetical to those of the other line: Spirit, promise, and freedom.

To yield to the Mosaic law is to align oneself with a lineage marked by slavery and human ingenuity. This option also fails to see that Christ stands within the lineage of Abraham, Sarah, and Isaac—the lineage of promise, which has been sustained by God's continuing Spirit. Being a true child of Abraham is not based on Torah observance. Rather, Christ is Abraham's seed and those "in Christ," both Jews and Gentiles, embody God's promise as direct descendents of Abraham. They do not need to pass through Sinai—observe Torah's commandments—to experience the fullness of God's original promise.

4. Paul sketches the Galatians' options as a choice between the law and Christ (5:1–12). The era of the law has given way to the era of Christ (4:4–5), and God's

grace has been displayed in Christ (1:6). If the Gentile Christians at Galatia opt for the law, even minimally, this implies lack of confidence in the full validity of Christ's death. They face an either/or choice: either Christ or the law, but not both. They must understand that submitting to circumcision symbolizes a commitment "to obey the entire law" (5:3). Since Christ is the channel through which God's grace has been displayed, to opt for the law is to "fall" from grace (5:4).

The full significance of Christ's death is understood only when one sees that "circumcised" and "uncircumcised" no longer have the valence they once had, either as markers of ethnic status or as indicators of salvation. With the passing of the era of the law, circumcision is a meaningless religious practice for both Gentiles and Jews; it has always been so for Gentiles, and is especially so now for Jews. What matters more than this ritual certifying one's status before God are practices in which faith is enacted as love (5:6)—God's preferred mode of being religious.

Paul Encourages Freedom and Life in the Spirit (5:13–6:18)

With such a strong final appeal based on the changes described in the didactic section (3:1–5:12), Paul can shift to encouragement in the *hortatory section* (5:13–6:18). Here the concern is expressly paraenetic: exhortation to adopt attitudes and exhibit behaviors that reflect one's status "in Christ." Typical of paraenesis, this section is marked with repeated imperatives and other forms of moral exhortation, but here Paul's exhortation resonates with the overall tone of Galatians. Since he previously characterized the law and Christ as promoting slavery and freedom respectively, he sketches the primary ethical choice confronting the Galatians as a choice between slavery and freedom (5:13).

Because the law was a central issue in the crisis at Galatia and figured prominently in Paul's earlier discussion, he grounds his appeal to love in the love command of Lev 19:18 (5:14). Earlier in the letter Paul had argued from the Law to contest a view of the law that sees circumcision as a requirement and Torah observance as the way of accessing God's righteousness. Here he shows, somewhat inconsistently, that Torah is inescapably revelatory, but that it is illuminated best when refracted through the Christ event.

Paul's sketch of moral options as a choice between the "works of the flesh" and the "fruit of the Spirit" (5:16–25) is also closely related to his earlier alignment of "flesh" with the law, and "Spirit" with the lineage of promise and freedom mediated through Sarah to Christ. By using these antithetical categories, Paul confirms the strong theology of the Spirit present within the Galatian churches. Their initial entry into the faith is described as "receiving the Spirit" (3:1–5), and they are explicitly designated as "the spirituals" (*pneumatikoi*, 6:1). Seen one way, the entire letter is a defense of the Spirit and a Spirit-oriented understanding of the Christian gospel. Moral choices, especially habitual forms of behavior, are rightly seen as "sowing to the flesh" and "sowing to the Spirit" (6:8).

Also recognizing the terrible toll such deeply fought controversies take on community life and the spiritual welfare of souls, Paul shapes his moral exhortation toward community building and responsible forms of mutual edification and support. Heading the list of moral exhortations is faithfully enacted love (5:13–15), the only true anti-dote to self-consuming, destructive congregational battles. Vices to be avoided include self-indulgence and other behaviors that threaten communal good will (5:16–21); virtues to be pursued are those that seek the common good and downplay self-aggrandizement (5:22–26). Mutual concern for each other's welfare and the willingness to share generously also figure prominently—doing what is right, doing what is good (6:1–10).

Even with all of these commendable exhortations, the final word is a word of warning: to be coldly realistic in the face of enemies (6:11–16).

The Truth of the Gospel

Galatians is unusual for the way the gospel functions as the pivot of the letter. This is seen by the sheer frequency of both the noun form "gospel" (*euangelion*, 1:6, 11; 2:2, 5, 7, 14) and the verb form "to gospel" or evangelize (*euangelizomai*, 1:8 [2x], 9, 11, 16, 23; 4:13). The crisis in Galatia stems from competing, antithetical construals of the gospel: the gospel Paul preaches and "another gospel" (1:6–9). Paul can differentiate his mission from Peter's as the gospel for the circumcised and uncircumcised respectively (2:7–10). He chastises Peter's behavior as being inconsistent with the "truth of the gospel" (2:14). Any effort to sketch the contours of Paul's theological vision in Galatians must take into account what Paul sees as the "truth of the gospel."

Christ, the Focal Point of the New Creation

Even though the overarching theological issue driving the letter is soteriological, at the center of Paul's theological vision stands Jesus Christ, both the historical person and the living reality. From this focal point Paul consistently argues; to it he constantly returns, appropriating traditional Christian language to summarize what God accomplished in Jesus Christ (see 1:1, 4; 2:20; 3:13; 4:4–5). From it he draws fresh implications, coining new metaphors and pushing the boundaries of old metaphors.

In recalling his initial encounter with the risen Christ, which resulted in his call/conversion, Paul speaks of the "revelation of Jesus Christ" that he received—literally, the "*apocalypse of Jesus Christ*" (1:12). More than the extraordinary quality of his encounter, this metaphor also suggests that Paul understood the content of the revelation in terms of his Jewish apocalyptic worldview. With its linear view of history, apocalyptic divided time between the "present evil age" and the "age to come." History was also seen as an unfolding divine drama in which God, the Prime Actor, and his designated vicegerent, the Anointed One, moved events toward their intended, divinely guided purpose.

Given this apocalyptic framework for Paul's understanding of the gospel, the coming of Christ is an apocalyptic event through which God has brought about the "new creation" (6:15). With all the force of a volcanic eruption within history, this event reconfigured national, ethnic, social, gender, and even religious boundaries (3:25–29). As in the first creation, God's Spirit is the energizing force behind this creative transformation, but this time the Spirit's energy is channeled through Jesus Christ, the one who challenges the "present evil age" (1:4) and moves it toward the "hope of righteousness" (5:5).

The "gospel of Jesus Christ" is both the story of this event and its ongoing, living performance. Through the proclamation of the gospel the cross is visibly displayed (3:1). To "hear [the gospel] in faith" is to receive it obediently. To participate in the gospel by ritual re-enactment of Christ's dying and rising is to experience death to the world's entire frame of reference and its capacity to control the human imagination, senses, and will. By doing so, one enters a new life of freedom from such enslavement.

Far from being a mere truth claim about Jesus Christ, the "truth of the gospel" reveals Christ as God's continuously enacted grace through which God summons humanity toward the life of faith. As its central pulsating force, Christ has both a punctiliar and linear dimension. As point, he marks the historic moment when God established the contours of the new creation. With him, a dramatic change occurred, creating residual effects whose cumulative power through time gives him linear embodiment in history.

Effects of the New Creation

Since the effects of God's new creation are interwoven into a complex tapestry of human and cosmic events, it is difficult to separate distinctive strands. For the purposes of analysis, we do so even at the risk of rupturing the whole.

1. *The Recovery of Faith as the Way of Accessing and Experiencing God's Righteousness.* Paul thinks of Jesus Christ standing at the junction of two eras: "before faith came" (3:23) and "now that faith has come" (3:25). With Christ, faith arrives not as a totally new way of relating to God but as an old way rediscovered. Jesus Christ reopens the way of faith as the normative mode of relating to God.

Paul finds the faith principle deeply embedded within Scripture as an old insight waiting to be recovered. It is there both as a general principle—"the righteous live by their faith" (Hab 2:4; cf. Gal 3:11)—and as a specific instance—"[Abraham] believed the LORD; and the LORD reckoned it to him as righteousness" (Gen 15:6; cf. Gal 3:6). The way of faith is as old as Abraham. It is a way of relating to God that was never revoked or superseded—overshadowed, perhaps, even obscured during the period of the law, but still latent within Scripture, waiting to be recovered in Jesus Christ.

The way of faith is reopened when Christ is seen as Abraham's true successor, the "seed" or progeny of Abraham through whom God's promise that "all the nations will be blessed" is kept. Christ is the one through whom God's promise is kept alive, and seeing this is itself an act of faith. This, among other things, is what it means to "believe in Christ Jesus" (2:16): to see him as the promised "seed" of Abraham, the one through whom God's promises finally come true. The arrival of faith ushers in an era when the capacity to receive God's promise, trust it, and lean into the future trusting in this promise becomes the hallmark of "those of faith," the true children of Abraham (3:7).

Since Jesus Christ is the critical link in the story—the one through whom God's original promise to Abraham comes to fulfillment—he becomes the one toward whom

A woodcut depiction of Saul's heavenly vision on the Damascus road (Acts 9); from a German translation of the Latin Vulgate, printed in 1477 in Augsburg. From the Digital Image Archive of The Richard C. Kessler Reformation Collection, Pitts Theology Library, Candler School of Theology, Emory University, Atlanta, Georgia.

faith is directed. As the enabler of God's promise, he is the object of faith. To "believe in Jesus Christ" means two things. First, that believers find the story of the gospel, and its interpretation of events, credible. Christ's death can be understood plausibly as a sacrificial death that benefits humanity (1:4). Second, that Christ himself is the prime actor in bringing about the new creation—the one who "set us free from the present evil age" (1:4).

Jesus Christ may be related to the era of faith in yet another way: as one who actively exercised faith. This is especially the case if the much disputed phrase *pistis Christou* (2:16; cf. Rom 2:23, 26) is understood in its more literal sense as the "faith of Christ"—the faith that Christ has or exercises ("of Christ" as a subjective genitive)—rather than its more traditionally understood sense "faith in Christ"—faith directed toward or placed in Christ ("of Christ" as an objective genitive). So understood, Jesus Christ is Abraham's "seed" in a double sense: he is the one through whom God's promise was fulfilled and the one who, like Abraham, faithfully trusted the promise of God. Like Abraham, Christ becomes an exemplar of faith.

2. *The Eclipse of Torah*. Faith's re-entry follows the era of the law (3:23), thereby exposing the law's ineffectiveness as a means of experiencing God's righteousness. As a response to the "other gospelers," for whom the law is both universal and absolute—universal because Torah is the full embodiment of God's revelation and its observance is required for anyone who wants complete access to God; absolute in the sense that literal adherence to Torah is an unconditional requirement—Paul's critique relativizes the law.

What once mattered ultimately—circumcision—is now a matter of indifference; and religious, ethnic, or national distinctions based on the presence or absence of circumcision are meaningless (5:6; 6:15). Since the law has been eclipsed by Christ, circumcision cannot be required of Gentile Christians. Now that restrictions about what to eat and with whom to associate no longer have exclusionary effect, there is no reason for Jewish Christians to refuse to eat with Gentile Christians. Since God has fully embraced Gentile Christians *as Gentiles*, Jewish Christians should do so as well.

In his critique of the law, Paul argues against the grain of much of the biblical witness and wider Jewish tradition that see the law as a sublime achievement, the jewel in the crown of God's revelation (esp. Ps 119; also cf. Ps 1:2; 19:7–11). For this reason, his sharp-edged critique is based on Scripture itself and has two distinctive elements: (1) the necessity of complete compliance (Gal 3:10, quoting Deut 27:26 and 28:58–59), and (2) the accent on performance (Gal 3:12, quoting Lev 18:5). Even more to the point, the dynamics of Torah observance conflict with the faith principle—"the law does not operate on the basis of faith" (Gal 3:12 REB).

Paul cannot find scriptural warrant for claiming that one accesses God's righteousness via the law. As the example of Abraham shows (Gen 15:6), faith is the way into God's righteousness. The cumulative effect of these criticisms is to expose fatal flaws in the way of law, or, as Paul puts it, the curse of the law (Gal 3:10). "No justification (or righteousness) through Torah" becomes Paul's mantra (Gal 2:15–16, 21).

Paul roundly criticizes the dynamics of Torah observance, but more significant is the larger framework within which these criticisms are set. In the extended argument that comprises the middle section of the letter (3:1–5:12), he proposes an alternative construal of God's story.

One way of reading the biblical story is to see the early Genesis narratives as the early stages of preparation for the giving of the law at Sinai and Israel's subsequent history as living within—sometimes successfully, more often unsuccessfully—this covenantal arrangement. Eras of prosperity are seen as times when Israel is obedient to the Mosaic covenant, whereas periods of turbulence and hardship reflect Israel's resistance and failure to keep God's law.

But Paul rewrites this version of the scriptural story. First, he accents Abraham and the pivotal significance of God's original promise to him eventually to "bless all nations," which extends God's promised blessings to include Gentiles. Second, Paul redefines the period of the law as a necessary detour that occurred as a prelude to the single most important figure after Abraham: Jesus Christ, Abraham's "seed." Far from being the zenith of the biblical story, the giving of the law at Sinai, Paul insists, launches a parenthetical period that placed Israel in a "holding pattern" in which it had to wait for the new messianic era to dawn.

What clinches this alternative version of the biblical story is the Abraham-Hagar-Sarah allegory (Gal 4:21–5:1). By sketching parallel lineages that provide two different options for constructing one's identity as a "child of Abraham," Paul further highlights Abraham as the pivotal, if not preeminent, OT figure for establishing one's pedigree. As a result, Paul diminishes the status of Moses and the law by linking God's covenant of promise exclusively with Abraham and his successors, "those of faith," and detaching it completely from the Mosaic law.

Paul's own personal narrative both conforms to and illustrates this reinterpreted scriptural narrative. In his experience of the "revelation of Jesus Christ" he recognized Christ as Abraham's true successor, his "seed," the one through whom God's blessings extend to the Gentiles, and himself as the apostle commissioned by God to enable that promise to be fulfilled.

What Paul meant by the cryptic phrase "through the law I died to the law" (2:19) is much debated; but it may refer both to his existential and exegetical experience. Through his own life under the law, he found the experience frustrating, finally even lethal, and thus gave it up as a way of experiencing God's righteousness. Through his own reading of the law, he became convinced that his alternative construal of the biblical story was more plausible, and thus the law's status as the preeminent chapter in the biblical story collapsed. Either way, in his encounter with Christ he experienced his own death to the law.

3. *Disclosing the Full Scope of God's Saving Activity.* When Paul read the Genesis account of God's promise to Abraham, he was struck by several features, especially the way the recipients of the promise are described: "all the Gentiles [or "nations"; *panta ta ethnē*] shall be blessed in you" (Gal 3:8; cf. Gen 12:3; esp. 18:18). While *ta ethnē* was a general term in the original promise, the phrase was a standard way of designating Gentiles in the Greek OT. Paul takes it in this more narrow sense and sees Gentiles at the center of God's vision for the future at this inaugural moment in Israel's story. Reaching out to them is not an afterthought; it was God's intention from the outset.

Something else was embedded in the scriptural promise from the outset: how they were to be included in God's promise. Like Abraham, Gentiles were to access God's righteousness by faith. In doing so, they become Abraham's heirs (Gal 3:6–9). Since this expectation is latent within the Genesis story, Scripture (God) "declared the gospel beforehand to Abraham" (Gal 3:8).

The gospel of full inclusion and God's righteousness accessed through faith, while enabled for the first time by Christ, is an ancient message, proclaimed by God to Abraham with the promised blessing! The gospel Paul preaches is not a message newly minted; it is rather an old message deeply embedded within Scripture to which he, as a prophetic messenger prepared by God even before his birth, is newly commissioned. What is new is that it is now encased in the story of Jesus Christ, whose time finally came.

Both the *who*—Gentiles—and the *how*—justification through faith—are explicitly envisioned in God's promise to Abraham. The full realization of this promise occurs as part of the new creation.

When God revealed Christ to Paul (Gal 1:15–16), Christ's true identity, his role as Abraham's successor, and the full scope of God's saving purpose were revealed. Paul's mission to the Gentiles—his (and his associates') work in reaching out to them—and the gospel he preached to them—the "gospel for the uncircumcised" (2:7), in other words, faith as the way of accessing God's righteousness—were both divinely authorized because they had full scriptural warrant. The thrust of his mission and the content of his gospel were corollaries. It was impossible for Paul to separate his apostolic calling, and thus his apostolic identity, from his mission to the Gentiles. For him, being an apostle meant preaching the gospel to Gentiles.

For this reason, Paul's defense of "the truth of the gospel" also serves as his brief for the Gentile mission. For him, two elements related to that mission are critically linked: (1) its legitimacy, and (2) the terms under which it is conducted. As the Jerusalem meeting showed (Gal 2:1–10), all parties were in agreement about the former. No one there seriously contested that the gospel of Christ should be preached to Gentiles. But what became clear in the Antioch episode were the divided opinions about the latter (2:11–14). For Paul's part, inviting Gentiles to participate in God's righteousness through faith conformed to the gospel God preached beforehand to Abraham; requiring them to be circumcised, and, by extension, to observe Torah invalidated the mission because it compromised the "truth of the gospel" (Gal 2:14).

4. *A Newly Configured Moral Vision.* Questions about specific behaviors figure prominently throughout Galatians: whether male Gentile Christians should be circumcised and whether all Gentile Christians, in turn, should adhere to other Jewish practices, such as the observances of holy days and the keeping of food and purity laws (Gal 2:11–14; 4:10). The "other gospelers" thought Torah observance would help establish beneficial behavioral boundaries for Gentiles who had turned away from practices deemed to be destructive and addictive, or, as Paul puts it, from "those feeble and bankrupt elemental spirits" (Gal 4:9 REB). By conceiving of the various demonic forces this way, Paul may mean the social structures to which Gentiles, as well as Jews, could easily be held captive. Those who promoted Torah observance as useful for Gentile Christians may have felt that a free-reigning Spirit gave way to uncontrolled behaviors and was certainly no match for curbing the desires of the flesh.

The eclipse of Torah that occurred with Christ removed the incentive for Torah observance, especially as a salvific activity, and probably even as a morally beneficial one. Paul saw Torah observance as the sure road to slavery. By ending the reign of Torah, Christ opened the way to freedom—freedom from the law as a "yoke of slavery" (5:1) and freedom to live in the Spirit.[6] In the new creation freedom is the existential space formed by Christ in which the Spirit reigns supreme, shaping new forms of individual and corporate existence that break through the world's oppressive structures to create newly imagined ways of being and living within the world.

Paul sketches the moral options open to Gentile Christians in terms of flesh and Spirit, another one of his frequently occurring polarities (5:16–26). These he sees as fundamentally opposed impulses that dictate two equally opposed realms of behavior (Gal 5:17). Especially significant is how these two impulses are identified with the two ways of understanding the lineage of Abraham. The way of Hagar and Sinai is the way of flesh, while that of Sarah, Isaac, and the Jerusalem above is the way of Spirit.

What typifies the former is the human inclination to self-serve, to interfere with God's purposes, an impulse that puts greater confidence in human ingenuity and in asserting one's self rather than waiting before God. Not surprisingly, the list of vices itemized under the "works of the flesh" (Gal 5:19–21) recalls behaviors associated with Israel both during the wilderness and afterward, or Israel living in the era of law. They are the vices of self-indulgence and mutually destructive social behavior.

In sharp contrast are the behaviors associated with the Spirit, the impulse characterizing the Abraham-Sarah-Isaac lineage. Here the lineage remains intact because people understood what it meant to live with the anxieties and unpredictability of a promise, but to trust in the Giver of the promise and view the future as an open-ended set of possibilities that God both controls and bestows. The behaviors characterized as the "fruit of the Spirit" (Gal 5:22–23), rather than being self-indulgent, self-destructive, and socially disorienting, are behaviors that occur with the death of "the flesh" (Gal 5:24), which is in some sense analogous to Christ's own death. The moral dynamic driving them is not "self-indulgence" but love as enacted faith (Gal 5:6), which captures the essence of the "whole law" (Gal 5:14). The overall effect of these behaviors is that people find themselves caring for each other, mutually reinforcing each other, and building constructive forms of social community (Gal 6:1–10).

When these contrasting sets of behaviors are seen as patterns of living before God that are aligned respectively with the two lineages of slavery and freedom outlined in the Abraham-Hagar-Sarah allegory, it becomes clearer why those in Christ respond to the impulse of the Spirit. To "live by the flesh" is to shape one's life by the expectations and behaviors of a bygone era. It is to live anachronistically.

Notes

1. For Marcion's treatment of Galatians, see Tertullian, *Marc.* 5.2–4. See A. von Harnack, *History of Dogma* (trans. Neil Buchanan; 7 vols. in 4 vols.; New York: Dover, 1961), 1:89–90. The quotation was originally made by Franz Overbeck. See Bruce M. Metzger, *The Canon of the New Testament* (Oxford: Oxford University Press, 1997), 93.

2. *Preachings of St. Peter* 17; also *Epistle of Peter to James* 2.1. See G. Strecker, "The Kerygmata Petrou," in *New Testament Apocrypha* (eds. E. Hennecke and W. Schneemelcher; trans. R. McL. Wilson. 2 vols. London: Lutterworth, 1965), 2:111–12, 121–23.

3. This rehearsal differs at substantial points from Luke's account of Paul's conversion and subsequent events in Acts. For example, Acts 9:19–30 reports Paul going to Jerusalem after his Damascus conversion experience, whereas Gal 1:16–17 excludes such a trip to Jerusalem. Galatians 1:22–23 reports that Paul was "unknown by sight to the churches of Judea," which is difficult to square with his reported preaching activity in Jerusalem in Acts 9:26–30.

4. Whether this meeting corresponds to the "Jerusalem Council" in Acts 15 is much debated. If so, they represent two quite different accounts of what happened. Some equate this meeting with Paul's trip to Jerusalem in Acts 11:27–30.

5. Old Testament passages or allusions cited in this section include Gen 15:6 (3:6); Gen 12:3; 18:18 (3:8); Deut 27:26 (3:10); Hab 2:4 (3:11); Lev 18:5 (3:12); Deut 21:23 (3:13); Gen 13:15; 17:8; 24:7 (3:16); Gen 16–21 (4:21–5:1); Isa 54:1 (4:27); Gen 21:10 (4:30). Paul's actual interpretive use of some of these OT passages is creative, if not downright baffling. For example, the conclusion he draws from Deut 27:26 appears inconsistent with the clear meaning of the text. He also cites a version of Hab 2:4 significantly different from standard Greek and Hebrew forms of the text.

6. Freedom is a more prominent theme in Galatians (2:4; 3:28; 4:22, 23, 26, 30, 31; 5:1, 13) than in Romans (8:21).

Bibliography

Commentaries

Betz, Hans D. *Galatians: A Commentary on Paul's Letter to the Churches in Galatia.* Hermeneia. Philadelphia: Fortress, 1979.

Bruce, F. F. *The Epistle to the Galatians: A Commentary on the Greek Text.* New International Greek Testament Commentary. Grand Rapids: Eerdmans, 1981.

Cousar, Charles B. *Galatians.* Interpretation: A Bible Commentary for Teaching and Preaching. Atlanta: John Knox, 1982.

Dunn, James D. G. *The Epistle to the Galatians.* Black's New Testament Commentaries. London/Peabody: Black/Hendrickson, 1993.

Hays, Richard B. "The Letter to the Galatians: Introduction, Commentary, and Reflections." Pages 181–348 in vol. 11 of *The New Interpreter's Bible.* Edited by Leander E. Keck. 12 vols. Nashville: Abingdon, 2000.

Longenecker, Richard N. *Galatians.* Word Biblical Commentary 41. Dallas: Word, 1990.

Lührmann, Dieter. *Galatians: A Continental Commentary.* Translated by O. C. Dean Jr. Minneapolis: Fortress, 1992.

Martyn, J. Louis. *Galatians: A New Translation with Introduction and Commentary.* Anchor Bible 33A. New York: Doubleday, 1997.

Ziesler, John A. *The Epistle to the Galatians.* Epworth Commentaries. London: Epworth, 1992.

Other Resources

Barclay, John M. G. *Obeying the Truth: A Study of Paul's Ethics in Galatians.* Studies of the New Testament and Its World. Edinburgh: T&T Clark, 1988.

Barrett, C. K. *Freedom and Obligation: A Study of the Epistle to the Galatians.* Philadelphia: Westminster, 1985.

Boers, Hendrikus. *The Justification of the Gentiles: Paul's Letters to the Galatians and Romans.* Peabody: Hendrickson, 1994.

Cosgrove, Charles H. *The Cross and the Spirit: A Study in the Argument and Theology of Galatians.* Macon: Mercer University Press, 1989.

Dunn, James D. G. *The Theology of Paul's Letter to the Galatians.* New Testament Theology. Cambridge: Cambridge University Press, 1993; repr. 2001.

Ebeling, Gerhard. *The Truth of the Gospel: An Exposition of Galatians.* Philadelphia: Fortress, 1985.

Martyn, J. Louis. *Theological Issues in the Letters of Paul.* Edinburgh/Nashville: T&T Clark/Abingdon, 1997.

Morland, Kjell A. *The Rhetoric of Curse in Galatians.* Emory Studies in Early Christianity 5. Atlanta: Scholars Press, 1996.

Nanos, Mark D., ed. *The Galatians Debate: Contemporary Issues in Rhetorical and Historical Interpretation.* Peabody: Hendrickson, 2002.

Chapter 15

Romans

". . . he was a herald both in the East and in the West, he gained the noble fame of his faith, he taught righteousness to all the world . . ."

1 Clement 5.6–7

"Paul would never have formed his characteristic doctrine of justification by faith had he not taken in hand the task of converting Gentiles."

William Wrede

More than any other Pauline letter, Romans presents a single, sustained argument. What constitutes the heart of the argument is much debated. For some, it is Paul's theology of justification by faith, certainly one of the prominent themes of the letter. For others, it is the mission to the Gentiles and how they relate to Israel within God's overall plan. But to reduce Romans to a single theme, even one as important as either of these, is to oversimplify a complex argument.

Romans presents a special challenge because of its length and complexity. Its complexity, in turn, stems from its many ambiguities, and yet these ambiguities help account for its enduring power. Although Romans did not always stand first among the Pauline letters in some canonical lists, it eventually did so, partly because of its length but mainly because of its sheer theological power.

As one of the most influential of Paul's writings, if not the entire NT, Romans has left a deep imprint on the church's thought and has even altered the course of its history. The metaphors of Romans may not have come to life in the church's hymns and art the way other NT images have, but the images of Romans have succeeded in conveying the letter's most powerful ideas. Through these ideas Romans has profoundly shaped how the church has thought about God, Christ, the Holy Spirit, and the way humans experience God's saving grace.

Compared with other Pauline letters, Romans exhibits a more reflective quality. Rather than addressing specific congregational concerns, as do the Letters to the Corinthians and Galatians, it adopts a much broader perspective. It may be addressed to Christians in a single city, but it is informed by Paul's experiences among churches in the Aegean region during the preceding years. This deeper fund of experience widens its angle of vision.

Probably written from Corinth at the conclusion of Paul's mission in the Aegean, Romans stands at a critical juncture in his life. Having completed an important phase of his mission to the Gentiles, and, even more important, having completed the collection for the poor Jerusalem Christians, he stands poised between two sets of anxieties: those connected with delivering the collection to Jerusalem and the usual anxieties of beginning a new phase of mission work that will extend the borders of his mission eventually to the coasts of Spain.

As one of Paul's later writings, Romans has been called his last will and testament, but this is a misnomer. It may be thought of as Paul's last word in the sense that it improves on, even refines, his earlier theological reflections. Yet because some notable Pauline themes are missing, it by no means represents the full and final statement of his theology. The Lord's Supper, for example, goes unmentioned. The term "church" (*ekklēsia*) is mentioned only a few times (significantly, they all occur in the final chapter: 16:1, 4–5, 16, 23), although much of what Paul says bears directly on the church, its mission, and its self-understanding. The letter accents the nearness of the end and reminds its readers of the sobering reality of God's future judgment, but it displays little interest in Christ's second coming and the sequence of events it triggers. Thus, while Romans has often been read as a comprehensive summary of Pauline theology, it is only a partial, albeit richly textured, statement of certain dimensions of his thought.

If we take into account the immediate context of the letter, as illumined by 1:1–16 and 15:14–16:27, we cannot read Romans without seeing how closely it is connected to Paul's missionary work among Gentiles. It may be a profound theological treatise, but its profundity has deep roots in his self-understanding as the "apostle to the Gentiles." Since Paul's mission among the Gentiles in the Aegean and its projected continuation in the West establishes the immediate context for writing Romans, we should read the letter as a position paper that explains and defends that mission. Because Paul's reputation precedes him in Rome, writing the letter enables him to establish credibility with a church whose goodwill he needs if he wants to go to Spain.

Internal tensions within the Roman church related to the success of the Gentile mission in Rome may be an additional motivation for writing Romans. It is possible that some well-established Gentile Christians were reluctant to welcome back to Rome returning Jewish Christians who earlier had been banished from the city by the emperor Claudius. If so, this was all the more reason for Paul to clarify God's purpose in extending the divine promise to Gentiles and to show how his own apostolic ministry related to that purpose. This in turn would have made the ticklish question of Israel's role within God's overall purpose even more pressing, given Israel's general reluctance to accept Jesus as God's Messiah.

Romans as an Argument

In Romans Paul adapts the widely known Cynic-Stoic diatribe, in which the argument unfolds in stages as the speaker engages in dialogue with an imaginary interlocutor. The argument is cast within Paul's usual epistolary form, with its standard greeting (1:1–7), opening thanksgiving (1:8–15), body (1:16–16:23), and benediction (16:25–27). It is a rhetorical argument in the form of a letter.

Because of some conspicuous literary breaks in the letter, chapters 1–4, 5–8, 9–11, and 12–16 are usually seen as discrete sections of the letter. Even within these units, further divisions are possible. After the greeting and thanksgiving, 1:16–3:31 forms a sensible thought unit, with chapter 4 serving as a natural extension of the argument. In the last section, chapter 16 stands on its own and is even considered by some to have been a separate letter perhaps addressed to the church at Ephesus. There also seems to be a break at 15:6–7, with 12:1–15:6 forming the concluding moral exhortation and 15:7–33 (perhaps 15:14–33) addressing more concrete concerns, including those relating to the delivery of the collection.

These divisions are usually marked by rhetorical devices that assist the reader in adjusting to shifts in the line of argument. The periodic uses of "Amen!" signal shifts (1:25; 9:5; 11:36; 15:33; 16:24, 27), possibly indicating points at which the hearers were expected to respond audibly. Even clearer are the highly rhetorical, often liturgically crafted passages that conclude individual sections on an upbeat (esp. 8:31–39; 11:33–36; 15:33; 16:25–27). Diatribal markers are perhaps the most effective device for moving the argument along. These include the direct forms of address to the imagined dialogue partner (2:1, 3; 9:20), the shift to the second person (2:17–25; 6:3, 12–14; 7:1–6, etc.), and the interlocutor's objections (3:1–9, 27–31; 4:1–10; 6:1–2, 15, 21; 7:7, 13; 8:31–36; 9:14, 19–21, 30, 32; 10:18; 11:1–4, 7, 11).

Rather than developing arguments and introducing objections in a highly formalized way, Paul employs the diatribe flexibly. This fluidity in his use of the diatribe gives the argument its liveliness. As the argument is unfolded, objections are raised and answered in a somewhat haphazard manner. The objections, for example, in 3:1–9 are hard to separate, or even to classify into categories. Nor are they taken up systematically as the letter unfolds. Chapters 9–11 take up the questions of 3:3 relating to Israel's disobedience; chapter 6 deals with the accusation of moral relativity introduced in 3:8; and the discussion of the law in 7:7–25 addresses the law-faith polarity introduced in 3:31. While the letter may seem to unfold in a zigzag pattern, the overall argument moves forward. The reader may experience frustration in trying to follow the argument in Romans, but ultimately a linear and finally coherent argument does unfold.

The argument of Romans closely coheres with its theology. In one sense we can distinguish between implicit theological assumptions within the letter and explicit theological reflection based on those underlying convictions. To use a distinction commonly made by modern theologians, we can distinguish between first order theological statements—basic confessional convictions—and second order theological reflection that systematically explores the implications of those primary convictions. Romans exhibits some of both. It is filled with short summaries of early Christian preaching and confession, yet it has second order theological reflection that explores more fully the implications of some early Christian beliefs. What sets Romans apart from many of the other Pauline letters is the way its theology is woven into the fabric of the argument. To get at the theology of Romans, we must follow the argument.

Romans reflects Paul's extensive missionary experience that has lasted some twenty years or more. The dialogue between speaker and interlocutor has been freshly formulated for this particular letter. Even so, it echoes Paul's lively conversations with friends and opponents alike in synagogues, private homes, shops, and public settings throughout the Mediterranean region. The argument in Romans represents the culmination of his thinking about the Gentile mission as it has developed over the years.

Paul's missionary work was driven by his own sense of apostolic calling, which required him to think through the implications of God's action in Christ and tackle a wide range of major theological questions. Romans may seem like a highly theoretical argument, but it addresses a concrete problem within the church's life: the Gentile mission. It is an instructive example of critical theological reflection being brought to bear on a practical issue.

Paul's argument in Romans is also deeply anchored in earlier Christian tradition. This is immediately evident in the opening greeting, in which he veers from his standard epistolary practice by including a capsule summary of Christian belief that places him squarely within the mainstream of the church. The repeated instances of formulaic summaries of Christian preaching and confession scattered throughout the letter underscore Paul's indebtedness to his predecessors (e.g., 3:25; 4:24–25; 5:8; 8:3, 34; 10:9). However distinctive the argument of Romans is—and it is quite distinctive in many respects—its substructure shows tight connections with earlier strands of Christian belief.

Another distinguishing feature of Paul's argument is its scriptural texture. No other NT writing, with the possible exception of Revelation or Hebrews, is so thoroughly scriptural in both its conceptuality and content. With more than fifty quotations from the Septuagint, many of them drawn from the Psalter and Isaiah, Romans exemplifies both the richness and diversity of Paul's argumentation from Scripture. While his use of Scripture is by no means uniform throughout the letter—Scripture argumentation is heavily concentrated in chapters 3–5 and 9–11—it is always central to his basic argument.

What to make of Paul's heavy dependence on Scripture in Romans is not altogether clear. Is the argument couched in scriptural terms because his target audience is primarily Jewish? Or is it because Paul himself is Jewish and that any case he would make for the legitimacy of the Gentile mission would have to derive its warrant from *his* Scripture? The answer is probably some of both, together with the fact that his argument has been hammered out in conversations over the years with his fellow Jews, both Christian and non-Christian. Paul's own Jewish background, the context of his ministry, and the background of his potential readers together account for the scriptural texture of Romans. **[See Expanded CD Version pp. 486–88: *Paul's Use of Scripture in Romans*]**

Plotting the Argument

While we should not equate the outline of the letter with the structure of Paul's argument, it is nevertheless useful to summarize how the letter unfolds:

1. After the opening greeting and thanksgiving (1:1–15), which concludes with a preliminary thesis statement (1:16–17), Paul first depicts the universal human dilemma: everyone lives within the grip of sin (1:18–2:29); this includes Gentiles (1:18–32), an unidentified group claiming to be religious (2:1–16), and Jews (2:17–29).

2. Paul then introduces a string of objections probably drawn from his mission experience that must be answered as he develops his argument in the letter (3:1–20). This prompts a further elaboration of his basic position (3:21–31).

3. In answer to one objection—that justification by faith challenges the principle of law, even undercuts the Mosaic law—Paul introduces Abraham as an example of justifying faith (ch. 4).

4. Paul then moves to a comprehensive description of how he understands "faith in Christ" or the life of faith enabled by Christ. With 5:1–11 serving as a transitional section, Paul introduces the Adam-Christ typology (5:12–21), then answers the objection that justification by faith actually encourages people to sin (ch. 6). Following this, he engages in a more detailed critique of the Mosaic law (ch. 7) and concludes by elaborating on the Spirit as the defining reality of Christian existence (ch. 8).

5. Once Paul finishes this extended exposition of his gospel, he then turns to the difficult question of Israel and the Gentiles. In particular, he seeks to account for Israel's largely negative response to the gospel and clarify its role in God's overall plan (chs. 9–11).

6. At 12:1, the letter shifts from a didactic to a hortatory mode, as Paul provides moral guidelines adapted for a Christian community comprising Jewish and Gentile Christians (12:1–15:13).

7. The concluding portion of the letter takes up practical matters relating to the collection, his impending visit to Jerusalem, and his eventual trip to Rome (15:14–33). The final chapter contains an extended set of personal greetings and a remarkably pointed warning against smooth-tongued troublemakers (16:17–20).

As we examine Paul's argument, we should distinguish between what Paul argues for—the telos, or overall purpose, of the letter—and his means of achieving that purpose—the network of sub-arguments that enables him to achieve this overall purpose. Three passages are pivotal to the argument: 1:16–17; 3:21–31; and 15:7–13. Of the three, the third states the purpose of the argument most succinctly.

Romans 15:7–9 introduces some key elements:

> Welcome one another, therefore, just as Christ has welcomed you, for the glory of God. For I tell you that Christ has become a servant of the circumcised on behalf of the truth of God in order that he might confirm the promises given to the patriarchs, and in order that the Gentiles might glorify God for his mercy.

First, Paul states the practical aim of the letter: to promote harmony within the Christian community at Rome. This has been the thrust of much of the moral exhortation in 12:1–15:6. It should be noted that the community's behavior is understood as a reflection of Christ's own behavior. Second, the work of Christ fulfills the covenant promise that was unfolded in Scripture. Third, this promise reaches its fulfillment through the mission to the Gentiles.

Seen as a whole, this passage reinforces our suggestion that the letter has a twofold purpose: to provide a rationale for the Gentile mission and to foster harmony within the Roman church.

The other two passages are closer to thesis statements, but they are connected with the argument itself. Rather than being the single thesis statement for the whole letter, 1:16–17 serves as a programmatic statement that is expanded in 1:18–4:25. This latter section is aptly titled *What Is Revealed in Christ*. Midway through this section, 3:21–31 further elaborates 1:16–17. In this tightly packed statement, Paul spells out the major points that he will develop throughout the letter. In their highly compressed form, 1:16–17 and 3:21–31 serve as the driving engines of the overall argument.

What is the ultimate point toward which Paul's argument moves? *The mission to the Gentiles is not only theologically defensible but also theologically necessary because of what has been revealed through the gospel.* As Paul's working thesis, this is a hard-edged argument with profound practical implications.

If this is the point toward which his overall argument moves, we might ask how Paul gets there. Briefly stated, Paul's argument can be sketched as follows: In 1:18–4:25, he unfolds what has been "revealed" or disclosed in the gospel. Having cracked open the "seed" of the gospel, Paul then describes what has actually occurred in Christ. He exposes a new set of realities that have been created by this foundational event (chs. 5–8). The implications of this new revelation are then developed in two directions: (1) understanding the church's mission (chs. 9–11) and (2) developing an appropriate form of ecclesial practice (chs. 12–15).

Having framed his argument as succinctly as possible, we can now delineate it more fully. Romans 1:16–17 is a programmatic statement:

> For I am not ashamed of the gospel; it is the power of God for salvation to everyone who has faith, to the Jew first and also to the Greek. For in it the righteousness of God is revealed through faith for faith; as it is written, "The one who is righteous will live by faith."

"Reveal" (*apokalyptō*) should be understood in the technical sense of unveiling a secret or mystery; it is not simply a synonym for "make known." The term "gospel" is Paul's shorthand expression for all that God has done through Christ; it refers both to the verbal account of God's action in Christ—what is preached—as well as the action itself—what occurred. Paul understands gospel as both story and event.

Two unveiled secrets are named. First is "God's righteousness." Taken as a reference to God's character, this expression can signify not only God's essential goodness but also God's integrity—God as One who acts justly and equitably in dealing with human beings. Understood as a divine action rather than solely as a divine attribute, it would imply something more: a righteous God who graciously bestows righteousness as a gift to sinful humanity. As such, it refers to God's *enacted character*.

The second revelation is the faith principle: *the appropriate way for people—all people in every time and place—to experience God's enacted righteous character is through faith.* The gospel exposes God's true character and intent for humanity; it is the prism through which this divine revelation is refracted clearly for the first time.

The implications of the first "revelation" are spelled out more fully in 1:18–2:29.[1] Through the gospel, several insights are more fully exposed:

1. The possibility that Gentiles, by observing the created order, can learn enough about God to develop sensitive consciences and moral standards;

2. God's extreme displeasure when enlightened Gentiles fail to live up to those moral standards and sink to indescribable levels of immorality, tied to the inevitability of God's future judgment and God's character as an impartial judge who does not tilt the scales of justice for anyone; and

3. The limits of the Mosaic law as a universal norm—it is possible to have the Mosaic law and be immoral or not have it and be moral; ethnicity (being Jewish) and morality (being religious) are not necessarily identical.

So radical are these insights that a string of objections follows (3:1–20), enough to prompt a further "revelation" that expands on the earlier thesis:

> But now, quite independently of the Law, God's righteousness has been disclosed. The law and the prophets bear witness to it: God's way of setting things right, effective through the faith of Jesus Christ for all who have such faith—everyone, without distinction. For all alike have sinned and are thereby deprived of God's splendor, and all are justified (or, made righteous) freely by God's grace through God's act of liberation in the person of Christ Jesus—the one whom God put forward as the means of expiating sin by his sacrificial death, effective through faith. This was a dramatic demonstration of God's righteousness since God had been unduly patient in overlooking the sins of the past. Even now, in the present, it occurs as a dynamic demonstration of God's righteousness in order to show that God indeed is righteous and regards as righteous the one who exemplifies Jesus' faith. (3:21–26 REB modified)

Several points introduced in 1:18–2:29 receive elaboration. They are now introduced as interlocking theses. Some were already introduced in 1:16–17, others are newly formulated:

1. God's righteousness so often spoken about in Scripture has now been fully disclosed (in the gospel).

2. This has occurred in a manner other than through the observance of the Mosaic law.

3. Being able to recognize this full disclosure occurs through faith.

4. The "eyes of faith" transcend ethnic boundaries—a good thing since everyone is infected with sin.

5. Christ is the pivotal event through which God's righteousness is disclosed.

All five theses directly challenge widely held assumptions about the Mosaic law. Because "faith" and "law" appear to be antithetical principles, Paul introduces Abraham to show that the "law of faith" is not only deeply embedded in the Mosaic law but also constitutes a prior principle. As a principle that was never abrogated, the faith principle is even more decisive than the covenant of circumcision.

Although chapter 4 focuses on Scripture's declaration that "Abraham believed God, and it was reckoned to him as righteousness" (Rom 4:3, citing Gen 15:6), Paul treats Abraham as the embodiment of Hab 2:4, "[T]he righteous will live by their faith." By the end of chapter 4, both parts of 1:16–17 have been amplified: the truly revelatory impact of the gospel in disclosing God's righteousness, and faith as the mode of being religious, through which those who aspire to be righteous relate to God.

If 1:18–4:25 elaborates *What Is Revealed in Christ*, chapters 5–8 unfold *What Has Occurred in Christ*. This section traces the implications of this revelatory event (note "therefore" in 5:1). The opening section, 5:1–11, serves as a transition introducing some of the basic themes to be explored: justification by faith through Christ, experiencing God's love through the Holy Spirit, and Christ's death as God's loving action on behalf of sinners. In an unfolding progression, Paul formally develops four themes:

1. *Adam and Christ: The Shift from Sin to Grace (5:12–21)*. By giving a *gospel* reading of Gen 3, Paul interprets Adam as a type of Christ (5:14). The central point of the comparison is Adam's disobedience and its counterpart, Christ's obedience (5:19). Each act may have been important in its own right; of greater significance are the consequences of these two acts. From Scripture, Paul concluded that "one man's trespass" (5:15, 17–18) introduced sin, condemnation, and death into the world. While Adam's "children" may not have sinned exactly as he did, in Paul's view they followed his general example of disobedience. Sin as a lethal force bedeviled humanity "from Adam to Moses" (5:14). Even after the "[Mosaic] law came in" (5:20), the problem of sin persisted. It even worsened, because the law not only raised humanity's consciousness of sin, but also, by naming sin, rendered it actual: "trespass multiplied" (5:20).

Moses proved to be no match for Adam. The effects of Adam's transgression could be offset only by an event of equally cosmic proportions. Like Adam, Christ is a truly representative figure who illustrates how the action(s) of one person can affect every person. As representative "types," Adam and Christ are not ordinary human beings but cosmic figures representing different orders of humanity. Because Christ's defining moment was an "act of obedience," a "free gift" disclosing God's grace, its universal effects are the radical opposite of those resulting from Adam's transgression. The era inaugurated by Adam was characterized by sin, condemnation, and death. The Christ era, by contrast, was triggered by an "act of righteousness" (5:18), introducing into the world a set of counteracting forces: grace, justification, and life, all universally available.

With this highly creative reading of Gen 3, Paul introduces a fresh reading of the larger biblical story. Adam finds his true counterpart not in Moses, but in another "larger than life" figure—Christ—who stands as the representative of a new humanity. Paul's exposition hinges on the assumption that a single human action can have universal consequences—for ill or good. It also provides a scriptural basis for Paul's earlier claim that sin is a universal human problem (1:18–2:29). In doing so, it introduces another way of reading the Mosaic law: as a narrative unfolding a tragic story of sin and death awaiting a successful conclusion. If Adam exemplifies the story of fallen humanity and humanity's desperate plight before God, Christ exemplifies the counterstory of enacted righteousness coming to humanity's rescue, inaugurating an era of grace and life that replaces the old era of sin and death.

2. *A Moral Paradigm Shift: Ritual Union with Christ (ch. 6)*. Paul now explores the implications of the Adam-Christ typology for believers. Because the Adam era was a time when "sin exercised dominion in death" (5:21), its distinguishing realities were sin and death. But with God's "free gift," the Christ era began, introducing a new

defining reality: "grace" that exercised "dominion through righteousness" and that eventually becomes "eternal life" (5:21*b*).

To imagine that the era of grace and life would actually produce more sin, Paul retorts, reflects a twisted logic that utterly fails to grasp what has occurred in the gospel. Rightly understood, Christ's "act of obedience" was shaped by the struggle between two opposing forces: sin/death on the one hand and God/life on the other. In Christ's death, he "died to sin, once for all"—emphatically—and by being raised, he "lives to God" (6:10). "Sin" and "God" become the two poles between which Christ's true identity was revealed; he said "No" to the one, "Yes" to the other.

Through baptism, the ritual reenactment of Christ's death and resurrection, believers relive Christ's own experience. The "the old self" (lit., "the old human," *ho palaios anthrōpos*, 6:6) is crucified and sin is left behind: one is "freed from sin" (6:7). The believer's new identity bears the imprint of Christ's identity: dead to sin, alive to God (6:11). Christ's own experience becomes the template of the believer's moral identity. But there is one critical difference: Christ already experiences life with God fully, while the believer does so only partly. The baptized believer begins to "walk in newness of life" (6:4) and begins to experience moral renewal. "Living fully with Christ" remains a future possibility (6:5, 8).

By being united with Christ ritually, the believer begins to experience the new era of grace. The cosmic drama of 5:12–21, in which the Adam era gives way to the Christ era, now becomes the believer's own story. Since "sin exercising dominion" characterizes life in the Adam era (5:21), this behavioral scheme is no longer appropriate for those "in Christ" who, like Christ, "live for God" (6:12–14). To "obey sin" is to behave as though one is living in another era—the era "under law." Now in the new era, one lives "under grace" (6:14), and the defining reality is righteousness (6:15–23).

If one understands what has truly occurred in Christ—a seismic shift from the era of sin to the era of grace—to "continue in sin" is tantamount to living in another era. By continuing in sin, one remains oblivious to the sea change that Christ's death triggered. Ritual union with Christ signals the believer's recognition of what a truly pivotal event Christ's death was. It also marks the beginning of a way of life characterized by a new set of defining realities: grace, righteousness, and life. Far from being motivated to "obey sin," citizens in the Christ era of grace live with a moral imperative driven by "life for God."

3. *Being Freed from the Mosaic Law* (ch. 7). What has been a minor theme so far now receives fuller treatment (5:13–14, 20; 6:15). The effect of the marriage analogy is clear: A woman whose husband dies is free to marry a new "living husband"; in the same way, one who has died to the law can be joined to the living Christ (7:1–6). The full force of Paul's illustration should not be muted: the death of Christ "discharges" us from the law that "held us captive" (7:6). A genuine shift of loyalty has occurred: from the oldness of the letter to the newness of the Spirit (7:6; cf. 2 Cor 3:6). For Paul, the Mosaic law and the living Christ are two opposing realities. They symbolize two different moral orders. One arouses "sinful passions" with truly destructive force, the other offers the possibility of "bearing [moral] fruit for God" (7:4–5).

In 5:13, 20, Paul introduced the distinction between sin and law. Now he exploits that distinction. To equate law and sin, he insists, is to collapse a vital distinction

(7:7). Rather than seeing law and sin as abstract principles, they are better seen as distinct personified forces struggling with each other. As the Adam story shows, sin is the prior force, but law was a force introduced later to cope with sin. In principle, the law is "holy and just and good" (7:12), even "spiritual" (7:14), but in practice it is ultimately ineffective in dealing with the power of sin.

But law has positive value. It identifies sin by naming it. By doing so, law raises sin to a level of consciousness that it does not possess otherwise. Yet ultimately the real moral struggle is not between sin and law, but between sin and God, between the "law of God"—what God wants us to do—and the "law of sin"—what sin wants us to do. These are the same polarities within which Christ's own moral struggle was set (6:10–11). Law was caught in the middle of this struggle, and rather than tilting the contest in God's direction, it became sin's tool.

The inner conflict depicted in 7:14–25, in which the mind and the flesh pull in opposite directions, is every human being's conflict. By moving from a portrayal of sin as a universal human experience (1:18–2:29) to a deeper psychological portrayal of the individual's inner struggle, Paul depicts the moral dilemma of everyone who lives in the Adam era. In theory, the Mosaic law is positively beneficial; in practice, it is ineffectual in coping with sin.

4. *Receiving God's Spirit: Present Gift, Future Hope (ch. 8)*. Earlier Paul contrasted life "under the old written code" with the "new life of the Spirit" (7:6). Having depicted humanity's predicament in the Adam era, he now turns to the defining experiential reality of the Christ era: the Spirit of life. Above all, the Spirit is seen as God's Spirit (8:9, 11, 14), a force unleashed in Christ's resurrection (1:4), now bestowed as a gift to believers (5:5; 8:11). Since God and the Spirit are so closely identified, they constitute a moral realm in direct opposition to the flesh (8:5–8). Ultimate loyalties can be expressed as mutually exclusive moral outlooks: the outlook of the flesh and the outlook of the Spirit. Because those in Christ have experienced God's life-giving Spirit, they have the "Spirit of [the risen] Christ" as their mark of identity (8:9). With the Spirit in their possession, believers can expect to experience full resurrection life even as Christ already has (8:11). Meanwhile, God's Spirit acts as moral catalyst enabling believers to become fully obedient children, even enabling them to utter Jesus' prayer, "Abba, Father!" (8:15). As adopted children rather than slaves (to the flesh), they share Christ's filial status (8:16–17).

The empowering effects of the Spirit are felt among believers at the microcosmic level, within individual lives and communities of believers; but they are also felt at the macrocosmic level. The entire creation feels the effects of the shift from the Adam era to the Christ era, struggling like a woman in labor to give birth to a new order that fully reflects God's transforming power. Yet the transformations of the cosmos and the believers are not separate but vitally linked processes. As those "in Christ" experience the painful tension between present suffering and future hope, they merely reflect the agony of all creation as it moves through suffering toward the restored glory that it lost in Adam.

To be ritually united with Christ has a twofold effect on believers. First, they receive the Holy Spirit as God's gift, a tangible expression of God's love. As the experiential expression of God's life-giving power, the "Spirit of life" becomes the energizing presence within believers, assisting them in their struggle with the Spirit's opposing force—flesh—and helping them conform to the pattern of obedience exemplified by Christ. The Spirit shapes a moral outlook appropriate to the "era of grace" and actively intercedes with God on behalf of believers. Even so, they experience only a partial measure of the Spirit, the "first fruits" (8:23), whose full effects are not felt until the final transformation.

The second effect is to become a participant in a much larger process—a cosmic transformation that the whole creation undergoes. While the "era of grace" may have begun with Christ's death and resurrection, its effects are only experienced gradually as the entire universe moves from bondage to freedom.

As a way of bringing the argument begun in 1:16 to a triumphant conclusion, Paul summarizes what God has achieved through Christ: by an emphatic display of overwhelming love, God tilted in humanity's direction and counteracted the effects of Adam's transgression. God's enacted righteousness is seen in the "free gift" of Christ, whose death, resurrection, and exaltation now position him as an active intercessor on behalf of God's elect. Neither extraordinary earthly calamities nor an array of cosmic forces can sever the tie between God's love and God's elect (8:35–39).

Now that the full impact of the "secret" unveiled in the gospel has been elaborated, Paul can trace its implications in two respects: (1) grasping the significance of the Gentile mission (chs. 9–11), and (2) shaping Christian community (chs. 12–16).

1. *Israel and the Gentiles (chs. 9–11).* Three Pauline convictions inform this discussion: (a) Gentile response to the gospel has exceeded Israel's response. (b) Israel's general failure to respond positively pains Paul though it does not surprise him. By failing to acknowledge Jesus as God's Messiah, Israel has failed to grasp "God's righteousness," but in doing so it has acted in character. (c) Israel's "disobedience" is temporary. Meanwhile, the Gentiles' enthusiastic response will make Israel jealous and eventually prompt it to see the light and respond positively. God's call is "irrevocable" and eventually "all Israel will be saved" (11:26).

It is one thing to argue that God's universal mission extends to Gentiles, quite another to account for Israel's unresponsiveness. Yet if Christ as God's Messiah has made it possible for God to make good on the original promise to include "all nations" as heirs of the divine blessings, how does one explain Israel's failure to accept this? Paul's answer has several components.

First, he fully acknowledges Israel's special role in salvation history by rehearsing their many privileges (11:4–5). In doing so, he fully affirms Israel's election.

Second, he insists that by moving beyond Israel (and beyond the law) to form a "new beloved people," God has exercised sovereign freedom and acted righteously. By acting in character, God maintains integrity. Furthermore, in taking the initiative to make good on the earlier promise to the Gentiles, God has acted in a manner fully consistent with Scripture. The God who chose Jacob over Esau and who later hardened Pharaoh's heart is the God who has chosen to chart a fresh course by reaching out fully to Gentiles. Once again, Paul finds full support for God's actions from his reading of Scripture.

Third, the Gentiles' positive response and Israel's largely negative response to the gospel can be explained by what has been "revealed" in the gospel:

(a) Israel's refusal to accept Jesus as God's Messiah signals its failure to recognize the death and resurrection of Christ as a truly revelatory moment disclosing God's enacted character.

(b) This in turn produces another level of blindness: failure to see that God brought the era of law to an end. Christ is the "end of the law" both in the sense that he brings God's promise to fulfillment and terminates the "old written code." This makes the old "way of righteousness"—Torah observance—passé.

(c) A third dimension of the new revelation has also eluded Israel: the principle of faith. This time-honored way of relating to God is as old as Abraham and deeply rooted in Scripture itself. It is through faith that one is "counted" righteous by God. Christ now makes it transparently clear that faith as a way of relating to God was established prior to the law. As such, faith takes precedence over performance of the law's demands as the scriptural way of relating to God. Grasping the principle of faith ultimately requires a reorientation of the human heart. As a mode of responding to God and thus as a way of life, faith has nothing to do with ethnic identity. As a universal capacity deeply embedded within every human being, faith transcends ethnic identity (10:1–17).

Far from being anticlimactic, chapters 9–11 show Paul bringing his critical theological reflections of chapters 1–8 to bear on a particular problem: the Gentile mission. At this juncture in Paul's ministry, the Gentiles' enthusiastic response to the gospel and Israel's tepid response have created a genuine dilemma requiring an extended explanation. Put quite simply, Paul's argument runs like this: *given (a) who God is, (b) the testimony of Scripture, and (c) what has actually occurred in Christ, the mission to the Gentiles is both theologically legitimate and necessary.*

By exposing sin as a universal human dilemma, the gospel has severed the connection between ethnicity and religiosity. It has exposed faith as the way every human being relates to God. Faith as a saving principle has been established since Abraham. The gospel has also exposed God's universal remedy—the "free gift" of Christ. That Gentiles have recognized the truly revelatory character of the gospel is not surprising, since Scripture itself anticipated their response (10:18–20); but neither should Israel's general failure to respond to God's initiative be surprising, given the testimony of Scripture (10:21). Yet, since God's call is irrevocable, Israel will eventually respond, however dim the prospects look at the moment.

2. *Shaping Christian Community (12:1–15:13)*. Even though this is a separate section, it is neither an afterthought nor simply an application of theological principles expressed in chapters 1–11. This concluding set of exhortations grows out of what precedes (cf. "therefore," 12:1). The call for believers to be "living sacrifices" (12:1–2) is rooted in Christ's death as an exemplary sacrifice (3:25). Developing renewed imaginations that challenge "this age" (12:2) resonates with the cosmic transformation under way and the conflict between the outlooks of the Spirit and flesh outlined in chapter 8. Although this section draws on what has already been said earlier in the letter, it does not develop those earlier themes systematically.

While general in scope and texture, Paul's exhortation in these chapters is directed in the first instance toward his readers in Rome. His remarks become quite concrete at 15:14. Prior to that, he is probably not more specific because he does not know more details about their situation.

Reminiscent of Paul's concluding moral exhortations elsewhere, chapters 12–15 contain miscellaneous admonitions. Many of these exhortations echo the teachings of Jesus. Not only do they echo the Gospel tradition, they are also typically grounded in Christ (15:3, 7). They also sound some distinctly Pauline themes, for example, the church as the body of Christ (12:4–8; cf. 1 Cor 12:12–30) and his instructions concerning the strong and the weak (ch.14; cf. 1 Cor 8–10).

While these exhortations may resemble a moral sampler, they have a common center: *what makes for harmony.* One indication of this is Paul's repeated use of "one another" (12:10, 16; 13:8; 14:13; 15:5, 7, 14; 16:16). He prays that they will "live in harmony with one another" (15:5; cf. 12:16) and become a people with "one voice" (15:6). With such consistent emphasis on their mutual responsibilities to each other, a strong social ethic emerges. This helps explain the prominence of 13:1–7, in which Paul insists that believers should respect civil authorities. What makes for order within the Christian community also makes for order within the larger society. This strongly worded exhortation is an extension of his other admonitions that promote social order.

Of special significance is the advice given in chapter 14 concerning the strong and weak. Clearly resonant with Paul's instructions in 1 Cor 8–10, in which he is responding to the problem of eating sacrificial meats, his advice here has a more general tone. Two practices are highlighted: the observance of food laws and the observance of special days (14:1–6). It is difficult to correlate these practices and the convictions that inform them with identifiable groups within the Roman church. The "strong" are not necessarily Jewish Christians any more than the "weak" are necessarily Gentile Christians. It is possible to imagine circumstances in which persons from both groups could be numbered among the "strong" and "weak."

The thrust of Paul's advice echoes that of 1 Cor 8–10:

- the strong should not run roughshod over the weak but defer to them;
- individual freedom should be balanced with communal interest;
- how one person feels about a particular practice is just as important as how another person professes some theoretical principle;
- one should behave in ways that edify the whole community; and
- no one is an island, and everyone lives under the Lord's sovereignty.

Also clear are some of Paul's own views, for example, that "nothing is unclean in itself" (14:14) and that "everything is indeed clean" (14:20). Even here, the faith principle is also at work: "whatever does not proceed from faith is sin" (14:23).

Paul's Theological Vision in Romans

Romans 3:21–31 compactly expresses several interlocking theses that are developed in the letter. Not every Pauline letter can be reduced to a set of theses, but Romans invites such analysis because of its distinctive argumentative texture.

God's Justifying Righteousness

Within the space of a few verses (Rom 3:21–31), Paul mentions God's righteousness four times (vv. 21, 22, 25, 26), "justify" four times (vv. 24, 26, 28, 30), and "righteous" once (v. 26). Such concentrated use of this language reminds us of how pervasive it is throughout the letter. Even the casual reader of Romans is struck by the number of times these two families of terms occur in the letter: "righteous" and "righteousness," on the one hand, and "justify," "justification," "justice," and "just," on the other hand. [See **Expanded CD Version p. 497: *Greek Semantics: Words of the dik- Root***]

In one sense, the web of relationships reflected in Paul's use of this word family illustrates the complexity of the letter as a whole. So heavily does this word family inform the way Paul thinks of God in Romans that some scholars see "God's righteousness" as the central theme of the letter (1:17; 3:5, 21, 22 [25, 26]; 10:3 [2x]; this expression only occurs elsewhere in Paul at 2 Cor 5:21 and Phil 3:9 and elsewhere in the NT at Jas 1:20 and possibly Matt 6:33). From the same cluster of terms also comes one of Paul's favorite metaphors in Romans for expressing the way God saves humanity: justification. One of the main axioms in Romans employs this root metaphor: "It is God who justifies" (8:33). God's saving action is thus seen as the justification of the sinner (3:26, 30; 4:5; 8:30).

The same word family is also used to characterize the newly acquired status of those who have been "justified": they have been "counted" righteous. "The one who is righteous," Paul declares (adapting Hab 2:4), "will live by faith" (1:17). *Dikaios* is also used of believers in 5:19; it characterizes human action in 2:13; 3:10; and 5:7. By using the language in this latter sense, Paul moves it beyond discourse about God and God's saving action in the direction of moral discourse. Not only does "righteous/just" characterize God and what God does in bringing humanity into a right relationship with God, but it is also used quite explicitly—and quite emphatically—of *human character and behavior*.

Drawing on a single semantic field, Paul sees three interrelated conceptions as part of the same continuum: what is being said about God ("God's righteousness"); how God's saving action is understood ("being made righteous" or "justification"); and the moral implications of such action (the believer as "righteous"). Even though these three elements are inseparable, for the purpose of analysis we distinguish them here.

While righteousness/justification is one of the most heavily accented themes in Romans, so is it one of the most ambiguous and controversial. [See **Expanded CD Version pp. 498–502: *Righteousness of God and Justification: History of Interpretation; Righteousness of God: Ambiguity within Biblical Thought***]

Apart from Law

Understood one way, Paul's second claim means that God's newly disclosed righteousness happened "independently of the Mosaic law." But since Paul develops his unfolding argument from the law itself, it is probably better to understand this claim as meaning "apart from the usual manner of law observance."

A woodcut depicting Phoebe, a deacon of the church at Cenchreae (Rom 16:1–2), receiving a letter from Paul the apostle; taken from a Low German dialect version of Martin Luther's translation of the New Testament (Magdeburg, 1547). From the Digital Image Archive of The Richard C. Kessler Reformation Collection, Pitts Theology Library, Candler School of Theology, Emory University, Atlanta, Georgia.

When Paul speaks of the "law of faith" and the "law of works" (3:27), he is differentiating between two distinct principles. That they represent polar opposites is clear from 9:32. Two options lay before Israel as it strove to live by the Mosaic law: it could have done so either "from faith" (*ek pisteōs*) or "from works" (*ex ergōn*). Israel's mistake, in Paul's view, was in assuming that it could be done the latter way. (An intriguing question is whether Paul envisions the former possibility: that Israel might have kept the law successfully "on the basis of faith.")

While the "way of faith" and the "way of works" are opposing principles expressing two different visions of life before God, "works" has a specific focus for Paul—"works of the law" (*erga nomou*). By this he means the various commandments found in the law and the set of religious practices prescribed therein (10:5). Paul affirms their salvific value: "'No human being will be justified in [God's] sight' by deeds prescribed by the law" (*ex ergōn nomou*, 3:20). This states his theology of salvation negatively; he states it positively when he asserts, "we hold that a person is justified by faith apart from works prescribed by the law" (3:28).

To apply a blanket condemnation to all "works of the law" might seem unusually harsh, especially considering the many positive behaviors the law requires. One need think only of the Decalogue for examples (see Exod 20:1–17; Deut 5:6–21). The specific requirement Paul may have in mind is circumcision, given the emphasis it receives in Romans (2:25–29; 3:1, 30; 4:9–12; 15:8). He may not be combating Judaizers who are insisting that Gentile males undergo circumcision to be saved, as is the case in Galatians, but he is combating a view of the law that would strengthen their claims.

In these remarks Paul is not targeting some specific requirement of the law, but a way of relating to the law, perhaps even a certain conception of the law. Such a conception sees the law's various prescriptions and commands as a system of requirements, which, if properly observed, somehow commend the one who observes them to God. The object of Paul's critique is a transactional view of the law in which one observes the law *in exchange for* certain benefits. Experiencing the benefits of law observance becomes a *quid pro quo*, literally "something for something": one receives God's blessing in exchange for one's faithful observance of the law. Such a view reflects the logic of the wage: someone engages in work and in exchange receives pay as "something due" (4:4).

While there may be positive benefits that accrue both to the person who so observes the law and to a society built around this conception, the logic of this conception of the law is fatally flawed: it leads to "boasting." If we relate to God primarily through our "works" and if we conceive of these "works" as obligations satisfied, we may think of our accomplishments as our own achievements.

Using this logic, Paul argues that Abraham would have had "something to boast about" if he had operated from the "works" principle (4:2). "Boasting," by contrast, is excluded when the "faith principle" dictates the way one relates to God (3:27). Circumcision provides a clear example. Seen as the fulfillment of a divine requirement, it tended to become a sign of ethnic, even spiritual, identity, and thus a mark of pride. As the sign that identified a Jewish male as an Israelite, circumcision signified privilege and status. Seen as the seal of "righteousness that comes by faith," it has a different valence (4:11).

Especially sinister is how this way of relating to the law eventually leads to arrogance. One may boast in the law (2:23), even while flagrantly violating it. And this way of relating to the law can produce a sense of ethnic identity inseparably tied to the law and one's perceived unique relationship to God through the law (2:17).

In Romans, "works of the law" acquires a technical sense. Out of Paul's discussion of the Mosaic law emerges his distinction between the principles of "faith" and "works." Yet it is a distinction that far transcends this discussion in Romans. If these terms symbolize opposed ways of being religious, they point to two different ways of envisioning one's relationship to God. To relate to God "through works" accents human performance and sees religious actions as satisfied requirements that prompt the bestowal of God's favor. Relating to God "through faith," by contrast, places the accent elsewhere. Rather than "doing in order to receive," the faith principle is motivated by a different impulse: "those who live 'in faith' do so *because they have received*." Or as Paul puts it, salvation is understood as gift rather than wage. In Luther's words, "one does not become just by doing good works, but by being just, one does just deeds."[2] [See Expanded CD Version pp. 503–6: *Paul's Critique of the Law in Five Key Passages: (1) 2:12–29; (2) 4:13–17; (3) Ch. 7; (4) 8:1–8; and (5) 9:13–10:5*]

The Faith Principle

A third critically important assertion is Paul's contention that God's righteousness is disclosed "for all who believe." For all its dynamic quality in Romans, faith can be thought of as a principle. The "law of faith," Paul insists, "excludes boasting" (3:27). To be true to Romans, we must think of faith as a dynamic principle. Faith is the fulcrum for Paul's theology of salvation: "we hold that a person is justified by faith apart from works prescribed by the law" (3:28). Occupying the space between the God who justifies and the one justified, faith is more an orientation than an action. And yet it is not merely a passive state in which one waits before God silently, suspended in a vacuum of inactivity. Faith signals recognition on the part of the believer. Faith "gets it," for example, when one sees the death of Jesus as an efficacious atoning sacrifice—it is "effective through faith" (3:25).

What can be grasped only by faith, above all, is the disclosure of God's righteousness. Whether the faith through which one recognizes God's righteousness is "faith *in* Jesus Christ" or "faith *of* Jesus Christ," it occurs "for all who believe" (3:22). But the righteousness of God, even when disclosed through something as dramatically conspicuous as Christ, is nevertheless elusive, as the history of biblical interpretation attests. Yet it is precisely this elusiveness, this lack of specificity of faith's object, that makes Abraham such a prime example of faith for Paul.

What commends Abraham to Paul is Gen 15:6: "Abraham believed God, and it was reckoned to him as righteousness" (4:3). Like Hab 2:4, "The righteous live by their faith," Gen 15:6 provides the critical linkage between "faith" and "righteousness," a connection rarely made in the OT.[3] Psalm 106:28–31 might have proved useful to Paul, since it characterizes Phinehas, who intervened to stop Israel's idolatry, as someone to whom righteousness was reckoned "from generation to generation forever." But the psalm does not connect Phinehas's "reckoned righteousness" to his faith. The Psalter speaks frequently of God's righteousness, but not as something accessed by human faith.

For Paul, it was critical that Abraham "believed in" a promise, even when the circumstances surrounding it were so palpably incredible. Paul sees the inner fabric of Abraham's faith fully exposed in his response to God's promise that he would have heirs. Seeing nothing but his own body "as good as dead" and an aging, barren wife (4:19), Abraham does not weaken in faith or experience distrust, but instead exhibits even stronger faith, fully convinced of both the integrity of the God who made the promise and the ability of God to make good on it (4:21). Abraham's capacity to lean into an open, uncertain future, clinging confidently to something as evanescent as a promise, constitutes the soul and fiber of his faith. What transformed the promise from being a flimsy, casually made pledge into a firmly grounded contract, even covenant, was the One who promised: it was the "promise *of God*" that Abraham believed in (4:20).

The way Abraham responded to this promise explains why "his faith 'was reckoned to him as righteousness'" (4:22). Paul observes that these words were written "not for his sake alone, but for ours also" (4:23–24). Paul sees a similarity between Abraham's faith and the faith of those who believe that God's righteousness has been disclosed in Jesus Christ. What they have in common is the capacity to believe in God as Creator— One who creates life where none otherwise exists (4:24–25). Abraham thus becomes an example not just of faith, but of *Christian* faith. Paul sees no difference between Abraham's capacity to believe in a life-giving God and the Christian believer's capacity to believe that God raised Jesus from the dead. They are analogous forms of faith.

Paul's capsule description of what Abraham displayed in this instance is "faith's righteousness" or "the righteousness he had by faith"—the inner disposition that the covenant of circumcision "sealed" or clinched. "Faith's righteousness" became the tracks on which God's promise to Abraham and his descendants would run. It embodied a principle—a way of relating to God—that antedated, and therefore did not depend upon, the Mosaic law (4:13). God's original promise to Abraham was launched on the "faith principle," which, Paul repeatedly insists, was never invalidated or repealed.

Who are Abraham's children? Those of his progeny who embody the "faith principle" as he did. This includes not only "adherents of the law," but also Gentiles, the "many nations" mentioned in the original promise (4:16–17). It is not the circumcised, but the faithful, who are Abraham's true heirs.

What God disclosed in Christ was the fulfillment of the original promise to Abraham. To have faith in God's righteousness as disclosed in Jesus Christ is to remember the original promise, to understand its basis as "grace"—it came to Abraham as a gift (4:16)—and to recognize Christ as the one through whom the fullness of the promise was brought to fulfillment. A crucial part of "faith's righteousness" is seeing the death of Christ as the pivotal event through which God was finally able to make good on the original promise. Equally important is to see the mission to the Gentiles as a central ingredient of the original promise.

In the gospel—the event and proclamation of Christ—God's righteousness is disclosed "through faith for faith," perhaps "faith pure and simple." Ever since Abraham, this is the authentic mode through which those who are righteous relate to God (1:17). Paul sees the "faith principle" as the way "righteous people" like Abraham have always, or should have always, related to God. As a principle, it was never repealed. Moreover, it was a principle lost on Israel, who strove for the "law's righteousness" but failed because they lived by the opposite principle: "works" (9:31–32). What is now clearly revealed, if not rediscovered, in Christ is not only the enduring validity of the "faith principle" but also its universality—that both Jews and Gentiles relate to God the same way, through faith (3:30). It is the permanence and singularity of the "faith principle" that is now disclosed in Christ. And if "faith of Christ" is the proper rendering of 3:22, 26, Christ becomes the embodiment of the "faith principle." As the counterexample to Adam, who exemplified disobedience, Christ embodies the opposite principle, the "obedience of faith," probably the "obedience that consists of faith" (1:5; 16:26). Christ restored what was lost in Adam by recovering what Abraham originally discovered.

There Is No Distinction

Paul's fourth thesis recalls his argument in 1:18–2:29, in which he insists that everyone, regardless of ethnic status, is infected with sin. This, too, Scripture fully attests: "There is no one who is righteous, not even one" (3:10). Being able to see the full disclosure of God's righteousness in the gospel requires the eyes of faith rather than some privileged status based on family pedigree. In an earlier section, we treated Paul's argument that sin is a universal human dilemma that prompted God's justifying righteousness, as well as its corollary that God's righteousness was disclosed in Christ and became a universally effective remedy.

Paul's insistence on faith as the primary way everyone should relate to God eliminates different ways of being religious for Jews and Gentiles. Paul also draws implications from God's oneness, insisting that if there is one God, there is only one way of relating to God (3:30).

The overall thrust of his argument is to eliminate distinctions within humanity. Sin is the universal leveler of humanity because it creates a universal need for God's saving action. As the second Adam, Jesus appears as the universal human who opens the way for everyone to relate to God equally. Perhaps one of the sharpest edges of Paul's argument in Romans is his firm insistence that there are no defining distinctions among human beings. Sin as a universal human experience causes everyone, Jew and Gentile alike, to become aware of their need for God's saving actions. While Jesus' death may be seen as the execution of a particular individual, in another, more profound sense it is the event that equalizes every human being.

Christ, the Pivotal Event

A fifth element in Paul's argument is the role of Christ within God's justifying righteousness. This involves two distinct considerations: (1) how the righteousness of God is disclosed through *pistis Iēsou Christou* (3:22, 26) and (2) how Christ becomes the effective agent of justification. We will consider them in reverse order.

Christ, the Effective Means of Justification. Paul's claims about Christ in Rom 3:22–26 are built on earlier Christian formulations. Even so, we should notice the different metaphors that he employs in speaking of Christ. They may be thought of as specific images for expressing what he means by "salvation" (*sōtēria*)—that which the gospel, as a dynamic expression of God's power, ultimately brings about (1:16). While salvation has both a present and future dimension (Rom 5:9–10; 8:24; 10:9–10, 13; 11:26; 13:11), it was triggered by the Christ event, which occurred in the past. Paul thinks of Christ as the effective agent through whom God brings about salvation.

As 3:21–26 shows, Paul does not distinguish sharply among the three metaphors of liberation/redemption, sacrifice/purification, and justification. Each metaphor expresses God's saving work differently, but the central focus of each is Jesus' death, which Paul sees as the singular event through which God's saving grace was displayed. Whether one sees Christ's death as liberating the sinner from bondage, purifying the sinner from ritual uncleanness, or justifying the sinner who stands condemned as guilty (either by declaring the sinner innocent or actually transferring innocence/righteousness to the sinner), in each case Christ is the effective agent through whom God's saving action occurs. **[See Expanded CD Version pp. 509–11: *Paul's Emphasis on Christ: Metaphors of Liberation and Sacrifice*]**

Faith in Christ/Faith of Christ. Paul's assertion that God's righteousness is revealed *dia pisteōs Iēsou Christou* (3:22) has long been thought to mean "through faith *in* Jesus

Christ." In this interpretation, the genitive form "Jesus Christ" is understood as an objective genitive. This means that the revelation occurs when Jesus Christ becomes the object of faith: when the believer directs faith toward Jesus Christ. But recently some interpreters have argued for the alternate meaning "faith of Jesus Christ," an expression which takes the genitive as a subjective genitive, thus referring to faith of which Jesus Christ is the subject—Christ's faithfulness or fidelity. In the latter interpretation, Christ's faithful obedience to God is seen as the lens through which God's own righteous action is disclosed.

The difference between these two formulations may appear to be slight, but a crucial distinction is being made. If God's justification of sinners occurs because of the trust a believer puts in Jesus Christ, this renders Christ as somewhat passive. Even though Jesus' death might be seen as a proactive event in which he willingly submitted to God, once Jesus' death occurred, the emphasis might easily fall on Jesus' death as a saving event rather than the person of Jesus as a Savior figure.

By reformulating *pistis Christou* as "Christ's faith," the emphasis falls on Jesus' active obedience—his own faithfulness before God. This need not refer only to the pattern of his obedient life, although this would be a powerful motivation in its own right, but it could also signify that Jesus' utter fidelity before God played an active role in bringing about God's justifying action. Seen this way, Jesus is an active participant with God in the act of salvation rather than as a passive figure through whom God acts.

The Ending of Romans

There is some uncertainty about where Romans originally ended. The long form of the letter (chs. 1–16), which is printed in our modern Bibles, has the strongest manuscript support, suggesting its widespread acceptance in the early church. Yet there is evidence that shorter forms of the letter also circulated. The shortest form, comprising chapters 1–14, is traceable to Marcion (died ca. 160 C.E.), but it was known outside the Marcionite churches. That another short form of the letter comprising chapters 1–15 circulated independently is suggested by $\mathfrak{P}^{46}$ (ca. 200 C.E.), in which the concluding doxology (16:25–27) occurs at the end of chapter 15, which is then followed by 16:1–23. This arrangement also suggests the possibility that 16:1–23 circulated independently and was later added to the main body of the letter. It now becomes clear why the concluding doxology (16:25–27) became something of a floating conclusion, sometimes occurring at the end of chapters 14, 15, and 16 respectively (or in one manuscript after both chapters 14 and 16!) and why an alternate, shorter conclusion (16:24) was introduced (see NRSV textual notes relating to 16:23–27).

Notes

1. The close connection between Rom 1:16–17 and the section that follows is indicated by the "for" in 1:18. Paul's exposé of humanity's sinfulness supports his opening thesis.

2. *LW* 25:3: "For in the presence of God this is not the way that a person becomes righteous by doing works of righteousness (as the foolish Jews, Gentiles, and all other self-righteous people proudly think), but he who has been made righteous does works of righteousness, as it is written . . . ."

3. Though see 1 Macc 2:52: "Was not Abraham found faithful when tested, and it was reckoned to him as righteousness?"

Bibliography

Commentaries

Achtemeier, Paul J. *Romans.* Interpretation: A Bible Commentary for Teaching and Preaching. Atlanta: John Knox, 1985.

Barrett, C. K. *A Commentary on the Epistle to the Romans.* Black's New Testament Commentaries. 2d ed. London: Black, 1991 (1957).

———. *Reading Through Romans.* Philadelphia: Fortress, 1977.

Barth, Karl. *The Epistle to the Romans.* Translated by Edwyn C. Hoskyns from the 6th edition. Oxford: Oxford University Press, 1968 (1st ed., 1919).

———. *A Shorter Commentary on Romans.* Richmond/London: John Knox/SCM, 1959.

Brunner, Emil. *The Letter to the Romans: A Commentary.* Translated by H. A. Kennedy from the 1956 German edition. Philadelphia: Westminster, 1959 (1938).

Byrne, Brendan. *Romans.* Sacra Pagina 6. Collegeville: Liturgical, 1996.

Cranfield, C. E. B. *A Critical and Exegetical Commentary on the Epistle to the Romans.* Reprinted with corrections. 2 vols. International Critical Commentary. Edinburgh: T&T Clark, 1980–1982 (1: 1975; 2: 1979).

———. *Romans: A Shorter Commentary.* Grand Rapids: Eerdmans, 1985.

Dodd, C. H. *The Epistle of Paul to the Romans.* Moffat New Testament Commentary. New York/London: Harper/Hodder & Stoughton, 1932.

Dunn, James D. G. *Romans.* 2 vols. Word Biblical Commentary 38. Dallas: Word, 1988.

Fitzmyer, Joseph A. *Romans: A New Translation with Introduction and Commentary.* Anchor Bible 33. New York: Doubleday, 1993.

Harrisville, Roy A. *Romans.* Augsburg Commentaries on the New Testament. Minneapolis: Augsburg, 1980.

Johnson, Luke T. *Reading Romans: A Literary and Theological Commentary.* Reading the New Testament. New York: Crossroad, 1997.

Käsemann, Ernst. *Commentary on Romans.* Translated by Geoffrey W. Bromiley from the 4th German edition. Grand Rapids: Eerdmans, 1980.

Nygren, Anders. *Commentary on Romans.* Translated by Carl C. Rasmussen from the 1944 Swedish edition. London: SCM, 1952.

Schlatter, Adolf. *Romans: The Righteousness of God.* Translated by Siegfried S. Schatzmann from the 1935 German edition. Peabody: Hendrickson, 1995.

Stuhlmacher, Peter. *Paul's Letter to the Romans: A Commentary.* Translated by Scott J. Hafemann from the 1989 German edition. Louisville: Westminster John Knox, 1994.

Wright, N. T. "The Letter to the Romans: Introduction, Commentary, and Reflections." Pages 393–770 in vol. 10 of *The New Interpreter's Bible*. Edited by Leander E. Keck. 12 vols. Nashville: Abingdon, 2002.

Ziesler, J. A. *Paul's Letter to the Romans*. Trinity Press International New Testament Commentaries. Philadelphia/London: Trinity/SCM, 1989.

Other Resources

Boers, Hendrikus. *The Justification of the Gentiles: Paul's Letters to the Galatians and Romans*. Peabody: Hendrickson, 1994.

Donfried, Karl P., ed. *The Romans Debate*. Rev. ed. Peabody: Hendrickson, 1991.

Grieb, A. Katherine. *The Story of Romans: A Narrative Defense of God's Righteousness*. Louisville: Westminster John Knox, 2002.

Hay, David M., and E. Elizabeth Johnson, eds. *Pauline Theology: Volume III: Romans*. Minneapolis: Fortress, 1995.

Lampe, Peter. *From Paul to Valentinus: Christians at Rome in the First Two Centuries*. Translated by Michael Steinhauser. Edited by Marshall D. Johnson. London: T&T Clark (Continuum), 2003.

Minear, Paul S. *The Obedience of Faith: The Purposes of Paul in the Epistle to the Romans*. Studies in Biblical Theology, 2d series, 19. Naperville: Allenson, 1971.

Morgan, Robert. *Romans*. New Testament Guides. Sheffield: Sheffield Academic Press, 1995.

Nanos, Mark D. *The Mystery of Romans: The Jewish Context of Paul's Letter*. Minneapolis: Fortress, 1996.

Robinson, John A. T. *Wrestling with Romans*. Philadelphia/London: Westminster/SCM, 1979.

Stendahl, Krister. *Final Account: Paul's Letter to the Romans*. Minneapolis: Fortress, 1995.

Stowers, Stanley K. *A Rereading of Romans: Justice, Jews, and Gentiles*. New Haven: Yale University Press, 1994.

Wedderburn, A. J. M. *The Reasons for Romans*. Studies of the New Testament and Its World. Edinburgh: T&T Clark, 1988.

Ziesler, J. A. *The Meaning of Righteousness in Paul: A Linguistic and Theological Enquiry*. Society for New Testament Studies Monograph Series 20. Cambridge: Cambridge University Press, 1972.

Chapter 16

Philippians

". . . you have welcomed the models of true Love and have helped on their way, as opportunity was given you, those men who are bound in fetters which become the saints . . . the firm root of your faith, famous from the earliest times, still abides and bears fruit for our Lord Jesus Christ."

Polycarp, *Letter to the Philippians*

". . . each soul should do as St. Paul says, and feel in himself what is in Christ Jesus."

Julian of Norwich

". . . that [the soul's] life is Christ is understood better, with the passing of time, by the effects this life has."

Teresa of Avila

Philippians is best read as a letter composed of at least two, possibly three, shorter letters, all written by Paul to the church at Philippi within a relatively short span of time. While it is impossible to know for certain, their probable order of composition was as follows: (1) a brief letter of thanksgiving (4:10–20); (2) a letter from prison explaining the circumstances of his imprisonment but also urging unity and solidarity within the church (1:1–3:1; 4:4–7, 21–23); and (3) a polemical letter warning against the threat of opponents (3:2–4:3; 4:8–9). Seeing the letter this way helps explain why Polycarp (ca. 69-155 C.E.), bishop of Smyrna, writing to the same church in the early second century, refers to the "letters" *(epistolas)* Paul had written to the Philippian church.[1] Understanding the letter's composite character helps account for its repetitive quality and the sharp change in tone at 3:2.

Whether we focus on the letter's individual parts or on the unified, edited form, we can easily detect several distinct catalysts prompting Paul to write the church, as well as his several aims in doing so: (1) to express appreciation for the financial gift the church has sent him by Epaphroditus (4:10–20); (2) to explain how his imprisonment, rather than obstructing the progress of the gospel, actually advances it (1:12–26); (3) to address internal tensions within the Philippian church by encouraging a spirit of unity, or, as Paul puts it more broadly, by promoting "conduct worthy of the gospel" (1:27–2:18; 4:2–7, 21–23); (4) to maintain contact with the church by sending Timothy and Epaphroditus (2:19–3:1a); and (5) to respond to the threat of opponents, those who "live as enemies of the cross of Christ," by countering their theological viewpoint (3:1b–4:1).

Typical of Paul's letters, the opening prayer of thanksgiving (1:3–11), which technically introduces only the second letter but still echoes the earlier letter, high-lights some of these concerns: (1) their "sharing in the gospel" (1:5–6); (2) "[his] imprisonment and . . . the defense and confirmation of the gospel" (1:7); (3) his prayer that their "love may grow ever richer in knowledge and insight of every kind, enabling [them] to learn by experience what things really matter" (1:9–10 REB); and (4) his longing for them (1:8), which anticipates both his sending of Timothy and Epaphroditus as his surrogate presence and his own expected personal visit (2:19–3:1a). The explicit threat of opponents is not mentioned, but by orienting his readers toward the "day of Christ" and anticipating the prospect of their "full harvest of righteousness that comes through Jesus Christ" (1:10–11 REB), Paul introduces motifs that are later developed in 3:1b–4:1.

More important than identifying separate literary pieces and the purpose of each is to see how Paul does theology as he interacts with the Philippian church. Philippians is especially illuminating in this regard because it shows how ordinary congregational and ministerial concerns—such as Paul's receiving a monetary gift, a co-worker's near fatal sickness, his co-workers' travel plans, his own incarceration and travel plans, deal-ing with enemies, or reconciling a strained relationship between two women in the church—become the occasion for theological insight and reflection. From these deep contingencies of life Paul's own theological convictions are forged and sharpened. To this ministerial situation he brings his own religious experience, thoughtfully articu-lated in terms of his faith in Jesus Christ. Yet his responses are not purely self-referential. Instead, they incorporate the faith of his Christian predecessors, most conspicuously in the pre-Pauline Christ hymn (2:6–11). Since Paul's own human experience serves as the medium through which God's revelation in Christ is conveyed, his ministerial experience acquires a sacramental character. He consistently interprets his ongoing ministerial experiences through the grand narrative of Christ. He can say, quite unself-consciously, that his own ministerial sufferings are an occasion for Christ to be "magnified" (KJV), in other words, for the cause of Christ to be glorified, through his body (1:20). Facing the prospect of death, he can realistically sketch his options as "living/Christ" versus "dying/gain" (1:21). What he commends as worthy of imitation about his own encounter with Christ is his letting go of one core religious identity, a way of being religious defined as "righteousness that comes through the law," and being engulfed by another identity in which God's righteousness is mediated through faith in/of Jesus Christ and is sustained by faith (3:9).

Expressing Thanks for Their Financial Gift (4:10–20)

As the only church from whom Paul accepted financial contributions in support of his own ministry, the Philippians occupied a unique place among the Pauline churches. Their role as Paul's supporting church began shortly after his founding visit in the early 50s, or, as Paul himself puts it, "in the early days of the gospel" (4:15; also cf. 1:5). While at his next stop, Thessalonica, the Philippians sent Paul money "more than once" (4:16). Their practice apparently continued during his eighteen-month stay in Corinth (2 Cor 11:8, 9).

The church's reputation for generosity is already hinted at in Luke's description of its founding (Acts 16:11–40), when Lydia, the dealer in purple cloth from Thyatira, extends hospitality to Paul and his entourage (Acts 16:15, 40). The Philippian church is not mentioned by name, but given its prominence among the three churches Paul established in the Roman province of Macedonia, it is surely included among the Macedonian churches recognized for their generosity (2 Cor 8:1–6). Nor was its spirit of liberality short-lived, for several decades later Polycarp cites the church's habit of extending hospitality to "those bound in fetters" because of the gospel.[2] Even the sad story reported by Polycarp about Valens, one of the Philippian church's presbyters, who along with his wife mismanaged some of the church's money and, as a result, had to be censured by the church, underscores the church's financial strength.[3]

Yet another financial gift, this time delivered by Epaphroditus to Paul in prison, prompts the brief note of thanksgiving located at the end of the letter (4:10–20). Elsewhere Paul tends to emphasize the hardships he has endured for the sake of the gospel, whereas here he balances the deprivations he has experienced with moments of abundance (cf. 1 Cor 4:10–13; 2 Cor 4:8–9; 11:23–29; 12:10; although cf. 2 Cor 6:4–7). Paul's response echoes the Stoic virtue of self-sufficiency (*autarkeia*, 4:11; cf. 1 Tim 6:6–8), but he gives it a distinctive twist by insisting that his true source of empowerment lies not within himself but comes from God (4:13; cf. 2 Cor 9:8). In keeping with his practice of using highly suggestive metaphors instead of the standard terms for money, Paul uses an image with rich OT associations to characterize their gift as a "fragrant offering, a sacrifice acceptable and pleasing to God" (4:18; cf. Gen 8:21; Exod 29:18; Ezek 20:41).

Explaining His Imprisonment (1:12–26)

Since the Philippians know where Paul is imprisoned, he does not specify his location. Because Paul mentions the "whole imperial guard," literally, the "whole praetorium" (1:13; see NRSV note), and "those who belong to Caesar's household" (4:22 NIV), early interpreters concluded that his Roman imprisonment was in view (Acts 28).[4] More recently, however, Caesarea and Ephesus have been proposed as possible locations. Acts 23:31–35 reports Paul's being taken as a prisoner from Jerusalem to Caesarea, where his defense before Felix occurred and where he languished in prison for two years (Acts 24:27); his subsequent defenses before Festus and King Agrippa reported in Acts 25–26 also occurred in Caesarea. Nowhere does the NT report that Paul was imprisoned at Ephesus (cf. Acts 19). Yet before Paul was imprisoned in either Caesarea or Rome, he mentions several imprisonments (2 Cor 11:23), which implies that he was imprisoned somewhere besides Philippi (Acts 16).[5] This, combined with his other references to severe ordeals at Ephesus (1 Cor 15:32; probably 2 Cor 1:8–11), has led some scholars to posit an Ephesian imprisonment and the likelihood that Philippians, and perhaps other Pauline "prison epistles," for example, Philemon and Colossians, were written from Ephesus.[6] **[See Expanded CD Version p. 523: *The Ephesian Imprisonment*]**

Perhaps the most important consequence of identifying the location of Paul's imprisonment when he wrote Philippians is how it affects our reading of the letter in relation to the other Pauline letters. If written from Ephesus during the eventful period of Paul's Aegean mission rather than in Rome toward the end of Paul's missionary period and probably shortly before his death, Philippians was composed in the mid-50s rather than around 60–61 C.E. Read with the Corinthian and Thessalonian correspondence, it then reflects many of the anxieties and concerns at the height of Paul's turbulent mission in the Aegean area. His concern for the unity of the Philippian church echoes similar concerns in 1–2 Corinthians. Preoccupation with his own form of ministry and its implications for the progress of the gospel reflects similar concerns in the Thessalonian letters. Since it is a period when he is already encountering other missionaries in the same region, his description of the mixed motives of such persons in 1:15–18 might reflect this concern. Similarly, his stern words against opponents who threaten the solidarity of the Philippian church (1:28; 3:2–4:1) may echo similar concerns in 2 Cor 10–13 and even Galatians. Framing his response around the issue of circumcision (3:2–6) probably anticipates the vituperative response in Galatians. The tightly compressed summary of his theological position in 3:7–16 becomes an embryonic statement that is more fully amplified, first in Galatians, and then in Romans.

If the letter falls within this earlier period, one of its oddities is the lack of any reference to the collection for the Jerusalem poor, which preoccupied Paul during this period (1 Cor 16:1–4; 2 Cor 8–9; Gal 2:10). But if the Philippian church had adopted a unique role in becoming Paul's sole supporting church, the letter probably reflects his interest in expressing thanks for their generosity rather than soliciting their participation in the larger charitable project. That the Philippians contributed generously to the collection for the Jerusalem poor is suggested by Paul's reference to the generosity of the Macedonian churches, of which they were certainly a vital part (2 Cor 8:1–2).

Framing Life or Death Choices in the Spirit of Jesus Christ

When discussing his imprisonment, Paul reveals little about the civil procedures that lie ahead. By referring to his "defense [*apologia*] and confirmation of the gospel" (1:7; cf. 1:16), Paul is perhaps anticipating formal judicial proceedings (also cf. 2:23). He envisions death as a possible outcome (1:20), and yet, possibly to buoy the Philippians' (and his own) hopes, he also speaks of visiting them again (1:19, 25–27).

By identifying the "progress of the gospel" (1:12 REB) as his overriding concern, Paul reflects his defensive posture. His imprisonment will provide a formal occasion for his "defense of the gospel" (1:16), probably in some public forum, but 1:12–26 is also his literary defense to his supporting church, which has a vested interest in his welfare. Since his imprisonment is "for Christ," it has had the effect of publicizing Christ in high places and making the church more confident in its public witness (1:13–14). Rather than obstructing the gospel, his imprisonment has served to advance it. Even with the clamor of Christian witness going on all around him, some ill-motivated, some nobly motivated, the gospel gets preached (1:15–18). Supported by the church's prayers and the "help of the Spirit of Jesus Christ" (1:19), Paul remains hopeful. He also sees his imprisonment as strengthening the already close bond between himself and the Philippians; through it he and they have jointly experienced God's grace (1:7).

Facing the prospect of his death realistically, Paul frames his options not simply as death or life; especially worth noting is how he interprets each option in light of the gospel. Rather than understanding "to live is Christ" as an expression of his Christ mysticism, we should see it quite pragmatically: "for me to live means that Christ continues to be preached." To die, however, is "gain" because it speeds Paul's ultimate union with the risen Christ. Either way, Christ is "magnified" (1:20 KJV); his message is written in larger, even bolder, type.

In Phil 1:12–26 Paul speaks as if both his persona—who he is as a preacher—and his message—the gospel he preaches—are a single medium through which the living reality of Christ is channeled. Because of this, his preaching—and his ministry—has a sacramental quality. So closely does he identify himself and his apostolic mission with the message of Christ that his circumstances, however hampered, and his ultimate fate, however it turns out, become occasions for mediating Christ's presence.

Paul's remarks in 1:12–26 are the words of a martyr—someone who dies for a person or cause nobler than one's self. Not surprisingly, later Christian martyrs, such as Ignatius (ca. 35–107 C.E.), drew on this text in shaping their own self-image and their perceptions of death.[7]

The issue in this passage is Paul's imprisonment: How will it turn out? Will it be a setback for the church? How is he doing? Yet Paul's remarks here redefine the issue, not as a question of his personal well-being, but as the viability and vitality of the gospel: Does his imprisonment arrest the "progress of the gospel"? Is Christ still preached? How is Christ present if Paul dies or if he lives? By insisting on the resilience and the sheer irrepressibility of the gospel, as well as the sustaining power of the church's prayers and the support of Jesus' own Spirit, Paul lays out his "defense of the gospel."

Conduct Worthy of the Gospel: Having the Mind of Christ (1:27–2:18; 4:2–7, 21–23)

Even a casual reading of Paul's carefully crafted exhortation to unity reveals tensions—perhaps quite serious—within the Philippian church. His repeated use of well-chosen terms hammers this point home: "one spirit" and "one mind" (1:27); "same mind," "same love," "full accord," "of one mind" (2:2). The Philippians' solidarity is threatened by their "opponents" (1:28), whose presence was bound to divide them. His call for them to be unified in spirit is part of a more broadly construed appeal: "let your conduct be worthy of the gospel of Christ" (1:27 REB). Here the gospel, broadly understood to include both the story and the person of Christ, becomes the norm by which Christian conduct is measured and thus the mold into which it is cast. To put it less rigidly, the gospel becomes a drama script enacted by those who are summoned and transformed by it. Since the phrase translated "let your conduct be . . ." translates the Greek term *politeuomai*, literally, "lead the life of a citizen," one is a worthy citizen of the gospel when its story establishes the contours of one's own living story.

Concretely, this means that when those who live by the gospel confront active resistance, they can reinterpret such resistance constructively rather than destructively, or, as Paul puts it, as an experience of "salvation" (1:28). In such moments one experiences true solidarity with Christ because one shares in Christ's suffering. One becomes a citizen of the gospel by "believing in Christ"; one becomes a *true citizen* of the gospel when one "suffer[s] for him as well" (1:29). The vital point of solidarity is between the citizen of the gospel and the Christ of the gospel. The besieged church is in closest solidarity with Paul at the point where their sufferings intersect (1:30)— when they are fellow sufferers for the gospel.

The Christ hymn in 2:6–11 is best understood within this larger framework, in which "gospel story" serves as the template for defining the church's "life story." The rhythmical character and strophic structure of this grand narrative have long been recognized. Whether structured as six separate stanzas (NJB) or as two main sections with three stanzas each (NRSV), the hymn is now widely regarded as an early Christian hymn composed either by Paul himself or taken over by him from already established liturgical practice. Even if it was composed earlier, which is probable, and thus should be designated as a pre-Pauline hymn, by incorporating it here Paul affirms its theology. Some have plausibly suggested that "even death on a cross" (2:8) is Paul's own editorial addition through which he gives his distinctive theological stamp to the hymn.

The scope of the grand narrative of Christ portrayed in the hymn is both epic and cosmic, moving from Christ's pre-existence through his voluntary descent to the earth, his full embrace of humanity reaching its nadir in his scandalous death, and then his journey upward, where his resurrection and ascension are fused into a single exaltation by God and he is given dominion over the three-tiered universe—heaven, earth, and the underworld. At the end comes universal confession. Those below who utter the confession "Jesus Christ is Lord" acknowledge the truth of the larger story. They demonstrate its truth by conforming the narrative of their lives to that grand narrative.

Especially noteworthy is Paul's choice of this grand, cosmic story, as opposed, for example, to the earthly story of Jesus. Typical of Paul is his studied indifference to the life of Jesus—what Jesus did on earth—as a resource for drawing moral lessons. What interests him far more is the story that extends from creation, or even before creation, to heavenly enthronement, and eventually to the Parousia and final judgment.

Also worth noting is how the Christ story is introduced by an ambiguous introductory line (2:5). "Let the same mind be in you *that was in* Christ Jesus" (NRSV, emphasis added) suggests that the Christ depicted in the hymn is a model. "Let the same mind be in you *that you have* in Christ Jesus" (NRSV note, emphasis added) shifts the accent from Christ the Exemplar to Christ the Enabler. In the first instance, the hymn delineates an exemplary form of behavior, or, perhaps more correctly, an exemplary disposition or frame of mind. In the alternative construal, the hymn depicts the story that makes it possible for the reconfiguration of our minds to occur. Either way, what Paul is calling for is quite clear: cultivating a frame of mind whose contours are shaped by the Christ story. He means more than mimicking the actions of Jesus.

Instead, the hymn depicts Christ as a second Adam who, in contrast to the prideful, presumptuous first Adam, displayed the disposition of humble obedience. Whereas the original Adam first rose and then fell, the second Adam fell and then rose. But in Christ's case it was voluntary descent and involuntary ascent. The hymn depicts the "mind of Christ" as the guiding disposition of faithful obedience before the Father rather than the grasping for power and dominion that characterized the first Adam.

Translating this cosmic ethical impulse into human action is a divinely bestowed gift. It is "God who is at work" (2:13), who enables both volition and action. God is the means through which salvation is worked out. Like Christ, those who are motivated by this overriding impulse are God's children shining "like stars in the world" (2:15). At the congregational level, such a disposition privileges the interests of others over one's own interests, and in doing so exhibits an "incentive in love" (2:1 NJB).

Maintaining Contact through Co-workers (2:19–3:1*a*)

Not only did Paul's letters serve as his surrogate presence within the churches that received them, but his co-workers did so as well. This was especially the case when a co-worker actually served as the courier of the letter. The co-worker would be expected to read the letter to the church just as Paul had instructed him. Of special concern to Paul are the moral qualities that commend Timothy and Epaphroditus to the Philippian church. Since self-transcending interest is a moral ideal for the church (2:4), one that was exemplified by Christ himself (2:6–11), Paul commends Timothy as the embodiment of that very ideal (2:20–21). Because Epaphroditus was the Philippian church's own "messenger" (*apostolos*, 2:25), he is their surrogate presence when he is with Paul (2:30).

The Identity That Comes with Knowing Christ (3:1*b*–4:1)

The threat of opponents elicits one of Paul's most theologically penetrating passages. It is remarkable for how it combines autobiographical review (3:5–6) with reflection on his encounter with Christ. Unlike Gal 1:13–24, in which Paul rehearses the course of his life to demonstrate the extraordinary nature of his prophetic call and his consequent independence from Jerusalem church authorities, this tightly compressed review accents the constitutive elements of his former core religious identity. It is so configured because the opponents would regard it as the ideal resumé. "Circumcised on the eighth day" heads the list (3:5), which suggests that it was the single symbol that captured the essence of the opponents' core identity. But Paul does not even grant them the use of the term; instead, he characterizes them as those who "mutilate the flesh" (3:2). The REB aptly catches his drift: "Be on your guard against . . . those who insist on mutilation—'circumcision' I will not call it" (3:2). Constructing one's core religious identity this way, in Paul's view, results in misplaced confidence. By grounding identity "in the flesh" or "in the physical" (REB), one creates a center of gravity for the self that is essentially human. Paul is playing on the double meaning of "flesh."

The term signifies the initiation rite in which physical flesh is cut away, but because circumcision creates a core religious identity that prizes other values, such as lineal descent, ethnic labels, and religious rectitude and achievement, it also signifies a whole way of being in the world.

If one must use "circumcision" to establish identity—as apparently the opponents must—Paul will lay claim to it—"we who are the circumcision"—but he will radically redefine it (3:3–14). The distinctive emphasis of these remarks is explained by the nature of Paul's opponents, probably Judaizers, although he does not use that label. It is even conceivable that he has non-Christian Jews in view. His remarks are primarily self-referential. Paul sketches his core religious identity and the process through which one construction of the self gave way to another. He focuses on who he was and who he has now become, primarily because he sees his own experience as extendable to others, in this case the Philippians. His own experience with Christ is a paradigm from which others can learn, which they can emulate, if not replicate.

Unlike other occasions on which Paul recalls his pivotal encounter with Christ, he does not highlight how Christ "appeared" to him (cf. 1 Cor 15:8–11; Gal 1:15–16; cf. 1 Cor 9:1). Here he is thinking less about the epiphanic moment itself and more about its consequences. Using economic metaphors of loss and gain, he sees the experience as a great exchange: "But all such assets [family pedigree, ethnic identity, etc.] I have written off because of Christ" (3:7 REB). Although he does not speak of the Christ he encountered in vivid, visual terms, such as those depicted in Luke's account of his conversion (Acts 9, 22, 26), or even as an apocalypse of Jesus Christ (Gal 1:12), this account is no less personal and certainly no less dramatic as a life-changing moment. He cannot think of the event apart from its central figure, Jesus Christ. Accordingly, Paul can speak of his "pride" in Jesus Christ (3:3 REB) and the great exchange that occurs "because of Christ" (3:7).

One of the most dominant motifs here is epistemological—"knowing" (3:8). Of special concern is how his way of knowing was redefined. Ostensibly the exchange was ludicrous: giving up a stellar core religious identity (3:4–6) for an apostolic life marked by shameful humiliation and suffering. It is ludicrous only if viewed in terms of "the flesh." Viewed another way, Paul exchanged an "earthly" construal of things for a "heavenly" one (3:19–20); or, as he puts it, what emerged in his encounter was the "surpassing value of knowing Christ Jesus my Lord" (3:8). The latter phrase renders the Greek literally (*to hyperechon tēs gnōseōs Christou Iēsou tou kyriou mou*). This phrase can have a double sense: knowledge whose object or content is Christ ("Christ" as objective genitive) or the knowledge Christ has of Paul ("Christ" as subjective genitive)— thus, either "knowing Christ" or "being known by Christ." That the accent probably falls on the latter is suggested by his later comment that he was "laid hold of," literally, "seized," by Christ Jesus (3:12), or that "Christ Jesus has made me his own" (NRSV). Paul's language suggests knowledge that is more than self-awareness, even a newly illuminated self-awareness. It is a way of knowing that transforms even as it reveals and illuminates the self. Such knowledge exposes the transparency of the self before Christ.

Because this form of knowing creates a new existential space in which to construct one's core religious identity, one who is so known is "in Christ." In one sense the relationship created is one of mystical union—"finding myself in union with him" (3:9 REB)—yet it is not reducible to the Christ mysticism some scholars find here.

The heart of this knowledge of Christ is the shedding of an old identity that saw "righteousness" as something that came "from the law" (*ek nomou*, 3:9). A new identity emerged for Paul when, through this divine revelation, "righteousness," the acknowledged goal of the sincere religious seeker, was experienced differently—as a gift from God that "comes through faith in/of Christ" and that is "based on faith" (3:9). Here, in the most succinct form imaginable, is the core of Paul's theological position that is more fully sketched in Galatians, and later, even more comprehensively, in Romans. God's righteousness is not experienced through Torah observance; hence the latter is not salvific. This "righteousness" rather occurs "through faith"—faith that sees Christ as the primary agent through whom God creates righteousness but also as the One who exemplifies such faith most fully.

Christ serves as the epistemological focus of Paul's remarks here. All cognitive, existential knowing becomes focused in him, and out of this newly acquired self-awareness emerges a correspondingly new frame of mind that sees Christ's death and resurrection not merely as things to be believed—although they are that—but also as templates for shaping behaviors. Christ's resurrection is not simply Christ's heavenly exaltation, but a power-emitting event whose residual force is actually appropriated by the one who is "in Christ." Paul can speak of the "power of his resurrection" (3:10). This is coupled with a way of thinking about human experience that sees Christ's death not just as a historic moment in the past, but as a primal, paradigmatic event toward which behavior "in Christ" can be conformed. Paul speaks of being "morphed" with Christ in his sufferings (3:10), or "being moulded to the pattern of his death" (3:10 NJB; cf. Gal 2:19).

As profound as this identity-creating experience is, it is future oriented, since the "resurrection of the dead" is the final event toward which it is directed. Even achieving that cannot be taken for granted, for Paul "somehow" hopes to attain it (3:11). Paul also emphasizes that the trajectory of a life so construed is both linear and upward. It is linear in the sense that it is not already achieved. The opponents may very well have operated with a notion of perfected knowledge that bordered on Gnosticism, and they may even have thought that resurrection or "being raised with Christ" should be thought of in fully realized terms. If so, Paul's insistence on the "not yet-ness" of the experience is apt. He thus accents the present and future tense, whereas the opponents may have turned the experience with Christ into a past or pluperfect experience, something that had already occurred, a way of relating to Christ that was not only fully realizable but already fully realized. Those who are properly "mature" or "perfect" (3:15), however, will understand how flawed this view is. A similar outlook is spelled out in 1 Cor 2:6–16.

Not only is the trajectory linear, it is also upward. Using the image of the sprinter, Paul conceives of the prize as heavenly and the primary thrust of the Christian's pursuit as heavenly citizenship (3:20). Conceiving the experience this way further trumps the alternative theological viewpoint of the opponents, whose emphasis on "the flesh" is earthbound.

Crafting Letters to Strengthen the Bonds of Affection

From the very beginning of the letter, we sense Paul's special affection for the Philippian church. Rather than identifying himself as an apostle of Jesus Christ, as he often does in his letters (cf. Rom 1:1; 1 Cor 1:1; 2 Cor 1:1; Gal 1:1; also, 1 Thess 2:7), he adopts a more deferential form of self-identification: he and Timothy are "slaves [*douloi*] of Christ Jesus" (1:1). The term "apostle" is used only once in the letter, not of Paul himself, but of Epaphroditus in the nontechnical sense of "messenger" (2:25). Unlike any other Pauline letter, he acknowledges the presence of "bishops and deacons" within the church (1:1). In sharp contrast to the Thessalonian letters, Paul's relationship with the Philippian church is of longer standing. No longer a fresh memory, as it is in other letters, his founding visit is a more distant moment in the past (see 1 Thess 1:9–10; 2:1–16; 1 Cor 2:1–5; also cf. Gal 3:1–5). This probably explains why he does not rehearse any details of his initial visit, except fleetingly. He does speak of it as "the early days of the gospel" (literally, "the beginning of the gospel," *en archē tou euangeliou*, 4:15), but he emphasizes the repeated contact that he has had with the church during the interim (4:15–16). What has especially strengthened the church's bond with him is its singular, steadfast financial commitment to his ministry; or, as he says in the opening prayer of thanksgiving, their "sharing in the gospel from the first day until now" (1:5). As much as anything else, this strong solidarity between Paul and the Philippian church, symbolized by its ongoing, active support of his ministry, shines through the letter. This probably accounts for his repeated use of language emphasizing their joint participation in his work.[8]

So close is the bond between Paul and the Philippian church that some have rightly seen a strong concentration of friendship language within the letter. Friendship letters (*philikai*) were a well-defined literary type within the ancient world, and handbooks giving instructions on how to write such letters noted their distinguishing characteristics. Since their purpose was to nurture friendship, they tended to recall the origin of the friendship and other circumstances that have strengthened it. Another recurrent motif is how the letter writer's physical separation from the recipient is offset by the spiritual or mental union that exists between them. The friendship letter serves as the means through which friends share in each other's presence. Language of affection was employed as a way of expressing the strong tie between friends and could take the form of the letter writer's expressing a longing to be with the recipient.

Several of the features that typified friendship letters occur in Philippians: the strong sense of solidarity between Paul and the Philippian church, especially seen in the language of "sharing" or "fellowship" (1:7); his longing for them (1:8; 4:1; cf. 2:26); shared experiences (1:30); affectionate language (4:1); sharing gifts (4:10–20); and familial forms of address ("brothers," *adelphoi*, is the most frequent form of address: Phil 1:12, 14; 3:1, 13, 17; 4:1, 8). But it is overly precise to classify the entire letter as a friendship letter.

The letter also displays many of the characteristic features of the hortatory (paraenetic) letter: the use of personal example as the basis of exhortation (most notably Christ, 2:5–11, but also Paul, 3:17; 4:9); the use of direct appeals (2:1–4; 4:2) and the frequency of moral directives;[9] and strong affective language. The concluding section could easily stand alone as a letter of thanksgiving (4:10–20), and the opening prayer exhibits the same literary form (1:3–11). More difficult to classify is the strongly worded warning of the polemical section (3:1*b*–4:1).

Given this mixture of epistolary features, it is better to see the letter as a mixed type rather than a single epistolary type. This is especially the case if our final edited version of the letter is composed of three smaller letters, each reflecting a distinctive shape to achieve its particular purpose. Drawing on several epistolary traditions, Paul has adapted their distinctive features in writing to the Philippians.

The Christ Hymn (2:6–11)[10]

One of the remarkable features of the Christ hymn is its detailed rehearsal of what was accomplished in the incarnation. Compared with the prologue to John's Gospel, in which the *Logos* "became" flesh (John 1:14), the tracking of Christ's "journey" here is considerably fuller. Christ moves from a pre-existent state, in which his relationship to God is sketched, downward to earthly existence, extending from his human birth to his "death on a cross." From the downward slope of this V-shaped Christology, the second half of the hymn traces Christ's movement upward. It poetically depicts his resurrection as exaltation and accents the universal worship that comes with his heavenly status. The Christ hymn can be read as a commentary on the Johannine prologue. [**See Expanded CD Version pp. 531–32: "*He Emptied Himself*": *The Christ Hymn in Christological Thought*]

Even though much biblical scholarship over the last two centuries has focused on the literary integrity of the letter, its place and circumstances of composition, its epistolary form, and the literary form and historical origin of the Christ hymn, it is still worth remembering how powerful Philippians, and especially the Christ hymn, has been in shaping the church's understanding of Christ and developing forms of piety appropriate to the Christ depicted in the hymn. The letter's buoyant emphasis on joy and hope has often offset its more somber dimensions; its call for unity has even drowned out the underlying tensions reflected in the letter. Such rosy readings occur at the expense of the more intractable, less attractive features of the text. Yet they too are part of the letter's history of reception, even if they illustrate the seemingly irresistible need for selective reading that accentuates the positive.

Notes

1. Pol. *Phil.* 3.2. Further evidence suggesting that the polemical letter was a separate composition is provided by the apocryphal Pauline *Epistle to the Laodiceans*, dated between the second and fourth century but possibly as early as the mid-second century, which depends heavily on canonical Philippians but shows no awareness of 3:2–4:3.

2. Pol. *Phil.* 1.1

3. Pol. *Phil.* 11.1–4.

4. The Marcionite Prologue to Philippians, dated between the early second and fourth centuries, reports: "The Philippians are Macedonians. They persevered in faith after [they] had accepted the word of truth and they did not receive false apostles. The Apostle praises them, writing to them from Rome from the prison, by Epaphroditus."

5. *1 Clem.* 5.6 reports of Paul, "Seven times he was in chains."

6. An Ephesian imprisonment of six days is mentioned in the apocryphal *Acts of Paul*. See W. Schneemelcher, "Acts of Paul," in E. Hennecke and W. Schneemelcher, eds., *New Testament Apocrypha* (ed. R. McL. Wilson; 2 vols.; London: Epworth, 1963–1965), 2:370.

7. Ign. *Rom.* 2; cf. Phil 2:17.

8. The language of joint participation is especially reflected in several terms: *koinōnia*, "sharing" or "fellowship" (Phil 1:5), and its verb form "shared" (Phil 4:15); also its cognate "joint sharers" (*synkoinōnous*) in God's grace (Phil 1:7); similarly, "jointly sharing" (*synkoinōnēsantes*) in Paul's distress (Phil 4:14). He also appeals to his "loyal companion," perhaps named Syzygus (itself a compound form employing the prefix *syn-*, literally "with"), to help arbitrate between Euodia and Syntyche, his "fellow strugglers" (*synēthlēsan*) in the work of the gospel (Phil 4:3). The same compound verb is used to describe the Philippians' "striving side by side [*synathlountes*] with one mind for the faith of the gospel" (Phil 1:27). Paul calls on the church to "join in imitating [*synmimētai*] me" (Phil 3:17). In his appeal for unity, he urges them to be "jointly souled" (*synpsychoi*) in their single mindedness (Phil 2:2). Given his close association with the church and with Paul, Epaphroditus is both "fellow worker" (*synergon*) and "fellow soldier" (*systratiōtēn*) of Paul (Phil 2:25).

9. This is seen especially in his repeated use of imperatives, e.g., Phil 1:27; 2:2, 12, 14, 18 (2x), 29; 3:1, 2 (3x), 17 (2x); 4:1, 4 (2x), 5, 6, 8, 9, 21; also cf. 3:16 and 4:2, in which infinitives are used imperatively. Altogether, there are twenty-three such directives.

10. For the following treatment, I draw on F. W. Beare, *Philippians* (London: Black, 1959), especially the essay on Kenotic Christology by Eugene R. Fairweather (pp. 159–74).

Bibliography

Commentaries

Beare, Francis W. *A Commentary on the Epistle to the Philippians*. 3d ed. Black's New Testament Commentaries. London: Black, 1973 (1959).

Bockmuehl, Markus. *A Commentary on the Epistle to the Philippians*. Black's New Testament Commentaries. 4th ed. London/Peabody: Black/Hendrickson, 1997.

Caird, George B. *Paul's Letters from Prison (Ephesians, Philippians, Colossians, Philemon) in the Revised Standard Version: Introduction and Commentary*. New Clarendon Bible. Oxford: Oxford University Press, 1981 [1976]. Pages 95–154.

Craddock, Fred B. *Philippians*. Interpretation: A Bible Commentary for Teaching and Preaching. Atlanta: John Knox, 1985.

Fee, Gordon D. *Paul's Letter to the Philippians*. New International Commentary on the New Testament. Grand Rapids: Eerdmans, 1995.

Gnilka, Joachim, and Franz Mussner. *The Epistle to the Philippians and The Epistle to the Colossians*. London: Sheed & Ward, 1971. Pages 9–74.

Hooker, Morna D. "The Letter to the Philippians: Introduction, Commentary, and Reflections." Pages 467–549 in vol. 11 of *The New Interpreter's Bible*. Edited by Leander E. Keck. 12 vols. Nashville: Abingdon, 2000.

Martin, Ralph P. *The Epistle of Paul to the Philippians: An Introduction and Commentary*. 2d ed. Leicester/Grand Rapids: InterVarsity /Eerdmans, 1987 (1959).

Osiek, Carolyn. *Philippians, Philemon*. Abingdon New Testament Commentaries. Nashville: Abingdon, 2000.

Witherington, Ben. *Friendship and Finances in Philippi: The Letter of Paul to the Philippians*. New Testament in Context. Valley Forge: Trinity, 1994.

Other Resources

Holloway, Paul A. *Consolation in Philippians: Philosophical Sources and Rhetorical Strategy*. Society for New Testament Studies Monograph Series 112. Cambridge: Cambridge University Press, 2001.

Marshall, I. Howard. "The Theology of Philippians." Pages 116–74 in Karl P. Donfried and I. Howard Marshall, *The Theology of the Shorter Pauline Letters*. New Testament Theology. Cambridge: Cambridge University Press, 1993; repr. 1999.

Oakes, Peter. *Philippians: From People to Letter*. Society for New Testament Studies Monograph Series 110. Cambridge: Cambridge University Press, 2001.

Peterman, G. W. *Paul's Gift from Philippi: Conventions of Gift Exchange and Christian Giving*. Society for New Testament Studies Monograph Series 92. Cambridge: Cambridge University Press, 1997.

Portefaix, Lilian. *Sisters Rejoice: Paul's Letter to the Philippians and Luke-Acts as Seen by First-century Philippian Women*. Coniectanea Biblica, New Testament Series 20. Stockholm: Almqvist & Wiksell, 1988.

THE CHRIST HYMN

Martin, Ralph P. *A Hymn of Christ: Philippians 2:5–11 in Recent Interpretation & in the Setting of Early Christian Worship*. Downers Grove: InterVarsity, 1997 [1967].

———, and Brian J. Dodd, eds. *Where Christology Began: Essays on Philippians 2*. Louisville: Westminster John Knox, 1998.

Sanders, Jack T. *The New Testament Christological Hymns: Their Historical Religious Background*. Society for New Testament Studies Monograph Series 15. Cambridge: Cambridge University Press, 1971.

Chapter 17

Philemon

". . . the church has done well in directing (Philemon) to be read at her public services. For it teaches with singular force and beauty several important lessons—moderation in the exercise of ecclesiastical authority, respect for the providential order of human society, the spiritual equality of the sexes, and the duty of Christian humility and brotherly love."

Theodore of Mopsuestia

"This letter gives us a masterful and tender example of Christian love."

Martin Luther

The shortest of Paul's letters, Philemon closely resembles an ordinary Hellenistic letter. Probably written in its entirety by Paul's own hand rather than dictated to a scribe (v. 19), the letter exhibits a straightforward structure.[1] An opening greeting (vv. 1–3) is followed by a prayer of thanksgiving (vv. 4–7), which establishes the deferential mood of the rest of the letter and signals its major theme: the unusual quality of Philemon's love and faith. The heart of the letter is Paul's appeal to Philemon on behalf of Onesimus (vv. 8–21). The letter concludes with an incidental appeal (v. 22), greetings from five named co-workers who are with Paul at the time of writing (vv. 23–24), and a benediction (v. 25).

In spite of its brevity, the letter displays considerable stylistic sophistication. So impressed with Philemon was the nineteenth-century French intellectual Ernest Renan that he called it a "little masterpiece" of the art of letter writing.[2] Not only is it a diplomatic masterpiece because of its sensitive handling of a delicate situation, but it also employs some typical Pauline literary devices and numerous characteristic Pauline phrases. These include his use of chiasm, the structuring of literary elements in an a-b-b-a pattern, to describe Philemon's (a) love and (b) faith toward (b¹) the Lord Jesus and (a¹) all the saints, which the NRSV correctly renders as "your love for all the saints and your faith toward the Lord Jesus" (v. 5); his well-known pun characterizing Onesimus (which literally means "useful") as formerly "useless" (*achrēstos*) but now "useful" (*euchrēstos*, v. 11; cf. 1 Cor 9:21); and his characteristic use of certain turns of phrase such as "not to mention that . . ." (v. 19 NIV) as a form of emphatic understatement (cf. 2 Cor 9:4). [See Expanded CD Version p. 540: "*A Prisoner of Christ Jesus": Paul's Location at the Time of Composition*]

Given the close connection between the letters of Philemon and Colossians, both letters probably stemmed from the same imprisonment.[3] The nature of the heresy combated in Colossae and the probability that Paul writes as an "old man" (*presbytēs*, v. 9)[4] increase the likelihood that this imprisonment occurred late in Paul's ministry. Even though Philippians was probably written during an Ephesian imprisonment, there is no compelling reason why Philemon and Colossians must have come from that same imprisonment. The thrust of Philippians is different from both of these prison letters, which were probably composed well after Paul's ministry in the East had been concluded. Philemon was most likely composed in Rome during the two-year imprisonment mentioned in Acts 28.

The Situation

Far more consequential for interpreting Philemon than determining the place of composition is reaching some clarity about the circumstances envisioned in the letter. Many of the details Paul leaves unexplained, since they were readily known to all the parties involved. From the letter itself, several things are clear:

(1) Onesimus is with Paul at the time of writing (v. 12). As Paul's "child" whom he fathered during his imprisonment, Onesimus had become a Christian through Paul's own efforts.[5] Since Paul speaks of Onesimus as "my own heart" (v. 12), the bond between them is close.

(2) The relationship between Onesimus and Philemon is one of slave (*doulos*) to master. Although some scholars have taken verse 16 to mean that Philemon and Onesimus are blood brothers, and that the slave language is being used metaphorically rather than literally, it is preferable to see Onesimus as Philemon's slave. Otherwise, it is difficult to understand why Paul would speak of Philemon's power to grant his consent in the matter (v. 14).

(3) Onesimus has been "separated" from Philemon (v. 15), and Paul is urging Philemon to welcome him back (v. 17). Onesimus appears to have caused his owner some loss, probably financial (vv. 18–19).

The exact circumstances surrounding the "separation" of Onesimus from Philemon are left unexplained. Traditionally, Onesimus has been viewed as a runaway slave[6] who fled (probably to Rome), eventually encountered Paul during his imprisonment, and became a convert to Christianity and an intimate associate of Paul. Since the consequences for fugitive slaves were dire, both for slaves and those who harbored them, Paul now takes the responsible step of returning Onesimus to his master, who is Paul's own close friend, Philemon. But because Onesimus's conversion to Christianity altered his relationship to Philemon, so that he is "no longer . . . a slave but more than a slave, a beloved brother" (v. 16), Paul intervenes as an interested third party who is willing to make good on any losses Onesimus has caused (v. 18) and who therefore urges Philemon to extend Christian love to Onesimus and receive him back.

While this construal of events long held sway,[7] it has given way recently to an alternative explanation that many scholars find more compelling. Those who adopt this latter view emphasize that Onesimus is nowhere identified in the letter as a fugitive. According to the first-century Roman jurist Proculus, when a slave had a grievance against a master, it was possible for the slave to seek out a third party to serve as a mediator between the two of them; moreover, a slave could go to another place to find such a mediator without technically becoming a fugitive.[8] As an *amicus domini*, a "friend of the master," the third party could hear the slave's complaint, judge its merit, then intervene on behalf of the slave with the master. In this way, wrongs (on either side) could be made right, and reconciliation could be achieved. Not only is this practice known from Roman law, but it is also attested in literary documents from the period that show how it actually worked.

The most notable instance is a letter from Pliny the Younger (61–112 C.E.) to a slave owner named Sabinianus.[9] In the letter Pliny writes in behalf of a freedman who incurred the displeasure of his master Sabinianus and subsequently sought out Pliny to intervene with his angry master. In vivid language Pliny describes the man's desperate entreaties, notes his penitent spirit, and in writing to Sabinianus exhibits a diplomatic spirit akin to that of Paul in Philemon. If anything, Pliny is more explicit than Paul in asking Sabinianus to forgive the man. Even more enlightening is a follow-up letter by Pliny[10] complimenting Sabinianus on his generosity of spirit in receiving the man back.

Read in the light of this practice of third-party arbitration, the letter of Philemon is Paul's letter of petition, or a letter of intercession, written to Philemon on behalf of Onesimus. In this construal Onesimus is not a fugitive slave but a slave whose relationship with his owner has become strained, possibly because of some loss for which he has been responsible. Using a well-established legal procedure, Onesimus has sought out Paul, a close friend of Philemon, to plead his case. The several allusions in the letter to Paul's close relationship with Philemon are seen as expressions of his status as *amicus domini*. There can be little doubt that Paul is trading on his intimate friendship with Philemon throughout the letter. In particular, his willingness to repay whatever losses Philemon has incurred is a concrete expression of his support of Onesimus (v. 18). As such, the letter can be read not merely as a personal letter, or even a personal petition, but as an apostolic letter in which Paul is exercising his own ministry of reconciliation (2 Cor 5:18–21).

Love as Enacted Faith

Read one way, Philemon is manifestly non-theological. It nowhere mentions the early Christian kerygma—the death and resurrection of Christ—or other familiar Pauline themes such as the Holy Spirit, justification by faith, or Christ's Parousia. It mentions God only twice (vv. 3, 4). Because of its ostensibly secular, seemingly ordinary, character, the letter apparently received little attention among early patristic and medieval interpreters.[11] As early as the fourth century, some even wondered whether the letter was written by Paul and thus whether it was inspired. This prompted a number of notable figures such as Jerome (ca. 345–420 C.E.),[12] John Chrysostom (ca. 347–407 C.E.),[13] and Theodore of Mopsuestia (ca. 350–428 C.E.)[14] to defend its Pauline authorship and commend its usefulness as an edifying document.

Philemon is unlike other Pauline letters. Here Paul is not explicitly thinking through the implications of God's action in Christ, and for this reason the letter betrays no signs of being reflective theology, certainly not in the sense that Galatians and Romans are. But if Philemon is read as a particular instance of lived theology, or even as an instance in which Paul does theology, it is profoundly theological.

Its focus is highly personal. Unlike the other Pauline letters we have treated so far, it is addressed primarily to one individual—Philemon. Admittedly, in the opening greeting Paul also addresses Apphia and Archippus, as well as the congregation meeting in Philemon's house (v. 2). But the heart of the letter (vv. 4–21) is addressed to Philemon himself, as seen by Paul's exclusive use in this section of the singular form of "you." While other individuals are mentioned, especially in the final greeting (vv. 23–24), the letter's primary focus is the triangular relationship among three individuals— Paul, Philemon, and Onesimus. Of the three, Philemon emerges as the most dominant figure, since he is the one being petitioned. He may be Paul's equal—his "partner," perhaps even his business associate (v. 17). He is certainly Onesimus's superior—his "lord," although this term itself is not used. He clearly has the patron's power to give or take away. This alone accounts for the deferential tone of the letter.

Especially instructive is how Paul shapes his petition to Philemon and what it reveals about how he understands life "in Christ." The sheer number of times Paul refers to Christ is itself suggestive—eleven times within the space of twenty-five verses. Paul himself is a "prisoner of Christ Jesus" (vv. 1, 9), a self-designation not found in the letters we have treated thus far.[15] This phrase may echo his self-understanding as one who was "seized by Christ" (Phil 3:12), but probably means that he is a "prisoner for the cause of Christ Jesus." Epaphras is probably Paul's "fellow prisoner in Christ Jesus" (v. 23) in a metaphorical sense, in other words, his "fellow campaigner" (cf. Col 4:10). Typical of his other letters, Paul delivers greetings in the name of Christ, specifically grace (and peace) from the "Lord Jesus Christ" (vv. 3, 25).

What characterizes Philemon's faith is that it is directed toward the "Lord Jesus" (v. 5), which suggests that he has confessed Jesus as Lord (cf. 1 Cor 12:3; Rom 10:9). No further reference is made to the content of the preaching to which he responded, nor even that it was Paul's preaching that brought him to faith, although this is implied (v. 19). As elsewhere, Paul's boldness derives from his own total immersion "in Christ" (v. 8; cf. 2 Cor 3:4). If this characteristic Pauline phrase denotes the newly created sphere within which those incorporated into Christ uniquely experience his creative power, this helps explain his highly provocative wording in v. 6: "that the sharing [*koinōnia*] of your faith might become concretely active by your becoming fully aware of all the good that we can do for Christ" (NJB modified). The "good to be done," which anticipates the action Paul hopes Philemon will take toward Onesimus, will further extend the "love for all the saints" (v. 5) that Philemon has shown through his unmentioned acts of generosity (v. 7).

This newly configured sphere is not merely mental or psychological. Rather than denoting one's mystical union with Christ, it has a concrete social dimension. Being "in the Lord" is as real as being "in the flesh" (v. 16). Existence "in the Lord" is more than a parallel track running alongside human relationships; it is, rather, a spiritual space that encloses human identity and, in doing so, transforms it. When one's status shifts from being a slave (*doulos*) to being a "beloved brother" (*adelphon agapēton*, v. 16), one experiences a doubly formed identity: "both on the natural plane and in the Lord" (NJB), or "both as a person and as a Christian" (REB modified).

Whether Philemon is willing to grant Paul's request depends on the depth and character of his being "in the Lord" (v. 20). Since "in the Lord" elsewhere specifies the agency through which, or the sphere within which, moral action is enabled, the underlying assumption may be that one's capacity to do good derives expressly from the depth of one's confession of Jesus as Lord. The Lord who is confessed becomes both the ground and agent of moral change. Paul's request that his heart be refreshed in Christ (v. 20) probably reflects the same conviction, although he appears to be asking for a measure of generosity that Philemon has shown on other occasions (v. 7).

It is not as though Paul simply peppers his appeal to Philemon with references to Christ. The letter rather exposes the internal texture of the network of relationships that Paul and Philemon have with Christ and thereby with each other. They are "partners" (v. 17) and "co-workers" (v. 1) by virtue of their common faith in Jesus Christ. This commonality of Christ-focused religious experience undergirds Paul's overall appeal.

Paul singles out Philemon's love and faith (v. 5) because he sees them as inseparable. Philemon is a concrete example of the principle Paul states elsewhere: what matters finally is "faith working through love" (Gal 5:6). What form Philemon's love has already taken is not known, but we can imagine various acts of generosity and hospitality. It is, after all, his home in which the church meets (v. 2), and his "love for all the saints" (v. 5) may have reached well beyond this one house church. Paul has been a recipient of Philemon's love, deriving both "joy and encouragement" from it (v. 7). Paul now asks Philemon to extend this same spirit of generosity toward Onesimus, not only by receiving him back without prejudice (v. 17), but also by allowing Paul to make good whatever losses are attributable to Onesimus (vv. 18–19), and probably by granting him freedom (v. 21).

The carefully crafted petition suggests that Paul was aware of the delicate dynamics of strained relationships as well as the subtle dynamics of his own relationship with Philemon. He knows, for example, that forced good is no good at all, and that for love to be genuine it must be voluntary (v. 14). Knowing that he can frame his request in terms of mutual obligation, Paul refrains from doing so (v. 19). Yet by his very mention of what Philemon owes him, Paul shows his willingness to play this card if he needs to. By anchoring his appeal "in the Lord," Paul seeks to move the underlying motivation to a higher, or deeper, level—or, at least, to another level than that of mutual human obligation.

What gives Paul confidence, finally, is Philemon's character—already demonstrated in his behavior toward "all the saints" (v. 5) and toward Paul himself. Confident that Philemon's faith in Christ is genuine because it has consistently taken the form of enacted love, Paul concludes his appeal on a confident note (v. 21). Presented with a deftly crafted appeal that resonates with the heart of the gospel for which Paul is in chains (v. 13), Philemon can be expected to act in character and welcome Onesimus as he would Paul himself (v. 17).

Where is the theology of Philemon? It is not found in creedal summaries or even in richly developed metaphors expressing Christ's saving work. It is rather seen within the texture of human relationships that have been transformed by the "grace of the Lord Jesus Christ" (v. 25), as well as within the texture of this Christ-focused petitionary letter itself. Philemon may not be a theologically explicit letter, but it is a theologically informed letter.

Slavery as a Theological Problem

While Paul may have thought of himself as a "slave of Jesus Christ" (cf. Rom 1:1; Phil 1:1; Gal 1:10), he had no firsthand experience of being a slave. For him, "slave" was a metaphor rather than a term describing his actual social status. This was not the case with Onesimus, whose claim to fame is that he is perhaps the best-known NT example of a slave who became a Christian. However enlightened his master Philemon might have been even before he became a Christian, Onesimus doubtless knew the opprobrium that was attached to slaves in the Roman world. According to one Roman proverb, "There are as many enemies as there are slaves."[16] Even as early as Aristotle (384–322 B.C.E.), a slave could be defined as "an ensouled piece of property,"[17] a view that helps explain how central the notion of ownership was to the ancient understanding of slavery. There were doubtless numerous slave owners throughout the Roman world who were enlightened and humane and who created conditions within their households under which slaves did not have to endure shameful, humiliating treatment. Yet the many evils and abuses associated with slave ownership are also well attested. Slavery could be a cruel, horrific way of life, even in the best of circumstances. Still, in spite of occasional enlightened critiques by both pagan and Jewish writers, slavery remained one of the fixed elements of Greek and Roman society.[18]

Philemon is an illuminating document because it is the one NT writing that deals with a specific case of slavery. Many interpreters have found Paul's treatment of the matter problematic because his response here, as elsewhere in his writings, does not take the form of an explicit, sharply worded critique of the institution of slavery. This perceived lapse has been judged especially unfortunate given the continuation of slavery in Western culture and the horrendous abuses often associated with it in the name of Christianity within the last few centuries.

When Christian interpreters struggle with Philemon, trying to understand what redemptive theological message, if any, can be deduced from the letter, we should try to be constructively critical. On the one hand, this calls for a sympathetic appreciation of the social situation and political realities within which Paul, Onesimus, and Philemon found themselves. On the other hand, this calls for a realistic appraisal of Paul's actual response. It does no good to read Paul uncritically, much less hastily spring to his defense.

As a start, we do well to recognize the complexity of the ancient situation, both the legal and social structures within which Paul operated as well as the ethical norms and theological warrants that informed his response. Even though Greek and Roman legal procedures were in place regulating the treatment of slaves, it is not at all clear that these were the primary considerations informing Paul in this case. We have no firm evidence, for example, that Philemon, probably a resident of the region of Phrygia within Asia Minor, was a Roman and would therefore have been bound by such regulations. Paul may have been appealing to the unwritten norms of honor and shame in constructing his petition to Philemon. Even the degree to which he might have been informed by his own Jewish heritage, most notably OT teachings pertaining to slavery, is not clear. Deuteronomy 23:15–16, which prohibits the extradition of slaves who had sought asylum in Israel, is often seen as the most relevant OT text, perhaps even affecting Paul's phrasing in Phlm 13–14. Yet neither Onesimus nor Philemon appears to have been Jewish, and the OT text may not even have been applicable in this particular case.

More germane are other Pauline texts, for example, 1 Cor 7:20–24, in which he appears to insist that one's social status as a slave, like one's ethnic status as a Jew or Gentile, is a matter of ultimate indifference. But in this text Paul does not critique the institution of slavery per se. And if Colossians is Pauline, as is probably the case, its inclusion of slaves and masters as part of the household code used for specifying expected forms of Christian behavior simply reinforces this point (Col 3:22–4:1; also cf. Eph 6:5–9; 1 Pet 2:18–25). The most pressing question in Philemon is whether Paul's cryptic remark in verse 21 is a veiled request for Philemon to grant Onesimus his freedom. And if Paul's main concern is to bring about reconciliation between alienated Christian brothers, his primary motivation may not have been legal or social, but theological. He may have been discharging his responsibility as a God-appointed "minister of reconciliation" (2 Cor 5:18–21), as he does elsewhere in his letters (cf. 1 Cor 6).

To Paul's credit, he does see Onesimus's newly acquired Christian status as a "beloved brother" (v. 16) modifying, even transcending, his social status as a slave. This is in keeping with his theological outlook expressed elsewhere that one's relationship "in Christ" transcends social, ethnic, and gender distinctions, even if it does not eliminate them (Gal 3:26–28; cf. 1 Cor 12:13–14; Col 3:11).

Notes

1. His customary practice of dictating to a scribe is reflected in Rom 16:22.

2. Ernest Renan, *St. Paul* (trans. Ingersoll Lockwood; New York/Paris: Carleton/Michel Lévy, 1869), 13.

3. Paul writes both letters from prison (Phlm 1, 13, 23; cf. Col 4:3, 10, 18). Timothy is the co-sender of both letters (Phlm 1; Col 1:1). Colossians 4:9 mentions Onesimus as a co-worker whom Paul is sending, along with Tychicus, to Colossae. Paul's five co-workers mentioned in Phlm 23 are also mentioned in Col 4:10–17; in both cases they are with Paul at the time of writing and send greetings to the respective addressees: Epaphras (Col 4:12–13); Mark (Col 4:10); Aristarchus (Col 4:10); Demas (Col 4:14); and Luke (Col 4:14). Archippus is mentioned in both letters: in Phlm 2 as one of the addressees of the letter, in Col 4:17 as an apparent member of the Colossian church.

4. This is the preferred translation of the NRSV, NJB, and NIV. An alternative form, *presbeutēs*, "ambassador," has been conjectured and is adopted in the REB; cf. Eph 6:20.

5. This is typically the language Paul uses when referring to people whom he has converted. Cf. 1 Cor 4:15.

6. The technical Latin term is *fugitivus*; the Greek equivalent is *phygas* or *drapetēs*.

7. This was the interpretation adopted by John Chrysostom in the late fourth century. It has been held by a continuous stream of interpreters ever since, and it is widely held today. As an alternative possibility, some have suggested that Onesimus was actually sent to Paul by Philemon himself, or by the Colossian church, perhaps as a courier bearing a message, gift, or some other form of assistance to the imprisoned Paul; and, that Paul writes hoping that Philemon will release Onesimus to render further service to him in his imprisonment and ministry.

8. Proculus's opinion is cited in Justinian's *Digest* 21.1.17.4; also cf. *Digest* 21.1.43.1.

9. *Ep.* 9.21.

10. *Ep.* 9.24.

11. It was by no means unread. Some see allusions to Philemon in Ign. *Eph.* 2; *Magn.* 12; *Pol.* 6. Ignatius (ca. 35–107 C.E.) also mentions an Onesimus, who is bishop of Ephesus (*Eph.* 1.3; 2.1; 6.2; also see Eusebius, *Hist. eccl.* 3.36.5), but does not identify him with the Onesimus mentioned in Philemon. Origen (ca. 185–254 C.E.) ascribes the letter to Paul (*Hom. Jer.* 19; *Comm. Matt.* tract. 33, 34). Tertullian (ca. 160–225 C.E.) wonders why Marcion accepted it but rejected the other Pauline letters addressed to individuals (*Marc.* 5.21).

12. *Comm. Phlm.*, preface.

13. *Argumentum, Hom. Phlm* (PG 62:702).

14. *In Epistolam B. Pauli ad Philemonem* in H. B. Swete, *Theodori Episcopi Mopsuesteni in Epistolas B. Pauli Commentarii* (2 vols.; Cambridge: Cambridge University Press, 1880–1882), 2:259–60.

15. In Philippians his imprisonment is mentioned explicitly (Phil 1:7, 13, 14, 17), but this particular self-designation is not employed. Cf., however, Eph 3:1; 4:1; 2 Tim 1:16.

16. The proverb is quoted in Seneca, *Ep. Morales* 47.5.

17. *Pol.* 1.2 § 1253b.

18. According to Josephus, members of the Essene sect did not practice slavery because it produced injustice (*Ant.* 18.1.5 § 21). Writings preserved from the Qumran community, however, mention slaves (cf. CD 11.12; 12.10–11). Philo agrees with Josephus that the Palestinian Essenes, as well as an Egyptian monastic group, the Therapeutae, did not own slaves because slavery produces injustices and is "against nature" (*Contempl.* 9 §§ 70–71; *Prob.* 12 § 79; *Hypoth.* 11.4). According to the Roman jurist Florentinus, writing in the late second century C.E., "Slavery is an institution of the law common to all peoples, by which, *in violation of the law of nature*, a person is subjected to the mastery of another" (Justinian, *Digest* 1.5.4; emphasis added). Somewhat later, the eminent Roman lawyer Ulpian (third century C.E.), wrote: "As far as Roman law is concerned, slaves are regarded as nothing, but *not so in natural law as well: because as far as the law of nature is concerned, all men are equal*" (Justinian, Digest 50.17.32; emphasis added). Quotations taken from Naphtali Lewis and Meyer Reinhold, *Roman Civilization: Selected Readings* (3d ed.; New York: Columbia University Press, 1990), 2:176–77. See Dio Chrysostom, *Or.* 14.

Bibliography

Commentaries

Barth, Markus, and Helmut Blanke. *The Letter to Philemon: A New Translation with Notes and Commentary*. Eerdmans Critical Commentary. Grand Rapids: Eerdmans, 2000.

Dunn, James D. G. *The Epistles to the Colossians and to Philemon: A Commentary on the Greek Text*. Carlisle/Grand Rapids: Paternoster/Eerdmans, 1996. Pages 291–349.

Felder, Cain Hope. "The Letter to Philemon: Introduction, Commentary, and Reflections." Pages 881–905 in vol. 11 of *The New Interpreter's Bible*. Edited by Leander E. Keck. 12 vols. Nashville: Abingdon, 2000.

Fitzmyer, Joseph A. *The Letter to Philemon: A New Translation with Introduction and Commentary.* Anchor Bible 34C. New York: Doubleday, 2000.

Lohse, Eduard. *Colossians and Philemon: A Commentary on the Epistles to the Colossians and to Philemon.* Hermeneia. Translated by William R. Poehlmann and Robert J. Karris. Philadelphia: Fortress, 1971. Pages 185–208.

Other Resources

Barclay, John M. G. *Colossians and Philemon.* New Testament Guides. Sheffield: Sheffield, 1997. Pages 97–126.

Bartchy, S. Scott. "Philemon, Epistle to." Pages 305–10 in vol. 5 of *The Anchor Bible Dictionary.* Edited by David N. Freedman. 6 vols. New York: Doubleday, 1992.

Callahan, Allan D. *Embassy of Onesimus: The Letter of Paul to Philemon.* The New Testament in Context. Valley Forge: Trinity, 1997.

Marshall, I. Howard. "The Theology of Philemon." Pages 175–91 in *The Theology of the Shorter Pauline Letters.* Edited by Karl P. Donfried and I. Howard Marshall. New Testament Theology. Cambridge: Cambridge University Press, 1993; repr. 1999.

Petersen, Norman R. *Rediscovering Paul: Philemon and the Sociology of Paul's Narrative World.* Philadelphia: Fortress, 1985.

SLAVERY

Finley, Moses I. *Ancient Slavery and Modern Ideology.* New York: Viking, 1980.

———. *Slavery in Classical Antiquity.* Cambridge: Heffer, 1968 (1960).

Martin, Dale B. *Slavery as Salvation: The Metaphor of Slavery in Pauline Christianity.* New Haven: Yale University Press, 1990.

Wiedemann, Thomas E. J. *Greek and Roman Slavery.* London: Croom Helm, 1981.

———. *Slavery.* Greece & Rome. New Surveys in the Classics 19. Oxford: Published for the Classical Association at the Clarendon Press, 1987.

Chapter 18

Colossians

"[Colossians] offers a vision of human victory in the face of an evil that can reach cosmic proportions."

Margaret MacDonald

"The one who comes into contact with grace knows, in faith, that it springs from the Father, the Son, and the Spirit; that grace, however, is not merely supposed to enrich [us] but give [us] insight, set [us] on a new path, show [us] something decisive for [ourselves] and for the church. [We] receive a mission."

Adrienne von Speyr

We do a double take when reading Colossians with the other Pauline letters firmly in mind. The world we encounter is Pauline, but it is different.

As in the other letters, Paul is a dominant image in Colossians. He is the co-sender with Timothy, and the early part of the letter is couched in the first person plural, although this soon shifts to the first person singular (1:23). From that point forward, Paul's authorial presence dominates the letter, all the way to the final verse, his own handwritten signature (4:18). Reminiscent of his other letters, the concluding set of extended personal greetings is full of details about Paul's co-workers (4:7–17). Similar personal details also occur earlier in the letter (1:7–8; 1:24–2:5). The letter is written from prison, with no indication of an expected release (4:3, 10, 18; cf. 1:24). Paul writes as an apostle whose influence extends to the Colossian church through its founder, Epaphras, one of Paul's co-workers (1:7; 4:12–13). Even though Paul has never visited Colossae (cf. 1:4; 2:1), his pastoral concern for the church is palpable (2:1–2; 4:13).

Colossians also exhibits epistolary features found in other Pauline letters. The form and content of the opening greeting (1:1–2) are vintage Paul, as is the following thanksgiving (1:3–8); the benediction is less so (4:18). We also encounter numerous images and turns of phrase found in Paul's earlier letters. **[See Expanded CD Version pp. 551–52: *Pauline Images and Phrases in Colossians*]**

Beyond these linguistic and stylistic indicators are broader conceptual similarities: Christ's death as God's redemptive act (1:14; cf. Rom 3:24); conversion as a radical transition from old to new (3:9–10; cf. Rom 6:4, 6); lists of vices and virtues (3:5, 8–9, 12; cf. Gal 5:16–26); existence in Christ that transcends ethnic, religious, and social distinctions (3:11; cf. Gal 3:28); and God as "our Father"(1:2–3; cf. Rom 1:7) and Creator (3:10; cf. 1 Cor 8:6).

A closer look at Colossians, however, reveals some features that distinguish it from the other Pauline letters. We encounter several new expressions: "the kingdom of his beloved Son" (1:13); "the hope of the gospel" (1:23 KJV); "Christ, the hope of glory" (1:27); "Christ who is your life" (3:4); and being "taken captive" (*sylagōgeō*) as a metaphor for accepting false teaching (2:8).

In addition to these new phrases, there is the rather provocative, if mystifying, claim that Paul in his flesh completes "what is lacking in Christ's afflictions for the sake of his body, that is, the church" (1:24). This language amplifies other Pauline statements that relate his own suffering to that of Christ (2 Cor 1:5–6; 4:10–12; also cf. 1 Pet 4:13). Moving well beyond anything we find in the undisputed Pauline letters is the claim that "in [Christ] the whole fullness of deity dwells bodily" (2:9; cf. 1:19; also John 1:14, 16).

We also find in Colossians some pronounced stylistic peculiarities that appear to be clumsy adaptations of characteristic Pauline phraseology. [See **Expanded CD Version pp. 552–53:** *Non-Pauline Style; Other Unusual Elements: The Christ Hymn (1:15–20); Cosmic Perspective;* and *Vision of the Moral Life*]

Another discernible advance beyond the undisputed Pauline letters relates to the "body of Christ." While other NT writings speak of Christ's body in terms other than his physical body or envision disciples as organically related to Christ (cf. John 2:21; 13:20; 15:1–11; Heb 10:5, 10; Matt 10:40; 25:40; Luke 10:16), the (local) church as Christ's body is a distinctively Pauline concept (1 Cor 12:27; also 12:12–13; Rom 12:4–5). In Colossians, however, this Pauline metaphor is developed in two directions: (1) it is applied to the universal church, and (2) Christ becomes the head of the body (1:18, 24). The church is thus envisioned as the cosmic "body of Christ" over which the exalted Christ presides as "head." As the one whose triumph over death founded the church, Christ is its "beginning" (1:18). He is also the reigning monarch (1:13) with whom the church is spiritually united (2:19). [See **Expanded CD Version p. 554:** *Distinctive Soteriology*]

Scholars have detected other differences between Colossians and the undisputed Pauline letters.[1] There are also numerous other instances in which the wording in Colossians echoes but slightly modifies Pauline idiom.[2] [See **Expanded CD Version p. 555:** *Pauline Motifs Absent in Colossians*]

Our double take, then, is reading Colossians and being struck by its Pauline char-acter; then reading it again and being equally struck by its conceptual distance from the undisputed Pauline writings.

Why the Difference?

Three explanations have been proposed to account for these differences:
1. *A Shift in Pauline Thought.* Those who hold this view believe that the historical

Paul wrote Colossians, that its similarities with the undisputed Pauline letters are greater than its differences, and that the changes reflect a fresh response to a newly encountered heresy. Colossians thus reveals Paul extending his theology in new directions. If the tone is more mellow, it is because the letter is written by an older, more mature Paul. [**See Expanded CD Version p. 555:** *Affinities with Philemon and the Dating of Colossians*]

2. *Non-Pauline Authorship.* Proponents of this view readily admit the Pauline texture of Colossians, but they weight the stylistic and conceptual differences more heavily. Consequently, they see the changes in baptismal theology and the strong, almost exclusive, orientation of believers toward the present rather than the future not as minor refinements in Paul's own thought but as major shifts. Similarly, the church as the body of Christ and the letter's vision of the moral life are seen as substantial theological shifts. In particular, the use of the household code is seen as a more regimented ethic than we find in the other Pauline letters.

Scholars who regard these changes as substantive assign the authorship of Colossians to a member of the Pauline circle, or the "Pauline school," probably writing in the late 60s or even later. This pseudepigraphical letter echoes the undisputed letters because its author was immersed in Pauline thought and thoroughly familiar with Pauline language and style. Even so, this "Paulinist" takes Paul's thought in a decidedly cosmic, even mystical, direction. The letter's explicit attribution to Paul, its mimicking of other Pauline letters, and its many personal references are explained as commonly accepted conventions used by disciples of an eminent thinker who write in his name. Analogues are seen in philosophical circles where, for example, the disciples of Aristotle (384–322 B.C.E.) wrote treatises under his name.

3. *Partial Pauline Authorship.* Some scholars think that portions of Colossians were written by the historical Paul himself, and that someone else, probably a Pauline disciple, shaped these into the present letter, while adding non-Pauline material. The more personal sections stem directly from Paul; sections reflecting theological shifts stem from someone else. Another version of this position, which is gaining favor, is that a Pauline disciple, probably Timothy, the co-sender of the letter, wrote the letter during Paul's lifetime and even under his supervision. Some envision that Paul's circumstances in prison had changed—that his situation had become more dire and that his movement had become more restricted. Yet, eager to address the threat posed by the "deceptive philosophy" in Colossae, he commissioned Timothy to compose a response. Timothy may have submitted the letter to Paul for his approval, at which point Paul added the personal greetings and made some editorial changes or additions. Once approved, it was then sent to Colossae from Paul and Timothy with Paul's full authorization.

Of the three options, the third, or some version of the third, is the most attractive. The differences between Colossians and the undisputed Pauline letters are too great—at all levels—for the letter as we have it to have been written by Paul, certainly in the same sense that he wrote Galatians or 1 Thessalonians. The stylistic and conceptual changes reflect a different fingerprint from the one we see in the other undisputed letters. The personal references, however, exude a sense of realism reminiscent of the historical Paul. The affinities with the Letter to Philemon also seem genuine,

even if Philemon envisions Paul's release and Colossians does not. Philemon was conceivably written when Paul expected to be released, but Colossians may have been written later when the prospect of release had vanished. This would explain the imploring tone in Col 4:18.

How the destruction of Colossae by an earthquake in 60–61 C.E. relates to the question of authorship remains a puzzle. The simplest explanation is that the letter was written prior to the earthquake, but some evidence suggests that a form of city life continued at Colossae after the earthquake. It is also difficult to imagine that someone writing years later would compose a Pauline letter addressed to Colossae unless there had been an actual connection between Paul and Colossae and some correspondence between them.

Given these considerations, Colossians reflects the voice of Paul rather than the actual words of Paul. Its value as a canonical witness to Christ does not depend on its direct Pauline authorship, although this was doubtless why it was originally included in the canon. The dispute about Pauline authorship may affect how we see the historical Paul and interpret Pauline theology, but the compelling theological vision of Colossians challenges readers, quite apart from the question of who actually penned the words. Colossians stands within the trajectory of Pauline writings and should be read as a probing theological letter extending the historical Paul's thought.

In the remaining discussion, Paul is referred to as the author, not as the historical Paul, but as the canonical or textual Paul whose image is projected in the letter.

The "Deceptive Philosophy"

That the "hollow and deceptive philosophy" (2:8 NIV) was a primary catalyst for the letter is seen by how much attention it receives and how the running description of the heresy is interwoven with theological counterclaims (2:4, 8, 16–23; also cf. 1:28: "warning everyone . . ."). The language is notoriously ambiguous not only because the syntax is complicated and often unclear, but also because some elements in the description are difficult to identify. Several questions emerge at the outset: Is it a single threat or a vaguely conceived set of threats? Does it come from inside or outside the church? What is the best way to characterize it? As some form of philosophy (2:8)? As a heresy? Or does such language imply a single, heterodox point of view that is more coherent than the description in chapter 2 allows?

The description suggests that a single point of view, however inchoate, is being opposed. Attitudes or practices are not linked with specific persons or groups to suggest the existence of different factions. To praise the Colossians for their "unbroken ranks and the solid front which [their] faith in Christ presents" (2:5 REB) sounds as though the opposing viewpoint has not infiltrated the church. Even so, the insistent tone attributed to its proponents makes them a serious threat. The warning in 2:16–19 suggests advocates not content with gentle persuasion but keen to "condemn" and "disqualify" (lit., "make an umpire's decision against") those who refuse to conform to their prescribed forms of religious practice and adopt the religious framework that supports them. That the church is being pressured is also reflected in the prohibitions against handling, tasting, and touching, in which we are probably hearing the demands of the opponents (2:20–21).

As we try to understand the outlook being opposed, we should remember the ancient rhetorical conventions governing polemic against false teaching. Typically, this rhetoric dismisses opponents through the use of caricatures. "Take captive" calls up the image of a false teacher capturing the Colossian believers and leading them away into slavery. Characterizing the threat as "philosophy" probably implies an organized system of thought, but it is hardly a complimentary term. "Empty deceit" suggests a hollow superficiality that distorts complex issues and resorts to heavy-handed arguments designed to persuade at all costs. A this-world outlook is further criticized when the viewpoint is pilloried as "the kind [of outlook] that human beings hand on, based on the principles of this world and not on Christ" (2:8 NJB).

Even allowing for rhetorical hyperbole, the description throws some light on specific practices and beliefs. The dietary practices and Sabbath observances mentioned in 2:16 have a decidedly Jewish cast, although similar practices were known outside Judaism. "False humility" (2:18 NIV) seems to imply ascetic practices, possibly fasting or other forms of abstinence. The food restrictions in 2:21 are quite open-ended. Characterizing them as regulations governing perishable things, with only human backing, does not sound as though such prohibitions are grounded in the Mosaic law.

Other elements of the description relate more directly to beliefs underlying the various practices being promoted. "Self-abasement" is linked with the "worship of angels" and visionary experiences (2:18). The worship of angels is attested in Phrygia, the region where Colossae was located, and long persisted as a form of worship opposed by the church (and the rabbis). The prominence of angels in the OT and early traditions relating to Jesus might have made the worship of angels attractive to Christians (e.g., Gen 19:1, 10; 32:1; Ps 91:11; Matt 4:11; 13:41, 49; John 1:51).

The "deceptive philosophy" possibly derived from the complex set of beliefs reflected in a variety of Jewish texts during the Hellenistic-Roman period. Possibly angels in mediating roles were thought to give access to Christ, who may have been regarded as a member, or even the archangel, of the angelic hierarchy.[3] "Dwelling on visions" (2:18), a highly problematic phrase, may imply ecstatic, visionary experiences (of angels?). These are dismissed as poorly grounded and self-inflating rather than self-confirming. The one claiming such access to the divine is "bursting with the futile conceit of worldly minds" (2:18 REB). **[See Expanded CD Version p. 559: *Possible Identities of the "Deceptive Philosophy"*]**

The "deceptive philosophy" may be difficult to identify, but we can readily discern how Colossians responds to it. One consistent theme is the illusory, human-based orientation of this competing worldview. The various restrictions are critiqued as superficial measures that fail to deal squarely with self-seeking human impulses. Read one way, 2:23 criticizes ascetic practices that mortify the flesh as having no benefit because they actually enliven the flesh and produce self-preoccupied, sensual forms of indulgence. To dismiss the opposing viewpoint as formed "according to human tradition" and "according to the elemental spirits of the universe" rather than "according to Christ" (2:8) invites the Colossians to choose between sharply opposed belief systems.

If we take the much debated phrase *ta stoicheia tou kosmou* ("elemental spirits of the universe," 2:8) as principles that constitute the world of the Colossians, it perhaps means "the structures of the world." As an alternative, Colossians presents a worldview whose central focus is Christ, whose creative, redemptive work has reconfigured the universe.

The Theological Vision of Colossians:
"The Mystery of God . . . Christ Himself"

Even at the risk of oversimplifying, we can locate the purpose of Colossians in 2:2–3: "so that [we] may have all the riches of assured understanding and have the knowledge of God's mystery, that is, Christ himself, in whom are hidden all the treasures of wisdom and knowledge." This passage identifies a core feature of the letter: at the heart of Christian faith lies the "hidden treasure" of God's mystery, whose content is Christ himself. Such language suggests a form of probing that encompasses the many ways of knowing—intellectual, aesthetic, emotional, physical, and spiritual. Framed this way, the "mystery" that ends in Christ begins with God, and it constitutes the primary resource for the moral life.

Becoming More Aware of God

Colossians gives depth to the character of God. To assert that God is "invisible" (1:15) might imply that God can easily fade from the view of believers. In one sense, God may be out of sight, but the God of Colossians can never be out of mind. The challenge is not to keep God in mind, as though knowing God were a mental game that one wins by developing the sheer power to concentrate on God. Colossians invites its readers to be properly informed about God, not in general, theoretical terms, but in vivid, memorable ways.

When Paul recalls the Colossians' initial response to the gospel, he commends them for having "truly comprehended the grace of God" (1:6). His choice of the verb *epiginōsko* is revealing, for it suggests a level of understanding that is both exact and thorough. While the noun form *epignōsis* (which occurs four times: 1:9, 10; 2:2; 3:10) may not necessarily have this same inflated sense, its several uses are equally revealing. Knowing God's will is a God-given capacity that comes in response to answered prayer. Since this knowledge is characterized by "all spiritual wisdom and understanding," it is a special gift of discernment (1:9). While such knowledge may be experienced in a flash of insight, it is a gradual process—knowledge that grows over time (1:10). That "knowing God" would take time—even a lifetime—is not surprising since the sole object of the quest is "God's mystery, that is, Christ himself" (2:2).

Conversion is viewed in similarly realistic terms. The transition from old self to new self may occur as a decisive moment, but more than acquiring a new identity is involved. Living out the new identity is a gradual process in which one's knowledge must be renewed constantly. The new self progresses "towards true knowledge the more it is renewed in the image of its Creator" (3:10 NJB).

In Colossians, Christ may be at center stage, but this does not mean that God is offstage. Far from being *deus absconditus* ("God concealed"), the God of Colossians is at the heart of the action. Especially accented is God's saving action, which is memorably formulated using OT imagery in 1:12–13. God has "qualified [the Colossians] to take [their] share in the territory allotted to God's people—that realm of light" (1:12 Moule's translation; cf. NIV, REB). They may have been naturally unfit, but through God's action they have been "made fit" (REB), just as God used Israel's wilderness experience as a training ground to equip them for life in the promised land. To speak of their destiny as an "inheritance" (NRSV) or "heritage" (REB) underscores its status as both gift and promise, something graciously bequeathed by God (cf. 3:24; also Acts 20:32; Wis 5:5). To speak of God's "rescue" probably recalls God's gracious deliverance of Israel first from Egypt and later from the wilderness. Such a divine rescue may represent an impressive show of strength, but it is not muscle-flexing for its own sake. It is rather power responsibly deployed to reflect God's true glory—salvific, constructive power rather than some destructive show of force (1:11).

The "light/darkness" imagery may also have OT resonance (cf. Isa 9:2; 49:6, 9; also 42:16; 60:1–22), although here, as elsewhere in the NT, especially in the Johannine writings, it is used to characterize contrasting moral domains (1 Thess 5:4–5; John 12:35, 46; 1 John 1:6; 2:11). "The ruling force of darkness" (1:13 NJB) is a pithy reminder that evil can exercise its own sinister control from which God delivers us. Its counterpart, however, is the "kingdom of [God's] dear Son" (1:13 REB), rather than the more usual "kingdom of God" (cf. Acts 26:18). As the sphere where Christ reigns supreme, it is the counterpart of the "domain of darkness" (REB). The unique attraction of this domain is the enlightening moral power to which it provides access.

Even when the focus shifts to the new life that the Colossians began to experience in Christ, God's role is still prominent. As the "truth of the gospel" declared, and as the readers had confessed, God "raised [Christ] from the dead" (2:12; cf. 1:5). Rather than stopping there, God extended similar life-giving power to the Colossians when they were morally and spiritually dead. From a Jewish perspective, their bereft condition was symbolized by their being "uncircumcised in the flesh," which placed them well outside the pale of God's redemptive action. For this reason, Paul interprets their baptismal initiation using the circumcision metaphor. The life abandoned in conversion is "the body of the flesh" (NRSV) or "sinful nature" (NIV), which has been stripped away like severed foreskin—this is "Christ's way of circumcision" (2:11 REB). Recalling the language of Rom 6, in which baptism is seen as a ritual re-enactment of Christ's death and resurrection, Paul once again stresses believers' co-participation with Christ. It is not that they die and rise *like Christ*; they do so *with Christ*. As before, God effects the change by bestowing complete forgiveness: God "made [them] alive together with [Christ]" (2:13).

If God (rather than Christ) is the subject of 2:14–15 (as reflected in NRSV, NIV, REB, and NJB), some astonishing images are used to portray what God accomplished in the death of Jesus. The arena of action is the cross, the defining moment when God extended universal forgiveness (2:13). Two images emerge.

First, God is the creditor who tears up the IOU stipulating humanity's debts. If this refers to God's cancellation of the Mosaic law, it is a cryptic reference indeed, since the usual Pauline word for law (*nomos*) is not used. Perhaps the most felicitous rendering of this verse is the NIV: "having canceled the written code, with its regulations, that was against us and that stood opposed to us" (2:14).

The second image envisions God's taking the cancelled note and nailing it to the cross. This startling image so defies literalism that we are prompted to think of a political cartoon depicting the crucified Christ with God hovering overhead, hammering a nail into the canceled note of indebtedness (perhaps sketched as a Torah scroll) somewhere above Jesus' head—the artist's way of depicting what *actually* happened at this seemingly tragic moment.

As if this piling up of images were not enough, God is finally depicted as a victorious emperor or general, who, having vanquished the "cosmic powers and authorities" (REB), forces them to lay down their weapons and then marches them as POWs displayed as a "public spectacle" in the victory parade (2:15 NIV; cf. 2 Cor 2:14–16). All of this is accomplished "in him" (Christ), or, more likely, "in it" (the cross). If the latter, the cross once again symbolizes the arena of God's action, where supernatural rather than natural forces and persons are the real adversaries. No mere human event, even a tragic human event, the death of Christ is rather the pivotal battle in a cosmic war. [See Expanded CD Version p. 562: *Other Images of God in Colossians*]

Christ's Supremacy

If Christ is the theological centerpiece of Colossians, the magnificent Christ hymn in 1:15–20 is the defining flower of the whole arrangement.[4] Perhaps most striking is the boldness of its christological claims. Roles or status previously reserved for God are now asserted of Christ. In an earlier confessional formula (1 Cor 8:6), God is the end toward whom the created order inclines, the One "for whom we exist." Now, Christ is the One "for whom" all things have been created (1:16). Earlier, God is "all in all" (1 Cor 15:28); now Christ is (3:11). Also remarkable is the cosmic canvas on which Christ is depicted. One measure of this is the sheer number of times "all" or "everything" occurs—eight times within the space of five verses ("all" and "everything" render the same Greek term *pas*).

While the Christ hymn in Phil 2 highlights Christ's pre-existence, it focuses more on his descent, his giving up the "form of God," and his subsequent ascent and exaltation. In Colossians, the cross is in view (1:20), not as the nadir of Christ's descent but as the sacrificial death through which God achieved universal reconciliation. Compared with Phil 2, the Christ hymn in Colossians displays greater interest in Christ's role at the beginning, thus marking a shift in emphasis from Omega to Alpha. This throws into bold relief the sole reference in Colossians to Christ's Parousia (3:4), thereby underscoring its slim interest in eschatology.

Whether we read 1:15–20 as a poem or a hymn (a poem chanted by worshipers), we are struck by its liturgical quality. For all its interest in cosmic origins and Christ as primal catalyst of "all things," the hymn makes claims about Christ in the present tense: "He *is* the image of the invisible God . . . he *is* before all things . . . and in him all things *hold together* . . . he *is* the head of the body . . . he *is* the beginning," etc. We hear the adoring language of devout believers bowed before the living Christ. The

Christ being worshiped may have been present at creation but he is experientially present in the believers' here and now, probably in some house church in the Lycus Valley. If we take seriously the hymn's soaring, poetic language, we will remember to interpret it as the language of worship—as if we were reading a psalm.

Different streams of thought inform the hymn. The poet draws on the popular two-story conception of the universe as comprising "the earth" and "the heavens" (1:16–20), but moves beyond it (cf. Eph 1:10; a three-level universe is envisioned in Phil 2:10; also Rev 5:3, 13). "Things seen and unseen" may reflect a Platonic outlook in which the world we experience—the world of sensible objects that we can see—has its counterpart in the unseen world of Ideas (cf. 2 Cor 4:18).

Yet another view of the world, which is informed by the apocalyptic imagination, sets in with the mention of "thrones, dominions, rulers, and powers," terms that are evocative precisely because of their ambiguity (cf. *1 En.* 61:10; *2 En.* 20:1; *T. Levi* 3:7–8; *Ascen. Isa.* 7–10, esp. the latter's portrayal of the seven heavens). Similar apocalyptic imagery is also reflected in other NT texts (e.g., Rom 8:38; 1 Cor 15:24; Eph 1:21; 3:10; 6:12; 1 Pet 3:22). Are we to think of cherubim (Ezek 1; Isa 6)? Angels (Dan 10:13, 20–21)? Or something roughly equivalent to Philo's heavenly "powers," variously named as creative, royal, merciful, and legislative, neatly aligned like filings around a magnet between the *Logos* and the World of Forms (*Cher.* 27–29)?

In one sense, it does not matter. The poetic imagination is at work here, drawing on several traditions whose origins are now obscure. It is the poet's way of saying that "all things"—reality understood in its most comprehensive sense, through whatever lens we view it—have Christ as their cause and end (1:16; Christ as God's agent of creation is also reflected in 1 Cor 8:4–6; also John 1:3; Heb 1:2; Rev 3:14).

Also evident is the poet's indebtedness to Jewish wisdom literature, in which Wisdom is personified as the pre-existent female figure Sophia (cf. Prov 8; Sir 24; Wis 6–12; also cf. Job 28). In this literature, Wisdom exists at the beginning with God (Prov 8:22–31), serves as agent of creation (Wis 9:2; also *2 En.* 30:8), and holds the universe together (Wis 1:7; cf. Sir 43:26). When the poet assigns similar roles to Christ—roles that are also assigned to such highly regarded treasures as Torah or to functions/figures close to God's inner circle, such as the *Logos*—it is a form of elevation that stems from deep springs of piety.

Had these images been read as poetry rather than literal theological assertions, the church might have been spared some controversy. For Arians in the fourth century, who believed that there was a time when Christ was not, "firstborn of all creation" (1:15) could only mean that Christ was the first created being. Orthodox defenders countered by insisting that Christ as "firstborn" differed qualitatively from everything created.[5] Accordingly, subsequent interpreters could take "firstborn" (*prototokos*) as an indicator of rank rather than time: in relation to "all creation," Christ enjoyed the status of the eldest child (cf. Rev 3:14; also Rom 8:29). This reading is supported by the logic of the hymn: how could Christ function as God's agent of creation if he were created? The piling up of "firsts" and other repeated claims of priority simply reinforce the point. He is "before all things" not only as a pre-existent figure, who like Lady Wisdom was there with God prior to creation; because of his priority he is, even now, still "before"—in other words, "above"—all things. If one looks for a primal person or principle, as the pre-Socratics did, Christ as God's agent in creation emerges as the *a priori* of the universe—the cosmic glue that holds everything together.

At this point the hymn shifts from creation to new creation. Christ as "the head of the body, the church," moves well beyond earlier Pauline conceptions of the local congregation as the "body of Christ" (cf. 1 Cor 12:12, 27; also 10:16–17; Rom 12:5).[6] In view is the universal church and Christ's "headship," which derives from his unique status as the "firstborn from the dead" (1:18).[7]

Because Christ experienced the end time in advance by being raised from the dead and was the only one to which this had happened, he is the church's *archē*, its "beginning." In one sense the church began before time; in another sense it began at Christ's resurrection, when his true primacy, his supremacy (1:18 NIV), was clinched (1:20). What qualifies Christ as "head" is his place at the beginning of a new order of humanity, a true counterpart to the first Adam (1 Cor 15:22, 45–49; Rom 5:12–21).

With the poem so clearly focused on the resurrected Christ as the reigning head of the universal church, this is perhaps the sphere in which "the fullness of God" dwells (1:19; cf. Col 2:9; also Eph 1:23; 3:19; 4:10, 13; John 1:16). If so, instead of giving a poetic rendering of Christ's incarnation, in which the full reach of God's deity is funneled into the earthly Christ, verse 19 envisions the church in its universal vastness as the sphere in which God is most fully experienced.

By visualizing Christ's sacrificial death as an event through which God "reconciles to himself all things"—as an event in which enmity and alienation give way to peace—the poet further extends Christ's cosmic reach.[8] His death is an event that somehow links the divine will with earthly reality. The warring parties who are brought together are not identified here, although Ephesians sees them as Jews and Gentiles (Eph 2:11–22).

As the one through whom God becomes palpable, Christ is the "image of the invisible God" (1:15). While this is by no means a unique claim, it is fully understandable in this context.[9] Living within a world in which emperors were regularly portrayed in inscriptions and paintings as images of the deity; in which moral people were regarded as express images of divine beings; in which the sun as Helios was seen as God's image; in which Philo of Alexandria could characterize the Divine *Logos* as God's image; and perhaps especially in which Wisdom is "a spotless mirror of the working of God and an image of [God's] goodness," the poet knew the force of depicting Christ as the "true likeness" of God.[10] Whether "image" has philosophical overtones suggesting that Christ is the seal that uniquely expresses God's essence or whether it recalls the creation account (Gen 1:26), Colossians invites us to see Christ as the visible, exact rendering of the "invisible God."[11] The created order may be God's handiwork, but God is most vividly displayed through the one responsible for the created order, Christ himself.

The Moral Life: "Walking Worthily of the Lord"

The moral vision of Colossians informs the whole letter, but its contours are sketched in 2:8–4:1. When we compare this sketch with similar advice in Rom 12–15,

Gal 5–6, and 1 Thess 4, we find a truly distinctive vision of the moral life. Moral options are defined by one's experience of Christ as a uniquely divine figure, exalted to God's right hand, reigning supreme over the cosmos and the universal church.

Three elements of this moral vision are worth noting. First, *it is anchored in a richly developed understanding of conversion.* One of the most well-known features of Colossians (and Ephesians) is its consistent stress on the way believers have "already been raised with Christ" (2:12; 3:1). Behaviors are neither recommended nor prohibited *primarily* because of their future consequences but in terms of how effectively they express one's identity here and now.

The root of Christian identity is traceable to one's conversion, and Paul pushes his readers to probe more deeply into this defining event. Conversion as a ritual re-enactment of Christ's own death and resurrection is resonant with Paul's theology of baptism sketched in Rom 6. The one who "enters" Christ's death and resurrection moves with him from one form of existence to a radically different way of life.

Coupled with the "dying/rising" metaphor in 2:11–13 is another provocative metaphor. Recalling the spiritualized circumcision of Rom 2:25–29 (cf. Deut 10:16), Paul sees conversion as a ritual analogous to cutting away the foreskin. Removing the "flesh" (*sarx*) symbolizes the elimination of a whole way of life. Equally provocative is "the circumcision of Christ" (2:11), a metaphor suggesting that in Christ's death his body was "stripped away" to symbolize his leaving behind an earthly mode of existence. His resurrection becomes a transition to a form of existence devoid of flesh in which God is the defining reality.

By analogy, the believer undergoes a similar transition: One form of "being human" is stripped away and replaced by another form of the self, which is free of "flesh." Since candidates for baptism probably disrobed before being baptized, "stripping away" could also be visualized as taking off old clothing. The "old self" (*palaios anthrōpos*) is stripped off like an old coat, and the newly baptized person is clothed with a "new self" (*neos anthrōpos*, 3:9–10). Like the first human, this "new self" is first formed in the image of God the Creator, then constantly renews this identity to conform to the divine image (3:10).

This deeper understanding of conversion, which extends metaphorically and theologically beyond Rom 6, enables the Colossians to combat the competing forms of religiosity facing them. Their choice involves more than selecting from among a smorgasbord of ascetic practices and assorted festivals, depending on one's predilections or the pressures of the moment. Living the moral life, instead, entails forms of behavior that reflect the shift in identity when one becomes a co-participant in Christ's death and resurrection or re-enacts Christ's "circumcision." One becomes fully incorporated with Christ by acquiring an identity that is fully formed "in Christ." The critical question for believers is whether their moral choices reflect an outlook that has been transformed by the Christ one has experienced and confessed, or whether their primary impulse arises from other sources.

Second, *the shape of one's moral universe is dictated by the shape of one's understanding of Christ.* Since Christ's death and resurrection are seen as a single event that marks a radical temporal transition, they redefine the temporal axis of one's moral universe. A heightened sense of "then" and "now" emerges, and competing identities associated with these eras are constructed accordingly. They are sketched in dramatic, even dualistic, terms—formerly dead, now alive; formerly uncircumcised (excluded), now circumcised (embraced), etc. Behaviors to be avoided are those associated with a former way of life (3:7). In this sense, one pursues the moral life in linear fashion—as a movement away from a state of death and despair toward a new path charted "in the Lord."

The Christ event is also understood spatially as his exaltation to God's right hand (3:1). The believer who is incorporated into Christ acquires a moral universe understood in spatial, even existential, terms. Moral options are now viewed as choices between "things above"—dispositions and behaviors associated with the exalted Christ—and "things below"—things that are "earthly" (3:1-2, 5), including well-known vices (3:5, 8-9) and certain religious practices (2:8, 18, 20-23).

It would be helpful if we knew more about the "elemental spirits of the universe" (*ta stoicheia tou kosmou*, 2:8, 20), since they are so closely identified with the "earthly" outlook and are inimical to Christ (2:8). If this elusive phrase is understood as "structures of the world," it would include the habits and structures of thought that become embodied in homes, communities, and nations as customs, laws, and other economic, political, educational, and social practices. In any case, the phrase identifies a set of attitudes, commitments, and practices that Paul dismisses as vicious, seductive, and ultimately ineffective in dealing with the primal impulse of "self-indulgence" (*sarx*, 2:23).

By contrast, behavior "above" entails impulses, dispositions, and actions that produce constructive social relationships. They reflect a radically redefined social order in which ethnic, religious, and social distinctions are transcended by the defining reality of a Christ who is "all in all" (3:11). Those "in Christ" may live "below," within the human arena, but the defining norms come from "above"—from the exalted Christ.

What is remarkable about this capsule description of the moral life in 3:12-17 is its christocentric focus. Those who are "God's chosen ones, holy and beloved" (3:12) take their moral cue from Christ: we forgive because Christ forgave us (3:13). The ruling disposition of the heart is the "peace of Christ" (3:15). The "word of Christ" (3:16), perhaps Christ's living voice as much as the church's teaching about Christ, becomes an indwelling disposition, which comes to life as the church learns and worships together. Every action is authorized "in the name of the Lord Jesus" (3:17), which suggests that the risen Christ is the ultimate warrant for all action that is done "in him." Prayers of thanksgiving are also offered to God through Christ (3:17). The household code of 3:18-4:1 reflects this framework of Christ-motivated behavior.

Third, *the moral life is an exercise in spiritual discernment*. Colossians stresses the need to grow in the knowledge of God. This emphasis on the cognitive dimension of the moral life is reflected in the frequent use of metaphors of knowing. Challenging us to see what we ordinarily would not see, Paul invites us to cultivate our powers of discernment, not by becoming mentally alert or even acquiring information per se, but by acquiring intellectual acuity for probing spiritual mysteries more deeply. Envisioned here is the capacity to think comprehensively, to see Christ not only as a personal Savior but also as cosmic Lord who embraces heaven and earth, animate and inanimate life, and people at enmity with one another. In view here is a disposition that relates Christ not only to one's self, or even to the several communities to which one belongs, but to the church universal—not just to the planet Earth, but to the furthest reaches of the universe. Colossians pushes us to an expansive vision—to see each thing in relation to every other thing and all things in relation to Jesus Christ.

Notes

1. In the following list, the English wording follows the Greek rather than the NRSV. (1) The Colossians' condition before conversion is one of being "estranged" or "alienated," literally "enemies in mind" (1:21). Such a description occurs only here and in Eph 2:12; 4:18. Sinners prior to being reconciled are called "enemies" in Rom 5:10. (2) In 1:22, Christ is said to have "reconciled [you] in the body of his flesh through [his] death to present you holy, blameless, irreproachable before him." Second Corinthians 5:18 also speaks of reconciliation, but it is God who reconciles us to himself through Christ. There are similar echoes in Rom 5:10. (3) In 1:23, Paul's qualifier is "if you continue in the faith [*tē pistei*]." Here "the faith" almost has the sense "deposit of faith," to which they are urged to be faithful (similarly 2:7); if so, it moves slightly beyond the similar expression in 2 Cor 13:5, "examine yourselves to see whether you are living *in the faith*" (cf. 2 Thess 2:15; also 1 Tim 6:10). (4) In 1:23, 25, Paul designates himself as a "servant [*diakonos*] of the gospel," which is not his usual way of describing his apostolic calling (though cf. 1 Cor 3:5; 2 Cor 3:6; 6:4; 11:23). Also, the way Paul speaks of his apostolic commission is a little unusual: "becoming a servant [*diakonos*] according to God's commission [*kata tēn oikonomian tou theou*] given to me for you, to make the word of God fully known" (1:25). (5) In 1:24, Paul's "rejoicing in his sufferings on their behalf" recalls, but moves beyond, Rom 5:3 by accenting the vicarious dimension of suffering. (6) In 1:26–29, the "mystery that has been hidden throughout the ages and generations but has now been revealed to his saints" is in apposition to the "word of God" or the gospel Paul is called to make known. The content of the mystery is Christ himself, the "hope of glory." This point is reinforced in 2:2: that you might reach "full knowledge of the mystery of God, that is, Christ." The aim is to make the mystery, that is, the gospel, known "among the nations." This clearly resonates with Rom 16:25–27, where the content of the "mystery that was kept secret for long ages but is now disclosed" appears to be the gospel, which is now made known to the Gentiles. Somewhat related is 1 Cor 2:1; the "mystery of God" is the gospel Paul proclaims. Yet, in Colossians, Christ himself constitutes the content of the mystery in a way that is not the case in Rom 16:25–27. (7) In 2:6, "receiving Christ Jesus as Lord" is a distinctive way of referring to the Colossians' reception of the faith, although it is quite close to 1 Cor 15:1, in which Paul speaks of "receiving" and "transmitting" the gospel. This may suggest that Col 2:6 should be understood in the sense of "receiving [the gospel that proclaims] Christ Jesus as Lord" (cf. Rom 10:9). As for "walking" in him, Paul frequently uses "walk" (*peripateō*) as a synonym for "live" (e.g., 1 Thess 4:1). (8) In 2:10 Christ is the "head of every ruler and authority," and thus has an already accomplished status that he now enjoys. In 1 Cor 15:24 Christ turns over dominion to God after "he [Christ] has destroyed every ruler and every authority and power." (9) Conversion as a form of spiritual circumcision (2:11) has clear echoes in Paul (cf. Rom 2:25–29). (10) In 2:13, the Colossians' former way of life is described as being "dead in [their] trespasses and the uncircumcision of [their] flesh." In Rom 6:11 Paul urges those baptized into Christ to consider themselves "dead to sin" and present themselves as having been "brought from death to life." The plural form "trespasses" is used in Rom 4:25: Christ "was handed over to death for our trespasses"; also 2 Cor 5:19: God in Christ "reconciling . . . not counting their trespasses against them." (11) The "elements of the world" (*ta stoicheia tou kosmou*) in 2:8, 20 recalls Gal 4:3: "while we were minors, we were enslaved to the elemental spirits of the world"; also Gal 4:9. (12) In 3:1, the Colossians' resurrection is already realized: "if you have been raised with Christ." In Rom 6, being "raised with Christ" (6:5) is a future prospect. (13) In 3:6, there is the prospect that immoral living will bring the wrath of God upon "those who are disobedient." Paul, too, knows of the wrath of God (Rom 1:18), and the "coming wrath [of God]" is envisioned in 1 Thess 1:10; 5:9.

2. Other instances in which the wording in Colossians echoes but slightly modifies Pauline idiom include: (1) 1:6, which speaks of the gospel "bearing fruit" (*karpophoreō*) and 1:10, which describes the Colossians "bearing fruit in every good work" (cf. Rom 7:4: "that we may bear fruit for God" [also Rom

7:5]); (2) "knowing fully" (*epiginōskō*) the grace of God in truth (1:6), which recalls other Pauline uses of the same verb, although this exact phrase is not used (cf. Rom 1:32; 1 Cor 13:12; 14:37; 2 Cor 1:13–14); (3) "to walk worthily of the Lord" (1:10; cf. 1 Thess 2:12; Phil 1:27); (4) "bearing fruit in every good work" (1:10), which echoes 2 Cor 9:8: "you may share abundantly in every good work" (cf. 2 Thess 2:17); (5) "the kingdom of the Son of his love" (1:13; cf. Rom 14:17; 1 Cor 4:20; 6:9–10; 15:24, 50; Gal 5:21; 1 Thess 2:12; 2 Thess 1:5); (6) "disarming the rulers and authorities, making public example of them, triumphing over them" (2:15), which recalls the image of the triumphal march in 2 Cor 2:14–16; (7) seeing conversion as the death of the "old self," literally the "old man" (*palaios anthrōpos* 3:9; cf. Rom 6:6); (8) the defining quality of this "new self" as Christ, not ethnic, religious, or social labels (3:11; cf. Gal 3:26–28); (9) "peace of Christ" (3:15; cf. Phil 4:7: "peace of God"); (10) being "called in one body" (3:15; cf. Rom 12:5); and (11) the "word of Christ dwelling in [them] richly" (3:16; cf. 1 Thess 1:8).

3. Angels as mediators of heavenly knowledge are standard fixtures in apocalyptic texts (e.g., *1 En.* 17–36; *Apoc. Ab.* 10–18; *4 Ezra* 3–14) as well other texts (e.g., *Jos. Asen.* 14–15; *Jub.* 1:27–29; 10:10–14). *First Enoch* 61:10 includes among heavenly powers "cherubim, seraphim, ophanim, all the angels of governance, the Elect One, and the other forces on earth [and] over the water." In *3 Baruch* the "angel of hosts" discloses the "mysteries of God" to Baruch (1:8; 2:6; 5:3); "angels over principalities" are mentioned in *3 Bar.* 12:3. Philo's elaborate view of angels is spelled out in *Gig.* 6–18 and *Somn.* 1.135–43 (commenting on Gen 28:12). Angels also figure prominently in Qumran texts (e.g., 1QSb 4:24–26; 1QM 9:15–16; 1QS 3:20–26; also *Songs of the Sabbath Sacrifice* [4Q/11QShirShabb]).

4. As with the Christ hymn in Phil 2:6–11, some basic questions arise: Is it poetic? If so, is it an early Christian hymn? The split opinions are reflected in the two major editions of the Greek New Testament. The NA[27] edition prints the text strophically, whereas the UBS[4] edition does not. Similar disparity is reflected in major translations: NRSV, NIV, NEB present it as straight prose, NJB as a poem "in the form of a diptych." Also, who composed it? Paul himself, wholly or partially? Some see 1:18 as an editorial addition by the author of Ephesians. Or is it an early Christian hymn, which Paul (or a Pauline disciple) has taken up and adapted for his own purposes?

5. Athanasius, *C. Ar.* 2.21.10.

6. Christ as head of the church is further developed in Eph 1:22–23; 4:15; 5:23. A different form of hierarchy is envisioned in 1 Cor 11:7. How later Gnostic thought, drawing on this image and its echoes in Ephesians, could envision a cosmic-sized body extending from the Head throughout the universe in gradually decreasing "aeons" or levels of being is quite understandable. The use of Colossians among Valentinian Gnostics is reflected in Irenaeus, *Haer.* 1.3.4; also cf. Clement of Alexandria, *Exc.* 69.1–74.1. Typically, Marcion rejected some parts (Col 1:15–16) and used others (Col 2:16–17, 21) to support his anti-Jewish views (cf. Tertullian, *Marc.* 5.19).

7. A similar phrase occurs in Rev 1:5; for other metaphors expressing his singular status as the first to be raised, cf. 1 Cor 15:20, 23 (first fruits); Acts 3:15 (author of life); also Acts 26:23.

8. Reconciliation is not conceived in quite the same way in 2 Cor 5:18; Rom 5:10. It is closer to the cosmic redemption depicted in Rom 8.

9. Paul calls Christ the "image of God" in 2 Cor 4:4. The same idea is expressed differently in Heb 1:3.

10. Ptolemy IV Philopator (221–203 B.C.E.) and Ptolemy V Epiphanes (203–181 B.C.E.) are so depicted in inscriptions; for the moral person (Diogenes the Cynic) as an image of God, see Diogenes Laertius 6.51; for Helios, see Plato, *Resp.* 508–9; for the *Logos* in God's image, see Philo, *Conf.* 97, 147; for Wisdom as the image of God, see Wis 7:26. Wisdom is similarly depicted in Philo, *Leg. All.* 1.43.

11. On God's invisibility, see Heb 11:27; John 1:18; 5:37; 6:46; 1 John 4:12.

Bibliography

Commentaries

Barth, Markus, and Helmut Blanke. *Colossians: A New Translation with Introduction and Commentary*. Translated by Astrid B. Beck. Anchor Bible 34B. New York: Doubleday, 1994.

Dunn, James D. G. *The Epistles to the Colossians and to Philemon: A Commentary on the Greek Text*. New International Greek Testament Commentary. Carlisle/Grand Rapids: Paternoster/Eerdmans, 1996. Pages 1–290.

Hay, David M. *Colossians*. Abingdon New Testament Commentaries. Nashville: Abingdon, 2000.

Lincoln, Andrew T. "The Letter to the Colossians: Introduction, Commentary, and Reflections." Pages 551–669 in vol. 11 of *The New Interpreter's Bible*. Edited by Leander E. Keck. 12 vols. Nashville: Abingdon, 2000.

Lohse, Eduard. *Colossians and Philemon: A Commentary on the Epistles to the Colossians and to Philemon*. Hermeneia. Translated by William R. Poehlmann and Robert J. Karris. Philadelphia: Fortress, 1971. Pages 1–183.

MacDonald, Margaret Y. *Colossians and Ephesians*. Sacra Pagina 17. Collegeville: Liturgical Press, 2000. Pages 1–189.

Martin, Ralph P. *Colossians and Philemon*. New Century Bible. London: Oliphants, 1974; Grand Rapids: Eerdmans, 1985 (1974). Pages 1–141.

Moule, C. F. D. *The Epistles of Paul the Apostle to the Colossians and to Philemon: An Introduction and Commentary*. Cambridge Greek Testament Commentary. Cambridge: Cambridge University Press, 1968 (1957). Pages 3–139.

O'Brien, Peter T. *Colossians, Philemon*. Word Biblical Commentary 44. Waco: Word, 1982. Pages xxv–liv, 1–261.

Pokorný, Petr. *Colossians: A Commentary*. Translated by Siegfried S. Schatzmann from the 1987 German ed. Peabody: Hendrickson, 1991.

Schweizer, Eduard. *The Letter to the Colossians: A Commentary*. Translated by A. Chester. Minneapolis: Augsburg, 1982.

Other Resources

Barclay, John M. G. *Colossians and Philemon*. New Testament Guides. Sheffield: Sheffield, 1997.

Furnish, Victor P. "Colossians, Epistle to the." Pages 1090–96 in vol. 1 of *The Anchor Bible Dictionary*. Edited by David N. Freedman. 6 vols. New York: Doubleday, 1992.

Wilson, Walter T. *The Hope of Glory: Education and Exhortation in the Epistle to the Colossians*. Supplements to Novum Testamentum 88. Leiden: Brill, 1997.

THEOLOGY OF COLOSSIANS WITHIN THE CONTEXT OF PAULINE THEOLOGY

Wedderburn, A. J. M. "The Theology of Colossians." Pages 3–71 in Andrew T. Lincoln and A. J. M. Wedderburn, *The Theology of the Later Pauline Letters*. New Testament Theology. Cambridge: Cambridge University Press, 1993; repr. 2000.

THE COLOSSIAN HERESY

Arnold, Clinton E. *The Colossian Syncretism: The Interface Between Christianity and Folk Belief at Colossae*. Wissenschaftliche Untersuchungen zum Neuen Testament, 2.77. Tübingen: Mohr (Siebeck), 1995; Grand Rapids: Baker, 1996.

Francis, Fred O., and Wayne A. Meeks, eds. *Conflict at Colossae: A Problem in the Interpretation of Early Christianity, Illustrated by Selected Modern Studies.* Rev. ed. Society of Biblical Literature Sources for Biblical Study 4. Missoula: Society of Biblical Literature (Scholars Press), 1975.

THE HOUSEHOLD CODE IN COLOSSIANS

Crouch, James E. *The Origin and Intention of the Colossian Haustafel.* Forschungen zur Religion und Literatur des Alten und Neuen Testaments 109. Göttingen: Vandenhoeck & Ruprecht, 1972.

Martin, Clarice J. "The *Haustafeln* (Household Codes) in African American Biblical Interpretation: 'Free Slaves' and Subordinate Women." Pages 206–31 in *Stony the Road We Trod: African American Biblical Interpretation.* Edited by Cain Hope Felder. Philadelphia: Fortress, 1991.

Chapter 19

Ephesians

"We believe in . . . one holy catholic and apostolic church."

The Nicene Creed

"Ephesians . . . the crown of Paulinism."

C. H. Dodd

R eaders of Ephesians are struck by several things: its Pauline frame of reference, its close similarity to Colossians, its faceless addressees, its majestic, liturgical-sounding language, and its grandly conceived vision of the universal church. Also evident is its reflective, even meditative theological outlook, with its wide-angle view of God's saving action, its highly refined sense of mystery, its strong devotion to tradition, and its heightened awareness of the church's separation from pagan culture. Its outlook also suggests an author who is somewhat distanced from the originating events of Christianity and who takes the long view of the church's future.

In one way, the mood of the letter is celebratory, a mood reinforced by richly formulated prayers and a carefully cultivated memory of what life was like before God's saving grace transformed death into life, desperation into hope, and enmity into peace. Yet by the letter's end, an ominous apocalyptic mood has set in, a mood fed by a vision of cosmic enemies who threaten the church's future and who can be overcome only by the church armed for spiritual warfare. But given the language of power and the metaphors of stability that pervade the letter, the dominant mood of the letter is one of confidence and hope.

The Pauline Frame of Reference

Formally, the letter bears some resemblance to other Pauline letters. Its opening greeting exhibits typical Pauline form, and like Romans, there is no co-sender. Its overall two-part structure—the first half predominantly prayers and instruction (chs. 1–3), the latter half exhortation heavily weighted with imperatives (chs. 4–6)—roughly corresponds to 1 Thessalonians and Galatians, though the proportions are different. The concluding section, with its mention of Paul's co-worker Tychicus and its reassuring tone (6:21–22), echoes Paul, as does the benediction (6:23–24).

Complementing these formal similarities is the Pauline voice we hear in the letter. Twice the author identifies himself as Paul (1:1; 3:1) and his form of self-description is familiar. He is an "apostle of Christ Jesus" (1:1), now imprisoned (3:1; 4:1; 6:20), charged with preaching to the Gentiles (3:8). He recalls his apostolic commission as an instance of divine grace extended to "the very least of all the saints" (3:8; cf. 1 Cor 15:9). Since the letter is singly written, we are expected to see the image of Paul, the apostle to the Gentiles who is now an ambassador in chains (6:20), behind the "I" who greets, prays, recalls, instructs, encourages, commands, and warns the readers. Yet the letter also frequently uses the first person plural (e.g., 1:3–14; 2:1–21; 4:7–16; 4:25–5:2). In these cases, the "we" is not Paul and his co-workers, but usually "we Christians," occasionally "we Jewish Christians." Paul is speaking not only *to* but also *for* all other Christians.

That Ephesians is operating within the world of Pauline thought is also evident in its theological idiom. The narrative of faith, which envisions "you" (Gentiles) and "all of us" (Jews) in the grip of sin (2:1–10), frames the universal human dilemma in terms reminiscent of Rom 1–3. Equally strong Pauline echoes are heard in its story of humanity's rescue—salvation by grace through faith, "not of works," solely initiated by a merciful, loving God, thus excluding boasting (2:4–10). Also central to its theological outlook is the core conviction that Christ's death was a redemptive sacrifice (1:7; 2:13).

While this is by no means a comprehensive list of similarities between Ephesians and the undisputed Pauline letters, it shows how deeply indebted the letter is to Pauline thought.

A closer look at the letter, however, reveals some basic differences in form and content. Instead of the usual prayer following the opening greeting, either a prayer of thanksgiving (e.g., Phil 1:3–11) or blessing (2 Cor 1:3–11), Ephesians has both, first a blessing (1:3–14), then a thanksgiving (1:15–23). The concluding section giving a personal touch to the letter is limp compared with its counterpart in Colossians (Eph 6:21–22; cf. Col 4:7–17). Whereas Ephesians mentions only Tychicus, Colossians mentions him along with nine other co-workers. Compared with other Pauline benedictions, Eph 6:23–24 is not only longer but also unusual.

Like Colossians, Ephesians exhibits some stylistic features that distinguish it from other Pauline letters. We encounter extraordinarily long, complex sentences, usually rendered by Greek editions and translators as several short sentences.[1] A distinctive compositional style is also reflected in the strings of genitive modifiers and synonymous expressions that occur throughout the letter.[2] Even though vocabulary usage is a notoriously subjective criterion for assessing a writer's literary style, Ephesians contains a number of remarkable expressions not encountered in other Pauline letters: "in the heavenly places" (1:3, 20; 2:6; 3:10; 6:12);[3] the devil (4:27; 6:11; cf. 1 Tim 3:6, 7; 2 Tim 2:26);[4] the "cosmic powers [*kosmokratoras*] of this present darkness" (6:12); and "blood and flesh" (6:12).[5]

Of greater import are the points at which the theological outlook of Ephesians differs markedly from that of the undisputed Pauline letters. Among the more notable differences are the following:

1. *The age to come is envisioned as a distant, final consummation rather than a cataclysmic event precipitated by Christ's coming.* Reflecting traditional Jewish eschatology, Ephesians divides time between "this age" and "the age to come" (1:21). It is also forward-looking in its expectation of a future inheritance (1:14, 18; 5:5) and a solidly grounded hope (1:18; 4:4). Believers may have fully realized salvation in one sense, but they still look to a future "day of redemption" (4:30; cf. 1:14), which serves as an incentive for good behavior in the ethical admonitions. The coming "wrath of God" (5:6) stands squarely within OT notions of the coming Day of the Lord (cf. Rom 1:18). A similar sense of future accountability is also seen in 6:8. The "evil day" of 6:13 may also refer to the end time.

In all these respects, Ephesians reflects a thoroughly Pauline outlook. Notably absent, however, is any reference to Christ's Parousia or any sense of urgency that the final consummation will occur soon—both standard fixtures in the undisputed letters (cf. 1 Thess 2:19; 3:13; 4:15; 5:23; 2 Thess 2:1, 8–9; 1 Cor 15:23; also Rom 13:11; 1 Cor 7:29; Phil 4:5). By contrast, Col 3:4 anticipates Christ's Parousia. A call to alertness is sounded (Eph 5:18), but not because Christ's return is imminent (cf. Mark 13:33; 1 Thess 5:6–7). Since there are "ages to come" (2:7), the church, looking to a long future, is urged to adopt a policy of slow growth as it matures toward perfection (4:13).

2. *The universal church, solidly anchored on its apostolic foundation, is broadly conceived as the "new humanity" unifying Gentiles and Jews in the body of Christ, which is obedient to its exalted Head.* When Paul uses the term "church" (*ekklēsia*), he normally has the local congregation in mind (though cf. Gal 1:13; 1 Cor 16:19). Ephesians, by contrast, focuses exclusively on the universal church. In Colossians, the universal church is also emphasized, but the local congregation is sometimes in view (cf. Col 4:15–16; also 1:2). This difference of perspective helps explain why Paul in the undisputed letters envisions ministerial roles as gifts primarily exercised within local churches (1 Cor 12:4–11; Rom 12:3–8; even 1 Cor 12:27–31 has a congregational focus). Similarly, duly appointed leadership roles are congregationally based (Phil 1:1). Reflecting a more comprehensive, historically distant perspective, Ephesians sees the universal church as having a foundation of "[holy] apostles and prophets," a previous generation of pacesetting founders who built a superstructure on Christ, the cornerstone (2:20; 3:5). Accordingly, roles of leadership and ministry in Ephesians are discrete activities that are viewed comprehensively and hierarchically (4:11–12).

Ephesians also displays considerable creativity in its use of metaphors for the church. Like Colossians, it extends the "body of Christ" to the universal church (4:12–13), moving beyond Paul's congregational application of the metaphor. Similarly, Christ as cosmic ruler is the head of the church, although the author of Ephesians is not as intrigued by Christ's pre-existence and his role in creation. Unlike Colossians, Ephesians displays a fascination with building metaphors for the universal church, most notably the temple of God (2:20–22; also cf. 2:14; 1 Cor 3:16–17; 6:19). The most innovative metaphor, however, is the church as the "new humanity" formed from the fusion of Jews and Gentiles reconciled by the death of Christ (2:15–16).

3. *Gentiles and Jews are now united in one church.* Ephesians is aware of the tense relationships, if not outright hostility, that had existed historically between Jews and Gentiles. It is also aware of the crisis created by the church's mission to Gentiles. Even so, it sees this as a past controversy, largely resolved, rather than a boiling caldron of unsettled issues. It is no less a matter of wonderment to the author of Ephesians that these two groups have been brought together through Christ, which is why the language of mystery is so apt for characterizing the union of Gentiles and Jews in the church. Ephesians shows no signs that there are sharply divided camps within the church still fighting about how the Mosaic law should figure in Christian belief and practice. Quite the opposite: the law was abolished with the death of Christ (2:15)— end of argument. Now the church moves forward as a unified group of Gentiles and Jews, relieved to have made the transition from death to life and confidently crafting an identity over against the pagan world. Gentiles have been fully embraced by Jews, and both live in "the promise in Christ Jesus through the gospel" (3:6).

Needless to say, this irenic perspective differs markedly from the heated controversies reflected in Galatians and Philippians and still not fully resolved in Romans. [See Expanded CD Version pp. 578–80: *Ephesians as an Expanded Version of Colossians*]

An Anomalous Letter

The puzzle of Ephesians begins with the opening verse. The phrase "in Ephesus" is absent in some of the earliest, most reliable manuscripts, which means that the letter circulated widely in a form addressed only "to God's holy people, faithful in Christ Jesus" (1:1 NJB; similarly RSV).[6] The lack of a specific addressee invited readers to fill in the blank. In the collection of Pauline letters assembled by Marcion in the early second century, the letter is identified as the Letter to the Laodiceans (cf. Col 4:16).[7] But by the end of the second century, the letter had acquired the title "To the Ephesians."[8] As often happened, this title gradually became expanded. One ninth-century manuscript titles the letter, "An Epistle of Paul the Apostle to the Ephesians written from Rome through Tychicus." Modern English translations usually adopt a shorter form of this title, for example, "The Letter of Paul to the Ephesians" (NRSV, REB).

Each element of this popular form of the title is problematic. Ephesians may exhibit some standard features of Pauline letters, but they have a rather different complexion. It may be a letter, but it is a most unusual letter. Similarly, the letter clearly operates within a Pauline framework, but there are enough structural, stylistic, and theological differences from Paul to raise substantial questions about its Pauline authorship. And finally, was it originally addressed to the church at Ephesus? If, as Acts reports, Paul was a major player in the early history of the church at Ephesus (Acts 18:24–20:1; 20:16–38), ministering there for three years (Acts 20:31) and, after leaving, maintaining close contact with the church, how could he write such an impersonal letter that revealed so little specific information about the church?

Because of the numerous questions about the epistolary structure of Ephesians, its stylistic features, and its overall complexion, it has been difficult to identify the genre of the letter with any precision. The prominence of moral exhortation, especially in chapters 4–6, and a number of individual motifs, for example, the call to imitate God and Christ (5:1–2), reflect concerns typically found in paraenetic letters. Its recurrent use of language praising God reflects Greek literary conventions related to the rhetoric of praise, whether directed to deities, persons, or other things worth celebrating. Since the Gentile readers are repeatedly commended for their conversion, the letter even resembles a "letter of congratulation." Some scholars, emphasizing content rather than form, see the epistolary framework as a literary "shell" containing a set of weighty theological reflections. Accordingly, they see the letter as an extended theological meditation in the form of an essay or treatise, embodying elements of early baptismal homilies as well as other liturgical features. Taken out of their epistolary setting, some portions of the letter (e.g., ch. 2) read like recitations of God's saving work addressed to newly baptized, Gentile converts. Still other portions read like prayers drawn directly from the church's worship (e.g., 1:3–14) or snippets of a hymn (5:14).

To explain the letter's unusual texture and contents, the text critical problem in 1:1, and its general outlook, some have suggested that Ephesians was originally a circular letter. As such, it would have been addressed not to any single congregation, but to several congregations within a single region, such as the Roman province of Asia (modern western Turkey). If so, the opening verse may have had a blank space that the reader of the letter would have filled in, depending on the congregation before whom it was being read aloud. Ephesus may have been one of the cities to which the letter circulated, yet because of its prominence as the largest, most well-known city in the province, and its importance as a Pauline church, its name was finally attached to the letter as the major addressee.

Still others have proposed that the letter served as a preface to the other Pauline letters, once they were gathered into a single collection. With its broad theological outlook firmly anchored within Pauline thought, Ephesians may have introduced the Pauline letters, much as Ps 1 does the entire Psalter.

While Ephesians presents a number of literary and theological puzzles, some scholars still read it as one of the prison letters (along with Philippians, Colossians, and Philemon) penned by Paul himself. But because of its literary, stylistic, and theological differences from the undisputed Pauline letters, it is best read as a pseudonymous writing, probably composed in the last third of the first century C.E. by a Pauline disciple thoroughly familiar with the apostle's thought and appreciative of its rich complexity. While this disciple certainly extends Pauline thought in new directions, Ephesians represents a reformulated theological vision that has been purchased at some cost. Paul's sense of apocalyptic urgency has given way to a more comfortable, though by no means naïve, view of the future. The moral vision in Ephesians is more inward-looking. Even though Paul emphasized the church's distinctive place within society, his outlook did not have the sharp sectarian edge we find in Ephesians. Romans 13, for example, presents the church relating to the state rather than standing against it.

But some things are gained in Ephesians as the author moves the church beyond its controversial past to a new future that is closer in spirit to Ignatius (ca. 35–107 C.E.), Irenaeus (ca. 130–200 C.E.), and even Nicaea (325 C.E.). With its emphasis on apostolic tradition and the apostolic foundation of the church, the letter prepares the way for apostolic succession as a way of establishing both historical continuity and theological legitimacy. Paul's theology of the cross gives way to a theology of glory in Ephesians, which accents Christ's exaltation and ascension. But the former remains present in the letter, even as the implications of the latter are more fully developed. By positioning the church in an obedient posture before the heavenly Christ, Ephesians creates the atmosphere and resources for deeply rooted spiritual sensibilities that find expression in the church's worship.

"The Church, the Wisdom of God in Its Infinite Variety"

Ephesians is remarkable for its expansive vision of the church, possibly the most fully developed such vision in the NT. One indication of this is the sheer frequency of the term "church" (*ekklēsia*), which occurs more times in Ephesians (nine) than in Galatians and Romans combined (eight). But more important than how often the term occurs in the letter is how it is used. In every instance, the term refers to the universal church, not a local congregation. When Ephesians speaks of the church, it envisions "God's holy people, faithful in Christ Jesus" (1:1 NJB) in the broadest possible sense—not those in a particular location or even in a particular region, and not even those at a particular moment in time. In Ephesians, the church transcends space and time. This does not mean that it is simply an idea in the mind of God or an abstract concept. It comprises human beings who confess common beliefs, who worship together, and who engage in distinctive behaviors. And yet, since the church experiences "spiritual blessings in the heavenly places" (1:3), it cannot be reduced to a set of empirical phenomena. Ephesians envisions the church in its sensory and suprasensory modes. To the extent that individual churches constitute the spiritual reality of Christ's body they are all in view. Far from presenting a theory of the church, Ephesians envisions the people of God embodied in Jesus Christ embracing both the realized experience of believers and the unrealized ideal toward which they aspire.

Rather than presenting a systematic doctrine of the church, Ephesians offers a distinctive vision of the church reflecting several closely connected convictions:

1. *The church is linked with God's eternal purpose*. In the opening prayer of blessing, God is celebrated for having chosen "us in Christ before the foundation of the world" (1:4). Worth noting is how heavily Ephesians accents God's action.[9] The repeated use of "pre-" words throughout the prayer locates the origin of God's redemptive purpose prior to creation; in doing so, Ephesians assigns to the church the pre-existent status Colossians ascribes to Christ.[10] Because the church existed before creation as an idea in the mind of God, as a definite though unrealized plan, it is in no sense an afterthought. With the coming of Christ, the church may have been an idea whose time had come, but it was an ancient idea, firmly in the Creator's mind well before anything else was created.

To the question "When did the church begin?" Ephesians answers, "Before the world began." Luke-Acts, by contrast, would answer, "On the day of Pentecost" (Acts 2). Yet another answer is provided by Matthew, who locates the church's founding at

Peter's confession at Caesarea Philippi (Matt 16:16–19). Ephesians may present a breathtaking theory of the church's origin, but it is remarkably undeveloped, especially compared with other NT writings that see the church as an expression of the divine purpose. In Ephesians, the church is not seen, for example, as the fulfillment of OT prophecies, nor even as the final chapter in the biblical story whose earlier chapters featured prominent OT figures, such as Abraham, Moses, or David (so Luke-Acts). The church may be a realized promise, but the intermediate stages of its fulfillment are not sketched in Ephesians. Instead, Ephesians fast-forwards from the time before creation to the time of redemption; God's original, pre-creation intention comes to full realization in Christ's death, resurrection, and ascension.

2. *The church exists only through God's redemptive work in Christ.* The salvific effects of Christ's death and resurrection figure prominently in NT writings. In Ephesians, these effects extend beyond individuals, even beyond individual communities of faith, to the catholic church. Since Christ is the exclusive locus of God's saving action, the one in whom God "gather[s] up all things . . . things in heaven and things on earth" (1:10), the direct beneficiary is his body, the church (1:22). Drawing freely on earlier tradition that understands Christ's death as a sacrifice whose purifying benefits extend to all those who are "in Christ," Ephesians repeatedly centers the church's identity in this defining, creative moment (cf. Eph 1:7; 2:13; 5:2, 25). If the idea of the church was conceived in the mind of God before creation, it was given birth in Christ's death and resurrection.

Christ's death is not an event in which Christ was a passive victim or one through which salvific benefits extended indirectly to the church. It is rather an event in which Christ himself acted consciously and lovingly on the church's behalf. Even though this close relationship between Christ and the church is elaborated most fully as part of the household code, as an analogy for the husband-wife relationship, its theological force is not thereby diminished. Remarkably, the fusion of husband and wife into "one flesh," as envisioned in Gen 2:24, is seen as a "great mystery" illuminating the indissoluble bond between Christ and the church. Such bold, unequivocal claims as "Christ loved the church and gave himself up for [the church]" (5:25) extend his relationship from being Head to being the Savior of the body (5:23). With this universalized ascription, the death of Christ is not only an event through which God worked to achieve the redemptive purpose, but also one in which Christ himself expressed and achieved his own purpose. [See **Expanded CD Version p. 583: *The Church as the "New Humanity" Comprising Jews and Gentiles***]

3. *The exalted Christ gives a distinctive imprint to the church's sense of identity and mission.* Whether Eph 1:20 envisions God's raising Christ from the dead and seating him at God's right hand as a single event in two stages or as two distinct events (resurrection and ascension) is not clear. What is clear is the distinctive emphasis Ephesians gives to Christ's exalted position "in the heavenly places." From beginning to end, the reader's attention is focused upward. In this respect, Ephesians shares the outlook of Colossians in seeing Christ at the apex of the cosmos. To drive home the point, the author unleashes a cascade of synonyms that extend the scope of Christ's dominion spatially and temporally—a poetic, perhaps liturgical, way of positioning Christ at the apex of the worshiper's own universe of meaning. As much as Christ presides over

space and time, however, his supremacy is most visibly and powerfully experienced in his role as the spiritual head of the church, his body, which somehow encompasses Christ's fullness as the one "who fills all in all" (1:22–23). [**See Expanded CD Version p. 584:** *The Vertical Axis in Ephesians*]

In Ephesians the church's ministry is constituted as a well-ordered set of discrete leadership roles authorized (and enabled) by the exalted Christ (4:7–16). Even if this way of legitimating the church's ministries is triggered by a highly unusual exegesis of Ps 68:18 in Eph 4:8, its overall force is clear. In sharp contrast to 1 Cor 12 and Rom 12, in which a variety of charismatic gifts characterizes each local community of believers, here the church's mission and ministry are envisioned comprehensively. Apostles, prophets, evangelists, pastors, and teachers may be part of local churches, but here they are agents of the universal church, discharged to nurture its overall growth, to maintain its steady course, to steer it clear of menacing threats and competing gospels, and especially to strengthen organic ties to its head, the true source of life, Christ himself. Their single mission, whether seen as their combined efforts or their singular form of contribution to the overall effort, is to cultivate its spiritual growth, and to do so constructively, that is, "in love" (4:16). It is the exalted Christ who both commissions and empowers the church's ministries, but who also directs the church's mission. As the head of the church, Christ is both source of the church's life and the goal toward which it pushes. He is both Alpha and Omega, not so much in a temporal sense but in an eternal sense that transcends both time and space.

4. *As the "new humanity," the church becomes a community unified through its singular commitment to shared beliefs and practices.* At the church's inaugural moment in Christ, two peoples are reconciled into one (2:14). To use the language of a slightly later period, it emerges as a "third race," a *tertium quid.*[11] Its singularity of essence and purpose takes different forms, such as the complete solidarity between Christ and the church symbolized as the "one flesh" comparable to husband and wife (5:31–32). Perhaps its most conspicuous expression comes in Eph 4:3–6, in which the church's overarching mission is to "maintain the unity of the Spirit in the bond of peace" (4:3). Since the Spirit is given as a blessing accompanying the church's response to the Gospel and serves as pledge of its future inheritance, it is both unifying goal and impulse (1:13–14). It is thus possible to think of the "unity which the Spirit gives" (4:3 REB).

Reflecting its strong embrace of tradition, Ephesians adduces the formalized pattern of beliefs and practices that constitute the church's unified identity (4:4–6). In doing so, it introduces yet another distinctive feature. However manifold the church's actual embodiment in time and space, its oneness derives from its singular focus on a commonly confessed Spirit, Lord, and God, a common initiation rite that expresses a common faith and hope, and a common acknowledgement of Christ as its head, which renders it one body. In 1 Cor 12 the unified congregation having diverse gifts is traceable to a common deity experienced as God, Christ, and Spirit; here, this conception becomes catholic as unity is the goal toward which the whole church must strive as well as the single purpose that motivates its striving.

5. *An inward-directed ethic gives the church a sharply profiled identity and a strong sense of solidarity against the world.* Well over half of Ephesians is devoted explicitly to moral exhortation (chs. 4–6), but a good portion of the first half of the letter addresses the

radical polarity between the world believers inhabit and the world they left behind. Like Colossians, Ephesians operates with a strongly developed sense of conversion informed by an equally strong sense of "then" and "now." But these are not merely temporal categories, for "then" also symbolizes the world of values that still threatens the church's identity. Ephesians operates with a strong "Christ against culture" ethic, drawing a sharp line between Gentile culture and the newly acquired moral universe of the church. The former is depicted in wholly negative, undifferentiated terms. Ephesians shows no appreciation for enlightened Greco-Roman moralists like Epictetus (mid-first to second century C.E.) or Plutarch (ca. 50–120 C.E.). Nor does it allow for the possibility that good moral people inhabit the ordinary households and shops of Roman cities or villages. Its contemptuous view of pagan life resonates with Paul's own moral sensibilities, heavily influenced by biblical perspectives, in which Gentiles can hardly be expected to behave morally since they are ignorant of the one God (1 Thess 4:5).

Perhaps this sharply sketched picture of the morally bankrupt life left behind derives from the strong sense of conversion; in any case, its deeply etched features stem from a negative, reactive impulse. Developing a positive ethic from such a negative portrayal of "the other" may represent an age-old moral strategy, but it is a moral view achieved at considerable cost. Even so, this is the dynamic that drives the moral view of Ephesians.

Drawing on the familiar imagery of darkness and light, which is well established in the Pauline letters (e.g., 1 Thess 5:5), in the Johannine writings (cf. John 1:5; 3:19; 8:12; 12:35, 46), and in both Jewish and non-Jewish ethical visions, Ephesians sharpens it even more. Darkness and light are not merely moral realms in which people live; people are actually said to have been darkness, or are now "light" in the Lord. The readers are charged to "live as children of light" (5:8).

Darkness and light may symbolize two antithetical moral realms, but their respective inhabitants are ordinary human beings. Urging readers to equip themselves in God's armor yields a picture of the church whose field of battle encompasses extraordinary, superhuman foes (6:12–13). The view of the world in this concluding call to arms may be more apocalyptic in texture, but its effect is the same: to solidify the identity of the church as a moral community firmly entrenched against a host of competing, threatening values.

The church's moral stance is filled out, first, by a highly structured view of its creedal commitments and ordered ministry (4:1–6), and, second, by an extended set of moral admonitions that often take the form of a single piece of advice first stated negatively, then positively. Much of the moral admonition here belongs to the common stock of early Christian teaching and finds parallels in the Pauline writings and the synoptic tradition. No uniform set of motivations undergirds this teaching, but several warrants surface: OT allusions and appeals, mutual responsibility, warnings linked with God's wrath or other forms of future accountability and punishment, imitation of God and Christ, character reflecting prior identity, and an appeal not to grieve the Holy Spirit. Compared with the ethical admonitions in Colossians, these miscellaneous instructions are more numerous and more pointed.

Like Colossians, the church's moral responsibilities are also structured using the household code, although the version in Ephesians is longer and more fully developed.

Particularly noteworthy is the intertwining of wife-husband responsibilities with the Christ-church analogy. As before, relationships are structured hierarchically—wives, children, and slaves are expected to be subordinate and obedient—but the overall expectations are cast in terms of mutual respect and love (5:21). This softens the effect to some extent, especially compared with Colossians. But it has the same effect: It gives Christian behavior a sharp profile vis-à-vis Gentile culture.

Notes

1. Ephesians 1:3–14 is rendered by NA[27] as four sentences, by NRSV as six sentences. The complexity of the passage is better captured by KJV, which still breaks it into three sentences. NA[27] renders 4:11–16 as a single sentence, NRSV as three sentences. Similarly long sentences also occur in 1:15–19; 2:1–7, 14–16, 19–22; 3:1–7, 8–12, 14–19; 5:17–20, 21–24.

2. Of the many examples, especially noteworthy are 1:18; 2:2; 3:2, although the piling up of genitive modifiers is more clearly seen in the Greek text than in English translations that smooth them out.

3. Paul employs the adjective "heavenly" (*epouranios*) several times (1 Cor 15:40–49; Phil 2:10; cf. 2 Tim 4:18), but not the exact prepositional form found in Ephesians. He does, however, speak of "in the heavens" (2 Cor 5:1; Phil 3:20).

4. Paul's more usual designation is Satan (Rom 16:20; 1 Cor 5:5; 7:5; 2 Cor 2:11; 11:14; 12:7; 1 Thess 2:18; 2 Thess 2:9), although he also employs other expressions, e.g., the tempter (1 Thess 3:5), the evil one (2 Thess 3:3; cf. Eph 6:16), and Beliar (2 Cor 6:15).

5. Paul's usual form of the phrase is "flesh and blood" (1 Cor 15:50; Gal 1:16 [in Greek]).

6. The phrase is absent in 𝔓[46] (ca. 200 C.E.), in the original, uncorrected form of Sinaiticus (mid-fourth century), Vaticanus (mid-fourth century), and also the text used by Origen (ca. 185–254 C.E.) and manuscripts mentioned by Basil of Caesarea (ca. 330–379 C.E.).

7. Tertullian, *Marc.* 5.17.

8. The title occurs in 𝔓[46] (see n. 6 above) and also occurs ca. 180 C.E. in Irenaeus, *Haer.* 5.2.3; 5.8.1; 5.14.3; 5.24.4.

9. In the "Great Blessing" of 1:3–14, the verbal actions attributed to God should be noted: "blessed [*eulogēsas*] us" (1:3); "chose [*exelexato*] us" (1:4); "destined [*proorisas*] us" (1:5); grace that [God] "bestowed [*echaritōsen*] on us" (1:6); "poured out [*eperisseusen*] on us" (1:8); "having made known [*gnōrisas*] to us the mystery of his will" (1:9); "set forth" (*proetheto*, 1:9); "having summed up [*anakephalaiōsasthai*] all things" (1:10); "we were given an inheritance [*eklērothēmen*] [by God]" (1:11); "having been destined" (*proristhentes*, 1:11); the one who "accomplishes [*energountos*]" (1:11); "were sealed [*esphragisthēte*] [by God]" (1:13).

10. The force of God's pre-creation actions is diminished in the NRSV, which renders *proorizō* "destined" (1:5, 11) rather than the preferred, though theologically troublesome, "predestined" (NIV) or "marked out beforehand" (NJB). Similarly, *protithēmi* (1:9), rendered as "set forth" in NRSV, emphasizes the temporal priority of God's action, which REB and NJB capture: "which [God] determined beforehand in Christ."

11. *Preaching of Peter* in Clement of Alexandria, *Strom.* 6.5.39.

Bibliography

Commentaries

Barth, Markus. *Ephesians*. Anchor Bible 34. 2 vols. Garden City: Doubleday, 1974.

Best, Ernest. *A Critical and Exegetical Commentary on Ephesians*. International Critical Commentary. Edinburgh: T&T Clark, 1998.

————. *Ephesians: A Shorter Commentary*. Edinburgh: T&T Clark, 2003.

Chadwick, Henry. "Ephesians." Pages 980–84 in *Peake's Commentary on the Bible*. Edited by Matthew Black and Harold H. Rowley. London: Nelson, 1962.

Dahl, Nils A., with Donald H. Juel. "Ephesians." Pages 1113–20 in *HarperCollins Bible Commentary*. Edited by James L. Mays. San Francisco: HarperCollins, 2000.

Hoehner, Harold W. *Ephesians: An Exegetical Commentary*. Grand Rapids: Baker, 2002.

Houlden, James L. *Paul's Letters from Prison: Philippians, Colossians, Philemon and Ephesians*. Pelican New Testament Commentaries. Harmondsworth: Penguin, 1970; Westminster Pelican Commentaries. Philadelphia: Westminster, 1977. Pages 235–341.

Lincoln, Andrew T. *Ephesians*. Word Biblical Commentary 42. Dallas: Word, 1990.

MacDonald, Margaret Y. *Colossians and Ephesians*. Sacra Pagina 17. Collegeville: Liturgical, 2000. Pages 191–354.

Muddiman, John. *A Commentary on the Epistle to the Ephesians*. Black's New Testament Commentaries. London: Continuum, 2001.

O'Brien, Peter T. *The Letter to the Ephesians*. Grand Rapids/Leicester: Eerdmans/Apollos, 1999.

Perkins, Pheme. *Ephesians*. Abingdon New Testament Commentaries. Nashville: Abingdon, 1997.

————. "The Letter to the Ephesians: Introduction, Commentary, and Reflections." Pages 349–466 in vol. 11 of *The New Interpreter's Bible*. Edited by Leander E. Keck. 12 vols. Nashville: Abingdon, 2000.

Schnackenburg, Rudolf. *Ephesians: A Commentary*. Translated by Helen Heron. Edinburgh: T&T Clark, 1991.

Other Resources

Arnold, Clinton E. *Ephesians, Power and Magic: The Concept of Power in Ephesians in Light of Its Historical Setting*. Society for New Testament Studies Monograph Series 63. Cambridge: Cambridge University Press, 1989.

Barth, Markus. *The Broken Wall: A Study of the Epistle to the Ephesians*. London/Chicago: Collins/Judson, 1960.

Best, Ernest. *Ephesians*. New Testament Guides. Sheffield: Sheffield Academic Press, 1997 (1993).

————. *Essays on Ephesians*. Edinburgh: T&T Clark, 1997.

————. *One Body in Christ: A Study in the Relationship of the Church to Christ in the Epistles of the Apostle Paul*. London: SPCK, 1955.

Lincoln, Andrew T. "The Theology of Ephesians." Pages 73–166 in *The Theology of the Later Pauline Letters*. Edited by Andrew T. Lincoln and A. J. M. Wedderburn. New Testament Theology. Cambridge: Cambridge University Press, 1993; repr. 2000.

Sampley, J. Paul. *"And the Two Shall Become One Flesh": A Study of Traditions in Ephesians 5:21–33*. Society for New Testament Studies Monograph Series 16. Cambridge: Cambridge University Press, 1971.

van Roon, A. *The Authenticity of Ephesians*. Supplements to Novum Testamentum 39. Leiden: Brill, 1974.

Chapter 20

The Pastoral Letters

"These [Titus, 1–2 Timothy] were written in personal affection; but they have been hallowed by being held in honor by the catholic church for the regulation of church discipline."

Muratorian Fragment

"This letter [2 Timothy] is Paul's testament and swan-song."

Johannes Albrecht Bengel

"Not every one can feign the heart of Paul."

Erasmus

I t was only natural for Paul's two letters to Timothy and the brief letter to Titus to be treated as a group by the early church and to be included in canonical lists, along with Philemon, after his letters to churches.[1] Not only were they addressed to individuals who were prominently mentioned co-workers of Paul during his Aegean ministry, but they also treated some common themes. Early readers of these letters were especially struck by their usefulness for regulating the practical affairs of the church. Tertullian (ca. 160–225 C.E.) reflected this viewpoint when he remarked that all three letters "treat . . . ecclesiastical discipline."[2]

Besides being read as general church orders, these letters were particularly beneficial to those engaged in Christian ministry. Thomas Aquinas (1224–1274) spoke of 1 Timothy as "resembling a pastoral rule" (*quasi pastoralis regula*)[3] and 2 Timothy as admonition to diligence in pastoral care and pastoral duty (*curam pastoralem ac pastorale officium*).[4] It was apparently not until the eighteenth century that they were formally called "pastoral letters."[5] Although this designation became widely accepted, its limitations were recognized. Some scholars, observing that the letters deal with other matters and that the treatment they give to the pastoral ministry is neither comprehensive nor particularly penetrating, insisted on calling them the "so-called pastoral epistles." Some also questioned whether the term "pastoral letter" was as fitting for 2 Timothy as it was for 1 Timothy and Titus. Other possibilities were suggested. In the early seventeenth century, they were referred to as the "pontifical epistles." A century later, they were characterized as the "ministerial epistles" (*epistolae ministeriales*). More recently, they have been called the "letters to Paul's delegates." Even though many still find the term "pastorals" problematic, no suitable substitute has received widespread acceptance.

The Church's Use of the Pastorals

How early the Pastorals were known, how widely they were read, and how they related to other Pauline letters are matters of some dispute. Echoes of the Pastorals are heard in some early second-century writings, but firm evidence of their usage does not emerge until the mid-second century.[6] By the end of the second century they were being cited explicitly as letters of Paul and confidently included in canonical lists among the Pauline writings.[7] Within another fifty years, they began to receive commentary treatment. Origen (ca. 185–254 C.E.) is said to have written a commentary on Titus, which has not survived. All three Pastorals were given extended homiletical treatment by John Chrysostom (ca. 347–407 C.E.).

We are on firm ground from about 200 C.E. forward, but on much shakier ground as we push back toward the beginning of the second century. Part of the problem is the uneven state of the evidence concerning the Pastorals as we move back through the second century. The earliest papyrus manuscript containing the Pauline letters ($\mathfrak{P}^{46}$), dated about 200 C.E., does not contain the Pastorals, but it is difficult to know the significance of this omission.[8] According to Tertullian, Marcion (died ca. 160 C.E.) rejected the Pastorals outright, but there is serious scholarly debate whether Marcion even knew them.[9] According to Clement of Alexandria (ca. 150–215 C.E.), some heretics (whom he does not name) rejected 1–2 Timothy because of the critique of "so-called knowledge [*gnōsis*]" in 1 Tim 6:20–21.[10] Later, Jerome (ca. 345–420 C.E.) reports that Tatian (ca. 160 C.E.), Justin Martyr's student who founded the ascetic Encratite movement, rejected 1–2 Timothy.[11]

With the stern words issued against false teachers in the Pastorals, their rejection by Christians who were not regarded as mainstream is understandable. But there is no indication that those who rejected the Pastorals questioned their Pauline authorship. Despite their uneven reception, by the end of the second century, and possibly much earlier, the Pastorals were known and used as authoritative Pauline writings in different parts of the Mediterranean world, from the westernmost edge (Irenaeus [ca. 130–200 C.E.] in Lyons) to Asia Minor (Polycarp [ca. 69–155 C.E.] in Smyrna), and perhaps Syria (Ignatius of Antioch, ca. 35–107 C.E.). Eusebius in his *Ecclesiastical History* (early fourth century) included the Pastorals with the other Pauline letters, characterizing them as "well known and undisputed" (with respect to their genuineness).[12]

The Puzzle of the Pastorals

Of all the letters attributed to Paul, the Pastorals are the least likely to have come directly from the pen of Paul himself. That they are Pauline in some sense, no one denies. Like every other Pauline letter, the first word in each of the Pastoral Letters identifies the person writing the letter as Paul (*Paulos*). The persona of Paul is writ large in each letter, and it resonates with the Paul known from the other letters. He is an "apostle of Jesus Christ," former persecutor of the church, commissioned by God to preach to the Gentiles. While carrying out this mission, Paul gathered around him numerous co-workers, including Timothy and Titus, well-known associates who worked closely with him during the Aegean ministry. The letters are saturated with images and turns of phrase familiar from Paul's other letters. Their overall literary shape closely resembles other Pauline letters, especially in the opening greetings, concluding instructions, and benedictions. Also, within the body of each letter, instructions and exhortations are formulated in ways that are characteristic of Paul. Along with these many stylistic resemblances, the theological outlook of the letters bears a distinctive Pauline stamp.

But the reader who is thoroughly familiar with the other Pauline letters notices a genuine shift in language, style, and outlook when moving to the Pastoral Letters. We encounter familiar Pauline vocabulary and phraseology, but we also encounter a large number of words and expressions that occur nowhere else in Paul.[13] Many of these words appear nowhere else in the NT outside the Pastoral Letters.[14] We also find a number of stylistic elements that are uncharacteristic of the other Pauline writings. These include certain formulaic expressions, but they have more to do with the overall style reflected in the letters. Along with these linguistic and stylistic shifts, we also detect some distinct conceptual shifts in the way central elements of Christian belief are articulated. Even allowing for differences that would normally occur when a new situation requires Paul to deal with new subject matter and formulate fresh thoughts, these changes in theological outlook are quite striking.

Especially remarkable is how the language of the Pastorals links the three letters together and sets them apart as a group from the other Pauline letters.[15]

In reading the Pastorals, we experience a shift similar to the one mentioned earlier in connection with Colossians and Ephesians. At one level, the world we encounter in the Pastorals is Pauline; at another level, it is not. Because the outlook has moved beyond Paul, it is post-Pauline. [**See Expanded CD Version pp. 595–600: *Unique Language, Outlook, and Situation: Details of the Post-Pauline Nature of the Pastorals***]

A Proposed Solution

Whatever form the solution to this puzzle takes, it must begin with what is widely recognized: that the language, style, and theological outlook of the Pastorals link them together as a group and set them apart from the other ten letters attributed to Paul. Still debated, however, is what to make of their distinctiveness. Do they differ from the other letters because Paul is writing not to a church but to individuals, and close associates at that? Or is it because they address a new situation? Does their unusual character, in other words, stem from the unusual circumstances they address?

The Eastern Mediterranean

© Copyright by HAMMOND INCORPORATED, Maplewood, N.J.

The Pastoral Letters of 1 Timothy and Titus are addressed to Pauline co-workers in the city of Ephesus in Asia and in the island of Crete respectively.

No one questions that the Pastoral Letters are all related to Paul in some way, but in what sense can we read them as Pauline?[16] Since they are full of Pauline terminology, expressions, and stylistic features, they exude his spirit. At one level, they are identifiably Pauline, and yet they reflect a different sensibility from the one we find in the other ten letters, especially the undisputed letters. That the Pastorals came directly from the hand of the Paul who penned (or dictated) Galatians and Romans, for example, is highly improbable. Impossible? Perhaps not, if we grant Paul an extraordinary degree of rhetorical versatility or theological flexibility. But the question is not whether Paul could have written these letters, but did he? Even granting some methodological weaknesses in some scholars' statistical analyses of language and style in the Pastorals, the cumulative weight of evidence is against direct Pauline authorship. Taking all the considerations into account—language, style, outlook, manner of expression, angle of vision toward the Christ event—many scholars believe that the mentality of the Pastorals is noticeably different from that of the other letters.

For the purposes of discussion, it may be helpful to distinguish between the textual Paul—the Paul whose image is projected in the text of the Pastorals—and the historical Paul—the Paul we know from the other (undisputed) letters. While the textual Paul of the Pastorals stands in continuity with the historical Paul, he has also moved beyond the Paul of the earlier letters.

Who wrote the Pastorals? When and under what circumstances? It is impossible to know for sure, and we will probably never know. Luke has been suggested. Some scholars have noted enough striking linguistic and stylistic similarities between the Pastorals and Luke-Acts to make this more than a fleeting possibility. That Luke might have written the Pastorals while Paul was still alive, even under Paul's authority, is not impossible. The fictive setting of Titus and 1 Timothy might easily be seen as a projected setting that would typify life among Pauline churches once Paul was gone. We know from Luke-Acts that Luke, or someone of equal literary sophistication, could exercise such poetic license. Numerous clues in the Pastorals signal to a discerning reader that these letters are more than simply letters from the historical Paul to his coworkers Timothy and Titus. The form of the concluding benediction is one clue: "Grace be to you [plural]"—a clear hint that the letters serve as more than instructions from Paul to two individuals, Timothy and Titus. They speak for Paul to a wider circle of (Pauline) churches—the whole "household of God."

How should we imagine the situation in the Pastorals? Even with the mention of "myths" and "so-called gnosis," and the various strands of false teaching—forbidding marriage, requiring abstinence from foods, fascination with Jewish law—nothing requires this configuration of beliefs and behaviors to be late. It could reflect a mixture of first-century ideas and inclinations that eventually surface in more fully developed Gnostic systems in the second century. Nor are the leadership roles and ministries envisioned necessarily late. There are enough analogues within contemporary Judaism, for example, a council of elders within a given community, to enable an early date.

More than anything else, what pulls the Pastorals toward the end of the first century are the similarities in ethos and outlook with texts such as the *Didache*, *1 Clement*, and even Ignatius and Polycarp. There is greater kinship between these two bodies of literature than between the Pastorals and the undisputed letters of Paul. An appreciation for tradition and its stabilizing power, the compelling power of creedal confession and its capacity for ordering individual and communal identity, the high premium placed on order, stability, and continuity—the Pastorals share all of these values with early Christian writings from the late first and early to mid-second century. It is better to view the Pastorals as letters that move the Pauline tradition along the trajectory toward the earliest full-scale church order, the *Didache*. How far along that trajectory they should be placed remains an open question.

Authorship and Authority

Although the Pastorals were included in the NT canon along with other Pauline writings and were doubtless read as authoritative because they were attributed to Paul, they can no longer be seen as Pauline in the same way they were within early Christian tradition. Admitting this shift in perspective possibly makes their more problematic features easier to digest, but it does not eliminate them. The Pastorals are still NT canonical writings even when detached from the historical Paul, and for this reason the church looks to them for inspired teaching. Their authority has been established through usage over the centuries, but this authority is also acknowledged functionally every time a church, either a local congregation or a denomination, privileges the NT over other religious writings by reading it in worship, preaching and teaching from it, and trying to live by it. The Pastorals may have moved beyond Paul in outlook, but not beyond the NT. They must be heard and read alongside the other NT witnesses to the Christ event.

In the following treatment, Titus is presented first, not because it was necessarily written first, but because it represents a less developed theological vision than 1 Timothy. Because of their close similarity in form and content, both Titus and 1 Timothy should be read together. Second Timothy, by contrast, represents a different situation and is written in a different genre. As Paul's farewell letter, it is treated last.

The Letter of Paul to Titus:
Continuing Paul's Work; Teaching What Is Sound

The Letter to Titus contains instructions to complete work left unfinished by Paul (1:5). The letter reflects concerns that had to be addressed in order to continue Paul's legacy and stabilize churches he left behind.

One of the letter's chief concerns is to promote order and stability within the church.[17] Foremost among these stabilizing forces are duly qualified church leaders—elders who exercise oversight and whose lives are acknowledged examples of rectitude and unswerving fidelity to the sacred tradition (1:5–9). Only with such strong leadership can there be stout, effective resistance of those who threaten the church's social fabric by upsetting its families with their misdirected teachings (1:10–16). A sense of order is also created when different groups within the church attend to their personal conduct and keep their obligations to others (2:1–15). More broadly, all believers are expected to be model citizens who honor civil authorities, respect other people, actively devote themselves to good works, and avoid useless disputes (3:1–11).

Stabilizing Strategies

Appointing Responsible Church Leaders (1:5–9). The form of leadership within the churches that Paul left behind is somewhat vague. Apparently envisioned is a group of elders (*presbyteroi*) who exercise oversight within each congregation.[18] No other roles of leadership or service, such as deacons, are mentioned (cf. 1 Tim 3:8–13; also Phil 1:1). Those who fill such roles are expected to display qualities typically associated with rulers or other public officials, although as "God's stewards" (1:7) they discharge their responsibilities with a higher allegiance. One of the qualities mentioned is self-control (*engkratēs*, 1:8), which identifies a common theme that runs through the list: restrained, disciplined behavior—the ability to control one's impulses, desires, and emotions. Besides avoiding excess and vices, leaders must possess virtues that reflect positive, loving impulses, for example, hospitality (lit., "love of stranger" [*philoxenos*]). To require that one love goodness (*philagathos*) and be prudent (*sōphrōn*), upright (*dikaios*), and devout (*hosios*) identifies qualities highly prized within Hellenistic culture.[19]

425

Besides displaying exemplary character, elders must be staunchly devoted to the gospel, clinging to it as "the trustworthy message" (1:9 NIV) that has been faithfully taught.[20] With a firm grasp of the Christian tradition they can discharge their double responsibility of (1) giving encouragement that is anchored in sound instruction, and (2) refuting those who contradict such instruction (1:9). As active interpreters who have been shaped by the gospel because they engaged it seriously, elders can nurture the faith of believers.

Dealing with False Teachers (1:10–16). Typical of rhetoric that pillories religious or philosophical opponents, this description assails the character of those who threaten the stability of Pauline churches. Especially noteworthy is its lack of specificity. In Pauline letters dealing with opponents, such as Galatians and 2 Corinthians, a fairly clear sense of the issues being debated and a relatively distinct profile of Paul's opponents emerge. Even with all of its lively imagery, the sketch of opponents in Titus remains rather general. That these "rebellious people" upset "whole families" (1:10–11) and are rebuked so that they "may become sound in the faith" (1:13) suggests that they are Christian adversaries who, with the proper teaching, can be straightened out. Since they are singled out as "those of the circumcision" (1:10), their Jewish identity is clear (see Acts 10:45; 11:2; Rom 4:12; Col 4:11).

But what aspects of Jewish teaching or tradition actually threaten these Pauline churches is not explicit. "Jewish myths" is notoriously vague; even more vague is which "commandments" are being promoted (1:14). Later warnings to avoid "stupid controversies, genealogies, dissensions, and quarrels about the law" (3:9) suggest Torah-centered disputes, but, once again, the language is disconcertingly opaque. From the overall tone of the warning, it sounds as though the threat is a highly esoteric form of speculation about fascinating but, in the author's view, ultimately unanswerable questions that have no practical benefit and drain away energies that could be channeled in far more constructive ways.

Quoting the disparaging proverb about inhabitants of Crete, usually attributed to the eccentric "prophet" Epimenides of Crete (late seventh, possibly late sixth-century B.C.E.) but possibly drawn from the Hellenistic poet Callimachus of Cyrene (third century B.C.E.), aligns the false teachers more closely with the Cretan context but also presents them as acting in character (1:12). But what incriminates them is the inconsistency between their actions and their professed beliefs (1:16). In Titus, knowing God is not a process of endless speculation but a form of enacted character. If the Cretan caricature is any indication of the actions that disqualify them, genuine knowledge of God would produce the exact opposite: people who are truthful, virtuous, and disciplined.

Teaching What Is Consistent with Sound Doctrine (2:1–3:11). The moral emphasis of the remaining instructions implies that "sound doctrine" (*hygiainousa didaskalia*, 2:1) should be understood not as well-formulated, systematically thought-out theological doctrines, for example, the doctrine of the incarnation or the Trinity, but as wholesome instruction—moral teaching that promotes the church's spiritual health and well-being. This is not to suggest that moral conduct is detached from theological convictions. Quite the opposite. The moral instructions are firmly grounded in creedal formulations, thereby reinforcing the causal connection between beliefs and behaviors.

The scheme of moral duties employed here reflects the household codes found in other letters, in which moral duties are spelled out for constituent groups within the household and in which the pairings are based on hierarchical relationships: husbands and wives, fathers and children, masters and slaves (see Eph 5:21–6:9; Col 3:18–4:1; 1 Pet 2:13–3:7). Here the groupings are more loosely conceived, based on age, gender, and social status: older men (2:2), older women (2:3–5), younger women (2:4–5), younger men (2:6–8), and slaves (2:9–10). In this scheme, each group has distinctive duties, which are conceived independently of the other groups. To this extent, this schematization is not as rigorously hierarchical in its conception as the household codes in Colossians, Ephesians, and 1 Peter. Even so, the scheme presupposes hierarchical relationships that typified ancient Roman society, which means that some of the duties involve being submissive to other persons (2:5, 9). Responsibilities of slaves are conceived exclusively in hierarchical terms (2:9–10).

While each group has some distinctive obligations, the virtues commended reflect the best of Hellenistic moral values. As with the qualities expected of elders (1:5–9), restraint and self-control are a common thread (2:2, 5, 6). Aristotle's classic definition of temperance (*sōphrosynē*) aptly captures the overall tone: "the temperate person [*ho sōphrōn*] desires the right thing in the right way at the right time."[21] Establishing the framework of each set of duties are the three virtues singled out in 2:12—being self-controlled (*sōphrōn*), upright (*dikaios*), and godly (*eusebēs*). These are root values that are expressed in different ways.

The moral instructions outlined in 3:1–3 are more broadly applicable, yet their call for loyalty to civil authorities, respect for others, and general civility in relating to other people reflects the letter's overall concern for order and stability. They also reflect an awareness that the church has a role within the larger society. The qualities that contribute to stability within the church are critical ingredients in knitting the fabric of the larger society. Located at the center of these concluding instructions is the strategically placed creedal summary of 3:4–8, the "sure saying" that anchors the moral advice in confessional conviction. Cautioning against enervating disputes that distract the church from its central mission, the concluding advice in 3:8b–11 takes a hard line against people bent on causing division. Whatever threatens cohesion within the church should be studiously avoided.

Practicing Virtue: The Pursuit of Godliness

While the pursuit of "good works" may seem like a superficial way of visualizing the life of faith, in Titus it is a central ingredient, if not the overall goal, of discipleship (3:8, 14; cf. 2:7). The moral rectitude expected of church leaders, which is so visibly absent in the lives of the church's detractors, and which different groups within the church are urged to embody, is spelled out in impressive detail. In crisp, unequivocal terms, the qualities of life that characterize believers are enumerated, with very little attention given to intellectual or emotional struggles that often accompany moral decision-making. Instead, the advice is straightforward and given in undiluted doses.

The moral dynamic informing the Letter to Titus is sometimes seen as overly simplistic, devoid of any real depth or compelling appeal, but this way of reading Titus overlooks some vital dimensions of its ethic. For all of its emphasis on living a good life, the letter does not merely promote goodness. From the outset, the letter accents "godliness" (*eusebeia*, 1:1), a theme to which it returns (2:12).[22]

However noble the pursuit of goodness, it is not goodness alone but disciplined godliness that becomes the church's defining goal in Titus. [See Expanded CD Version pp. 604–5: *The Emphasis on Godliness in Titus*]

Paul's First Letter to Timothy: Preserving Paul's Legacy

Except for the mention of Paul's being en route to Macedonia, Timothy's location in Ephesus (1:3), and Paul's intention to rejoin Timothy at Ephesus (3:14; 4:13), the Letter of First Timothy is devoid of concrete details about its historical setting. Two lapsed Pauline followers are mentioned—Hymenaeus and Alexander—but their geographical location is not identified (1:20). With such a loose connection to a specific church, the letter should be read as a set of instructions outlining what is required to preserve Paul's legacy anywhere and at any time. Referring to Timothy as Paul's loyal follower and representative in the church at Ephesus may help pinpoint the historical situation envisioned in the letter, but its general tone and the broad applicability of its teachings made it a useful guidebook for Pauline disciples regardless of their location.

The letter reveals an extremely close bond between Paul and his "loyal child" Timothy (1:2; cf. 1:18). Apart from a reference to Timothy's ordination service (4:14; cf. 1:18) and his youth (4:12), we gain hardly any information about Timothy as a person. Even so, the letter presupposes knowledge of Timothy as a devotee of Paul and his connection with the church at Ephesus.[23]

Broadly speaking, the letter has two main divisions: (1) general instructions outlining what is required to preserve Pauline Christianity (1:3–4:5), and (2) the behavior expected of a minister representing Paul (4:6–6:19). These are bracketed by an epistolary greeting (1:1–2) and benediction (6:20–21).

What Is Required to Preserve Pauline Christianity

Paul's instructions in the first section of the letter develop six main themes: (1) recognizing threats to the Pauline gospel (1:3–11); (2) honoring Paul's example (1:12–20); (3) capturing the universal vision of Paul's gospel in worship (2:1–7); (4) clarifying gender roles in worship (2:8–15); (5) appointing responsible leaders (3:1–13); and (6) holding fast to the mystery of the faith (3:14–4:5).

Dealing with Detractors (1:3–11). What must be preserved at all costs is the "glorious gospel of the blessed God" that was entrusted to Paul (1:11). This alone forms the basis of "sound teaching" (*hygiainousa didaskalia*, 1:10). Another way of characterizing Paul's gospel is the unusual phrase "God's plan of redemption which is founded on faith" (NJB modified; *hē oikonomia theou en pistei*, 1:4).[24] The speculative "myths and endless genealogies" that threaten the pristine Pauline gospel are unspecified, although they have some connection to the Jewish law (1:7). Perhaps the opponents were fascinated with genealogical lore around certain OT figures that was preserved in such Jewish writings as *1 Enoch* or *Jubilees*. Most surprising, however, especially considering Paul's penetrating critique of the law in Galatians and Romans, is the positive view of the law expressed here. Its value is established on utilitarian grounds: it is good because it prevents egregious forms of socially destructive behavior (1:9–10). As a beneficial force within society, the law is aligned with Paul's gospel, which also has the same ends in view. Any would-be "teachers of the law" (1:7) must see that the law can be understood properly only when unobscured by confusing speculations. So understood, law and gospel are friends, not foes.

Paul the Exemplar (1:12–20). When Paul reflected on how he became an apostle, he recalled his earlier life as a persecutor of the church (Gal 1:13; 1 Cor 15:9; Phil 3:6). He could hardly think about the redirection of his life except as an experience of divine grace (1 Cor 15:9–10; cf. 3:10). If this image of violent persecutor tamed by God's mercy formed a central element of his memory of the past, it received unforgettably dramatic portrayal in the skillful hands of Luke (Acts 8:3; 9:1–19; 22:1–21; 26:2–23). This image is further enhanced here but in language uncharacteristic of Paul. Now he becomes the "chief of sinners" who epitomizes the goal of Christ's mission to the world and becomes a model for every potential convert (1:15–16). He becomes an example of the misdirected sinner, acting "ignorantly in unbelief" (1:13), to whom Christ's "utmost patience" (1:16) extends and who finally yields to God's overflowing grace. The only adequate response is gratitude (1:12) that bursts forth in praise (1:17). Paul's exemplary behavior encourages Timothy to "fight the good fight" and display similar "faith and a good conscience." It also serves as a counter-model for people like Hymenaeus and Alexander who, by "rejecting conscience," shipwreck their faith (1:18–20).

Although Paul was ordinarily reluctant to relate the circumstances of his apostolic call except when under attack, the story of his conversion became a solidifying element within Pauline Christianity. Pauline churches remembered Paul this way and even nurtured this memory as they sought to proclaim the Pauline gospel. Not only did Paul's conversion help counter negative images of Paul circulated by his enemies, but it also linked Paul's gospel with the memory of Paul himself.

Worship That Expresses the Universal Scope of Paul's Gospel (2:1–7). Chapter 2 can be read as instructions primarily about prayer and worship. Prayer is encouraged (2:1, 8), and liturgical prayer may even be in view, but the instructions serve a broader purpose. If there is a single concern expressed in this section, it is the universal scope of the gospel: "God our Savior . . . desires everyone to be saved and to come to the knowledge of the truth" (2:4). Every form of prayer should reflect this universal vision, which embraces everyone, beginning with "kings and all who are in high positions" (2:2). The creedal formulation in 2:5–6, with its crisp, confessional claim that "Christ Jesus . . . gave himself a ransom for all," provides the theological basis for this universal vision. The connection is clear: how the church prays should express what the church confesses. Paul's own example reinforces the point: as "teacher of the Gentiles" he embodied this universal vision. His apostleship expressed the universal scope of God's saving work that the church believes in, confesses, and prays for (2:7).

This universal vision has practical effects: Paul's legacy is best preserved when the implications of his gospel are fully understood and then translated into an effective mission. The universalism advocated here has a distinctive focus: the "one mediator . . . Christ Jesus." God's universal purpose embraces both Jews and Gentiles, and Christ is the effective means through which this purpose is achieved. Churches that adopt this mission and shape their lives together by this vision will embody the Pauline gospel. If this becomes the mission and vision of the church universal, Paul's gospel will become universalized.

Clarifying Gender Roles in Worship (2:8–15). These instructions seemingly clarify the respective liturgical roles of men and women within Pauline churches. But with such scant attention given to men's roles (2:8), the more pressing question was the role women should play within worship. Paul had already dealt with the question at Corinth, but even then his advice had broader implications for "all the churches of the saints" (1 Cor 14:33b–36). The tone and content of the instructions in 1 Timothy suggest that, if anything, the question had become more widespread and required a more definitive answer.

The focus of the discussion is probably worship.[25] Two main issues are addressed: what women should wear (2:9–10) and whether they should exercise a visible teaching role when the church met together (2:11–12). The advice given here, especially in response to the second question, is more restrictive and far-reaching than Paul's instructions in 1 Cor 11 and 14. This teaching has become especially problematic for today's church at a number of levels. Even if we strongly disagree with what is said here, we should nevertheless try to understand its logic.

Reflecting the overall tone of the letter, the advice in 2:9–10 emphasizes restraint and sobriety: women should dress "modestly and decently" (*meta aidous kai sōphrosynēs*; see Titus 1:8; 2:2, 5, 6, 12). Also reflecting the broader vision of the letter, "reverence for God" (*theosebeia*) is the overall moral aim (2:10). Still further, single-minded devotion to God is best expressed through "good works" (*erga agatha*). In view is the practice of virtue in its many, unspecified forms. The fundamental point of this uncomplicated vision of practical piety is clear: genuine devotion to God occurs through doing good, not by dressing well.[26]

The injunction that women should remain silent in the assembly conforms to Paul's advice in 1 Cor 14:33b–36, which already anticipates the emphasis here on "full submission" and the threat women teachers pose to men's authority. What is new, however, is the use of the creation story—Adam's being created before Eve, and Eve's transgression—to justify woman's submission to man as a permanent social role within liturgical settings.[27] Asserting that the woman "will be saved through childbearing" (2:15) creates a legitimate social role, but one linked to the household rather than the gathered community of faith. Her conduct must conform to the virtues of "faith, love, and holiness." "Modesty" (*sōphrosynē*), or moderation, establishes the broader moral horizon. Silence in worship and refraining from activities that threaten man's authority are commended as proper exercises of moral discipline.

The difficulties of seeing this teaching as a genuine expression of Pauline theology are well known. It contradicts his theological vision of union in Christ as a relationship that transcends ethnic, gender, and social boundaries (Gal 3:26–27; though cf. 1 Cor 11:3). It reinforces a hierarchical view of the world that has often taken demonic forms. In grappling with this difficult passage, interpreters should note two things. First, both parts of the advice are seen as expressions of *sōphrōsynē*—moderation—a cherished Hellenistic virtue embraced within this stream of the Pauline church. Second, roles are advanced that have biblical warrant. Apart from this highly problematic use of the Genesis story, the hermeneutical challenge is to honor both the appeal to a deeply rooted, widely honored virtue, on the one hand, and the appeal to Scripture for shaping appropriate behavior, on the other hand, recognizing that the concrete form this takes in a modern setting might be different.

Appointing Responsible Leaders (3:1–13). Compared with the Letter to Titus, which only envisions a group of elders who oversee a congregation (1:5–9), the leadership structure sketched here is more elaborate. Like the two-pronged polity of the church at Philippi (Phil 1:1), these instructions see bishops (*episkopoi*) and deacons (*diakonoi*) as separate roles. In the former role, one exercises general oversight as a servant leader; in the latter role, one exercises a particular ministry of service. [**See Expanded CD Version pp. 608–9: *The Roles of Elders and Deacons*]**

Holding Fast to the Mystery of Faith (3:14–4:5). This section is best read as the concluding section of the first part of the letter. Verse 15 is an apt summary of everything that has preceded. All the instructions to this point will assist Timothy, and by extension, all Pauline churches, in knowing "how one ought to behave in the household of God, which is the church of the living God, the pillar and bulwark of the truth" (3:15). But these instructions are read too narrowly as mere protocols for worship. They are instructions to guide the general conduct of Pauline churches. Worth noting is how the household (*oikos*) is a metaphor for the church. Both here and in the Letter to Titus the Roman household supplies analogies for ecclesial practice. Also worth noting are the vivid architectural metaphors "pillar" and "bulwark," which carried particular weight with inhabitants of the Aegean surrounded by Greek and Roman buildings. Such metaphors had powerful stabilizing effect: the church, whose foundation is the Pauline gospel and that is nurtured through these instructions, is a firm structure that houses the faith and ensures its permanence. [**See Expanded CD Version pp. 609–10: *The Critical Elements of the Faith: Paul's Creedal Summary*]**

What Is Required of Ministers of the (Pauline) Gospel

For the most part, the instructions in the second half of the letter (4:6–6:19) are couched in the second person singular. They express what is required for Timothy, and, by extension, any minister among the Pauline churches, to be a "good servant of Christ Jesus" (4:6). Much of the instruction is personal advice directed to Timothy himself. It includes seemingly mundane advice pertaining to his physical health (5:23), but more attention is given to the pursuit of godliness (*eusebeia*), a recurrent theme (1 Tim 4:7, 8; 6:3, 5, 6, 11; cf. 5:4; also Titus 1:1; 2:12). At the center of Timothy's spiritual formation is undiluted commitment to "the faith" (*hē pistis*), core convictions repeated in the several creedal summaries in the letter (1 Tim 2:5–6; 3:16; cf. 1:17; 4:10; 6:7–8, 15–16), and the "sound teaching" (*hygiainousa didaskalia*, 4:6) that amplifies this faith. Timothy's ordination was a defining moment when his gifts were formally recognized by prophetic discernment within the council of elders (4:14). The vocational formation that began at his ordination is a gradual process that must be carefully nurtured (4:15). Such formation occurs within the regular performance of his ministerial duties—exhortation, teaching, and the reading of Scripture in worship (4:13). His personal demeanor must also exhibit qualities of life that reflect his maturity and make his ministry credible (4:12, 16). Also required is knowing how to fit one's speech to different audiences and occasions in a manner reflecting pure motives (5:1–2).

Ministers must also attend to various groups within the church, including widows (5:3–16), elders (5:17–19), and slaves (6:1–2). The minister must know when to rebuke sinful behavior (5:20) and must, like a good judge, discharge one's duties impartially (5:21). Prudence means not ordaining other ministers prematurely (5:22) and sorting out the difference between sins and good works (5:24–25).

Returning to the threat posed by false teachers introduced earlier, these personal instructions also call for a vision of godliness (*eusebeia*, 6:3) based on "the sound words of our Lord Jesus Christ" (6:3). Godliness so conceived will be refined enough, and deep enough, to enable the minister to spot useless disputes and the ill motives that often prompt them (6:4–5). Ministers must see the difference between godliness and financial gain, recognize the distorting quality of wealth, and understand the truth of the proverb, "the love of money is a root of all kinds of evil" (6:10). Ministers, in other words, must negotiate their way through false teachers and false gods.

These instructions are aptly summarized in the concluding summary of 6:11–16. Timothy, the "man of God," is urged to pursue "righteousness, godliness, faith, love, endurance, gentleness" (6:11). The basis of his call is the "good confession" that he made at his ordination, whose essential elements are rehearsed in the creedal summary (6:13–16). The eventual "manifestation of our Lord Jesus Christ," the Parousia (6:14), determines the horizon within which all ministry is carried out. The God who is confessed in such liturgically resonant terms establishes the Presence before whom ministry is actually done (6:15–16). The concluding instructions sound like words of benediction the minister pronounces over the congregation (6:17–19). They ask the congregation to orient its life according to the same standards that have been set for the "good servant of Christ Jesus."

Paul's Second Letter to Timothy:
Passing the Torch; Moral Exhortation as Testament

Second Timothy exhibits the following epistolary structure: an opening greeting (1:1–2), the body of the letter (1:3–4:8), concluding instructions and reassurances (4:9–18), and final greetings and benediction (4:19–22). Within the body of the letter are three main sections: (1) an initial statement of Paul's appeal to Timothy (1:3–18); (2) a series of exhortations elaborating his initial appeal (2:1–3:9); and (3) a restatement of the appeal and Paul's final charge to Timothy (3:10–4:8).

Rather than unfolding in neatly contained units, each of the main sections is somewhat loosely constructed. Even so, certain recurrent themes emerge and an overall logic can be detected. The first main section begins with an elaboration of Paul's close personal relationship with Timothy (1:3–7). This carefully crafted recollection of Paul's close ties with Timothy forms the basis of the following appeal (1:8–18), in which Timothy is urged to reaffirm his allegiance to Paul's gospel. The object of his allegiance is twofold: (1) "the testimony about our Lord," in other words, the content of Paul's gospel, which is elaborated in the creedal summary (1:9–10), and (2) Paul himself, the Lord's prisoner (1:8), whose impeccable credentials are rehearsed (1:11–12). Urged to remain loyal to Paul (1:13–14), Timothy is given contrasting examples of disloyalty (1:15) and loyalty (1:16–18) by which to measure his own conduct.

The miscellaneous exhortations in the second main section range from short pieces of advice to longer clusters of advice gathered around certain themes. Here, Timothy is given the following imperatives: (1) faithfully transmit the sacred tradition he had received (2:1–2); (2) like a good soldier, athlete, or farmer, be fully committed to suffer on behalf of the larger enterprise (2:3–7); (3) emulate the way Paul embodied the gospel (2:8–13); (4) exercise discernment in weighing and using words (2:14–21); (5) shun youthful passions and pursue virtuous behavior (2:22); (6) avoid useless quarrels (2:23–26); and (7) avoid false teachers (3:1–9).

In the final section, the overall appeal is restated (3:10–17) in order to undergird the final solemn charge to Timothy to be a faithful, responsible evangelist (4:1–5) who remembers the endurance and fidelity of Paul (4:6–8).

Paul's Testament as a Letter of Exhortation

Second Timothy is written as a personal letter from Paul to Timothy his "beloved child" (1:2). The overall tone of the letter is set by Paul's imprisonment (1:16; 2:9) and the prospect of his impending "departure" (4:6), which prompt him to review his life as he confidently faces an uncertain future (4:7–8). Timothy is the faithful disciple in whose hands the future of Paul's legacy rests. As one personally ordained by Paul to the ministry, Timothy has been carefully nurtured in the ways of the Pauline gospel. Now that Paul's death is imminent, Timothy is the carrier of the Pauline tradition who is responsible for transmitting it faithfully to the next generation of disciples. The combination of these elements—Paul's impending death, his preview of the future even as he reviews the past, and his preoccupation with preserving his legacy—results in a farewell letter in the form of a testament. In this well-known literary genre, the aged letter writer typically gives advice to prospective heirs. Such advice can include positive exhortations to ensure that the accomplishments and values of the writer will continue. It can also include warnings that envision threats and opposition to the writer's legacy. The addressee is urged to pursue the former while avoiding the latter.

By their very nature, testaments place a high premium on the transmission of moral values. Reflecting this emphasis, 2 Timothy contains many elements typically found in paraenetic letters, in which exhortation draws heavily on what is already known and adduces examples of commendable moral behavior. When these paraenetic elements are cast in the form of a testament, the one bidding farewell becomes the exemplar of the virtues to be preserved. Also typical of paraenetic letters is carefully crafted hortatory language designed to strengthen the already close bond between writer and addressee. In such letters, where the legacy being transmitted is moral rather than financial or material, moral suasion matters more than anything else.

Appeal to the Familiar. Especially prominent in 2 Timothy are frequent appeals to remember certain things. Paul's memory of Timothy and the personal memory that shaped Timothy's faith through his mother Eunice and grandmother Lois are prominently mentioned at the outset, thus setting the tone for the letter (1:3–5). Timothy's memory of his own ordination by Paul also becomes a resource for renewed moral strength (1:6–7).

If there is a single focus for Timothy's memory, it is most succinctly expressed in 2:8: "Remember Jesus Christ, raised from the dead, a descendant of David." "That," Paul assures Timothy, is "my gospel." While this formulaic memory is expected to stick with Timothy, its behavioral implications are amplified in the "sure saying" that follows (2:11–13). The extent of Timothy's creedal memory is broadened by the fuller summary of the Pauline gospel in verses 9–10. What is believed and confessed anchors Timothy's faith. Because these core memories have received further elaboration in the "sound teaching" that Timothy has received from Paul (1:13–14), the sacred tradition containing these teachings is also to be remembered. Likewise, sacred Scripture should inform Timothy's memory (3:15–16).

When Timothy is encouraged to "continue in what you have learned and firmly believed, knowing from whom you learned it" (3:14), he is reminded of the value of what he already knows: Jesus proclaimed in the gospel and confessed in worship, the sacred tradition through which this faith is nurtured and transmitted, and the sacred text that informs the understanding of both Jesus and the tradition. This reminder also signals the importance of those who have transmitted the tradition, most notably Timothy's own spiritual father and teacher, Paul himself.

Moral Examples. Throughout the letter, the moral exhortations to Timothy are closely intertwined with appeals to Paul's own exemplary behavior. Paul's exhortation that Timothy should not be ashamed of the gospel (1:8) is grounded in his own unashamed embrace of the gospel and the firm confidence in God that it has given him (1:12). Timothy is invited to become a fellow sufferer with Paul in the gospel (1:8; 2:3; 4:5), but this invitation is given credibility by Paul's own willingness to "suffer hardship" (1:12; 2:9) and "endure everything" (2:10). Timothy is also invited to adopt images that have shaped Paul's own self-understanding—good soldier (2:3; cf. 4:7), good athlete (2:5; cf. 4:7), and faithful evangelist (4:5; cf. 1:11).

What gives Paul's exhortations special force is Timothy's close-range experience with Paul. It is not as though Paul's exemplary behavior is merely a literary portrait that Timothy is expected to emulate. Rather, Paul's behavior has been displayed visibly before Timothy in a wide range of settings. "Now you have observed my teaching," he writes, "my conduct, my aim in life, my faith, my patience, my love, my steadfastness, my persecutions and suffering the things that happened to me in Antioch, Iconium, and Lystra" (3:10–11).

While Paul's example provides the primary mold for shaping Timothy's behavior, other examples are given as well. The opening appeal inviting Timothy to be firm in his allegiance to Paul is buttressed by two contrasting examples (1:15–18). Phygelus and Hermogenes symbolize disloyalty and stand in sharp contrast to Onesiphorus, who epitomizes true loyalty. The latter's extreme devotion is reflected in the lengths to which he went to find Paul and alleviate his suffering. A similar pattern of exemplifying both positive and negative behaviors is seen throughout the letter: the apostates Hymenaeus and Philetus (2:17); their earlier counterparts Jannes and Jambres, who opposed Moses (3:8); the deserter Demas (4:10), and perhaps Crescens and Titus as well (4:10); the opponent Alexander the coppersmith (4:14–15); and the several loyalists mentioned at the letter's conclusion, beginning with Luke, Paul's sole companion at the time of writing (4:11–13, 19–21).

Moral Instructions. Although miscellaneous moral instructions cluster within the second main section (2:1–3:9), they occur throughout the letter. They are easily spotted as clear directives, usually expressed as imperatives. Typical of such instruction is the exhortation in 2:22: "Shun youthful passions and pursue righteousness, faith, love, and peace, along with those who call on the Lord from a pure heart." Self-discipline (*sōphronismos*, 1:7), sexual restraint, pure motives, and active pursuit of well-known virtues establish the moral horizon of the letter. False teachers who threaten to undermine the faith are portrayed in vivid detail as the complete antithesis of these values (3:2–4). Their general moral failure is their inconsistent practice: they profess godliness (*eusebeia*), but their lives betray their real values (3:5).

Also prominent is an emphasis on fidelity to the tradition and steadfast endurance (2:10–13; 3:14; 4:2, 5, 7, 17–18). One of the overarching concerns of the letter is the moral instruction related to speech. Since false teaching receives such prominent attention, there are the expected warnings against "wrangling over words" (2:14) and "stupid and senseless controversies" (2:23). Many of these warnings reflect the standard boilerplate used to pillory opponents, but especially emphasized is the connection between how one speaks and how one lives. Timothy's capacity to "rightly explain the word of truth" is a function of his moral character. The implication is that his ability to interpret the gospel meaningfully and credibly derives from his moral standing before God (2:15). By contrast, the case of Hymenaeus and Philetus, who claim that "the resurrection has already taken place" (2:18), is seen not merely as doctrinal deviance but as a moral failure deriving from intellectual laziness. Their misconstrual of the resurrection reflects a failure of language with profound moral consequences (2:16–19). While portraying the victims of false teachers as "silly women" (3:6) reinforces stereotypes that offend us, linking "corrupt minds" with "counterfeit faith" also implies that enduring patterns of faith can only derive from disciplined patterns of thinking and speaking. What is finally exposed is the "folly" (*anoia*, lit., "mindlessness") of false teachers (3:9).

The appeals to Scripture within 2 Timothy should be seen within this broader framework. The "sacred writings" are not only "inspired by God" but also the most valuable resource for moral instruction relating to "salvation through faith in Christ Jesus" (3:15–16). Over against the fickleness of false teachers stands the clear testimony of Scripture (2:19; the OT passages quoted are Num 16:5 and probably a combination of Job 36:10 and Isa 26:13). [See **Expanded CD Version pp. 614–15:** *Pauline Christianity as Envisioned in 2 Timothy*]

The Theological Vision of the Pastorals

The Pastoral Letters are often seen as theologically arid, devoid of any real spiritual vitality or compelling moral urgency. Since Paul's name is attached to them, they are often measured alongside the other Pauline letters and found wanting. Many have viewed their preoccupation with matters of church order and stability as the nemesis of dynamic faith. Quite the contrary is true. All three letters are steeped in the language of faith, and much of this language bears the imprint of Paul's gospel. And yet we also hear occasional echoes in the Pastorals from other streams of early Christian tradition, suggesting that the Pauline gospel has been expanded to embrace the wider church.

Frequent creedal summaries punctuate all three letters. Some are fairly extensive and formally distinctive (1 Tim 2:5–6; 3:16; 4:9–10; Titus 2:11–14; 3:4–7; 2 Tim 1:9–10; 2:11–13), while others are less so (Titus 1:1–3; 2 Tim 2:8). The manner in which they are interwoven throughout the letters is far from wooden. Whether they elaborate an opening greeting, reinforce some image of Paul, or constitute the basis for extended instructions, these carefully placed summaries reveal the world of faith in which the letters operate.

Throughout the letters we detect a consistent distinction between these core convictions of the faith, sometimes simply referred to as "the faith," and teachings (*didaskalia*) elaborating that faith. This distinction surfaces clearly when Paul instructs the elders to hold fast to "the sound teaching that conforms to the glorious gospel of the blessed God" (1 Tim 1:10–11). Here the gospel is a centering force that must be faithfully taught, but around which a body of "sound teaching" develops to provide the basis for exhortation. This same distinction also surfaces in Paul's advice that Timothy be "nourished on the words of the faith and of the sound teaching [he has] followed" (1 Tim 4:6).[28] The distinction may appear slight, but it is real. With this distinction between first order convictions and second order reflection, we are witnessing the birth of doctrine. Since the foundational convictions expressed in the creedal summaries have authority, they are properly designated as normative faith. By extension, the "sound teaching" that amplifies these core convictions also acquires normative force.

Four aspects of the theological outlook of the Pastorals can be noted: (1) the gospel as foundational truth and normative faith; (2) the churches' strategy for dealing with doctrinal deviations; (3) ordering the church's life; and (4) salvation understood as instruction (*paideia*).

Paul's Gospel as Foundational Truth and Normative Faith

So grounded are the Pastorals in the church's faith that certain truths of the gospel acquire an a priori quality. That "Christ came into the world to save sinners" is so self-evident as to need no further demonstration. Another truism is that "everything created by God is good." Such bold assertions spring from deep levels of confidence in the church's faith. Their forthrightness and unqualified character suggest convictions that have been sharpened and internalized by frequent repetition. The clarity of such claims is itself revealing. These are firmly held, non-negotiable convictions that establish a core identity for believers.

The core set of beliefs is never spelled out clearly, although the creedal formulations provide a rough outline. It goes under different names: "gospel" (1 Tim 1:11; 2 Tim 1:8, 10; 2:8), perhaps "word of God" (2 Tim 2:9; 4:2; Titus 1:3, 9), "word of truth" (2 Tim 2:15), "mystery of the faith" (1 Tim 3:9; cf. 3:16), or even "faith that is in Christ Jesus" (1 Tim 3:13). These core beliefs possibly included some of Jesus' own teachings, depending on what we make of "the sound words of our Lord Jesus Christ" that are distinguished from "the teaching that is in accordance with godliness" (1 Tim 6:3). Whether the "standard of sound teaching" (2 Tim 1:13) that Timothy had heard from Paul refers to Paul's own ministerial conduct or to a more fully developed framework of teaching is unclear. The latter seems more likely, but the ambiguous language suggests that the line between "words of faith" and "words of instruction about the faith" is blurred. However fluid the boundary between gospel and teaching about the gospel in the Pastorals, they frequently mention "the faith" and "the truth."[29] These expressions acquire a technical meaning and designate a set of beliefs that constitute a normative body of teachings that define and demarcate the church's faith.

Whether understood in its narrow sense—the faith of the gospel—or in a broader sense—the "sound teaching" based on the faith—"the faith" gives structure to the theological outlook of the Pastorals. While no single, definitive statement of "the faith" is given, its outlines are clear enough. It has a distinctive Pauline flavor, and at times the Pauline version of the gospel is seen as the purest expression of the faith. And yet, "the faith" heralded in the Pastorals reaches beyond Paul to embrace early catholic Christianity. Now that the faith has become normative, it establishes the church's center of gravity. Or, to use the Pastorals' own metaphor, the church is now the "pillar and bulwark of the truth" (1 Tim 3:15).

Since "the faith" shapes and stabilizes the church, its transmission and preservation receive special attention in the Pastorals. Far from being a formalized set of beliefs that are simply recited or even defended, "the faith" has an inescapably human dimension. It takes shape in grandmother Lois, mother Eunice, and child Timothy; in Paul the teacher and Timothy the disciple; in Timothy the evangelist and those faithful disciples to whom he hands it on. "The faith" is taught, nurtured, lived, and shared. Paul and Titus are joined by "the faith [they] share" (Titus 1:4). These human impulses give rise to its defense. Since we defend ardently what we cherish most, we understand why the Pastorals are so fiercely protective of "the faith." Reflecting a coldly realistic sense about what threatens "the faith," the Pastorals assume that defense is a prerequisite to survival.

Dealing with Deviance and Dissent

One indicator of the faith's normative status is the metaphors used to signal opposition and dissent. Opponents can "deviate" (or swerve) from the faith (1 Tim 1:6; 2 Tim 2:18); they can "turn away" (2 Tim 1:15), "oppose" (2 Tim 3:8), "renounce" (1 Tim 4:1), or refuse to "put up with sound doctrine" (2 Tim 4:3); they can "miss the mark" (1 Tim 6:21) or even shipwreck their faith (1 Tim 1:19–20). While "another gospel" (Gal 1:6–9) is not used of the opposition, they are said to "teach other things" (1 Tim 1:3). Such language only makes sense when some definable body of normative teaching is presupposed.

Because references to opponents are scattered throughout the letters, it is difficult to tell whether the faith is being threatened by a single, coherent theological position. Regardless of the vague contours of the threat, the Pastorals' strategy for dealing with deviance and dissent is clear. More than anything else, it is a strategy of caricature and dismissal. There is little head-on argumentation, in which issues are identified and then debated. Would-be teachers of the law are given a crash course in what the law is really about, and ascetics who impose food restrictions are told that all of God's creation is good. Such brief responses do not really join the fight, much less allow for any real argument. Instead, the Pastorals display a palpable distaste for debate that quells the spirit of controversy. In their view, nothing is gained by pursuing truth through argument since this only leads to quarrels and division, and nothing is ever finally settled (see 1 Tim 6:4–5; 2 Tim 2:14, 23–26; Titus 3:9).

This same straight-arrow mentality is at play elsewhere in the Pastorals. Hierarchical structures both within society and the church are not only recognized but also honored. Kings, princes, and those in high places must be honored, respected, and obeyed. Utilitarian motives for doing so are transparently clear: to ensure a quiet, peaceful existence. Just as caricatures are used to shape the images of opponents, so do they contribute to the superficial portrait of women in the Pastorals. The same impulse that silences opponents also silences women into subjection. Even men are urged to pray, not so much to honor God, but to suppress anger and argument. Slaves too are expected to be obedient to their masters. Within these hierarchical structures, however, there is room for mutuality of relationships. The world of the Pastorals not only allows for but also invites spontaneous generosity. Not every duty must be prescribed.

A truly authoritarian spirit pervades the Pastorals, even if it derives from a good source. Creedal clarity may produce an enviable confidence that is necessary to make a place for the church's faith within the larger society. The presence of mean-spirited detractors constantly nipping at the heels of orthodox teachers justifies taking a hard line against them, even to the point of being dismissive of them. And yet, this spirit of confident orthodoxy is purchased at a price. While this strategy of dealing with dissent may appeal to some, its limitations are obvious.

Ordering the Church's Life

An organizational impulse informs the Pastorals. Perhaps the single most revealing image of the church is the "household of God" (1 Tim 3:15). True to the Roman domestic household, with its extended family and complex network of relationships, the church is an institution with clearly differentiated roles and responsibilities. In contrast to other NT writings, household codes do not provide a rigid framework for delineating the duties of various groups. Even so, people are grouped loosely according to age, gender, marital, and social status. The church is not an organic collection of charismatic ministries in which differently gifted people work together toward a common purpose (see 1 Cor 12 and Rom 12). Nor is it a hierarchy of ministries consisting of apostles, prophets, evangelists, pastors, and teachers (Eph 4:11–13). Instead, the most visible roles are occupied by elders/bishops, deacons, and ministers who provide leadership within local congregations.

Rather than delineating the responsibilities of elders/bishops and deacons, the Pastorals enumerate the qualities of life they should possess. Drawing on Hellenistic values, these lists place a high premium on sobriety, restraint, and respect for others. Sketching such character profiles is more valuable than giving procedures for selecting such persons.

Guidelines for conduct mostly take the form of directives—straightforward, unqualified advice about how to behave and think. While most of the directives are instructions to Paul's co-workers Timothy and Titus, they also extend to the church as well. Subgroups within the church may be singled out for particular instructions, or the church as a whole may be in view. Some attention is given to protocols for worship, which are neither extensive nor detailed. The space devoted to caring for widows suggests a complicated situation that requires widows to be classified into groups based on demonstrated need. The lengthy instructions bring order to the church's life by asking families to assume responsibilities that rightly belong to them and by requiring widows themselves to display responsible conduct. Plenty of attention is given to dealing with opponents and detractors, even to the point of shaping future expectations to guard against external threats.

Seeking to ensure that the church's faith will be transmitted faithfully to future generations, the Pastorals reflect a consistent concern for order, stability, and continuity. Since ministers like Timothy will bear the main responsibility for carrying out these directives, he must exercise caution about whom he ordains. It helps to recall what a defining moment his own ordination was. To perpetuate the Pauline gospel, the Pastorals present a well-honed image of the memory of Paul, a heroic figure, who is portrayed with a certain grandiosity. The entire story of salvation history came to its rightful culmination in the gospel Paul preaches (Titus 1:3). He is its "herald, apostle, and teacher," and no other collaborators are envisioned apart from the circle of co-workers whom Paul has gathered around himself. Timothy is urged to be ashamed neither of the Lord nor of Paul himself, almost as if they were equal objects of loyalty.

Salvation through Moral Education: Christian Paideia

Timothy is urged to pursue "instruction in righteousness" (*paideia en dikaiosynē*, 2 Tim 3:16). In a similar vein, God's grace was manifested for the purpose of instructing (*paideuousa*) recipients of divine grace in how to live morally (Titus 2:12–13). "Sound instruction" (*hygiainousa didaskalia*) or similar expressions become something of a mantra in the Pastorals. While translators frequently render the phrase "sound doctrine," this suggests a higher degree of doctrinal formulation than was likely present during the first century. Probably in view are teachings that elaborate certain theological beliefs, for example, insistence that the resurrection of believers has not already occurred but remains a future possibility. The "sound instructions" in Titus 2 relate to behaviors rather than beliefs.

When scholars speak of the Pastorals' unusual interest in practical piety, they usually mean the repeated mention of "good works" as the goal of Christian living. Doing good, which is a stated priority of the Pastorals, can take such concrete forms as caring for widows and providing for one's household. Failure to do the latter is equivalent to apostasy and renders one worse than an unbeliever.

How the gospel is actually lived constitutes one of the overarching themes of the Pastorals. Living the gospel occurs through education. The believer's life story is closely correlated with the gospel story. Young wives must be subject to their husbands to keep the word of God (probably the gospel) from being discredited (Titus 2:5). Slaves should display obedient behavior "so that in everything they may be an ornament to the doctrine of God our Savior" (Titus 2:10). Since moral renewal is a function of God's saving work, it is possible to speak of the moral effects of the gospel. Merely recalling life prior to receiving the gospel and the sense of desperation that accompanied it calls to mind the grand narrative of God's saving action through Christ. It is in this sense that the Pastorals construe salvation as a form of Christian *paideia*. One manifests God's saving grace by displaying the palpable effects it brings about: renouncing "impiety and worldly passions" and pursuing "lives that are self-controlled, upright, and godly'" (Titus 2:12).

By speaking of the life of faith as "godliness" (*eusebeia*), the Pastorals reveal the close connection between devotion to God and the practice of goodness. A common expression in Hellenistic religion, *eusebeia* means "life devoted to the gods." Such a life was expected to be morally exemplary. In the Pastorals, "sound instruction" is essential to achieving such devotion. When the full force of the health metaphor is recognized, such instruction is seen as wholesome. If false teaching is gangrene, fidelity to the gospel is enjoying full health. It may even be worth recalling that the Greek word "save" (*sōzō*) could also mean "heal." If this therapeutic dimension of the word family is given full play, salvation may mean experiencing eternal life but also wholeness in this life.

Seen in this larger context, the Pastorals' insistence that believers must have a good conscience, pure hearts, and a sincere faith takes the discussion of morality beyond external forms of behavior to underlying motives. By no means do the Pastorals probe the psyche, but neither do they ignore motivations for behavior. The Pastorals understand the dynamics of wealth and the urge to acquire possessions well enough to display a healthy skepticism toward the accumulation of riches. It may be proverbial wisdom to observe that the "love of money is a root of all kinds of evil" (1 Tim 6:10; cf. 1 Tim 3:3; 2 Tim 3:2), but by citing it the Pastorals pinpoint a motivation universally recognized as sinister.

It would be claiming too much to suggest that the Pastorals offer a comprehensive moral vision. They do not. But neither can their outlook be easily dismissed as a bourgeois ethic. Much of their moral teaching takes the form of directives, but they are not completely devoid of subtlety. Practical piety is understood as "good works," but the Pastorals do not confuse godliness and goodness. Rather than being acquired through human effort, goodness flows from genuine devotion to God, prompted by the transforming experience of God's goodness and mercy. "Instruction in righteousness" does not occur automatically, much less casually. Instead, it is a process of formation carefully nurtured over time. The church, with its differentiated roles and responsibilities, is the context in which such nurturing can occur. As the locus of salvation, the church also serves as the instrument of *paideia*. [**See Expanded CD Version pp. 620–25: *The Core Theological Vision* and *Widows*]**

Notes

1. Although Philemon was also addressed to Apphia, Archippus, and the "church in [Philemon's] house" (vv. 1–2), it was thought of as a letter to an individual. The current canonical arrangement (1–2 Timothy followed by Titus) and the placement of the Pastorals before Philemon is regularly found in early canonical lists, although there are some exceptions. In the Muratorian Fragment (ca. 200 C.E.), the four letters to individuals follow the letters to churches, but the two single letters are mentioned first (Philemon, Titus), then the two letters to Timothy.

2. *Marc.* 5.21. This same sentiment is reflected in the Muratorian Fragment, which is quoted above: ". . . *in honore tamen ecclesiae catholicae, in ordinatione ecclesiasticae disciplinae sanctificatae sunt.*"

3. *In Omnes S. Pauli Apostoli Epistolas Commentaria* (Turin: Marietti, 1929), 2:183–258, esp. p. 184.

4. *S. Pauli Apostoli Epistolas Commentaria*, 2:230.

5. In 1726–1727 Paul Anton delivered lectures at the University of Halle, which J. A. Maier edited and published in 1753–1755 under the title "Exegetical Treatment of the Pastoral Letters of Paul (Pastoral-Briefe Pauli) to Timothy and Titus." But Anton did not limit the term "pastoral" to these three letters. He also thought of the seven letters to the churches of Asia in Rev 2–3 in the same way, since they offered equally useful instructions for those exercising pastoral leadership of churches.

6. Faint echoes are heard around 96 C.E. in *1 Clem.* 1.3 (Titus 2:4, 5); 2.7 (Titus 3:1); 34.4 (2 Tim 2:21; 3:17). Stronger echoes are heard in Ignatius (ca. 35–107 C.E.), bishop of Antioch. Knowledge of 1 Tim 1:3–5 appears to be reflected in *Eph.* 14.1; *Magn.* 8.1. There are also possible reminiscences of 1 Tim 1:1 in *Eph.* 21.2; *Magn.* 11; *Trall.* 2.2; *Phld.* 5.2; 11.2 and of 2 Tim 1:16 in *Smyrn.* 10.2. It is also possible that *Magn.* 8.1 echoes Titus 1:14; 3:9, and that *Pol.* 4.3 reflects knowledge of 1 Tim 6:2. Fainter echoes appear elsewhere: *Rom.* 9.2 (1 Tim 1:13); *Eph.* 17.1 (2 Tim 3:6); *Trall.* 7.2 (2 Tim 1:3); *Rom.* 2.2 (2 Tim 4:6); *Pol.* 6.1 (Titus 1:7). Some echoes are also heard in *Barn.* 5.6 (1 Tim 3:16; 2 Tim 1:9–10); 5.9 (1 Tim 1:15); 7.2 (2 Tim 4:1). We are on much firmer ground when we come to Polycarp (ca. 69–155 C.E.), bishop of Smyrna: *Phil.* 4.1 appears to reflect 1 Tim 6:10 and 6:7, though it may be drawing on widely known proverbial material (Polycarp does not attribute the material to any source); *Phil.* 9.2 may reflect knowledge of 2 Tim 4:10. Other possibilities include: *Phil.* 4.3 (cf. 1 Tim 5:5); 5.2 (cf. 1 Tim 3:8; 2 Tim 2:12); 8.1 (1 Tim 1:1); 11.4 (2 Tim 2:25); 12.3 (1 Tim 2:1–2). More remote possibilities: *Phil.* 6.3 (cf. Titus 2:14); 11.2 (1 Tim 3:5); 9.2 (2 Tim 4:10); 12.1 (2 Tim 1:5); 12.3 (1 Tim 4:15). There are some possible echoes in the *Epistle to the Apostles* (last quarter of the second century C.E.); thus, *Ep. Apos.* 3 (1 Tim 6:15); 16 (2 Tim 4:1); 38 (1 Tim 2:7); 39 (Titus 1:16). First Timothy 3:16 may be reflected in *Diogn.* 11.3, which dates to the second, and possibly the third, century. While each of these instances should be weighed carefully, it is highly probable that Polycarp knew 1–2 Timothy. Evidence that *1 Clement*, Ignatius, and *Epistle to the Apostles* knew the Pastorals is much weaker.

7. In the late second century 1 Tim 2:2 is quoted as the "divine word" by Theophilus (*Autol.* 3.14, also echoing Titus 3:1 and quoting Rom 13:7–8); it is also quoted by Athenagoras, *Leg.* 37.1 (ca. 177 C.E.). The Pastorals are cited several times as Pauline texts by Irenaeus (ca. 130–200 C.E.) in his refutation of heresies (*Haer.* Pref. 1 [1 Tim 1:4]; 1.16.3 [Titus 3:10]; 2.14.7 [1 Tim 6:20]; 3.3.3 [2 Tim 4:21]; 3.3.4 [Titus 3:10]; 3.14.1 [2 Tim 4:10–11]; cf. 4.16.3 [1 Tim 1:9]; 5.17.1 [1 Tim 2:5]). They are included among the Pauline writings in the Muratorian Fragment (ca. 200 C.E.). Tertullian (ca. 160–225 C.E.) cites them as authoritative Pauline writings (e.g., *Ux.* 1.7; cf. 1 Tim 3:2; 5:9; Titus 1:6; also cf. *Praescr.* 6 & 7; cf. Titus 3:10–11). According to Eusebius (ca. 260–340 C.E.), the Roman presbyter Gaius (early third century) accepted thirteen Pauline letters, excluding Hebrews (see *Hist. eccl.* 6.20.3); also cf. Jerome, *Vir. ill.* 59.

8. $\mathfrak{P}^{46}$ contains extended portions of Romans, Hebrews, 1–2 Corinthians, Ephesians, Galatians, Philippians, Colossians, and 1 Thessalonians, but is incomplete from that point forward. Since

1 Thessalonians is identified as such, the original manuscript likely included 2 Thessalonians. There appears to have been no room in the unpreserved portion of the papyrus to have included Philemon and the Pastorals, although this is debated. Possibly the manuscript only included Pauline letters (including Hebrews) to churches, thus explaining the absence of Philemon and the Pastorals. The Pastorals are also absent from the fourth-century uncial manuscript Vaticanus (B), an incomplete manuscript that breaks off in the middle of the Letter to the Hebrews and thus lacks everything from Heb 9:14 onward: 1–2 Timothy, Titus, Philemon, and Revelation.

9. *Marc.* 5.21. Had Marcion known the Pastorals, presumably he could have edited them by removing portions that he regarded as offensive, e.g., 1 Tim 1:8. Moreover, if the later Marcionite churches accepted the Pastorals, as seems likely since some manuscripts contain "Marcionite prologues" to the Pastorals, their acceptance is easier to explain if Marcion, rather than rejecting them outright, did not know them at all. Some scholars who date the Pastorals well into the second century even suggest that they might have been written to refute Marcion.

10. *Strom.* 2.11. Origen also reports that some rejected 2 Timothy (*Comm. ser. Matt.* 117; Migne PG 13:1769c).

11. *Comm. Tit.* Prologue.

12. *Hist. eccl.* 3.3.5.

13. Of the total number of separate vocabulary words (excluding proper names) used in the Pastorals, over one-third occur in none of the other ten letters attributed to Paul.

14. Roughly 20 percent of the total vocabulary in the Pastorals does not occur elsewhere in the NT.

15. The more prominent instances will be treated below, e.g., *eusebeia*, "piety" or "religion" and *hygiainō*, "be sound" or "be healthy." Other examples of terms used in the Pastorals but not in the other Pauline letters include: "myth" (*mythos*, 1 Tim 1:4; 4:7; 2 Tim 4:4; Titus 1:14); "genealogy" (*genealogia*, 1 Tim 1:4; Titus 3:9); "deny" (*arneomai*, 1 Tim 5:8; 2 Tim 2:12, 13; 3:5; Titus 1:16; 2:12); "lord" (*despotēs*, 1 Tim 6:1, 2; 2 Tim 2:21; Titus 2:9); "avoid" (*paraiteomai*, 1 Tim 4:7; 5:11; 2 Tim 2:23; Titus 3:10); and "valuable" (*ōphelimos*, 1 Tim 4:8; 2 Tim 3:16; Titus 3:8).

16. Some scholars find certain portions of the Pastorals especially reminiscent of Paul, e.g., 2 Tim 1:1–18. Other passages in which Pauline language tends to cluster and that contain a lower percentage of words used infrequently in other Pauline letters or the rest of the NT include 2 Tim 4:5b–22; Titus 3:12–15; also 2 Tim 1:16–18; 3:10–11; 4:1–2a. Other passages, however, are virtually devoid of Pauline echoes, e.g., 1 Tim 5:6–12, 21–25; 6:6–10, 15–21; 2 Tim 2:23–3:9; Titus 1:6–14; 2:1–10; 3:8–11.

17. This overall concern is captured in Paul's opening instruction to Titus to "put in order [*epidiorthoō*] what remained to be done" (1:5).

18. "Bishop" (*episkopos*, 1:7) is best understood here as a functional description of what elders do rather than as an alternative title for the office or position.

19. See Aristotle, *Mag. mor.* 2.14.1212b; *Eth. nic.* 3.12.1119b.9–10; Plato, *Leg.* 2.663b; *Gorg.* 507a–b.

20. Literally, "clinging to the faithful word according to the teaching" (v. 9).

21. *Eth. nic.* 3.12.1119b.9–10.

22. *Eusebeia* suggests "living as God would have us live."

23. Acts 19:22 reports Paul's sending Timothy and Erastus from Ephesus to Macedonia. In 1 Cor 4:17, Paul calls Timothy his "beloved and faithful child in the Lord," who is being sent to Corinth as the one authorized to teach and interpret his "ways in Christ" to the Corinthian church (cf. 1 Cor 16:10–11). It is widely agreed that Paul is in Ephesus when he writes 1 Corinthians. Other NT references reinforce the picture of Timothy as Paul's devoted disciple (Acts 16:1–5; 17:14–15; 18:5; 20:4; 1 Thess 3:2; Rom 16:21; Phil 2:19–22).

24. *Oikonomia* can also be understood as instruction or training, hence NRSV: "the divine training that is known by faith." *Oikonomia* signifies "God's plan of salvation" in Eph 1:10 (cf. Eph 3:2, 9; Col 1:25; also 1 Cor 9:17). *Oikonomia theou* could be rendered literally as "God's economy" or the "divine economy" as long as it is understood as the arrangement or plan through which God's overall redemptive purpose is achieved.

25. Here again, Corinth offers a parallel: the question of appropriate attire at worship is one of the major issues in 1 Cor 11:2–16.

26. For similar caution about adopting society's dress code, see 1 Pet 3:3.

27. See Gen 2 for Adam's being created first; Gen 3:13 for Eve's transgression; also cf. 2 Cor 11:3.

28. The same distinction is evident in Titus 1:9.

29. For "the faith," see 1 Tim 3:9; 4:1, 6; 5:8; 6:10, 12, 21; 2 Tim 4:7; Titus 1:13. For "the truth," see 1 Tim 2:4; 3:15; 4:3; 6:5; 2 Tim 2:18; 3:8; 4:4; Titus 1:1, 14.

Bibliography

Commentaries

Barrett, C. K. *The Pastoral Epistles*. New Clarendon Bible. Oxford: Oxford University Press, 1963.

Bassler, Jouette M. *1 Timothy, 2 Timothy, Titus*. Abingdon New Testament Commentaries. Nashville: Abingdon, 1996.

Collins, Raymond F. *1 & 2 Timothy and Titus: A Commentary*. New Testament Library. Louisville: Westminster John Knox, 2002.

Dibelius, Martin, and Hans Conzelmann. *The Pastoral Epistles*. Hermeneia. Edited by Helmut Koester. Translated by Philip Buttolph and Adela Yarbro. Philadelphia: Fortress, 1972.

Donelson, Lewis R. *Colossians, Ephesians, First and Second Timothy, and Titus*. Westminster Bible Companion. Louisville: Westminster John Knox, 1996. Pages 115–89.

Dunn, James D. G. "The First and Second Letters to Timothy and the Letter to Titus: Introduction, Commentary, and Reflections." Pages 773–880 in vol. 11 of *The New Interpreter's Bible*. Edited by Leander E. Keck. 12 vols. Nashville: Abingdon, 2000.

Fee, Gordon D. *1 and 2 Timothy, Titus*. New International Biblical Commentary. Peabody: Hendrickson, 1988.

Kelly, J. N. D. *A Commentary on the Pastoral Epistles*. Black's New Testament Commentaries. London: Black, 1963.

Lock, W. *The Pastoral Epistles*. International Critical Commentary. 3d ed. Edinburgh/New York: T&T Clark/Scribners, 1952 (1924).

Marshall, I. Howard, with Philip Towner. *A Critical and Exegetical Commentary on the Pastoral Epistles*. International Critical Commentary. Edinburgh: T&T Clark, 1999.

Quinn, Jerome D. *The Letter to Titus*. Anchor Bible 35. New York: Doubleday, 1990.

———, and William C. Wacker. *The First and Second Letters to Timothy: A New Translation with Notes and Commentary*. Grand Rapids: Eerdmans, 2000.

Other Resources

Davies, M. *The Pastoral Epistles*. New Testament Guides. Sheffield: Sheffield Academic Press, 1996.

Donelson, Lewis R. *Pseudepigraphy and Ethical Argument in the Pastoral Epistles*. Hermeneutische Untersuchungen zur Theologie 22. Tübingen: Mohr (Siebeck), 1986.

Harrison, P. N. *Paulines and Pastorals*. London: Villiers Publications, 1964.
————. *The Problem of the Pastoral Epistles*. Oxford: Oxford University Press, 1921.
Thurston, Bonnie B. *The Widows: A Women's Ministry in the Early Church*. Minneapolis: Fortress, 1989.
Verner, David C. *The Household of God: The Social World of the Pastoral Epistles*. Society of Biblical Literature Dissertation Series 71. Chico: Society of Biblical Literature (Scholars Press), 1983.
Wilson, S. G. *Luke and the Pastoral Epistles*. London: SPCK, 1979.
Young, Frances. *The Theology of the Pastoral Letters*. New Testament Theology Series. Cambridge: Cambridge University Press, 1994.

Chapter 21

Hebrews

"Kepe thiselfe as a pilgryme and a geste vppon yerthe, to whom longeth nothinge of worldely bisinesse. Kepe thi herte free and rered vppe to thi God, for thou hast here none abydynge cite."

Thomas à Kempis, *On the Imitation of Christ*

"But truly there are many that go upon the Road, that rather declare themselves Strangers to Pilgrimage, then Strangers and Pilgrims in the Earth."

John Bunyan, *The Pilgrim's Progress*

"[Hebrews] is not a theological treatise in cold blood, but a statement of the faith, alive with practical interest . . . [and] nothing is more practical in religion than an idea, a relevant idea, powerfully argued."

James Moffatt

"The author of Hebrews ranks with Paul and the Fourth Evangelist as one of the three great theologians of the New Testament."

Barnabas Lindars

"O ratory is good," wrote the fifth-century B.C.E. Greek rhetorician Isocrates, "only if it has the qualities of fitness for the occasion, propriety of style, and originality of treatment."[1] Hebrews succeeds on all three counts.

Convinced that much is at stake when believers lose heart, the author of Hebrews composed a finely crafted "word of exhortation" (13:22) with a simple premise: faith matters; in fact, it matters ultimately. We do not know the identity of the addressees, but a specific community of faith is clearly in view. Every carefully crafted line, every well-chosen word was written for them. How appropriately Hebrews responded to the needs of its original addressees can be gauged by the larger church's eventual embrace of the letter, even without knowing who wrote it and for whom it was written. Hebrews was judged as an apt response to believers anywhere whose faith was shaky.

What made Hebrews an especially fitting sermon was not only its seriousness of purpose but also its refined oral style. Knowing that the art of persuasion is more than having a way with words, the author of Hebrews reveals a broadly informed understanding of rhetorical style. His respect for style is everywhere apparent—in the grandly conceived plan of the work; in its finely turned phrases and carefully chosen words; in its musical sounds and lively images; and in its richly exploited deep metaphors. But unlike the ancient Sophists, our author was guided by an overarching moral vision that required him to exercise restraint in his use of style.

It would be impressive if Hebrews were just a stylistic tour de force, but it also passes the test of originality. It is well within the framework of the early Christian kerygma, but its deep probing of Jesus' role as high priest, combined with its finely balanced blending of Jesus' dual roles as eternal Son of God and the obedient Son who suffered "in the days of his flesh" (5:7), distinguishes it from other NT writings. To achieve such a brilliantly rendered vision of Christ, some bold interpretive moves were required. Who would have imagined the fertile christological possibilities of the enigmatic priest Melchizedek (5:5–10)? Who else would dare call Christ "God" without demur (1:8–9; cf. Rom 9:5; 2 Thess 1:12; Titus 2:13; 1 John 5:20; 2 Peter 1:1; also John 1:1)? Others knew "apostle" as an esteemed title applied to a select few, but no one else saw how well this title captured God's unique commissioning of Christ (3:1). We see similar creative impulses when a newly coined title (perfecter) is joined with a rarely used one (pioneer; Heb 12:2; cf. Acts 3:15).

Other indications of the author's originality are evident, none more remarkable than his use of the OT. Whether his overall understanding of the OT reflects standard typological interpretation or a quasi-philosophical way of reading the OT akin to Philo of Alexandria's heavily Middle Platonic exegesis of the Pentateuch, or whether it is a christianized blend of both, is much debated. What is scarcely denied, however, is the result—a highly creative reading of the OT that undergirds the richly developed vision of Christ as the eternal Son of God, the exalted high priest. Even the rehearsal of biblical figures who exemplified faith (ch. 11) has a distinctive imprint that sets it apart from similar lists, such as the "Let us now sing the praises of famous men" eulogy in Sir 44–50.

When scholars rank the author of Hebrews with Paul and John as the third great NT theologian, they are acknowledging this remarkable theological creativity. That this was accomplished in fewer pages than Romans and in a work a third as long as the Gospel of John underscores how much the author's rhetorical giftedness contributed to this monumental achievement.

The Church's Use of Hebrews

Through the centuries, the church was often impressed but also disturbed by what it read in Hebrews. Read one way, the letter brims with spiritual meaning as it nudges readers forward in their journey of faith, while looking upward to their final destination, the heavenly city. However differently readers understood the portrayal of Jesus in Hebrews, no one doubted its richness and depth. Its wide appeal notwithstanding, other readers had difficulty accepting its pessimistic claim that lapsed believers cannot be "restored again to repentance" (6:4). Despite many nagging questions about its teaching and its apostolic status, Hebrews has figured prominently in ecclesiastical disputes and has heavily influenced the church's life and thought.[2] **[See Expanded CD Version pp. 636–37: *The Church's Reading of Hebrews*]**

The Riddle of Hebrews

The story of the church's relationship with Hebrews reads like the story of a couple finding an orphaned child, not quite knowing what to do with him, soon discovering his brilliance, embracing him, and spending the rest of their days trying—unsuccessfully—to identify him. Through it all they are dazzled by what they learn from him, never quite sure where to seat him among their other children. Finally they yield to his wise counsel, even if they must live with some of his more prickly pronouncements.

Hebrews probably originated in the last quarter of the first century, or perhaps earlier, since it was used in *1 Clement*, a letter written from the Roman church to the church at Corinth about 96 C.E.[3] Even though Clement of Rome mentioned 1 Corinthians and attributed it to Paul,[4] he did not refer to an "Epistle to the Hebrews," much less attribute it to Paul. What happened next to this anonymous writing remains a mystery.[5] A firm clue comes a century later, when Hebrews was included in an Egyptian papyrus, 𝔓[46], the earliest surviving manuscript containing a collection of Paul's letters, dated about 200 C.E. By then, it had acquired a title, "To Hebrews" (*Pros Hebraious*). It had also found a home—in second position in the Pauline corpus, wedged between Romans and 1–2 Corinthians. Its anonymous author now had an identity. It was a letter of Paul.

Why it received the title "To Hebrews" is puzzling. The Greek word "Hebrew" (*Hebraios*) does not occur in the letter, nor does any of its cognate forms (see Acts 6:1; 2 Cor 11:22; Phil 3:5; also Acts 21:40; 22:2; 26:14; John 5:2; 19:13, 17, 20; 20:16; Rev 9:11; 16:16). Neither does the term "Jew" (*Ioudaios*) or any of its cognate forms appear. "Israel" (*Israēl*) occurs only three times, two of which are in an OT quotation (Heb 8:8 = Jer 31:31; 8:10 = Jer 31:33; 11:22). Someone thought that only readers who bore the honorific if somewhat archaic title "Hebrews" and presumably spoke Hebrew or Aramaic could understand the technical OT argumentation or appreciate its fascination with the Levitical sacrificial system. Such a general title may mean that the writing was originally addressed to a relatively obscure church. If the letter had been written to a well-known church, the title would have contained that church's name. However the title originated, it has influenced the church's perception of the writing. Based on the title, readers usually assume that its addressees were Jewish Christians. But some scholars, observing that the author explains Hebrew terms and sometimes speaks as though his readers came from Gentile backgrounds (7:1–2; 9:1–5), have argued that the letter addressed Gentile Christians.

Why it was included with Paul's letters is an equally fascinating question. The brief concluding reference to Timothy and the greeting from "those of Italy" (13:22–25) provided one link to Paul, however slight, and this may explain why it was placed immediately after Romans. Since Paul referred to himself as a "Hebrew born of Hebrews" (Phil 3:5), the title "Hebrews" strengthened the Pauline connection. Even so, baptizing the letter into the name of Paul proved to be difficult.

At roughly the same time that $\mathfrak{P}^{46}$ circulated in Egypt, Clement of Alexandria made repeated use of Hebrews, quoting it as a Pauline letter.[6] Easily recognizing the letter's non-Pauline style, Clement proposed that it was originally written by Paul "for Hebrews in the Hebrew tongue" but was translated into Greek by Luke.[7] Origen reflected similar ambivalence. Despite its non-Pauline quality, Origen attributed Hebrews to Paul some 200 times.[8] He noted that "not without reason have the men of old handed down [Hebrews] as Paul's."[9] Acknowledging that Hebrews lacks "the apostle's rudeness in speech" and displays "better Greek in the framing of its diction," Origen still insisted that it had close affinities with Pauline thought.[10] Eventually Origen drew his now famous conclusion: "Who wrote the epistle? Only God knows."[11] **[See Expanded CD Version pp. 639–41: *The Church's Search for the Author of Hebrews*]**

The church's perennial fascination with the question of authorship testifies to its insatiable historical curiosity. But the emergence of an anonymous writing that quickly gained popularity and eventually overcame dubious certification and even strong resistance in the West well into the fifth century severely tested the church's capacity for spiritual discernment. Early on, the church recognized that it could hardly ignore Hebrews, even had it wanted to do so. Its witness to the gospel was too profound, its rhetoric too powerful. Hebrews extended the horizon of the gospel in ways no other NT writing did. It exercised profound influence on the church's understanding of Christian ministers as priests and the Eucharist as a sacrifice, even as it proved pivotal in deciding major christological controversies. Through its powerful language, Hebrews shaped the church's prayer and worship. The church's use of Hebrews in lectionaries at moments of high celebration confirmed its need to hear the Word of God through the letter's memorable cadences and images. The letter's authority ultimately derived not from the name of its author, but from its inspired message.

Rhetoric in the Service of the Gospel

Hebrews has been called a literary puzzle for several reasons. Except for the benediction (13:20–21) and concluding exhortation and greeting (13:22–25), it lacks the usual epistolary features that characterize other NT letters. Perhaps most striking is how it begins—a highly rhetorical, stately introduction rather than the familiar epistolary greeting followed by a prayer of thanksgiving or blessing.[12] Neither the author nor the addressees are identified—an equally puzzling feature. And yet it has commonly been referred to as the Letter or Epistle to the Hebrews and confidently attributed to Paul.

No one can deny the obvious—that Hebrews is a written document. But what kind of discourse was written down? The author's concluding remark, "I have written [*epesteila*] to you briefly" (13:22) does not necessarily imply that the writing should be classified as a letter in the strict sense.[13] Since the author consistently uses verbs suggesting oral speech, it is better to think of this "word of exhortation" (13:22) as a discourse composed for the ear more than the eye.[14]

A close look at the text of Hebrews, especially the Greek text, suggests an author who used rhetoric in the service of the gospel. One gauge of his originality is the impressive vocabulary. Hebrews contains over 150 NT *hapax legomena*—words found in no other NT writing. Among these are ten words found in no other Greek writing from antiquity, or if so, only rarely—words that the author himself seems to have coined.[15] Not only this, but some ninety other terms used in Hebrews occur in only one other NT writing, yet another indication of the author's distinctive vocabulary. Since many of these terms do not occur in our author's favorite text, the Greek OT, we know that he read widely and had a particular fondness for philosophical texts.

His rhetorical savvy is evident from the way he framed his intricate (some would say labyrinthine) argument. Reflecting classical Greek sensibilities, he constructed long, complex literary periods, but rather than concentrating them in one section, he wisely distributed them throughout the writing.[16] To offset their cumbersome effect, he also peppered the discourse with crisply formulated, short sentences. "Where there is forgiveness of these, there is no longer any offering for sin" (10:18) and "It is a fearful thing to fall into the hands of the living God" (10:31) are welcome pauses in the intricate argument about Christ's sacrifice in chapter 10 (also cf. 2:16, 18; 4:9; 11:1; 12:29; 13:1, 8). His interweaving of exposition and exhortation throughout the narrative is also a nod to stylistic variety.[17] As the texture of the writing fluctuates, so does the tone. The lofty grandeur of the opening section, which takes us back to the remote past while lifting our vision to the heavenly throne of the "Majesty on high," introduces the world of angels as the arena within which the Son of God's pre-eminence is most conspicuously displayed. Yet this sharply contrasts with the intricate arguments of the central exposition (6:13–10:39), which in turn give way to the epic rehearsal of Israel's faithful heroes and heroines in chapter 11, culminating in its most recent exemplar, Jesus (12:1–2). Exhortation includes both direct imperatives and gentler "let us" appeals, even though the former tend to cluster toward the end of the writing.[18]

The author wrote prose, but he had a poet's instincts. How words sound was as important to him as what they mean, sometimes more so. His stylistic sensibilities conform to Isocrates's strong preference for discourses adorned "with striking thoughts and clothed in flowing and melodious phrase"[19] that are "more akin to works composed in rhythm and set to music than to the speeches which are made in court."[20] Like his rhetorical teachers, the author of Hebrews knew the importance of framing literary periods that begin and end with memorable cadences. He followed Aristotle's advice to conclude sections using the paeonic rhythm in which three unaccented (short) syllables were followed by one accented (long) syllable.[21] Yet he was confident enough to use the same cadence as an introductory device.[22] The closer we look at the language of Hebrews, the more evident it becomes that the author not only agonized over words but syllables as well, giving special attention to how they sounded together.

Also impressive is the author's masterly use of rhetorical conventions. Incurably alliterative, the author opens the letter with a burst of five *p*'s, a pattern that recurs elsewhere.[23] His use of anaphora, the repetition of a word or phrase to introduce successive units of thought, is evident in chapter 11, with its eighteen uses of "by faith" (*pistei*) that march the parade of faithful witnesses before our eyes. Given the contrasts within the writing, the frequent use of antithesis is hardly surprising: "there is, on the one hand . . . there is, on the other hand" (7:18–19; cf. 7:28; 10:11–12); "we are not among those who shrink back and so are lost, but among those who have faith and so are saved" (10:39). The staccato effect of asyndeton, a series of structurally similar units without intervening conjunctions, is also put to good use: "they were stoned to death, they were sawn in two, they were killed by the sword," and so forth (11:37; cf. 11:33–34). His use of paronomasia—play on words—is often obscured in English translation but is quite apparent in Greek: "to distinguish good [*kalou*] from evil [*kakou*]" (5:14); "he learned [*emathen*] . . . through what he suffered [*epathen*]" (5:8). Astute listeners would hardly miss the rich resonances of the latter, since "learning through suffering" (*pathei mathos*) had proverbial status in Greek antiquity.[24] Aesop's form was *pathēmata mathēmata*, "sufferings are teachings." Isocolon, the use of equally balanced parallel clauses, also occurs: "the reflection of God's glory . . . the exact imprint of God's very being" (1:3). Sometimes the author achieves emphasis through the use of a double negative: "God is not unjust" (6:10; cf. 4:15; 9:18). Closely related is his fondness for terms (twenty-four in all) that describe through negation, a device Aristotle recommended as having special rhetorical power.[25] Melchizedek, for example, was "without father, without mother, without genealogy" (7:3). The author also understood the rhetorical power of a series of carefully formulated, rapid-fire questions (3:16–18). Equally arresting are well-placed questions that sometimes give the writing a diatribal effect (1:5, 13–14; 2:3–4; 7:11; 10:29; 11:32; 12:7, 9). Transitions from one section to another are well managed on the whole, thus edging the argument forward. One way of achieving this is to introduce an idea or motif, such as high priest, then develop it later (2:17; 5:5–6).

Like every skilled rhetorician, the author of Hebrews employed vivid images drawn from everyday life. These include memorable metaphors and examples of proverbial wisdom: "You need milk, not solid food" (5:12); "What child is there whom a parent does not discipline?" (12:7); "Ground that drinks up the rain falling on it repeatedly . . . receives a blessing from God" (6:7); "not laying again the foundation" (6:1); "the city that has foundations, whose architect and builder is God" (11:10); "this hope, a sure and steadfast anchor of the soul" (6:19); "An oath given as confirmation puts an end to all dispute" (6:16); "Let us also lay aside every weight and . . . run with perseverance the race that is set before us" (12:1); "Lift your drooping hands and strengthen your weak knees" (12:12); and "The word of God is . . . sharper than any two-edged sword" (4:12). The author also exploits cultic images, such as "high priest" and "sacrifice," as root metaphors.

While many of these literary conventions were associated with Greek and Roman rhetoric, the author's grounding in biblical traditions is everywhere apparent. His indebtedness to the Septuagint is reflected in such phrases as "in these last days" (1:2; cf. Jer 23:20), "heart of unbelief" (3:12; cf. Jer 16:12; 18:12), "throne of grace" (4:16; cf. Jer 14:21; 17:12), or "prayers and supplications" (5:7; cf. Job 40:27 LXX; 41:3 NRSV). His extensive use of the argument known in Greco-Roman circles as *a minore ad maius* and in Jewish circles as *qal wahomer*, "from the lesser to the greater," supports his emphasis on the "better way." According to its logic, if something is true in a lesser instance, it is even truer in a greater instance. If disregarding the message delivered *through angels* had penalties, even greater penalties will befall those who ignore the message from one *greater than angels* (2:2–4). Or, if we accept the discipline of a human father, should we not submit even more willingly to the discipline of our heavenly Father (12:9)? That our author drew from a wide range of rhetorical and exegetical traditions is evident in his use of the rabbinic interpretive method *gezera shawa*, in which an unclear term in one passage is illuminated by its clear use in another passage. The use of God's "rest" in the Genesis story of creation clarifies the full meaning of "rest" in the story of Israel's wilderness wandering (4:1–11).

What emerges from this minutely planned, methodically executed rhetorical strategy is anything but monotonous. From the well-trained mind of an author who had a preacher's heart and a rhetorician's ear comes one of the liveliest, most vigorous sermons from the early church. Yet this writing is far more than a rhetorical decathlon; it is a deeply probing meditation on basic Christian convictions—a manifesto declaring that intellectually grounded theological depth is the best antidote for spiritual lethargy.

The Central Argument: Discerning Scripture's Voices

Like many other NT writings, Hebrews displays a form of messianic exegesis in which the OT is seen through the lens of Jesus Christ. Early Christians were so transformed by their faith in Christ that they sometimes read Scripture to confirm beliefs they already held. But not all early Christian reading of Scripture can be dismissed so easily. Hebrews is one such case.

Even a superficial reading of Hebrews reveals a writer who was thoroughly immersed in Scripture.[26] He read widely beyond Scripture, but the world of Scripture primarily shaped his world of meaning. To understand his particular reading of Scripture, we must discern its internal logic. To understand *what Hebrews argues* we must grasp *how it argues*.

Jesus the Pivot

All exposition of Scripture in Hebrews stems from a single conviction: Jesus, the eternal Son of God, came to earth, suffered, died, and was exalted to God's right hand. Although elements of this formulation are expressed distinctively in Hebrews, it conforms to the early statements of Christian belief found elsewhere in the NT. Still, this conviction forms the base line of scriptural interpretation in Hebrews. It not only establishes the hermeneutical principles for our author, it *is* his hermeneutical principle. It shapes his understanding of past, present, and future, and consequently gives him a Christ-defined sense of time. Since he cannot think of heaven and earth apart from Christ, this conviction also defines his sense of space.

While the author of Hebrews affirms that Christ "came into the world" (10:5), he also believes that Christ has existed eternally with God (1:1–4). Blind to anachronism, he writes that Moses considered "abuse suffered for the Christ" (11:26) in deciding to leave Egypt. Since Christ is an active presence in the past, he is present everywhere in Scripture—at least, theoretically—not only as the One spoken about, but also as the One spoken to (by God), and even as the One who speaks! Reading Scripture as a multiple set of voices suggests another sense in which it is "living and active" (4:12). The author of Hebrews experiences Scripture as a chorus of voices bearing testimony about Christ, the Eternal Now.

In Hebrews the Scriptures often speak about Christ, but three texts lie at the heart of its argument: Ps 110, Jer 31, and Ps 40.

Psalm 110

By the time Hebrews was written, Christians had already used Ps 110:1 as a favorite proof text in different settings. For them, "The LORD says to my lord" meant that God was speaking, not to David or some other Israelite figure, but to Jesus, God's Anointed One. And what he said to this Anointed Lord—"Sit at my right hand until I make your enemies your footstool"—was read as God's promise to exalt the risen Christ within his heavenly court and vanquish his earthly foes.

Unlike other NT writers, the author of Hebrews read further to Ps 110:4: "The LORD has sworn and will not change his mind, 'You are a priest forever according to the order of Melchizedek.'" The author's use of this verse was remarkable for several reasons. First, he believed that verse 4, like the opening verse of Ps 110, spoke of Christ. Second, he noted that God is not just speaking under oath but making an *eternal oath*. Third, he concluded that God commissions Christ as an "eternal priest" in the special priestly order of Melchizedek.

As scriptural testimony about Christ, Ps 110:4 supplies a fresh metaphor for interpreting Christ. The notion of Christ's priesthood triggered many questions, for example, when did Christ become a priest? Oddly enough, the author of Hebrews does not pursue this red herring, probably because he understood "forever" to mean just that—it is an eternal status. But it prompted a complete re-evaluation of the Levitical priesthood. Because of Psalm 110:4 the author reread the entire book of Leviticus, especially Lev 16, if not the whole Pentateuch. Since God's promise was made under divine oath, it could not be dismissed casually. Christ's priesthood took priority over the Levitical priesthood, the author of Hebrews reasoned, because Gen 14 presents Melchizedek as a greater figure than Abraham. Not only did Abraham bow before Melchizedek, he even paid the mysterious priest a tithe of his possessions. Since Melchizedek is greater than Abraham, he must be greater than all of Abraham's descendants, including Levi, Aaron, and Moses. Hence, the playful exegetical point: since Levi was in the loins of Abraham, he actually paid tithes to Melchizedek even before he was born! Because Melchizedek enjoyed genealogical priority over Abraham's descendants, most notably Levi, his priesthood trumped the Levitical priesthood.

Convinced that Jesus' eternal priesthood was confirmed by God under oath, the author of Hebrews takes conventional Christian notions about Jesus' life and work, his death and exaltation, in new directions. He knew that the earthly Jesus was not a priest and that people whom he encountered did not regard him as one. On the contrary, the early tradition about Jesus was full of negative images of priests who actively resisted him. To complicate matters further, Jesus did not descend from the tribe of Levi but from the tribe of Judah. Yet this did not keep the author of Hebrews from using the priestly metaphor to interpret Jesus. If God under oath said that Jesus is an eternal high priest, the question was not whether this was the case but how it should be understood.

Christians had already interpreted Jesus' death as a sacrificial offering. That Jesus was crucified meant that he was slaughtered, like a sacrificial victim; it also meant that special significance was attached to the shedding of his blood. The one ritual act within the Levitical system that provided the most fruitful analogy was the annual sacrificial offering made by the high priest on the Day of Atonement (Yom Kippur). The detailed description of this ritual in Lev 16 supplied early Christians rich imagery for understanding Jesus' sacrificial death.

Leviticus 16 depicts the high priest's procession into the tabernacle, first through the holy place, the outer tent, then through the curtain into the most holy place, the inner sanctuary. This stately procession known both from the biblical account and Israel's own experience provided a vivid metaphor for interpreting the death and exaltation of Christ. Assisted by cultural assumptions in Jewish and other religious traditions that earthly shrines had heavenly counterparts, the author of Hebrews envisioned Jesus' life on earth as proceeding through the outer court of the tabernacle, his death as the high priest passing through the curtain, and his exaltation as entry into the heavenly, inner sanctuary. Leviticus 16 provided a narrative template visualizing what other early Christians expressed as Jesus' death and resurrection. With one rare exception (13:20), our author studiously avoids speaking of Jesus' "resurrection." His reluctance to use such language may derive from his Christology. To claim that Jesus experienced a new form of life after death might have implied that he had not experienced eternal life prior to his coming into the world. Probably influenced by Ps 110:1, the author of Hebrews prefers to speak of Jesus' exaltation rather than his resurrection.

Hebrews exploits cultic symbolism in two ways: Jesus is both *sacrifice* and *high priest*. Strictly speaking, such double appropriation is inconsistent since Lev 16 does not present the high priest as both officiant and sacrifice. While this blending of images might seem inconsistent, it is understandable in the world of religious symbolism, in which metaphorical images can be remarkably fluid.

Whether Jesus' death is seen as a sacrifice whose blood purifies the whole people of God, or whether his transition from death to exaltation is envisioned as a high priestly procession from the earthly "outer court" into the heavenly "inner court," a reevaluation of the Levitical system was called for. The interpretive move is from the death and exaltation of Christ *backward* to the biblical account. When the two priesthoods—that of Christ and that of Levi—are compared, serious flaws in the latter are exposed. For one thing, the stipulation that only members of the tribe of Levi are qualified to officiate must be rethought. God's oath in Ps 110:4 abrogates the "legal requirement concerning physical descent" (Heb 7:16), rendering the "earlier commandment" as "weak and ineffectual" (7:18). Because God, under oath, designated an "eternal priest" of an entirely different order—the order of Melchizedek—both the Levitical priesthood and the Mosaic law were flawed.

The more Jesus' priesthood is contrasted with the Levitical priesthood, the more distinctive it becomes. Jesus received his priestly appointment through a divine oath, but the Levitical priests did not (7:20–22); Jesus' priesthood was "forever," but theirs was not; when Jesus died, his priesthood began (formally), but when the Levitical priests died, their term of office ended (7:23–24); Jesus was "holy, blameless, unde-filed," but the Levitical high priest had to offer sacrifice for his sins; Jesus' sacrifice was "once for all," but the Levitical sacrifice occurred annually (7:26–27).

Recognizing that the Levitical priesthood was a central part of the scriptural record and thus had divine approval, the author of Hebrews nevertheless saw Jesus as the only sensible referent for Ps 110:4 and his priesthood as having prior claim over the Levitical priesthood. But did this way of reading Ps 110:4 have scriptural support? This was the interpretive challenge facing the author of Hebrews. [See Expanded CD Version pp. 647–49: *Two More Examples of the Author's Use of Scripture: Jer 31 and Ps 40*]

Summary

This way of reading Scripture may appear arbitrary, and yet it has its own inter-nal logic. Given the world of Scripture that the author of Hebrews inhabits and his construal of Jesus as God's eternal Son designated by God, under oath, as an eternal priest after the order of Melchizedek, this form of messianic exegesis yields a compre-hensive, yet distinctive, vision of the biblical story. It produces bold claims: Jesus, an eternal priest duly ordained by God, came into the world, exposed imperfections in the old covenant, and as high priest launched God's new covenant. The author leaves no doubt that the new covenant is better than the old one. Like the Levitical priesthood, the closely linked Mosaic law is rendered obsolete by the arrival of the new priesthood and the new covenant. This cannot mean that the revelatory significance of Scripture, including the Pentateuch, has ended, because the argument throughout Hebrews is based on Scripture. The One through whom God is speaking "in the last days" himself speaks through Scripture, but he does so in ways that transcend the old covenant. The new covenant that he inaugurated is itself part of the scriptural vision. The argument of Hebrews does not render Scripture obsolete, but it does offer a fresh reading of Scripture—one that recognizes both continuities and discontinuities between the old and new covenants. It sees Jesus as continuing the story of Scripture, but only because he is the One through whom God's revealing word has finally found its voice. And Jesus is also heard as God's own voice. [See Expanded CD Version pp. 649–54: *Hebrews and Paul Compared*]

Why Endure? Making the Case for Remaining Faithful

For all of its complexity, Hebrews has a single, driving purpose: to encourage faint-hearted believers. Their precise identity is not known, nor is their location. They have a special bond with "those of Italy" who send greetings (13:24), but we do not know whether the author is writing from Italy or to Italy. Since Hebrews is first cited by Clement of Rome about 96 C.E., there is a strong probability that it was addressed to Italian Christians. From the author's anxious concern for his listeners, the way he closely identifies with them, the sometimes harsh, sometimes endearing tone of the letter, and his expectation of rejoining them soon, we can surmise that they enjoyed a close rela-

The author of the Letter to the Hebrews at his writing desk, envisioning Jesus as high priest and the crucifixion as Jesus' sacrificial death. From *Biblia ectypa*, a book of biblical images by Christoph Weigel published in 1695. From the Digital Image Archive of The Richard C. Kessler Reformation Collection, Pitts Theology Library, Candler School of Theology, Emory University, Atlanta, Georgia.

tionship with each other. The author hopes that their mutual friend Timothy, recently released from prison, will accompany him when he returns to his beloved church (13:23). Nowhere does he speak as if he were the church's founder, nor does he identify himself as one of its leaders whom he repeatedly calls the church to respect. Instead, he closely identifies with the church and includes himself as one of those who received the gospel from those who had heard the Lord directly (2:3). The air of authority reflected in his censure of the church in 5:11–6:12 and elsewhere in the letter may suggest that he was their preacher or teacher, but he does not identify himself this way.

That the church has encountered resistance, even active persecution, is evident from several passages (10:32–34; 13:3). But no one has suffered to the point of death (12:4). Enough pressure has been applied to make "shrinking back" a live possibility. In the author's view, some of the members are on the verge of giving up their faith (3:12–13; 6:12; 10:39). Characterizing them as lethargic and fatigued suggests the image of battle-weary soldiers or exhausted athletes who do not have the energy to go forward (12:12–13). Inertia has slowed their momentum. They are experiencing ennui because they have grown weary in well-doing and now lack spirit and will.

The author seeks to counter this spirit of malaise. To the extent that his discourse makes a sustained argument for the listeners to stay the course, it is deliberative rhetoric. As such, it invites the readers to follow a recommended course of action. And yet the discourse also exhibits features of epideictic rhetoric, whose overall aim was to praise and blame. Either way, the letter has a practical purpose: to shore up the faith of discouraged believers. The author does so by making the case for faithful endurance. The discourse seeks to answer a single question: Why should believers in Christ endure? His answer has several interlocking components.

1. *To live in faith, one must negotiate two constant perspectives—moving forward and looking upward.* To concentrate on one to the exclusion of the other distorts both. There is an undeniably linear character to the theological perspective of Hebrews. Reflecting the overarching framework of early Christian belief, Hebrews establishes a horizontal axis that moves from creation to final judgment. This linear perspective is already set in the opening verses: "long ago . . . but in these last days." Since the unfolding revelation occurs in time, it has temporal markers. "Jesus Christ is the same yesterday and today and forever" (13:8). To the extent that this temporal axis moves toward the end of time, the vision of Hebrews is eschatological.

While this horizontal axis forms a basic presupposition for the argument of Hebrews, it is not simply conceived. In one sense, Israel's history from creation to the Hasmonean period constitutes this time line, which is continued by Jesus and his "church of the first-born" (12:23). The author positions himself and his listeners along this axis, perhaps one generation removed from Jesus himself (2:3). He is keenly aware that certain things must still be accomplished by God before Christ's second coming, which is expected soon. The contrast between the old and new covenants is predicated on this horizontal, temporal axis. Otherwise, one cannot speak sensibly of past and present. Nor can anything be obsolete unless there is a meaningful sense of then and now, old and new.

The presence of this horizontal axis accounts for the forward movement in Hebrews. This is vividly captured by the pilgrimage metaphor, in which the people of God are moving toward a destination: Abraham toward the city of God; Israel toward the promised "rest"; the church toward the heavenly Jerusalem; or the church following Jesus "outside the camp" through uncharted vistas toward its own "rest." It is also reinforced by the metaphor of the athletic race (12:1–4).

There is also an upward movement in Hebrews. Numerous metaphors establish a vertical axis, none more graphically than the author's use of "exaltation" to express the cardinal Christian belief in Jesus' resurrection. While he does not employ the language of ascent and descent, which is characteristic of the Gospel of John, there is no doubt that the location of Jesus' exaltation is "at the right hand of the Majesty on high" (1:3). By introducing the world of angels, the litany of OT citations in 1:5–14 lifts the listeners' imaginations upward. Being made "lower than the angels" (2:7, 9) suggests downward movement from Jesus' exalted heavenly state. This vertical axis is also reinforced by the author's cosmological dualism, in which a sharp distinction is drawn between earth and heaven. Accordingly, the tabernacle is envisioned as an earthly tent, which has a heavenly counterpart—the heavenly tabernacle that Jesus enters after his exaltation. So pervasive is this dimension that the label "heavenly" describes the calling of believers (3:1), the gift of the gospel (6:4), the "better country" (11:16), and Jerusalem (12:22).

Although the correlation is not as precise, the distinction between seen and unseen also reflects this spatial outlook. Generally, earth is the world of the seen, and heaven the world of the unseen. What many see as a strong Middle Platonic outlook in Hebrews—the recurrent contrast between shadow and reality, between the phenomenal and noumenal world, and between the earthly and heavenly tabernacles—easily aligns with the vertical axis.

The community of faith stands at the intersection of these two axes. On the one hand, it derives its sense of continuity with the past and its vision of the future from the conviction that God's revelation embraces time and history. The church moves forward inexorably through time, drawn into the future by God. But it is not severed from its past. The church also positions itself along a vertical axis whose outer points are earth and heaven, the seen and the unseen, humanity and God. The church especially positions itself along the vertical axis when it worships, not only as a gathered community of faith but also as individual worshipers. In these moments of worshipful pause, the church experiences God's presence. Not that the church cannot experience God in its forward-moving history, but it experiences God differently when it looks upward.

If we see only the horizontal movement in Hebrews, we will miss its emphasis on the church as a worshiping community defined by its acute sense of God's heavenly presence. If we see only the vertical dimension, we will easily overlook the tension caused by living in the interim between now and not yet, or as Hebrews puts it, between the "today" of God's summons and the future "rest" toward which the church moves. To ignore the peculiar dynamic created by simultaneously moving forward and looking upward is to ignore the church's conscious engagement of Time and Eternity. The church expresses its identity most authentically when it embraces the tension created by their intersection.

2. *The life of faith cannot be sustained unless believers grasp the true significance of Jesus' sacrificial death.* It was by no means novel to use images from the sacrificial cult to interpret the death of Jesus. Since Jesus was crucified, it made sense to think of him as a slaughtered, sacrificial victim. This was so not only because the cult played such a central role in Israelite life and thought but also because the sacrificial system was such a fixed feature of the ancient world. Sacrificial symbolism was well known in Greek and Roman religions, as well as in ancient Near Eastern religions. Rituals involving the slaughter of animals and the sprinkling of their blood on altars for the purposes of ritual purification were familiar features of religions throughout the Mediterranean world. Even the ritual sacrifice of humans was an accepted part of some ancient religions.

Drawing on this universally understood symbolism, the author of Hebrews probes even further the sacrificial effects of Jesus' death. Informed most directly by the practice of ancient Israel as described in the book of Leviticus, our author makes scattered references to various sacrificial offerings. He draws most heavily on the Day of Atonement (Yom Kippur) ritual performed by the high priest, as described in Lev 16. As an annual ritual, it ranked as one of the highest holy days in Israel's life. As the name suggests, its core element was the ritual atonement for sins, both the sins of the people and those of the high priest himself. Since it required the high priest to go through the outer court of the tabernacle, then pass through the veil into the inner sanctuary that housed the ark of the covenant, the ritual provided symbolism that dramatized the high priest's gradual movement through increasingly holy spaces until he arrived in the very space where God's presence was localized. There he performed ritual actions on his own behalf, through which his own sins were purified. Having achieved ritual purification for himself, he then sprinkled the blood of the slaughtered sacrificial animal(s) on the ark of the covenant, an action that had the mysterious effect of purifying the sins of all the people of Israel. Once this somber ritual event was completed and both the high priest and the entire people were ritually cleansed, they felt the renewal that naturally comes with the removal of guilt.

Like his earlier Christian counterparts, the author of Hebrews saw an analogy between Jesus' death and the slaughter of the sacrificial victim on the Day of Atonement. In both cases, blood was shed and its purifying effects extended to the people of God, whose identity and continued existence were vitally linked to this single sacrificial event. Yet it was their similarities that pointed up the differences between these two ritual sacrifices. Most conspicuously, in one instance, animals were slaughtered; in the other, the blood of a human being was shed. While the former symbolized the loss of something valuable, the latter, by comparison, was an infinitely greater loss.

As the author of Hebrews probed the significance of this analogy, he was especially struck by two things about the death of Jesus: (1) the identity of the One who was sacrificed, and (2) the qualities of his sacrificial death. As to the first, it was the eternal Son of God, the One duly commissioned as God's Messiah, who was slaughtered—no ordinary human being, in other words. Equally important was the nature of the life sacrificed. Jesus displayed two crucial qualities. First, he was an innocent victim who was seen as blameless, perfect, and sinless. Second, he was an obedient Son, which meant that his death was not only voluntary but also intentional. It expressed his active will. Both elements are critically significant for our author, because the one underscores Jesus' clean conscience, and the other a human heart fully disposed toward God—the two expectations of God's new covenant in Jer 31. Because Jesus' death embodied both elements in their purest form, it marked the official beginning of God's new covenant. As the perfect sacrifice, Jesus' death became the sacrifice-ending sacrifice. By extending to the deepest reaches of the human heart, Jesus' death rendered all forms of animal sacrifice primitive and, by comparison, ineffectual.

The saving effects of Jesus' death are experienced as purification (1:3). If human sinfulness is understood primarily as a stained conscience, which creates distance between the sinner and the holy God, we can understand the appeal of portraying salvation as a purification that gains unmediated access to God. When we grasp the full force of this cultic metaphor, we can better appreciate the difference between the symbolism of redemption/liberation, on the one hand, and purification/cleansing, on the other. In the former, the sinner is released from chains; in the latter, the sinner is cleansed from stains.

Closely related to the symbolism of purification is the language of sanctification, which draws its metaphorical power from the religious understanding of holiness. To be sanctified is to be set apart, and therefore rendered as separate and holy. Moving from a state of ritual impurity to a state of ritual purity becomes spatial movement from the ordinary to the holy. Since God is the purest form of being holy, human sinfulness is experienced as distance from God. Access to God becomes the purest expression of salvation as well as its greatest benefit.

Within this thoroughly cultic frame of reference Hebrews probes more deeply into the significance of Jesus' death. As a rhetorical strategy designed to bolster the faith of the fainthearted, this line of argument receives its compelling force from the universal need to deal satisfactorily with a troubled human conscience and enjoy fellowship with God. If failure to endure means relinquishing access to God and with it any viable means of dealing with the stain of human guilt, Jesus' sacrifice, properly understood, provides a strong incentive to remain faithful.

3. *To "shrink back" from faith means relinquishing the access to God that Jesus alone provides as God's duly appointed high priest.* No other NT writing portrays Jesus as high priest, at least not in the way, or to the extent, that Hebrews does. Jesus' priestly intercession is perhaps implied by Paul's remark that the Christ who "died . . . was raised . . . [and] is at the right hand of God . . . [and now] intercedes for us" (Rom 8:34). Some have also seen the image of priest behind Jesus' intercessory prayer in John 17. But Hebrews alone traces the implications of reading Ps 110:4 as God's promise to appoint Christ a priest after the order of Melchizedek. Because of its pivotal role in the overall argument, some have even suggested that Hebrews should be read as an extended midrash on Ps 110:4. While such a broad claim is an overstatement, it contains an element of truth. **[See Expanded CD Version p. 659: *The Image of Melchizedek in Early Jewish and Christian Writing*]**

In Hebrews, it is not Jesus' role as eschatological high priest that is of central interest; it is rather his intercessory role on behalf of the church living "between the times" of Christ's first and second comings. What Jesus as high priest does for believers in the present is emphasized more than what he will do for them in the future. By being exalted to the right hand of God, Jesus has opened up a permanent way of access to God.

While believers have constant access to Jesus' intercessory powers, they probably experience Jesus as high priest most powerfully when they are gathered for worship. Given the importance Hebrews attaches to the regular assembly (10:25), its calls to "approach the throne of grace with boldness" (4:16), to "approach with a true heart in full assurance of faith, with our hearts sprinkled clean from an evil conscience and our bodies washed with pure water" (10:22), and to "hold fast to the confession of our hope without wavering" (10:23) resonate with the context of worship. Similarly, the exhortation to "continually offer a sacrifice of praise to God . . . the fruit of lips that confess his name" (13:15), while imaginable as private prayer, has clear liturgical echoes.

If the church experiences the ongoing intercessory benefits of Jesus the high priest as it worships together, there is a double incentive for believers to hold fast in solidarity with fellow believers. When the author of Hebrews portrays Jesus as high priest, he is exploiting a very powerful metaphor. Yet it is a mistake to think of the church's experience of Jesus as intercessory high priest at the purely metaphorical level. Not only does this ignore the powerful role metaphors play in both expressing and shaping experience, but it also misunderstands the nature and function of metaphorical language. For the author of Hebrews and his fainthearted believers, at some inescapable, deeply religious level, Jesus *is* high priest.

4. *Every believer lives as part of a larger community of faith that embodies the transcendent vision of God, its ultimate source of strength and hope.* Most immediately, believers

experience the community of faith as those who assemble to worship in a particular location—the local church. To neglect this seemingly ordinary gathering is to cut oneself off from a vital source of fellowship and strength (10:25). Not only does mutual exhortation occur there, but in such gatherings believers are also reminded regularly of the commitments they have made and the ultimate values by which they have ordered their lives. As they "see the day approaching," they distinguish peripheral and central matters and refocus energies. Since the church at worship is where Jesus' priestly intercession is experienced acutely, the community of believers serves as source and resource for spiritual renewal.

Also evident from the exhortations in chapters 12–13 is the church's role as a community of moral formation. The author repeatedly reminds the church to be attentive to its common life together. While the pursuit of peace (12:14) and mutual love (13:1) are moral commonplaces, they are not for that reason trivial. Rather, their value for nurturing community is universally recognized. And when members are urged to help each other "obtain the grace of God" (12:15), they are probably being reminded to strengthen weaker members.

Believers must also be self-monitoring so that "no root of bitterness springs up and causes trouble" (12:15). In view is probably the defilement that comes with teaching that threatens the vibrancy of the faith. Being alert to "strange teachings" is called for, with the reminder that grace gives more strength than worrying about food regulations (13:9). Warnings against immorality and godlessness abound, with Esau serving as a useful reminder of seriously misplaced values and woefully bad judgment (12:16–17). Honor and fidelity in marriage are also valued among the highest virtues (13:4).

Equally praised is a generous spirit demonstrated by acts of hospitality (13:1–3). Doing good and sharing possessions are twin virtues that constitute their own form of sacrificial worship (13:16). The church is urged to visit those in prison, to attend to those who are tortured, and to identify fully with their suffering (13:3). The universal evil—love of money—and its attendant vices are also rejected. Readers are reminded that the insatiable desire to acquire possessions actually implicates God (13:5). Respect for the church's leaders is twice called for, advice grounded in the recognition of the debt students owe to teachers (13:7, 17). The stabilizing effect of such grateful behavior is also obvious. Underlying these several exhortations is the assumption that a decision to leave the church's fellowship will inevitably have adverse moral consequences—perhaps not immediately, but eventually.

Transcending the local church is a much larger community of faith, which the author of Hebrews depicts in several ways. As chapter 11 shows, every local community is expected to see itself as part of the people of God in every time and place. Using the vivid image of the gallery of witnesses, the author invites his listeners to construct a "community of the mind" inhabited by worthy exemplars of faith. While it is a highly stylized rehearsal of the biblical story, it derives its rhetorical power from the initial definition of faith (11:1). Here the author crisply—and memorably—encapsulates his view that faith has two defining elements: it serves as the ground of hope and it affirms the truth of transcendent reality.

Recognizing that faith is a way of living based on a way of seeing, our author adduces examples of those who shaped their lives by a vision of God's future that altered their present experience of life. As the author puts it, they believed in God's promises even though they did not live to see them fulfilled. Jesus is the defining exemplar, the "pioneer and perfecter" of faith, since he exemplified completely what his predecessors had experienced partially (12:1–4).

The larger community of faith is not confined to the description in 11:1–12:4. In chapters 2–4, the contrast between Jesus and Moses serves the same purpose. Both are utterly faithful—Moses faithful in God's house, Jesus faithful over God's house—even though Jesus, because of his heavenly position, surpasses Moses in rank. Though it is a negative example, Israel's experience in the wilderness is a powerful reminder of the importance of faithful obedience (3:16–19; 4:11).

Sketching the multi-dimensional character of the community of faith functions as part of the author's overall rhetorical strategy. By enlarging the horizons of the individual believer's understanding of the community of faith, the author constructs a more complex network of support, one that transcends time and space. Nowhere is the author's strategy clearer than in the highly rhetorical, poetically rendered vision of 12:22–24:

> But you have come to Mount Zion and to the city of the living God, the heavenly Jerusalem, and to innumerable angels in festal gathering, and to the assembly of the first-born who are enrolled in heaven, and to God the judge of all, and to the spirits of the righteous made perfect, and to Jesus, the mediator of a new covenant, and to the sprinkled blood that speaks a better word than the blood of Abel.

Through this cluster of well-chosen images, the author has constructed an unforgettable vision for believers. Taken together, its several elements sketch a transcendent community with a fully human dimension. This vision also bridges past, present, and future, even as it links heaven and earth; and it identifies the "living God," "God the judge of all," "Jesus, the mediator of the new covenant" and Jesus' "sprinkled blood" as the central realities of the vision—realities that are jointly experienced and confessed.

To underscore the transcendent nature of this vision, the author contrasts the alternative vision of Sinai, whose distinguishing features are palpable, even empirical—what can be "touched, a blazing fire, and darkness, and gloom, and a tempest, and the sound of a trumpet, and a voice …" (12:18–19). The effect of the contrast is clear: the way of faith is to pursue the transcendent vision rather than to be seduced by the physical world we see and experience. To exchange the former for the latter is to commit Esau's folly (12:16–17).

5. *While the new covenant initiated by God through Jesus' death opens new possibilities for believers, it also establishes solidarity with the faithful witnesses in Israel's past.* Hebrews shares with other NT writings the conviction that the coming of Jesus marks a pivotal moment in the story of God's dealings with humanity. Elsewhere in the NT, different metaphors are used to express this, for example, new creation or the turning of the ages (2 Cor 5). In Hebrews this conviction is expressed in yet another way.

In the prologue, the dominant metaphor is God's speaking. Opening the discourse with this oral/aural metaphor, the author expects his listeners to think of the different ways God has spoken during the past—through the prophets, to be sure, and in the view of early Alexandrian interpreters, through philosophers as well. Envisioned is a chorus of voices, with their many sounds and harmonies all singing God's narrative tune. Yet as the chorus moves forward, there emerges a clearer, louder voice—a solo sung against the background of the chorus of voices who preceded it.

Reinforcing this bold claim of Jesus' unique role in revealing God is the chorus of scriptural voices that come to life in the chain of OT quotations in 1:5–14. Jesus is superior to angels, but these passages should be read for what they are—*testimonia*, the technical term used to describe OT passages that spoke of Jesus. In them we hear God's voice testifying to Jesus' unique role as God's duly appointed Messiah, God's agent of creation, the one exalted to God's right hand. These highly adorational claims enhance Jesus' role as messianic revealer and mark the arrival of a new day in God's dealings with humanity.

The other major way in which this claim is developed in Hebrews is through the contrast between the old and new covenants. As already noted, the author's exposition of Jer 31 in chapter 8 functions as part of the extended middle section, in which he explores the implications of Ps 110:4. The death of Jesus is a unique instance in which the two expectations articulated by God in sketching the new covenant were fulfilled: a completely pure conscience free from the stain of guilt and a human heart on which God's will was fully inscribed. Because these two expectations achieved full, perfect expression in the death of Jesus, this marked the beginning of God's new covenant.

Coupled with this was the conviction that Jesus' appointment as high priest, while made earlier and constituting an eternal covenant, officially took effect with his death and exaltation in the heavenly sanctuary. A new high priest officially marks the arrival of the new covenant. A will takes effect, argues our author, when the person making the will, the testator, dies. The death of Jesus thus marks the moment when the new covenant takes effect.

The contrast between old and new, which is developed extensively in Hebrews, merely reinforces the momentous change that occurred with Jesus—a shift from old priesthood to new priesthood, from earthly tabernacle to heavenly tabernacle, and from the Mosaic law to the new covenant initiated by Christ. In marking this shift, Hebrews shares with other NT writings the conviction that Christ redefined the order that was in place when he arrived. Yet the way in which Hebrews expresses this redefinition is quite distinct. It lacks the agonizing ambivalence we find in Paul's nuanced critique of the Mosaic law in Romans and Galatians. It also differs from Paul's appropriation of the old and new covenant language in 2 Cor 3, especially the contrast between letter and spirit and the alignment of the ministries of Moses and Christ with each of them respectively. Paul's bold claim that the "letter kills and the spirit gives life" or that the old covenant was a ministry of death while the new covenant brings life constitutes a different claim from the one we find in Hebrews. Like Paul, Hebrews insists that the loyalty of believers in Christ shifted from the Mosaic law to Christ. The more emphatic language of Colossians and Ephesians that the Mosaic law was "taken out of the way and nailed to the cross" does not occur in Hebrews.

The particular form of the contrast in Hebrews should be noted: the old that is surpassed is the Levitical system of offerings and sacrifices, while the new that replaces it is the obedient spirit that does the will of the Lord. Hebrews is more pointed than Paul and other NT witnesses in its critique of the ineffectiveness of the Levitical sacrificial system—"it is impossible for the blood of bulls and goats to take away sins" (10:4). In lodging such a sustained critique of the Levitical sacrificial system, the author of Hebrews insists that he is on good scriptural grounds. In his view, God's own critique of this system is made abundantly clear in Jer 31. If it has become obsolete— and it has—it is owing to Israel's own unfaithfulness and to God's recognition of the broken covenant.

The continuity Hebrews sees between the new covenant and Israel's past is the enduring principle of faith and its manifestation in doing the will of God. In one sense, this is a slight variation on Paul's insistence in Romans and Galatians that justification by faith has always been the way the people of God have experienced God's righteousness, beginning with Abraham. Yet Hebrews places the accent on faith at a slightly different point. Rather than seeing faith as trusting in God in the Pauline sense, and linking this sense of trust with experiencing God's righteousness, the author of Hebrews sees faith in slightly different terms—as the absolute conviction of things unseen and the ultimate ground of hope. But rather than finding its most exemplary expression in Abraham, the author of Hebrews sees faith as the distinguishing characteristic of the notable figures in Israel's history from the time of Abel forward. And what each of them experienced in quite different circumstances, even through the horrific trials of the Maccabean period, Jesus experienced in its purest form.

Seen this way, the understanding of Jesus' faith in Hebrews is a more fully developed understanding of what many scholars now understand Pauline "faith of Christ" to mean—the absolute fidelity of Christ to the will of God and its fully exemplary character for other believers. Even if this is not the case, it is still clear that the author of Hebrews sees Jesus Christ not merely as one in a long succession of faithful witnesses but as the pinnacle of faith—or, as he puts it, as the "pioneer and perfecter of our faith." In this sense, Jesus stands in close solidarity with Israel's past, even Moses, who was just as faithful in his own way within God's order. Jesus surpasses Moses in Hebrews, and even surpasses the angels, given his heavenly status. But Hebrews affirms a strong sense of continuity between the new covenant Jesus inaugurated and Israel's past. It is a mistake to see the contrast between the old and the new covenants as an undifferentiated contrast between Judaism and Christianity, or even between law and gospel. Hebrews confirms that God's witness as revealed through Scripture continues into the new covenant; indeed, the scriptural witness is one of the main underpinnings of the new covenant.

And how does this overall construal of Jesus and the new covenant offer encouragement to believers? It reminds them of the seismic shift that occurred in Jesus' coming, life, death, and exaltation. The new covenant symbolizes the new possibilities that he brought about, even as it reminds believers of the solution it offers to the perennial problem of human sinfulness. The anti-ritualistic critique reinforces this point, but it is just as heavily reinforced by the cosmic dualism of Hebrews and its insistence that access to God's presence and closing the gap between human stain and God's holiness are genuine possibilities for those with enduring faith in Christ.

Notes

1. *Soph.* 13.

2. For the following rehearsal of the church's use of Hebrews and other aspects related to its history of interpretation, I am indebted to Craig Koester, *Hebrews: A New Translation with Introduction and Commentary* (AB 36; New York: Doubleday, 2001), esp. 19–63.

3. *1 Clem.* 36.1–6, drawing heavily on Heb 1:1–13 but also on Heb 2:17–18; 3:1; 4:15. Clement's dependence on Hebrews is noted by Eusebius in *Hist. eccl.* 3.38.1–3. Some scholars prefer to date *1 Clement* more flexibly, sometime between 90 and 120 C.E.

4. *1 Clem.* 47.1.

5. Possible echoes of Hebrews are heard in Polycarp, *Phil.* 6.3 (Heb 12:28); 12.2 (Heb 6:20; 7:3); Ignatius, *Smyrn.* 8.2 (Heb 6:19); Hermas, *Mand.* 4.3.1–2 (Heb 6:4–6); and Irenaeus, *Haer.* 2.30.9 (Heb 1:3). On Irenaeus's use of Hebrews, see Eusebius, *Hist. eccl.* 5.26.

6. Frequent quotations from Hebrews occur, for example, in *Strom.* He attributes quotations from Hebrews to "the apostle (Paul)" in *Strom.* 4.16 & 20 (cf. ANF 2:427–28, 432).

7. From Clement of Alexandria's *Hypotyposes* as cited by Eusebius in *Hist. eccl.* 6.14.1–4; also cf. 3.38.2. Similarly, from Cassiodorus's Latin translation of fragments from Clement: ". . . Luke also may be recognized by the style both to have composed the Acts of the Apostles and to have translated Paul's Epistle to the Hebrews" (ANF 2:573). Later interpreters spotted the flaw in this ingenious solution. Throughout the letter the author uses the Septuagint and at several points the argument would make no sense in Hebrew. In 9:15–17, the argument hinges on the Greek term *diathēkē* and its double sense "covenant" and "will," which the Hebrew term *bĕrît* does not convey. Similarly, in 10:5–10 the exposition of Ps 40:6–8 depends on the phrase "body you have prepared [for me]" (5b), which is based on the LXX instead of the Hebrew Bible, in which the term for "body" is "ear."

8. E.g., *Princ.* Pref. 1; *Comm. Jo.* 2.72; 10.84.

9. Eusebius, *Hist. eccl.* 6.25.13. Origen also reports earlier suggestions in the tradition that the author was Clement of Rome or Luke (see Eusebius, *Hist. eccl.* 6.25.14; also cf. 3.38.2).

10. See Origen's *Homilies on Hebrews* as cited in Eusebius, *Hist. eccl.* 6.25.11–14.

11. Eusebius, *Hist. eccl.* 6.25.14. Cf. *The Greek Anthology* 9.135 (LCL 3).

12. Hebrews shares this feature with 1 John, and to some extent with 2–3 John. Some have even conjectured that Hebrews had an original epistolary greeting that has been lost. Alternatively, others have explained the exclusive epistolary features at the end of the work by suggesting that ch. 13 was a later addition. Neither is probable.

13. In the NIV rendering, "I have written you only a short letter," the term *epistellō* is taken in a very specific sense. While the term can mean to "send a letter" or "instruct or inform by a letter," it can have the more general sense "to write" or "to send something to someone." Cf. Acts 15:20; 21:25.

14. The author typically uses phrases like "what we are speaking [or saying]," e.g., 2:5; 5:11; 6:9; 8:1; 9:5; 11:32. Except for 13:22, he does not refer to what he "writes" (*graphō*); cf. 1 Cor 4:14; 5:9, 11. His use of personal forms of address, e.g., "brothers" (*adelphoi*) in 3:1, 12; 10:19; and 13:22 is less decisive, since this is a typical form of address in letters. Cf. 1 Cor 2:1; 3:1, etc. It should also be noted, however, that Paul frequently uses oral verbs in his letters, e.g., 1 Cor 9:8; 15:34—an apt reminder that letters were written to be read aloud and thus served as substitutes for the letter writer's own oral speech.

15. For example, "without genealogy" (*agenealogētos*, 7:3); "[sin that] clings so closely" (*euperistatos*, 12:1); "recompense" (*misthapodosia*, 2:2; 10:35; 11:26); "rewarder" (*misthapodotēs*, 11:6); and "perfecter" (*teleiōtēs*, 12:2).

16. These are constructed in Greek as single, complex sentences, consisting of extended clauses connected by various coordinating devices. Since English translations typically break them up into several shorter sentences, it is often impossible to spot them. Among the longest are 1:1–4; 6:16–20; 9:6–10; 10:19–25. Others include 2:2–4, 8–9, 14–15; 3:12–15; 4:12–13; 5:1–3, 7–10; 6:4–6; 7:1–3; 8:4–6; 9:2–5, 24–26; 10:11–13; 11:24–26; 12:1–2, 18–21, 22–24.

17. The opening exposition of chapter 1 gives way to the exhortation in 2:1–4. Intermittent exhortations, often marked by the use of the hortatory subjunctive, "let us . . .," punctuate the remaining exposition, e.g., 4:1–2, 11, 14–16; 6:1–12; 10:19–25; 12:1–2.

18. Imperatives occur at 3:13; 10:32, 35; 12:3, 7, 12, 14, 25; 13:1, 2, 3, 7, 9, 16, 17, 18, 24. Hortatory subjunctives, typically translated "let us . . .," occur at 4:1, 11, 14, 16; 6:1; 10:22–24; 12:1, 28; 13:13, 15.

19. *Soph.* 16–17.

20. *Antid.* 46–47; also *Phil.* 27; *Panath.* 2. Also see Cicero, *Or. Brut.* 52.174–76; 56.187–57.196; 69.229 (critical of using poetic rhythms); *De or.* 1.33.151.

21. *Rhet.* 3.8.1409ª. Examples include *gĕgŏnĕnāi* [11:3] and *ĕtĭ lălēi* [11:4].

22. E.g., *pŏlŭmĕrōs* (1:1); *ŏthĕn ădĕlph* (3:1); *ĕtĭ găr ēn* (7:10).

23. Five *p*'s in 11:28, four *p*'s in 11:17.

24. Aeschylus, *Ag.* 177.

25. *Rhet.* 3.6.1408ª.

26. While it is difficult to get a precise count, Hebrews contains some thirty-five OT quotations: 1:5*a* (Ps 2:7); 1:5*b* (2 Sam 7:14; 1 Chr 17:13); 1:6 (Deut 32:43 LXX; Ps 96:7 LXX); 1:7 (Ps 104:4); 1:8–9 (Ps 45:6–7); 1:10–12 (Ps 102:25–27, esp. LXX); 1:13 (Ps 110:1); 2:6–8 (Ps 8:4–6); 2:12 (Ps 22:22); 2:13 (Isa 8:17–18; 12:2, esp. LXX); 3:5 (Num 12:7, esp. LXX); 3:7–11, 15; 4:3, 5, 7 (Ps 95:7–11); 4:4 (Gen 2:2); 5:5 (Ps 2:7); 5:6 (Ps 110:4); 6:14 (Gen 22:17); 7:1–2, 4 (Gen 14:17–20); 7:17, 21 (Ps 110:4); 8:5 (Exod 25:40); 8:8–12 (Jer 31:31–34); 9:20 (Exod 24:8); 10:5–9 (Ps 40:6–8); 10:16–17 (Jer 31:33–34); 10:28 (Deut 17:6); 10:30 (Deut 32:35–36); 10:37–38 (Isa 26:20; Hab 2:3–4, esp. LXX); 11:18 (Gen 21:12); 11:21 (Gen 47:31, esp. LXX); 12:5–6 (Prov 3:11–12); 12:15 (Deut 29:18); 12:21 (Deut 9:19); 12:26 (Hag 2:6, 21); 12:29 (Deut 4:24; 9:3); 13:5 (Deut 31:6, 8; Gen 28:15); 13:6 (Ps 118:6). The distribution is striking: almost half are from the Pentateuch; about a third are from the Psalter (from eleven different psalms); one is from the book of Proverbs; the rest are from the prophets. While it is not explicitly quoted, Leviticus heavily informs Heb 9. Use is also made of other writings included in the Septuagint (2 Macc 5–7 in 11:35–38; Wis 7:25 in 1:3). Add to these the dozens of OT allusions and we get a sense of what constitutes the author's understanding of the "oracles of God" (5:12; cf. Acts 7:38; Rom 3:2; 1 Pet 4:11). Also remarkable is the absence of the usual NT designations for Scripture, e.g., *hē graphē*, or the familiar introductory formula, "it is written" (*gegraptai*; though cf. 3:15; 7:17). Instead, quotations are usually attributed directly to God (e.g., 1:5), the Holy Spirit (e.g., 10:15), or Christ (e.g., 10:5).

Bibliography

Commentaries

Attridge, Harold W. *The Epistle to the Hebrews*. Hermeneia. Philadelphia: Fortress, 1989.

Bruce, F. F. *The Epistle to the Hebrews*. New International Commentary on the New Testament. Rev. ed. Grand Rapids: Eerdmans, 1990 (1964).

Buchanan, George Wesley. *To the Hebrews*. Anchor Bible 36. Garden City: Doubleday, 1972.

Craddock, Fred B. "The Letter to the Hebrews: Introduction, Commentary, and Reflections." Pages 1–173 in vol. 12 of *The New Interpreter's Bible*. Edited by Leander E. Keck. 12 vols. Nashville: Abingdon, 1998.

deSilva, David. *Perseverance in Gratitude: A Socio-Rhetorical Commentary on the Epistle to the Hebrews*. Grand Rapids: Eerdmans, 2000.

Héring, Jean. *The Epistle to the Hebrews*. Translated from 1st French ed. by A. W. Heathcote and P. J. Allcock. London: Epworth, 1970 (1954).

Jewett, Robert. *Letter to Pilgrims: A Commentary on the Epistle to the Hebrews*. New York: Pilgrim, 1981.

Koester, Craig R. *Hebrews: A New Translation with Introduction and Commentary*. Anchor Bible. New York: Doubleday, 2001.

Lane, William L. *Hebrews*. Word Biblical Commentary 47. 2 vols. Dallas: Word Books, 1991.

Long, Thomas G. *Hebrews*. Interpretation: A Bible Commentary for Teaching and Preaching. Louisville: Westminster John Knox, 1997.

Moffatt, James. *A Critical and Exegetical Commentary on the Epistle to the Hebrews*. International Critical Commentary. New York: Scribner, 1924.

Montefiore, Hugh W. *A Commentary on the Epistle to the Hebrews*. Black's New Testament Commentary Series. London: Adam & Charles Black, 1964.

Pfitzner, Victor C. *Hebrews*. Abingdon New Testament Commentaries. Nashville: Abingdon, 1997.

Thompson, James W. *The Letter to the Hebrews*. Austin: Sweet, 1971.

Other Resources

deSilva, David A. *Despising Shame: Honor Discourse and Community Maintenance in the Epistle to the Hebrews*. Society of Biblical Literature Dissertation Series 152. Atlanta: Society of Biblical Literature (Scholars Press), 1995.

Greer, Rowan A. *The Captain of Our Salvation: A Study in the Patristic Exegesis of Hebrews*. Beiträge zur Geschichte der biblischen Exegese 15. Tübingen: Mohr (Siebeck), 1973.

Horton, Fred L. *The Melchizedek Tradition: A Critical Examination of the Sources to the Fifth Century A.D. and in the Epistle to the Hebrews*. Society of New Testament Monograph Series 30. Cambridge: Cambridge University Press, 1976.

Hughes, Graham. *Hebrews and Hermeneutics*. Society for New Testament Studies Monograph Series 36. Cambridge: Cambridge University Press, 1979.

Käsemann, Ernst. *The Wandering People of God: An Investigation of the Letter to the Hebrews*. Translated by Roy A. Harrisville and I. L. Sandberg. 2d ed. Minneapolis: Augsburg, 1984 (1938).

Lindars, B. *The Theology of the Letter to the Hebrews*. New Testament Theology. Cambridge: Cambridge University Press, 1991; repr. 2001.

Thompson, James W. *The Beginnings of Christian Philosophy*. Catholic Biblical Quarterly Monograph Series 13. Washington, D.C.: Catholic Biblical Association of America, 1982.

Young, Frances M. "Letter to the Hebrews." Pages 488–91 in vol. 1 of *Dictionary of Biblical Interpretation*. Edited by John H. Hayes. 2 vols. Nashville: Abingdon, 1999.

Part 5

THE
CATHOLIC
LETTERS

The Catholic Letters

In Athanasius's well-known *Thirty-Ninth Festal Letter*, issued in 367 C.E., he enumerates the twenty-seven NT writings that he regarded as canonical. Included among them are the "seven so-called catholic epistles of the apostles": James, 1–2 Peter, 1–2–3 John, and Jude. Writing some thirty or forty years earlier, Eusebius reported that James, the brother of Jesus, was "the author of the first of the epistles which are entitled catholic" (*Hist. eccl.* 2.23.24). He also called Jude one of the "seven catholic epistles" (*Hist. eccl.* 2.23.25). Eusebius went on to say that James and Jude "as well as the others, have been read in public in most churches" (Hist. eccl. 2.23.25).

As this patristic testimony shows, by the fourth century these seven NT writings were grouped together and described as "catholic." With his concluding comment, Eusebius suggests one sense in which these letters were catholic—they were read and accepted by the church at large. This echoes the sentiment of the Muratorian Fragment, which probably reflects the situation in the West around 200 C.E., when it reports that Jude and two Johannine letters were "accepted in the catholic [church]."

But these seven writings were catholic in another sense. In contrast to Paul's letters, which were addressed to churches in specific locations or to named individuals, these letters envisioned a wider audience. Both James and 1 Peter are addressed to Christians in the "Dispersion." In the former, they are the "twelve tribes in the Dispersion" (Jas 1:1); in the latter they are the "exiles of the Dispersion" located in named provinces of Asia Minor (1 Pet 1:1). The addressees of 2 Peter, 1 John, and Jude are described in general terms, while 2 John is addressed to "the elect lady and her children" (v. 1) and 3 John is addressed to "the beloved Gaius" (v. 1). While these greetings represent a range of addressees, these letters were seen as "catholic" or "general" because their audience was the church universal rather than congregations in one city or locale.

Before these letters were grouped together and accepted as canonical, their individual status within the church varied. James, 1 Peter, and 1 John won early acceptance, while the status of 2 Peter, 2–3 John, and Jude was more seriously contested. A distinction was made between the major (James, 1 Peter, & 1 John) and minor (2 Peter, 2–3 John, and Jude) Catholic Letters.

While the designation "catholic" is a convenient label for an otherwise disparate set of writings, it can easily mask the particularity in some of the letters. This is especially true of the three Johannine letters, which address a theological crisis within the Johannine church. The letters of Jude and 2 Peter also reflect theological tensions among communities of believers. While it is difficult to identify the actual situation addressed by 1 Peter, the circumstances were by no means vague or nonspecific. Of the seven, James is perhaps the most general in its overall orientation.

Regardless of the particular circumstances reflected in the various letters, they were "catholic" because they were worthy witnesses of the gospel to the church at large.

Chapter 22

James

"Therefore St. James's epistle is really an epistle of straw . . . for it has nothing of the nature of the gospel about it."

Martin Luther

"If the Epistle is 'of straw,' then there is within that straw a very hearty, firm, nourishing but as yet uninterpreted and unthrashed grain."

Johann Gottfried Herder

"Me thynketh it ought of ryght to be taken for holye Scripture."

William Tyndale

Jerome's *Lives of Illustrious Men*, a work devoted to "all those who have published any memorable writing on the Holy Scriptures from the time of our Lord's passion until the fourteenth year of the Emperor Theodosius" (392 C.E.), treats 135 distinguished men. Second in the list—after Peter—is James, the brother of Jesus, who receives twice as much space as Peter and more space than any of the four evangelists. Noting that James was ordained by the apostles as bishop of Jerusalem, Jerome (ca. 345–420 C.E.) reports that he "wrote a single epistle, which is reckoned among the seven catholic epistles." He further observes that "even this [epistle] is claimed by some to have been published by some one else under [James's] name, and gradually, as time went on, to have gained authority."[1] [**See Expanded CD Version pp. 677–79: *The Church's Debate Over the Letter of James*]

Identifying James: The Person and the Letter

Like 1–2 Peter and Jude, the Letter of James receives its name from the author named in the opening greeting. Calling himself "a servant of God and of the Lord Jesus Christ" (1:1), this James was early identified as James the apostle, son of Zebedee and brother of John (cf. Matt 4:21; 10:2; 17:1 and parallels; Acts 1:13; according to Acts 12:2, James the apostle was killed by Herod Agrippa I ca. 44 C.E.). He was also identified with another James—the brother of Jesus—who emerged as the leader of the Jerusalem church and who, according to tradition, died as a martyr just before the destruction of the Jerusalem temple in 70 C.E. (cf. Matt 13:55; Mark 6:3; 1 Cor 15:7; Gal 1:19; 2:9, 12; Acts 12:17; 15:13; 21:18; also Jude 1).[2] Also remembered in the tradition for his courageous piety and frequent prayer that gave him calloused knees like a camel, he became known as James the Just.[3]

Questions about the authenticity of the letter surfaced early. Eusebius (ca. 260–340 C.E.) reports that "[James] is considered spurious," noting that "certainly not many of the ancients mentioned it."[4] His perception squares with what we now know from ancient sources: no undisputed usage by any second-century writer;[5] lack of inclusion in the Muratorian Fragment (ca. 200 C.E.); first explicit mention by Origen;[6] apparent neglect in the West until the mid-fourth century.[7] Thanks to Origen, who regarded James as apostolic scripture, the letter gained acceptance in the East and was included in the canonical list of Athanasius's *Thirty-Ninth Festal Letter* (367 C.E.). It was eventually embraced in the West, accepted as canonical by the Council of Hippo (393 C.E.) and the Councils of Carthage (397, 419 C.E.). Although the Syrian churches generally rejected the Catholic Letters, James gained wider acceptance by being translated (along with 1 Peter and 1 John) into Syriac and included in the Peshitta version in the early fifth century. By the beginning of the fifth century, doubts about James in most regions of the church had been assuaged.

With no clear mention of James by the earliest Christian writers, it is difficult to date or locate the writing. Probably the earliest allusion comes in the opening greeting of the Letter of Jude, who is identified as a "brother of James," but Jude is equally elusive. If the letter were definitely attributable to James, the brother of Jesus, and if the reports of his martyrdom were reliable, it would have been written prior to 70 C.E. This would also ensure its Palestinian provenance. Some scholars think the reference to early and late rains (5:7) points to a Palestinian or Syrian setting. Some prefer an early dating, about 50 C.E., raising the possibility that it could be the earliest NT writing. There is nothing to preclude this, but there is no hard evidence to support it. At a number of points, the letter echoes the Jesus tradition, for example, the Sermon on the Mount. This might suggest connections with the earliest stages of the Gospel tradition, but this is only conjecture. No firm connection with historical persons or datable events in the first century C.E. is evident in the letter. James reflects no awareness, for example, of the Jew-Gentile controversy that preoccupied Paul in the early 50s and that is prominently reported in Acts.

How best to characterize the Letter of James depends on the framework of comparison one uses. Its fondness for proverbial wisdom and its pervasive moralistic emphasis align it closely with Jewish wisdom literature, especially Sirach, and to some extent Wisdom of Solomon, *Testaments of the Twelve Patriarchs*, and Proverbs. Yet it also reads well alongside Greco-Roman moral writings, displaying an interest in themes commonly treated in such writings: the value of wisdom, how to cope with hardships, the danger of riches, vices relating to speech, and the cultivation of virtuous behaviors such as patience. Since the letter is couched in the form of an oral discourse in which the speaker develops topics in conversation with an imaginary interlocutor, it bears close resemblance to the Cynic-Stoic diatribe. Given this blend of interests and its distinctive formal features, it is best seen as a Jewish Christian wisdom tractate presented in sermonic form.

While the Greek style of James is by no means elegant, neither is it inelegant. Instead, the letter reveals an author at home with Greek, with an impressive vocabulary and skill in the use of Greek stylistic conventions, and familiar with the language of the Septuagint and that of the wider Hellenistic world.

How Christian Is James?

At first glance, James seems superficially Christian. Frequently noted are its two lone references to Jesus Christ (1:1; 2:1), its neglect of the Holy Spirit,[8] the absence of distinctive Christian terms, such as gospel (*euangelion*), and its failure to mention central elements of early Christian belief, most notably the death and resurrection of Jesus. Some scholars have even wondered whether James was originally a Jewish composition later embroidered here and there with bits of Christian lace.

But this is an optical illusion. Explicit Christian language may be hard to find, but it is not totally absent. The "elders of the church" (5:14, *hoi presbyteroi tēs ekklēsias*) who are summoned to pray over the sick are doubtless leaders of Christian communities (the same expression is used of the Ephesian church leaders in Acts 20:17; cf. Acts 14:23; 1 Tim 5:17–19; Titus 1:5). Their anointing the sick "with oil in the name of the Lord" (5:14) should be seen as a rite of Christian unction performed under the authority of the Lord Jesus. Accordingly, the prayers, songs of praise, and mutual confessions mentioned in 5:13–16 should be understood as practices carried on within Christian communities. While unidentified, the Lord who "raises up" the sick is probably the Lord Jesus whose healing power elsewhere extends to Christian communities (cf. Acts 3:6; 9:34). The repeated use of "[beloved] brothers" as a form of address (1:2, 16, 19; 2:1, 5, 14; 3:1, 10, 12; 4:11; 5:7, 12, 19) and the presence of "brothers and sisters" (2:15) within the community of believers reflect standard Christian practice.[9]

It is just as reasonable to see Jesus behind other unspecified references to "the Lord." While the OT knows of the coming Day of the Lord (Ezek 30:1–4; Joel 2:1–2; Amos 5:18–20; Zeph 1:14–18), the "coming of the Lord" (*hē parousia tou kyriou*), which establishes the future horizon of James, is probably Jesus' Parousia (5:7, 8; cf. 1 Thess 2:19; 3:13; 4:15; 5:23; 2 Thess 2:1; 2 Pet 1:16; also Matt 24:3, 27, 37, 39).

While the exact relationship between the treatment of faith and works in Jas 2:14–26 and Paul's elaboration of justification by faith in Galatians and Romans continues to be debated, both discussions reflect a larger debate within early Christianity.

Also striking are the numerous echoes of Jesus' teaching known from the Gospel tradition. One of the most remarkable instances is the prohibition against swearing (5:12), which closely resembles Jesus' wholesale prohibition against oaths in the Sermon on the Mount (Matt 5:33–37).[10]

A Miscellany of Teachings or an Ordered Discourse?

Interpreters have found it difficult to outline James or to find a clear organizational principle. Topics seem to shift abruptly, themes introduced at one point are picked up later in the letter, and key words that conclude one section seem to introduce another section. Such apparent lack of organization often characterizes wisdom writings. But this is not surprising, given the self-contained nature of wisdom sayings and the difficulty editors of wisdom writings experienced in arranging such teachings into coherent collections. Part of the explanation may relate to the sermonic quality of James. Such loose thematic development could also characterize oral discourses composed in diatribal style. More important than neat, sequential development of a single topic was the overall rhetorical impact of a cumulative set of images, brief arguments in the form of dialogue, and aphoristic teachings.

Even with this kaleidoscopic movement from topic to topic in James, we can propose a discernible sequence in the overall argument.

The discourse opens with teaching about how to face trials (1:2–15). Trials produce patience and should be faced prayerfully and confidently (1:2–8). Proper perspective is provided by remembering the false security of the rich. Faced with trials, we tend to think that the rich and privileged are better off; they are not (1:9–11). More important is to recognize the true source of life's trials—they are not from God, but are part of the human condition, and are often of our own making (1:12–15).

In order to face trials, we must learn to be responsive to God's message (1:16–27). God, the source of blessings, is our true Parent, giving birth to us through the "word of truth" (1:16–18). Instead of being angry about trials, we should develop positive strategies in dealing with them. Human anger works at cross-purposes with God's righteousness. The proper attitude is to be receptive to God's "implanted word" (1:19–21). The faithful response is doing the word, not just hearing it (1:22–25). Concretely, this means practicing "pure religion," caring for widows and orphans (1:26–27).

Required of all believers is faith that eliminates class distinctions (2:1–13). The basic principle is to hold to the glorious faith of the Lord Jesus Christ without discriminating on the basis of class (2:1). Believers' actions toward people of different social class, especially in worship, betray their true attitudes (2:2–4). God affirms the poor and condemns the abusive practices of the rich (2:5–7). Showing favoritism based on class violates the "royal law" of Lev 19:18 (2:8–11) and brings severe penalties (2:12–13).

Faith properly understood eventuates in actions (2:14–26). Faith without action is dead (2:14–17). Actions are the true sign of faith (2:18–19), as seen in the examples of active faith, Abraham and Rahab (2:20–26).

Among the greatest challenges of the faithful life is controlling the tongue (3:1–12). This begins by accepting responsibility for what we say (3:1–2) and learning from nature (the horse's bridle, the ship's rudder, the spark that ignites a forest fire) the importance of taming the tongue (2:3–8). Equally necessary is speaking with integrity, also something nature teaches (3:9–12).

Division and strife are to be avoided (3:13–4:12). This requires distinguishing between earthly and heavenly wisdom (3:13–18) and recognizing that quarrels and strife stem from wrong desires (4:1–3). Living peaceably as a community involves choosing between friendship with the world and friendship with God (4:4–10) and avoiding slanderous speech (4:11–12).

Among the most defining decisions believers can make is how to view the future. Two visions of the future are possible (4:13–5:12). Believers can view the future arrogantly and thereby entertain false hopes (4:13–17). Yet this view of the future is dashed when they realize the impermanence of wealth and the injustices done by the wealthy (5:1–6). Alternatively, the future can be understood in the light of the Lord's coming (5:7–9). The future so understood means living patiently and faithfully (5:10–12).

No final reminder is more appropriate than an exhortation to prayer (5:13–18). There are different ways and different reasons to pray (5:13–16), but Elijah's example shows prayer to be indispensable to faithful living (5:17–18).

As a final appeal, hearers are exhorted to recover wayward believers (5:19–20).

Faith and Works

For good or ill, the discussion of faith and works in Jas 2:14–26 has invited comparison with Paul's treatment of justification by faith in Romans and Galatians. It is easy to understand why. The contrast between faith (*pistis*) and works (*erga*), which runs throughout Jas 2:14–26, resonates with Paul's distinction between the "law of faith" (*nomos pisteōs*) and the "law of works" (*nomos tōn ergōn*) as two diametrically opposed principles (Rom 3:27; 9:32; cf. 3:20, 28; 4:2). Moreover, both James and Paul cite the example of Abraham and even draw on the same proof text, Gen 15:6 ("Abraham believed God, and it was reckoned to him as righteousness"), to support their positions (Jas 2:23; Rom 4:9; Gal 3:6).

Interpreters have employed various strategies to relate the theological viewpoints expressed by James and Paul. Some see them as mutually contradictory theologies of salvation, while others see them as different but theologically compatible viewpoints.[11] Given the close similarity of language and their common appeal to Abraham, reading James and Paul in light of each other is not only inevitable but also illuminating. When comparing them, we should let each speak for himself rather than listening to one only through the voice of the other.

If James has a distinctive viewpoint, it is his insistence that faith and actions are inseparable.[12] If we take the body/spirit analogy seriously (2:26), his point is not that faith gives life to actions, but that actions enliven faith. Faith may define actions, even give them shape. Feeding and clothing the poor may be charitable deeds, but when they are done in the name of Christ, they are more than acts of charity; they are actions of faith. James cannot separate faith and actions any more than he can conceive of inhaling without exhaling. Or, to frame his theological viewpoint in terms of Gen 15:6, righteousness for James has an inescapably practical dimension—righteousness can only be lived; theoretical righteousness is an oxymoron.

The phrasing in 2:22 is especially revealing: "[Abraham's] faith was active along with his works, and faith was brought to completion by the works." Here faith and actions are seen as symbiotic. Actions do not follow faith as a separate, sequential stage; rather, faith is actively channeled through actions. To restate the verse literally: Abraham's faith "acted together with his actions and through those very actions his faith was completed." Actions prompted by faith display the texture of faith.

Of the two complementary halves, actions are more heavily accented than faith. "Justified by actions" aptly captures James's emphasis (2:21, 24, 25). Abraham and Rahab are exemplary because each embodies the truth of this claim. Readers are expected to follow suit. James is not opposing hypocritical faith—claiming one thing and doing another—but empty faith—professing, then doing nothing.

Paul also insists on enacted faith: "the only thing that counts is faith working through love" (Gal 5:6). When Paul speaks of faith and actions together, he neither values actions nor accents their importance as James does. Instead, he invariably favors faith over actions. He never comes close to James's formulation: that we are "justified by actions." In sharp contrast, "justified by faith" compactly expresses Paul's view. What Paul finds revelatory about Gen 15:6 is the way faith and righteousness are linked in the figure Abraham. Rather than seeing Abraham's willingness to sacrifice Isaac as his finest hour (as James does), Paul sees his earlier willingness to believe in God's promise (Gen 12) as a far more defining moment. In Paul's view, Scripture identifies this earlier moment as the time when Abraham, through his faith, was reckoned by God as righteous. What Paul sees as especially instructive about Abraham's example was not so much his willingness to act on his faith but rather his initial capacity to have faith.

Paul and James are neither expressing diametrically opposed theological viewpoints nor saying the same thing in a different way. One of the chief differences between them is that the controversy over Torah observance by Gentiles, which fundamentally shapes the discussion in Paul, is absent in James. In the preceding discussion about fulfilling the law (2:8–13), James mentions the "royal law" (2:8) and the "law of liberty" (2:12). Parts of this discussion resonate with Paul, for example, the law's requirement to love neighbor as self (2:8, citing Lev 19:18; cf. Gal 5:14) and the principle of wholesale accountability to the law (2:10; cf. Gal 3:10). But James is not prompted by the same set of questions that prompted Paul to write Galatians and Romans.

When seen within the context of the controversy over Torah observance, in which the main issue was whether Gentiles were obligated to keep the law, Paul's contrast between faith and actions takes on a different hue. Like James, he speaks of faith and actions as a pair of opposites, but unlike James, he opposes a theological viewpoint that regards "works of law" (*erga nomōn*) as salvific. Consequently, other pairs of opposites surface in Paul's discussion: the law versus faith or the law versus Christ. To this extent, Paul's theological viewpoint is more fully elaborated, which is not surprising considering that most of Romans and Galatians is devoted to it. By contrast, James's discussion is more focused and limited in scope. James combats faith that has no social conscience, not even the capacity to translate belief into the simplest acts of kindness, while Paul combats a view of faith that values good deeds as inherently salvific.

For James, the central issue is whether authentic faith can exist without expressing itself in action; for Paul, it is whether humans can authentically experience God's righteousness apart from faith.

The Theological Vision of James

Compared with other NT moral instruction, James is remarkable for its thoroughly Jewish outlook. Offering a blend of Torah-based piety, prophetic rage, and practical wisdom, James draws on all three sections of Scripture—the law, prophets, and writings;[13] he also refers to several OT episodes.[14] His firm embrace of Torah aligns him closely with the spirit of Ps 119:97, "O how I love your law!" His relentless critique of the rich and their abusive treatment of the poor places him directly within Israel's tradition of socially conscious prophetic witness (cf. Amos 4:1–3; 8:4–8). Equally clear is his indebtedness to Israel's sages who traded heavily on the lessons from everyday life as they collected and dispensed wisdom.

Monotheistic Piety

Believing that "God is one" is the central axiom of James (2:19; cf. Deut 6:4). Devotion to "God the Father" (1:27) establishes the overarching religious framework of James. On the whole, James uses positive, endearing images of God, the source of wisdom, who gives generously to those who ask (1:5). As the Father of lights, perhaps the One who created the heavenly luminaries, God is not only the source of every good gift, but also of generosity itself (1:17). Much is made of God the Creator, the One in whose likeness humans are created (3:9). As One in whom there is no variation (1:17), God is utterly reliable. God can be expected to carry through on his promises: lovers of God will be rewarded with the crown of life (1:12); they will also receive the promised kingdom of God (2:5).

God's reliability is also reflected in an unerring sense of justice. God's righteousness becomes a standard for evaluating human anger (1:20). God also sets the expectations for pure and undefiled religion: caring for orphans and widows is a duty before God (1:27). God takes up the cause of the poor against the rich and makes the poor rich in faith (2:5), but also hears the cries of the oppressed (5:4). God also reverses the roles of the proud and the humble (4:6). Followers of God are expected to submit to God (4:7) and to do so with humility (4:10).

God's rectitude serves as a steadying force. God is both lawgiver and judge (4:12) and is probably the eschatological judge who stands at the door (5:9). Such a God is not amenable to being tested, nor does this God tempt, or play games with, any human being (1:13). Time and history are in God's hands. All human plans have a universal qualifier: "if the Lord wishes" (4:15).

Far from being a distant figure, God is not only Lord but also Father (3:9), the One who births believers through the word of truth (1:18). As Abraham showed, friendship with God is possible, although it is a function of faith (2:23). But this exclusive form of friendship precludes friendship with the world (4:4). The reassurance of God's own nearness prompts humanity to draw near to God (4:8), and such mutual attraction repels the presence of evil (4:7). God probably has an insatiable yearning to commune with the human spirit (4:5). If so, Augustine's "the soul does not rest until it rests in God" is reformulated in James: "God cannot rest until finding residence in the human soul."

Torah Observance

Nowhere are James and Paul more different than in their respective attitudes toward the Mosaic law. In James, Torah is neither passé nor problematic. Nor is James's attitude toward Torah ambivalent. Torah is in full effect for believers in Christ (2:10), and they are expected to revere it as the "perfect law, the law of liberty" (1:25; cf. 2:12) and the "royal law" (2:8). Christians are also expected to observe Torah scrupulously: "whoever keeps the whole law but fails in one point has become accountable for all of it" (2:10). When Paul cites this principle of 100 percent accountability in his critique against "Judaizers," he distances himself from it (Gal 3:10). For James, it is an utterly firm principle that informs Christian practice. Embrace of one's neighbor must take the form of impartial treatment of everyone (2:8). Complying with the Decalogue's prohibitions against adultery or murder must be matched with impartial behavior within the assembly, which is seen as a concrete example of loving neighbor as self (2:8). The law's intent is clear: one cannot treat the rich well and mistreat the poor. To do so places one under the law's judgment.

Torah has a similarly pivotal role in James's prohibition of judgmental conduct (4:11–12). Speaking evil of another believer (probably slandering the person) places one in flagrant violation of Torah. To judge another believer is to judge the law. Here, as in Jesus' Sermon on the Mount in Matthew, Torah serves as a defining norm for Christian behavior. Like Matthew, James regards the law (and the prophets) as fully in force and permanently binding for Christian conduct (cf. Matt 5:17–20).

James delivering his letter to a courier, possibly accompanied by representatives of the Dispersion (Jas 1:1). Woodcut from a Low German dialect version of Martin Luther's translation of the New Testament (Magdeburg, 1547). From the Digital Image Archive of The Richard C. Kessler Reformation Collection, Pitts Theology Library, Candler School of Theology, Emory University, Atlanta, Georgia.

This *halakic* understanding, in which Torah is read and interpreted to provide ethical norms for conduct, informs James's consistent call for "doing the word" (1:22–25). Although the word of the gospel may be in view, probably "word" is meant in the same sense it is used in Ps 119—the word of God. To comply with Torah is to comply with God's word as revealed in Scripture. When God implants the word within receptive hearts, it takes root and grows into appropriate actions (1:21).

Further evidence of the binding force of Torah is seen in James's pervasive use of Scripture argumentation. Not only does Torah prescribe a code of conduct, it also serves as a form of revelation from which a scribal teacher can argue. It is both moral guide and revelatory text. Whereas Paul critiques Torah yet argues from Scripture, James is more consistent in upholding both.

While Torah is uniformly binding in James, no cultic requirements are specified for Christian practice. Nor are distinctive practices such as circumcision, food laws, or Sabbath observance mentioned as binding on the Christian community.

Practical Wisdom

Sharing the outlook of Jewish Wisdom literature and the Greco-Roman moralists, James targets universally recognized vices and virtues. Trials are one of life's inevitabilities traceable more to human misguidedness than to God's mischievousness. They are valuable for teaching patience (1:2–4, 12–16; cf. Sir 2:1–6; 15:11–20). Strife, bitterness, envy, and quarreling are perennial threats to community harmony, stemming primarily from ill-conceived desires and fractious spirits (4:1–3; cf. Sir 28:8–11; 40:5, 8–9). Tensions between rich and poor also beset human society and thus religious communities as well (2:1–7; 5:1–6).[15] The rich tend to live with inflated views of themselves and to exploit the poor; by contrast, the poor must cultivate their own self-esteem. They must not be intimidated by the rich but live with the confidence that even wealth is illusory and short-lived. Vices related to speech are also targeted, especially loose, slanderous speech (1:26; 3:1–12).[16] Closely related is the standard theme of "saying and doing," or "words and deeds," with the accent falling on the practical benefits of doing good and the hypocrisy of hearing and not doing (1:22–25; cf. Matt 7:26; Deut 28:15; also cf. *m. 'Abot* 1.15, 17; 5.14; Philo, *Praem.* 14.79). This theme has a distinctive religious connotation in the contrast between "*faith* and deeds," or in its more familiar form, "faith and works."

One of the hallmarks of Wisdom literature is its belief that the everyday world is one of life's best teachers. Wisdom draws on the world of ordinary experience to teach moral lessons and illustrate character traits, both positive and negative. Lavish use of such images occurs in James: the indecisive person who is like a wind-tossed wave of the sea (1:6); the rich withering like a wild flower in the scorching sun (1:9–11); the God who does not change like shifting shadows (1:17); our failure to act on what we hear as being like looking in the mirror and immediately forgetting the image we saw (1:23–24); keeping a tight rein on the tongue (1:26); the hypocrisy of a finely attired rich man getting the best seat in church while a shabbily clothed poor man sits on the floor (2:2–3); the spectacle of the rich dragging the poor into court (2:6); curbing speech as being like putting bits in horses' mouths (3:3); the tongue as a small rudder guiding a ship (3:4–5); careless speech as being like the spark igniting a forest fire

(3:5–6); the loose tongue full of deadly poison (3:8); the absurdity of fresh and salt water flowing from the same spring (3:11) or a fig tree bearing olives, and a grapevine bearing figs (3:12); life as brief as a vanishing mist (4:14); and the patient farmer waiting for the autumn and spring rains (5:7).

Typical of Wisdom literature, James derives its force from the authoritative voice of the sage, who is identified as "a servant of God and of the Lord Jesus Christ." The only other time the author reveals his identity, he includes himself among the teachers (*didaskaloi*), warning them not to enter the profession casually (3:1–2). Nowhere does he feel compelled to trace his teachings to an apostolic voice, nor even to Jesus himself, although we hear some faint echoes of Jesus' teachings from the Gospel tradition.

Only in the most general sense are the teachings given in the name of Jesus. Individual instructions do not receive their warrant because they come from Jesus or come with authority traceable to him. [**See Expanded CD Version p. 688: *Ethical Teaching in James Compared with Rom 12–15***]

Neither does James undergird his teachings by appealing to tradition, recent or early. The one warrant repeatedly drawn upon is the voice of Scripture. But even the scriptural voice is less dominant than the authoritative voice of the author himself.

By identifying himself as a teacher, James places himself within the tradition of sages and scribes, whose authority to teach derives from their mastery of Scripture and their stature within the community as wise, perceptive readers of everyday life and human experience. This is the tradition of the rabbis, whose charge is to interpret Torah and apply it to life through compelling, authoritative teachings by which communities of the faithful can negotiate the moral dilemmas of life. There is a hard practicality to these teachings, since they draw on the cumulative experiences of life and its myriad decisions, both good and bad. These teachings have a pragmatic character, for it is not in the nature of these sages to speculate about life but to learn from it. They may draw on popular philosophical notions here and there—the teachings of other sages—but they are less interested in theorizing than in achieving hard, practical results. Noting inconsistencies between word and speech, between profession and practice, is the sages' stock-in-trade, and they are relentless in pointing them out. They also observe human behaviors and the ravaging effects such vices as slander and envy can have on people trying to live together as a community. They see through the pretensions of the wealthy and appreciate the hardscrabble lives of the poor. In James we hear the voice of practical experience steeped in the wisdom traditions of several cultures, all brought to bear on Christian practice to form the one NT writing that can rightly be called Christian Wisdom literature.

Notes

1. *Vir. ill.* 2 (NPNF[2] 3:361).

2. As Jesus' brother, James is thus distinguished from (although sometimes confused with) the other apostle, James the son of Alphaeus (Matt 10:3 and parallels; Acts 1:13), sometimes identified with "James the younger," the son of Mary mentioned in Matt 27:56; Mark 15:40; 16:1; Luke 24:10. Yet another James, the father of Judas the apostle, is mentioned in Luke 6:16 and Acts 1:13. Josephus reports the stoning of James, the brother of Jesus, by Ananus the high priest ca. 62 C.E. (*Ant.* 20.9.1 § 200; similarly, Josephus

as cited in Origen, *Cels.* 1.47). Drawing on the second-century account of Hegesippus, Eusebius also reports the martyrdom of James and even sees the siege of Jerusalem as vengeance against the Jews for "their guilty crime against James" (*Hist. eccl.* 2.23.19; also 2.1.4–5 citing the account of James's death in Clement of Alexandria [ca. 150–215], *Hypotyposeis*; similarly Origen, *Comm. Matt.* 10.17 on Matt 13.55 [ANF 9:424]).

3. Hegesippus (second century), as reported in Jerome, *Vir. ill.* 2; cf. *Gos. Heb.*, frg. 7 (Hennecke-Schneemelcher, *NTA* 1:165).

4. *Hist. eccl.* 2.23.25. Commenting on the canonical status of the various NT writings, Eusebius includes James, along with Jude, 2 Peter, and 2–3 John among the disputed writings (*Hist. eccl.* 3.25.3).

5. Possible knowledge of James in the late first and second century includes *1 Clem.* 10.1 (2:23); 12.1 (2:25); 23.3 (1:8); 30.2 (4:6); 46.5 (4:1); 49.5 (5:20); *2 Clem.* 15.1 (5:19, 20); 16.4 (5:20); *Barn.* 21.9 (2:1); Ign. *Eph.* 5.3 (4:6); Pol. *Phil.* 12.3 (1:4); *Diogn.* 9.3 (5:20); *Ep. Apos.* 40 (5:16). More probable is usage in the Shepherd of Hermas (mid-second century), especially *Mand.* 9.1–12 (1:5–8, double-mindedness); *Sim.* 1.8 (1:27, caring for widows and orphans; cf. *Mand.* 8.10); also *Vis.* 1.1.8 (1:15, desire brings death); 2.2.7 (1:8, double-mindedness; 1:12, blessedness of enduring affliction); 3.9.1–6 (5:1–6, responsibility of the rich toward the poor; cf. *Sim.* 1.8–11); *Mand.* 2.2 (4:11, speaking evil of no one); 12.4.7; 12.5.2 (4:7, resisting the devil); *Sim.* 6.1.2; 9.21.3 (1:8, double-mindedness). Echoes are also heard in Irenaeus (ca. 130–200 C.E.), *Haer.* 4.13.4; 4.16.2 (2:23, Abraham, friend of God); 4.34.4 (1:25, law of liberty); 5.1.1 (1:18, 22, doers of the word). The earliest clear, though unattributed, citation of James (3:1–2) occurs in the Pseudo-Clementine epistle *Concerning Virginity* 1.11 (ANF 8:59), a writing from southern Syria or Palestine dated in the first half of the third century. Portions of James are also preserved in two Egyptian papyri: 𝔓²³ (P. Oxy. 1229, late second or early third century, containing 1:10–12, 15–18) and 𝔓²⁰ (P. Oxy. 1171, third century, containing 2:19–3:9).

6. James is unmentioned by Clement of Alexandria. Origen, on the other hand, quotes the Letter of James frequently, attributing it to James the apostle (*Sel. Ps.* 65, citing 5:13 with the phrase "as the apostle says"); also cf. his cautious comments in *Comm. Jo.* 19.152 (2:17); 20.66 (2:17); *Sel. Ps.* 30 (2:26); *Sel. Ps. 118* (4:10); *Sel. Exod.* 15 = PG 12:287–88d (1:13).

7. James goes unmentioned by Irenaeus (though cf. *Haer.* 4.13.4; 4.16.2; 5.1.1; 5.10.1), Tertullian (ca. 160–225 C.E.), Cyprian (died 258 C.E.), the African Mommsen Canon (359 C.E.), and Ambrose (ca. 339–397 C.E.). When James was included among the Scriptures translated into Latin in the mid-fourth century, it became known to Latin readers in the West. The first Latin author to quote James is Hilary of Poitiers, writing ca. 356–358 C.E. while exiled in the East (*Trin.* 4.8, quoting 1:17). It is cited frequently by Jerome (ca. 345–420 C.E.) (*Jov.* 1.39; 2.3; *Epist.* 51.6; 79.9; *Pelag.* 1.19). It is also cited by Augustine (*Civ.* 11.21; 14.9; 21.22; 21.26; 21.27 [2x]; cf. 19.27), in fact, with comparatively greater frequency than a number of other NT writings, e.g., Hebrews and 1–2 Thessalonians.

8. The term "spirit" (*pneuma*) only occurs twice in the letter (2:26; 4:5). The latter is notoriously difficult: ". . . that the spirit [God] caused to live in us envies intensely" (NIV). Two alternative renderings are given in the NIV notes: ". . . that God jealously longs for the spirit that he made to live in us" (similarly, NRSV); and ". . . that the Spirit he caused to live in us longs jealously." In any case, the phrase "Holy Spirit" (*hagion pneuma*) does not occur in James.

9. While the use of kinship language in designating community members was not unique to early Christians, they commonly referred to each other as brothers and sisters. This is amply illustrated in Paul (e.g., Rom 1:13; 7:1 passim); also cf. Matt 23:8–10; Heb 13:22.

10. Other notable echoes of the Gospel tradition occur in 1:4 (striving for perfection; Matt 5:48); 1:5 (asking and receiving; Matt 7:7; Luke 11:9); 1:22–25 (not only hearing but also doing the Lord's word; Matt 7:26–27); 2:5 (the poor as heirs of the kingdom; Matt 5:3); 2:10 (scrupulous observance of the law; Matt 5:19); 2:13 (the merciless receive no mercy; Matt 18:23–35, esp. 33); 3:11–12 (integrity illustrated by a fig tree unable to produce olives and a grapevine that cannot bear figs; Matt 7:16–20); 3:18 (making peace; Matt 5:9); 4:11 (speaking evil of or judging another; Matt 7:1); 5:1–2 (clothes moth-eaten; Matt 6:19); and 5:1–6 (woes to the rich; Luke 6:24).

11. Augustine's statement remains classic: ". . . the statements of the two apostles Paul and James are not contrary to one another when the one says that a man is justified by faith without works, and the other says that faith without works is vain. For the former is speaking of the works which precede faith,

whereas the latter, of those which follow on faith, just as even Paul himself indicates in many places" (*Div. quaest. LXXXIII*; trans. David L. Mosher, *Saint Augustine: Eighty-Three Different Questions* [The Fathers of the Church; Washington, D.C.: Catholic University of America Press, 1982], 196).

12. Throughout the discussion, I typically render *erga* as "actions," not only to move the discussion beyond the familiar categories of the Reformation debate, but also because "actions" better captures the dynamic dimension of *erga*.

13. James 2:8 (Lev 19:18); 2:11 (Exod 20:13–14; Deut 5:17–18); 2:23 (Gen 15:6); 4:6 (Prov 3:34, esp. LXX; cf. Job 22:29); 5:4 (Isa 5:9 LXX); 5:5 (Jer 12:3); 5:20 (Prov 10:12).

14. Abraham's offering of Isaac (2:21; cf. Gen 22:1–19); Abraham's being reckoned righteous because of his faith (2:23; Gen 15:6); Rahab's assisting the spies (2:25; Josh 2:1–21); the prophets who spoke in the name of the Lord (5:10; Jer 26:20–23; cf. 2 Chr 24:20–21); Job's endurance (5:11); and Elijah's fervent prayer (5:17; 1 Kings 17:1; 18:41–45).

15. Sirach amply treats this theme: obligations to the poor (4:1–10; 7:32); how the rich oppress the poor (13:18–20); privileging the rich over the poor (13:21–24); beware the rich (13:3–7); the need to care for orphans (4:10); God attuned to the needs of the poor (21:5); avoidance of luxury (18:32–19:1); and wealth's addictive power (31:1–11).

16. For an illuminating parallel of Jas 1:26; 3:1–12, see the critique of sins of the tongue in Sirach, especially slander (Sir 28:12–26). Sirach also treats gossip (19:4–12); the wisdom of knowing when to speak (20:5–8, 18–20); controlling the tongue (22:27); hypocritical speech (being double-tongued) (5:9–6:1); prudent speech (32:7–9); appropriate speech (4:23–25; 6:5; 18:15–18); foul language (23:12–15); and how speech reveals character (27:4–7).

Bibliography

Commentaries

Dibelius, Martin. *A Commentary on the Epistle of James*. Revised by Heinrich Greeven. Translated by Michael A. Williams. Philadelphia: Fortress, 1975.

Johnson, Luke T. *The Letter of James: A New Translation with Introduction and Commentary*. Anchor Bible 37A. New York: Doubleday, 1995.

———. "The Letter of James: Introduction, Commentary, and Reflections." Pages 175–225 in vol. 12 of *The New Interpreter's Bible*. Edited by Leander E. Keck. 12 vols. Nashville: Abingdon, 1998.

Laws, Sophie. *The Epistle of James*. Harper's (Black's) New Testament Commentaries 16. San Francisco: Harper & Row, 1980; repr. Peabody: Hendrickson, 1993.

Martin, Ralph P. *James*. Word Biblical Commentary 48. Waco: Word, 1988.

Moffatt, James. *The General Epistles: James, Peter, and Judas*. The Moffatt New Testament Commentary. New York/London: Harper & Row/Hodder & Stoughton, 1928.

Other Resources

Adamson, James B. *James: The Man and His Message*. Grand Rapids: Eerdmans, 1989.

Bauckham, Richard. *James: Wisdom of James, Disciple of Jesus the Sage*. New Testament Readings. London: Routledge, 1999.

Chester, Andrew. "The Theology of James." Pages 1–62 in Andrew Chester and Ralph P. Martin, *The Theology of the Letters of James, Peter, and Jude*. New Testament Theology. Cambridge: Cambridge University Press, 1994; repr. 1996.

Johnson, Luke T. *Brother of Jesus, Friend of God: Studies in the Letter of James*. Grand Rapids: Eerdmans, 2004.

Penner, Todd C. *The Epistle of James and Eschatology: Re-reading an Ancient Christian Letter*. Journal for the Study of the New Testament Supplement Series 121. Sheffield: Sheffield Academic Press, 1996.

Wachob, Wesley H. *The Voice of Jesus in the Social Rhetoric of James*. Society for New Testament Studies Monograph Series 106. Cambridge: Cambridge University Press, 2000.

Chapter 23

First Peter

"Yea, and know well, this debt is thine to pay,
Through suffering to make glorious thy life."

Sophocles, *Philoctetes*

"I asked them whether they were Christians, and if they confessed, I asked them a second and third time with threats of punishment. If they kept to it, I ordered them for execution; for I held no question that whatever it was that they admitted, in any case obstinacy and unbending perversity deserve to be punished."

Pliny, the Roman governor of Bithynia,
to the emperor Trajan

"Nowhere in the New Testament can we see more clearly than in 1 Peter how the eschatology of the Gospel becomes the teleology of the Church's life."

Edward Gordon Selwyn

By its own account, the "short letter" of 1 Peter was written "to encourage [Christians in Asia Minor] and to testify that this is the true grace of God [in which they stood]" (5:12). Since the letter's purpose is both hortatory and kerygmatic, it can be read as a sermon in the form of a paraenetic letter. This helps explain one of the most distinctive features of the letter: the close interweaving of moral exhortation and theological exposition. What God has done in Christ for believers (1:3–12) easily gives way to how believers are expected to behave (1:13–16). Yet the reverse occurs just as easily (and more often): moral injunctions are given, then anchored in a rehearsal of basic theological convictions (1:17–21).[1] Such close linkage between exhortation and theological exposition suggests that genuine exhortation occurs through informed, authentic witness to God's grace.

The letter also exhibits other elements that contribute to its distinctive form of witness among NT writings. Perhaps one of its most remarkable features is the numerous echoes of other NT writings. Some turns of phrase are strikingly Pauline, as are certain clusters of OT texts and metaphorical expressions.[2] So extensive are these

"Paulinisms" that some scholars plausibly believe the author of 1 Peter knew Romans, and possibly Ephesians.[3] Less generous critics have accounted for these similarities by positing 1 Peter's direct, even extensive, literary dependence on the Pauline letters, thus seeing its author as a rather unimaginative drudge. Still others, insisting that 1 Peter should be read on its own terms rather than through Paul, have fought to liberate 1 Peter from Pauline captivity. For all of its Pauline echoes, however, 1 Peter also has close affinities with the synoptic tradition[4] and to a lesser extent with the Gospel of John,[5] Hebrews,[6] and James.[7] There are also remarkable convergences with Peter's speeches in Acts.[8] Since 1 Peter resonates with such a wide spectrum of early Christian witnesses, some scholars have suggested, only half jokingly, that its author knew the whole NT!

Similar breadth of outlook is also seen in the remarkable variety of literary forms and traditions found in 1 Peter. The abundance of baptismal language has led some scholars to see a baptismal homily behind the letter, or perhaps even the remnants of a baptismal liturgy that have been incorporated virtually unchanged into the letter. Just as prominent are other liturgical elements, including prayers, hymnic fragments, and creedal formulae. Among the most prominent prayers is the opening blessing (1:3–12). Portions of 1 Peter that have been seen as hymnic include 1:18–21 (esp. the couplet in v. 20); 2:1–10, in four strophes (vv. 1–3, 4–5, 6–8, 9–10); 2:6–8, as a hymnic fragment, based on Isa 8:14, known to both Peter and Paul; 2:21–25; and 3:18–22. Creedal elements are visible, whether they were originally part of hymns or not, for example, "put to death in the flesh, but made alive in the spirit" (3:18; cf. 1 Tim 3:16); "destined before the foundation of the world, but . . . revealed at the end of the ages" (1:20); and portions of 2:22–25 (similarly, 3:18–19, 22).

Also evident are catechetical elements, most notably the abbreviated household code (2:18–3:7), not to mention the numerous ethical injunctions, proverbial sayings, and other forms of instruction found throughout the letter. One way of explaining such variety is to think of the author as a mere collector and transmitter of traditions. While the variety and abundance of the author's sources are evident, so is his creativity in shaping them into a coherent, powerful form of witness. Part of 1 Peter's enduring appeal stems from the breadth and depth of the common tradition on which it draws and its appropriation of the earlier, apostolic consensus in giving authority to its distinctive voice.

Of all the literary sources and traditional elements informing 1 Peter, none is more prominent than the OT, whose pervasive presence gives the letter another distinctive mark. In a manner reminiscent of Hebrews and Revelation, 1 Peter reveals an author whose mind was thoroughly steeped in the OT. This is evident from the many OT citations and allusions scattered throughout the letter,[9] as well as in certain sections in which the author makes use of a tightly clustered set of OT images or themes. Among the most noticeable is the "living stone" exhortation in 2:4–8, which is reinforced by a uniquely configured chain of three "stone" passages (Isa 28:16; Ps 118:22; Isa 8:14),[10] followed by the impressive cluster of honorific, ecclesial designations drawn from the OT (Exod 19:6; Isa 43:20–21; Hos 1:6–7, 9; 2:23). In a similar vein, the advice to slaves in 2:18–21 is based on an appeal to Christ's exemplary behavior, which is amplified in 2:22–25 by lavish use of various images from Isa 53. This midrashic exposition is remarkable for its explicit appropriation of Isa 53 in making sense of the death of Jesus.[11] Yet another form of OT usage occurs in 1 Pet 3:9–12, with the extensive citation of Ps 34:12–16 to reinforce the appeal for non-retaliatory behavior. The length of this passage and its apparent echoes elsewhere in the letter have led some to see Ps 34 as the central text informing the extended baptismal homily lying behind the letter.

Yet another distinguishing feature of 1 Peter is its emphasis on suffering. The sheer frequency of the language of suffering in 1 Peter underscores the prominence of this theme. More important, of course, it surfaces the readers' ongoing experiences of suffering. [See Expanded CD Version p. 697: *The Language of Suffering in 1 Peter*]

The readers addressed in 1 Peter were living under the shadow of suffering. There is no firm evidence that their suffering resulted from widespread, state-sponsored persecution, as was once thought. This did not happen until much later, during the persecution under Decius (ca. 250 C.E.). The tone of 1 Peter's repeated references to suffering suggests that the readers were being ridiculed and perhaps ostracized by persons within their local communities or regions. We cannot identify these "cultured despisers" who were bringing social pressure against the readers, but they probably included neighbors and even family members.

Even if the form of suffering encountered by the readers was social pressure, this does not mean that they had not experienced bodily harm. First Peter nowhere mentions that any of its readers had died for the faith, as Revelation reports had happened to Antipas at Pergamum (Rev 2:13). Yet it by no means follows that those who were addressed in 1 Peter were only experiencing psychological pressure. There is ample evidence from the first century to suggest that riots in which local folks were pitted against religious groups such as Jews and Christians could turn nasty and that people could go home bloody.

This picture is reinforced by Acts (also cf. 1 Thess 2:14–16). Though later than 1 Peter, the letter of Pliny the governor of Bithynia, written to the emperor Trajan about 112 C.E., still offers valuable insight into the situation that Christians in Bithynia-Pontus might have faced a few decades earlier. It shows how Christians suffered at the hands of local provincial leaders, even though there was no official, imperial policy against Christians throughout the empire. Christians endured all sorts of social pressure and verbal abuse, but they were also brought before the authorities and even killed.

The suffering in 1 Peter appears to have been going on for some time (1:6), and it related to the readers' distinctive Christian identity. What caused them to be "reviled for the name of Christ" (4:14) is not stated, but their practices were different enough from other religious cults in the region to justify their being called "Christian" (4:16). At the very least, enduring grief because of this name could be seen as a disgrace (4:16). While the author admits that the readers' detractors might "malign [them] as evildoers" (2:12), there is no mention of specific practices that their non-Christian neighbors may have found offensive.

Given what we know about Roman suspicions of foreign religious groups, especially recently founded ones, we can surmise that the readers' neighbors would have seen them as a potential political threat to Roman order. Numerous experiences throughout the empire also demonstrated the destabilizing effect new religious cults could have within domestic settings, especially among women and slaves, who often experienced the debilitating effects of hierarchical structures. Converting to new religions could easily fuel their desire to redefine their conventional responsibilities within the household and perhaps even throw off the yoke of domestic oppression.

The Purpose and Structure of the Letter

First Peter possesses the standard features of an ancient letter: initial greeting (1:1–2), opening prayer of blessing (1:3–12), body of the letter (1:13–5:11), and concluding greetings and benediction (5:12–14). It also displays elements that characterize paraenetic letters: (1) recalling the familiar, which helps explain its heavy use of traditional elements; (2) the use of examples to illustrate behaviors being recommended, for example, the suffering Christ as the paradigm for suffering Christians (2:21); and (3) the use of affective, reassuring language to shape moral exhortations and to bolster the confidence of the readers, for example, the carefully formulated language of divine election and numerous images that instill pride and confidence—chosen people, royal priesthood, holy nation, and God's own people (2:9).

While the structure of the letter is still debated, scholars usually see clear breaks at 2:11 and 4:12. The resulting threefold division is closely related to the overall purpose of the letter: to encourage the readers and to testify to God's grace (5:12).

Faced with constant resistance, readers would have experienced doubts about their decision to become Christians. Such adverse pressure would also threaten their identity, causing nagging questions about who they really were. Accordingly, the first main section (1:3–2:10) reaffirms the readers' identity and might be appropriately titled *Remembering Who You Are*.

An identity shaped around the readers' distinctiveness as a "holy community" (1:15–16) would reinforce their alien status within Gentile society. This, in turn, calls for instruction about how they should conduct themselves as "resident aliens." The second main section (2:11–4:11) might be titled *Living Honorably Among Gentiles*. After some initial remarks (2:11–12), the author gives instructions to all Christians concerning their conduct before civil authorities (2:13–17). Then individual instructions are given to slaves (2:18–25), wives (3:1–6), and husbands (3:7). Then follows a set of extended instructions profiling how Christians should conduct themselves before outsiders. Called for are solidarity with each other (3:8), non-retaliatory conduct (3:9–12); doing good (3:13); enduring unjust suffering (3:14–22); moral rectitude as a distinctive form of witness (4:1–6); and disciplined spirituality within the eschatological community (4:7–11).

Since the readers' ongoing suffering prompted the letter, the third section (4:12–5:11) focuses on *Coping with Suffering*. What it means to suffer without shame is spelled out (4:12–19), as is the role that responsive leaders should play in helping suffering communities (5:1–4). Concluding instructions call for yielding to God's protection, and the need for humility, mutual submission, and recognition of the universal fellowship of Christian suffering (5:5–11).

Given the unusual form of the greeting, in which the addressees are identified by provincial regions in Asia Minor, the letter should be read as a circular letter.[12] Since it addresses such a broadly defined audience rather than believers in one city or local

First Peter is addressed to "the exiles of the Dispersion in Pontus, Galatia, Cappadocia, Asia, and Bithynia" (1 Pet 1:1). This implies the apostle Peter's widespread influence throughout Asia Minor.

region, it has regularly been read as one of the Catholic Letters, along with James, 2 Peter, 1–2–3 John, and Jude, addressed to the larger church.[13] While the letter is attributed to the apostle Peter, its impressive Greek literary style, its use of the Greek OT,[14] a date late enough to allow for the mission presupposed in regions of Bithynia-Pontus and Cappadocia—areas not reached by the Pauline mission—and its paucity of personal details linking it to Petrine traditions all suggest a pseudonymous author. Silvanus, identified as the author's amanuensis (5:12), was probably responsible for collecting traditions associated with Peter and drafting them as a letter of exhortation from the Roman church, where Peter was a well-known figure, to Christians in Asia Minor. Quite possibly, 1 Peter along with 2 Peter and Jude stemmed from a circle of Peter's followers in Rome. If so, this would help account for the conspicuous literary and material differences among the letters.

A Baptismal Homily?

The prominence of baptismal language in 1 Peter has long been noted. Not only does the technical designation for this early initiation rite occur (*baptisma*, 3:21), but related imagery also abounds (cf. 1:3, 22–23; also note the abundance of conversion language, e.g., 1:14, 18–19, 21; 2:2; 4:3–4). While the use of baptismal imagery is by no means unique to 1 Peter (cf. Rom 6), it is pervasive enough for a number of scholars from the early twentieth century onward to think that the letter is best understood when read in the light of ancient baptismal practices. [See Expanded CD Version pp. 700–1: *Proposals to Account for the Baptismal Language in 1 Peter*]

Living as Christians within a Non-Christian Society

First Peter's reminder that its addressees have "brothers and sisters in all the world [who] are undergoing the same kinds of suffering" (5:9) may be rhetorical hyperbole in one sense, but it correctly suggests that Christians by this time were scattered throughout the Mediterranean world. Christianity may have been a vast network of small communities linked by their common faith in Jesus Christ and a common set of aspirations inspired by that faith, but with Christians numbering well under 1 percent of a larger population of some sixty million, it was still a tiny blip on a very large screen.[15]

Even so, Christianity had begun to register as a distinctive presence throughout the Roman Empire, and 1 Peter offers some illuminating insight into the dynamics that were created when Christians began to establish a separate identity among non-Christians. They are distinguishable by the name "Christian" (4:16), perhaps given to them as a pejorative, although aptly descriptive, label by their neighbors. Like other designations with similar suffixes, for example, Herodian, Augustinian, Ciceronian, it referred to someone who was associated with, or was even a devoted follower of, the person named in the proper noun, in other words, Herod, Augustus, or Cicero; in this case, a Christian is a Christ-partisan.

First Peter's readers have also adopted a lifestyle that separates them from undisciplined, indulgent, and excessively dissolute behaviors (4:3). These are now replaced by "good conduct in Christ," whose ethical profile is sufficiently distinct to prompt ridicule and abuse (3:16). Outsiders are "surprised that [Christians] no longer join them in the same excesses of dissipation," and consequently "blaspheme" them (4:4). We can easily imagine that such banter would occur between newly converted Christians and their former "drinking buddies." Somewhat surprising, however, is the suggestion that others would "malign [Christians] as evildoers" (*kakopoiōn*, 2:12).[16] Even if such language has a polemical edge, it still implies that Christians were in some sense a negative force within Roman society. These scattered clues in 1 Peter reveal the newly created social distance between Christians and their non-Christian neighbors, and also some of the tensions created by such separation.

What we find in 1 Peter is merely a microcosm of a larger social reality found throughout the Roman Empire. [See **Expanded CD Version pp. 702–5:** *Roman Suspicion of Nontraditional Religious Groups*]

First Peter had to help its readers justify their existence as Christians living as a "holy community" within society. It was a single strategy with two interlocking components: creating an identity that separated them from Roman culture, and yet showing how they, as a "community of the elect," upheld the best of Greek and Roman values by "living honorably among Gentiles." First Peter does not urge its readers to reject the larger society wholesale. Instead, it urges a policy of selective accommodation. Those values that contribute to moral ruin it rejects wholeheartedly; those that foster political stability and social order it upholds steadfastly and encourages vigorously.

First Peter's Theological Vision

Addressed to readers who live in remote parts of the Roman Empire and who are undergoing suffering, 1 Peter draws on the common faith of early Christianity to sketch its vision of "living hope" (1:3). As a paraenetic letter, rather than introducing what is novel, it instead rehearses what is familiar. In doing so, it reaffirms core convictions, although it does so in a distinctive mode.

The God Who Calls

First Peter operates with a strong, well-developed understanding of God, who is "Father of our Lord Jesus Christ" (1:3), probably the Father of humanity as a whole, but especially of all believers (1:2, 17). First Peter sharpens the image of God's fatherhood by presenting Him as the One who regenerates (*anagennaō*) believers, giving them a "new birth" (1:3, 23). God revivifies believers "not of perishable but of imperishable seed" (*spora*, 1:23)—divinely empowered, life-giving and life-sustaining proclamation.[17] In view is the gospel, the "good news that was announced to [them]" (1:25). It is rightly called the "gospel of God" (4:17), since it originated with God and was carefully nurtured by God through the ages. God's calling of believers, far from being an afterthought, expresses God's original intention. In this sense, believers were elected "according to God's foreknowledge" (*kata prognōsin theou*, 1:2), or "chosen and destined by God" (NRSV; cf. Rom 8:29).

God's election of believers is not just an original desire that remains latent; God makes good on this intention by actively calling believers "out of darkness into his marvelous light" (1:15; 2:9; cf. 5:10). This powerful sense of divine summons establishes a firm basis for ethical action. Believers who suffer unjustly can react in a way that receives "God's approval" (2:20), literally, that displays the "grace" of God. They are reminded of that to which they have been called (2:21): the story of Christ who suffered unjustly but reacted with grace rather than vengeance. An equally strong motivation is God's character as uniquely holy, which believers are expected to experience as well as emulate by pursuing moral lives (1:15–16).

God's redemptive action toward humanity is an expression of mercy (1:3). Even before the time of Christ, God could display patience "in the days of Noah" (3:20). At the "end of the ages" (1:20) stands the "God of all grace, who has called [believers] to his eternal glory in Christ" (5:10). Perceptive OT prophets spoke of the grace that believers were to experience (1:10). Since God's grace has been experienced in many different ways, believers are expected to be "good stewards of the manifold grace of God" (4:10). Finally, 1 Peter is a letter written about "the true grace of God," in which believers can "stand fast" (5:12). As the defining foundational experience for believers, God's grace has a permanent anchoring effect.

The Apostle Peter. A woodcut by Lucas Cranach, the Elder (1472–1553), from *Hortulus animae*, an early Lutheran prayer book (Wittenberg, 1550). From the Digital Image Archive of The Richard C. Kessler Reformation Collection, Pitts Theology Library, Candler School of Theology, Emory University, Atlanta, Georgia.

It is this pervasive sense of God's grace that accounts for God's overarching care. Through faith, believers experience God's protective power as they look toward their future hope (1:5). The God who calls also restores, supports, strengthens, and establishes (5:10). Believers are able to serve because of the "strength that God supplies" (4:11). They can live anxiety-free because God cares for them (5:7). If God, rather than Christ, is the "shepherd and guardian of [believers'] souls" (2:25), divine protection is reinforced even further.

God's protection is rendered meaningful by a carefully calibrated sense of God's justice and might. Under the "mighty hand of God" believers humble themselves (5:6). The God who "gives grace to the humble" also "opposes the proud" (5:5, citing Prov 3:34, esp. LXX). Evildoers can expect to experience God's stern side: "the face of the Lord [God] is against those who do evil" (3:12, citing Ps 34:16). God is rightly to be feared (2:17). God does not act capriciously or prejudicially; instead, God judges justly (2:23), in other words, impartially (1:17). For this reason, judgment that begins "with the household of God" is fair and equitable, even for those "who do not obey the gospel of God" (4:17). In the "day of visitation" (2:12), outsiders who have been impressed by the moral character of believers (and have followed suit) can "glorify God" (2:12). While God's actions at the end of time are not spelled out in detail, God is pictured as the one who will "judge the living and the dead" (4:5). This balanced sense of God's justice and power makes "God's will" a determinative force within human life (2:15; 3:17; 4:2, 19). "As God would have you do it" (5:2) becomes a meaningful motivation for elders—and, by extension, all believers—as they discharge their duty.

Possessing a finely balanced blend of mercy, grace, power, and justice, God can be trusted (1:21). Believers can call upon God (1:17), and entrust themselves to the "faithful Creator" (4:19), even as the suffering Christ could commit his cause to the "one who judges justly" (2:23). This eminently trustworthy God, who raised Jesus from the dead (1:21), is ultimately the basis of Christian hope (1:3). Believers' faith and hope are "set on God" (1:21).

For all of these reasons, believers can rejoice in God (1:6). They can be challenged positively by reflecting on whether they "have tasted that the Lord [probably God] is good" (2:3). This means that believers can experience God as sheer delight. As those who belong to God, they can feel embraced as God's own people (2:9–10), as "servants of God" (2:16). Their conduct, both toward civil authorities and within the household, occurs "for the Lord's sake" (2:13) and in full awareness of God (2:19; 3:4). Whoever speaks (probably a Spirit-inspired, prophetic utterance) must do so as one speaking the very words of God (4:11).

The Christ Who Suffered

First Peter typically refers to Jesus Christ (1:1, 2, 3, 7, 13; 2:5; 3:21; 4:11; once to the Lord Jesus Christ, 1:3), or more often simply to Christ (1:11 [2x], 19; 2:21; 3:15, 16, 18; 4:1, 13, 14; 5:1, 10, 14), which tends to be used as a personal name rather than as a christological title. Confession is thus expressed as "sanctifying Christ (rather than Jesus) as Lord" (3:15). Unlike Hebrews, 1 Peter nowhere refers to Jesus alone. Nor is Jesus Christ ever said to be "Son of God" in 1 Peter, although God is called the "Father of our Lord Jesus Christ" (1:3).[18] Only one other time does 1 Peter use "Lord" of Christ, which distinguishes the letter sharply from Paul, for whom "Lord" was a frequent christological designation. Ordinarily, "Lord" in 1 Peter refers to God (1:25; 2:3, 13; 3:12 [2x]). Other christological titles found elsewhere in the NT, for example, Savior, are absent in 1 Peter.

First Peter's Christology stands squarely within early Christian tradition. Brief mention is made of Christ's pre-existence: "he was marked out [*proegnōsmenou*] before the world was made" (1:20 NJB), but this dimension of Christ remains undeveloped. Nothing is made of Christ's eternal nature (as in Hebrews), his status with God prior to creation (cf. Phil 2), or his role in creation (cf. Col 1; Heb 1). His coming into the world is expressed as his being "revealed at the end of the ages" (1:20). No mention is made of the circumstances of his birth, for example, that he was "born of a woman" (cf. Gal 4:4). No events or sayings from his earthly ministry are recalled. Instead, almost exclusive focus is given to Christ's death and resurrection: he was "put to death in the flesh, but made alive in the spirit" (3:18). His resurrection is expressed in conventional creedal language: "resurrection of Jesus Christ from the dead" (1:3; 3:21);

God "raised him from the dead and gave him glory" (1:21; also 1:11); and Christ has "gone into heaven and is at the right hand of God, with angels, authorities, and powers made subject to him" (3:22). First Peter moves well beyond conventional creedal language, however, in depicting the resurrected Christ as the "living stone" (2:4).

Of greatest interest to 1 Peter is Christ's death, which is seen as a sacrificial offering: Christ was an unblemished lamb whose blood has redemptive power (1:19).[19] First Peter can speak of Christ's "death" (3:18), but much prefers to speak of "Christ's suffering(s)" (1:11; 2:21, 23; 3:18; 4:1, 13; 5:1). Heavily influenced by Isa 53, 1 Peter sees Christ's death as the redemptive death of the Suffering Servant, the sinless, guileless, non-retaliating, faithful servant who "bore our sins in his body on the cross" (2:21–25). His death was vicarious—"Christ . . . suffered for you" (2:21)—and redemptive—"Christ also suffered for sins once for all" (3:18). He died as a sinless figure on behalf of sinful humanity: "the righteous for the unrighteous, in order to bring [them] to God" (3:18).

Christ's suffering in the flesh somehow finally deals with sin: "for whoever has suffered in the flesh has finished with sin" (4:1).[20] Coming close to the view of Luke-Acts that Christ's sufferings were a divine necessity prescribed by Scripture, 1 Peter sees the OT prophets, prompted by the "Spirit of Christ within them," testifying "in advance to the sufferings destined for Christ" (1:11).

Apart from its redemptive value, Christ's suffering is also prototypical and exemplary: in his suffering, he leaves them "an example, so that [they] should follow in his steps" (2:21). He is particularly noteworthy as a righteous figure who suffered unjustly. As such, he serves as the prototype of the one who experiences unjust suffering with equanimity. Consequently, believers who experience undeserved suffering "share Christ's sufferings" (4:13). It may not diminish the pain of suffering, but such close identification between suffering believers and the suffering Christ can actually become an occasion for rejoicing (4:13).

Other images of Christ also surface: (probably) the "chief shepherd" (5:4) and the "shepherd and guardian of [believers'] souls" (2:25). Christ may also be the Unseen One whom believers love, in whom they believe, their source of delight (1:8). Believers can take comfort that, like Christ, the rejected stone who became "the very head of the corner" (2:7), they too can be rejected by humanity yet be "chosen and precious in God's sight" (2:4). The stone metaphor also gives additional solace: those who refuse to accept the gospel "stumble" over Christ, the stone. Believers, on the other hand, become "living stones," the materials from which God's "spiritual house" is built (2:5). A thoroughly Pauline note is struck when believers are greeted as those "in Christ" (5:14).

Christ's role at the end of time is expressed as the "revelation of Jesus Christ" (*apokalypsis Iēsou Christou*), which the NRSV renders as "when Jesus Christ is revealed" (1:7, 13). The end is expected soon (4:7). Nowhere does 1 Peter refer to Christ's "coming" (*parousia*), nor does it expand on Christ's role at the end of time, for example, as judge. The One who judges humankind impartially according to their deeds is God (1:17; cf. 2:23), who is probably the one who will "judge the living and the dead" (4:5).

Among the most unusual features of 1 Peter's Christology—and unique in the NT—is its claim that, having been made "alive in the spirit," Christ "went and made a proclamation to the spirits in prison" (3:18–19). The meaning of this enigmatic creedal element remains an unsolved puzzle. The imprisoned spirits are envisioned as having been disobedient "in former times . . . in the days of Noah" (3:20). These may be the infamous disobedient "sons of God" of Gen 6, who had sexual intercourse with earthly women, a sinful act egregious enough to bring about the flood as God's universal punishment of humankind (cf. *1 En.* 6–16). If they were elusive heavenly figures who escaped the flood's destruction, presumably they still needed redemption. Christ's elevation to the realm of the spirit would have given him access to this heavenly realm. Christ's preaching to these captive spirits, and presumably converting them, would symbolize the far-reaching effects of his death and resurrection, as well as declare emphatically his dominion over the heavenly realm.

The Spirit Who Sanctifies

Compared with God and Christ, the Spirit is mentioned infrequently in 1 Peter. But this does not mean that 1 Peter operates with a flattened view of the Spirit.[21] In certain ways, 1 Peter conceives the Spirit quite subtly, even surprisingly. Only once is the Holy Spirit (*pneuma hagion*) mentioned. Those who originally evangelized the believers in the Dispersion scattered throughout Asia Minor did so "by the Holy Spirit sent from heaven" (1:12). If this is understood in the Pauline sense, it suggests that their preaching was empowered by the Holy Spirit, perhaps even accompanied by signs and wonders (cf. 1 Thess 1:5–6; 4:8; 5:19; 1 Cor 2:4; 2 Cor 12:12). In any case, the evangelistic preaching that converted them was not merely human persuasion. However the Spirit was conceived in the initial evangelistic preaching, its effects did not end there. The "spirit of glory [and power?]" understood as the "Spirit of God" (*pneuma theou*) continues to be present, notably when believers are being "reviled for the name of Christ" (4:14). This may reflect the conviction, expressed elsewhere, that God's Spirit would assist disciples in knowing what to say when facing resistance and persecution (Luke 12:11–12).

The Spirit as the enlivening power of Jesus' resurrection may be in view in 3:18: "[Jesus was] put to death in the flesh, but made alive in the spirit." The two-part parallel structure may suggest that while Jesus died physically, his own spirit experienced new life when he was raised from the dead. Closely related is the curious reference to the gospel being "proclaimed even to the dead," possibly those from earlier centuries who discerned the true meaning of the OT or, more likely, Christians who had already died. In either case, it was done so that, "though they had been judged in the flesh as everyone is judged, they might live in the spirit as God does" (4:6). Apparently implied is their experience of the resurrection, in which they enjoy an existence "in the spirit" comparable to that of God. "Spirit" thus defines God's exclusive realm. Old Testament prophets, eager to know the future form God's grace would take, ascertained in advance (and testified to) Christ's death and resurrection, or "the sufferings destined for Christ and the subsequent glory" (1:11). And how did they discern this? Through the promptings of "the Spirit of Christ within them" (1:11). In ways comparable to Hebrews, Christ's Spirit is a fully active presence within OT witnesses, not merely a divine capacity limited to the time of Jesus and the church. Even so, since believers, "chosen and destined by God" are "sanctified by the Spirit" (*en hagiasmō pneumatos*), the Spirit is also the ongoing source of believers' moral renewal (1:2). Here again, 1 Peter reflects the Pauline conviction that believers experience God's sanctifying power through the agency of the Spirit (cf. 1 Cor 6:11; 1 Thess 4:3, 8; 2 Thess 2:13).

The Church as Exiled Community

Although 1 Peter nowhere uses the term *ekklēsia*, it presents a richly textured view of the church. Using the image of "exile" (*paroikos*), 1 Peter sketches a vision of the church that both fits its social location and enables it to establish a distinct behavioral profile within that location. The readers are literally "exiles of the Dispersion" (1:1), especially when considered from the point of view of "Babylon," a code word for Rome (5:13). Unlike many of the large urban centers reached by the gospel, such as Antioch of Syria, Ephesus, Corinth, and especially Rome, most of the villages and towns in the provinces listed in the opening greeting were located in rural settings. The readers were exiled geographically and socially. First Peter offers plenty of clues suggesting conventicles of Christians who were experiencing social alienation because of their newly acquired faith.

Trading on the exile image, 1 Peter urges its readers to be "aliens and exiles" (*paroikous kai parepidēmous*, 2:11) in a moral sense—to adopt a way of life that displays honorable conduct among their non-Christian neighbors, but that distances themselves from their neighbors' values and behaviors. In the former case, they would bear powerful witness to the gospel by showing that they posed no threat to political stability (2:13–17), maintained orderly households (2:18–3:7), and displayed a sense of communal unity and harmony (3:8–12). As to the latter, their lives were to be above reproach, since they had left behind the worst forms of self-indulgence (4:2–4). They were not to be found guilty of major crimes, such as murder, thievery, and other forms of mischief (4:15). So also were they to conquer the lesser vices of malice, guile, insincerity, envy, and slander (2:1). Holy living, which moved beyond the impulsive desires of their former lives, was to mark their existence (1:13–16).

This sense of newly created distance between the readers and the world they inhabit is reinforced by 1 Peter's repeated emphasis on their conversion. Probably reflecting patterns of early catechesis, the author reminds the readers of who they once were and who they now are (2:10, 25). The description of their transition from darkness to light reflects similar conversional language (2:9). Their "obedience to the truth" also harks back to their initial reception of the gospel, which began the process of moral purification (1:22). Drawing on well-established Christian imagery, 1 Peter portrays its readers as once "going astray like sheep" but now returning to "the shepherd and guardian of [their] souls" (2:25). Reminders that they were ransomed by the blood of Christ (1:18–21) echo the same theme, as do the repeated references to their "renewed birth" (1:3, 23). The cumulative force of these repeated references to their conversion is to draw the line even more firmly between their past and present existence, marking them off from their non-Christian neighbors, who are surprised at the change they have undergone (4:3–4).

To the extent that they were practicing a way of life that transcended their geographical location and their social alienation, they were living "during a time of exile"

(1:17). While 1 Peter does not fully exploit the notion of "heavenly citizenship," as Paul does (Phil 3:20), or develop the pilgrimage motif of Hebrews, it is moving in that direction.

To offset any sense of social deprivation created by the resistance encountered by Asian believers, 1 Peter appropriates a powerful set of competing images drawn from Israel's rich history, all brimming with honor and pride: "royal priesthood and holy nation" (Exod 19:6); "chosen people [NIV], God's own people" (Isa 43:20–21); and a "spiritual house" and "holy priesthood" (2:5, 9). An even more emphatic reversal of fortunes is implied in 1 Peter's use of imagery from Hosea: "not a people" becomes "God's people"; "not having received mercy" becomes "having received mercy" (2:10; cf. Hos 2:23). Like the image of alien and exile, which recalled Abraham (Gen 23:4; also cf. Ps 39:12), these images tap into Israel's past and give 1 Peter's readers a sense of history rich enough to instill pride and deep enough to stabilize them against assorted threats and abuse. Equally important, these images established a counter-identity to their surrounding culture. By reminding them of God's elective initiative, which continues in the form of sustaining grace, protective assurance, and vindicating judgment, the church experiences God's firm embrace. They are, in the fullest sense, "God's own people" (2:9). As such, believers can operate with a vibrant sense of being "servants of God" (2:16), God's household (4:17), and the "flock of God" (5:2).

The Church's Use of 1 Peter

First Peter was embraced quickly by the church, which quoted it early and often.[22] [See Expanded CD Version pp. 711–12: **More Discussion of the Church's Early Use of 1 Peter**]

It is easy to understand the church's warm embrace of 1 Peter. Not only was it read as apostolic testimony from Peter himself, who, as Origen reports, was the "one on whom the Church of Christ is built, against which the gates of Hades shall not prevail,"[23] but it also connected with the experience of churches in various parts of the Mediterranean. Given 1 Peter's thoughtful attention to the sufferings that Christians had to endure for the sake of Christ and how these were seen as replications, if not extensions, of Christ's own suffering, it was readily applicable when Christians in other settings underwent similar sufferings.

Echoes of 1 Peter are heard in the unforgettable report of Christian suffering recorded in the letter of the martyr churches of Vienne and Lyons in southern Gaul, written to Christians in Asia and Phrygia.[24] Reporting an outbreak of violence against Christians in the summer of 177, the letter, drawing heavily on the stories of the Maccabean martyrs, rehearses episodes of valiant Christian courage in the face of excruciating torture and death. Describing Biblis, a woman who under pressure had denied the faith but who changed her mind, resisted her torturers, and reasserted her Christian identity, only then to die as a martyr, the letter appropriates the image of the devil as a "roaring lion [who] prowls around, looking for someone to devour" (1 Pet 5:8). Accordingly, Biblis is characterized as one whom "the devil *supposed* that he had already devoured."[25] Reflecting on the fate of those martyred, the letter draws on 1 Pet 5:6 to describe their now exalted status: "They humbled themselves under the mighty hand by which they are now greatly exalted."[26] The case of Sanctus, who was tortured to the point that his body was "one whole wound and bruise, contracted, having lost the outward form of a man," provides an occasion to recall Christ's exemplary suffering in 1 Pet 2:21, "bringing the adversary to nought and showing an example for those that remained."[27]

First Peter figures regularly in early Christian discussions of suffering and martyrdom.[28] Since the devil as a roaring lion stalking his prey was such a memorable way of symbolizing evil as a moving target and the violence that inevitably accompanies evil, we can well understand why 1 Pet 5:8 was the passage most frequently cited by early Christian writers. [See **Expanded CD Version pp. 713–14:** *The Church's Use of 1 Peter in the Medieval and Reformation Periods*]

Notes

1. One gauge of 1 Peter's pervasive moral emphasis is the number of imperatives (more than fifty) that occur in the letter. For other examples of ethical imperatives followed by theological indicatives, see 1:15–16, 17–21; 2:4–8, 13–15, 18–25; 3:8–12, 16–20; 5:5, 7.

2. Prominent examples include the use of "in Christ" (3:16; 5:10, 14; cf. 2 Cor 5:17, one of over 150 uses in Paul); not repaying evil for evil (3:9; cf. Rom 12:19); offering spiritual sacrifices (2:5; cf. Rom 12:1); the christological use of the two "stone" passages from Isa 28:16 and 8:14 (2:6–8; cf. Rom 9:33); the use of "not my people/my people" from Hos 1 & 2 (2:10; cf. Rom 9:25–26); submission to civil authorities (2:13–17; cf. Rom 13:1–7); discipleship as mutual service using allotted gifts (4:10; cf. Rom 12:3–8; 1 Cor 12:4–11); rejoicing in suffering (4:12–13; Col 1:24). Especially worth noting are similarities of form and content between 1 Pet 3:8–12 and two Pauline texts: Rom 12:9–21 and 1 Thess 5:12–22. There are also some close parallels with the Pastorals, including instructions to women concerning proper attire (3:3–4; cf. 1 Tim 2:9–10); conversion as rebirth and renewal (1:3–5; cf. Titus 3:4–5); similarities in creedal formulations (3:18; 1 Tim 3:16); and the church as the household of God (4:17; 1 Tim 3:15; cf. Eph 2:19).

3. First Peter's resonances with Romans are evident in the passages cited in the previous note. Some resonances with Ephesians include God's prior election of the saints (1:2; Eph 1:4–5; also cf. Rom 8:28–30); the promised inheritance and the resultant hope in Christ (1:3–5; Eph 1:11–12); moral distance from Gentile life (4:3–4; Eph 4:17–18); moral instruction in the form of household codes (2:18–3:7; cf. Eph 5:21–6:9; also Col 3:18–4:1); and Christ's exaltation to the right hand of God (3:22; cf. Eph 1:20–23).

4. Christ's death as a ransom for many (1:18; cf. Mark 10:45); Christ the rejected stone of Ps 118:22–23 (2:7; cf. Mark 12:10–11 and parallels); especially echoes of Christ's sayings, e.g., OT prophets' longing to see the future as unfolded in Christ (1:10–12; cf. Matt 13:17); praying to God as Father (1:17; cf. Matt 6:9; Luke 11:2); good (honorable) deeds as witness to God's glory (2:12; cf. Matt 5:16); dealing with suffering and abuse (2:19–20; Luke 6:27–36); being reviled and rejoicing (4:13–14; cf. Matt 5:11–12); the humble exalted (5:6; Luke 14:11; 18:14); and turning anxiety over to a caring Lord (5:7; cf. Matt 6:25–34).

5. E.g., conversion as rebirth (1:3, 23; cf. John 3:3, 7); loving one another (1:22; 3:8; 4:8; cf. John 13:34; 15:12; also 1 John 3:11); Jesus as shepherd (2:25; 5:4; cf. John 10:11, 14); and instructions (to Peter, and by extension, to other elders) to tend the flock (5:1–3; cf. John 21:15–17).

6. Obedience to Jesus Christ (1:2; cf. Heb 5:9); the pilgrim motif (1:1; 2:11; cf. Heb 11:9, 13–16); Jesus the chief shepherd (5:4; cf. 2:25; cf. Heb 13:20); Christ suffering for sins "once for all" (3:18; Heb 7:27; 9:26); and discipleship as a life of offering sacrifice (2:5; cf. Heb 13:15–16).

7. Addressees in the Dispersion (1:1; cf. Jas 1:1); joy in tribulation (1:6–7; cf. Jas 1:2–4); the word's capacity to generate life (1:23–25; cf. Jas 1:18); resisting the devil (5:8–9; cf. Jas 4:7); love covering a

multitude of sin (4:8 = Prov 10:12; cf. Jas 5:20); fleeting life as a fading flower (1:24–25 = Isa 40:6–8; cf. Jas 1:10–11); and God's opposing the proud and strengthening the humble (5:5 = Prov 3:34; cf. Jas 4:6).

8. E.g., christological use of Isa 53 (2:21–25; cf. Acts 3:13, 26; also 4:27, 30; 8:32–33); Christ as judge of the living and the dead (4:5; cf. Acts 10:42); God as impartial judge (1:17; cf. Acts 10:34; 15:9); and Christ as the rejected stone of Ps 118:22 (2:7; cf. Acts 4:11).

9. Since the OT is so closely interwoven with the theologically based ethical exhortations throughout the letter, it is difficult to get an exact count of the number of OT citations and allusions. Editors of Greek editions and English translations differ as to what they include in this category. According to my count, 1 Peter contains nine OT citations and a dozen or so allusions. In the first group are the following: 1:16 (Lev 11:44–45; 19:2); 1:24–25 (Isa 40:6–8); the three "stone" passages: 2:6 (Isa 28:16); 2:7 (Ps 118:22); 2:8 (Isa 8:14); 2:22 (Isa 53:9*b*); 3:10–12 (Ps 34:12–16); 4:18 (Prov 11:31, esp. LXX); 5:5 (Prov 3:34, esp. LXX). Included among the allusions are: 2:3 (Ps 34:8); 2:9 (the cluster of images drawn from Exod 19:6 and Isa 43:20–21); 2:10 (Hos 1:6–7, 9; 2:23); 2:11 (Gen 23:4; Ps 39:12); 2:12 (Isa 10:3); 2:17 (Prov 24:21); 2:24–25 (images drawn from Isa 53:4–6, 12); 3:14 (Isa 8:12); 4:8 (Prov 10:12); 4:14 (Isa 11:2); 5:8 (Ps 22:13). The references to Sarah (3:6; cf. Gen 18:12, esp. MT, LXX; cf. NIV) and Noah (3:20; cf. Gen 6–8) belong in a separate category. While the range of biblical usage is remarkable, including texts from the law, prophets, and writings, there is a conspicuous preference for Isaiah, Psalms, and Proverbs.

10. Other OT "stone" passages include Isa 51:1–2; Dan 2:34; Zech 12:3; possibly Gen 49:24. As indicated in the notes above, appropriation of the "rejected stone" image (Ps 118:22–23) occurs on the lips of Jesus at the end of the parable of the wicked tenants (Mark 12:10–12; Matt 21:42–44; Luke 20:17–18). It also occurs as part of early Christian preaching in Peter's sermon before the Jerusalem authorities (Acts 4:11). The other pair of "stone" passages (Isa 28:16; 8:14) occurs in Paul's explanation of Israel's unbelief (Rom 9:33).

11. Elsewhere in the NT, Isa 53 is interpreted christologically, but nowhere quite like this; cf. Acts 8:32–33.

12. Ordinarily, one would expect Bithynia to be linked with Pontus, since the two formerly distinct territories formed a single Roman province in the late first century C.E. The order given probably reflects the route that couriers followed when traveling from the West and entering Asia Minor on the northern coast next to the Black Sea.

13. Origen appears to be the first to identify 1 Peter as one of the Catholic Letters; cf. Eusebius, *Hist. eccl.* 6.25.5.

14. Most of the OT passages cited or alluded to conform to the LXX, although some seem closer to the Hebrew Bible (MT), e.g., 1:24 (Isa 40:6*b*–7). Some OT quotations or allusions vary from both the LXX and the MT, e.g., 1:25; 2:6*a*, 8, 22, 24.

15. R. Wilken, *The Christians as the Romans Saw Them* (New Haven: Yale University Press, 1984), estimates that the "total number of Christians within the empire [in the early second century] was probably less than fifty thousand" (31). For the following sketch, I am dependent on Wilken's treatment.

16. REB, "wrongdoers"; NJB, "criminals"; NIV, "doing wrong."

17. Thus taking 1:23 as "through the living and enduring word of God," although "living and enduring" may describe God. Cf. NRSV note.

18. In this respect, 1 Peter conforms to the pattern in the Pastoral Letters.

19. The "slain Passover Lamb" does not appear to be in view (cf. John 1:29). The imagery is rather drawn from Isa 53: the innocent, slain lamb whose death was redemptive.

20. Perhaps this reflects the outlook of Hebrews that Christ's death deals with sin once and for all (Heb 7:27; 9:28). It resonates, in certain ways, with Paul's view that one's dying with Christ ends the dominion of sin (Rom 6:7); or possibly 2 Cor 5:14: "one has died for all; therefore all have died [to sin?]."

21. The term "spirit" (*pneuma*) is mentioned eight times. Six of these arguably refer to the Holy Spirit (1:2, 11, 12; 3:18; 4:6, 14). Two clearly do not (3:4, 19).

22. Perhaps the earliest witness is 2 Peter, which appears to presuppose 1 Peter's existence (cf. 2 Pet 3:1). Second Peter seems to rank the testimony of 1 Peter along with the authoritative, scriptural status of the Pauline letters (3:15–16).

23. *Comm. Jo.* cited in Eusebius, *Hist. eccl.* 6.25.8.

24. It is preserved in Eusebius, *Hist. eccl.* 5.1–3.

25. *Hist. eccl.* 5.1.25. The same passage is appropriated again in 5.2.6.

26. *Hist. eccl.* 5.2.5.

27. *Hist. eccl.* 5.1.23.

28. Clement, *Strom.* 4.7, a section discussing the blessedness of the martyr, in which relevant texts, especially from Rom 8 and 1 Peter are interwoven with classical citations to show how it is possible for "feeble flesh to resist the energies and spirits of the Powers." Also, Tertullian, *Scorp.* 12, citing 1 Pet 2:20–21; 4:12–16. Similarly Polycarp, *Phil.* 8.1–2, appropriating 1 Pet 2:21, 22, 24; *Acts of the Scillitan Martyrs* (1 Pet 2:17).

Bibliography

Commentaries

Achtemeier, Paul J. *1 Peter*. Hermeneia. Minneapolis: Fortress, 1996.

Bartlett, David L. "The First Letter of Peter." Pages 227–319 in vol. 12 of *The New Interpreter's Bible*. Edited by Leander E. Keck. 12 vols. Nashville: Abingdon, 1998.

Beare, Francis Wright. *The First Epistle of Peter: The Greek Text with Introduction and Notes*. 3d ed. Oxford: Blackwell, 1970 (1947).

Best, Ernest. *1 Peter*. New Century Bible. Rev. ed. London/Grand Rapids: Oliphants/Eerdmans, 1982 (1971).

Elliott, John H. *1 Peter: A New Translation, with Introduction and Commentary*. Anchor Bible 37B. New York: Doubleday, 2000.

Goppelt, L. *A Commentary on I Peter*. Edited by F. Hahn. Translated and augmented by J. E. Alsup. Grand Rapids: Eerdmans, 1993 (1978).

Kelly, J. N. D. *A Commentary on the Epistles of Peter and Jude*. Black's/Harper's New Testament Commentaries. New York: Harper & Row, 1969.

Perkins, Pheme. *First and Second Peter, James, and Jude*. Interpretation: A Bible Commentary for Teaching and Preaching. Louisville: Westminster John Knox, 1995.

Selwyn, Edward Gordon. *The First Epistle of St. Peter: The Greek Text with Introduction, Notes, and Essays*. 2d ed. London: Macmillan, 1947; repr. 1964.

Other Resources

Balch, David L. *Let Wives Be Submissive: The Domestic Code in 1 Peter*. Society of Biblical Literature Monograph Series 26. Chico: Society of Biblical Literature (Scholars Press), 1981.

Brown, Raymond E., Karl P. Donfried, and John Reumann, eds. *Peter in the New Testament*. Minneapolis: Augsburg Fortress, 1973.

Cullmann, Oscar. *Peter: Disciple—Apostle—Martyr: A Historical and Theological Essay*. Translated by F. V. Filson. Philadelphia: Westminster, 1962.

Elliott, John H. *A Home for the Homeless: A Sociological Exegesis of 1 Peter, Its Situation and Strategy*. Philadelphia: Fortress/London: SCM, 1981. Expanded as second edition, *A Home for the Homeless: A Social-Scientific Criticism of 1 Peter, Its Situation and Strategy, With a New Introduction*. Minneapolis: Fortress, 1990.

Martin, Ralph P. "1 Peter." Pages 87–133, 166–67 in Andrew Chester and Ralph P. Martin, *The Theology of the Letters of James, Peter, and Jude.* New Testament Theology. Cambridge: Cambridge University Press, 1994; repr. 1996.

Martin, Troy W. *Metaphor and Composition in 1 Peter.* Society of Biblical Literature Dissertation Series 131. Atlanta: Society of Biblical Literature (Scholars Press), 1992.

Selwyn, Edward Gordon. *The Epistle of Christian Courage: Studies in the First Epistle of St. Peter.* London: Mowbray, 1940.

Talbert, Charles H., ed. *Perspectives on First Peter.* National Association of Baptist Professors of Religion Special Study Series 9. Macon: Mercer University Press, 1986.

Volf, Miroslav. "Soft Difference: Theological Reflections on the Relation Between Church and Culture in 1 Peter." *Ex Auditu* 10 (1994): 15–30.

Wilken, Robert L. *The Christians as the Romans Saw Them.* New Haven: Yale University Press, 1984.

Jude and Second Peter

In early canonical lists, 2 Peter typically followed 1 Peter, and Jude came at the end of the Catholic Letters. While this arrangement is also reflected in our current canonical arrangement, in the following presentation Jude and 2 Peter are treated together because of broad scholarly agreement that they are literarily dependent. Here, Jude is read as the earlier of the two and 2 Peter as a "second edition" of Jude.

Since scholarship on these two letters is closely linked, bibliography relating to them is placed at the end of the chapter on 2 Peter.

Chapter 24

Jude

"Jude's language about the Faith is highly dogmatic, highly orthodox, highly zealous. His tone is that of a bishop of the fourth century."

Charles Bigg

"[Jude] is a plain, honest leader of the church who knows when round indignation is more telling than argument. . . . [The letter] denounces rather than describes the objects of its attack, and there is a note of exaggerated severity in it."

James Moffatt

Struck by Jude's beguiling brevity, Origen (ca. 185–254 C.E.) called it "a letter of a few lines . . . but filled with robust words of heavenly grace."[1] Not everyone has agreed with Origen's assessment. Because the letter is short, some have ignored it. Its "robust" language some have seen as overly harsh, if not downright offensive. Not only does Jude exude the spirit of controversy, but it has also created controversy far out of proportion to its length.

Before it began to be grouped with the other six Catholic Letters, usually in the seventh position, Jude was read in its own right. It came to be regarded as catholic not because it addressed the church at large, but because it addressed an unidentified group of readers whose faith was being seriously threatened. It is this specificity—a community of believers trying to cope with ungodliness masquerading as godliness—that makes Jude catholic. Every church eventually confronts some version of this problem.

Unlike other NT writings, such as the Pastoral Letters, which confront false teaching as one of several concerns, this is Jude's sole focus. Its overarching concern is to expose "certain intruders" (v. 4) who have gained entry among the readers. Besides denouncing "these people" (vv. 5–16),[2] Jude also gives positive advice to his "beloved" readers on how to cope with these threats (vv. 17–23). While the identity of the false teachers and the contours of their teaching remain elusive, we catch some intriguing glimpses into their activity. The rare reference to "love feasts" (v. 12) suggests that Christian fellowship meals, probably connected with eucharistic observance, were used as occasions to promote their views.[3] It is not difficult to imagine what forms this promotion took, especially if we take "feeding themselves" in its more proper sense of shepherds who abuse their sacred trust by caring only for themselves rather than their flocks.[4]

Of particular interest is the rhetorical texture of Jude's response to a threat that was serious enough to interrupt his plans to address his readers on more positive matters (v. 3). For all of its bombast, the letter is a carefully crafted, rhetorically sophisticated composition. Displaying a moderately grand rather than grandiose style, Jude uses well-chosen, often graphic images. In a tightly organized fashion, he also employs conventional rhetorical devices that strengthen and decorate the argument. His fondness for groups of threes (see vv. 2, 5–7, 8, 11) and fives (vv. 12–13, 16) is evident. Also worth noting is Jude's careful use of catchwords as a device for linking different sections and establishing thematic coherence. One of the clearest examples is the use of the "ungodly"/"ungodliness" word family (*asebēs, asebeō, asebeia*) in verses 4, 15, and 18. Far more than street Greek, Jude's language reflects a refined literary style with some close affinities to polished Attic Greek.

The veneer may be Greek, but the content of the argument is an intriguing mixture of familiar, even conventional, biblical examples and non-biblical apocalyptic traditions (similar lists occur in Sir 16:5–10; 3 Macc 2:3–7; *T. Naph.* 3:1–4.3; *m. Sanh.* 10:3; CD 2:14–3.12). Jude's willingness to break with convention and quote explicitly from otherwise marginal works, which some scholars see as an indication of his naïve, uncritical judgment, actually reflects an admirable independence of spirit, if not a gift for originality. The clearest instance is verses 14–15, in which he quotes directly from *1 En.* 1:9. Less clear is verse 9, which refers to Michael the archangel's dispute with the devil concerning the burial of Moses. This episode, which is nowhere recorded in the Bible, was probably drawn from the *Testament of Moses,* an apocryphal work relating to Moses.[5] [See Expanded CD Version p. 726: *The Church's Response to Jude's Use of 1 Enoch*]

In Jude we see a mixture of prophetic rage and apocalyptic fervor brought into the service of the Christian gospel. Giving the letter its sense of urgency is the threat of an imminent, divine judgment that will be unleashed against those who dare to oppose God's purposes (see vv. 6, 13, 15; cf. 21, 24–25). What gives the argument its special power is the world shared by Jude and his readers: the biblical story enhanced with non-biblical, explicitly apocalyptic, traditions in which memorable events and figures serve as instructive examples for future generations of God's people—but, more than that, a story in which prophecies by eminent figures like Enoch anticipate the actions, both good and ill, of later generations. The archangel Michael's dispute with the devil over the burial of Moses, while not part of the official biblical story, has as much instructive value as the biblical stories of disobedient Israel in the wilderness or Sodom and Gomorrah. The story of the sons of God "coming down" to the daughters of men in Gen 6, now read through the apocalyptic lens of *1 Enoch,* has as much moral force as the three unforgettable OT examples of arrogance, greed, and rank insubordination: Cain, Balaam, and Korah. [See Expanded CD Version p. 727: *Evidence for Jude's Palestinian Origin*]

Taken together, these distinctive features reveal a pastoral directive couched in quasi-epistolary form, attributed to Jude, a well-placed member within early Christian circles, who has the authority to speak a word of warning to a group of beloved fellow believers. Since he acknowledges the apostles as a group distinct from himself (v. 17), he does not speak as an apostolic voice. Nor is he identified with any title other than "servant of Jesus Christ and brother of James" (v. 1). There is no indication that he is the founder of the community of believers that he addresses, even though he relates to them in intimate, endearing terms. But he speaks with a firm, authoritative voice that is fully aligned with the "faith that was once for all entrusted to the saints" (v. 3).

To think of this faith as a rigid creedal statement that has hardened over time and has lost its existential punch is to misconstrue what drives Jude to defend it. In spite of the brevity of the letter, the contours of this faith are visible. Indeed, in so short a space Jude touches on virtually every major element of early Christian belief. That this faith, whose centerpiece is Jesus Christ, has been revealed with dramatic finality is quite clear—it has been entrusted to the saints "once for all." Since it is the faith that the apostles warn others to protect, it can be called the apostolic faith, although the apostles are not its sole, authentic bearers.

It is Jude's confidence in the faith as superlatively holy (v. 20) that explains his moral outrage toward those who would threaten it with cheap grace. Unlike later Christian apologists who delineate the position of their opponents, answer their objections, and then present a positive, well-reasoned statement of the faith, Jude is unwilling to give even the faint outlines of his opponents' teachings. To do so would give them undeserved publicity. They must be excoriated, not treated as serious intellectual equals.

Jude's unwavering confidence in the faith also explains his free use of unconventional sources. He is not threatened by writings with dubious canonical status because of his confidence in the faith he has received. Instead, he reads Scripture and the traditions that have accumulated around it through the lens of the Christ event. Where he finds Christ revealed, even in the most obscure writings or traditions, there he finds revealed truth that can be instructive for the life of faith. Jude probably appropriates *1 Enoch* because he thinks it speaks of Jesus Christ. If so, the "coming Lord" of *1 En.* 1:9 who will execute judgment on all is the Lord Jesus Christ whose mercy will bring the faithful to eternal life (v. 21).

In Jude, then, we find a vigorous orthodoxy blended with an independent spirit confident enough in its faith to embrace the seemingly unorthodox; a work with a sharply defined apocalyptic outlook whose preemptive strike against opponents enabled it to outlive its imminent eschatology; and a writing addressed to a single church with particular needs, whose value to other churches was acknowledged by putting it at the end of the Catholic Letters. So positioned as the prelude to the Johannine Apocalypse, this writing, with its fervent, apocalyptic view of Christianity, turned out to be well placed.

The Letter's Purpose and Structure

Jude opens with a standard epistolary greeting (vv. 1–2) but concludes with a doxology rather than personal remarks and a formal benediction (vv. 24–25). In this regard, Jude more closely resembles James and 2 Peter than 1 Peter. Even so, it should be read as a genuine letter.

A note of urgency is struck by the author's omission of a transitional prayer of thanksgiving or blessing (cf. 1 Pet 1:3–12) and an immediate move to his stated purpose for writing (vv. 3–4). Employing conventional paraenetic language (*parakaleō*), Jude formulates his appeal using a strong athletic metaphor: "to contend [*epagōnizomai*] for the faith that was once for all entrusted to the saints" (v. 3). Here the life of faith is seen as a fierce athletic contest requiring the strength, stamina, and courage of dedicated contestants. What prompts the struggle is faith understood as a sacred trust—not a set of beliefs or values still in a state of flux but given and received as definitive revelation. Those who threaten this faith are exposed as its fraudulent representatives (v. 4).

The heart of the letter (vv. 5–16) is a tightly structured attack in which Jude denounces these unnamed "intruders" (v. 4). The first set of examples is arranged not according to their biblical sequence but in the order of ascending depravity. What disobedient Israel in the wilderness, the rebellious angels, and Sodom and Gomorrah have in common are insolent actions that were decisively punished by God. Since the opponents' licentiousness is singled out (v. 4), the last example underscores the grievous consequences of egregious sexual misconduct.

The restrained behavior of Michael, who as archangel had every right to slander his rival the devil but yielded the floor to God, serves as an example of controlled speech for the immoral, insubordinate, loose-tongued opponents (vv. 8–10). Then follows a second set of three memorable OT cases of people who led others astray—Cain, Balaam, and Korah—again arranged in ascending order of culpable participation: the opponents first "walk," then "abandon themselves to," and finally "perish" (v. 11). A cluster of vivid images depicting the instability of the unpredictable opponents links them with the negative examples already introduced (vv. 12–13). Finally comes the citation from Enoch's prophecy, in which Jude insists that the opponents' behavior was anticipated long ago; they can expect to experience the full force of God's wrath (vv. 14–16).

Having amply illustrated what fighting for the faith entails, Jude then turns to advice directed to the readers (vv. 17–23). Here he spells out what their struggle will require. First is confronting ungodliness directly (vv. 17–19). This involves remembering apostolic warnings about those who would undermine the faith. Readers must take these warnings seriously and not be naïve in dealing with such people. Second is cultivating true godliness (vv. 20–23). This involves listening to positive instruction about the faith and practicing disciplined spirituality: praying in the Holy Spirit, living within God's love, and framing a hopeful future shaped by the mercy of Christ. Faith practiced this way will be directed toward others and find ways to extend them mercy (v. 23).

The concluding doxology (vv. 24–25) firmly anchors the readers' existence within the faith they confess. This prayer centers and stabilizes them within the turmoil they are experiencing.

The Threat

The strong polemical tone of the letter suggests caution in developing a profile of the opposition. Much of the language reflects the rhetoric often used in ancient philosophical debates to depict one's opponents in the worst possible terms. Typically opponents are caricatured as flatterers, slanderers, and self-indulgent, unpredictable people who waver in their opinions and create havoc wherever they go.

Even so, Jude is not tilting at windmills. Those who are threatening the faith and stability of his readers are itinerant, charismatic teachers. Characterizing them as "certain intruders [who] have stolen in among you" (v. 4) suggests that they have arrived from somewhere else and gained entry into the Christian community in covert ways. Their behavior at Christian "love feasts" is fearless and calculating (v. 12). Calling them "dreamers" (v. 8) probably implies their use of ecstatic visions and revelations, perhaps comparable to those often depicted in apocalyptic writings, to back up their claims. That they "reject authority" (v. 8) need not mean that they are actively opposing the Mosaic law, even though the dispute between Michael and the devil involves the burial of Moses. Nowhere in the letter is the Mosaic law (*nomos*) mentioned, nor are issues related to its practice identified. The opponents' conduct is antinomian only in the sense that they defy conventional forms of authority and commonly accepted behaviors.

References to their licentiousness suggest conduct involving sexual immorality (vv. 4, 8, 18). Perverting "the grace of our God into licentiousness" (v. 4) sounds like a version of the behavior Paul refutes: God's grace misconstrued as freedom to indulge the desires of the flesh (Rom 6:1).

Behind these scattered references some commentators have seen Gnostic patterns of behavior, either incipient or well developed, for example, the Carpocratians. The spirit of libertinism seen in the letter sometimes characterized Gnostic groups. Calling the opponents "worldly people" (v. 19, *psychikoi*) employs a stock term for a certain grade of Gnostic achievement. The term occurs in Paul in a more neutral sense (1 Cor 2:14), but it could have a quasi-technical Gnostic sense in Jude. Opponents who "deny our only Master and Lord, Jesus Christ" (v. 4) resemble the "deceivers" in the Johannine letters who deny that Jesus "has come in the flesh" (2 John 7). In Jude, however, the form of denial is not specified; it may refer to the failure to understand fully the confession that Jesus is Lord and the form of behavior such allegiance requires. Jude's double accent on Jesus Christ as the "only Master and Lord" (v. 4) and the "only God" (v. 25) need not be seen as countering a Gnostic hierarchy of deities or even some form of Marcion's sharp distinction between the deities of the OT and NT. If "dreamers" (v. 8) implies the opponents' claims to special inspiration, Jude's heavy use of apocalyptic traditions may be a way of countering the opponents' exclusive claims to esoteric knowledge. Accordingly, his charge that they are "devoid of the Spirit" (v. 19) may reflect a similar questioning of their claims to unique access to God's revelation.

While many of these elements have strong resonance with various strands of Gnostic thought, they are too vague to identify the opposition with one stream of Gnosticism or any single Gnostic figure. But they do reveal attitudes and behaviors that are later found in some Gnostic groups. To this limited extent, the position being opposed is incipient Gnosticism.

The Faith Worth Fighting For

In formulating a response to this threat, Jude adopts a strategy that differs from the Pastorals. Rather than recite various creedal statements, Jude constructs a response heavily based on Scripture, yet also strongly informed by non-biblical traditions. Instead of drawing out the fuller implications of elements of Christian belief, Jude uses the full weight of the biblical story and accompanying Jewish traditions to construct a sharply worded condemnation of those who threaten the stability of Christian communities.

Here, doing theology takes the form of polemical denunciation of opponents coupled with reassuring instruction to the church itself. In following this strategy, Jude anticipates in some respects later Christian apologists, but his protective, even episcopal, instincts are everywhere evident. For this reason, Jude can be compared more beneficially with Basil the Great (ca. 330–379 C.E.) than with Athenagoras (second century) or Tertullian.[6]

The Church's Use of Jude

Through patristic comments made about Jude from the early third century onward, several themes emerge. First, Jude tended to be ignored by early Christian writers.[7] Second, Jude is consistently mentioned with the other Catholic Letters. Because a clear divide appears between the "major" (James, 1 Peter, 1 John) and "minor" (2 Peter, 2–3 John) Catholic Letters, Jude is typically included with the latter group. Third, its disputed status is frequently noted. It is usually included among the other writings whose authorship, content, or apostolic authority is disputed (*antile-gomena*). Sometimes the dispute pertains to the identity of the author, but some also objected to Jude's endorsement of apocryphal writings. Quite often, these are named: the writings of Enoch (*1 Enoch*) and the *Assumption* (or *Testament*) *of Moses*.[8] Fourth, even though writers mention some of the church's objections to Jude, its inclusion with the other canonical NT writings is justified because of its antiquity and the authority it acquired through usage.[9] **[See Expanded CD Version pp. 731–32: *The Church's Use of Jude: Further Discussion*]**

Notes

1. *Comm. Matt.* 10.17. The Greek expression rendered by "robust words" is *errōmenoi logoi*. The phrase might be translated literally as "healthful" or "sound" and thus by extension "powerful" or "formidable" words. "Robust" is intended to retain the health metaphor yet convey the idea of strength and power.

2. This pejorative designation of the opponents almost acquires a technical sense in Jude. See esp. vv. 10 and 19; also the use of "these" in vv. 8, 12, 14, 16.

3. Only here in the NT does the familiar Greek term *agapē* mean "love feast" or "fellowship meal" (also in a variant reading of 2 Pet 2:13). It also occurs in this sense in Ignatius, *Smyrn.* 8.2 (probably *Rom.* 7.3); also cf. Clement of Alexandria, *Paed.* 2.1 (ANF 2:238–39).

4. See NRSV note on v. 12 for the alternate rendering.

5. Some ancient testimonies (e.g., Clement, *Annotations*, on v. 9 [ANF 2:573]; Origen, *Princ.* 3.2.1) refer to Jude's source as the *Assumption* (or *Ascension*) *of Moses*. Other ancient sources refer to a *Testament of Moses*. Whether these were separate works or two parts of the same work is not certain. Possibly, the episode referred to by Jude in v. 9 was drawn from the conclusion of *T. Mos.*, which is no longer extant.

6. See, e.g., Basil, *Epist.* 125 (*NPNF*[2] 8:194–96).

7. Eusebius reported of James, and also of Jude, that "not many of the ancients mentioned it" *(Hist. eccl.* 2.23.24–25).

8. Origen, *Princ.* 3.2.1 refers to *The Ascension of Moses,* which he calls "a little treatise of which the apostle Jude makes mention in his epistle" *(ANF* 4:328). In an ambiguous passage, Didymus the Blind of Alexandria (ca. 313–398 C.E.) mentions Jude's use of the *Assumption of* Moses, but whether he does so in order to defend himself against his critics is not at all clear. See his comments on v. 9 in PG 39:1815; also Peter R. Jones, *The Epistle of Jude* . . . (Texts and Studies in Religion 89; Lewiston: Mellen, 2001), 68. Jerome, *Vir. ill.* 4, singles out Jude's use of "the apocryphal book of Enoch" as the reason it was "rejected by many."

9. Jerome, *Vir. ill.* 4.

Chapter 25

Second Peter

"When I speak of a long period I mean it relatively to ourselves . . . for the gods any length of human life is but nothing."

Plutarch

"Above the dogmatic eschatological necessity . . . there stands the omnipotence of God, which is bound by no limitations."

Albert Schweitzer

Second Peter gives extended attention to a single, contested element of early Christian belief: Christ's Parousia. It does so in a way that distinguishes it from other NT writings. The form of the question it addresses is distinctive, as is the form of its response.

The sharply polemical tone of 2 Peter suggests that it confronts a serious crisis of confidence within the early church—one with profound implications for the church. To use the language of Christian doctrine, the issue is the relationship between eschatology—how the church understands the end time—and ethics—its view of the moral life. Second Peter's overriding moral concern is reflected in its references to Christianity as "the way of truth" (2:2), "the straight road" (2:15), and "the way of righteousness" (2:21)—expressions that accent codes of behavior rather than codes of belief.

Considered by most scholars to be a pseudonymous writing, probably stemming from a circle of Peter's followers in Rome from the late first or early second century, 2 Peter is written in the form of a testament. Like two other Catholic Letters, James and Jude, it opens with a standard epistolary greeting (1:1–2) but exhibits few other distinctive epistolary elements, such as a concluding section with personal greetings and benediction (cf. 1 Pet 5:12–14). Even so, it exhibits enough of an epistolary character to be judged a testamentary letter.

Second Peter is predicated on the impending death of the apostle Peter (1:12–15). Perhaps the best literary representative of the testament genre is the *Testaments of the Twelve Patriarchs*, a Jewish writing from the second-century B.C.E. that went through various redactions and eventually included Christian elements. The genre draws on OT farewell addresses by such figures as Jacob (Gen 49), Moses (Deut 31–33), and Joshua (Josh 23–24). Many scholars classify Jesus' farewell address in John 13–17 in the same manner and find a shorter example in Paul's speech to the Ephesian elders (Acts 20:17–35). In many ways, 2 Timothy, the "testament of Paul," conforms to the same genre.

Typical of the testament genre, the anticipated death of a revered figure becomes an occasion to address a circle of beloved followers, often comprising family and friends. When formulated as a letter, the testament was intended to embody the revered figure's legacy for a wider audience, even succeeding generations.

Testaments exhibit distinctive literary characteristics, but they usually reflect two sets of concerns. First, they recall the revered figure's legacy, with particular emphasis on virtues exemplified in the person's life. Second, the person's impending death inevitably invites a look at the future. Things that might threaten the continuation of the person's legacy are identified, and attention is given to what is required to preserve that legacy. Typically this entails defining ways to "pass the torch" to the person's successors in a manner that ensures the continuation of values the person stood for.

Since 2 Peter exhibits many of these elements, an apt title for the letter would be "The Testament of Peter." No such writing is known from antiquity, although a number of apocryphal writings were produced under the name of Peter, including *Acts of Peter, Apocalypse of Peter, Gospel of Peter, Preaching of Peter, Martyrdom of Peter, Martyrdom of Peter and Paul,* the Gnostic *Letter of Peter to Philip* (VIII.2), and the Gnostic *Apocalypse of Peter* (VII.3).

Responding to the Crisis Created by the Delay of the Parousia

Responding to an unnamed group of overly skeptical Christian believers, 2 Peter unfolds in a logically coherent manner. After the initial greeting (1:1–2), Peter's legacy is presented in the form of a majestic summary of early Christian faith (1:3–11). In keeping with the testament genre, Peter's impending death is mentioned (1:12–15). This in turn prompts reference to two items that underpin his apostolic testimony: (1) his presence at Christ's transfiguration (1:16–18), when he experienced direct access to God by hearing the same voice that Christ did (1:18); and (2) his resulting credentials as an authentic representative of the "prophetic message" (1:19–21).

In one sense, the focus of these remarks in chapter 1 is on Peter (esp. 1:12–15). Unlike the synoptic accounts of the transfiguration, which identify Peter, James, and John as the primary apostolic participants, the account in 2 Peter mentions no one else besides Peter. But the shift to the first person plural, especially in 1:16–21, along with the reference to the testimony of the apostles (3:2), suggests that Peter is speaking for all of the apostles. The scope of the apostolic witness is broadened even further by introducing Peter's "beloved brother Paul" (3:15).

While Peter's legacy is the majestic vision to which he was privy, and which sustained him through his apostolic witness, two elements of his summary of this experience are prominent: (1) a vision of the future filled with promise; and (2) the present viewed as a time of moral transformation.

The first element is distinctively formulated as the promise of "entry into the eternal kingdom of our Lord and Savior Jesus Christ" (1:11). The "precious and very great promises" (1:4) that God (or possibly Christ) entrusted to Peter (as well as his apostolic colleagues, and, by extension, to the readers) doubtless refer to the promise of Christ's Parousia, which is mentioned more explicitly elsewhere in the letter (cf. 1:16; 3:4, 9–10, 12). The prospect of sharing in the divine nature is also an eschatological benefit for those who are morally upright (1:4).

Closely connected with a meaningful sense of the future is the second element, a vision of Christian vocation—one's "calling and election" by God (1:10), enacted as a life of progressive moral development (1:5–8). The eight virtues, which are seen as successive steps of moral progress beginning with faith and ending with love, reflect highly prized Hellenistic values. As a defining feature of Peter's legacy, active pursuit of the moral life is required to participate in the divine nature. By framing moral expectations in this manner, 2 Peter reflects the sophisticated Hellenistic outlook expressed by the moral philosopher Plutarch (ca. 50–120 C.E.): "Divinity, to which [humans] are eager to adapt and conform themselves, seems to have three elements of superiority—incorruption, power, and virtue; and the most impressive, the divinest of these, is virtue" (*Arist.* 6.2).

The remainder of the letter takes up each element of Peter's legacy in reverse order. Chapter 2 delineates the threat posed by false teachers, whose behavior is sketched as a direct antithesis of the moral ideal in 1:5–8. Chapter 3 confronts the false teachers by showing how their skepticism about the future undercuts a Christian view of the future informed by the promise of Christ's coming.

Having certified his apostolic credentials, Peter now turns to what threatens the continuation of his legacy—and by extension, the broader apostolic legacy: the presence of "false teachers" (2:1) who stand in direct opposition to "the Master who bought them" (2:1). Chapter 2 is devoted to this threat. While these remarks exhibit many of the standard elements found in ancient descriptions of philosophical and religious opponents, they concentrate on the false teachers' moral failures. Several features of their conduct are repeatedly mentioned: gross sexual misconduct, arrogance, greed, disregard for authority, and deceit. The opponents also promote their own conduct as worthy of emulation, all in the name of "freedom" (2:19).

Interwoven with this rehearsal of the false teachers' reprehensible conduct is a series of biblical examples illustrating that gross misconduct in the past raised God's ire and brought severe punishment (the misbehaving angels [2:4], Noah's contemporaries [2:5], and Sodom and Gomorrah [2:6]). Other examples show that those who displayed exceptional righteousness, such as Noah (2:5) and Lot (2:7), were rescued by God. The deceptive ways of the false teachers also prompt comparison with Balaam (2:15–16). Their inability to remain faithful to their original Christian commitment recalls the OT proverb of the dog returning to its vomit (2:22; cf. Prov 26:11), which is paired with another ancient proverb just as disgusting—the washed sow returning to the mud.

Skepticism about the Future

While the author has referred briefly to the future in his assault on the false teachers' ethical lapses (2:9–10), his main concern in chapter 3 is to respond to their disillusionment about the future. The language of "scoffing" (3:3) suggests a deep level of cynicism, if not outright denial. That Christ's Parousia is the focus of their doubts is clear from Peter's formulation of their position in 3:4: "Where is this 'coming' he promised? Ever since our fathers died, everything goes on as it has since the beginning of creation" (NIV).

Elsewhere, the NT reflects puzzlement about Christ's expected coming. From Luke's reinterpretation of the synoptic tradition, it is evident that some Christians wondered whether Jesus would ever return, and, if so, how soon. Paul's letters also deal with eschatological misunderstandings, which included questions about the timing of Christ's Parousia. None of these other NT passages, however, is quite so blunt in reporting believers' skepticism about this central Christian belief.

By the time 2 Peter was written, enough time had elapsed for Christians to doubt seriously whether Christ would actually deliver on his promise to return—a promise reported in different versions in the Gospels (e.g., Mark 9:1 and parallels). The prospects were dim enough to suggest an alternative view of history, which understood time as having begun with creation and then moving forward as an ongoing flow of events unaffected by divine providence. Looking back, the false teachers could see no time when God had intervened decisively, much less visibly, in human affairs. Looking forward, they could see no prospect that this would ever occur.

Such skepticism about the future was known throughout the Mediterranean world in a variety of settings. Its Jewish form was most conspicuously represented in Sadducean thought, which denied the notion of a resurrection of the dead and a general judgment of all humanity. On the non-Jewish side, one of the most visible representatives was Epicureanism, which operated with a view of the universe that excluded the possibility of divine intervention in human life. Not surprisingly, in some texts Sadducees and Epicureans are confused with each other. Whether either of these traditionally well-known forms of eschatological skepticism was operative in the situation addressed by 2 Peter is uncertain. The attitude attributed to the false teachers may reflect a more widespread sense of malaise that typified the culture. Neither Jewish apocalyptic visions of the end time nor Christian views about Christ's Parousia were particularly intelligible, much less convincing on first blush, to many people in the Greco-Roman world.

Envisioning a Hopeful Future

Second Peter responds to this eschatological skepticism with three arguments followed by a final appeal.

First, the author reasserts the biblical view of history that extends from creation to final judgment. Both events occur "by the word of God" (3:5). If the world came into being through God's agency, Peter argues, why is it so difficult to imagine that it will come to an end "by the same word" (v. 7)? If at an earlier time the world was "deluged with water and perished" (3:6), why not envision its final destruction in a similar manner? The implication is clear: to deny the possibility of a final, fiery destruction of the world and a following judgment that brings about the "destruction of the godless" (3:7) is to question the credibility of the biblical view of history. Much is at stake, then, in the false teachers' skeptical view of how the world will end. A critical theological point is being made: how one envisions the end of history reveals much about one's overall philosophy of history.

Second, the author formulates a theological—as opposed to a chronological—view of time. The "scoffers" have interpreted the non-occurrence of Christ's Parousia as an instance of God's tardiness. To draw such a conclusion, Peter insists, is to judge God's plans according to human time. The force of the "thousand years as a day" equation is to remind the readers that since God transcends time, God cannot be held to a human timetable (3:8). Rather than implicating God for being slow in making good on divine promises, it is better to see the perceived delay as an opportunity to repent that will not last forever (3:9). This was by no means an idiosyncratic response, as seen in Plutarch's tractate "On the Delays of the Divine Vengeance," which stems from roughly the same period:

> . . . it is far more likely that when we see that God, who knows no fear or regret in anything, yet reserves his penalties for the future and awaits the lapse of time, we should become cautious in such matters, and hold the gentleness and magnanimity displayed by God a part of virtue that is divine, which by punishment amends a few, while it profits and admonishes many by the delay. . . . When I speak of a long period I mean it relatively to ourselves, as for the gods any length of human life is but nothing, and to put the evildoer on the rack or hang him now, and not thirty years ago, is like doing it in the evening and not in the morning, especially as he is shut up in his life as in a prison-house affording no removal or escape. . . .[1]

Third, the author reasserts the prophetic promise of the coming Day of the Lord, an expectation deeply embedded within the biblical witness (among the many OT references, see Ezek 30:1–4; Joel 2:1–2; Amos 5:18–20; Zeph 1:14–18). That its arrival will be as unexpected as a thief draws on a common metaphor (Matt 24:43–44; Luke 12:39–40; 1 Thess 5:2; Rev 3:3; 16:15). Likewise, the highly graphic vision of cosmic destruction draws on familiar biblical imagery but also resonates with other views of a final conflagration that were current in the ancient world (Isa 34:4 LXX; Joel 3:15).[2]

Once these three responses are articulated, the author moves to a final appeal in which he reaffirms the link between one's view of the future and one's behavior in the present. Insisting once again on the firm Christian conviction that a point of future accountability before God provides a powerful incentive for "leading lives of holiness and godliness" (3:11), the author reasserts the vision of a transformed heaven and earth "where righteousness is at home" (3:13).

To set this final exhortation within the broader context of early Christian belief, the author makes the highly unusual reference to Paul, who also insisted on a strong connection between eschatology and ethics (e.g., 1 Thess 5:1–11; 1 Cor 15:30–34). Especially intriguing is the author's presumed familiarity with "all his letters" and the implication that they were already being read like "the other scriptures" (3:16). Which Pauline letters were in view is not known, although since 2 Peter probably originated from Rome we can imagine that the Letter to the Romans and some of the other major Pauline letters were included. Besides documenting the broader perception that Paul's writings were difficult to understand, this passage also provides some basis for dating

2 Peter toward the end of the first century or possibly at the beginning of the second century. Such a date would allow a reasonable interval of time for the Pauline letters to be collected, then begin to acquire scriptural status comparable to other canonical writings, such as the OT and possibly other Christian writings like the Gospels.

The final charge (3:18) reiterates two recurrent concerns of the letter: (1) acquiring complete, authentic knowledge of "our Lord and Savior Jesus Christ," a way of referring to Christ unique to 2 Peter (1:11; 2:20; cf. 1:1; 3:2); and (2) holding fast to a meaningful sense of the future.

Recasting the Message of Jude

Close readers of 2 Peter and Jude instantly sense similarities of phraseology within the two letters. This is especially the case in two sections of Jude (vv. 4–13 and 16–18) and two sections of 2 Peter (2:1–18; 3:1–3).[3] Although we do not find extended sections with verbatim phraseology comparable to what we find in the Synoptic Gospels (e.g., John's preaching of repentance in Matt 3:7–10 and Luke 3:7–9), there are enough common terms and phrases to suggest some form of literary dependence between 2 Peter and Jude. Common authorship of the two letters is not a convincing explanation because of the pronounced differences in their vocabulary and literary styles. This was already noticed by Jerome (ca. 345–420 C.E.), who defended Peter's authorship of both letters but explained the stylistic differences by positing his use of different secretaries (*Ep.* 120.11). The resemblance between the two letters is too close and the situations of both the implied authors and readers are too different to think that two separate authors are drawing independently on a common document or oral tradition.

Direct literary dependence, which is a simpler solution, is preferred by most scholars. Such a connection has long been recognized. Martin Luther (1483–1546), for example, thought that Jude was a digest of 2 Peter. Commenting on verse 2, Luther writes, "Nor does [Jude] contain anything special beyond pointing to the Second Epistle of Saint Peter, from which it has borrowed nearly all the words."[4] Others who held this view thought it more probable that Jude would have drawn from the apostle Peter than vice versa. More recently, the scholarly consensus has favored 2 Peter's dependence on Jude. [See **Expanded CD Version pp. 740–42:** *Evidence for 2 Peter's Literary Dependence upon Jude*]

The Church's Use of 2 Peter

Compared with other NT writings, with the possible exception of Jude, 2 Peter's acceptance by the church was characterized by reluctance, qualification, and even resistance. Unlike the anonymous Letter to the Hebrews, 2 Peter was attributed to a named apostle, but this apostolic attribution did not prevent it from being questioned repeatedly. Unlike the Apocalypse of John, which enjoyed initial acceptance generally, but then had to contend with divided loyalties as the East rejected it and the West embraced it, 2 Peter enjoyed strong endorsement neither in the East nor the West, at least not initially. Unlike James, whose origins and authorship were debated yet was strongly endorsed and frequently quoted by Origen, 2 Peter appears never to have been quoted with such enthusiasm. For these reasons, its eventual acceptance into the NT canon is the story of overcoming resistance in a way that no other single NT writing had to do. The early church rightly saw Petrine authorship of the letter as an easily recognizable, transparent fiction, and, accepting the letter for what it was, embraced it anyway as authentic testimony from the apostle Peter. **[See Expanded CD Version pp. 742–43:** *The Church's Use of 2 Peter: Further Discussion***]**

Notes

1. *Sera* 5 & 9 (*Moralia* 551 b–c and 554 d; LCL 7:199 & 217–19); also cf. *4 Ezra* 7:74.

2. For other references to an anticipated cosmic destruction, see *Sib. Or.* 4:175–78; 1QH 11:24–36 (F. G. Martínez, *The Dead Sea Scrolls Translated* [2d ed.; trans. G. E. Watson; Grand Rapids: Eerdmans, 1996], 332–33); *1 En.* 52:6; 83:3–5; Plato, *Tim.* 22b–23c; Zeno, Frg. 98; Berosos as reported in Seneca, *Nat.* 3.29.1.

3. Among the similarities between these respective sections of Jude and 2 Peter, the following are noteworthy: those who "deny the Master" (2 Pet 2:1; cf. Jude 4); God's punishment of sinful angels, committing them to "chains of deepest darkness to be kept until the judgment" (2 Pet 2:4; cf. Jude 6); turning the cities of Sodom of Gomorrah to ashes and condemning them to extinction (2 Pet 2:6; cf. Jude 7); the false teachers characterized as "those who indulge their flesh in depraved lust . . . despise authority . . . slander the glorious ones" (2 Pet 2:10; cf. Jude 8); angels not bringing against [their opponents] "a slanderous judgment from the Lord" (2 Pet 2:11; cf. Jude 9); characterization of the false teachers as "irrational animals, mere creatures of instinct . . . [who] slander what they do not understand" (2 Pet 2:12; cf. Jude 10); false teachers as "blemishes, reveling in their dissipation while they feast with you" (2 Pet 2:13; cf. Jude 12), as "following the road of Balaam" (2 Pet 2:15; cf. Jude 11), as "waterless springs . . . mists driven by a storm; for [whom] the deepest darkness has been reserved" (2 Pet 2:17; cf. Jude 12–13), and as those who "speak bombastic nonsense . . . with licentious desires of the flesh . . . [who] entice people who have just escaped from those who live in error" (2 Pet 2:18; cf. Jude 16); and the prediction that "in the last days scoffers will come . . . indulging their own lusts" (2 Pet 3:3; cf. Jude 17–18).

4. *LW* 30:203; also cf. *LW* 35:397–98.

Bibliography

Jude & 2 Peter

Commentaries

JUDE AND 2 PETER

Bauckham, Richard. *Jude, 2 Peter*. Word Biblical Commentary 50. Waco: Word, 1983.
———. *Jude, 2 Peter*. Word Biblical Themes. Dallas: Word, 1990.
Kelly, J. N. D. *A Commentary on the Epistles of Peter and Jude*. Black's/Harper's New Testament Commentaries. New York: Harper & Row/London: Adam & Charles Black, 1969; repr. Grand Rapids: Baker, 1981.

Kraftchick, Steven J. *Jude, 2 Peter*. Abingdon New Testament Commentaries. Nashville: Abingdon, 2002.

Neyrey, Jerome H. *2 Peter, Jude*. Anchor Bible 37C. New York: Doubleday, 1993.

Perkins, Pheme. *First and Second Peter, James, and Jude*. Interpretation: A Bible Commentary for Teaching and Preaching. Louisville: John Knox, 1995. Pages 141–94.

Watson, Duane F. "The Letter of Jude: Introduction, Commentary, and Reflections." Pages 471–500 in vol. 12 of *The New Interpreter's Bible*. Edited by Leander E. Keck. 12 vols. Nashville: Abingdon, 1998.

———. "The Second Letter of Peter: Introduction, Commentary, and Reflections." Pages 321–61 in vol. 12 of *The New Interpreter's Bible*. Edited by Leander E. Keck. 12 vols. Nashville: Abingdon, 1998.

Other Resources

JUDE AND 2 PETER

Gerdmar, Anders. *Rethinking the Judaism-Hellenism Dichotomy: A Historiographical Case Study of Second Peter and Jude*. Coniectanea Biblica: New Testament Series 36. Stockholm: Almqvist & Wiksell, 2001.

Watson, Duane F. *Invention, Arrangement, and Style: Rhetorical Criticism of Jude and 2 Peter*. Society of Biblical Literature Dissertation Series 104. Atlanta: Society of Biblical Literature (Scholars Press), 1988.

JUDE

Bauckham, Richard. *Jude and the Relatives of Jesus in the Early Church*. Edinburgh: T&T Clark, 1990.

Charles, J. Daryl. *Literary Strategy in the Epistle of Jude*. Scranton: University of Scranton Press/London: Associated University Presses, 1993.

Jones, Peter Russell. *The Epistle of Jude as Expounded by the Fathers—Clement of Alexandria, Didymus of Alexandria, The Scholia of Cramer's Catena, Pseudo-Oecumenius, and Bede*. Texts and Studies in Religion 89. Lewiston: Edwin Mellen, 2001.

Martin, Ralph P. "Jude." Pages 65–86 in Andrew Chester and Ralph P. Martin, *The Theology of the Letters of James, Peter, and Jude*. New Testament Theology. Cambridge: Cambridge University Press, 1994; repr. 1996.

Reese, Ruth Anne. *Writing Jude: The Reader, the Text, and the Author in Constructs of Power and Desire*. Biblical Interpretation Series 51. Leiden: Brill, 2000.

2 PETER

Fornberg, Tord. *An Early Church in a Pluralistic Society: A Study of 2 Peter*. Coniectanea Biblica: New Testament Series 9. Lund: CWK Gleerup, 1977.

Martin, Ralph P. "2 Peter." Pages 134–63 in Andrew Chester and Ralph P. Martin, *The Theology of the Letters of James, Peter, and Jude*. New Testament Theology. Cambridge: Cambridge University Press, 1994; repr. 1996.

Starr, James M. *Sharers in Divine Nature: 2 Peter 1:4 in Its Hellenistic Context*. Coniectanea Biblica: New Testament Series 33. Stockholm: Almqvist & Wiksell, 2000.

GENERAL

Smith, Terence V. *Petrine Controversies in Early Christianity: Attitudes Toward Peter in Christian Writings of the First Two Centuries*. Wissenschaftliche Untersuchungen zum Neuen Testament 2.15. Tübingen: Mohr (Siebeck), 1985.

Chapter 26

The Letters of John

"Love is a sweet word, but sweeter the deed."

We begin by putting "Letters of John" in quotation marks since none of them claims to have been written by a person named John. In 2–3 John, the writer simply identifies himself as "the elder" (2 John 1; 3 John 1), but otherwise does not name himself. First John reveals even less about its author. We are left to guess the identity of the opening "we." The "I" who several times claims to be writing the letter also remains unidentified. With no named author, the Letters of John are unique among the Catholic Letters, since the others—Peter, James, and Jude—were written under identifiable names. Were it not for the Letter to the Hebrews, whose author also remains anonymous, the Letters of John would be unique among the NT epistolary writings in not naming their author.

In spite of their anonymity, all three letters quickly became identified with the name "John." Early readers of these letters recognized how similar they are in language, style, and outlook to the Fourth Gospel.[1] By the late second century, the Muratorian Fragment was attributing the Fourth Gospel to "John, one of the disciples" and quoting 1 John as one of "his epistles." The Fragment even mentions two epistles said to be "of John," but we are not sure whether this refers to 2–3 John or 1–2 John.[2] From this point forward, we find 1 John especially and 2–3 John occasionally attributed to John, the author of the Gospel. Typical are the sentiments of Origen (ca. 185–254 C.E.), who mentions John "who reclined on the breast of Jesus" as the author of the Gospel and the Apocalypse, but who also wrote "an epistle of a very few lines" and "possibly a second and a third, for not all say that these are genuine."[3] A century later Eusebius (ca. 260–340 C.E.) echoes Origen's views, including among the "treatises of John" the Gospel and the three letters (and the Apocalypse), yet widening the gulf between 1 John and 2–3 John by including "the extant former Epistle of John" (along with 1 Peter) among the undisputed writings. Eusebius relegated the "so-named second and third [epistles] of John, whether they happen to be of the Evangelist or even of another [author] of the same name as he" to the disputed writings, along with James, Jude, and 2 Peter.[4]

Of the three letters, 1 John was the most warmly received by the church, no doubt because of its sheer rhetorical power, its emphasis on love, and its capacity to enrich the church's faith even as it warned against false teachers. In the prologue to his *Ten Homilies on the Epistle of John to the Parthians*,[5] which covers 1 John 1:1–5:3, Augustine (354–430 C.E.) says that in the "Epistle of the blessed John," the author (who also wrote the Gospel) "has spoken many words, and nearly all are about charity." Some manuscripts amplify the title and identify the letter as the "Epistle of John About Charity." Whether it was because the letter captivated the church's attention as an "Epistle of Love" or because it spoke to a wider range of pressing issues, 1 John emerged fully in the church's consciousness by the mid-second century, probably even earlier. Eusebius reports that Papias (ca. 60–130 C.E.) "used testimonies drawn from the former epistle of John,"[6] and we find it being quoted by Polycarp (ca. 69–155 C.E.), bishop of Smyrna,[7] and Justin Martyr (ca. 100–165 C.E.).[8] Not far behind were 2–3 John, although the former seems to have been more widely accepted than the latter; at least, it tends to be mentioned with 1 John.[9] Clement of Alexandria (ca. 150–215 C.E.), for example, claims to have examined all the "catholic epistles,"[10] but cites only 1–2 John.[11] The church may have found the refutation of false teachers in 2 John more useful in combating Gnostic teaching. With its specific focus on Diotrephes, 3 John may have had more limited value in addressing the wider needs of the church.

Not until the fourth century do all three Letters of John begin to be mentioned together in canonical lists among the "seven so-called Catholic Epistles of the Apostles,"[12] usually following James and Peter but preceding Jude. Sometimes the seven Catholic Letters are placed after the Gospels and Acts and before Paul's letters (e.g., in Codex Vaticanus, mid-fourth century), which is understandable since their presumed authors are either mentioned in Acts or relate to the earliest period of the church. This suggests that even though the church recognized how closely the Letters of John and the Fourth Gospel were connected, it saw them, along with the other Catholic Letters, as addressing the general needs of the church. Their audience was the church universal. While 2–3 John may not have enjoyed the early popularity of 1 John and had the dubious distinction of being included by Eusebius among the "disputed writings," all three letters eventually came to be treated as a group, especially by expositors and commentators in the church. [See **Expanded CD Version pp. 752–53: *The Johannine Letters and the Lectionary; The Johannine Letters in the Medieval, Reformation, and Modern Periods***]

Some Questions to Decide

Recent scholarship has focused on three sets of issues relating to the Letters of John: (1) authorship, (2) relationship to the Fourth Gospel, and (3) their order. [See **Expanded CD Version pp. 753–54: *How the Johannine Letters Relate to Each Other and to the Fourth Gospel***]

The position adopted here is that the Letters of John were probably written after the Gospel in response to conflicting interpretations of the Johannine "gospel," that is, the theological view or version of the early Christian gospel that came to be expressed in the Fourth Gospel. Even granting that the Gospel of John went through several stages of editorial redaction, it appears unlikely that its author(s) also wrote the three letters. It is more probable that all three letters were composed by someone other than the author(s) of the Fourth Gospel. It is quite conceivable that 1 John was written by someone other than "the elder" who penned 2–3 John, although it is impossible to know for certain. There is good evidence to suggest that the author of 1 John knew the Fourth Gospel and that the author of 2 John knew 1 John (1 John 2:7–8 reflects John 13:34; 1 John 1:1–4 reflects John 1:1–4; 2 John 7 reflects 1 John 4:1–6). Third John may have preceded 2 John, but this is only a guess. The three letters are best read as efforts to address a conflicted Johannine church. First John represents a general response by someone steeped in the theology of the Johannine "gospel" who was probably a long-time member of the Johannine church. This person was so closely connected with the church and its traditions that his anonymous voice speaks authoritatively for them. Second and Third John, by contrast, address the difficult question of how to establish boundaries of fellowship in the aftermath of the split within the Johannine church.

Given this construal of the Letters of John and their relationship to the Fourth Gospel, they can be read as a case study of doing theology within the Johannine church. While Acts, as the sequel to Luke, allows us to see the direction that Luke's set of traditions about Jesus took, the Letters of John give us another angle of vision on the trajectory of John's Gospel. But whereas Acts reveals very little about the actual situation it addresses, the Letters of John yield many details about the church's situation. Although we are left to wonder how the Gospels of Matthew and Mark, even Luke, were read and interpreted within their respective churches or regions, we can think of the Letters of John as the earliest interpretive reflections on the Gospel of John.

Seen this way, the Letters of John may be read as a specific instance of practical theology. They allow us to see a particular moment (or moments) in the history of the Johannine church. [**See Expanded CD Version p. 755: *"Doing Theology" in the Johannine Letters*]**

The Catalyst: A Crisis of Belief

Passages that speak to the crisis of faith within the Johannine community include 1 John 2:18–27 and 1 John 4:1–6 (also 2 John 7–9). That "crisis" is not too strong a word is suggested by the apocalyptic language used in 1 John 2:18. To speak of the arrival of "many antichrists" as a sign of the "last hour" sounds a note of urgency that moves well beyond John's Gospel. We may be inclined to think of the "antichrist" as some mythological figure like Leviathan who threatens the stability of the social order, but ordinary human beings—other members of the Johannine church—are in view. The "antichrist," we are told, is "the one who denies the Father and the Son" (2:22; 2 John 7).

Another formulation of the dissenting viewpoint helps explain the appropriateness of the label "antichrist": To deny "that Jesus is the Christ" (2:22) is an "anti-Christ" viewpoint. But what does this actually mean? That Jesus did not have the qualifications of the expected Jewish Messiah? Or that the Messiah cannot be equated with the human figure Jesus? Yet another formulation accents Jesus' humanity: "Every spirit that confesses that Jesus Christ has come in the flesh is from God, and every spirit that does not confess Jesus [lit., "dissolves Jesus"] is not from God" (4:2–3). If the same set of dissenters is in view, this formulation suggests doubts about Jesus' complete humanity. The dissenters may have been willing to think of Jesus as the pre-existent Logos, even the Son of God who exists eternally with the Father, but not as someone who became fully human and accepted the limitations of existence "in the flesh."

Efforts have been made to link these dissenters with other known groups or figures in early Christianity. Among later Gnostic groups that typically drew a sharp distinction between flesh and spirit and between body and soul, the Docetists claimed that Jesus' humanity was an illusion; he was really a divine Christ figure who only "seemed" (Greek *dokeō*) to be human. Cerinthus, who flourished around 100 C.E., distinguished between the human figure Jesus and the divine power, "the Christ," which descended upon Jesus at his baptism but left before he was crucified. According to Irenaeus (ca. 130–200 C.E.), John's Gospel was written against Cerinthus. While it is difficult to connect either of these viewpoints with the dissenters of 1 John, they show how the seemingly simple confession "Jesus is the Christ" posed problems for some early Christians.

The confession raised a number of questions: In what sense can the human figure Jesus be called the Messiah? When did he become Messiah? Prior to his birth? At his birth? At his baptism? At his resurrection? How long did he remain Messiah? It is possible that some believed in Jesus' messiahship but denied his pre-existence as the divine *Logos*. They might have conceded that Jesus met the popular expectations of a messianic prophet—that he was a new Moses perhaps, or even a messianic king in David's succession—but could not bring themselves to believe that he had existed with the Father before creation, much less that he was a figure who enjoyed the unique status of God's Son and was to be equated with God. If, as we saw in the chapter on John's Gospel, each of these elements was central to Johannine Christology—Jesus as pre-existent *Logos*, present at creation; God's "only begotten Son," sent to the earth "in the flesh" as God's Messiah; the Son of Man who connected heaven and earth, whose mission as "Savior of the world" was to redeem humankind—we can understand what a tall order it was for some early Christians to subscribe to such a "high" Christology.

Basic differences about this core belief—Jesus' messiahship—created such a rupture within the Johannine church that a group broke away. First John gives us the perspective of those who stayed behind. Those who "went out from us," we are told, were never really a part of the group: "they did not belong to us" (2:19). Perhaps they had never subscribed fully to the Johannine "gospel." From 1 John's perspective, their refusal to confess Jesus as the Christ made them "liars" (2:22), and presumably their efforts to get other church members to see things their way made them "deceivers" (2:26). Whether 1 John includes them among the "many false prophets [who] have gone out into the world" (4:1) is uncertain, but seems probable, since "false prophet" is a standard label used in ancient religious controversies to characterize one's opponents.

[See Expanded CD Version pp. 756–57: *The Identity of Those Who Left*]

The Response of 1 John: Nurturing Community

First John responds to the crisis by standing squarely within the framework of the Johannine "gospel." Operating with the strongly dualistic thought-world reflected in John's Gospel, 1 John divides reality into two opposing spheres: light and darkness (1:5–10). God is wholly aligned with light; indeed, "God is light" (1:5), which allows light and darkness to serve as moral categories. There are thus two options for human behavior: "walking in the light" or "walking in darkness" (1:6–7; 2:9, 11). Since these are the realms of God and the devil respectively, people fall into one of two groups: children of God or children of the devil (3:10). Similarly, there are only two possibilities for human discourse: truth and falsehood (1:6; 2:4, 21; 4:6).

Other elements of the Johannine "gospel" are also prominent in 1 John:

- Jesus the Messiah who is Son of God (1:3, 7);
- referring to Jesus and God as "the Son" and "the Father" (2:23);
- eternal life (1:2; 2:25; 3:15; 5:11, 13, 20);
- disciples understood as "children of God" (3:1–2, 10; 4:4; 5:2, 19);
- the commandment to "love one another" (4:7–21);
- "abiding in" the Father/Son as a metaphor for discipleship (2:6, 24, 28; 3:6; 4:13, 16);
- the devil as "the evil one" (2:13–14; 3:12; 5:18, 19; see 3:8, 10);
- a strong stance against "the world" (2:15–17; 3:1; 4:3–5); and
- the disciples' possession of the Spirit (3:24; 4:13).

First John is not bound strictly to the categories and language of the Johannine "gospel." Whereas John's Gospel uses "Paraclete" exclusively of the Spirit (John 14:16, 26; 15:26; 16:7), 1 John speaks of Jesus as the Paraclete who advocates on behalf of sinners to the Father (2:1). In John's Gospel, Jesus is the light (John 1:4–9), but in 1 John God is light (1:5). For 1 John, "the beginning" is not the beginning of creation, but a later beginning, either the beginning of Jesus' life and ministry or the beginning of the Johannine community (1:1). Rather than minutely analyzing these differences to decide whether the same person wrote the Gospel and 1 John or to detect a shift in theological position from one document to the other, we are better off seeing the author of 1 John as someone operating with a Johannine construal of the world—the Johannine "gospel"—yet being free to extend it in new directions. What can hardly be denied is 1 John's staunch alliance with the Johannine "gospel." It speaks from and for that gospel.

The Voice of Tradition

Also worth noticing is the author's perspective reflected in 1 John. It may worry us that the author never names himself, but this silence may be significant. Rather than identifying himself with the Beloved Disciple of John's Gospel or with some named figure such as the apostle John, the son of Zebedee, the author of 1 John is content to let his words be the voice of the Johannine tradition. This becomes evident in several ways, perhaps most visibly in the way he alternates between the first person plural and the first person singular.

As 1 John unfolds, a single individual addresses the readers. There are numerous indications that 1 John is a written, not an oral, discourse (1:4; 2:1, 7, 8, 12–14, 21, 26; 5:13). Even though the author speaks as an "I," more frequently he speaks as "we," and there is strong reason to believe that this is more than an editorial "we." In speaking this way, he aligns himself with the larger Johannine community, both its earliest leader(s), who had direct links with Jesus himself, and those who came later. This suggests that we should understand the voice of 1 John as speaking authoritatively on behalf of the Johannine tradition.

Another indication of this is the way 1 John speaks of "what was from the beginning" (1:1). Twice 1 John speaks of "the beginning" as if it were the beginning of the world (2:13–14; 3:8). More often, though, 1 John speaks of a more recent beginning, probably the earliest period of the Johannine community's existence, which went all the way back to the period of Jesus' ministry (2:7, 24; 3:11). By appealing to this early formative period and to what "we heard, saw, and touched with our hands" (1:1), the author of 1 John is linking the Johannine church's existence directly to Jesus' ministry.

The author of 1 John can even claim that the message (*angelia*) he proclaims to his readers is a message "we have heard from him," presumably Jesus himself (1:5). The author may be presenting himself as an eyewitness who was a member of the original circle of Jesus' disciples. Because the Johannine church thought Jesus' voice transcended time and space, the author may not be referring to a time during Jesus' ministry when he gave this message to his circle of disciples, but to a much later time, well after Jesus' death, when the Spirit instructed the Johannine church (John 16:13; 1 John 2:27).

Still another indication of 1 John's distinctive perspective—and it represents a shift in perspective from John's Gospel—is its view of faith as assent rather than decision. If the primary focus of John's Gospel is "believing in"—the existential encounter between Jesus and the disciples—the primary focus of 1 John is "believing that"— assent to a confessional statement. Given the nature of the crisis within the Johannine church and the way the wording of the confession figured in the controversy, it is only natural for 1 John to be preoccupied with the content of faith—what is believed— rather than the object of faith—the one in whom they believe. [See Expanded CD Version p. 759: "Tradition" in the Johannine Church]

Being Obedient Children

Much is said in 1 John about beliefs and behaviors, but both are rooted in an underlying identity: being children of God. Although the metaphor of being "born again," which occurred in the Nicodemus story (John 3), does not appear in 1 John, the promise in the Gospel prologue that believers can become "children of God" through divine conception (John 1:12–13) provides one of 1 John's basic images for the believer's self-identity.

The metaphor is stretched to its limits with 1 John's claim that "God's seed abides in" believers (3:9–10). The force of the metaphor should be noted: Believers are not God's children by adoption (as in Paul; see Gal 4:5–7; Rom 8:15), but by divine insemination that comes as an expression of the Father's love (3:1). Through such a divine begetting, the ordinary parent-child relationship is displaced by something extraordinary: a relationship in which adults once again become children who owe their "life" to a divine parent, to whom they primarily respond through obedience.

Although 1 John's repeated insistence that believers should keep God's commandments is not specifically seen as a duty of obedient children, the metaphor of being "children of God" establishes the framework within which this expectation of discipleship is set (2:3–4; 3:22–24; 5:2–3). Especially to be noted are the expectations that accompany this fundamental identity: "doing right" (2:29; 3:10); not sinning (3:9; 5:18); and loving (4:7). The underlying psychological and ethical assumption here is that who we are is expressed in how we behave, or alternatively, how we behave reflects who we are. By their behavior, children of God reflect who God is: God is righteous, and God's children are righteous or do not sin (2:29); God is love, and God's children love each other (4:7); and so on. It is assumed throughout that believers' behavior is ultimately rooted in the character of God.

Clarifying Belief and Testing the Spirits

Since conflicting christological beliefs triggered the crisis within the church, 1 John reflects a concern for right belief. While there is not detailed discussion of what qualifies as right belief, we can safely assume that the issue was primarily christological and that one point of contention was the phrase "in the flesh" (4:2). If those who left the church had difficulty affirming Jesus' true humanity, we can understand better why 1 John makes this a test of genuine faith. Skepticism about Jesus' incarnation probably also explains why 1 John opens with an emphatic declaration that links the readers with Jesus' earthly ministry (1:1–3) and concludes with a strong, though enigmatic, affirmation of Jesus as one "who came by water and blood" (5:6–7). If this two-pronged phrase recalls Jesus' baptism and crucifixion, then 1 John is asserting the importance of Jesus' earthly ministry, which began with his baptism and ended with his crucifixion.

But is there more to it than simply affirming Jesus' full humanity? First John's heavy emphasis on Jesus as "the atoning sacrifice for our sins" (2:2; 4:10) suggests that the dissenters also questioned the salvific purpose of Jesus' death. While the author of 1 John does not develop the Fourth Gospel's image of Jesus as the "Lamb of God who takes away the sin of the world," he does recall the image of Jesus as "the Savior of the world" (4:14; cf. John 4:42).

By using the technical sacrificial term *hilasmos* (1 John 2:2; 4:10; cf. Lev 16:16, 30), which does not occur in the Fourth Gospel, 1 John actually pushes the sacrificial image in a new direction. Whether the term is best translated "propitiation," which would suggest that Christ's death somehow placated or appeased an offended God, or "expiation," which would suggest a death that somehow cleanses or removes defilement, is much debated. The latter is more probable, given 1 John's insistence that "the blood of Jesus his Son cleanses us from all sin" (1:7).

Even with its strong emphasis on Jesus' actual humanity and the salvific purpose of his life and death, 1 John is not content to push for right belief; it also pushes the Johannine church to be discerning, even skeptical, as it seeks to clarify what it believes

525

(4:2–6). Urging its readers to "test the spirits to see whether they are from God" (4:1), 1 John recognizes the broad marketplace that operates under the name of Christian faith. It also urges its readers not to be naïve as they shop in this marketplace. Genuine and counterfeit goods lie side by side, often bearing the same label. How, then, does the discerning believer tell the fake from the real thing, or, to use 1 John's words, "the spirit of truth" from "the spirit of error" (4:6; cf. 1QS 3:18–19)?

Since John's discussion is couched in terms of "spirits," "false prophets," and the "antichrist," the dissenters seem to have authorized their theological positions by making various appeals to the Spirit. They may have even claimed that God's Spirit was speaking through them. It is difficult, of course, either to confirm or disprove such appeals, and this may be one reason why 1 John says so little about the Spirit, especially given its prominence in the Fourth Gospel.

First John insists that the Spirit resides within the church that remained behind (1 John 3:24; 4:13; 5:6–7). Yet, interestingly enough, in offering advice that might help his readers tell the difference between true and false prophets, 1 John gives priority to what had defined the Johannine community: its confession "that Jesus Christ has come in the flesh" (4:2). This may seem like nothing more than an appeal to a creedal statement, and in one sense it is; yet it was the statement that captured the essence of the Johannine community's faith and accounted for its historical linkage to Jesus' ministry. The creed had become embodied in the community itself. In making this confession, the church expressed both what it believed and who it was.

The Apostle John sending a letter by a courier. A woodcut from a Low German version of Martin Luther's translation of the New Testament (Magdeburg, 1547). From the Digital Image Archive of The Richard C. Kessler Reformation Collection, Pitts Theology Library, Candler School of Theology, Emory University, Atlanta, Georgia.

Cultivating Moral Behavior

First John calls upon the Johannine church to recognize two commandments from God: "that we should believe in the name of his Son Jesus Christ and love one another" (3:23). It might appear that one commandment relates to belief, and the other to behavior. Yet by joining them, 1 John suggests that proper belief, or authentic faith, involves more than getting the words of the confession right. It also involves understanding the relationship between "the Father" and "the Son" as one of reciprocal love and seeing God's sending the Son as a concrete expression of love (4:10).

Proper belief also entails seeing Christ's "being sent" not as a compelled action motivated by some sense of blind obedience, but as a willing, indeed willful, self-giving, as an action of "lived love" (3:16). So understood, the confession, or what is believed, "gets lived" when it is expressed in patterns of behavior that reflect the same dynamic interplay of self-giving love and informed obedience.

Recognizing this close interplay between belief and behavior enables us to appreciate 1 John's overarching concern for ethics. Its treatment of sin is remarkable, considering the brevity of the writing. Its treatment of the love command goes well beyond the Fourth Gospel. No doubt 1 John's ethical concern is prompted by the crisis within the community. When conflict turns friends into enemies and fellow believers into antichrists, the rhetoric of hate all too easily replaces the rhetoric of love, thereby corrupting the attitudes, words, and actions of all parties. Although the author of 1 John does not always identify who is doing the hating, he perceives the need to encourage those who remain behind to "love each other."

Sin. Perhaps the crisis had brought out the worst in everyone or perhaps those who left thought of themselves as sinless, but for some reason the author of 1 John is prompted to name sin as an ongoing Christian problem, to provide an elementary vocabulary for thinking about sin, and to reassure his readers that their sins can be forgiven. First John's discussion of sin reveals an undeniable tension between the reality of sinfulness and the possibility of sinlessness. The author sees sin as a part of everyday Christian experience (1:6–10; 2:1–2; 5:16). He writes to help his readers avoid sin, yet he realistically recognizes that they will sin (2:1).

Not only does he allow for the possibility of sinning, but he also emphatically disallows claims to be sinless (1:8–10). To deny sin in our lives, he insists, makes us liars because it exposes our refusal to see ourselves as we really are; it also makes God a liar by implying that God wrongly diagnosed the human condition in sending Christ as Savior of the world. First John adopts a pragmatic view: Ideally, we will not sin; realistically, we will. Consequently, the readers are reassured that between sinners and God stands Jesus Christ the righteous Advocate, someone with impeccable character, who is "without sin" (3:5). Jesus' death is a *hilasmos*—not an event in which Christ appeased an angry, offended Deity, but one in which he appealed to a merciful God on behalf of all sinners, both church and world, and effected their purification.

Alongside this hard, practical side of 1 John, which sees Christians as fragile, sinful human beings, is the idealistic side that envisions sinlessness as a possibility for those "born of God" (3:9; 5:18). Such an audacious claim is conditional: "No one who abides in him sins" (3:6). In these passages, 1 John may be thinking of sin as a way of life—habitual sin—that vanishes (eventually) when people are "born of God." Thus, "those who have been born of God do not [continue to] sin . . . they cannot [continue to] sin, because they have been born of God" (3:9).

Even if 1 John is thinking of the cessation of habitual sin, we should not resolve the difficulties in the text too quickly. In one breath, the author denies the possibility of sinlessness, and in the next breath he leaves it open. Recognizing fully that "the whole world lies under the power of the evil one" (5:19), 1 John sees those who have been "born of God" as a unique company of people in whom "God's seed abides" (3:9). Somehow inoculated from evil in a way others are not, God's children are protected from "the evil one" by "the one who was born of God," probably Christ himself (5:18). Everyday Christian experience may contradict 1 John's assertions about the possibilities of "not sinning," but we should let his claim stand as a bold formulation of the ethical ideal that shapes the Johannine church's identity.

Even with this undeniable tension in 1 John between the reality of sin and the ideal of not sinning, there emerges a fairly well-developed "theology of sin." First John thinks of sin (*hamartia*) or sins (*hamartiai*) in general terms (1 John 1:9; 2:1, 12: 3:5, 8, 9; cf. the opposite notion of "doing what is right," 3:7, 10). Sin is not a personified force with a capital "S" as it is in Paul (e.g., Rom 7:7–25). As behavior that reflects an alliance with darkness, sin is ultimately traceable to the devil, the eternal sinner and father of all sinners (3:8), the one who now holds the world in his grip (5:19). As a frontal assault on sin, God sent "the Son" to break the devil's stranglehold on the world (3:8). **[See Expanded CD Version pp. 763–64: *The Practical Application of the "Theology of Sin" in 1 John*]**

Loving Each Other. It is one thing for Jesus to instruct his disciples to "love one another" (John 13:34–35; 15:12, 17). It is another thing to "live out" the love command, especially in a crisis that has split the church. First John illustrates how a single ethical imperative, mentioned only briefly in the Gospel but deeply rooted in the Johannine "gospel" (1 John 3:11), becomes amplified in response to a congregational crisis. Given the prominence of "love" in 1 John (the noun occurs eighteen times, the verb twenty-eight times), especially in 4:7–5:5 (also 2:7–11; 3:11–17), we understand why Augustine says of 1 John that "nothing in it is so commended as charity."[13]

The heart of 1 John's appeal is succinctly summarized in 4:7: "Beloved, let us love one another." What distinguishes the Johannine version of Jesus' love command is its accent on "one another." In sharp contrast to the Matthean saying, in which Jesus requires his disciples to "love your enemies and pray for those who persecute you" (Matt 5:43–48; see Luke 6:27–36), or to Paul's appeal to the Galatians to "work for the good of all, and especially for those of the family of faith" (Gal 6:10; cf. 5:14; Rom 13:9), the thrust of the Johannine love command is inward. The place where this command is carried out (or not) is the Johannine community. **[See Expanded CD Version pp. 765–66: *How Love Is Understood in 1 John*]**

The Responses of 2–3 John: Defining Boundaries of Fellowship

More closely resembling an actual letter, 2 John expands themes found in 1 John. Speaking as a mature voice, perhaps even as the representative of the Johannine church, "the elder" addresses "the elect lady and her children" (v. 1), conceivably a distinguished woman and her family who belong to a Johannine congregation in a nearby town, but probably a metaphor for the congregation itself. If so, the "children of your elect sister" (v. 13) who send greetings are the elder's own congregation.

The elder's call for his sister congregation to "love one another" echoes 1 John (2:7–11; 3:11; 4:7–21) and may be seen as a general exhortation rather than an indication of strife between the two congregations. The elder's mood is precautionary rather than polemical. Fearing that the dissidents who have left the Johannine community (1 John 2:18–19; 4:1) will extend their reach to other congregations in the region, the elder issues a pastoral warning. He characterizes the dissidents with the same epithets—"deceivers," "the deceiver and the antichrist" (v. 7; cf. 1 John 2:18, 26)—and attributes the same theological position to them: They deny that Jesus has come in the flesh (v. 7; cf. 1 John 4:2).

First John's emphasis on "right belief" gets sharpened in 2 John. "The teaching of Christ" (v. 9, *hē didachē tou Christou*) might even be rendered "the doctrine about Christ," the confessional belief that Jesus actually came "in the flesh." To abide in such teaching has a behavioral component; the readers are expected to "walk in" the commandment of love (v. 6). But 2 John's accent falls more heavily on belief rather than behavior. "The teaching" (v. 9) or "this teaching" (v. 10) has a much sharper creedal edge, and we detect a similar shift, however subtle, in how "the truth" (vv. 1, 4) is now being understood. "The truth" is now more "the true belief" about Jesus than belief in the figure Jesus (John 8:32; 14:6). To "walk in the truth" (vv. 4, 6), while not completely divorced from the "lived life" of love, now means to accept the Johannine church's construal of Jesus.

Apart from "loving one another," the primary behavior called for in 2 John is "negative hospitality": refusing to extend fellowship to those who hold unacceptable views about Jesus (vv. 10–11). Such exclusion is the natural extension of 1 John's advice to "test the spirits" (4:1–6). Once a "false prophet" is identified, the appropriate response is to withhold fellowship. Overt expressions of hospitality symbolize deeply held attitudes toward others; thus to welcome such people is to collude with them. Seen one way, such refusal is in tension with the love commandment, but excluding false teachers here becomes an expression of the love command. To "love one another" means not being naïve about the motives of those whose views threaten the solidarity of the church's fellowship and taking responsible action in defining the boundaries of fellowship.

Third John also looks like a genuine letter, even more so than 2 John. Also brief, it is addressed to a named individual, "Gaius" (v. 1), and its concluding greetings conform to the pattern of contemporary letters. It also deals with a specific issue: the arrogant behavior of Diotrephes, presumably a member of Gaius's congregation. The general outline of the letter also follows typical epistolary form.

One of the distinctive elements of 3 John is its references to "the church" (vv. 6, 9), the only such occurrences in all the Johannine writings. In 3 John we get a clearer picture of personalities in the church: Gaius, a prominent member commended for his hospitality and his loyalty to "the truth" (vv. 3–4, 8); Diotrephes, probably the host of this Johannine house church, clearly not in good graces with the elder, and overly protective of his house church (vv. 9–10); and Demetrius, perhaps the courier of the letter, whom the elder commends to Gaius (vv. 11–12).

In 3 John there is no indication that false teachers pose a threat to the church, nor is there any concern expressed about conflicting theological views and the need for right belief. In 2 John, the threat comes from outside; in 3 John it comes from within. Issues of authority are central; the elder's authority within the church, exercised from a distance, is sharply contested by Diotrephes, who establishes his turf by challenging the elder's leadership within the church and by serving as an overly eager gatekeeper for the church. Third John represents the opposite extreme of 2 John. In the latter instance, the church was failing to draw boundaries sharply enough; in the former, it is drawing them too sharply. Second John combats a tendency to be overly inclusive; 3 John resists being overly exclusive.

No specific guidelines are offered in 3 John for countering Diotrephes's actions. We are not told, for example, that right confession should be the basis for allowing people into the fellowship. This suggests that the situation envisioned in 3 John is distinct from that of 2 John. Third John reflects an intra-congregational conflict in which issues of authority are being worked out, in which an external authority figure is being challenged by an internal authority figure, and in which the social dynamics are those of an early Christian house church.

One plausible scenario concerning the composition of the letters of John is as follows: First John is written as a general letter intended to address Johannine congregations throughout the region. At an earlier stage, the Gospel of John had already been written and was read as the definitive Gospel among those churches. First John responds to a crisis created by conflicting interpretations of the Johannine "gospel." Third John is written next, perhaps but not necessarily by the same person who wrote 1 John, primarily to address an internal conflict within a Johannine congregation in the region. It is a genuine letter dealing with a specific authority issue. Its thrust is: "Don't be too exclusive." Second John is written last because the elder has learned that the dissidents now threaten another Johannine congregation, perhaps even Gaius's church. The thrust of 2 John is: "Don't be too inclusive." The church is now urged to follow the love command but also to be discerning as it deals with the threat of false teachers, and even to refuse fellowship as an expression of its conformity to the Johannine "gospel" and its commitment to "love one another."

Notes

1. Strong thematic connections include: unity of Father and Son (1 John 1:3; 2:22–24; 2 John 9; cf. John 5:20; 10:30, 38; 14:10); Jesus' coming in the flesh (1 John 4:2; 2 John 7; cf. John 1:14); a dualistic outlook (1 John 2:15–17; 4:3–6; 2 John 7; cf. John 14–17); divine begetting (1 John 2:29; 3:9; 4:17; cf. John 1:13; 3:3–8); knowing God (1 John 2:3–5, 13–14; 3:1, 6; 4:6–8; cf. John 1:10; 8:55; 14:7; 16:3); abiding in God, et al. (1 John 2:6, 24, 27; 4:12–15; 2 John 2, 9; cf. John 8:31; 14:17; 15:4–10); Jesus' water and blood (1 John 5:6–8; cf. John 19:34–35); the love command (1 John 2:7–10; 3:11; 2 John 4–6; cf. John 13:34–35); truth (1 John 2:21; 3:19; 2 John 1; 3 John 3, 8; cf. John 8:32; 18:37); being of God (1 John 3:10; 4:1–6; 3 John 11; cf. John 8:47); and keeping the commandments (1 John 2:3–4; 3:22, 24; 5:2–3; cf. John 14:15, 21, 23; 15:10). See Udo Schnelle, *The History and Theology of the NT Writings*

(Minneapolis: Fortress, 1998), 434–35.

2. Irenaeus (ca. 130–200 C.E.) also attributes the Fourth Gospel and 1–2 John to "John, the disciple of the Lord" (*Haer.* 3.16.5 & 8).

3. Quoted by Eusebius, *Hist. eccl.* 6.25.9–10. Origen makes extensive use of 1 John, but does not cite 2–3 John. Similarly, Clement of Alexandria cites 1 John, John's "longer epistle," but he does not cite 2–3 John. See *Strom.* 2.15.66.

4. *Hist. eccl.* 3.24.17–18; 25.2–3.

5. According to the Venerable Bede, "Many ecclesiastical authors, and among them St. Athanasius, bishop of the Church of Alexandria, witness that the First Epistle of John was written *ad Parthos.*" Some later manuscripts also include *pros parthous* as part of the superscription to 2 John. The idea that 1(2) John was addressed to the Parthians possibly arose from confusion about the wording in the superscription, which may have read *pros parthenous*, "To the Virgins," or perhaps even *tou parthenou*, "of the Virgin," i.e., "The Epistle of John the Virgin." John was referred to this way quite early, for example, in one superscription of the Apocalypse: "The Apocalypse of the holy, most glorious Apostle and Evangelist, 'the Virgin,' the Beloved, who lay in the bosom [of the Lord], John the Theologus." Thus, conceivably, "to the Parthians" arose from misreading the phrase "of the Virgin." (See *NPNF*[1] 7:459 n. 1).

6. *Hist. eccl.* 3.39.17.

7. Pol. *Phil.* 7.1, alluding to 1 John 4:2–3.

8. *Dial.* 123.9, referring to 1 John 3:1–2. Supposed references in earlier writings, including *Didache*, *1 Clement*, Ignatius, and Shepherd of Hermas, cannot be confirmed.

9. Pol. *Phil.* 10.3 alludes to 3 John 8.

10. Eusebius, *Hist. eccl.* 6.14.1.

11. Similarly, Irenaeus cites 1–2 John but not 3 John. Cf. *Haer.* 1.16.3; 3.16.5 & 8.

12. Athanasius, *Thirty-Ninth Festal Letter* (367 C.E.). They are also included as a group in the Mommsen Catalogue (ca. 359 C.E.), Codex Sinaiticus (mid-fourth century), the canonical list of Cyril of Jerusalem (ca. 315–387 C.E.), the Canon of the Council of Laodicea (ca. 363 C.E.), the Canon of the Council of Carthage (397 C.E.), and by Epiphanius (ca. 315–403 C.E.).

13. *Tract. ep. Jo.* 5.7 (*NPNF*[1] 7:490).

Bibliography

Commentaries

Black, C. Clifton. "The First, Second, and Third Letters of John: Introduction, Commentary, and Reflections." Pages 363–469 in vol. 12 of *The New Interpreter's Bible*. Edited by Leander E. Keck. 12 vols. Nashville: Abingdon, 1998.

Brooke, Alan E. *A Critical and Exegetical Commentary on the Johannine Epistles*. International Critical Commentary. Edinburgh: T&T Clark, 1921; New York: Scribner, 1964.

Brown, Raymond E. *The Epistles of John*. Anchor Bible 30. Garden City: Doubleday, 1982.

———. *The Gospel and Epistles of John: A Concise Commentary*. Collegeville: Liturgical, 1988.

Bultmann, Rudolf. *The Johannine Epistles: A Commentary on the Johannine Epistles*. Hermeneia. Translated by R. Philip O'Hara, Lane C. McGaughy, and Robert W. Funk. Philadelphia: Fortress, 1973.

Dodd, C. H. *The Johannine Epistles*. Moffatt New Testament Commentary. London: Hodder & Stoughton, 1966 (1946).

Kysar, Robert. *I, II, III John.* Augsburg Commentaries on the New Testament. Minneapolis: Augsburg, 1986.

Painter, John. *1, 2, 3 John.* Sacra Pagina. Collegeville: Liturgical, 2002.

Perkins, Pheme. *The Johannine Epistles.* New Testament Message 21. Wilmington: Glazier, 1984 (1979).

Rensberger, David K. *1 John, 2 John, 3 John.* Abingdon New Testament Commentaries. Nashville: Abingdon, 1997.

Schnackenburg, Rudolf. *The Johannine Epistles: Introduction and Commentary.* Translated by Reginald and Ilse Fuller. New York: Crossroad, 1992 (1975).

Smalley, Stephen S. *1, 2, 3 John.* Word Biblical Commentary 51. Waco: Word, 1984.

Smith, D. Moody. *First, Second, and Third John.* Interpretation: A Bible Commentary for Teaching and Preaching. Louisville: John Knox, 1991.

Strecker, Georg. *The Johannine Letters: A Commentary on 1, 2, and 3 John.* Hermeneia. Translated by Linda M. Maloney. Minneapolis: Fortress, 1996.

Other Resources

Brown, Raymond E. *The Community of the Beloved Disciple.* New York: Paulist, 1979.

Bultmann, Rudolf. "The Theology of the Gospel of John and the Johannine Epistles." Pages 3–92 in vol. 2 of *Theology of the New Testament.* Translated by K. Grobel. 2 vols. New York: Scribner, 1951–1955.

Cullmann, Oscar. *The Johannine Circle.* Translated by John Bowden. Philadelphia/London: Westminster/SCM, 1976.

Culpepper, R. Alan. *The Johannine School: An Evaluation of the Johannine-School Hypothesis Based on an Investigation of the Nature of Ancient Schools.* Society of Biblical Literature Dissertation Series 26. Missoula: Society of Biblical Literature (Scholars Press), 1975.

Edwards, Ruth B. *The Johannine Epistles.* New Testament Guides. Sheffield: Sheffield Academic Press, 1996.

Hengel, Martin. *The Johannine Question.* Translated by John Bowden. London/Philadelphia: SCM/Trinity, 1989.

Kysar, Robert. "John, Epistles of." Pages 900–12 in vol. 3 of *The Anchor Bible Dictionary.* Edited by David N. Freedman. 6 vols. Garden City: Doubleday, 1992.

Law, Robert. *The Tests of Life: A Study of the First Epistle of St. John: The Kerr Lectures for 1909.* 3d ed. Grand Rapids: Baker, 1968 (1909).

Lieu, Judith. *The Second and Third Epistles of John: History and Background.* Studies of the New Testament and Its World. Edinburgh: T&T Clark, 1986.

———. *The Theology of the Johannine Epistles.* New Testament Theology. Cambridge: Cambridge University Press, 1991; repr. 1997.

Segovia, Fernando F. *Love Relationships in the Johannine Tradition: Agape/Agapan in I John and the Fourth Gospel.* Society of Biblical Literature Dissertation Series 58. Chico: Society of Biblical Literature (Scholars Press), 1982.

Smith, D. Moody. *Johannine Christianity: Essays on Its Setting, Sources, and Theology.* Columbia: University of South Carolina Press, 1989 (1984).

von Wahlde, Urban C. *The Johannine Commandments: 1 John and the Struggle for the Johannine Tradition.* Theological Inquiries. New York: Paulist, 1990.

Part 6

JESUS IN THE APOCALYPTIC IMAGINATION

Chapter 27

Revelation

"Now in the Book called the Apocalypse, there are, to be sure, many obscure statements, designed to exercise the mind of the reader; and there are few statements there whose clarity enables us to track down the meaning of the rest, at the price of some effort."

St. Augustine

"We all thirst so after beauty, after openings into the vault of heaven, after sights and sounds capable of transcending the all-too-human sizes and shapes we assume, the well-defined and measured restrictions on what is possibly human."

Hildegard of Bingen

"I confess Apocalyptic Studies are fittest for those Raised Souls whose Heart Strings are made of a Little Nicer Clay than other mens."

Cotton Mather

"Where a book, through thousands of years, stirs up the heart and awakens the soul, and leaves neither friend nor foe indifferent, and scarcely has a lukewarm friend or enemy, in such a book there must be something substantial, whatever anyone may say."

Johann Gottfried Herder

"Reading the Book of Revelation has tended to be more of an obsession than a pastime."

Bernard McGinn

R evelation gets its name from its opening words, "the revelation of Jesus Christ" (*apokalypsis Iēsou Christou*), an expression occurring elsewhere in the NT (Gal 1:12; cf. 2 Thess 1:7; 1 Pet 1:7, 13), but not to describe the contents of a literary work. The expression carries a double sense: The writing is both a revelation about Jesus Christ—the central figure in the book—and a revelation that Jesus Christ received from God and transmitted through an interpreting angel to "his servant John" (1:1). The superscription later added to the work became "The Revelation of John," referring to the revelation that John received from God through Christ.[1]

As a literary work belonging to the genre "apocalypse," Revelation is unique among NT writings. Its sole counterpart in the OT is Daniel, especially chapters 7–12, written during the mid-second century B.C.E. in the context of the Maccabean revolt. It also resonates with other OT writings from as early as the sixth century B.C.E.: Isa 24–27 (the Isaiah Apocalypse), Isa 56–66, Ezekiel, Joel 2:28–3:21, and Zech 9–14 (esp. ch. 14).

Revelation also shares much in common with the non-biblical Jewish apocalypses that began to be written in Palestine as early as the third century B.C.E. Most notable among these is *1 Enoch*, a collection of five separate works associated with the antediluvian figure Enoch, written and compiled between the third century B.C.E. and the first century C.E. With the exception of the *Similitudes of Enoch* (chs. 37–71), which may have been written early in the first century C.E., portions of all sections of *1 Enoch* were found among the writings of Qumran. This suggests that apocalyptic literature figured prominently within this separatist Jewish group in Palestine prior to the Christian period.

Another pre-Christian apocalyptic text is *Testament of Levi 2–5*, probably written in the second century B.C.E. While *1 Enoch* is the only comprehensive non-biblical Jewish apocalypse written earlier than Revelation, others were produced at roughly the same period, toward the end of the first century C.E. These include *4 Ezra* (= 2 Esd 3–14), *2 Enoch*, the *Apocalypse of Abraham*, *2 Baruch*, *3 Baruch*, and the partially preserved *Apocalypse of Zephaniah*. Other writings, which are not technically apocalypses but reflect strong apocalyptic elements, include *Jubilees*, the *Testament of Abraham*, and the *Sibylline Oracles*.

While Revelation has long been recognized as an apocalyptic writing whose language and outlook resonate with these other biblical and non-biblical apocalyptic writings, which were produced between 200 B.C.E. and 200 C.E., scholars in the nineteenth and twentieth centuries focused especially on its apocalyptic features. As the vast body of Jewish and Christian apocalypses became available in critical editions and translations, scholars were able to gain a better understanding of how apocalyptic literature worked, what symbols and images it tended to use, how it related to biblical prophetic books, and what circumstances produced such writings. Understanding the "rules" of apocalyptic writing and how apocalyptic thinkers construed their world enabled scholars to interpret Revelation within the broader context of the ancient world. [See **Expanded CD Version pp. 776–77:** *The Literary Structure of Apocalyptic Writings*]

The Apocalyptic Worldview

Using these basic narrative frameworks and a combination of literary devices to structure discourses and visions, writers of apocalypses produced a fascinating variety of works. Regardless of their many differences in literary structure and overall emphasis, these writings reveal a distinctive worldview, which is characterized by several recurrent themes:

1. *God's Sovereignty over History and the Cosmos*. God is consistently portrayed as the One who controls history or the One who holds the key to the mysteries of the universe. In the first instance, God stands at both the beginning and the end of history, which is understood as a story that moves through time from creation to judgment. In the latter instance, God sits enthroned, presiding over a cosmic hierarchy. Proximity to God is understood in spatial rather than temporal terms.

2. *Access to Divine Revelation through Intermediary Heavenly Beings*. Access to God may be mediated through heavenly figures, usually angels, or obstructed by malevolent beings, either the chief obstructer himself, Satan, or his demonic minions. Either way, the human being down below does not have direct access to God. True knowledge about God must be provided by heavenly intermediaries.

3. *Ultimate Vindication*. The apocalyptic mind firmly believes that the cause of God will eventually triumph. This often takes the form of a divinely overseen, universal judgment that will happen at the end of time. If an apocalypse focuses on the end of time and accompanying events, it is eschatological in orientation. But not every apocalypse is preoccupied with eschatology. This is a distinction worth noting, since the terms "apocalyptic" and "eschatological" are sometimes used interchangeably as though they are synonymous. Such imprecision only confuses an already complex topic.

4. *Symbolic Language*. Apocalyptic writers also assume that these heavenly mysteries—who God is, what God has done in the past, how God relates to the present, and what God intends to do in the future—can be expressed only through graphic images that convey symbolic meaning. Ordinary language and genres are inadequate for capturing the sense of ineffable mystery that relates to God's will.

5. *Enduring Optimism as the Basis for Exhortation*. The apocalyptic view of the world is ultimately hopeful. Apocalypses that forecast the future, either short-term or long-term, often sketch a progressive worsening of conditions that produces a mood of hopelessness. They may view history as a downward spiral of events, but they typically envision a moment of divine intervention that ensures the continuation of God's purpose for humanity. In spite of their dire predictions and seemingly unremitting pessimism, apocalypses offer encouragement that yields a theology of hope.

Revelation Compared with Other Apocalypses

The close family resemblance between Jewish apocalyptic writings and Revelation is undeniable. But it is a mistake to think of the Jewish apocalyptic tradition as a firmly fixed tradition, the Jewish apocalypse as an equally fixed literary genre, and both as some fixed standard by which Revelation must be evaluated. Apocalyptic writings can reflect different historical and social situations. Depending on the circumstances and the name around which the apocalyptic writings develop, each writing or group of writings can exhibit distinctive features.

This accounts for some of the apparent anomalies we find in Revelation. The entire apocalypse is cast in the form of a letter with a formal greeting (1:4–5) and benediction

(22:21) similar to what we find in other NT letters. Since Revelation was addressed to several Christian communities in Asia Minor, adapting the Christian letter to address this situation was an entirely plausible move. Another anomaly: While most Jewish apocalyptic writings employ pseudonyms that lend greater authority to the work, Revelation does not. The Christian movement was too young to have acquired a gallery of venerable figures comparable to Enoch, Abraham, or Ezra. Had its author wanted to employ a pseudonym, John the apostle would have been an obvious choice, since his name would have linked the work to Jesus' closest followers. Neither the epistolary form of Revelation nor the absence of a pseudonymous author makes it any less apocalyptic. Both elements reflect the peculiarity of the Christian situation out of which it arose.

But Revelation does contain many elements that typify apocalyptic writings. John experiences both visions and auditions, as seen by the repeated use of the phrases, "And I saw. . .," and "And I heard. . . ." Unlike Daniel, John's revelatory experiences do not occur during a dream but rather "in the spirit," which suggests some form of ecstasy. Revelation is not easily classified as a "historical review" or an "otherworldly journey," although it reflects aspects of both. Rather than reviewing the periods of history that preceded the coming of Christ, Revelation displays greatest interest in the events after Christ's death and resurrection. Even then, its primary focus is on the end of history and how cycles of crisis, judgment, and vindication will lead to the end. The closest Revelation comes to a historical review is the beast with the "seven heads and ten horns" (17:6–14; cf. 13:1–4). A thinly veiled interpretation equates the "seven heads" with the "seven mountains on which the woman is seated," which readers would recognize as the seven hills of Rome. The seven kings would be easily recognized as seven Roman emperors, even if interpreters found it challenging to decide which five kings had already passed and who the sixth, seventh, and eighth kings actually were. Although this imperial calculus is vague, it is intended to help the readers identify where they are in God's timeline.

John's mode of receiving his divine revelation does not readily conform to the otherworldly journeys that we find in many of the Jewish apocalypses. He does not ascend through a series of numbered heavens, as is the case in *2 Enoch*. Instead, John is taken up "in the spirit" into heaven (4:2), where he is shown God's throne and where he reports seeing and hearing many marvelous things. Rather than descending to earthly reality again, John remains in this elevated visionary state throughout the work. At the conclusion of the book, he bows before his interpreting angel in gratitude, only to be chastised for daring to worship someone besides God (22:8–9).

One of the most significant points of resemblance between Revelation and other Jewish apocalypses is the extent to which it shares the apocalyptic worldview described earlier. God straddles history as the "Alpha and Omega" (1:8; 21:6). The line of God's divine purpose running through history from creation until judgment is unbroken, even if it is seriously threatened and disturbed by the archenemy Satan. Assured that the "mystery of God will be fulfilled" (10:7), readers are reminded that God's overall purpose stretches from the beginning until the end of time and encompasses God's people.

Conforming to many Jewish apocalypses that anticipate a period of turmoil and stress, Revelation envisions an "hour of trial" (3:10) that will be a "great ordeal" (7:14). The cast of the eye is forward and the anticipated time is short (1:1, 3; 3:11; 22:10, 20). Belief in God's firm purpose is so strong that final vindication has already been assured in heaven. This is seen most vividly when the blast of the seventh trumpet introduces the heavenly chorus proclaiming the victory of God and the Messiah, along with the twenty-four elders singing of God's power and victory over those who oppose God's elect, the prophets, the saints, and all the faithful (11:15–19). Also reflecting a true apocalyptic perspective are the many assurances that God's ways are "just and true" (15:3; 16:7; 19:2) and that God will take vengeance on those who afflict the saints (16:5–6).

Revelation stands squarely within the Jewish apocalyptic tradition, which looks to the end of history for the final vindication of God's cause. Because of its focus on the "last things," Revelation is thoroughly eschatological. It reports the events that will constitute a crisis for the believing community: the deteriorating conditions accompanied by disasters both natural and unnatural; the continuing struggle between the forces of good and evil; and the final set of events that brings closure to the crisis. John sketches a distinctive scenario for the future: a final battle led by Christ and his forces against the "beast and the kings of the earth" (19:19); the defeat of Satan and his imprisonment for a thousand years while the martyred saints reign with the Messiah; the release of Satan, who joins with Gog and Magog against the saints; and Satan's final and decisive defeat. Then follow universal judgment, a reconstituted heaven and earth, and finally paradise restored—an eternal city, the new Jerusalem.

Some of these features are found in other Jewish apocalypses, some of which foresee periods of varying length when God's Messiah will reign on earth. In *4 Ezra* 7:26–33, for example, a 400-year reign of the Messiah is envisioned (cf. *2 Bar.* 29–30). Such writings can also envision some form of universal judgment in which God's cause is finally vindicated. In these writings, resurrection may be viewed as one of the events of the end time, but Revelation's two resurrections (cf. 20:5, 12) are distinctive, even when compared with other NT sketches of the end time.

The symbolism of Revelation, which draws heavily from the OT as well as other sources, is also thoroughly apocalyptic. One only has to read the Animal Apocalypse of *1 Enoch* to appreciate the creativity of the apocalyptic mind in using images from everyday life in highly unusual ways. We find similar ingenuity in Revelation, not only in its portrayal of evil through the use of horrific symbolism but also in its sketch of the new heaven and the new earth and the paradisal reality of the new Jerusalem. The rich set of images already found in OT prophetic writings and in other biblical and non-biblical apocalyptic writings enriches John's mind, but he is not bound to them. As an inspired artist, he uses them freely to produce an astonishingly original work.

When compared with other apocalyptic writings from the ancient world, Revelation displays many similarities in both literary form and content. Even so, it stands out within this body of literature as an unexcelled exemplar of both the apocalyptic genre and the apocalyptic outlook.

A copper engraving by Caspar Luiken (1672–1708), depicting the New Jerusalem (Rev 21). In the foreground are the angel bearing a "measuring rod of gold" (Rev 21:15) and John. The rays of light symbolize the absence of sun and moon, since "the glory of God is its light" (Rev 21:23). In the lower right is an eagle (representing John) with a book and a writing feather. From a work published in 1712 in Nuremberg, Germany, containing illustrations of biblical scenes with didactic poems in Latin and German. From the Digital Image Archive of The Richard C. Kessler Reformation Collection, Pitts Theology Library, Candler School of Theology, Emory University, Atlanta, Georgia.

540

Interpretive Yield

By reading Revelation as an apocalyptic writing within a much broader tradition, interpreters learn how apocalyptic works. We become attentive not only to what the text says but to what it does. Since symbolic language is such a central feature of apocalyptic texts, interpreters must allow the language to do its work rather than try to find some allegorical referent for every single symbol. As the Seer advises, the reader must develop an ear to "listen to what the Spirit is saying to the churches" (3:22).

Familiarity with apocalyptic literature requires us to recognize what a critical role the senses play in interpreting the text. When early interpreters criticized Revelation for its sensuousness, they were calling attention to how its images and symbols activate the full range of our senses. It challenges our imaginations visually, especially through its use of color. A veritable rainbow unfolds in Revelation—white, green, red, purple, scarlet, black, emerald, and gold—and does so with kaleidoscopic effect. Our auditory senses are also activated. Our ears have to be open to the "sounds of many waters," to thunder and lightning, and to silence. To appreciate the effect of the opening of the seventh seal, we should imagine a packed stadium crowd in total silence for half an hour (8:1)! Attuning our senses to the language and the imagery of Revelation is perhaps more crucial than using a dictionary to look up every unfamiliar term.

The Occasion and Setting of Revelation

The rhetoric of Revelation suggests that it was written in response to a crisis. Whether the crisis derives primarily from the author's perception or whether it reflects the readers' lived experience is a matter of scholarly debate.

That Revelation originated in Asia Minor seems certain. The seven churches addressed in the opening vision identify the sphere of John's influence, and the letters are detailed enough to suggest that John knew these churches. Urban life in Asia Minor establishes the social matrix within which Revelation should be understood.

Since the time of Irenaeus (ca. 130–200 C.E.), Revelation has been dated toward the end of the reign of Domitian (81–96 C.E.).[2] Some have dated it earlier, during the reign of Claudius (41–54 C.E.)[3] and Nero (54–68 C.E.).[4] By the time Revelation was written, the church at Smyrna appears to have been a settled Christian community (Rev 2:8–11). Yet Polycarp (ca. 69–155 C.E.), bishop of Smyrna, reports that no church existed in Smyrna when Paul wrote his letter to the Philippians (mid- to late 50s).[5] This would suggest that Revelation was composed later than Nero's reign. If the ambiguous reference in Rev 11:1–2 implies that the Jerusalem temple was still standing at the time John wrote the letter, this would point to a pre-70 date. Some scholars have suggested that John's use of "Babylon" to refer to Rome reflects a post-70 practice (see 14:8; 16:19; 17:5; 18:2, 10, 21). The "king list" in Rev 17:7–14, while probably referring to a succession of Roman rulers, is too ambiguous to decide the question, although there is good reason to believe that the "eighth king" (17:11) refers to Nero. This possibility is rendered more plausible by the Nero *redivivus* myth, which envisioned his return to life after his assassination in 68 C.E. (cf. 13:3).

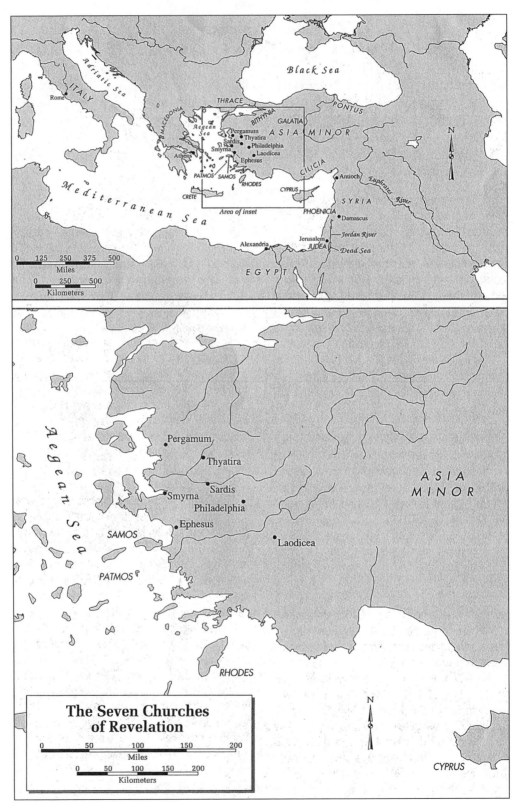

The Seven Churches
of Revelation

These considerations suggest that Revelation was probably composed during the reign of Domitian in the mid-90s. This does not mean that it was written because Christians were being persecuted for refusing to submit to the imperial cult and to confess Domitian as "our Lord and God" (*dominus et deus noster*).[6] When Irenaeus dates Revelation to the time of Domitian, he does not report persecution of Christians by Domitian. Connecting the composition of Revelation with Christian persecution under Domitian occurs for the first time in Eusebius of Caesarea (ca. 260–340 C.E.), although Clement of Alexandria (ca. 150–215 C.E.) reports a tradition of John's departure from Patmos after "the tyrant," presumably Domitian, died.[7] Tertullian (ca. 160–225 C.E.) writes that Domitian was "a man of Nero's type of cruelty."[8] From Pliny's *Letter to Trajan* (ca. 112 C.E.), we know that Christians in the regions of Bithynia and Pontus had experienced pressure from the Roman government,[9] but there is no evidence of systematic persecution of Christians in Asia Minor under Domitian. [See **Expanded CD Version pp. 784–85:** *The Imperial Cult and Roman Treatment of Christians*]

But whatever prompted John to compose Revelation, it need not have been a single event. His perception of affairs may have developed over years, or even decades, since Revelation was not written overnight. It is more probable to imagine that the work grew out of an extended process of reflection, which included years of scriptural meditation, study, and prophetic experiences. As someone engaged in prophetic activity (1:3; 10:11; 22:7, 10, 18, 19), John may have been part of a wider circle of prophets in Asia Minor (22:6). If so, he stood in the tradition of OT prophets who responded to political and social crises by both speaking to them and about them.

A Unified Vision

One of the challenges facing every reader of Revelation is finding a way to grasp the entire work. This is difficult because of the length and complexity of the book. As is evident from the numerous interpretations of Christ's 1000-year reign based on Rev 20:1–6, rather than seeing the work as a whole, readers tend to seize on one passage, one image, or one theme and then use it to interpret the rest of the book. Readers often experience difficulty finding an organizing principle or a coherent logic that runs consistently throughout the book. Like other apocalyptic writings, Revelation may have gone through stages of compilation and editorial redaction that resulted in the interruptions or digressions found throughout the work.

Regardless of Revelation's seemingly chaotic literary structure, the writing reflects the mind of an inspired artist rather than a confused fanatic.

One indication of this is the use of numbers as an organizing principle. John is especially fond of groups of seven, either as a numbered set, for example, the seven seals, trumpets, and bowls of wrath, or as an unnumbered series, for example, seven churches (chs. 2-3) and seven blessings (1:3; 14:13; 16:15; 19:9; 20:6; 22:7, 14). Other numbers also serve as structuring devices, for example, four—four living creatures and four horsemen; twelve and its multiples—the twelve tribes and 144,000; and three—the three woes.

A close analysis of the literary arrangement also reveals that the individual parts of the work have been carefully pieced together. The words of Christ introducing each of the seven letters (2:1–3:22) draw on motifs introduced in the opening vision (1:9–20), thus making a theological point: The risen Christ is more than a radiant vision; each church directly experiences some aspect of his heavenly persona.

- Ephesus: seven stars in his right hand (2:1; cf. 1:16, 20); walking among the lampstands (2:1; cf. 1:13);
- Smyrna: first and last (2:8; cf. 1:17); dead and came to life (2:8; cf. 1:18);
- Pergamum: sharp two-edged sword (2:12; cf. 1:16);
- Thyatira: eyes like a flame of fire (2:18; cf. 1:14); feet like burnished bronze (2:18; cf. 1:15);
- Sardis: seven stars (3:1; cf. 1:16, 20);
- Philadelphia: key of David, opening and shutting (3:7; cf. 1:18); and
- Laodicea: Amen, origin of God's creation (3:14; cf. 1:17).

The messages to the seven churches are also linked literarily with the rest of the book, which means that the first section (chs. 1–3) should not be read as a self-contained section, detached from the remaining chapters.

Another unifying literary device is also used elsewhere in the book: Motifs are introduced at one point and then developed later. The bowls of incense representing the prayers of the saints, for instance, are introduced in 5:8 and then become part of the preparatory vision in 8:3–5. The angel announces the fall of Babylon in 14:8, anticipating the fuller account in chapter 18.

Interpreters sometimes fail to notice one of the most conspicuous signs of literary unity: Revelation reports a *single*, continuous vision. Everything from the opening vision of Christ (1:9–20) until the concluding vision of the new Jerusalem (21:9–22:7) is presented as a vision John experienced on the isle of Patmos on the Lord's day. This is reinforced by recurrent interchanges between John and his guiding angel (17:7–18; 19:9–10; 21:9; 22:6–9).

John's unified vision is also reflected in the way he links a new section to the previous one. The heavenly throne vision of chapter 4 is introduced, "After this [the opening vision and the messages to the seven churches] I looked." Continuity is underscored even further by John's mention of the "first voice, which I had heard speaking to me like a trumpet" (4:1), in other words, in the opening vision (1:10). Toward the end of the book, after the vision of the seven angels and the seven bowls of wrath (15:1–16:21), the vision of the great whore and the beast in chapter 17 is introduced by "one of the seven angels who had the seven bowls" (17:1). Similar linkage is seen when the final vision of the new Jerusalem is also introduced by one of the "seven-bowl" angels (21:9). In this way, John links the final major section of the book (chs. 17–22) with the previous section.

One of the most complex parts of the Revelation is the large middle section comprising chapters 6–16 (see diagram). In spite of the complexity of this section, we see an overarching pattern of organization. One of its most dominating features is the three sets of seven: the seven seals, the seven trumpets, and the seven bowls of wrath. In the diagram, these are listed in separate columns to highlight their unified structure.

Some scholars also see the set of "miscellaneous visions" as a group of seven visions, but John is perfectly capable of numbering his visions when he wants to. For this reason, we should leave unnumbered what he does not number. The most striking pattern within these sets of visions is his literary technique, variously called interweaving, overlapping, or interlocking. Put simply, one set of visions is interwoven with another set. The seventh seal (8:1–2) introduces the seven trumpets (8:2–11:19), and the seven angels of the seven bowls of wrath introduce visions in chapters 17–22.

Even more noticeable in this section are the two sets of interludes or "digressions": the vision of the 144,000 (7:1–17), which occurs between the sixth (6:12–17) and seventh (8:1–2) seals, and the two visions of the angel and the little scroll and the two witnesses (10:1–11:14), which occur between the sixth (9:13–21) and seventh (11:15–19) trumpets. As one reads the visions, their purpose becomes clear: they are introduced to heighten the drama. By the end of the sixth seal, the reader has experienced a gradually intensifying set of catastrophes. Wondering what will come next, the reader is required to take a momentary breather, one that introduces a note of comfort, before proceeding to the final seal. Even then, John keeps the reader at bay, observing a period of "silence in heaven for about half an hour" (8:1), during which the angel offers incense and the prayers of the saints on the altar before the throne (8:2–5). Only then do the seven angels begin to blow their trumpets. The dramatic effect of this literary structure is powerful, especially when we remember that Revelation was written to be *heard* (1:3).

The second interlude also creates dramatic effect through another literary technique: the three woes. The first four trumpets are uniformly brief, but the next three are more detailed as they depict worsening woes. To highlight this, John pauses at 8:13 to announce the three coming woes, and after each of the next trumpets, the woes are numbered (9:12; 11:14). In this way, the interlude of 10:1–11:14 is incorporated more smoothly into the seven trumpets.

The miscellaneous visions in chapters 12–14 create the same effect, for they provide a similar "interlude" between the first two series of sevens and the final set of seven, the seven bowls of wrath. Here again we detect a similar pattern: The visions of chapters 12–13, which reek with war and violence, are counterbalanced by three visions of hope in chapter 14.

Also worth noting is how the visions of this large middle section are tied to the earlier heavenly vision of chapter 4, which was accompanied by "flashes of lightning, and rumblings and peals of thunder" (4:5). Echoing what was heard at Sinai (Exod 19:16–19), these sounds are heard again at the beginning and the conclusion of the seven trumpets (8:5; 11:19) and at the conclusion of the seven bowls of wrath (16:18–21).

One of the most vivid examples of John's careful structuring occurs at the end, where the fall of Babylon (17:1–19:10) and the vision of the new Jerusalem (21:9–22:7) are presented as parallel occurrences. Clear literary markers at the beginning and the end of each section (cf. 17:1–3 and 21:9–10; 19:9–10 and 22:8–9) establish the parallel structure of the sections. Especially noteworthy is how the structural parallelism reinforces the theological message. In each section two cities are portrayed as women—the whore of Babylon represents the fall of Rome, and the bride of the

Prologue & Opening Vision of Christ (1:1-3:22)	Opening Heavenly Vision (4:1-5:14)	The Lamb Opens the Seven Seals (6:1-8:5)	The Seven Trumpets (8:2-11:19)
Prologue (1:1-8)	God enthroned in heaven (4:1-11)	Opening the Seven Seals (6:1-8:5)	Angel's preparatory offering: altar of incense (8:3-5)
Opening vision of Christ (1:9-20)	- God's throne surrounded by 24 thrones with 24 elders - seven spirits of God - four living creatures: lion, ox, human, eagle sing Trisagion	Seal # 1: White horse: rider, bow, crown, conquering (6:1-2) Seal # 2: Red horse: rider warrior with sword (6:3-4)	Preparation (8:6) Trumpet # 1: Hail, fire, blood: earth scorched (8:7) Trumpet # 2: Burning mountain thrown into the sea, devastates sea (8:8-9)
- John's vision (1:9-11) - Son of Man among the churches (1:12-16) - Christ's charge to John (1:17-20) Christ speaks to the seven churches (2:1-3:22)	Scroll with seven seals Challenge: Who can open? (5:1-5) Enter: The slain Lamb of God (5:6-14)	Seal # 3: Black horse: rider with pair of scales, famine (6:5-6) Seal # 4: Pale green horse: rider: Death, followed by Hades: given power to devastate ¼ of earth (6:7-8)	Trumpet # 3: Star fallen from heaven: wormwood, makes rivers, springs bitter (8:10-11) Trumpet # 4: 1/3 Sun, moon, stars darkened: (8:12) Note: Three woes to come (8:13)
1. Ephesus (2:1-7) 2. Smyrna (2:8-11) 3. Pergamum (2:12-17) 4. Thyatira (2:18-29)	- 7 horns, 7 eyes - 4 living creatures & 24 elders praise the Lamb - heavenly chorus praises the Lamb - heavenly host bow in worship before God & Lamb	Seal # 5: Martyrs under altar: "How long?" (6:9-11) Seal # 6: Earthquake, cosmic catastrophes engulf earth (6:12-17)	Trumpet # 5: Star fallen from heaven; key to bottomless pit (9:1-12) First Woe: smoke, locusts, torture of non-elect Trumpet # 6: Angels from Euphrates released (9:13-21)
5. Sardis (3:1-6) 6. Philadelphia (3:7-13) 7. Laodicea (3:14-22)		*Interlude*: 144,000 (7:1-17) - 4 angels + 1 angel (7:1-3) - 12 tribes x 12,000 sealed (7:4-8) - vision of universal crowd before throne (7:9-17) Seal # 7: Silence in heaven: seven angels, seven trumpets (8:1-2)	Second Woe: 200,000,000 cavalry slaughter 1/3 humankind; others worship idols *Interlude*: Two visions Vision # 1: Angel & the little scroll; seer eats little scroll (10:1-11) Vision # 2: The two witnesses testify, die & rise (11:1-14) Trumpet # 7: Worship of enthroned God in heaven (11:15-19) Third Woe: Divine judgment vs. nations

Miscellaneous Visions (12:1-14:20)	Seven Angels, Seven Plagues, Seven Bowls of Wrath (15:1-16:21)	The Fall of Babylon (17:1-19:10)	Final Visions and Epilogue (19:11-22:21)
Woman, child, dragon (12:1-17) - Pregnant woman bears son, snatched by dragon (12:1-6) - Outbreak of war in heaven: Michael & angels vs. dragon, who is expelled from heaven (12:7-9) - Victory over dragon announced in heaven (12:10-12) - Dragon wars with woman on earth (12:13-17) Dragon by seashore (12:18): Two beasts who serve the dragon: Beast from the sea (13:1-10) - Beast with 10 horns, 7 heads given power by dragon (13:1-4) - Beast wars vs. saints (13:5-10) Beast from the earth (13:11-18) - Ravages earth on behalf of first beast - Magic number: 666 Three visions of hope: 1. Lamb atop Mt. Zion w/ the 144,000, faithful & redeemed (14:1-5) 2. Three angels announce coming judgment, fall of Babylon, wrath vs worshippers of beast (14:6-13) 3. Final judgment: Son of Man enthroned, angels reap vengeance over earth (14:14-20)	Seven angels with seven plagues (15:1) Opening vision: faithful triumphant, worshipping (15:2-4) Angels given seven bowls of wrath (15:5-8) Pouring out seven bowls of wrath (16:1-21) **Bowl # 1**: Upon earth: sores upon those with mark of beast (16:2) **Bowl # 2**: Into sea: becomes blood, creatures died (16:3) **Bowl # 3**: Into rivers, springs: become blood (16:4-7) **Bowl # 4**: On sun: scorching heat (16:8-9) **Bowl # 5**: On throne of beast: darkness, pain, cursing (16:10-11) **Bowl # 6**: On Euphrates: dried up, prepare kings from east; 3 foul spirits prepare kings for final battle at Armageddon [Possible Interlude?] (16:12-16) **Bowl # 7**: Into air: voice from throne: "it is done" – cosmic signs, destruction of Babylon (16:17-21)	Vision of the great whore (17:1-6) - wilderness, woman on beast with 7 heads, 10 horns - woman dressed like a whore, name on her head: Babylon the great, woman drunk with saints' blood Mystery of beast explained (17:7-18) - 7 heads = 7 hills (of Rome): 5 down, 1 living, 1 to go; maybe an 8th (17:9-11) - 10 horns = 10 kings, alliance with the beast vs. Lamb, Lamb wins (17:12-14) - Beast and 10 horns (kings) destroy the whore (17:15-18) Dirge over fallen Babylon (18:1-24) - Angel's dirge (18:1-3) - People called to flee (18:4-8) - Three dirges: kings, merchants, shippers (18:9-19) - Saints, apostles, prophets' joy (18:20) - Angel's gesture: stone (Babylon) thrown into sea (18:21-24) Heavenly rejoicing over Babylon's fall (19:1-8) - Heavenly chorus (19:1-3) - 24 elders, 4 creatures, throne voice (19:4-5) -Multitude's hallelujah (19:6-8) Angel's interchange with seer (19:9-10)	Vision of Christ with heavenly armies: Christus victor (19:11-21) - Open heaven, white horse ridden by Faithful & True, Word of God (19:11-16) - Slaughter of God's adversaries (19:17-21) Binding of Satan in bottomless pit, 1000 years (20:1-3) The millennial kingdom; first resurrection: martyred saints (20:4-6) Satan's final defeat (20:7-10) Final judgment; Second resurrection, universal judgment (20:11-15) New heaven & new earth (21:1-8) - Jerusalem descending (21:1-4) God enthroned, sinners excluded (21:5-8) New Jerusalem (21:9-22:5) - Heavenly Jerusalem described (21:9-27) - River & tree of life (22:1-5) <hr> Epilogue (22:6-21) Sayings (22:6-20) - Vision validated, concluding words of Jesus, warnings, blessings and curses Benediction (22:21)

Lamb represents the new Jerusalem. They are also depicted as polar opposites: The whore dressed in scarlet and laden with jewelry is set over against the bride dressed in fine linen to symbolize her virginity. Once Babylon/Rome is destroyed, she is replaced by the new Jerusalem. The intervening material (19:11–21:8) shows how this transition occurs: The victorious Christ appears to do battle with Satan; Satan is finally defeated; next comes universal judgment; then appear the new heaven and the new earth, and finally the new Jerusalem. Thus unfolds John's version of the "tale of two cities."

Reading Strategy: Linear or Cyclical Reading?

One interpretive decision the reader must make is whether to read the three sets of visions—the opening of the seals, the seven trumpets, and the seven bowls of wrath—in a linear or a cyclical fashion. Do they unfold a series of events that rehearse in successive, chronological stages what will occur in the future? Or do they essentially rehearse—recapitulate—the same cycle of events several times from slightly different perspectives? The latter way of reading Revelation, usually referred to as a "recapitulation" reading, emerged quite early and was reflected most clearly in the commentary by Victorinus of Pettau (died ca. 304 C.E.). It was also used by Tyconius (died ca. 400 C.E.) and Augustine (354–430 C.E.).

If read in a linear fashion, the seven seals unfold one chronological period of history, the seven trumpets another chronological period that follows immediately, and the seven bowls of wrath yet another. Those who read the visions this way find greater difficulty explaining why the interludes occur and how they function. Proponents of this view usually explain the presence of these interludes as later editorial insertions into the narrative. The linear reading also has difficulty explaining why some visions seem to violate neat chronological boundaries. The vision of the woman, child, and dragon (chs. 12–13) reaches back to the birth of the Messiah (12:1–5), and maybe even earlier (12:9), and thus can hardly be fitted into a sequence of end-time events depicted in the seven seals or the seven trumpets. Moreover, what appear to be the same events are depicted several times; for example, the destruction of Babylon in 16:19 cannot be different from the one depicted in chapters 17–18.

The cyclical method of reading the visions is preferable because it helps the reader see a pattern that recurs throughout the book: a progressively worsening series of catastrophes that lead to a climactic moment when the forces of evil and the forces of good clash, evil is defeated, and divine judgment brings history to an end. We see this pattern not only in the three sets of seven numbered visions and in several of the miscellaneous visions, but also in the book as a whole.

Revelation actually exhibits both cyclical and linear features. Taken as a whole, the narrative unfolds a single vision that moves toward a grand climax. From the standpoint of the Seer, the visions unfold in linear succession. What is unfolded in the visions, even if the three major sets of visions recapitulate the same events in the apocalyptic drama, exhibits a linear progression. Certainly, the visions of chapters 17–22 represent the culmination of all that has preceded. One should also distinguish between the linear movement of the narrative and a linear interpretation of the narrative. It is possible, for instance, to see the story of Revelation unfolding in a linear fashion but interpret the meaning of the story in a non-linear way.

John's Theological Task

Sometime toward the end of the first century C.E., John the Seer was prompted to do something no other Christian had done: write a full-scale apocalypse. How did he make this choice? By his own account, he was "in the Spirit on the Lord's day" (1:10) when he experienced the opening vision of the risen Son of Man standing "in the midst of the lampstands" (1:13), in other words, the seven churches. He was also lifted "in the spirit" to see God's throne and report the several visions he experienced "in heaven" (4:2).

John's Prophetic Consciousness

While John does not use the language of his prophetic predecessor Ezekiel, who reported that a "spirit entered into me" and "I heard him speaking to me" (Ezek 2:2), he probably experienced a similar moment of prophetic inspiration. John wants us to read Revelation as "the words of the prophecy" (1:3), a point he reinforces by presenting himself as the voice of prophecy (10:11). A similar point is made toward the end of Revelation, when John is reminded by the angel that "the testimony of Jesus is the spirit of prophecy" (19:10). It is the "God of the spirits of the prophets" (22:6) who is ultimately the prompting voice of this work (1:1) and who is also guiding future events. What has been unfolded—"the words of the prophecy of this book"—is to remain open and is to stand as it is, without addition or subtraction (22:10, 18–19).

John operates with the self-consciousness of a prophet. His most frequent conversation partners are two OT prophets, Daniel and Ezekiel, but he is also heavily influenced by other OT prophetic figures, including Isaiah, Jeremiah, Zechariah, and Zephaniah. John is doing for his own time what they did for theirs. Calling Revelation a "prophetic apocalypse" may seem redundant, since Jewish apocalyptic was deeply rooted in the OT prophetic tradition. Yet the prophetic dimension of John's work establishes his central frame of reference. What prompts him to write an apocalypse is the "spirit of prophecy" as it bears testimony to Jesus (19:10).

Early Christian Worship as the Context for John's Prophetic Activity

By setting his vision on "the Lord's day" (1:10), John signals the context within which his prophetic imagination has been shaped: early Christian worship. His use of songs and prayers is too lavish for us to ignore their central role within the overall work. By drawing on a rich collection of liturgical materials to portray how God and the Lamb are praised in heaven, John not only validates his readers' experience of worship within the seven churches, but he also uses this liturgical experience as one of his most powerful rhetorical resources. God and the Lamb, and even the Spirit to some extent, are praised in the heavenly visions as those who empower the churches to be "faithful unto death" (2:10).

Early Christian worship was probably the context in which John's reading of Scripture was shaped. The biblical texts on which he draws so heavily were probably read within the seven churches. John's creative use of those texts may reflect the exegetical practices of these churches. Should we imagine a solitary John poring over the Scriptures, working out intricate connections among their various passages, every now and then sharing an insight or provocative reading with a fellow prophet? Perhaps. But why not imagine a much wider exegetical conversation in which John and the churches were participants? This seems more probable than imagining the lone prophetic genius John, who labored on his magnum opus for years and finally published it to be "read aloud" among the churches (1:3). John's apocalyptic version of the Christian story may be fantastically conceived, but it probably reflects not only his own theological outlook, but also that of his fellow prophets in the seven churches.

John and the Jesus Tradition

John and his churches were deeply rooted in traditional Christianity. Revelation's resonance with the Gospel tradition suggests a close relationship between John the Seer's understanding of the Jesus tradition and the one(s) reflected in the four Gospels. (The details of John's understanding of Jesus are spelled out in a later section.) There are also enough echoes in Revelation of other NT voices, including that of Paul, to suggest that John's theology was connected with other parts of the Christian tradition.

If the Gospel tradition showed an interest in pushing the origins of the Jesus story backward in time, from John the Baptist (Mark), to Abraham (Matthew), to Adam (Luke), and finally to Creation (John), Revelation moved in the opposite direction, pushing the story of Jesus forward to the end of time. Revelation extends an important trajectory already found in the Gospel tradition, but it does not simply extend it horizontally into the future; it also extends it spatially by opening up the heavens far beyond what the Fourth Gospel ever imagined. Circumstances in the churches prompted John to think from the Christ event forward, to reflect on Jesus this side of Easter and what he does as the Davidic Messiah and the Danielic Son of Man. This explains why Revelation presents one of the most fully developed eschatologies in the NT. The churches' experience of oppression, persecution, and martyrdom caused John to do what Jews writing in the aftermath of the Maccabean revolt did: think about life after death and how the cause of those who had been martyred would be vindicated.

John's construal of the Jesus story should not be understood as an implicit critique of narrative traditions about Jesus found in the Gospels. Nor does his thoroughly apocalyptic portrait of Jesus compete with other NT writings. Rather, it complements them. John takes the image of Jesus as the "slaughtered Lamb" in a direction that no other NT writer does. In doing so, he is extending an image found in both Paul and John. Like them, John thinks that the Lamb's death was an act of love that "freed us from our sins" (1:5).

John's Conversation with Scripture

If we can glimpse the form of the conversation John was having with the Jesus tradition, what about his conversation with Scripture? John is so thoroughly steeped in Scripture—its language, its images, its overall story—that it is often difficult to distinguish his voice from the voice of Scripture. This is evident by his failure to cite Scripture as such. Scripture functions for John more as a sacred voice than as a sacred text.

We do injustice to John if we think that he used Scripture simply as a treasury of images and motifs to be exploited creatively in crafting a fresh version of the Christian story. John does some of this, but he also does more. While John is not a midrashic interpreter who ponders a single text or biblical theme and tries to explain how it relates to Jesus, he does find patterns in the OT story that help him make sense of Jesus and the experiences of his followers in Asia Minor. Thus the risen martyrs' triumph through Jesus the Lamb can be understood as a new exodus, comparable to Israel's deliverance through Moses.

What especially characterizes John's reading of the OT is his stunning creativity. Certain parts of the OT have been enormously influential in shaping his work. He is heir to a tradition of biblical interpretation already present within the biblical writings and other Jewish apocalypses. By subtle appropriation of the scene from Dan 7, John makes explicit theological claims. He attributes to the risen Son of Man qualities of the Ancient of Days in Dan 7 and thus elevates Jesus to divine status comparable to what we find in the Fourth Gospel. John does not go quite as far as the second century B.C.E. Jewish author Ezekiel the Tragedian, who portrays Moses as part of the heavenly court seated on the throne vacated by God. Rather, God remains enthroned in Revelation, with the Lamb close by, sharing dominion with God, not usurping it.

The OT is a rich resource for John, but it is not the only written source that informs his theological vision. For all of the similarities between motifs in Revelation and those we find in other Jewish apocalypses (besides Daniel), there is no firm evidence that he knew these other writings. But he made ample use of ancient Jewish and pagan stories relating to Satan's fall from heaven, the birth of Apollo, the combat myth, and imagery known from Greek and Roman architecture and iconography. John had a broad literary vision and was aware of the material culture of the Roman world as he knew it in Asia Minor.

Not every apocalypse was written in response to a crisis, and not every religious crisis prompted the writing of an apocalypse. The crisis of the Maccabean revolt prompted the writing of Daniel, an apocalyptic work, but it also produced Sirach, a work of a completely different genre. The Jewish revolt in 66–70 C.E. prompted the writing of apocalyptic works like 4 Ezra, the Apocalypse of Abraham, 2 Baruch, and 3 Baruch, yet the Palestinian rabbis came to terms with the aftermath of the destruction of Jerusalem in a wholly non-apocalyptic manner. Out of their efforts emerged the rabbinic tradition that gave rise to the Mishnah and the Talmud. John stands in the tradition of Daniel and the post-70 Jewish apocalyptists. Like them, he found in the apocalyptic tradition a way of looking at the world, a construal of the biblical story, and a compelling literary genre, all of which suited his purpose. By blending these elements, John devised a powerful rhetorical strategy for recasting the Jesus tradition. In choosing this strategy he exemplified a wonderfully independent spirit, but one full of both risk and promise.

John's Use of the Old Testament

Nowhere in Revelation do we find the formula "It is written," followed by an OT citation. Yet the OT is written all over Revelation. One of the first to see this was Marcion (died ca. 160 C.E.), who rejected it as canonical. John has blended OT citations, allusions, and echoes into his narrative so skillfully that it is difficult to identify them. Depending on how one defines allusion, estimates of the number of OT allusions in Revelation have ranged from 200 to 1,000. It is not as though John nowhere cites the OT, for in a number of places verbatim OT phraseology is found.[10] Close comparative analysis of John's OT allusions reveals that he used both the Septuagint and the Hebrew Scriptures, and there are strong indications that his native language was Hebrew or Aramaic. His allusions cover the entire range of the OT, although the majority of them come from the Psalter, Isaiah, Jeremiah, Ezekiel, and Daniel. Considering its relative brevity compared with the other OT writings he uses, Daniel supplies a disproportionately high percentage of the allusions. Even so, Ezekiel appears to have exercised the greatest influence on John.

In addition to supplying many of the images and metaphors in Revelation, the OT informs the structure of the narrative. The heavenly vision of chapters 4–5 is heavily influenced by the vision of the Ancient of Days and the Son of Man in Dan 7:9–14. John also makes lavish use of the throne vision in Ezek 1. The motif of the scroll containing a prophetic message, which is introduced in 5:1–5 and repeated in 10:1–11, derives from Ezek 2:8–3:3. The measuring of the temple in 11:1–3 is informed by Ezek 40:3–42:17. The eschatological scenario sketched in chapters 20–22 draws on Ezek 37–48. The vision of the new Jerusalem in 21:9–22:5 is based on John's rereading of Ezek 40–48, which explains why the temple and city sketched there are literary rather than historical realities.

The story of the plagues in Exod 7–14 informs the series of catastrophes unfolded in the vision of the seven trumpets (8:7–11:19) and especially the seven bowls of wrath (15:5–16:21). Like his prophetic predecessor Amos, John creatively appropriates the symbolism of the plagues to address a new situation (Amos 4:10; cf. 8:9), leaving no doubt that the God who afflicted Egypt will again unleash divine wrath in the last days (also see Wis 11–19). The influence of Zech 14 can be seen in Rev 7, perhaps also in chapters 20–22.

In addition to these structural influences, we also detect major OT themes, for example, the image of the divine warrior, if not the larger "holy war" theme. Revelation has even been called the "Christian War Scroll."

When we compare Revelation with other NT writings that draw heavily on the OT, we are struck by how differently John positions himself vis-à-vis the OT. We find nothing in Revelation resembling the formula quotations of Matthew or the promise fulfillment scheme of Luke-Acts and the Gospel of John. Nor do we find John engaged in the midrashic exposition of Scripture attributed to Peter and Paul in Acts 2 and 13. Although John's use of the OT differs considerably from other NT writers, he firmly believes that Jesus is the messianic Son of David who fulfilled the expectations of Scripture. [See Expanded CD Version pp. 795–97: *John's Use of the OT: A Case Study—Rev 15:3–4*]

John's Theological Vision

The Sovereign God

Revelation's opening line introduces "the revelation of Jesus Christ, which God gave." Revelation is a set of visions about God and Jesus Christ. Its perspective on God is succinctly expressed in the epilogue: "Worship God!" (22:9). As the angel's utterance to John, Revelation comes with heaven's authority. This is a wonderfully compact way of expressing one of Revelation's most central concerns: belief inevitably expresses itself in worship. By accenting worship, John also exposes one of the central issues in the book: living within the tension created by two competing loyalties, both of which are regarded as ultimate and absolute. Whether John's readers were being pressured to participate in the emperor cult, in which Caesar was confessed as Lord, or to accept other forms of idol worship, their belief in one sovereign God was being challenged.

Perhaps even more threatening to this belief was their own experience of suffering. The cry of the saints under the altar is, "Sovereign Lord, holy and true, how long will it be before you judge and avenge our blood on the inhabitants of the earth?" (6:10). Their plaintive prayer captures their dilemma: It is offered to a God whom they confess as "Sovereign Lord, holy and true," yet it comes from those who look at the bodies of the slain and say, "Our blood." This tension between belief in a sovereign God and the undeniable reality of unjust human suffering prompts the writing of Revelation.

This tension also helps explain why God plays such a central role in the book. Part of John's response is to picture God so vividly that this image becomes a fixed point in the readers' mental universe. The chief symbol for accomplishing this is God's enthronement. By repeatedly depicting God's throne with lavish symbolism, John makes it the focal center of the book. Even with all of the interludes, the visions keep returning to the enthroned God. We can easily understand why John chose this strategy, since God's throne had to compete with both the image and the reality of the enthroned Roman emperor, whom the readers constantly encountered in coins and iconography as part of their daily experience. John knew the struggle created by the two images of God's throne and the emperor's throne.

John's strategy resonates with the tradition of Scripture, in which the enthroned God is a recurrent image (1 Kgs 22:19–23; Isa 6:1–5; Ezek 1:22–28; Ps 9:4; 103:19; cf. *1 En.* 14:18–24; *T. Levi* 5:1–2). John's throne imagery is especially informed by Dan 7, in which the enthronement of God, the Ancient of Days, follows a vision of the four beasts that symbolize the four successive empires of the Babylonians, the Medes, the

A copper engraving by Caspar Luiken (1672–1708), depicting the opening of the seventh seal (Rev 8). Winged angels with trumpets are assembled on the clouds around an altar with fire. One angel pours out the contents of a censer, raining destruction on the earth. Two angels are blowing their trumpets, while another angel shouts, "Ve, Ve, Ve" (Woe, Woe, Woe). Above the altar is a triangular sun. From a work published in 1712 in Nuremberg, Germany, containing illustrations of biblical scenes with didactic poems in Latin and German. From the Digital Image Archive of the The Richard C. Kessler Reformation Collection, Pitts Theology Library, Candler School of Theology, Emory University, Atlanta, Georgia.

Persians, and Alexander the Great. The implications are clear: Four earthly, temporary thrones are being contrasted with God's heavenly throne. What makes Dan 7 even more appropriate for John is that it was written in the context of the Maccabean revolt, when Jews died as martyrs in the name of the Sovereign God. In Daniel, with the destruction of the fourth throne (7:11–12) come the night visions in which the Ancient of Days transfers authority to the one "like a Son of Man," who receives universal dominion (7:13–14). Revelation sees Jesus as the Son of Man exercising such dominion (1:9–20; 14:14–20).

Echoes of Dan 7 are heard in the opening vision of Christ (Rev 1:9–20), in which the Son of Man has head and hair "white as white wool, white as snow," imagery used of the Ancient of Days in Dan 7:9. Following Jesus' messages to the seven churches, the opening vision of God in chapter 4 is the first of a series of visions of God's enthronement (7:9–17; 8:1–5; 11:15–19; 14:2–3; 15:2–8; 19:1–10; 21:3–8; cf. 20:11–15). "In heaven stood a throne," John tells us (4:2), and his throne imagery (4:3–6) draws heavily on yet another well-known OT throne vision: Ezek 1. So overpowering is this opening vision of the heavenly court both visually and aurally that the reader (hearer) can hardly forget it. Equally unforgettable is the worship that occurs there. The enthroned God is praised as triply holy, all-powerful, and eternal (4:8). As the Creator, God is worthy of lavish praise (4:11). The heavenly throne remains the scene for the Lamb's appearance and the opening of the seven seals in chapters 5–6. [See Expanded CD Version pp. 798–99: *The Role of the Throne Image in Revelation*]

The Slaughtered Lamb

The Jesus of Revelation is deeply rooted in early Christian tradition but exhibits features that distinguish him from other NT portraits. Several times he is designated simply "Jesus" (1:9; 12:17; 14:12, et al.) and even "Jesus Christ," which is used as his name rather than a title (1:2, 5; 22:21 [variant]). Virtually no interest is shown in his earthly life, except for a few scattered references. Revelation mentions "the twelve apostles of the Lamb" (21:14) and twice refers explicitly to his passion: the bodies of the two slain witnesses lie in the street of "Sodom and Egypt" (Jerusalem), "where also their Lord was crucified" (11:8). Echoing the Fourth Gospel, John refers to "those who pierced him" (1:7; cf. John 19:34, 37). The "male child" born to the woman being threatened by the dragon is probably Jesus (12:5), but this is likely not an allusion to the tradition of Jesus' virgin birth. If anything, it is a symbolic statement of Jesus' birth from Israel, since the woman's other children also had to fend off the dragon's attacks while holding fast to God's commandments and "the testimony of Jesus" (12:17). The life, deeds, and words of the historical Jesus are presupposed rather than cited or elaborated.[11]

Positioned at a point far removed from the ministry of Jesus, John has an angle of vision set well this side of Easter. The moment of the Jesus story that looms largest for the Seer is Jesus' death. This is seen by the way he focuses on Jesus as the "slaughtered Lamb." Most of his creative energies have been concentrated on this image. John has thought long and hard about Jesus' death, not so much as a miscarriage of justice—the

A copper engraving by Caspar Luiken (1672–1708), depicting John's vision of the slain lamb receiving the scroll from God on his throne (Rev 5). God and the lamb are surrounded by four creatures (man, lion, ox, eagle), representing the four evangelists. Above them is an angel, and below them are crowned elders with harps and golden bowls full of incense. From a work published in 1712 in Nuremberg, Germany, containing illustrations of biblical scenes with didactic poems in Latin and German. From the Digital Image Archive of The Richard C. Kessler Reformation Collection, Pitts Theology Library, Candler School of Theology, Emory University, Atlanta, Georgia.

death of an innocent man, as in Luke-Acts—but rather as a saving event. The "slain Lamb" emerges as the predominant image of Christ in Revelation and serves as one of the main interpretive categories used by the Seer for making sense of Jesus' death.

John operates with the basic conviction of early Christian preaching that Jesus died and was raised, but his formulation of the kerygma differs markedly from what we find in other NT writings. Standard NT language for describing Jesus' resurrection is absent in Revelation. Jesus is not said to have been raised by God (cf. 1 Cor 15:4; Acts 2:24). The term "resurrection" (*anastasis*) occurs only twice (20:5–6; cf. 20:13), neither time in reference to Jesus' resurrection. John's belief in Jesus' resurrection is not weaker than that of other NT writers; it is simply expressed with a different set of metaphors.

In the opening vision (1:9–20), in which John experiences the equivalent of the disciples' Easter morning encounter with the Risen Lord or Saul's Damascus road experience, we hear Jesus the Son of Man telling John, "I am the first and the last, and the living one. I was dead, and see, I am alive forever and ever; and I have the keys of Death and of Hades" (1:17–18). To the church at Smyrna, Jesus identifies himself as the one "who was dead and came to life" (2:8). Here Jesus speaks from the other side of death, expressing the distinctive element of early Christian belief: Jesus, having died, now lives "forever and ever." Unlike Enoch and Elijah, he actually *died*, and now as "the living one" (*ho zōn*) who participates fully in life as only God knows it (Deut 5:26; Sir 18:1), he "places his right hand on" John, who is in a visionary trance.

The living Jesus can say that he now holds the "keys of Death and of Hades"—a metaphor drawn from a common Hellenistic understanding of the goddess Hekate as the holder of the keys to the gates of Hades (though cf. Job 38:17)—because he has "conquered" death (3:21; 5:5). Whereas other NT writings, drawing on the imagery of Ps 110:1, can speak of Jesus' exaltation to God's right hand (cf. Acts 2:33), a status attained because of God's raising him from the dead, in Revelation Jesus boldly asserts, "I myself conquered" (3:21). The victory over death was his, not God's. As the first one to experience this form of new life, Jesus is the "firstborn of the dead," resurrection's eldest son (1:5; cf. Col 1:18; 1 Cor 15:20).

Because of Jesus' victory over death, he now stands "in the midst of the seven golden lampstands." Jesus is actively present within his churches, walking among them and addressing them directly (2:1). Fully aware of their triumphs and defeats, he reminds them, "I know your works. . . ." As the one who "searches minds and hearts" (2:23), the risen Lord displays a pastoral concern arising from intimate knowledge of his churches. This same knowledge enables him to discipline wayward churches. The concluding refrain "To the one who conquers . . ." is credible reassurance because it comes from the one who himself has conquered (2:7, 11, 17, 26; 3:5, 12, 21).

Revelation is also remarkable for the many visions in which the "slaughtered Lamb," rather than sitting passively at God's right hand, works actively on behalf of his beleaguered people (6:9; 12:11, 17; 19:10; 20:4). If the male child's being "snatched away and taken to God and to his throne" (12:5) is a metaphorical description of Jesus' resurrection (or his exaltation and ascension), it would be unique among NT writings (see Luke 24:51; Acts 1:6–11; 2:32–33; 1 Tim 3:16; Heb 8:1; 10:12).

In the visions, Jesus is in the heavenly court by virtue of his resurrection, or as John puts it, his "conquest" of death. Because we are repeatedly invited into God's exclusive space, usually depicted as a throne room (4:2–6:17; 7:9–17; 11:16; 14:1–19; 19:1–8), but also as a tabernacle (15:5) and as a temple with an altar of incense (8:3; cf. 11:19), we are given a visionary interpretation of what the living Jesus does. Above all, he shares dominion with God, not just as another member of the heavenly court— the twenty-four elders all have their places in the circle of thrones surrounding God's throne, as do the four living creatures, one on each side of the throne—but in a unique position close beside the enthroned God.

The Lamb is positioned at the "center of the throne" (7:17) so that God's power and majesty extend to him. Honor is given to "the one seated on the throne and to the Lamb" (5:13; 7:9–10) or to God and "his Messiah" (12:10). So closely is the Lamb joined to God that he assumes God's titles, most notably, "Alpha and Omega" (1:8; 21:6; 22:13; cf. 2:8) and "King of kings and Lord of lords" (17:14; 19:16), who becomes "ruler of the kings of the earth" (1:5). Through these visionary images, John depicts Jesus' exalted status to amplify the image of enthronement envisioned in Ps 110:1. Revelation might even be read as an extended visionary midrash on Ps 110:1.

In his heavenly status, Jesus' messianic role is duly acknowledged: "The kingdom of the world has become the kingdom of our Lord and of his Messiah" (11:15; cf. 12:10). Asked who Jesus is, John would undoubtedly respond with traditional language: The Jesus now exalted is none other than the "Lord's Messiah." Rather than reflecting on how the earthly Jesus became Messiah or even adducing proofs of his messianic status such as we find, for example, in Luke-Acts, John instead assumes Jesus' messiahship as a given. True to early Christian tradition, John links Jesus especially with David (Matt 1:1; Luke 1:32; John 7:42; Acts 13:22–23; Rom 1:3; 15:12; 2 Tim 2:8). In Revelation, Jesus is not the "Son of David," as is frequently the case in the synoptic tradition. Jesus is rather the "Root of David" (5:5) and the "root and the descendant of David" (22:16), John's way of expressing the OT image of the "shoot from the stump of Jesse" (Isa 11:1, 10; cf. Jer 23:5; 33:15; Rom 15:12). As the one who has the "key of David" (3:7; cf. Isa 22:22), Jesus exercises royal authority. Combined with the Davidic image are other messianic titles: "Lion of the tribe of Judah" (5:5; cf. Gen 49:9–10); the morning star (2:28; 22:16; cf. Num 24:17); the holy one (3:7); and especially the Son of Man (1:12–16; 14:14–20; cf. 1:7).

In his depiction of Jesus as Son of Man, John echoes the Gospel tradition, although he develops the image of the Son of Man only as eschatological judge. The Son of Man as the one who must suffer, die, and be raised, or as the one who exercises authority in word and deed during the ministry of Jesus, is absent in Revelation. Instead, drawing directly on Dan 7:13–14, John envisions the Son of Man's "coming with the clouds" (1:7) as an imminent expectation. The Son of Man, who stands "in the midst of the lampstands" (1:13), has already been exalted, yet he is now present among the churches. In the vision of 14:14–20, the Son of Man swings his sickle over the earth to reap the final harvest, in which God's wrath will be revealed in all its awful force (14:19–20).

The claim that the triumphant Jesus will "strike down the nations, and . . . rule them with a rod of iron" (19:15; 12:5; cf. 2:26–27) takes John's understanding of Jesus' messiahship in a decidedly militant direction. This is much closer to the messianic vision found in the *Psalms of Solomon* (first century B.C.E.), in which the expected Messiah's rule is seen as aggressive warfare (*Pss. Sol.* 17:21–25). In this respect,

Revelation diverges sharply from the synoptic understanding of Jesus' Davidic messiah-ship, which considerably mutes militaristic expectations that were normally associated with messianic rule.

If frequency of usage is any gauge, the image that most vividly captures the essence of Jesus in Revelation is Lamb (*arnion*), a term used twenty-nine times, all but one (13:11) as a symbol for Jesus.[12] John's theology of the cross is reflected in the recur-rent image of the "slaughtered Lamb" (5:6, 12; 13:8) and the related expression "blood of the Lamb" (7:14; 12:11; also cf. 1:5). This ambiguous symbol possibly recalls Isa 53:7, "like a lamb that is led to the slaughter," but it is doubtless informed by Jewish sacrificial practice, whether the daily Tamid offering, Passover observance, or other sacrifices more explicitly for the purpose of purification.

Even though the background of the image may be obscure, John's own under-standing is clear: Jesus inhabits the heavenly court not simply as one who died, but as one who experienced a violent death (1:7; 11:8). Martyred saints are able to identify with him (5:9; 6:9; 18:24). Jesus' death was an act of love (1:5; cf. John 15:12–13), and his shed blood is the price through which a new, universal people was purchased or "ransomed" for God (5:9; 14:4; cf. 1 Pet 1:18–19).

Those responsible for Jesus' death are not identified in Revelation. Who killed Jesus is not a pressing question for John, for the real force behind Jesus' death was Satan himself (12:4–6). What Jesus has experienced—violent death at Satan's hands—he overcame through his resolute character as the "faithful witness" (1:5; 3:14; cf. 19:11), a form of faithfulness that tilts saints toward lives of steadfast endurance (14:12; cf. "faith of Jesus" in Rom 3:22, 26; Gal 2:16, 20; 3:22). By shedding blood, Jesus, like the sacrificial lamb, gives up life for the benefit of the one needing purifica-tion. Those who are slaughtered like him acquire "white robes"—resurrected bodies like his. By suffering a fate like his, they have been bathed in the Lamb's blood (7:14). Saints who exhibit Jesus-like fidelity conquer Satan "by the blood of the Lamb and by the word of their testimony." Like Jesus, they see "clinging to life" as the lesser good when given the choice between living faithlessly and dying faithfully (12:11).

Blended with the sacrificial image of the Lamb is another image: the Lamb as messianic leader. As the one who shares fully in God's heavenly dominion, the Lamb receives all of the relevant privileges: "power and wealth and wisdom and might and honor and glory and blessing" (5:12–13; cf. 7:9–10; 14:4; 21:22; 22:1, 3). In a reversed metaphor, the Lamb can also become the shepherd who guides the vindicated saints to "springs of the water of life" (7:17). In this respect, the Lamb functions in a mes-sianic pastoral role. The 144,000 saints who are redeemed gather around the "Lamb, standing on Mt. Zion" (14:1), and they "follow the Lamb wherever he goes" (14:4). The Lamb's role as messianic leader also has a hard edge, since he can show his wrath (6:16; 14:10) and discharge his responsibility as the messianic warrior who fights, and wins, the holy war against the kings of the earth (17:14). By no means is the Lamb in Revelation a wholly gentle image. Just as Jesus can rule with an "iron rod" as the "Lion of Judah and Root of David," so can he make war as the Lamb.

With Revelation's fully developed messianic Christology built around the image of Jesus as Lamb and undergirded by faith in Jesus as God's Davidic Messiah and the Danielic Son of Man, we can perhaps understand why christological images that are so dominant in other NT writings play a relatively minor role in Revelation. John knows Jesus as Son of God, but compared with the Fourth Gospel, this image hardly figures in his understanding of Jesus (2:18; cf. 1:6; 2:28; 3:5, 21; 14:1). Even less prominent is Lord as a christological title (11:8; 22:20–21; cf. 1:10; 14:13; 17:14; 19:16). John shows little interest in Jesus' pre-existence. Jesus as the "origin of God's creation" (3:14) perhaps echoes the tradition assigning Jesus a role in creation (John 1:2–3; Col 1:15–16). Other echoes of the prologue in the Fourth Gospel may be heard when Jesus, the triumphant warrior, is called "The Word of God" (19:13). Yet another image emerges in the opening vision in which the Son of Man is clothed in priestly attire (1:13). Images prominent in other NT writings, such as Savior or Teacher, or reworked OT images such as the new Moses, do not figure in Revelation. Their absence does not make John's Christology any less compelling, just more distinctive.

The Contest with Evil

For a book that is so preoccupied with evil, Revelation is remarkably devoid of the usual NT vocabulary for evil. Individual vices are targeted (21:8; 22:15), and the special lure of idolatry and its twin vice sexual immorality are singled out more than once (2:14, 20). Otherwise unexplained practices, teachings, individuals, social groups, or institutions judged to be deviant or threatening are also marked for attention, but what they all have in common is their cryptic character. These include the "works [and teaching] of the Nicolaitans" (2:6, 15); the "synagogue of Satan" (2:9; 3:9); "Satan's throne" (2:13); and "that woman Jezebel" (2:20). We know they are to be avoided, but the specifics remain largely unknown, at least to us.

Of far greater importance in Revelation is the symbolism of evil used throughout the book. In Revelation, the ordinary Greek words for evil occur just a few times. The most common NT words for evil are *ponēros* and *kakos*. The only time *ponēros* occurs in Revelation, it is used with *kakos* to describe a "foul and painful sore" (16:2). The other use of *kakos* is more conventional: "evildoers" (2:2). The term *adikeō* occurs several times, usually in the sense "to do harm" or "damage" (2:11; 6:6; 7:2, 3; 9:4, 10, 19; 11:5), but twice in the final admonition, "Let the evildoer still do evil" (22:11). The usual word for sin (*hamartia*) occurs three times (1:5; 18:4–5).

By contrast, the primary symbol for evil—beast (*thērion*)—occurs thirty-nine times. The related symbol "dragon" (*drakōn*) occurs thirteen times! (Within the NT, the term *drakōn* occurs only in Revelation.) For John, when evil is experienced in its rawest form, ordinary language is inadequate; it can be expressed only symbolically.

At one level, John and his readers are caught in a political-social maelstrom, the details of which remain vague. Domitian's rule sets the political context and urban life in Asia Minor forms the social context in which Christians are being tested. How they are being tested we know only through the Seer's eyes. Antipas has died (2:13), and probably so have others as well (6:9–11; 7:14; 12:11; 16:6; 19:2; 20:4). For John, the churches are involved in more than a social-political struggle for their religious rights, or even in a fight for their lives. They are called to exercise discernment in sorting out various teachings and practices, but through it all, their own mythic story is being tested. Does the Christ story remain credible? Does it still make sense to view reality through the window of the cross?

Viewed one way, Jesus' life, death, and resurrection formed a story that could be understood as a part of the larger story of salvation history, a story punctuated periodically by divine intervention but one that always proceeded under providential care. But this was inadequate for John, who saw the Jesus story in rather different terms. It could be properly understood only against a much different backdrop, graphically depicted in the visions of chapters 12–14 and chapters 17–22. Here John draws on ancient mythic stories in which a dragon or some sinister figure threatens the life of a royal child and is later slain by the grown child. The classic account is the story of the dragon Python threatening the child Apollo, born to Zeus and Leto, only later to be slaughtered by Apollo himself. Variations of the story existed in Egyptian and Iranian mythology.

With the mention of the pregnant woman who gives birth to the male child, John telescopes the Jesus story into a single metaphorical moment. Who is the mother? Mary? The church? Israel? Probably Israel, or even Israel's heritage broadly understood as the one who "gave birth" to Jesus the Messiah, as well as his followers, her other "faithful children" who had to carry on after the "male child" had been "snatched away and taken to God and to his throne" (12:5). Unlike any other NT metaphorical depiction of Jesus' death, resurrection, and exaltation, this metaphor is truly revealing, for it sees Jesus at the time of his death caught in the middle of a cosmic struggle between God and the dragon, "that ancient serpent, who is called the Devil and Satan, the deceiver of the whole world" (12:9). As the only human figure, the woman wears the face of humanity, who must continue to contend with Satan, fleeing for safety, looking to nature for rescue, but all the while her life—human life lived out as Christian witness—must contend with Satan's ongoing anger, and her children find themselves gripped in an ongoing war with him (12:13–17).

And why does life on earth have such an ongoing demonic dimension? Because Satan and his angels were expelled from heaven in a titanic struggle with the archangel Michael and his angels (12:7–9). Evil does not exist naturally in the world, but occurs as a piercing eruption from outside, and the human struggle with evil should be seen as a continuing, though temporary, struggle that has already occurred in heaven. So proclaims the heavenly chorus (12:10–12). The world of earth and sea finds itself contending with the devil's "great wrath" but takes some heart in knowing that his "time is short" (12:12). Ahead lies a severe, though short-lived, struggle.

To achieve his purposes, Satan co-opts two servants: Rome and the religious institutions supporting the imperial cult. In John's view, both are the quintessence of evil, which is why they too can be depicted only symbolically: Rome as the sea monster Leviathan—the first beast from the sea (13:1–10; cf. Ezek 29:3; 2 Esd 6:49–52; 1 *En.* 60:7–10, 24)—and the imperial cult as the land beast Behemoth, the second beast that arose "out of the earth" (13:11–18; 2 Esd 6:49–52; 1 *En.* 60:7–10, 24). Only through beastly imagery can the devouring, bloodthirsty power of Rome be depicted, but its corruption must be seen as the result of conspiracy with Satan himself (13:4). These are not civil, human beings, acting in the cause of justice, peace, and good order, who are "making war on the saints" (13:7), but carnivorous animals, a blend of leopard, bear, and lion (13:2).

A copper engraving by Caspar Luiken (1672–1708), depicting Satan's defeat (Rev 20). Holding the key to the bottomless pit and a great chain, an angel seizes the dragon, the ancient serpent, a symbol for the Devil, binds him for a thousand years, and throws him into the pit. From a work published in 1712 in Nuremberg, Germany, containing illustrations of biblical scenes with didactic poems in Latin and German. From the Digital Image Archive of The Richard C. Kessler Reformation Collection, Pitts Theology Library, Candler School of Theology, Emory University, Atlanta, Georgia.

562

John's mythic depiction continues in chapter 17 with the vision of the great whore and the beast. Such unforgettable imagery of excess and unbridled lust underscores Rome's political alliances and military expansions as arising from ambitions bred by a lust for power and unremitting self-indulgence. Rome itself is depicted as a mindless machine of warfare and corruption in which those unwilling to yield their loyalties are finally crushed (17:6).

But it will eventually end. Just as Babylon fell and its mourners sang dirges lamenting its fall, so will Rome. The victory of the armies who conquer Rome, however, is not a political victory, for even here the purpose of God is being carried out (17:17). As the final set of visions shows, the real victory is cosmic. It is only through the appearance of God's Messiah, the "Faithful and True" (19:11), that the "armies of heaven" (v. 14) are marshaled to bring about the defeat of the "beast and the kings of the earth" (19:17–21). Even the final defeat of Satan is achieved by the key-bearing angel from heaven (20:1), who binds him for a thousand years while the saints enjoy their reign with Christ (20:4–6). Released for a final spurt of deception, Satan and his hosts are consumed by fire from heaven before he is finally banished to eternal torment together with the "beast and the false prophet" (20:10).

What had begun as a temporary victory when Michael expelled Satan from heaven now becomes a permanent expulsion, which clears the way for life free of Satanic power: the new heaven and the new earth (chs. 21–22).

By drawing on ancient mythic stories found in Greece, Egypt, and other parts of the Near East and a dazzling array of biblical images, motifs, and themes, John constructs a story that provides a broad interpretive framework for himself and his readers, a larger story within which they can set their specific story. More than this, however, he provides a story that squarely confronts evil as it is being experienced within the churches of Asia Minor. He is less interested in explaining the origin of evil than in showing how it manifests itself in visible, human form, and also in showing something of the magnitude of the church's struggle in coming to terms with evil.

While evil takes many forms, spelled out graphically as sins of excess, exploitation, and lust for power, at its core is deception, as epitomized by Satan himself, "the deceiver of the whole world" (12:9). The point of John's counterstory is to reveal an alternate way of viewing reality whose truth can be easily obscured, especially since it is visible only to the eyes of faith. The lie John fights is the lie of tyranny and oppression, the lie of brute force embodied in seemingly legitimate political and social institutions, the lie that eliminates the voices of resistance. The truth he reveals is the ultimate futility, even banality, of evil. For all of his terrifying power, often unleashed through the savage force of political and religious authorities, Satan eventually yields to the power of heaven and is finally banished from the scene. Evil may be horrific, John insists, but it is not permanent.

Revelation as a Problematic Writing

Because of its checkered history, Revelation poses a special problem for readers who wish to take it seriously. If the history of interpretation teaches us anything, it is

Revelation's potential for producing unusual or even dangerous readings. Over time, the church has learned that Revelation can appeal to the best, but also to the worst, in us. While some early interpreters eagerly embraced Revelation, others emphatically rejected it. The debate about its authorship often boiled down to the question: Could an apostle of Jesus possibly have produced a work this bizarre, this frightening, this violent? In his critique of the Egyptian chiliasts, Dionysius, bishop of Alexandria (died ca. 264 C.E.), mentions critics who were mystified by the contents and arrangement of Revelation. While Dionysius was unwilling to reject it as they did, he nevertheless remained puzzled by the work. Jerome (ca. 345–420 C.E.) expressed a similar view in his letter to Paulinus, bishop of Nola: "The Apocalypse of John has as many secrets as words. I am saying less than the book deserves. It is beyond all praise; for multiple meanings lie hidden in each single word."[13]

Others were not so gentle. In the preface to his 1522 edition of the New Testament, Martin Luther (1483–1546) wrote, "My spirit cannot accommodate itself to this book. For me this is reason enough not to think highly of it: Christ is neither taught nor known in it."[14] Ulrich Zwingli (1484–1531) also rejected it. While many literary figures have acknowledged the imaginative boldness and dramatic power of Revelation, they have also been among its severest critics. D. H. Lawrence (1885–1930), who exorcised the demons of his fundamentalist upbringing in the Midlands of England by writing a short work titled *Apocalypse*, called it a tedious, uninspiring allegory, "the work of a second-rate mind" that appealed to "second-rate minds in every country and every century."[15] For Lawrence, Revelation was to the NT what Judas was to the Twelve; it "had to be included in the New Testament," he said, "to give the death kiss to the Gospels."[16] Some biblical critics have been just as critical of the work. Among the more well-known is Rudolf Bultmann (1884–1976), who characterized the Christianity of Revelation as a "weakly Christianized form of Judaism."[17]

The legacy of lingering doubts about Revelation can be traced to the early controversy surrounding the work, which is reflected in its uneven acceptance within canonical lists. Though finally accepted in both East and West and though it found a place in the major canonical lists, its emphatic exclusion from certain canonical lists, for example, that of Cyril of Jerusalem (ca. 315–387 C.E.), underscored these doubts. A similar reluctance is reflected in the Orthodox Church's long-standing practice of excluding Revelation from use in church. Revelation provides no lectionary readings in the Orthodox liturgy, although as a canonical writing it is read by Orthodox Christians privately or in other non-church settings. In the Protestant and Roman Catholic lectionaries, by contrast, Revelation occupies an important, though not highly influential, position.

Counterbalancing these negative reactions is Revelation's influence on the church through music and art. Some of the most memorable choruses from Handel's *Messiah* are drawn from Revelation, even as it has inspired some of the most memorable works of visual art through the centuries. What Lawrence called its "splendiferous imagery"[18] captured the imagination of poets, artists, and writers in every age and from every quarter. Any assessment of Revelation must account for this aesthetic dimension of the work and its lasting artistic legacy. [See **Expanded CD Version pp. 809–15: *The Church's Reception of Revelation* and *Ways of Reading Revelation*]**

Notes

1. The book is referred to as the "Revelation of John" (*apokalypsis Iōannou*) in the Muratorian Fragment (ca. 200 C.E.) and in Codex Sinaiticus and Codex Alexandrinus. Other variations also occur: "Revelation of [the holy] John, the Theologian" and "Revelation of John the Theologian and Evangelist." In the Authorized Version, it carries the title "The Revelation of St. John the Divine." In the RSV and NRSV, the work is titled "The Revelation to John (The Apocalypse)."

2. *Haer.* 5.30.3; cf. Eusebius, *Hist. eccl.* 3.18.3. Elsewhere, Irenaeus reports that John the apostle, to whom he attributes Revelation, lived until the time of Domitian's successor, Trajan (98–117 C.E.). Both statements could be true (cf. *Haer.* 2.22.5; 3.3.4; reported in Eusebius, *Hist. eccl.* 3.23.3–4). Later writers agreed with Irenaeus's dating to the time of Domitian (Jerome, *Vir. ill.* 9.6–7). Eusebius is even more specific in dating Revelation in the fourteenth year of Domitian's reign, thus 95 C.E., (*Chron.*, PG 19:551–52). Of that year, Eusebius reports "persecution of Christians" and says that "under him [Domitian] the apostle John is banished to Patmos and sees his Apocalypse, as Irenaeus mentions" (*Chron.*, PG 19:551–52).

3. Epiphanius, *Pan.* 51.33.9.

4. Theophylact of Ohrid (died after 1125), preface to his commentary on John (PG 123:1133–34).

5. Polycarp, *Phil.* 11.3: "we [the Smyrnaeans] had not yet known him [Christ]."

6. According to the Latin writer Suetonius (ca. 70–130 C.E.), Domitian enjoyed being addressed as "Lord" by the crowds in the amphitheatre (*Dom.* 13.1; cf. Pliny the Younger, *Pan.* 33.4) and required that he be identified as "Our Lord and God" in letters sent out under his name by procurators (*Dom.* 13.2). Suetonius goes on to report that "the custom arose of henceforth addressing him in no other way even in writing or in conversation" (*Dom.* 13.2; cf. Dio Cassius 67.4.7; 67.13.4; also cf. Martial 5.8). Reports of Domitian's love for statues of himself also circulated widely (Pliny the Younger, *Pan.* 52.3; Dio Cassius 67.8.1). But these and other unflattering reports about Domitian must be read critically; their negative portraits may reflect court propaganda that sought to contrast the good qualities of later emperors, such as Trajan, with the "tyrannical and corrupt" rule of Domitian. Writings closer to Domitian's time that reflect court policy do not confirm his insistence on being called "Lord and God," nor is such language used of Domitian in any of the coins, inscriptions, or medallions from his era. On one occasion, according to the Roman poet Statius, Domitian forbade his being acclaimed "Lord" (*Silv.* 1.6.81–84).

7. Eusebius, *Chron.* PG 19.551–52. Clement of Alexandria, *Quis div.* 42; also cf. Eusebius, *Hist. eccl.* 3.23.5–19.

8. Tertullian, *Apol.* 5.

9. Pliny the Younger, *Epist.* 10.96–97.

10. The passages that come closest to being direct citations are: 4:8 (Isa 6:3; Amos 3:13); 6:16 (Hos 10:8); 7:16 (Isa 49:10); 7:17 (Isa 25:8); 14:5 (Zeph 3:13; Isa 53:9); 15:3–4 (Ps 86:9–10; 98:1–2; Jer 10:7); 20:9 (2 Kgs 1:10, 12); 21:4 (Isa 25:8). The following passages, while using language from the OT, are allusions: 1:7 (cf. Dan 7:13; Gen 12:3; 28:14); 2:27 (cf. Ps 2:9); 11:11 (cf. Ezek 37:5, 10); 19:15 (cf. Ps 2:9); 21:3 (cf. Ezek 37:27–28; Zech 2:10–11); 21:7 (cf. 2 Sam 7:14).

11. Echoes of the Gospel tradition are heard several times: Jesus' coming like a thief (3:3; 16:15; cf. Matt 24:42–44; Luke 12:39–40; 1 Thess 5:2; 2 Pet 3:10); calling on the mountains, "Fall on us . . ." (6:16; Luke 23:28–31; cf. Hos 10:8); the circling eagle (8:13; cf. Luke 17:37); trampling of the temple court by the nations (11:2; cf. Luke 21:24); Son of Man seated on the cloud (14:14; cf. Mark 13:26–27); mouth of the false prophet (16:13; cf. Mark 13:22); millstone thrown into the sea (18:21–23; Luke 17:2); shedding the blood of the prophets (18:24; cf. Luke 11:49–51); gathering for the great supper of God (19:17; cf. Matt 8:11; Luke 13:29); birds gathering for the feast (19:17; cf. Matt 24:28; Luke 17:37); let the one who has ears to hear listen (2:11, 17, etc.; cf. Matt 11:15; 13:9; Mark 4:9 etc.).

12. The Greek term *arnion* is the diminutive form of *arēn*, "lamb" or "sheep," thus technically "little lamb," but by NT times it does not necessarily retain this diminutive sense. In John's Gospel it is used of the disciples whom Peter is urged to care for (John 21:15). The term used in John 1:29, 36, "the Lamb of God who takes away the sin of the world" is *amnos*.

13. Jerome, *Epist.* 53.8.

14. *LW* 35:399. In the 1530 Preface, Luther modified his view that Revelation was neither "apostolic nor prophetic." He still denied its apostolic authorship but conceded that the writing had some prophetic value if it were rightly understood. Even so, he found it valuable in denouncing the papacy as the antichrist (see *LW* 35:399–411).

15. D. H. Lawrence, *Apocalypse* (Harmondsworth: Penguin, 1979; originally published in 1931), 14.

16. Lawrence, *Apocalypse*, 18.

17. Rudolf Bultmann, *Theology of the New Testament* (trans. K. Grobel; 2 vols.; New York: Scribner's, 1951–1955), 2:175.

18. Lawrence, *Apocalypse*, 6.

Bibliography

Commentaries

Aune, David E. *Revelation*. 3 vols. Word Biblical Commentary 52. Dallas: Word, 1997–1998.

Barker, Margaret. *The Revelation of Jesus Christ: Which God Gave to Him to Show to His Servants What Must Soon Take Place (Revelation I.I)*. Edinburgh: T&T Clark, 2000.

Beale, Gregory K. *The Book of Revelation: A Commentary on the Greek Text*. New International Greek Testament Commentary. Grand Rapids/Carlisle: Eerdmans/Paternoster, 1999.

Caird, George B. *A Commentary on the Revelation of St. John the Divine*. Black's New Testament Commentaries. 2d ed. London: Black, 1984 (1966).

Charles, R. H. *A Critical and Exegetical Commentary on the Revelation of St. John: With Introduction, Notes, and Indices, also the Greek Text and English Translation*. International Critical Commentary. 2 vols. Edinburgh/New York: T&T Clark/Scribner, 1920.

Collins, Adela Yarbro. *The Apocalypse*. New Testament Message 22. Wilmington: Glazier, 1979.

Farrer, Austin M. *The Revelation of St. John the Divine*. Oxford: Clarendon, 1964.

Giblin, Charles H. *The Book of Revelation: The Open Book of Prophecy*. Good News Studies 34. Collegeville: Liturgical Press, 1991.

Kovacs, Judith L., Christopher Rowland, with Rebekah Callow. *Revelation*. Blackwell Bible Commentaries. Oxford: Blackwell, 2003.

Roloff, Jürgen. *The Revelation of John*. Translated by J. E. Alsup. Continental Commentaries. Minneapolis: Fortress, 1993.

Rowland, Christopher. "The Book of Revelation: Introduction, Commentary, and Reflections." Pages 501–743 in vol. 12 of *The New Interpreter's Bible*. Edited by Leander E. Keck. 12 vols. Nashville: Abingdon, 1998.

Thompson, Leonard. *Revelation*. Abingdon New Testament Commentaries. Nashville: Abingdon, 1998.

Other Resources

Barr, David L. *Tales of the End: A Narrative Commentary on the Book of Revelation*. Santa Rosa: Polebridge, 1998.

————, ed. *Reading the Book of Revelation: A Resource for Students.* Resources for Biblical Study 44. Atlanta: Society of Biblical Literature, 2003.

Bauckham, Richard. *The Climax of Prophecy: Studies on the Book of Revelation.* Edinburgh: T&T Clark, 1993.

————. *The Theology of the Book of Revelation.* New Testament Theology. Cambridge: Cambridge University Press, 1993; repr. 2002.

Carey, Frances, ed. *The Apocalypse and the Shape of Things to Come.* Toronto: University of Toronto Press, 1999.

Collins, Adela Yarbro. *Crisis and Catharsis: The Power of the Apocalypse.* Philadelphia: Westminster, 1984.

Court, John M. *Myth and History in the Book of Revelation.* Atlanta: John Knox, 1979.

Ellul, Jacques. *Apocalypse: The Book of Revelation.* Translated by George W. Schreiner. New York: Seabury, 1977.

Emmerson, Richard K., and Bernard McGinn. *The Apocalypse in the Middle Ages.* Ithaca: Cornell University Press, 1992.

Farrer, Austin M. *A Rebirth of Images: The Making of St. John's Apocalypse.* Westminster: Dacre, 1949.

Grubb, Nancy. *Revelations: Art of the Apocalypse.* New York: Abbeville, 1997.

Hemer, Colin J. *The Letters to the Seven Churches of Asia in Their Local Setting.* Journal for the Study of the New Testament 11. Sheffield: JSOT Press, 1986.

Lawrence, D. H. *Apocalypse.* Penguin Twentieth-Century Classics. New York: Penguin, 1976 (1931).

Minear, Paul S. *I Saw a New Earth: An Introduction to the Visions of the Apocalypse.* Washington, D.C.: Corpus, 1968.

————. *New Testament Apocalyptic.* Interpreting Biblical Texts. Nashville: Abingdon, 1981.

Pippin, Tina. *Apocalyptic Bodies: The Biblical End of the World in Text and Image.* London: Routledge, 1999.

————. *Death and Desire: The Rhetoric of Gender in the Apocalypse of John.* Literary Currents in Biblical Interpretation. Louisville: Westminster/John Knox, 1992.

Price, S. R. F. *Rituals and Power: The Roman Imperial Cult in Asia Minor.* Cambridge: Cambridge University Press, 1984.

Schüssler Fiorenza, Elisabeth. *The Book of Revelation: Justice and Judgment.* 2d ed. Minneapolis: Fortress, 1998.

————. *Invitation to the Book of Revelation.* Garden City: Doubleday, 1981.

————. *Revelation: Vision of a Just World.* Proclamation. Minneapolis: Fortress, 1991.

Thompson, Leonard L. *The Book of Revelation: Apocalypse and Empire.* Oxford: Oxford University Press, 1990.

van der Meer, Frederick. *Apocalypse: Visions from the Book of Revelation in Western Art.* London: Thames and Hudson, 1978.

Wainwright, Arthur W. *Mysterious Apocalypse: A History of the Interpretation of the Book of Revelation.* Nashville: Abingdon, 1993.

Apocalyptic

Burridge, Kenelm. *New Heaven, New Earth: A Study of Millenarian Activities.* New York: Schocken Books, 1969.

Cohn, Norman R. C. *Cosmos, Chaos, and the World to Come: How the Wait for Heaven on Earth Began.* New Haven: Yale University Press, 1993.

————. *The Pursuit of the Millennium: Revolutionary Millenarians and Mystical Anarchists of the Middle Ages.* Rev. ed. Oxford: Oxford University Press, 1970.

Collins, John J. *The Apocalyptic Imagination: An Introduction to Jewish Apocalyptic Literature.* 2d ed. Grand Rapids: Eerdmans, 1998.

Cook, Stephen L. *The Apocalyptic Literature.* Interpreting Biblical Texts. Nashville: Abingdon, 2003.

Hanson, Paul D. *The Dawn of Apocalyptic.* Philadelphia: Fortress, 1975.

————, ed. *Visionaries and Their Apocalypses.* Issues in Religion and Theology 4. Philadelphia/London: Fortress/SPCK, 1983.

Himmelfarb, Martha. *Ascent to Heaven in Jewish and Christian Apocalypses.* Oxford: Oxford University Press, 1993.

————. *Tours of Hell: An Apocalyptic Form in Jewish and Christian Literature.* Philadelphia: University of Pennsylvania Press, 1983.

McGinn, Bernard. *Antichrist: Two Thousand Years of the Human Fascination with Evil.* San Francisco: HarperSanFrancisco, 1996.

————. *Visions of the End: Apocalyptic Traditions in the Middle Ages.* New York: Columbia University Press, 1998.

————, John J. Collins, and Stephen J. Stein, eds. *The Encyclopedia of Apocalypticism.* 3 vols. New York: Continuum, 1998.

Minear, Paul S. *New Testament Apocalyptic.* Interpreting Biblical Texts. Nashville: Abingdon, 1981.

Rowland, Christopher. *The Open Heaven: A Study of Apocalyptic in Judaism and Early Christianity.* New York: Crossroad, 1982.

Rowley, Harold H. *The Relevance of Apocalyptic.* 3d ed. New York: Association, 1964 (1944).

Russell, David S. *The Method and Message of Jewish Apocalyptic: 200 BC–AD 100.* Philadelphia: Westminster, 1964.

————. *Prophecy and the Apocalyptic Dream: Protest and Promise.* Peabody: Hendrickson, 1994.

Part 7

THE FORMATION OF THE NEW TESTAMENT CANON

Chapter 28

The Christian Scriptures: Witnesses to Christ and the Church's Faith

"Scripture . . . can be understood only in relation to a community of persons."

Wilfred Cantwell Smith

". . . the word of God was the gospel message of the risen Christ long before it was a book or collection of books."

William A. Graham

W hen someone stands before the church, reads from the Bible, then declares, "This is the Word of God for the people of God," and the congregation responds, "Thanks be to God," this exchange calls attention to the sacred character of the reading. We may read poetic or other secular literary texts in worship, but we do not use the same liturgical formulae in referring to them that we pronounce over biblical texts. As profound as their message might be, we do not declare them the "Word of God for the people of God." In churches, this language is reserved for the Christian Scriptures, the collection of writings that we designate the Old and New Testaments.

Now that we have dealt with each of the twenty-seven writings of the NT, it is appropriate to ask how they, along with the OT writings, became the church's Scriptures. Why are these writings "the church's books" in a way that other Jewish and Christian writings are not? It is important not only to understand how these writings acquired unique authority for the church, but also to explore the implications of this for contemporary readers of the Christian Scriptures.[1]

Clarifying Terms

While the terms "Scripture(s)," "Bible," and "canon" are often used interchangeably, each of them has a slightly different nuance. We should also clarify what

571

we mean by Old Testament and New Testament, since these designations signify different things to different people.

Scripture

"Scripture" transliterates the Latin *scriptura*, which renders the Greek *graphē*, meaning "writing" or "something written." At its most basic level, Scripture thus designates a written text. In religious communities, however, the term acquires special meaning, referring not to any written text but to a text, usually a collection of texts, considered uniquely authoritative for members of that religious community. In such contexts, "Scripture" means an authoritative religious text and hence is usually preceded by the term "holy." While the written form of scriptural texts often receives close attention from religious specialists, including preachers, rabbis, and biblical commentators, the oral form of the text should not be ignored. Scripture may be written, but it is written to be read and heard aloud. It has an indispensable oral dimension. Some would even give higher priority to how Scripture is experienced orally than to Scripture in its written form.

When a text, for whatever reason, is cited within a religious community as an authoritative text distinguishable from other texts, it functions as Scripture for that community. Typically, these texts are introduced with such formulae as "It is written" or "Scripture says," which frequently happens when NT writers introduce citations from the OT. In 2 Pet 3:16 Paul's letters are accorded the same authority as "the other [OT] scriptures," implying, of course, that the author regarded Paul's letters as Scripture. **[See Expanded CD Version p. 830: *"Scripture" in the Post-Apostolic Period*]**

Canon[2]

The term "canon" is a transliteration of the Greek *kanōn*, whose root meaning is "straight rod" or "bar." The related Greek terms *kanna* or *kannē*, meaning "pole-reed," have close counterparts in the Hebrew *qāneh*, Akkadian *qanû*, and Latin *canna*, meaning "reed." *Kanōn* understandably acquired the metaphorical sense "standard" to designate that by which other things were measured, such as a carpenter's plumb line, a ruler or straightedge, or even a musical monochord. Aristotle (384–322 B.C.E.) speaks of the virtuous person as the "standard [*kanōn*] and measure [*metron*]" of all that is noble and pleasant.[3] Pliny the Elder (ca. 23–79 C.E.) refers to Polyclitus's famous statue *Doryphorus*, "Spearbearer," as the canon other sculptors should emulate because it so perfectly rendered the proportions of the human body.[4] Polyclitus (ca. 460–410 B.C.E.) even wrote a book with the title *Canon* in which he expounded the mathematical principles of his art. As historians, Herodotus (fifth century B.C.E.) and Thucydides (ca. 460–400 B.C.E.) could be spoken of as the "perfect model(s)" (*aristos kanōn*) of literary style.[5]

The term *kanōn* passes into Christian usage when Paul in Gal 6:16 gives a concluding blessing to "those who will follow this rule [*kanōn*]," that is, adhere to the revolutionary implications of the new creation.[6] Among early patristic writers, *kanōn* was used of the faith transmitted through early Christian tradition. In Clement of Rome (fl. ca. 96 C.E.) the "glorious and venerable rule of our tradition" (*kanōn tēs paradoseōs*) serves as an exemplary standard for believers.[7] Clement of Alexandria (ca. 150–215 C.E.) speaks of "the rule of the faith" (*ho kanōn tēs pisteōs*) to which Christian conduct should conform.[8] In the fourth century, *kanōn* acquired further ecclesiastical nuance when it was used to designate the decisions reached by church councils relating to matters of doctrine and conduct. At that time, it became commonplace to speak of the canons issued by a particular synod or council.

It was not until the late fourth century that the term *kanōn* and its cognate forms "canonical/non-canonical" (*kanonikos/akanonikos*) and "canonize" (*kanonizō*) were used in connection with a designated list of Christian writings. About 350, Athanasius (ca. 296–373 C.E.), bishop of Alexandria, characterized the Shepherd of Hermas as "not belonging to the canon" (*mē ōn ek tou kanonos*).[9] In his well-known *Thirty-Ninth Festal Letter*, issued in 367, Athanasius calls the twenty-seven NT writings "canonical books" (*biblia kanonizomena*) that are to be distinguished from apocryphal works (*apokrypha*).[10] This is the first time that the term *kanōn* is applied to this collection of twenty-seven writings.[11] Around 380, Amphilochius (ca. 340–395 C.E.), bishop of Iconium, spoke of the writings of the Old and New Testaments as "the canon . . . of the divinely inspired scriptures" (*kanōn tōn theopneustōn graphōn*).[12] Somewhat later, Macarius Magnes (fourth–fifth centuries) used the expression "canon of the New Testament" (*kanōn tēs kainēs diathēkēs*).[13]

When the term "canon" is used to designate a specific list of writings, it has a slightly different nuance from the term "Scripture." Rather than signifying that a writing is sacred, and thus to be read as Scripture, canon signifies a collection of such texts from which other highly regarded, even sacred, texts are excluded. Canon as a concept implies that certain writings are included, while others are explicitly excluded. **[See Expanded CD Version pp. 831–32: "Canon" in Fourth-Century Writers]**

If "Scripture" designates a sacred writing, "canon" refers to a defined collection of such writings. *The church, we might say, possessed Christian Scriptures before it possessed a Christian canon of Scripture.*

New Testament

The English term "testament" derives from the Latin *testamentum*, which ordinarily refers to a document in which people specify what they wish to be done after their death—their "last will and testament." In the Latin Vulgate, *testamentum* renders the Greek *diathēkē*, "covenant," signifying commitment to an agreement or promise made in good faith between two parties. In the synoptic accounts of the institution of the Lord's Supper, Jesus employs the language of covenant when speaking of the benefits that his death would convey to his followers. He speaks of the "blood of the covenant, which is poured out for many" (Matt 26:28; Mark 14:24). In the Lukan account (Luke 22:20) and the earlier tradition preserved by Paul in 1 Cor 11:25, Jesus speaks of the "new covenant in my blood." The phrase "new covenant," which is rendered by the Vulgate as *novum testamentum*, probably recalls the promise of Jer 31 that one day God would establish a "new covenant" with the people of God. So understood, Jesus' death marks the beginning of this new arrangement. Similar appropriation of Jer 31 occurs in Paul's midrashic exposition of the giving of the Mosaic law in 2 Cor 3, in which he contrasts the "old covenant" (v. 14) with the "new covenant" under which he conducts his ministry (v. 6). Drawing explicitly on Jer 31, the author of Hebrews (ch. 8) develops the contrast between the "old covenant" and the "new covenant" in a different direction.

When Paul says that the people of Israel during his time "hear the reading of the old covenant" (2 Cor 3:14), he has in mind the written Mosaic law. This gives force to his strong contrast between "letter" (*gramma*) and "spirit" (*pneuma*). Nowhere in the NT, however, does "new covenant" refer to anything written, certainly not to any Christian writings. The use of "old covenant" and "new covenant" in the NT paves the way for later developments when these expressions designate, respectively, the Jewish Scriptures as adopted and read by Christians, and a specific set of Christian writings.[14] When this first occurred is difficult to say, but it was perhaps with an anonymous, anti-Montanist writer in the second century.[15] **[See Expanded CD Version pp. 832–33: "New Testament" in Second- and Third-Century Writers]**

Since "new testament" or "new covenant" as a designation for a defined collection of Christian writings appears to be a second-century development, when we use "New Testament" to characterize earlier writings, we are being anachronistic. Yet we do so for the sake of convenience.

We should recognize that Old Testament and New Testament are distinctively Christian designations. By characterizing each set of writings as a "testament," early Christians underscored the covenantal dimension of each set of writings. By designating the Jewish Scriptures as "old" and the Christian canon as "new," the church signaled its conviction that Jesus represented a pivotal shift in God's dealings with humanity. In one sense, the "old/new" contrast signaled this shift and to some extent set them against each other. Yet it also bound both sets of writings together as two parts of a continuous story that reached from creation to final judgment.

For Christians, the Old Testament usually meant the Greek Old Testament rather than the Hebrew Scriptures. When Jesus referred to Scripture, he doubtless had in mind the Hebrew Scriptures. Although some NT writers knew and even used the Hebrew Scriptures, for the most part the Old Testament used by the four evangelists, Paul, and the other NT writers is the Greek Old Testament, which in some respects differs significantly from the Hebrew Scriptures. When in the interest of ecumenical good will, modern Christians speak of the Old Testament as the Hebrew Scriptures, they are ignoring the historical reality that for Christians, from the second century onward, "Old Testament" usually meant the Septuagint. Not only that, but "Old Testament" also meant the Jewish Scriptures read through a Christian lens. In this sense, "Old Testament" is a Christian designation for a distinctively Christian book.

Bible

In contrast to the terms mentioned so far, "Bible" derives from the Greek *biblos* and *biblion*, meaning "book" or "writing." The latter term actually derives from *byblos*, the term used for Egyptian papyrus, the material from which writing sheets were manufactured. Both terms are used in the NT in different senses, sometimes designating a sacred scroll (Luke 4:17, 20; John 20:30; 2 Tim 4:13). What makes "Bible" an appropriate designation for the Christian canon is that its plural form *biblia*, "books," con-notes a collection of writings. Whereas we can use "Scripture" and "Scriptures" more or less interchangeably, we cannot do the same with "Bible" and "bibles." Implicit within the former is the notion of a collection of sacred writings or Scriptures brought together under one cover. The plural form "bibles," by contrast, suggests something quite different. We do not think of the individual writings or groups of writings with-in the collection as "bibles."

Some Considerations

The formation of the Christian Scriptures was a gradual process that occurred over many centuries. While we can identify certain stages of development, we should not see the overall process as a neatly unfolding, inevitable set of developments.

One way of envisioning this process is as follows: Initially, Christian writings were composed by persons who wrote without any consciousness that they were writing Scripture. A second stage occurred when certain of these "ordinary" Christian writings were ascribed special status and acquired a sacred character through extensive usage. Gathering these sacred writings into special, though loosely defined, collections was a third stage. This was then followed by a final, delimiting stage in which other writings, even other sacred writings, were excluded. Thus emerged a collection of Scriptures with a limited number of writings—a closed canon of Christian Scriptures. It is some-times assumed that from the end of the fourth century the question of the canonical limits of the Christian Bible had finally been resolved by the church, making it possi-ble to speak confidently of canonical and non-canonical writings—those that belong to the definitive collection of NT writings and those that were excluded from it.

While this linear, even evolutionary, scheme is attractive in many ways, it both oversimplifies and distorts the complex historical process through which the Christian Bible was formed.

We can begin by questioning the initial assumption that all of the NT writings were originally composed without any consciousness on the part of the author(s) that their writings would eventually be read as Scripture. It may be technically correct to say that none of the NT writings is a self-styled "scripture" and that they were not referred to in this way until several decades or even centuries after their composition. The NT writings, however, display different levels of prophetic self-consciousness. The author of Luke-Acts would probably be more surprised than the author of the Johannine Apocalypse that his two-volume work was later read as Scripture. And yet, given the style and overall purpose of Luke-Acts, it may well have been intended as a continuation of the biblical story. Neither author was writing merely for the moment. Similarly, the letters of Paul and 2 Peter presume a higher level of inspired authority than, say, the Letter of James or the Gospel of Mark. Since Paul regarded himself as an inspired apostle, his letters possess an aura of apostolic authority traceable to Christ himself. To the extent that any of the NT writers expected their works to function as authoritative texts, this created the possibility that these writings would be read as Scripture within the communities to which they were addressed.

Even when the church began to decide which writings it considered most authoritative or which ones possessed enduring value, the process was often messier than we sometimes imagine. In early patristic writers, we often hear echoes, allusions, or even citations from the four Gospels, but should we assume that these reflect *written* gospels? These references may be drawn from oral tradition. When a second-century Christian writer introduces a NT quotation with the formula "It is written," or characterizes a NT writing as "scripture," what does this imply? Are we to imagine a single text that is read as Scripture or should we think of a collection, or canon, of such texts?

We experience a similar difficulty evaluating judgments about NT writings made in different regions of the church. Decisions in the East are not necessarily honored in the West, and vice versa. In some regions, such as Syria and Egypt, we find localized preferences for and against certain writings. These traditions may be associated with single cities. A NT writing that is highly regarded in Alexandria may not be so honored in Antioch of Syria. Or a text revered in Rome may not be equally revered in Ephesus or Damascus.

Regional preferences may reflect the influence and tastes of certain individuals. The opinions of Clement of Alexandria and Origen (ca. 185–254 C.E.) carried great weight in Alexandria, although Origen's influence also shaped attitudes in Palestine, where he spent the latter part of his life. Irenaeus (ca. 130–200 C.E.) may have written from Lyons, but he spoke for Rome and the West. Even when an influential bishop rendered a decisive judgment about the Christian Scriptures, what was the extent of its applicability? Did the decision apply only within his episcopal jurisdiction, or was it also honored elsewhere?

Amid these many variables, some generalizations are nevertheless possible. The second and third centuries are a period of sifting and consensus building. Early in the second century, an emerging consensus developed around the four Gospels and most of the letters attributed to Paul. Worth noting is how quickly this happened. *After the first Pauline writings appeared in the mid-first century, it took only 70–100 years for Christians to make the basic choices about which writings would constitute the core of their canon.*

Even so, some qualifications are in order. Different regions of the church seem to have preferred one or more of the four Gospels, and in some areas these Gospels had to compete with other gospels that were later excluded from the NT, such as the *Gospel of Peter*. Another regional difference is found in Syria. Instead of adopting the four Gospels as a collection of separate writings, the Syrian church initially used Tatian's *Diatessaron* (ca. 150–160 C.E.), which wove the four Gospels together into a single story. This continued to be the practice in the Syrian church until the fifth century, when influential Syrian bishops replaced Tatian's single gospel, which in its Syriac version was called the "Gospel of the Mixed" (i.e., the Gospels mixed together), with the "Gospel of the Separated" (i.e., the Gospels as separate works).

If the second and third centuries were a time of sorting out which Christian writings would be read as the church's Scriptures, the fourth century represents a defining moment. The fourth century can be called "the century of canonical lists." It was not only a time when church councils and synods formulated definitive lists of OT and NT writings, but individual bishops and other influential figures also drew up their own lists. Compilation of canonical lists within the church doubtless reflects mutual influence among individual leaders and regions of the church.[16] Some scholars have suggested that the church's practice was also part of a larger cultural phenomenon, in which literary classics throughout the Mediterranean world began to be identified and collected.

Even though the working consensus of the second and third centuries reached greater definition in the fourth century, not all of the questions relating to the limits of the NT canon were fully resolved. The status of Hebrews in the West and Revelation in the East remained cloudy. As the *Doctrine of Addai* shows, Syrian Christianity about 400 C.E. still rejected the Catholic Letters and Revelation. Over the next two centuries, the Syrian church moved toward the adoption of a twenty-seven book NT canon, but it was a gradual, uneven process. While Hebrews tended to be read as Pauline in the Syrian churches, Philemon was contested and in some cases rejected. Even then, certain anomalies pertaining to the Syriac NT persisted for centuries. The Peshitta, the "vulgate" translation of the NT in Syriac that appeared at the beginning of the fifth century, possibly earlier, consisted of a twenty-two book canon. It included the four Gospels, Acts, James, 1 Peter, 1 John, thirteen letters of Paul (Romans, 1–2 Corinthians, Galatians, Ephesians, Philippians, Colossians, 1–2 Thessalonians, 1–2 Timothy, Titus, Philemon) and Hebrews; it excluded 2 Peter, 2–3 John, Jude, Revelation, and 3 *Corinthians*. Later, after the Syrian church split, a revision of the Peshitta was authorized in 508 by Philoxenus (ca. 450–523 C.E.), bishop of Mabbug (Hierapolis). Not only did the Philoxenian Syriac version produce a closer translation, but it also included Syriac translations of the four minor Catholic Letters and Revelation. In the seventh century, the Philoxenian version underwent extensive revision by Thomas of Harkel at Alexandria. While this expanded twenty-seven book NT began to be used among the Western Syrians, the five "new books" were accepted slowly and somewhat reluctantly.[17] The seven Catholic Letters and Revelation are not found in some NT lists dating to the ninth and tenth centuries that appear to reflect practices among Syriac-speaking churches.[18]

In certain respects, the consensus reached by the fourth century was firm; in other respects, it was still fragile. This became evident during the Reformation when the status and authority of individual writings, such as Hebrews and the Letter of James, were seriously contested.[19] One indication of this fragility is the decisions beginning in the sixteenth century among various Christian confessions relating to the limits of the OT and NT canons. In 1546, at its fourth session the Council of Trent declared that the books contained in the Latin Vulgate were "sacred and canonical" and issued an Anathema on "anyone . . . [who] knowingly and deliberately rejects" this decision. By this action, the biblical "table of contents" became an article of Roman Catholic faith—a decision that was reaffirmed by the First Vatican Council (1870). Similar decisions were reflected in other confessional statements, such as the Gallican Confession of the French Reformed Churches (1559), the Belgic Confession (1561), which was adopted by the Reformed Churches in the Netherlands in the 1560s and 1570s, The Thirty-Nine Articles of the Church of England (1563), and the Westminster Confession of Faith (1647).[20] By affirming the OT and NT lists of the Synod of Laodicea (ca. 363 C.E.) and ruling in favor of several OT "apocrypha," the Synod of Jerusalem (1672) defined the biblical canon for the Orthodox Church.[21]

Consensus and Fluidity

One way of grasping some of the complexities of the canonical process is to identify areas of consensus and disagreement.

Consensus

A high regard for the four Gospels is already reflected in Tatian's *Diatessaron*, in which he wove the Synoptic Gospels into the chronological framework of the Fourth Gospel. Tatian also made appreciative, though by no means uncritical, use of Paul's letters.[22] He used several of the letters, including Hebrews, but rejected 1–2 Timothy.[23] In his apologetic work *To Autolycus*, Theophilus of Antioch (late second century) made use of three of the four Gospels (Matthew, John, and Luke), according them status comparable to the OT prophets. Like Tatian, he also made use of several Pauline letters, including the three Pastoral Letters. In one instance, Theophilus refers to a conflated passage drawn from 1 Tim 2:2 and Rom 13:7–8 as "the divine word" (*ho theios logos*).[24]

An emphatic endorsement of the four Gospels occurred with Origen, who referred to them as "the only indisputable [Gospels] in the Church of God under heaven."[25] Origen explicitly rejected other gospels, although he read them to expand his breadth of knowledge.[26] Origen made extensive use of Acts and the Pauline letters. He also quotes Hebrews frequently, initially as a Pauline writing, though in his later writings he finesses the question of its Pauline authorship.[27] Origen is aware of the doubts pertaining to several of the Catholic Letters and fails to make use of 2 Peter and 2–3 John.[28] [See Expanded CD Version pp. 837–38: **Consensus Reflected in Hippolytus and Later Christian Thinkers**]

Perhaps the most comprehensive statement of the consensus at the beginning of the fourth century is given by Eusebius (ca. 260–340 C.E.), who classifies Christian writings into several categories: the agreed-upon writings (*homologoumena*; the four Gospels, Acts, the fourteen letters of Paul [including Hebrews], 1 Peter, 1 John, and possibly Revelation); the disputed writings (*antilegomena*), in two groups, those widely recognized (James, Jude, 2 Peter, 2–3 John), and the spurious (*notha*; Acts of Paul, Apocalypse of Peter, Shepherd of Hermas, Barnabas, Didache, and perhaps Revelation and the Gospel of the Hebrews); and, finally, the senseless and impious writings (*atopa . . . dussebē*) of the heretics (Gospel of Peter, Gospel of Thomas, Gospel of Matthias, Acts of Andrew, Acts of John, and acts of the other apostles).[29]

Fluidity

Even within the emerging consensus there was fluidity. The status of some NT writings remained uncertain. In some cases, other writings were read as Scripture.

The *Epistle of Barnabas*, an early Christian writing composed sometime between 70 and 150 C.E., and reflecting a strong anti-Jewish outlook, introduces a statement from *1 Enoch* with the formula "For the scripture says."[30] *First Enoch* was held in equally high regard by Tertullian, who cited it as Scripture.[31] The author of the *Epistle of Barnabas* also regards the authors of Wisdom of Solomon[32] and *4 Ezra*[33] as prophets.

The Shepherd of Hermas, a three-part work from the second century that commended repentance and the pursuit of virtue and also promised forgiveness for post-baptismal sin, achieved widespread use. Its popularity is reflected in the relatively large number of manuscripts in which it is preserved. It was a frequently quoted work that in some quarters served as a textbook for catechumens.[34] In the work, Hermas says that he received divine revelations, and this claim is taken seriously by a number of early Christian writers. The Shepherd of Hermas appears to have been regarded as Scripture by Irenaeus,[35] was apparently considered inspired by Clement of Alexandria,[36] and was cited in a third-century pseudonymous Latin text as "divine scripture."[37] Writing in the 240s, Origen called the Shepherd a "scripture that seems to me very useful, and, in my opinion, divinely inspired."[38] Another indication of the church's high regard for the Shepherd is its inclusion, along with the *Epistle of Barnabas*, after the NT writings in the fourth-century Codex Sinaiticus. In the sixth-century Codex Claromontanus is a list of biblical books that includes the Shepherd, along with the *Epistle of Barnabas*, *Acts of Paul*, and *Apocalypse of Peter*. Some scholars think the list predates the codex manuscript and should be dated about 300 C.E. According to Jerome (ca. 345–420 C.E.), in some Greek churches the Shepherd was read publicly.[39] While the Shepherd was widely used and read as Scripture by some Christian writers, its authority was by no means uncontested. Tertullian criticized the Shepherd's liberal position toward penitent adulterers and thus called Hermas the "shepherd of adulterers."[40] The Muratorian Fragment, probably reflecting opinion in Rome near the end of the second century, allows the Shepherd to be read for private edification but disallows its official use in church, since that would imply a status equivalent to the prophets and apostles. Eusebius included it among the disputed writings that are spurious and thus not to be accepted by the church.[41] The Shepherd was often included in Latin manuscripts of the Bible well into the medieval period. **[See Expanded CD Version pp. 839–41:** **Fluidity: Other Examples: (1) Apocalypse of Peter; (2) Agrapha—Noncanonical** **Sayings of Jesus; (3) Other Gospels; (4) Writings of Influential Christians;** **(5) Third Corinthians; (6) Epistle to the Laodiceans; (7) The Trullan Synod in the** **Seventh Century]**

The NT canon of the Ethiopian (Abyssinian) church, whose origins are obscure but are traceable to the efforts of St. Frumentius (ca. 300–380 C.E.) and Edesius of Tyre in the fourth century, also exhibits some interesting variations. Owing to the rise of Islam, the fortunes of the Ethiopian church shifted as it became increasingly isolated. From the thirteenth century onward, however, it experienced renewed growth and visibility. With historical ties to Coptic Christianity, the Ethiopian church acquired its own patriarch in 1959, thus becoming fully independent. Much about the limits of the eighty-one book Ethiopian Bible remains unclear, although *1 Enoch* and *Jubilees* are regularly reckoned among the "broader canon" of its OT. In addition to the usual twenty-seven writings, its "broader canon" of the NT includes four other works: *Sinodos*, which contains materials relating to church order; *Clement*, a seven-part work containing instructions Peter gave to Clement of Rome (not to be confused with *1 and 2 Clement*, or other writings from western Clementine literature); *The Book of the Covenant*, a two-part work with materials relating to church order and a post-resurrection discourse by the risen Lord to his disciples; and the *Ethiopian Didascalia*, a book on church order with some overlap with the fourth-century Apostolic Constitutions. The case of the Ethiopian (Abyssinian) church, with its somewhat looser conception of the limits of the NT canon, challenges the usual perception that Christianity, while operating with different versions of the OT canon, nevertheless uses the same NT canon. [See **Expanded CD Version pp. 842–44: *Other Variables: Clement of Alexandria and Irenaeus***]

Catalysts: Conflicting Theological Visions and the Emergence of Orthodoxy

A series of theological crises prompted the church to clarify the nature and limits of authentic witness to Christ. While these controversies differed in important respects, they forced the church to ask which writings bore the most reliable, compelling testimony to the gospel of Christ. This prompted other questions: What is the relationship between the oral gospel—the Christ who is known and experienced through the church's preaching and confession—and the written records that report and amplify this gospel? Or, what is the relationship between Holy Word and Holy Writ? Invariably, the authority of influential leaders at the center of these controversies was closely linked to the authority of the written texts to which they ascribed scriptural status.

These disputes surfaced issues that had not been addressed previously, at least not with such urgency. On what basis could an individual church leader decide which writings should be accorded scriptural status? Once such a decision was made, to what extent did it apply to individual congregations and the larger church? When individuals claimed to speak under prophetic inspiration, how were these claims to be assessed? To what extent should churches yield to such claims? What authority did these persons possess and how far did this authority extend? Were their claims qualitatively similar to those closer in time to Jesus, such as his apostles, family, or other disciples? Or were they of a different order and to that extent less compelling?

With such a proliferation of literary activity within the Christian movement, much of it attributed to those who had been among Jesus' closest followers, judgments had to be made about the relative worth of early Christian writings associated with these figures. One of the most pressing questions was deciding what could be read in worship. If Scripture is a relational concept, meaningful only if a community recognizes it as an authoritative witness to the gospel of Christ, the community gathered for worship constitutes Scripture's audience in its purest form. Because hearing the word of God in such settings forms the identity of the people of God over time, deciding whether a text can be read in worship is one of the most critical choices churches make. Even further, deciding the number of such texts has equally far-reaching consequences. The basic impulse of the canonical principle is deciding which writings constitute the church's definitive collection of texts, or which Scriptures constitute its Bible.

Among the considerations that prompted the church to refine and formalize its understanding of Scripture, three important catalysts can be singled out: Marcion, Gnosticism, and Montanism.

Marcion

When Marcion arrived in Rome about 140 C.E., no one could have foreseen the impact he was destined to have on the church. Within a hundred years Marcionite churches would be scattered throughout the Roman Empire, and Marcion's radical gospel would prompt fierce replies from major theologians ranging from Irenaeus, Hippolytus, and Tertullian in the West to Clement and Origen in the East. His sharply formulated gospel of grace and his rejection of the Mosaic law, both stemming from a narrow, highly idiosyncratic reading of Paul, had broad appeal. Unable to reconcile the many troubling images of God he found in the OT with the God of Jesus Christ, Marcion found it easier to reject the Jewish Bible totally rather than rescue it through allegorical exegesis or other exegetical schemes that somehow vindicated the Creator God, or Demiurge. His impressive organizational skills, which perhaps explain his earlier success as a wealthy shipowner in Pontus near the Black Sea, were redirected toward planting and nurturing a broad network of churches that eventually reached as far as northwest Mesopotamia.

No one denies that Marcion was an enormously influential figure within the second-century church and beyond. His followers were too numerous and his many critics too prominent for anyone to question his catalytic role in shaping the church's agenda on several fronts. Evaluating the role that Marcion played in the formation of the Christian Bible, however, is not an easy task.

According to one view, the idea of a fixed canon—a defined collection of *Christian* writings that would serve as the church's normative text—originated with Marcion. This would imply that prior to him the church possessed no clearly formulated notion of a fixed set of Christian writings, either a group of four Gospels or even a group of Pauline letters, that were exclusively definitive in matters of belief and practice. Other scholars argue, however, that the idea of a Christian canon existed earlier but that it was inchoate, implicit rather than explicit in Christian writers who preceded Marcion. In Marcion, these scholars insist, the canonical principle became formalized in a way that had not been the case earlier. Whether the idea of a Christian canon originated with Marcion or whether his innovative efforts merely accelerated a process that was already under way, he must figure nevertheless in any account of the formation of the Christian Bible.

His sharply formulated version of the Christian gospel supplied the critical edge that produced his distinctive two-part biblical canon comprising Gospel ("Evangelion") and Apostle ("Apostolikon"). His theological vision and his set of Scriptures were mutually reinforcing. Under the first heading belonged an edited, or what Tertullian called a "circumcised,"[42] version of Luke's Gospel, which lacked almost all of the first four chapters because of Marcion's elimination of conspicuously Jewish elements. Comprising "Apostle" were ten Pauline letters, with Galatians heading the list. Not included were the three Pastoral Letters.

How Marcion arrived at this arrangement is not altogether clear. Since Marcion drew so heavily on Paul, whom he regarded as the one interpreter who truly grasped the essence and significance of Christ, it is conceivable that he took Paul's references to "my gospel" (Rom 2:16; 16:25; cf. 2 Tim 2:8) to refer to Luke's Gospel. Since

Marcion does not attribute the Gospel that he uses to Luke (he refers only to "the Gospel of Christ"), and indeed criticizes Luke for corrupting the original story of Jesus by incorporating many Jewish features, "Gospel" for Marcion may not have referred in the first instance to an altered version of our Gospel of Luke, but to Paul's gospel—the narrative account of Jesus that informed Paul's preaching.

Marcion's radically conceived gospel of grace was provocative and in some respects without precedent. Unlike several Gnostic interpreters, who also saw the Jewish Bible as problematic but who developed interpretations that allowed them to retain it as part of the Christian Bible, Marcion excised it completely. None of his Christian predecessors had proposed the complete rejection of the Jewish Bible as a hermeneutical solution. Limiting the number of Gospels to one heavily edited version of Luke's Gospel represented another bold move. This may not have been an unprecedented move. Other Christian groups seem to have favored, perhaps even fixated on, one Gospel. Individuals had their favorites, as we know from Ignatius's fondness for Matthew. As for heavy editing of a Gospel text, Luke's use of Mark could be seen as a precedent.

Marcion's ten-letter "Apostolikon" may not have been a radical new departure. Second Peter 3:15–16 indicates that Paul's letters had begun to be collected prior to Marcion and that they were already being read as Scripture. Novel features are present in Marcion, however, such as placing Galatians first and excluding the Pastoral Letters (assuming that he knew them). Consistent with his ideological editing of the Gospels, Marcion also eliminated passages from the Pauline letters that seemed too "Jewish" (e.g., Gal 3:16–4:6; 2 Thess 1:6–8).

There was also some precedent for Marcion's designating the two parts of his collection as "Evangelion" and "Apostolikon." Earlier references to "the Lord and the apostles" suggest a two-pronged base of authority that is roughly comparable,[43] although Marcion's attaching specific texts to each category develops the idea.

Just as prior developments make it difficult to portray Marcion as a true innovator—as the first person to introduce the idea of a Christian canon—it is equally difficult to establish a causal connection between his innovative, critically edited set of Scriptures, and subsequent decisions made in the church relating to which Christian Scriptures should be part of a canonical collection. Irenaeus's ingenious arguments for four Gospels suggest that such a case had to be made, but that he did so to counter Marcion's insistence on one Gospel is by no means certain. Later references to the Pauline writings, whether as a thirteen-book collection or as a fourteen-book collection that included Hebrews, become fairly standard. That this expanded Pauline corpus should be seen as a direct response to Marcion's ten-letter "Apostolikon" is hard to prove. It also requires some effort to show that Marcion's abbreviated canon motivated the church to add writings, such as Acts and the Catholic Letters, to broaden the circle of apostolic witness.

In summary, a larger collection of canonical Christian Scriptures emerged after Marcion; that this happened directly in response to Marcion is difficult to establish. Marcion's provocative gospel posed a serious challenge to more orthodox forms of Christianity, as seen by his excommunication by the church at Rome in 144 C.E. There are strong indications that the overall shape of the Christian Bible was already forming by the time Marcion appeared on the scene. Yet he still must be seen as an important catalyst who prompted the church to clarify how it would regard the Jewish Scriptures and the extent to which any one person, however charismatic and influential, could lay claim unilaterally to a selected set of Scriptures, even highly edited ones, to bolster a compelling, radically simplified version of the gospel.

Gnosticism

In one respect, Gnostic Christianity shares Marcion's practice of adopting only one Gospel to the exclusion of all others. Just as Irenaeus objected to Marcion's exclusive use of Luke, so does he criticize the sole use of Matthew among the Ebionites, of Mark among an unnamed Gnostic group (Docetists), and of John among the Valentinians.[44] In another respect, however, Gnostic Christianity illustrates the opposite tendency, the practice of producing other gospels to supplement, if not replace, the four canonical Gospels. The Valentinians, Irenaeus complains, "put forth their own compositions" and "boast that they possess more Gospels than there really are."[45] In particular, Irenaeus objects to the Valentinian *Gospel of Truth*, a "comparatively recent writing" that diverges conspicuously from "the Gospels of the Apostles."[46] Another Valentinian work, the *Gospel of Philip*, dated by some scholars as early as the second or third century and possibly referred to by Epiphanius,[47] is an anthology of excerpts reflecting various types of literary materials drawn from other works. Another non-narrative Gnostic writing, the *Gospel of Thomas*, which contains 114 sayings and parabolic teachings of Jesus, was probably composed in the mid-second century, though possibly earlier. Given the close affinities between some of these sayings and similar ones in Matthew and Luke, some scholars have suggested that the *Gospel of Thomas* reflects very early traditions, possibly traceable to the decades immediately following Jesus' death.

Although Irenaeus does not provide a complete catalog of the numerous Gnostic gospels that circulated during the second century, his spirited defense of catholic orthodoxy against the threat of various heretical groups is revealing. His arguments for the necessity of four Gospels may sound far-fetched to us. "It is not possible," he writes, "that the Gospels can be either more or fewer in number than they are."[48] Just as there are "four zones of the world" and "four principal winds," so must there be "four pillars [of the Gospels], breathing out immortality on every side, and vivifying men afresh."[49] Accordingly, Christ "the Word, the Artificer of all . . . who was manifested to [humanity] has given us the Gospel under four aspects, but bound together by one Spirit."[50] The four Gospels correspond to the images of the four living creatures of Rev 4:7: John as lion, Luke as calf, Matthew as a man, and Mark as eagle. Since the "living creatures are quadriform" so "the Gospel is quadriform."[51] In this way, Irenaeus also explains why there are "four principal covenants given to the human race: the first from Adam to the flood; the second from Noah until Moses; the third from Moses to Christ; and the fourth initiated with Christ, "raising and bearing [humanity] upon its wings into the heavenly kingdom."[52]

The strongly apologetic thrust of Irenaeus's several ingenious arguments for a fourfold Gospel has a double-edged character. Against those committed to using only one Gospel, Irenaeus argues for the use of four, not one. To counter those bent on pro-ducing additional gospels, he insists on no more than four. Four becomes his magic number, not because it constitutes some Platonic ideal, but rather because of the wide-spread use and orthodox reputation of the four established Gospels.

A similar form of canonical sharpening is also reflected in Irenaeus's treatment of other NT writings. By insisting that the Gospel of Luke and Acts are linked by their common authorship, Irenaeus extends the fourfold Gospel to include Acts. In a simi-lar manner, he finds Acts and the Pauline letters to be in full harmony. What Acts reports about Paul is reinforced, Irenaeus insists, by what Paul reports in his own let-ters. Through this close alignment of Acts and Paul's letters, Irenaeus underscores Paul's close connections with Peter, John, and other members of the apostolic circle. This has the effect of countering Marcion's exclusive privileging of Paul as well as answering Ebionite resistance to Paul. This strategy of aligning Acts with Paul also combats Gnostic interpretations that drive a wedge between Paul and the apostolic circle. [See Expanded CD Version p. 848: *The Use of Paul by the Gnostics*]

The Gnostic appropriation of Paul during the second century was matched by efforts among orthodox theologians to reclaim Paul. Champions of Paul, such as Polycarp (ca. 69–155 C.E.), bishop of Smyrna, who spoke endearingly of "the blessed and glorious Paul" who "taught the word of truth accurately and reliably,"[53] consis-tently voice support for Paul. By linking Paul's letters with the apostolic teaching con-tained in the four Gospels and Acts and the sayings of the Lord, Irenaeus counters the claims made on Paul's legacy by Marcion and Gnostic groups. Such wrangling over the legacy of Paul doubtless forced orthodox theologians to refine their understanding of the Pauline writings, perhaps even to define their limits more precisely. At some point, they had to decide whether writings attributed to Paul, such as *3 Corinthians* or the *Epistle to the Laodiceans*, belonged with the rest of the Pauline corpus. But it is more dif-ficult to establish that such efforts to delineate the Pauline corpus were done to com-bat the use of Paul's letters among Gnostic groups than it is to show that appeals were made to the fourfold Gospel against the "one-gospel" canon of Marcion or Tatian or the "many-gospel" principle of various Gnostic groups. The relatively free use of Christian writings—both the Gospels and the Pauline letters—among Gnostic groups doubtless prompted orthodox theologians to clarify their understanding of the canon-ical limits of the NT. But the precise connection between Gnostic use of Christian writings and orthodox delimitation of these writings remains largely undefined.

Montanism

As with the Marcionite controversy, a single individual—the self-styled prophet Montanus—was at the center of another controversy within the second-century church. Hailing from Phrygia in west-central Asia Minor, Montanus claimed to be endowed with the Spirit of prophecy. Reported to have experienced moments of ecstatic inspiration, Montanus uttered numerous prophetic oracles that were collected and written down by his followers. Attracted to his charismatic leadership were two women, Priscilla and Maximilla, who reportedly left their husbands to become follow-ers of Montanus. From its earliest stages, the "Phrygian heresy" developed a reputation for allowing women to exercise the gift of prophecy and play prominent leadership roles. The movement's strong eschatological thrust was reflected in prophecies anticipating that the new Jerusalem would soon descend to the earth and be located at Pepuza, a small town northeast of Hierapolis near the Maeander River. This eschatological fervor was accompanied by a strong ascetic emphasis that eventually took an even more rigorous form in North Africa, where second marriages were forbidden and other forms of lax behavior were condemned. Whether Montanus began to prophesy around 156 C.E. or some years later is disputed,[54] but the movement spread quickly, reaching Rome and North Africa, where, around the year 206 C.E., it attracted Tertullian to its ranks. [See Expanded CD Version pp. 849–51: *The Threat of Montanism*]

Numerous strategies were used to combat the claims of the Montanists. Their opponents pointed to the non-fulfillment of their predictions[55] and charged them with behavior that did not conform to that of earlier prophets like Agabus or the daughters of Philip.[56] Critics also noted their numerous moral shortcomings, such as their mercenary interests and love for fine clothing, which directly violated Jesus' instructions that prophets should travel light and live simply.[57] While the Montanist controversy may not show the church appealing to an already well-formulated Christian canon as a direct strategy for responding to claims of new prophetic revelation, it does reveal some of the dynamics that were at work when traditional sources of authority were challenged by charismatic individuals operating with a strong sense of prophetic authority. If, as the evidence suggests, Montanist churches produced their own writings that contained the prophetic oracles of their leaders, and if these writings functioned as Scripture within those communities, to that degree a competing view of Scripture was present. Given the use made of the Gospel of John, Revelation, and Hebrews within Montanist circles, and the efforts of anti-Montanist writers to disqualify these Christian Scriptures in various ways, we know that the debate in some cases focused on the question of which writings belonged to the canon. From the anonymous anti-Montanist author mentioned by Eusebius we can also conclude that a fairly well-defined sense of the Christian canon was operative within the debate and that this "canon" was functioning as a norm by which other Christian writings were being measured. To some degree, the writings of the "new covenant" were an inhibiting force against more recent revelations attributed to the Spirit. In this limited sense, the Montanist controversy was a catalyst that prompted the church to refine its understanding of the nature and limits of authentic prophetic witness.

Criteria of Canonicity

Viewed theologically, the process through which the church clarified the nature and extent of authentic witness to the apostolic gospel may be seen as *an exercise in ecclesial discernment.* Displaying the complexity that typically accompanies theological controversies, the church's debates and decisions about what should constitute the Christian Scriptures surfaced several criteria of canonicity. These criteria were expressed in different ways and in different settings. In some senses, they are interrelated and overlap. Sometimes they are implicit, at other times more explicit. From the tangle of controversy, however, they emerge as discrete criteria. At least four can be identified: (1) inspiration; (2) apostolicity; (3) orthodoxy; and (4) universality.

Inspiration

While inspiration may not have been the sole differentiating criterion for determining the canonical status of a particular writing, it was a crucial consideration. Numerous early Christian writings, such as the Shepherd of Hermas and the *Apocalypse of Peter*, claimed to be divinely inspired. Some NT writings (Revelation) claimed explicit inspiration in a way that other NT writings (Luke-Acts) did not. Claims of inspiration were notoriously difficult to authenticate. If someone claimed to be speaking or writing under the impulse of the Spirit, who could deny it? Since the early church operated with such a strong sense of the Spirit's possession, one of its constant challenges was to distinguish between true and false prophets.

Even so, claims of inspiration were commonly made about the NT writings.[58] Theophilus of Antioch speaks of the "holy prophets who were possessed by the Holy Spirit of God"[59] and includes the Fourth Evangelist as one of "the spirit-bearing men."[60] He also regards both the OT prophets and the Gospels as "inspired by one Spirit of God."[61] Origen's exposition of Scripture presupposes as a matter of principle that the same Spirit who inspired the writings of the OT "did the same thing both with the evangelists and the apostles."[62] In the fourth-century canonical list composed by Amphilochius, bishop of Iconium in Lycaonia, the writings listed are "the most reliable [lit., "unfalsified"] canon of the divinely inspired scriptures" (*houtos apseudestatos kanōn an eiē tōn theopneustōn graphōn*).[63]

While this is only a selection of authors who characterized the NT writings as inspired, it represents a widely held view. Inspiration may not have been the only decisive criterion, but it was a prerequisite for canonicity. *No writing could have been included in the NT canon had it not been regarded as inspired.*

Apostolicity

None of the four Gospels names its author. Of the four, Luke names its addressee—Theophilus—but neither it nor its sequel, the book of Acts, names its author. The thirteen Pauline letters, of course, name the apostle Paul as the letter writer. Hebrews is anonymous. Of the seven Catholic Letters, only two are attributed to an apostle—1–2 Peter. None of the three Johannine letters mentions the name John. The John mentioned as the author of the Apocalypse is identified not as an apostle but as the Seer.

By the second century, however, two of the Gospels are attributed to two of the twelve apostles, Matthew and John. The other two Gospels, Mark and Luke, are attributed to persons closely associated with apostles—Peter and Paul respectively. The anonymous Letter to the Hebrews becomes incorporated into the Pauline corpus and eventually read as a Pauline letter. The Johannine letters and the book of Revelation are attributed to John the apostle, the author of the Fourth Gospel.

The early emergence of these apostolic ascriptions to anonymous writings and the tenacity with which they were defended show the importance of apostolic authorship as a means of vouching for the authority of a given writing. As some of the church's early theological disputes show, apostolicity and canonicity were closely linked. In the Montanist controversy, the apostolic authorship of writings that were heavily used by Montanists, such as the Fourth Gospel, Revelation, and Hebrews, was contested by anti-Montanist writers. Origen rejects the *Gospel of Peter* because it was not composed by the apostle Peter—a clear appeal to the criterion of apostolicity. Acceptance or rejection of the Letter to the Hebrews often hinged on how strong a case could be made for its Pauline authorship, or at least its authorship by someone closely linked with Paul, such as Luke, Apollos, or Priscilla.

Apostolic authorship was closely related to canonical credibility. If a writing were demonstrably apostolic, it could be linked more closely with Jesus himself, the one who called the Twelve and made an appearance to Paul. Besides establishing a direct connection between apostolic witness and Christ himself, the criterion of apostolicity is a test of chronological and geographical proximity. Determining apostolic authorship was often a matter of deciding how close in time and place a writing (or the traditions lying behind a writing) was to the originating figure, Christ.

Orthodoxy

It also mattered whether a writing conformed to what was variously referred to as the "canon of faith," the "rule of faith," or the "truth of the gospel." Since "orthodoxy" literally means "straight teaching or belief," what is envisioned here are theological beliefs that conform to the teachings of Jesus and the apostles, and to the original form of the gospel that gained widespread acceptance across a range of churches.

An appeal to orthodoxy has already been mentioned: the decision by Serapion, bishop of Antioch, to disallow the use of the *Gospel of Peter* in the churches under his jurisdiction because it contained Docetic teaching. Convinced that the apostolic rule of faith was preserved by a succession of apostles, teachers, evangelists, and bishops, Irenaeus applied the test of orthodoxy with a vengeance. The four Gospels, he insisted, conformed to and embodied the apostolic faith, whereas the gospels used among heretical groups did not.

The criterion of orthodoxy sought to determine a writing's *theological cogency*. Was the writing theologically acceptable to the faith of the church? Did it constitute a persuasive, powerful statement of the faith? The Letter to the Hebrews was finally accepted in both the East and West because it made a convincing case for the faith.

Catholicity or Universal Usage

Writings that gained early and wide acceptance in all regions of the church, both East and West, such as the Gospels, the Pauline letters, 1 Peter, 1 John, and Revelation (initially), were read as Scripture, cited as authoritative, and included in canonical lists. Those that were unable to pass the test of universal usage, such as Hebrews and Revelation (after its status became disputed), had a more difficult time achieving the authoritative status of the writings that were widely accepted. Augustine provides one of the clearest statements of the criterion of catholicity. To the Christian reader, he writes,

> Now, in regard to the canonical Scriptures, [the skillful interpreter] must follow the judgment of the greater number of catholic churches; and among these, of course, a high place must be given to such as have been thought worthy to be the seat of an apostle and to receive epistles. Accordingly, among the canonical Scriptures he will judge according to the following standard: *to prefer those that are received by all the catholic churches to those which some do not receive*. Among those, again, which are not received by all, he will prefer such as have the sanction of the greater number and those of greater authority, to such as are held by the smaller number and those of less authority. If, however, he shall find that some books are held by the greater number of churches, and others by the churches of greater authority (though this is not a very likely thing to happen), I think that in such a case the authority on the two sides is to be looked upon as equal.[64]

[See Expanded CD Version pp. 855–56: *Employing the Criteria: A Case Study— The Muratorian Fragment*]

Canon: Some Implications for the Church

Biblical scholarship over the last century or so has called for reading the NT like any other ancient writing. Placing the NT writings within their larger Greco-Roman context arose out of the Renaissance and Enlightenment as a corrective to dogmatic construals of the NT. While this has been a helpful corrective, in its more extreme forms this approach downplays the sacred character ascribed to these texts within Christian communities. By including Christian writings within a canonical list, the church ascribes to them a sacred character that enables believers to regard these texts as "Holy Writ." When Theophilus of Antioch cites the Gospel of Matthew as "holy word" (*hagios logos*), he affirms the sacred quality of this text for himself and his community at Antioch.[65]

Once a community of faith accepts the OT and NT writings as canonical, several implications follow:

1. *By recognizing the overall structure of the Christian canon, the church acknowledges its multiple sources of authority.* The Christian Scriptures comprise the Old and New Testaments. With this two-part canon, the church firmly embraces the Jewish Scriptures as read through the lens of Christian experience and faith. By adopting the Scriptures of the synagogue, the church made an extraordinarily novel move—without parallel in any other major religion. But more than that, the church decided to supplement the Jewish Scriptures with a carefully selected set of Christian writings. By joining these two sets of writings, the church formed a unique set of Scriptures. By insisting that Christ cannot be understood apart from the OT narrative, the church embraced the OT as the pre-history to Christ.

Each testament also comprises several parts. The OT is designated as "law and prophets" or "law, prophets, and writings," or sometimes simply as "the prophets."

Similarly, the NT consists of "Gospel" and "Apostle," a distinction apparently intro-duced by Marcion but also found in Irenaeus, Origen, and other Christian writers.[66] By "Gospel" is meant the four canonical Gospels; by "Apostle" is usually meant every-thing else, especially the writings of Paul. In either case, Jesus Christ is the primary subject matter of all twenty-seven writings. [**See Expanded CD Version pp. 856–57: *Plurality of Witnesses: Patristic Evidence*]**

These examples suggest that *the church listens to (and for) the word of God through a plurality of canonical voices.*

2. *The church listens to the Jewish Scriptures as a prophetic witness to Christ and looks to them for guidance in the life of faith.* From Judaism, the church inherited the "scripture principle" of appealing to a sacred text as a source of authority. "As the scripture has said . . ." is a defining principle for Jesus himself (John 7:38; cf. Mark 12:24). Paul echoes the sentiments of other NT writers when he claims that "whatever was written in former days" is relevant for Christian instruction (Rom 15:4; cf. 1 Cor 10:11). The consistent practice of appealing to the Jewish Scriptures established the identity of the church as a "people of the book."

By drawing from all parts of the Jewish Scriptures, NT writers represent the sen-timents of the risen Lord who embraces "the law of Moses, the prophets, and the psalms" (Luke 24:44). Even so, some NT writers reflect distinct preferences for certain books or sections of the Bible. The "scripture principle" was firmly established within early Christianity even though the exact limits of the Jewish canon were probably still undefined in the first century C.E. The NT Letter of Jude cites *1 Enoch* as an authori-tative prophetic text (vv. 14–15). The unknown author of the *Epistle of Barnabas* regards the Septuagint texts Wisdom of Solomon and *4 Ezra* as prophetic writings. Epiphanius, bishop of Salamis, concludes his list of NT books by placing the "Wisdoms, I mean Solomon's [Wisdom of Solomon] and Sirach's [Ecclesiasticus]" after the Revelation of John.[67]

Among some early patristic writers, we find a tendency to cite the OT more fre-quently than the NT. The *Epistle of Barnabas* repeatedly refers to OT texts, using over a hundred introductory formulae, and makes scarce use of the NT. In his *Dialogue with Trypho*, Justin relies more heavily on the OT than the NT. Polycarp, bishop of Smyrna, by contrast, cites the NT almost ten times more frequently than the OT. In Clement of Alexandria's thousands of biblical citations, the NT is represented twice as often as the OT. Irenaeus also cites the NT more frequently than the OT.

Whether the citation index among patristic writers favors the use of the OT or the NT, we find them listening to the Jewish Scriptures as an authoritative voice. The OT serves as both a prophetic witness to the Christian gospel and, in the words of Paul, a source of encouragement and hope for Christian readers (Rom 15:4).

3. *The NT canon presupposes Christ as the ultimate norm of Christian belief and prac-tice.* While decisions about the limits of the canon were finally about Christian writings, the decision makers knew that the gospel of Christ is not reducible to words written on a page. The written text may have been the medium of revelation, but it could not be equated simply with the revelation itself. By distinguishing between "gospel" in its primal sense of early Christian preaching and the "rule of faith" that arose out of that preaching, Irenaeus drew attention to the gospel behind the Gospels.

"Gospel," for Irenaeus, did not represent in the first instance the writings of the four evangelists, but something beyond, or behind, the fourfold Gospel. When these writings were titled "The Gospel According to . . ." an apostle or apostolic associate, this meant that each evangelist was rendering a separate account of a common gospel. "Gospel" was not so much a written genre as the living message to which each evangelist bore witness.

There are three senses in which the canon shows the church acknowledging Christ as its ultimate source of authority. First, *the church hears the voice of Christ throughout the NT canon, especially in the four Gospels.* By collecting and recording the sayings and teachings of Christ in their many forms, the early church recognized the a priori authority of "what the Lord says. . . ." Even Paul, who rarely draws on material from the life and ministry of Jesus, acknowledges the primacy of the voice of Christ (1 Thess 4:15; 1 Cor 7:10; 9:14). Echoes of the teachings of Christ are heard throughout Paul's moral teachings (e.g., Rom 12). Christ's teachings are often just below the surface in other NT writings as well (e.g., James 5:12; 1 Pet 2:19–20). At other times, explicit appeal is made to what Christ taught (Acts 20:35).

The pattern that begins in the NT period is also evident in the post-apostolic period. Twice *1 Clement* urges its readers "to remember the words of the Lord Jesus."[68] Ignatius urges the Philadelphians to "do nothing in factiousness," but to behave "after the teaching of Christ."[69] Several times the *Didache* refers to what the Lord commanded.[70] In Ptolemy's *Letter to Flora* (ca. 160 C.E.), the "words of the Savior" are cited as authoritative.[71] Similar respect for "what the Lord taught" is found in Polycarp.[72] The generous use of agrapha among early Christian writings attests the same fondness for citing the voice of Christ, even beyond what is found in the canonical Gospels.

There is a second sense in which Christ is seen as a norm for the church: *The person or character of Christ is regarded as exemplary.* Besides appealing to Christ's teachings, the *Didache* also adduces the "ways of the Lord" as instructive for its readers.[73] Similarly, Polycarp commends Jesus' exemplary endurance.[74] Whether Christ's story was portrayed as a cosmic narrative (Phil 2:6–11) or as an earthly story, as is the case in the four Gospels, it was understood by the church as a defining norm by which the life of discipleship could be measured. Luke constructs the story in Acts to show that the lives of leading figures in the church correspond to the life and character of Jesus in the Gospel of Luke. The action of Christ at the Last Supper becomes determinative for the church's eucharistic practice (1 Cor 11:23–26).

By canonizing the four Gospels, with their lavish supply of stories about Jesus interwoven with his teachings, the church sketched a character profile of Jesus that became normative. The "faith of Jesus" also becomes a recurrent emphasis in the other NT writings. In the Letter to the Hebrews, for instance, Jesus' sufferings "in the days of his flesh" serve as an experience with which the readers of Hebrews, who have also suffered (10:32–34), can identify. Standing at the end of a long line of heroic figures, Jesus becomes the epitome of faithful endurance (12:1–2). First Peter proposes the suffering of Christ as an example for its readers, so that they might "follow in his steps" (2:21).

Christ also functions as the church's norm in a third way: *He is the One to whom the gospel of Christ bears witness.* Whether the gospel of Christ is summarized in brief formulations expressing what was originally preached and confessed in the church, or whether it is understood in its more fully elaborated, narrative form found in the four Gospels, it is experienced as saving event and saving story. In some cases, the gospel of Christ concentrates on the web of events around his death and resurrection. Often the formulaic summaries of the gospel found in the Pauline letters focus on this part of the "Christ event." At other times, the gospel of Christ can encompass all that preceded and followed his death and resurrection. So understood, the "story of Christ" can be told and experienced as a grand salvation narrative.

Early Christian writers underscore this distinction between the written Gospels and the *living gospel* to which they bear witness. In a highly revealing passage, Ignatius insists that, for Christians, the gospel experienced as saving event has priority over the written record that rehearses that event. For his Jewish Christian readers at Philadelphia, the Jewish Scriptures were the "charters" or "archives" to which one should make final appeal. "If we do not find it in the charters [lit., "archives," *archeia*]," they argued, "we do not believe it in the gospel [*euangelion*]." To them Ignatius retorted, "As for me, the charters [*archeia*] are Jesus Christ; the inviolable charters [*ta athikta archeia*] are his cross and death and resurrection, and the faith that is through them."[75]

Something similar is at stake in Papias's insistence that the oral tradition was a more valuable form of witness than the written tradition. "For I did not think that information from books," he writes, "would help me so much as the utterances of a living and surviving voice."[76] Tertullian also recognizes the priority of the oral gospel by insisting that the "rule of faith," the common, fundamental belief of the church, was orally received by the churches from the apostles and transmitted from generation to generation as the baptismal creed.[77]

By acknowledging the full range of NT writings, the church embraces both "Gospel" and "Apostle," not in the early sense of a two-part collection but in a redefined sense. "Gospel" stands behind all of the writings, either in the narrative form of the Gospels or the kerygmatic form that often serves as the presupposition of the epistolary writings. "Apostle" no longer means one of the Twelve in the strict sense, but designates a faithful transmitter of the gospel of Christ. As such, it can refer to an individual author, an anonymous editor, or even to a community of believers who faithfully collected, shaped, and transmitted the Jesus tradition.

4. *Even with all of their variety of literary forms and theological perspectives, the NT writings display recognizable patterns of theological coherence without imposing a gray monotony of theological uniformity.* By limiting the NT canon to these twenty-seven writings, the church excluded some unacceptable theological viewpoints. Numerous Gnostic gospels are attacked and rejected by Irenaeus and Epiphanius because they stood outside the pale of orthodox belief. When Serapion, bishop of Antioch, finally decided against the *Gospel of Peter* for use in worship because of its Docetic teachings, he established a clear doctrinal boundary.

And yet the twenty-seven canonical writings reflect considerable theological diversity. Clement's characterization of the Fourth Gospel as "the spiritual gospel" over against the other three Gospels is a tacit recognition of the theological distance separating John from the Synoptic Gospels. Nor was the early church naïve about the theological differences reflected in other parts of the canon. The distinctiveness of the

Pauline gospel was easily recognized, as were the many different forms in which it was appropriated by both orthodox and heretical claimants of the Pauline legacy.

By choosing writings that represented a broad spectrum of theological diversity, the church embraced the principle of *limited theological pluralism*. Even with the variety of theological perspectives reflected in the NT canon, there is an overall pattern of theological coherence discernible throughout the writings.

5. *The Christian Scriptures and the Christian church are symbiotically related.* Under the influence and guidance of God's Spirit, the church produced the NT. Yet the church submits to the NT as a uniquely authoritative set of writings that bear witness to Christ. As such, they provide resources for spiritual renewal and moral guidance. The Christian Scriptures acquire *functional authority* for the church as the church acknowledges their *intrinsic authority* as normative witnesses through which it hears the word of God. Scripture has an inescapable relational dimension. A text can function as Scripture only when it is recognized as authoritative within a prescribed community of faith. By adopting a canon of Scriptures, a community of faith agrees to live by them and embody their vision of life.

6. *As the written form of apostolic witness to the gospel, the Christian Scriptures have a unique role in the church's worship and ministries.* Justin's description of an early Christian service reflects the central role that Scripture plays within Christian worship: ". . . the memoirs of apostles or the writings of the prophets are read, for as long as time permits. Then the reader stops and the leader instructs by word of mouth, and exhorts to the imitation of these good things. Then we all stand together and pray."[78]

When the Scriptures are read, proclaimed, expounded, and studied as the living Word for the people of God, the possibility is created, once again, that the Christ of faith can be experienced anew. Even though the gospel of Christ may be encoded in the written words of Scripture, it is not reducible to the printed page. The community of faith may embody the gospel in its various practices, but it regularly gathers for worship to hear the words of Scripture activate the Living Word.

By acknowledging the OT and NT, and the multiple components of each, and reading them as one book relating a single coherent story, the church continues to listen to the several voices that guided the apostolic church: the voice of God as heard through Jewish Scripture; the voice of Christ as heard through the Gospels; and the voice of Christ's apostles and earliest disciples as they bore witness to Christ. Through these several voices, the church heard (and hears) the voice of God's Spirit as mediated through the law, prophets, and writings; through Christ as both incarnate and living Word; and through Christ's church, both its original, influential prophetic witnesses and succeeding generations of discerning witnesses. In these several senses, the Christian Scriptures comprising the OT and NT function as the church's book.

[See Expanded CD Version pp. 871–89: *Appendix 1: Canonical Lists in the Ancient Church* and *Appendix 2: Patristic Comments on the Gospel*]

Notes

1. For the following treatment, I rely heavily on (and draw liberally from) Bruce M. Metzger, *The Canon of the New Testament: Its Origin, Development, and Significance*. Clarendon paperbacks. Oxford: Clarendon Press, 1997 (1987).

2. The following section draws from Metzger, "History of the Word Κανών," Appendix 1 in *Canon of the NT*, 289–93.

3. *Eth. nic.* 3.4.5 (1113ᵃ34).

4. *Nat.* 34.55.

5. Dionysius of Halicarnassus, *Pomp.* 3.16.5.

6. Paul also uses the term three other times in a single passage (2 Cor 10:13–16) to refer to the geographical area of his missionary assignment. *Kanōn* also occurs in Phil 3:16 in some manuscripts.

7. *1 Clem.* 7.2.

8. *Strom.* 4.15.98. Elsewhere, Clement speaks of "the rule of the truth" (*kata ton tēs alētheias kanona*, *Strom.* 6.15.124). Also see Irenaeus, *Haer.* 3.2.2; Eusebius, *Hist. eccl.* 3.32.7; 4.23.4; 5.24.6; 28.13; 7.30.7.

9. *Decrees of the Synod of Nicaea*, No. 18.3.2.

10. *Epist. Fest.* 39.

11. See, however, Eusebius, *Hist. eccl.* 3.25.6; also 5.28.13.

12. *Iambi ad Seleucum*, line 319.

13. *Apocriticus* 4.proem.

14. For the use of "(new) testament," see Irenaeus, *Haer.* 4.28.1–2; also 4.15.2; Clement of Alexandria, *Strom.* 2.6 (*ANF* 2:354), Tertullian, *Pud.* 1; *Prax.* 15, and Origen, *Comm. Jo.* 5.8.

15. The text is preserved in Eusebius, *Hist. eccl.* 5.16.2–17.4.

16. Influential figures, such as Hilary of Poitiers (ca. 315–367 C.E.) and Lucifer of Calaris (died ca. 371 C.E.), who were banished to the East, appear to have been influenced positively toward writings otherwise suspect in the West, such as Hebrews, James, and 2 Peter. Through Jerome's efforts, the Athanasian canon (367 C.E.) was accepted in the West, where it was probably adopted formally by Pope Damasus (382 C.E.), certainly by Pope Innocent I (405 C.E.), and also embraced by Augustine (*Doctr. chr.* 2.13).

17. Yet another anomaly occurs in the twelfth century, when a Syrian scribe prepared a copy of the Harclean Syriac NT that presents another variation. It includes the four Gospels, Acts and the seven Catholic Letters, and the Pauline letters, including Hebrews. Inserted after the Gospels, however, is an account of Christ's passion based on the four Gospels. More surprising is the inclusion of *1–2 Clement* between Acts and the Pauline letters. The scribe's system of dividing and numbering *1–2 Clement* suggests that he regarded them as canonical. Not surprising, however, is his omission of Revelation. How widely this particular configuration was recognized or used is not known.

18. See Metzger, *Canon of the NT*, 220–21.

19. Luther placed Hebrews, James, Jude, and Revelation in a separate section at the end of his NT, an ordering that was continued in early English translations, beginning with William Tyndale's English translation of the NT (1525).

20. In the Lutheran tradition, by contrast, no formalized statements concerning the limits of the biblical canon occurred in creedal formulations—a theologically understandable decision, given Lutheran reluctance to equate divine revelation with the biblical writings themselves.

21. Although Revelation is omitted from the Synod of Laodicea's list of NT writings, it was included by Cyril Lucar (1570–1638), patriarch of Constantinople.

22. Eusebius, *Hist. eccl.* 4.29.6.

23. Jerome, *Comm. Tit.* Prologue.

24. *Autol.* 3.14.

25. *Comm. Matt.* as quoted by Eusebius, *Hist. eccl.* 6.25.4. Cf. *Hom. Luc.* 1.

26. In *Hom. Luc.* 1, Origen also affirms exclusive use of the four canonical Gospels and rejects several heretical gospels: *According to the Egyptians, According to the Twelve Apostles, According to Thomas, According to Matthias*, and a gospel written by Basilides.

27. Eusebius, *Hist. eccl.* 6.25.11–14.

28. Origen knows the doubtful status of 2 Peter and 2–3 John (Eusebius, *Hist. eccl.* 6.25.8–10); also of James (*Comm. Jo.* 20.66) and Jude (*Comm. Matt.* 17.30).

29. Eusebius, *Hist. eccl.* 3.25.1–7.

30. *Barn.* 16.5–6, citing *1 En.* 89:56, 66–67.

31. *Cult. fem.* 1.3; also *Res.* 32.1.

32. *Barn.* 6.7.

33. *Barn.* 12.1.

34. Eusebius, *Hist. eccl.* 3.3.6; Athanasius, *Ep. fest.* 39.7.

35. *Haer.* 4.20.2, introducing Herm. *Mand.* 1.1 as *graphē* (confirmed by Eusebius, *Hist. eccl.* 5.8.7).

36. *Strom.* 1.29.181 (*ANF* 2:341) introduces Herm. *Vis.* 3.4.3, "Divinely, therefore, the power which spoke to Hermas by revelation, said. . . ."

37. The reference occurs in a sermon against dice-throwers (*Adversus Aleatores*) attributed to Cyprian (died ca. 258 C.E.), bishop of Carthage. In chapter 2, the text cites Herm. *Sim.* 9.31.5–6.

38. *Comm. Rom.* 10.31; also cf. *Hom. Luc.* 35.3; *Princ.* 1.3.3; 4.1.11. Origen thinks that the Hermas of Rom 16:14 is the author of the Shepherd. Also, see Eusebius, *Hist. eccl.* 3.3.6.

39. *Vir. ill.* 10.

40. *Pud.* 20; also cf. *Pud.* 10.

41. *Hist. eccl.* 3.25.5; cf. 3.3.7.

42. *Marc.* 4.2.

43. Pol. *Phil.* 6.3; see Tertullian, *Prax.* 15.

44. *Haer.* 3.11.7.

45. *Haer.* 3.11.9.

46. *Haer.* 3.11.9.

47. *Pan.* 26.13.2.

48. *Haer.* 3.11.8.

49. *Haer.* 3.11.8.

50. *Haer.* 3.11.8.

51. *Haer.* 3.11.8.

52. *Haer.* 3.11.8.

53. Pol. *Phil* 3.2.

54. Epiphanius, *Pan.*48.1.2 supports 156–57; Eusebius, *Hist. eccl.* 4.27.1 implies a date in the 170s C.E.

55. Eusebius, *Hist. eccl.* 5.16.19; 18.1.

56. Eusebius, *Hist. eccl.* 5.17.2–3.

57. Eusebius, *Hist. eccl.* 5.18.2–14; see Matt 10:9, 10; cf. Matt 12:33.

58. See, e.g., *1 Clem.* 47.3; Irenaeus, *Haer.* 2.28.2.

59. *Autol.* 3.17 (*ANF* 2:116).

60. *Autol.* 2.22, citing John 1:1 (*ANF* 2:103).

61. *Autol.* 3.12.

62. *Princ.* 4.16; also Preface 8.

63. *Iambi ad Seleucum* 318–19.

64. *Doctr. chr.* 2.8.12 (*NPNF*[1] 2:538), emphasis added.

65. *Autol.* 3.13.

66. See Tertullian, *Prax.* 15.

67. *Pan.* 3.1. (6.) 76.5 (See Frank Williams, trans., *The Panarion of Epiphanius of Salamis* [2 vols.; Leiden: Brill, 1994–1997], 2:522).

68. In *1 Clem.* 13.2 we find a cluster of phrases echoing Matt 5:7; 6:14–15; 7:1–2, 12; and Luke 6:31; *1 Clem.* 46.7–8 recalls Mark 9:42; Matt 18:6–7; and Luke 17:1–2.

69. Ign. *Phld.* 8.2.

70. *Did.* 8.2; see 15.4.

71. See Ptolemy, *Letter to Flora* 33.3.5; 33.3.8; 33.4.1; 33.4.3.

72. Pol. *Phil.* 2.2, 3; 7.1, 2.

73. *Did.* 11.8.

74. Pol. *Phil.* 8.2.

75. Ign. *Phld.* 8.2.

76. Eusebius, *Hist. eccl.* 3.39.4.
77. *Praescr.* 13; also *Virg.* 1; *Prax.* 2.
78. *1 Apol.* 67.3–5.

Bibliography

Abraham, William J. *The Divine Inspiration of Holy Scripture.* Oxford: Oxford University Press, 1981.

Achtemeier, Paul. *The Inspiration of Scripture: Problems and Proposals.* Philadelphia: Westminster, 1980.

Aland, Kurt. *The Problem of the New Testament Canon.* Contemporary Studies in Theology 2. London: Mowbray, 1962.

Auwers, J.-M., and H. J. de Jonge. *The Biblical Canons.* Bibliotheca Ephemeridum Theologicarum Lovaniensium 163. Leuven: University Press/Peeters, 2003.

Barr, James. *Holy Scripture: Canon, Authority, Criticism.* Philadelphia: Westminster, 1983.

Barton, John. *Holy Writings, Sacred Text: The Canon in Early Christianity.* Louisville: Westminster John Knox, 1997.

———. *People of the Book? The Authority of the Bible in Christianity.* Louisville: Westminster John Knox, 1988.

Bruce, F. F. *The Canon of Scripture.* Downers Grove: InterVarsity, 1988.

Campenhausen, Hans von. *The Formation of the Christian Bible.* Translated by John Austin Baker. London: Black, 1972 (1968).

Childs, Brevard S. *The New Testament as Canon: An Introduction.* London: SCM, 1984; Philadelphia: Fortress, 1985.

Evans, C. F. *Is 'Holy Scripture' Christian? and Other Questions.* London: SCM, 1971.

Gamble, Harry Y. *Books and Readers in the Early Church: A History of Early Christian Texts.* New Haven: Yale University Press, 1995.

———. *The New Testament Canon: Its Making and Meaning.* Guides to Biblical Scholarship. Philadelphia: Fortress, 1985.

Gnuse, R. *The Authority of the Bible: Theories of Inspiration, Revelation, and the Canon of Scripture.* New York: Paulist, 1985.

Goodspeed, Edgar J. *The Formation of the New Testament.* Chicago: University of Chicago, 1926.

Graham, William A. *Beyond the Written Word: Oral Aspects of Scripture in the History of Religion.* Cambridge: Cambridge University Press, 1987.

Grant, Robert M. *The Formation of the New Testament.* New York: Harper, 1965.

———. "The New Testament Canon." Pages 284–308 in vol. 1 of *The Cambridge History of the Bible: From the Beginnings to Jerome.* Edited by P. R. Ackroyd and C. F. Evans. Cambridge: Cambridge University Press, 1970.

Hahnemann, Geoffrey Mark. *The Muratorian Fragment and the Development of the Canon.* Oxford Theological Monographs. Oxford: Clarendon, 1992.

Harnack, Adolf. *The Origin of the New Testament and the Most Important Consequences of the New Creation.* Translated by J. R. Wilkinson. Crown Theological Library 45. New Testament Series 6. London: Williams & Norgate, 1925.

Kelsey, David H. *The Uses of Scripture in Recent Theology*. Philadelphia: Fortress/London: SCM, 1975.

Knox, John. *Marcion and the New Testament: An Essay in the Early History of the Canon*. Chicago: University of Chicago, 1942.

Kümmel, Werner G. "The Formation of the Canon of the New Testament." Pages 475–510 in *Introduction to the New Testament*. Rev. ed. Translated by Howard C. Kee. Nashville: Abingdon, 1975.

Levering, Miriam, ed. *Rethinking Scripture: Essays from a Comparative Perspective*. Albany: State University of New York Press, 1989.

Marxsen, Willi. *The New Testament as the Church's Book*. Translated by James E. Mignard. Philadelphia: Fortress, 1972 (1966).

McDonald, Lee M. *The Formation of the Christian Biblical Canon*. Rev. ed. Peabody: Hendrickson, 1995.

Metzger, Bruce M. *The Canon of the New Testament: Its Origin, Development, and Significance*. Oxford: Clarendon Press, 1997 (1987).

Moule, C. F. D. *The Birth of the New Testament*. Black's New Testament Commentaries. 3d edition. London: Black, 1981 (1966).

Smith, Wilfred Cantwell. *What Is Scripture? A Comparative Approach*. Minneapolis: Fortress, 1993.

Sundberg, Albert C., Jr. *The Old Testament of the Early Church*. Harvard Theological Studies 20. Cambridge: Harvard University Press, 1964.

Trobisch, David. *The First Edition of the New Testament*. Oxford: Oxford University Press, 2000.

Westcott, Brooke Foss. *The Bible in the Church*. 2d ed. London: Macmillan, 1913 (1st ed., 1864).

———. *A General Survey of the History of the Canon of the New Testament*. 7th ed. London: Macmillan, 1896 (1st ed., 1855).

Index

Acts of Andrew: 578

Acts of the Apostles:
apologetic (answering charges), 239–40;
and apostolic roles, 233–34;
ascension of Christ, 244 (references);
authorship, 34, 158–59, 584, 586;
and Baur, F C, 226;
canonical function, 34;
and the church, 243–44, 248–51;
Christology, 244–48;
date, 227;
deistic views of, 225–26;
as divine drama, 228;
ecclesiology, 243–44;
genre of, 227–32;
geography of, 233–34;
as history, 229–32;
and Israel, 242–43;
and Jesus, 241–42, 244–47;
and *kerygma*, 238–39;
and lectionary usage, 227;
and literary structure, 233;
and messianic vision, 247–48;
modern views of, 226–27;
and novels, ancient, 229, 232;
and OT interpretation, 239, 241–43, 246;
patristic views of, 225;
and Paul, 251–54;
and Pentecost, 249–50;
prosōpopoeia, 238;
purpose of, 227, 229–32;
and sermons, 246–47;
sources of, 226, 228–29;
and speeches, 236–38;
and the Spirit, 240, 248–51;
and textual traditions, 227;
as a theological narrative, 228, 240, 248, 251;
"we" passages, 158 (references), 226
(Acts of) John: 578
(Acts of) the other apostles: 578–79
Acts of Paul: 578
Addai, Doctrine of: 577

Aesop: 450
Agrapha: 579, 590
Ambrose of Milan: 285n6; 481n7
"Ambrosiaster": 283, 301n7
Amphilochius of Iconium: 190, 573, 586
Angel worship: 397
Annet, Peter: and Acts, 226
"Antioch episode": 335–36, 345
Anton, Paul: and the Pastorals, 441n5
Apocalypse of Abraham: 536, 551
Apocalypse of Peter: 29, 31, 36n10, 511, 578–79, 586
Apocalypse of Zephaniah: 536
Apocalyptic: 536–41;
and Galatians, 337–38, 340;
and Revelation, 537–39, 551–52;
worldview of, 536–37
Apollonius of Tyana: 265
Apostles' Creed: 227
Aquinas, Thomas: 420
Aristotle: 388, 394, 449, 572
Athanasius of Alexandria: 406n5;
canonical list in *Thirty-Ninth Festal Letter*, 27–28;
and the Catholic Letters, 469;
and the Johannine letters, 531n12;
and 1 John, 531n5;
and the Letter of James, 472;
and Romans, 32;
and the Shepherd of Hermas, 30, 573, 594n34;
and the Thessalonian letters, 301n8
Augustine of Hippo:
and the Athanasian canon, support of, 593n16;
and the book of Revelation, 535, 548;
and canon, criterion of catholicity, 588;
and faith and works, Paul and James, 481–82n11;
and the Gospel of John, 54, 192;
and the Gospel of Matthew, 192;
and the Gospels, 40–41, 47, 54nn1&9;
Harmony of the Gospels, 40;
and the Johannine letters, 519–20, 528;
and the Letter of James, 477, 481n7, 481–82n11;
and Paul, 281–83;
and Pelagius, 281;
and relationship of the Gospels (chart), 41

Index

Barth, Karl: 104, 282, 368
2 Baruch: 536, 551
3 Baruch: 536, 551
Baur, Ferdinand Christian: 47, 80, 225–26
Bede (the Venerable): 517, 531n5
Belgic Confession: 577
Bengel, Johannes Albrecht: 420
"Bible," etymology: 574–75
Bigg, Charles: 503
Bonaventure, St: 78
Bornkamm, Günther: 90–91, 94, 99;
  and historical–critical method, 90
Bultmann, Rudolf: 58, 64, 71, 81, 87–89, 89–92, 94, 282;
  and the book of Revelation, 564;
  and dialectical theology, 89;
  and form criticism, 88–89;
  and Gentile Christianity, 92;
  and Jesus, 87–89;
  and theological vision of, 89
Bunyan, John: 445

Cadbury, Henry: 98
Caird, George B: 158
Callimachus: 426
Calvin, John:
  and the Gospel of John, 192;
  and Gospels harmony, 40
Canonization, process of:
  and *Addai, Doctrine of*, 577;
  and agrapha, 579;
  and *Apocalypse of Peter*, 579, 586;
  and apostolicity, 586–87;
  and authorial consciousness, 575;
  "canon," etymology of, 572–73;
  and catholicity, 587–88;
  and Christ, 589–90;
  and confessional statements, 577;
  and consensus, 576, 578;
  and *3 Corinthians*, 579;
  criteria for determining, 585–88;
  developmental stages, theory of, 575–76;
  and ecclesial discernment, 585;
  and the *Epistle to the Laodiceans*, 579;
  and Ethiopian Christianity, 579–80;
  Eusebius's fourfold classification of early Christian writings, 578;
  and fluidity, 578–80;
  and the fourth century, 576–77;
  and functional authority, 592;
  and Gnosticism, 583–84, 591;
  and inspiration, 586;
  and "localized preferences," 576;
  and Marcion, 581–83;
  and Montanism, 584–85;
  and non-canonical Gospels, 579;
  and orthodoxy, 587;
  and the Reformation, 577;
  and the Shepherd of Hermas, 579, 586;
  and Syrian Christianity, 577;
  and theological cogency, 587;
  and theological crises, 580–85;
  and the Trullan Synod, 579
Catholic Letters: 469–70;
  canonical arrangement, 35;

canonical position, 31–32
Cerinthus: 522
Chrysostom, John: 333
  and the Acts of the Apostles, 225;
  and Galatians, 333;
  and the Gospel of Matthew, 129, 131;
  and the Pastoral Letters, 421;
  and Philemon, 386, 390n7;
  and slavery, 390n18;
  and the Thessalonian letters, 301nn6&7
Cicero: 265, 267, 489
Claudius (the Emperor): 349, 541
1 Clement, 305, 348:
  and the Ethiopian canon, 579;
  and Hebrews, 464n3;
  and the Johannine letters, 531n8;
  and Jesus' words, 590;
  and the Pastorals, 424, 441n6;
  and Paul, 348;
  and the Syrian church, 593n17
Clement of Alexandria: 190;
  and the Acts of the Apostles, 258n4;
  and the *Apocalypse of Peter*, 36n10;
  and biblical citations, 589;
  and the book of Revelation, 543;
  and the failure to cite the Letter of James, 481n6;
  and Hebrews, 448;
  and the Johannine letters, 520;
  and John as the last Gospel written, 199;
  and John as the "spiritual gospel," 190, 192, 199, 591;
  and the Letter of Jude, 508n5;
  and Marcion, 581;
  and the Pastoral Letters, 421;
  and Paul, 282;
  and 1 Peter, 499n28;
  and the rule of faith, 573;
  and the Shepherd of Hermas, 579;
  and a theory of Gospel origins, 41;
  and the use of Colossians by Gnostics, 406n6
Clement of Rome:
  and the Ethiopian canon, 579;
  and Hebrews, 447, 454, 464nn3&9;
  and the rule of faith, 573
Codex Claromontanus: 220n3, 579
Colossians, Letter to the:
  authorship of, 393–96;
  and the Christ hymn, 400–2, 406n4;
  Christology, 400–2;
  cosmic perspective of, 393–94, 400, 402, 404;
  and Ephesians, 34, 412;
  epistolary features of, 392;
  and Gnosticism, 406n6;
  imagery of, 399–402;
  and opponents, 396–98;
  purpose of, 398;
  and polemical rhetoric, 397;
  stylistic features of, 392–93;
  theological features of, 393;
  theological vision of, 398–405;
  and Timothy as author, 394
Corinthian letters (as a group):
  and the Acts of the Apostles, 306–7;
  and Apollos, 306;
  Christ's death, 324–26;
  and the collection, 326;

and compositional problems, 305;
and congregational ministry, 317–30;
and the Corinthian congregation, 303–7;
and corporate identity, 314–16;
and the correspondence, 304;
covenants, old and new, 320–22;
epistemology of the cross, 311–13;
historical reconstruction, 308–10;
historical setting, 304;
and letters of recommendation, 319;
literary structure, 269 (1 Cor);
and new creation, 325;
and Pauline theology, 305, 310–13, 317–18;
Paul's founding visit, 306;
Paul's opponents, 308, 321, 324, 326–29;
and Paul's personality, 304;
and Paul's theology of ministry, 318–26;
and "proto–Gnosticism," 307;
and resurrection, 316;
and sociological analysis, 305, 307;
and Titus, 308
3 Corinthians: 577, 579, 584
Council(s) of Carthage:
  acceptance of the Letter of James, 472;
  canonical list, 28;
  and Johannine letters, 531n12
Council, First Vatican: 577
Council of Hippo: acceptance of the Letter of James, 472
Council of Laodicea:
  canonical list, 28, 577;
  and Johannine letters, 531n12;
  omission of Revelation, 32, 593n21;
  and Thessalonian letters, 301n8
Council of Trent: decision about canon, 577
Cullmann, Oscar: 39
Cyprian of Carthage: 594n37
Cyril of Jerusalem: omission of Revelation in his
  canonical list, 32, 564

Deissmann, Adolf: 266–67
Demetrius *(On Style)*: 263
Deuteronomic History: 231
Diatribe: 265, 270, 349–50, 472
Dibelius, Martin: 64, 71, 225
Didache: 28, 32, 424, 531n8, 578, 590
Dionysius of Alexandria:
  and the book of Revelation, 564
Dionysius of Halicarnassus: 230
Docetism/Docetists: 89, 211, 522, 583, 587, 591
Dodd, C H: 409
Domitian: 541, 543, 560, 565nn2&6

Early Christian centers: *see* Jesus Tradition
Ebionites: 583
Edesius of Tyre: 579
Eichhorn, Johann Gottfried, 71; originator of sayings
  source idea, 55–56n28
1 Enoch:
  angels as heavenly mediators in, 406n3;
  and apocalyptic, 536, 539;
  and *Epistle of Barnabas,* 578;
  and Ethiopian Bible, 579;
  and opponents in Pastorals, 429;
  Tertullian's high regard for, 578;

use in the Letter of Jude, 504–5, 508, 509n8, 589;
use in Renan's *Life of Jesus,* 82
2 Enoch:
  and apocalyptic, 536;
  and heavenly ascents, 538
Ephesian imprisonment hypothesis: 34; 372–73; 381n6
Ephesians, Letter to the:
  addressees, 275, 412;
  authorship of, 280, 413;
  and the church, 411–12, 414–18;
  as circular letter, 412–13;
  and Colossians, 34, 409–11, 414–15, 417–18;
  distinctive vocabulary, 410;
  eschatology of, 403, 411;
  and exaltation, 415–16;
  function within the Pauline corpus, 413;
  genre of, 412–13;
  and Gnosticism, 406n6;
  "in the heavenly places," 410 (references), 415, 418n3;
  Jews and Gentiles in, 401, 412;
  literary structure, 270, 409–10, 416–17;
  and Marcion (=Letter to the Laodiceans), 412;
  mood of, 409;
  moral vision of, 413, 416–18;
  and the "new humanity," 411, 416;
  post-Pauline perspective, 413;
  sectarian outlook, 416–18;
  stylistic features of, 410;
  time of composition, 277;
  title of, 412
Epictetus: 417
Epicurus: letters of, 265
Epicureans/Epicureanism: 513
Epimenides: 426
Epiphanius: 583, 591;
  and his NT canon list, 589;
  and testimony for Montanism, 594n54
Epistle of Barnabas: 578–79, 589
Epistle to the Laodiceans: 380n1, 579, 584
Erasmus of Rotterdam: 420
Ethiopian Church: canon of, 36n1, 579–80
Eusebius of Caesarea: 30–31
  and anonymous anti–Montanist writer, 585, 593n15;
  authorship of Hebrews (Clement of Rome or Luke),
    464n9;
  and the book of Revelation, 32, 543, 565nn2&5;
  and the Catholic Letters, 469;
  classification of early Christian writings, 578, 594n29;
  Clement of Rome's use of Hebrews, 464n3;
  Clement's *Hypotyposes,* 464n6;
  Clement's testimony about the Gospels, 220n8;
  Irenaeus's use of Hebrews, 464n5;
  Jerusalem's destruction as divine vengeance against
    Jews for the death of James, 481n2;
  Letter of martyr churches in Vienne and Lyons to
    Christians in Asia and Phrygia, 496, 498n24;
  and the martyrdom of James, 481n2;
  Matthew originally written in Hebrew, 131;
  and the NT canon, 481n4, 593n11;
  order of Gospels composition, 54n8;
  Origen's *Homilies on Hebrews,* 464n10;
  Origen's testimony about the Gospels, 220n2; 593n25;
  Origen's testimony about 2 Peter and 2–3 John,
    594n28;

Origen's testimony about the unknown authorship of Hebrews, 448, 464n11; 593n27;

Papias's testimony about Mark, 126n2;

Papias's testimony about Matthew, 156n2;

Papias's testimony about the value of oral tradition, 595n76;

and 1 Peter, 496, 498n13;

and the Shepherd of Hermas, 579, 594nn34,35&38;

Tatian's use of Paul's letters, 593n22;

testimony about the Johannine letters, 519–20;

testimony about the Letter of James, 469, 472;

testimony about the Letter of Jude, 509n7;

testimony about Montanus, 594nn54–57;

testimony about the Pastorals, 421;

testimony about the rule of faith, 593n8;

testimony about thirteen Pauline letters (Gaius), 441n7;

theory of Gospels composition, 53;

use of the Acts of the Apostles, 225

4 Ezra: 536, 551, 578, 589;

and a 400–year messianic interregnum, 539

Farrar, Frederic W: 83–84

Fidati, Simon: medieval Life of Jesus, 78

Florentinus, Roman jurist: on slavery, 390n18

Form criticism:

model explaining formation of the Gospel tradition, 72;

and the Pauline letters, 272–74;

pioneers, 71;

principles, 71

Fredriksen, Paula: 96

Frei, Hans: 77, 97

Frumentius, St: 579

Galatians, Letter to the:

and allegory, 334, 338, 343, 346;

and apocalyptic, 337–38, 340;

"canon within the canon," 282, 284;

"faith of Christ," 342;

literary structure, 269, 271;

and Marcion, 333, 346n1;

moral vision, 339–40, 345–46;

and new creation, 333, 340–46;

occasion, 264, 334;

opening prayer omitted, 269;

opponents, 334;

and Pauline chronology, 276, 279–80, 346nn3&4;

role in Reformation, 282, 333–34;

and Romans, 348, 363;

structure of, 334–35;

use of OT, 337, 343, 346n5

Gallican Confession: 577

Gallio/Gallio inscription: 276, 279

Gender roles (Pastorals): 428, 430

Gerhardsson, Birger: 73, 75n7

Gnosticism: 50, 77, 87, 91, 301n4, 333;

and the Acts of the Apostles, 225;

and canon, 583–84;

and Colossians, 406n6;

and the Corinthian letters, 307;

and the Gospel of John, 191;

and Irenaeus, 283, 591;

and the Johannine letters, 522;

and the Letter of Jude, 507;

and non-canonical Gospels, 591;

and the Pastorals, 424;

and Paul, 584;

and Petrine traditions, 511;

and Philippians, 378;

Valentinians, 583

Gospel of the Egyptians: 593n26

Gospel of the Hebrews: 44, 46, 578

Gospel of John, *see* John, Gospel of

Gospel of Luke, *see* Luke, Gospel of

Gospel of Mark, *see* Mark, Gospel of

Gospel of Matthew, *see* Matthew, Gospel of

Gospel of Matthias: 578

Gospel of Peter: 576, 578, 587, 591

Gospel of Philip: 583

Gospel of Thomas: 50, 578, 583, 593n26

Gospel of Truth: 583

Gospels, general:

and apostolic attribution, 66–67;

and criteria of authenticity, 89, 91–94;

and the early church, 77;

and the four living creatures of Rev 4:7, 583;

and the Enlightenment, 78, 95;

Gospel genre, 229;

harmonizations of, 39–40;

and the Jesus tradition, 66;

John and the Synoptics, 52–53;

literary dependence among, 40, 45–46, 55n22;

locations of, 69;

Papias's testimony, 104, 107, 126n2, 131, 150, 156n2;

synoptic, meaning, 39;

in Syrian Christianity, 576

Graham, William A: 571

Griesbach, Johann Jakob: 46–47, 55n27

Gunkel, Hermann: 71

Hadrian: 265

Harkel, Thomas of: 577

Harnack, Adolf: 98, 263, 333, 346n1

Hebrews, Letter to the:

and addressees, 445, 447–48, 455;

alliteration, use of, 449;

anaphora, use of, 449–50;

antithesis, use of, 450;

argumentative features of, 454–55;

asyndeton, use of, 450;

and "axes," horizontal and vertical, 456–57;

canonical placement, 27–31, 587, 593n19;

and the Christian community, 459–61;

context of, 454;

and covenants, old and new, 461–63, 574;

cult, critique of, 462–63;

date of, 447;

ecclesiology, 459–61;

eschatology of, 456;

exhortation, 449;

and faith, 445–46, 449–50, 456–57, 463;

genre of, 448–49, 456, 464nn13&14;

gezera shawa, use of, 451;

and *hapax legomena*, 449;

imagery, use of, 450;

imperatives, use of, 465n18;

"Italy, those of," 447, 454;

and Judaism, 463;

and the law, 461–63;

legacy of, 446–47;
"lesser to greater," use of, 450–51;
and Levitical priesthood, 452–54;
and literary periods, 449, 464n16;
and Melchizedek, 446, 450, 452–54, 459;
and messianic exegesis, 451, 454;
and Middle Platonism, 446, 457;
modern views of, 448;
and Montanism, 585;
and morality, 446, 460;
negation, use of, 450;
originality of, 445–46, 449;
OT, use of, 446, 450, 451–54, 465n26 (list of OT
    quotations);
paronomasia, use of, 450;
patristic views of, 447–48, 464nn5–11, 454, 577–78,
    585, 587, 593n16;
and Paul, 35, 445, 447–48, 454, 459, 462–63, 464nn6,
    7&14, 582, 586–87;
pilgrimage metaphor, use of, 445, 456;
Psalm 110, use of, 452–54;
purification imagery, use of, 458;
qal wahomer, 450–51;
questions, use of, 450;
and repentance, 447;
rhetoric of, 446, 448–51, 455–56;
rhetorical conventions, use of, 449–50;
sacrificial imagery, use of, 457–58;
stylistic features of, 445–46, 449;
and *testimonia*, 462;
theological perspective of, 445–46, 456;
title, 447;
transitions, use of, 450;
vocabulary of author, 449;
as "word of exhortation," 445, 449;
and Yom Kippur, 453, 457
– and Jesus:
death of, 457–58, 462;
as exemplar of faith, 449, 461, 463, 590;
as hermeneutical principle, 451;
as high priest, 446, 453–55, 459, 462;
as Son of God, 446, 449, 451, 458
Hegel, Georg Wilhem Friedrich: 80–81
Hellenistic-Jewish fragmentary authors: 231
Heracleon: 191, 220n6
Herder, Johann Gottfried: 71, 471 (Letter of James), 535
Herodotus: 230, 232, 572
Hilary of Poitiers: 593n16
Hildegard of Bingen: 535
Hippolytus of Rome: 578, 581
Historical literary genre: 229–32
Holtzmann, Heinrich Julius: 48
Hybrid stories (in Mark): 108

Ignatius of Antioch:
and *agapē*, "love feast," 508n3;
and "charters," Jesus Christ, 591;
and Ephesians, 413;
and Jesus' teachings, 590;
and 1 John, 531n8;
Matthew, use of, 129, 137, 582;
and Onesimus, bishop of Ephesus, 390n11;
and Philippians (martyrdom), 374;
and the Pastoral Letters, 421, 424, 441n6;
and Thessalonian letters, 289, 300n3, 301n9

Irenaeus of Lyons:
and the Acts of the Apostles, 225, 258n2;
and the book of Revelation, 541, 543, 565n2;
and canon, 576, 580, 587 (criterion of orthodoxy), 589
    (twofold division, "Gospel" and "Apostle");
Colossians, Gnostic use of, 406n6;
and Ephesians, 413, 418n8;
and four Gospels, arguments for, 583–84;
and Gnostic use of Gospels, 583–84, 591;
and Gnostics, polemic against, 283;
and "gospel" behind the Gospels, 589–90;
and the Gospel of John, 190–91, 199, 522, 531n2;
Gospels, order of composition, 54n8;
and Hebrews, 464n5;
and the Johannine letters, 531nn2&11;
and the Letter of James, 481nn5&6;
and Marcion, 581–82;
Matthew, written in Hebrew, 131;
and NT, frequency of citation, 589;
and "new testament," use of, 593n14;
and Pastorals, 421, 441n7;
and Paul, 282–83, 584;
and the "rule of faith," 593n8;
and Shepherd of Hermas, 579
Isocrates: and Hebrews, 445, 449

James, Letter of:
Abraham, example of, 475–76;
argument of, 473–75;
authenticity of, 471–73;
author of, 471–73, 480–81n2;
canonical status, 27–29, 31, 472, 577–78, 593n16,
    594n28;
and the Catholic Letters, 32, 35, 469–70;
Christian content, 473;
date of, 33, 472;
faith and works, 475–76, 481–82nn11&12;
genre of, 472;
on God, 477;
Gospel tradition, echoes of, 473, 478, 481n10, 590;
and Graeco–Roman moralists, 472;
and the Holy Spirit, 473;
legacy of, 471;
literary unity, 473–75;
and Luther, 471, 593n19;
and moral teachings, 479–80;
and OT, 477–79, 482nn13&14 (references);
patristic views of, 472, 481nn4–7;
and Paul, 475–76, 481–82n11;
principle of 100% accountability, 478;
and Sirach, 482nn15&16;
and "spirit," 481n9;
summary of content, 473–75;
and Syriac Christianity, 577;
and Torah, 477–79;
and Wisdom literature, 479–80
Jerome:
and the book of Revelation, 564, 565n2;
and canon, 593n16;
and the Gospel of Mark, 104;
and the Gospel of Matthew, 129;
and James, 471, 480nn1, 3, 7;
and the Letter of Jude, 509nn8&9;
and the Pastorals, 421, 441n7;
and 2 Peter, 515;

and Philemon, 386;
and the Shepherd of Hermas, 579;
and the Thessalonian letters, 301n7
Jerusalem collection:
and the Corinthian letters, 303–5, 308, 310, 314, 316,
326–27;
and Galatians, 336;
and Romans, 349–50, 352
Jerusalem Conference/Council: 233–34, 236–38, 241,
250, 252–53, 276–78, 346n4
Jesus Seminar: 94
Jesus Tradition: 89–94, 203;
apocalyptic teachings, 63;
and the apostles, 66–67, 70;
centers for, 58–60;
commissioning stories, 64;
controversy stories, 64;
formation of the Gospel tradition, models of: 69–70
(traditional model), 71–72 (form critical model),
72–73 (rabbinic transmission model);
hero stories, 64;
and Jesus stories, 63–64;
and literary forms, 62–65;
logia (sayings), 62;
midrash (Scripture interpretation), 63;
miracle stories, 63–64;
mobility and speed of transmission, 67;
parables, 62–63;
Passion Narrative, 65;
and preaching, 61;
pronouncement stories, 64;
and prophecy, 66;
and settings in life, 60–62;
and the Spirit, 66;
and teaching, 61;
three–stage development, theory of, 58–59;
the twelve apostles, role of, 66–67;
and worship, 60
John, Gospel of:
and "above/below" terminology, 207;
authorship, 35, 70, 83, 199–200, 531n2, 586;
and the book of Revelation, 550–52, 555, 560;
canonical status, 27–29, 31, 39, 531n12, 578;
and Cerinthus, 522;
chronological framework, 193–95, 194 (chart);
composition, theories of, 30, 40, 53–54, 199–201;
context of, 205–6;
date of, 198–99;
dualism of, 207, 212–15;
eternal life in, 211–12, 217;
and "ethical dualism," 212;
geographical framework, 192–93;
Gnostic reception of, 191, 583;
historicity of, 81 (Strauss), 83 (Renan), 85
(Schweitzer), 88 (Bultmann), 95–96, 99, 201–2;
and "I am" sayings, 196, 198, 210;
and "the Jews," 213–15;
and the Johannine letters, 521, 530;
and the lectionary, 191, 220n7;
literary structure of, 195–96;
location of, 69, 190, 199, 205;
and Matthew, 79, 190–91, 192, 198, 203, 206, 208–9,
213–15, 586;
modern views of, 191;

and Montanism, 585;
and OT, 203–5;
and parables, absence of, 63;
and Passover lamb, 204, 212;
patristic views of, 191;
prologue of, 198, 201, 209–10, 212, 220n7;
purpose of the Gospel, 65;
and Qumran, 199, 212–13;
and sectarianism, 213–14, 217;
and the seven signs, 198, 210;
and sources, 53–54;
and the Spirit, 216;
the "spiritual Gospel," 39, 41, 190, 192;
and the Synoptic Gospels, 34, 39, 41, 51–54, 69, 99,
191–98, 591;
and the twelve apostles, 66
– and Christ: 207–12;
as heavenly Savior, 211–12;
as Lamb of God, 212, 565n12;
as *Logos*, 209–11;
and messianic identity, 195–96;
as Son of God, 208–9;
speech of, 197–98;
titles of, 293–98
1 John: *see* John, Letters of
2 John: *see* John, Letters of
3 John: *see* John, Letters of
John, Letters of:
and the "antichrist," 521, 526, 529;
authorship, 519–20, 523, 531n2, 586;
and the Catholic Letters, 520;
context of, 521–22;
and dissenters, 522, 525–26;
and Docetism, 522;
and Eusebius, 519, 578;
and Gnosticism, 520;
and the Gospel of John, 519–21, 523–24, 530, 530n1;
and Jesus, 521–22;
order of composition, 753–754;
and Origen, 578;
patristic views of, 519–20, 531n8;
and the Syrian church, 577
– 1 John:
and Augustine, 519–20, 528;
and "children of God," 524–25;
and community, 523–28;
dualism of, 523–24, 530n1;
and faith, view of, 524;
and Jesus, 525–26;
and the Johannine "gospel," 521, 523, 528, 530;
incarnation of Jesus, 525–26;
and love command, 528–30, 530n1;
and moral expectations, 527–28;
sacrifice of Jesus, 525;
and sin, 527–28;
and tradition, 523–24
– 2 John:
and dissenters, 529;
and faith, 529;
and "negative hospitality," 529
– 3 John:
and authority, 530;
and the church, 529–30;
and Diotrephes, 529–30
Johnson, Luke Timothy: 94

Josephus: 66;
  and the Acts of the Apostles, 231;
  and the death of James, 480n2;
  and Luke's preface, 159;
  and Renan, 82;
  and slavery among the Essenes, 390n18
Jubilees: 17;
  and apocalyptic, 536;
  and the Ethiopian canon, 579;
  and the Pastoral Letters, 429
Jude, Letter of:
  and apocalyptic traditions, 504–5, 507;
  authorship, 27, 31–32, 504–5, 508;
  canonical status, 27–29, 469–70, 481n4, 578, 593n19,
    594n28;
  and Catholic Letters, 28, 35, 469–70, 508;
  and *1 Enoch*, 504, 508, 589;
  and "the faith," 503, 505, 507–8;
  and false teachers, 503, 506–7, 508n2;
  and Gnosticism, 507;
  and the Letter of James, 472;
  and "love feasts," 503, 507, 508n3;
  Michael, the archangel, 506;
  and paranaesis, 506;
  patristic views of, 503, 508, 508n5, 509nn7&8,
    594n28;
  and 2 Peter, 35, 501, 515, 516n3;
  and sexual immorality, 506–7;
  structure of, 505–6;
  stylistic features of, 504;
  and Syrian Christianity, 577
Julian of Norwich: 370
Justin Martyr:
  and the Acts of the Apostles, 225;
  and the Bible in early Christian worship, 592;
  and the Bible, use of, 589;
  and 1 John, 520;
  Tatian's teacher, 421

Kähler, Martin: 86–87, 96, 100
Käsemann, Ernst: 89–91, 94
Keck, Leander: 77
à Kempis, Thomas: 445
Kierkegaard, Søren: 282

L, Luke's special source: 51
Lawrence, D H: and the book of Revelation, 564
Lessing, Gotthold Ephraim: 79
Letters, ancient: 266–71; *see also* Paul, letters of;
  scholarship on, 266–67;
  structure, 267–71;
  types, 271–72
Lindars, Barnabas: 445
Literary dependence theories: *see* Synoptic Gospels
Livy: 230
Ludolf of Saxony: 78–79
Luke, Gospel of:
  and the Acts of the Apostles, 34, 158–59, 225, 246–48,
    584, 590;
  addressees, 30, 169–70;
  authorship of, traditions about, 26, 29–30, 34, 66, 70,
    158–59, 169, 225, 424, 584, 586;
  biblical "echoes," 168–69;
  birth stories, 43, 64, 83–84, 161–63, 198, 209;
  blessings and woes, 181–83;

canonical status, 27–29, 31, 40, 190;
  Christology, 176–78, 246–47;
  composition, theories of, 41, 68, 160–61, 169;
  context of, 169–70;
  date of, 169–70;
  and discipleship, 183–85;
  doublets, 50, 56n31;
  ecclesiology, 175–76, 242, 415;
  eschatology, 170–72, 217, 513;
  and the Galilean ministry, 163;
  and Gentiles in God's plan, 175–76;
  genre of, 229;
  and the Gospel of John, 53, 199;
  and the Gospel of Mark, 41, 47–49, 51, 54n9, 55nn14,
    15, 17, 19, 20, 24, & 27, 107, 111, 131, 160–61,
    162 (chart), 163, 165–66, 167, 171–72;
  and the Gospel of Matthew, 42–43, 46, 48, 56n29, 131,
    133, 143;
  and the Holy Spirit, 249–50;
  and the Jerusalem section, 165–66;
  and Jerusalem's destruction, 170;
  "Jew"/"Jews," use of the term(s), 213;
  and kingdom of God, 178–81;
  and L source, 47, 51, 93, 160, 162, 229;
  location, 69, 169;
  and Marcion, 581–82;
  and OT, use of, 68, 167–69, 175–76, 243, 552, 575;
  parables, 63;
  parables unique to Luke, 165;
  and the Parousia, 170–72;
  patristic use, 190–91, 578;
  place of composition, 69, 169;
  preface, 46, 51, 65, 68, 159–60, 227;
  Proto–Luke, composition theory, 160;
  purpose of, 159–60, 170, 226–28, 575;
  and Q, 50, 68;
  as "second edition" of Mark, 33–34, 131–33;
  Sermon on the Plain, 181–82, 195;
  and sources, 33, 69, 160–61, 229;
  theological work of, 170–85;
  Theophilus, 65, 159, 586;
  and the Travel Narrative, 43–45, 50–51, 162, 163–65,
    186–87, 192;
  wealth, attitude toward, 183–85, 247
  – and Christ: 172–78;
  ascension, 43, 244, 299;
  birth narrative(s), 161–62, 208;
  death of, significance, 172–75, 207, 246;
  innocence of, 65, 557;
  as interpreter of Scripture, 16, 63, 173, 589;
  as king, 176–77;
  as Lord, 176;
  as master, 176;
  as messiah, 176–78, 558;
  mission of, 174–75;
  as prophet, 174–75, 177;
  resurrection appearances, 43;
  as Son of David, 176–77;
  as Son of God, 176;
  as Son of Man, 176–77, 246;
  suffering of, 172–73, 493;
  suffering servant, Isaianic, 173–74, 242;
  as teacher, 176;
  teaching of, 164–65, 178–85;

titles, Christological, 176;
trial of, 166
Luther, Martin:
and the book of Revelation, 564, 566n14, 593n19;
and canon, 593n20;
faith and works, 284, 363;
and Galatians, 282, 333;
and the Letter to the Hebrews, 593n19;
and the Letter of James, 471, 593n19;
and the Letter of Jude, 515 (as digest of 2 Peter), 593n19;
and Paul, 281–82, 284;
and 2 Peter, 515;
and Philemon, 383;
and Romans, 282, 363;
and the Thessalonian letters, 301n7

M, Matthew's special source: 51
Macarius Magnes: NT canon, 573
MacDonald, Margaret: 392
Malherbe, Abraham J: xiv, 289
Mani (Manichaeism): and Galatians, 333
Marcion:
and the book of Revelation, 552;
and canon of the NT, 580, 581–83;
and Colossians, 406n6;
and Ephesians, 412;
Epistle to the Laodiceans, 29;
and Galatians, 333, 346n1;
"gospel" and "apostle," two–part NT canon, 581, 589;
and the Gospel of Luke, 77, 161, 581–84;
and Harnack, 333;
and a letter to the Alexandrians, 29;
and the Muratorian Fragment, 29;
and the OT, 149, 507;
and the Pastoral Letters, 421, 442n9;
and Paul, 284, 333, 581, 584;
and Philemon, 390n11;
and Romans, 367;
and Tertullian, 190
Mark, Gospel of:
and apocalyptic discourse (ch 13), 107, 112–13, 118, 120;
Christology, 119;
commentary on Mark, earliest, 32;
and controversy stories, 107, 111–12, 115, 119;
and disciples/discipleship, 112, 119–23;
distinctive features, 107;
doublet, use of, 56n31;
ending of, 43, 104, 107, 123;
as epitome of Matthew (Augustine), 41;
Gnostic use of, 583;
as first Gospel (Markan priority), 47–51, 67–68, 95, 107;
and historicity, 95;
and "hybrid stories," 108;
"immediately," use of, 108;
and Jerome, 104;
and Jesus tradition, 68–69;
and literary dependence theories, 45–46;
literary style, 107;
location, 69, 169;
and "messianic secret," 84, 106, 121;
and "narrative arrows," 108–9;

organization, perceived lack of, 107–9;
and OT, 67–68, 104, 115–17;
and parables, 63, 106, 111–12, 114, 121–22;
patristic views of, 104;
and Peter (reminiscences), 69–70, 586;
place of composition, 69;
plot of, 109;
and pronouncement stories, 110–12;
simplicity of, 104;
sources of, 67–68;
structure of, 107;
"summaries," use of, 108;
theological achievement, 121–23;
use (%) by Matthew and Luke, 55n24
 – and Christ: 110–19;
as charismatic teacher, 110;
deeds and sayings of, 110–15;
and discipleship, 119–21;
as Elijah, 114–15, 117, 119;
as eschatological judge, 118;
and the kingdom of God, 106, 110–13, 115;
as messianic king, 115–16, 118, 122;
ministry of, 107–8, 120–23;
miracles of, 110, 112–15;
as Moses, 114–15, 117, 119;
portrait of, 115–19;
as preacher, 110;
as Son of David, 114–16, 119;
as Son of God, 104, 106, 107, 114, 116–18, 121;
as Son of Man, 117–18;
suffering of, 107, 112–13, 118, 121–22;
as Teacher, 116;
teaching of, 107, 110–13;
transfiguration of, 106, 107, 112, 114–16, 120, 121
Martyn, J Louis: 333
Marxsen, Willi: 9
Mashal: figurative speech in OT, 62
Mather, Cotton: 535
Matthew, Gospel of:
and Augustine, 40, 54n9, 192;
authorship, 26, 30, 66, 70, 190–91, 586;
birth narrative(s), 43, 64, 83, 161, 163, 198, 209;
and the book of Revelation, 565n11;
and Calvin, John, 40;
canonical status, 27 (Athanasius), 28–31, 190;
as Christian Pentateuch, 138;
Christology, 142–49;
and the church, 128–29, 130, 135, 137, 140–43, 146, 148, 150, 151, 153, 414;
as "church handbook," 137, 141–42;
church and Israel, 149;
church and synagogue in, 135, 137, 140, 142, 146, 148, 150, 214;
as "community rule," 141;
context of, 135–38, 140, 150;
didactic quality of, 130–33;
and discipleship, 141, 143, 145–47, 151–53;
doublets in, 56n31;
and the Ebionites, 583;
editorial strategy of, 131–33, 140;
and the five discourses, 44, 130, 133, 137–38, 147, 152, 164;
and formula quotations, 68, 134 (references), 135, 141–42, 203, 552;

as foundation narrative, 140–42;
and genealogy of Christ, 128, 130, 140–43, 550;
and the Gospel of Luke, 31, 39, 42–43, 46 (Griesbach hypothesis), 49, 55n15; 160–61, 164–65 (Travel Narrative), 166, 169, 172–73, 178, 181, 184, 515, 583;
and the Gospel of Mark, 31–33, 39, 43, 46–49, 55n14 (significant agreements), 55n18, 55n24, 107, 131–33, 132 (chart), 142, 145, 151, 160, 167;
and historicity, 83, 91;
as "holy word" (Theophilus of Antioch), 588;
and Ignatius, 129, 137, 582;
"Jew"/"Jews," use of, 213–14;
and the Johannine letters, 528;
and Judaism, 130, 135, 137, 149, 150, 213;
"kingdom of heaven/God" in, 149–50, 197;
language of composition, 131, 150;
"law and prophets," 128, 141, 147–49, 150, 152, 478;
and the Letter of James, 473, 478, 481n10;
literary structure of, 61, 137–38;
literary style, 49, 107;
location of, 69, 137, 169;
and M source, 47, 51, 93, 133–34;
and Origen, 578;
and OT, use of: 61, 68, 134–35, 139–40, 167, 169, 203, 206;
and Papias, 131, 150;
parables in, 63, 111;
patristic use, 28–30, 41, 129–31, 190, 578, 583, 588;
and pesher interpretation, use of, 61;
and 1 Peter, 497n4;
and Q, 47, 49–50, 68, 133–34, 143;
and Qumran, 137;
and righteousness, 139–40, 148, 152–53;
"school of St Matthew," 61, 75n2, 170;
as "second edition" of Mark, 33–34;
and the Sermon on the Mount, 44, 130, 140, 147, 152, 181, 195, 215;
sources of, 68–69, 133–34;
theological vision of, 21, 140–53
– and Christ: 142–49;
baptism of, 133, 139, 143, 147;
birth of, 128, 135, 139, 142;
and disciples, 134, 141, 143–47, 151–53;
as eschatological judge, 144;
as Lord, 144–45;
as Lord of the church, 142–46;
as messianic king (*see* Son of David);
as messianic teacher, 146–47, 152;
miracles of, 49, 145;
as model for the church, 151–52;
as Moses, 138–40, 147, 206;
as Pantocrator, 128, 146;
as perfecter of the law and the prophets, 147–49;
as "rabbi" of the church, 214;
rhetorical power of, 139;
as Son of David, 142–43, 558;
as Son of God, 143–45, 208;
as Son of Man, 143–45, 176;
as teacher of righteousness, 152–53
McGinn, Bernard: 535
Medieval lives of Jesus: 78–79
Melanchthon, Philipp: and the Thessalonian letters, 301n7
Messianic secret: 84 (Wrede), 85, 106 (references in Mark), 121

Metzger, Bruce M: 26
Midrash: 61, 63, 68, 170, 204, 246, 320, 337, 459, 485, 551, 553, 558, 574
Miscellaneous source theories: *see* Synoptic problem
Mitchell, Margaret M: 303
Moffatt, James: 445, 503
Montanism/Montanus:
and the NT canon, 584–85, 587
Montgomery, William: 85, 100nn21&24
Morgan, Thomas: and Acts, 225–26
Moule, C F D: xiv, 399
Multiple Stage Development theories:
see Synoptic problem
Muratorian Fragment:
and the book of Revelation, 565n1;
and canon of the NT, 28–30, 31, 36nn7&8;
and the Catholic Letters, 469;
and the criteria of canonicity, 588;
date of, 36n7;
discovery of, 28;
and the Gospel of John, 519;
and the Johannine letters, 519;
and the Letter of James, 472;
Muratori, Lodovico Antonio, 28;
and the Pastoral Letters, 420, 441nn1&2, 441n7;
and the Shepherd of Hermas, 579;
and the Thessalonian letters, 301n8

Nag Hammadi Library: 50
Nero: 541, 543
New Testament, general:
as "canon," 572–73;
canonization of, 576–77, 580–92; *see also* Canonization;
and extra–canonical writings, 29;
and history of interpretation, 2;
modern canon of, 26–27;
origin of the phrase, 573–74;
as "scripture", 572;
and theological angle of vision, 13–15
Nicene Creed: 409
Nock, A D: 289

Ogden, Schubert: 9
Origen of Alexandria:
and the Acts of the Apostles, 30, 578;
and allegorical interpretation, 40;
and the book of Revelation, 30, 519;
canon of NT, his, 30;
and canonization, 576, 586;
and the Catholic Letters, 30, 578, 594n28;
and Ephesians, 418n6;
"gospel" and "apostle," use of, 589;
and the Gospel of John, 30, 190–92, 199, 220n6, 519;
and the Gospel of Matthew, 129–30, 131;
and the Gospels, 30, 40, 54n8, 190–92, 578, 593n26;
and inspiration as a criterion of canonicity, 586;
and the Johannine letters, 30, 32, 519, 531n3, 578;
and the Letter to the Hebrews, 30, 448, 464nn9&10, 578;
and the Letter of James, 30, 472, 480–81n2, 481n6, 516;
and the Letter of Jude, 503, 508n5, 509n8;
and Marcion, 581;
and "new testament," use of, 593n14;

and non–canonical Gospels, 578, 587, 593n26;
and the Pastoral Letters, 421, 442n10;
and Paul, 282;
and the Pauline letters, 30, 578;
and 1 Peter, 30, 496, 498n13;
and 2 Peter, 30, 578, 594n28;
and Philemon, 390n11;
and the Shepherd of Hermas, 579, 594n38;
and the Thessalonian letters, 301n7

Papias of Hierapolis: 104, 107, 131, 591
Papyri:
  and ancient epistolography, 266–67;
  Letter from Theon to his father, 267;
  Oxyrhynchus Papyrus No 115: 266;
  $\mathfrak{P}^{20}$, 481n5;
  $\mathfrak{P}^{23}$, 481n5;
  $\mathfrak{P}^{46}$, 301n8, 367, 418nn6&8, 421, 442n8, 447, 448;
  $\mathfrak{P}^{52}$, 198, 200;
  $\mathfrak{P}^{66}$, 199;
  $\mathfrak{P}^{75}$, 158, 199, 200
Paraenesis: 293–95, 339, 379–80, 413, 433–35, 484, 487,
  506
Parousia, Christ's:
  delay of, 170–71;
  in Paul, 411 (references);
  and 2 Peter, 510–15
Paschal, Blaise: 104
Pastoral Letters (as a group):
  authorship of, 35, 421–25;
  and canonical arrangement, 441n1;
  and Christ, 436;
  and church structure, 438–39;
  dating of, 424;
  distinctive vocabulary, 422, 442n13;
  and God, 427–28: as savior, 440;
  historical situations of, 428;
  and moral instruction, 439–41;
  and $\mathfrak{P}^{46}$, 442n8;
  patristic views of, 420–21, 441nn6–12;
  post–Pauline perspective, 35;
  stylistic features of, 422;
  theological features of, 436–41;
  title, 420;
  on widows, 439, 441
Paul of Tarsus: [BOLDFACE REFLECTS ITEM FOUND IN DIS-
  PUTED LETTERS]
  on Abraham, 337–38, 341–46, 354, 364–65, 475–76;
  and the Acts of the Apostles, 275–78, 292–93;
  and Adam Christology, 283, 355–57, 365;
  on the body of Christ, 310, 316–17, **392, 402**;
  on Christ, 283, 297, 337–38, 340–41, 354–56, 365–67,
    371, 375–76, 378, 380, 385–87, **400–5, 415–16**;
  on the Christian community, 312–16, 352–53, 359–
    60, **416**;
  and chronology of ministry, 275–81;
  on the church, **411–12, 414–18**;
  on circumcision, 338–39, 343, 363, 365, 376–77;
  call/conversion of, 335;
  on conversion, **398–99, 403**;
  and creedal statements, 265, 273, 324, **431–32, 436**;
  dialectical thinker, 284;
  and dialogical theology, 264–65;
  and earlier Christian traditions, use of, 273–74;
  and Eastern Christianity, 282;

and Egyptian papyri, 266–67;
epistemology of, 311–13, 377–78;
and epistolography, 266–71, 379–80;
eschatology of, 290, 298–300, **411;**
on ethnicity, 359, 365–66;
on faith, 341–42, 364–67, 386–87, **431, 436–37**;
and the faith principle, 364–65;
on Gentiles, 282, 343–45, **410–12**;
and Gnosticism, 584;
on God, 296–97, 311, 317, 321–22, 325–26, 337–39,
  361, **398–400, 414–15, 441**;
on the gospel, 321–24, 329, 340, 353–54, 373–74,
  428–29, 431–32;
on grace, 355–56;
on the Holy Spirit, 298, 357–58;
on the Incarnation, 380;
interpretation of, 281–85;
and "introspective conscience," 282;
and the Jerusalem collection, 303, 316, 326, 349, 352,
  373;
on Judaism, 358–59, 362–63;
on the law, 337, 339–40, 356–57, 361–64, **428–29**,
  454;
legacy of, 275, 281–85;
letters, disputed and undisputed, 280–81;
on marital relations, 313–14;
and metaphors, 283, 348, 366, **393, 403**;
on ministry, 318–26;
  defense of, 328–29, 335–36;
  description of, 318–19;
  methods of, 321–22;
and "missionary journeys," 278;
on morality, 339–40, 345–46, 355–58, 387, **402–5,
  416–18, 427–28, 433–35**;
on the "new creation," 340–46;
on opponents, 326–27, 334, **396–98, 424, 426, 432,
  435**;
and OT, 343–44, 351;
on the Parousia, 290, 298–300, 411 (references), **432**;
and patristic attitudes toward, 281–82;
and Platonism, 282;
and pre–Pauline tradition(s), 58, 272–74, 277–78, 324,
  351, 375;
on the resurrection, 316–17, 378, 380;
on righteousness, 336–39, 361–67, 378;
on sacrificial food, 314–16;
on salvation, 336–37, 364, 366, **399**;
"second founder of Christianity," 283;
on sin, 355, 366;
and situational theology, 264;
and slavery, 388–89;
on spiritual gifts, 316;
and state, attitude toward, 283–84;
and *theologia crucis*, 310–13;
and theology in, 265, 277, 281, 283–85;
on Torah, 342–46, 504;
and the two covenants, 442–44;
on worship, 316
– letters of:
canonical arrangement, 34–35, 274–75;
chronological order, 275–77, 278 (chart);
dialectical dimension of, 284;
and editions of the collection, 274–75;
and issues of authorship, 280–81, 289–90, 392–96,
  409–14, 421–25;

occasional quality of, 264, 270;
and a "second" imprisonment, 280;
structure of, 267–71;
types of, 271–72
Pelagius: 281, 301n7
Perrin, Norman: 92–93;
and criteria of authenticity, 92–93;
and Two Source Hypothesis, 93
Pesher: 61, 68
Peshitta, the Syriac "vulgate": contents, 577
1 Peter:
authorship of, 488;
catechetical features of, 485, 495;
on Christ, 492–94;
and the church, 495–96;
and exile, 495–96;
on God, 490–92;
literary features of, 485;
liturgical dimension of, 485, 488–89;
and martyrdom, 496–97;
and moral conduct, 489;
and OT, 485–86, 498n9 (list of OT citations or allusions), 498nn10&11, 498n14;
patristic views of, 496–97;
and Paul, 484–85;
purpose of, 487–88;
and Rome: 495;
on the Spirit, 494–95;
structure of, 487–88;
on suffering, 486–87
2 Peter:
authorship of, 510, 515–16;
and biblical view of history, 513–14;
eschatological skepticism, 512–13;
and false teachers, 512;
genre of, 510–11;
and Jude, 35, 515, 516n3;
literary structure, 511–12;
and moral expectations, 512, 514;
and OT, 512, 514;
and the Parousia, 510, 513–14;
and Paul, 514–15;
and "the prophetic message," 511;
and theological view of time, 514;
and the transfiguration, 511;
use of, the church's, 515–16
Philemon, Letter to:
context of, 384–85;
location of, 384;
patristic use, 385–86, 390nn11–14;
as a petition, 385;
and slavery, 388–89;
structure of, 383–84
Philippians, Letter to the:
and the Christ hymn, 375, 380;
and the congregation, 379;
and co-workers, 376;
epistolary characteristics of, 379–80;
and financial contributions, 371–72;
integrity of, 370–71;
and kenotic Christology, 380;
koinōnia, and language of joint participation, 381n8;
and martyrdom, 374;
and the "mind of Christ," 374–76;
and opponents, 376–77;

paraenetic features, 379;
and Paul's imprisonment, 34, 370, 372–74;
purpose of, 370–71
Philo of Alexandria: 66, 264
Philodemus: 265
Philoxenus of Mabbug: 577
Pirke Aboth, 273
Plato: 83, 99, 265, 282
Pliny the Elder: 572
Pliny the Younger: 385, 484, 486, 543
Plutarch: 265, 417, 510, 512, 514
Polybius: 230
Polycarp of Smyrna: 370, 372, 520, 541, 584, 589
Ptolemy the Valentinian: 590

Q: 47, 49–51, 55n28, 68, 133–134, 143–144;
and doublets, 50, 56n31;
Eichhorn, J G, originator of sayings source idea, 55n28;
as hypothetical source, 50, 55n28;
meaning of, 55n28;
redaction of, 50–51;
theology of, 50;
and sayings material, 60–61;
Weisse, C H, originator of sayings source common to Matthew and Luke, 55n28
Qumran: 11–12, 61, 137, 199, 212–13, 536;
and apocalyptic literature, 536;
and behavioral expression of theology, 11–12;
and Scripture, 61

Reimarus, Hermann Samuel: 79–80, 84–85, 91, 112–13;
and ecclesiastical response to, 80;
legacy of, 80;
and rationalism, 79–80;
and understanding of Jesus, 79–80
Renan, Ernest: 81–83, 96, 99, 128, 131, 383;
and portrayal of Jesus, 110–11;
and responses to, 111
Revelation, book of:
authorship, 536, 541, 543, 549, 564, 565n2, 566n14;
Babylon, Rome as, 541;
and the bride of Jerusalem, 545, 548;
canonical position, 32;
canonical status, 564;
catalyst for, 541–43;
cyclical reading of, 548–49;
dating of, 541–43, 549, 565nn2-4;
eschatology of, 539, 550;
on evil, 560–63;
and Rome, 561–63;
genre of, 536; *see also* Apocalyptic;
on God, 553–55;
history of interpretation, 563–64, 566n14;
and the imperial cult, 543;
legacy of, 563–64;
and the Jesus tradition, 550, 565n11 (passages echoing the Gospel tradition);
linear reading of, 548–49;
and literary devices, 543–44;
literary technique of, 543–44;
location of, 541;
and martyrs, 550;
and Montanism, 585;
and numbers, 543;
occasion, 541–43, 560;

and OT, 551–53, 565n10 (list of passages);
patristic views of, 564, 565n2;
and prophecy, 549–50;
recapitulation theory of reading, 548–49;
suffering and death, as occasion, 560;
symbolism of, 539;
throne imagery, 553, 555;
title of, 536, 565n1;
unified vision of, 543–48;
and the whore of Babylon, 545, 548, 563;
and worship as formative context of, 549–50, 553
– on Jesus: 550, 555–60;
death of, 555–57, 559;
as Lamb, 557–59, 565n12;
as messiah, 558–59;
as slaughtered Lamb, 555, 557, 559;
story of, 561
Riesenfeld, Harald: 74
Robinson, James M: 90–91
Roman Empire: population, 489, 498n15
Romans, Letter to the:
Abraham, role of, 364–65;
apocalyptic dimension, 353–54;
argument of, 349–60;
canonical position, 32, 348;
community formation, 359–60;
context of, 349, 351;
and the diatribe, 349–50;
dikaios word family, 361;
ending of, 367;
the faith principle, 364–65;
Holy Spirit, 357–58;
impartiality, divine toward humans, 365–66;
Israel and the Gentiles, 358–59;
and justification, 348, 361; *see* Paul, on righteousness;
law, critique of, 356–57, 361–64;
moral vision, 359–60;
OT, use of, 351;
as Paul's "last will and testament," 349;
pivotal passages (1:16–17; 3:21–31; 15:7–13), 352;
purpose of, 352–53;
righteousness of God, 348, 361, 365;
scriptural texture, 351;
setting, 349, 351;
Spirit as moral catalyst, 357–58;
and "strong/weak" distinctions, 360;
structure of, 269, 350, 352;
summary of argument, 352;
theology of, 350, 360–67;
theses, five interlocking, 354
– and Christ:
as Adam, 355–56;
"faith of/in," 364, 366–67;
liberation/freedom, metaphors of, 366;
means of justification, 366;
sacrifice, metaphors of, 366;
union with, 355–56

Sabinianus: 385
Sadducees: 513
Sallust: 230
Sanders, E P: 96
Schleiermacher, F D E: 45, 71, 96
Schmidt, Karl Ludwig: 71
Schubert, Paul: 268, 272

Schweitzer, Albert: 77, 84–86, 94–96, 98, 129, 131, 134, 510;
and messianic consciousness of Jesus, 99;
and "mirror syndrome," 86, 94, 98;
and Parousia, 85;
and Paul, 284
Selwyn, Edward Gordon: 484
Seneca: 263, 267
Serapion of Antioch: 587, 591
"Scripture," etymology: 572
Shepherd of Hermas: 28–29, 31–32, 573, 578–79
Sibylline Oracles: 536
Single source theories: *see* Synoptic problem
Sirach: 28, 551, 589
Slavery: 385, 388–89, 390nn16–18 (ancient attitudes toward, references)
Smith, William Cantwell: 571
Sophocles: 484
Stanton, Graham: 93
Strauss, David Friedrich: 47, 80–81, 94, 96;
and form criticism, 81;
and rationalistic interpretations, 81
Streeter, Burnett Hillman: 48
Synod of Jerusalem: 577
Synoptic Gospels (as a grouping): 39
Synoptic problem: 42–51;
and agreement of wording in gospels, 42, 55n14;
and differences in Gospels, 43–44;
and the Double Tradition (Q), 49–50;
and doublets, 50, 56n31;
and literary dependence theories, 45–46;
and miscellaneous source theories, 45–46;
and multiple stage development hypotheses, 51;
and passion narratives, 51;
and Q; 47, 49–51; *see* Q;
sequence of events, 42–43;
and single (common) source theories, 44–46;
and the Triple Tradition, 47, 49;
and the Two Gospel Hypothesis, 46–47;
and the Two Source Hypothesis, 47–51;
major features of, 48–51;
and Markan priority, 48–49

Tacitus: 231
Tatian: 40, 161, 421, 576, 578, 584
Teresa of Avila: 303, 370
Tertullian of Carthage:
and the book of Revelation, 543;
and *1 Enoch*, 578;
and the Gospels, 190;
and the Letter of Jude, 508;
and Marcion, 289, 301n8, 581;
and Montanism, 585;
and the Pastoral Letters, 420;
and the rule of faith, 591;
and the Shepherd of Hermas, 579;
and the Thessalonian letters, 289, 301n8
Testament of Abraham: 536
Testament of Levi: 536
Theodore of Mopsuestia: 383, 386
Theodosius, Emperor: 471
Theology, model for doing: 15–24;
catalysts, 22–23;
context, 18;
interpreter(s), 18–19;

tetrahedron (diagram), 20;
text, 16–17;
theology, etymology, 24n1;
tradition, 17–18
Theophilus of Antioch: 578, 586, 588
Thessalonians, Letters to the:
  and the Acts of the Apostles, 292–93;
  and apocalyptic, 295–96, 300–1, *see also* Paul, on eschatology;
  authenticity of 2 Thessalonians, 34;
  and authorship, 289–90;
  canonical status, 301n8;
  date, 34, 278, 301n10;
  genre of, 293–96;
  OT, use of, 293, 301nn11&12 (references);
  patristic use, 301nn4–8;
  and psychagogy, 301n6;
  rhetoric of, 293–96;
  structure of, 293–94;
  on text of, 291–92;
  theology of, 296–300
Thirty-Nine Articles of the Church of England: 577
Thucydides: 230, 232, 236, 572
1 Timothy: 428–32;
  on church leaders, 431–32;
  on gender roles, 430–31;
  as instructions, 431–32;
  and ministers, 431–32;
  and Paul as exemplar, 429;
  and universal vision, 429–30
2 Timothy: 432–35;
  as exhortation, 433–35;
  and memory, 434;
  and moral examples, 433–34;
  and moral instructions, 435;
  structure of, 432–33
Titus, Letter to: 425–28;
  on church leaders, 425–26;
  on false teachers, 426;
  on "sound doctrine," 426–27
Tobit: 28
Toland, John: 225
Trullan Synod: 579
Two Gospel Hypothesis: *see* Synoptic problem
Two Source Hypothesis: *see* Synoptic problem
Tyconius: 548
Tyndale, William: 471

Ulpian, Roman lawyer: on slavery, 390n18

Valentinus: 583
Vatican Council, First: 577
Victorinus of Pettau: 548
von Speyr, Adrienne: 392

Weiss, Johannes: 85
Weisse, Christian Hermann: 48, 55n28, 190
Westcott, Brooke Foss: 26
Westminster Confession: 577
Wisdom of Solomon: 29–30
Worship, early Christian: patristic references, 75n1
Wrede, William: 84–85, 283, 348
Wright, N T: 96, 101n66

Xenophon: 83, 230

Zwingli, Ulrich: 564